THE ROMANTIC REVOLUTION
IN AMERICA

Vernon Louis Parrington was born in Aurora, Illinois, in 1871, and was graduated from Harvard University. In 1908 he became Professor of English at the University of Washington. He died suddenly in 1929, at the height of his critical powers. His masterpiece, MAIN CURRENTS IN AMERICAN THOUGHT, in two volumes, *The Colonial Mind* (1620–1800) and *The Romantic Revolution in America* (1800–1860), appeared in 1927. The final volume, *The Beginnings of Critical Realism* (1860–1920) was published posthumously and in fragmentary form in 1930.

VERNON LOUIS PARRINGTON

Main Currents
in American Thought

VOLUME TWO · 1800–1860
THE ROMANTIC REVOLUTION IN AMERICA

A Harvest Book

HARCOURT, BRACE & WORLD, INC.

NEW YORK

Copyright, 1927, by
Harcourt, Brace & World, Inc.

Copyright renewed, 1954, by Vernon L. Parrington, Jr.,
Louise P. Tucker, Elizabeth P. Thomas

Q.4.66

Printed in the United States of America

FOREWORD

In justification of the choice of writers and allotment of space in the following pages, let it be said frankly that I have been guided by what I conceived to be the historical significance of the several documents. With aesthetic judgments I have not been greatly concerned. I have not wished to evaluate reputations or weigh literary merits, but rather to understand what our fathers thought, and why they wrote as they did. This will serve to explain the considerable number of pages devoted to southern letters, as well as to certain well-nigh forgotten figures. For the purpose I had in view such a method was inevitable. Lost causes have a way of shrinking in importance in the memory of later generations, and the historian must go back to the days before their overthrow, and view them in the light of their hopes. Time is not always a just winnower; it is partial to success and its verdict too often inclines to the side of the biggest cannon or the noisiest *claque*. The exhuming of buried reputations and the revivifying of dead causes is the familiar business of the historian, in whose eyes forgotten men may assume as great significance as others with whom posterity has dealt more generously. Communing with ghosts is not unprofitable to one who listens to their tales. To our fathers John Taylor and Beverley Tucker and Fisher Ames were living figures; they spoke for their generation, and they may have something still to say to a later generation. For dealing at length with such men as Hugh Legaré and Gilmore Simms and John P. Kennedy and Herman Melville, no apologies need be offered. They have too long been slighted. Walt Whitman I have chosen to regard as the forerunner of a later school, and have reserved the consideration of his work for another study. Certain other men I have omitted regretfully out of regard to space—diverse figures such as Orestes Brownson,

Albert Brisbane, and John Esten Cooke, together with a group of poets and essayists, who though they have long been reckoned ghosts are nevertheless well worth knowing. Even echoes imply substance somewhere.

V. L. P.

Seattle, February 22, 1926.

INTRODUCTION

The present volume is the second in a proposed study of the main tendencies of American thought as expressed in our literature. In the preceding volume I have considered the incoming into America of certain old-world ideals and institutions, and the subjection of those ideals and institutions to the pressure of a new environment, from which resulted the overthrow of the principles of monarchy and aristocracy, and the setting up of the principle of republicanism. In the present study I purpose considering certain new growths that sprang up in the land thus cleared—what particular forms they assumed and why they assumed such forms. The delimitations of the period to be treated of are fixed by two wars that disturbed the normal unfolding of national experience: the War of 1812 that hastened the development of nineteenth-century ideals, and the Civil War that uprooted certain of the crasser growths of those vigorous years. The half century that lay between these dramatic episodes was a period of extravagant youth, given over to a cult of romanticism that wrought as many marvels as Aaron's rod. In the South, in New England, and on the western frontier, it laid hold of men's minds, consuming the stubble of eighteenth-century harvests, sweeping away the drab realisms of a cautious past, and offering in their stead more alluring ideals. Revolutions, greater and lesser, trod on each other's heels; the common adventure led into unexplored paths; and the final outcome for which it was all preparing was the emergence of a new middle class that in the succeeding half century was to subdue America to middle-class ends.

Such drastic overturnings of the customary and familiar, such swift ruptures with the past, quite evidently do not come from trivial causes. Men do not put off the old before the new is ready; and if in those credulous years they turned romantic and refused to heed the counsels of experience, it was because the soil had been new-plowed for the growing of such crops as their fathers had not known. The grapes from which the wine of romance is vinted, it must not be forgotten, are rooted in the common earth. The loveliest romantic dreams spring from a parentage that is humbly prosaic. There is no more fruitful source of romantic hope than a fluid economics that overflows all narrow preëmptions and sweeps away the restrictions that hamper free endeavor. With fresh economic realms to conquer, the dullest plodder discovers a stimulus in anticipation that sets him upon creating a Utopia. The breaking up of the static, the bold adventuring upon new worlds, is the fertile soil in which romance springs most luxuriantly. It needs no uncommon eyes, surely, to discover in the swift changes that came to America in the wake of the second English war, the seedbed of those ebullient romanticisms which in politics and economics, in theology and literature, turned away so contemptuously from the homespun past. Of a sudden America was becoming a new world with potentialities before undreamed of; and this new America was no longer content with the narrow ways of a more cautious generation. The older America of colonial days had been static, rationalistic, inclined to pessimism, fearful of innovation, tenacious of the customary. It conceived of human nature as evil, and accounting men incurably wicked, it opened no doors to Utopian dreams of a golden future. The round of daily life was confined within a narrow domestic economy, with few and rare changes in social status. Growth in population came mainly from natural increase. Exploitation was laborious, and such wealth as was laid by was gained in shop and field, in fisheries and shipping. With its expectations cramped by a drab agrarianism, it was content to remain primitively self-sufficient, not given to seeking riches by speculative short-cuts, clinging to the habitual, distrustful of change.

During the thirty-odd years between the Peace of Paris and the end of the War of 1812 that older America was dying. The America that succeeded was a shifting, restless world, youthfully optimistic, eager to better itself, bent on finding easier roads to wealth than the plodding path of natural increase. It conceived of human nature as acquisitive, and accounting acquisitiveness a cardinal virtue, it set out to inquire what opportunities awaited it in the unexploited resources of the continent. The cautious ways of earlier generations were become as much out of date as last year's almanac. New commonwealths were rising in the wilderness; immigration from war-torn Europe was pouring in; wild lands were daily coming on the market. Money was to be made by the enterprising, and the multitude of the enterprising was augmenting with the expansion of the settlements. The ideal of a static society having been put away, progress was assumed to be the first law of nature, and innovation was accepted as the sign and seal of progress. It was our first great period of exploitation, and from it emerged, as naturally as the cock from the mother egg, the spirit of romance, gross and tawdry in vulgar minds, dainty and refined in the more cultivated. But always romance. The days of realism were past, and it was quietly laid away with the wig and smallclothes of an outgrown generation.

Unfortunately economic romance is more imperious in its demands than literary romance. Its dreams follow objective desires, and in America of those days of new beginnings the desires of diverse economic groups conducted straight to antagonistic imperialisms. The major interests of the three great sections of the country differentiated more and more sharply. The East was discovering its Utopia in an industrial capitalistic order. With the flocking of immigrants to the factories began the extraordinary expansion of the cities and the movement of centralization that was eventually to transform America from a rural to an urban society, supplanting the farmer by the business man and disintegrating the traditional psychology. The new manufacturing and the new finance were subjecting an agrarian people to the dislocations and readjustments implied in the industrial revolution, the outcome of which no man could foresee. The reaction of this new industrialism upon the South was immediate. With the improvements in textile manufacturing came greater demands upon the new southern staple, and an agriculture that had long been static with its traditional crops of indigo, rice, and tobacco, began to look forward confidently to a Utopia founded on cotton, and conceived an imperialistic dream of expanding fields of white bolls and black slaves, reaching into Mexico and embracing the West Indies. The new South left off apologizing for slavery and hoping for its ultimate extinction. Slavery had become enormously profitable and it proposed to exploit the Negro as frankly as New England was exploiting the Irish immigrant, but more humanely if possible, in something of the patriarchal spirit.

Meanwhile in the Inland Empire was arising an economics

that looked with little favor on the imperialisms of eastern capitalism or southern slavery; an economics equalitarian in temper, decentralizing in impulse; nourished on the idealism of the Declaration of Independence, but interpreting it to mean the natural right of every free citizen to satisfy his acquisitive instinct by exploiting the national resources in the measure of his shrewdness. Democratic in professions, it was middle-class in spirit and purpose. Discovering the inflowing tide of immigration to be favorable to speculation, it sought its Utopia in county-seat towns where land holdings mounted in value with every new wave. No narrow horizons bounded a realm that stretched to the Pacific and into the remote Northwest, and no stodgy ways of money-getting could satisfy men whose imaginations ranged through such spaces. This country was theirs to do with as they chose, and if eastern capitalism or southern slavery interfered with their inalienable rights, their Sharp's rifles were at hand for defense. In the vast territory drained by the Mississippi—the "Valley of Democracy," a recent writer has chosen to call it—was conceived what may be accounted the most romantic dream that ever visited the native mind of America. It impressed de Tocqueville, who discovered the poetry of America in this romance of a moving frontier, in the vision that led the pioneer on his conquering way westward, hewing at an interminable wilderness that was matched only by his ambitions.

Such swift expansions, such mounting romanticisms of temper, must inevitably provide themselves with correspondent philosophies to phrase the new aspirations. The nineteenth century was not content to think in the narrower terms of the eighteenth, but must refashion its thought to suit the romantic style. The modes which it came to accept were for the most part of European origin, adapted to new-world needs. From France and England, and later from Germany, came variant schools of romantic theory that at bottom were a common glorification of the ideal of individualism; and this very diversity of interpretation made possible in America an appeal to different classes and diverse interests, the sum total of which was a many-sided contribution to social theory, but a contribution which carried within it the seeds of later conflict.

The first stage in the romanticization of American thought resulted from the naturalization of French revolutionary theory. Its devious progress through the country can be traced fairly accurately. Landing first in Virginia in the early seventeen-seventies, it met with a hospitable reception from the generous planter society and spread widely there the fashion of Physiocratic agrarianism. Traveling thence westward into the Inland Empire it domesticated itself in frontier log cabins under the guise of an assertive individualism, to issue later as the coon-skin democracy of the Jacksonian revolution. Eventually reaching New England, the last haven and refuge of eighteenth-century realism, it disarmed Yankee antagonism by assuming the dress of Unitarianism and preached the doctrine of human perfectibility with such conviction as to arouse the conscience of New England to an extraordinary enthusiasm for reforming man and society. And coming finally to New York it inoculated the mind of the emerging proletariat with its doctrine of the rights of man, with Fourieristic and other Utopias, and turmoiled contemporary politics with equalitarian Locofoco programs. No other philosophy assumed so many and such attractive disguises, or wrought such changes in American ideals, as this French romanticism with its generous humanitarian impulses. The ground was ready for the seed it was to sow, and if in the judgment of a hostile philosophy the crop turned out to be tares, increasing thousands believed it to be excellent wheat, to the growing of which America was to be dedicated henceforth.

The rival philosophy, which came to view with increasing dislike the doctrines of French romanticism, was of English middle-class origin and sprang from the long struggle of that class to loose the hands of the landed gentry from control of the state. Phrased persuasively by Adam Smith, it embodied the principle of liberalism as that principle was understood by men of affairs. It conceived of a social Utopia that must result if economic forces were given free play; if governmental restrictions on trade were done away with and individual enterprise were free to buy and sell in the open market. Springing from the same root of individualism that brought forth French romanticism, it flowered in an economics that denied the aspirations of the French school. Assuming as its determining principle the common instinct of acquisitiveness, it set up the economic man as the criterion of conduct and proposed to reorder society to the single end of trade. Thus sanctioned and given free rein, the principle of acquisitiveness set forth on its triumphant march through western civilization. Accepted by the English middle class as the ultimate social philosophy sufficient to all needs, it presented to willing eyes the ideal of exploitation as the goal of social progress.

But transported to America, the new philosophy soon discovered unforeseen obstacles in its path. The acquisitive instinct was here enormously strengthened by the vast unpreëmpted resources lying all about, but unfortunately those resources were too great or too speculative to be exploited by individual effort. Capital was wanting, and unless collective funds were available, exploitation must be slow and inadequate. There was need of the state to further the opening up of western lands and to throw its guardianship about an infant industrialism. Roads and canals could not wait on individual enterprise; tariffs and subsidies could flow only from the government. Hence arose a modification of *laissez faire*, from which resulted the theory that a democratic state stands *in loco parentis* to the economic interests of its citizens, and should guarantee the progressive well-being of strategic groups on whose prosperity depended the common well-being. It was this modification of the English philosophy that the Whig party came to embody in its platform, and which by pooling the interests of western speculators, eastern financiers and New England industrialists, sponsored the "American Plan," a curiously ingenious scheme to milk the cow and divide the milk among those who superintended the milking.

Meanwhile in the imperialistic South was arising a distinctive philosophy, native to the special conditions imposed by slavery, that was to set it apart from both eastern and western economics and draw it inevitably into a narrowing isolation. Frankly defensive in purpose, rejecting alike French equalitarianism and English individualism, it sought to justify the institution of slavery by an appeal to realism and square it to the theory of democracy by analogy with northern industrialism. The conception of a Greek democracy, which was the last citadel of the southern mind, was a skillful compromise between the antagonistic principles of aristocracy and democracy, the most romantic ideal brought forth by our golden age of romance. Assuming the middle-class principle of exploitation as the creative source of every civilization, it proposed to erect a free state on the basis of a slave proletariat after the model of ancient Athens. A democracy, it argued, is possible only among equals. In every society hitherto the inevitable inequality between economic classes has nullified every democratic program.

Master and man, exploiter and exploited, are necessarily opposed in vital economic interests; and this potential clash, this fundamental antagonism of classes, has been intensified by the rise of industrialism. Exploitation has been brutalized by the impersonal wage-system, and the proletariat has been reduced to sodden and embittered beasts. If now as honest realists we recognize frankly that equality cannot exist between inferior and superior races, if we accept the inevitable proletarian status of the Negro, if finally we concede the truism that the lifelong relations between master and slave are more humane than the temporary relations between wage-giver and wage-earner, we shall concern ourselves less with a romantic equalitarianism and more with a rational conception of a democracy of equals that may conceivably erect a civilization worthy of the name.

It was an ingenious theory, but unfortunately it left out of account the ambitions of the middle class, and it was this class that in the end destroyed it. Whether they will it or not, imperialisms have a way of clashing with rival imperialisms. Reality persists though romance may deny it, and in their several programs the three diverse sections of America were driving blindly to a collision. In that bitter collision the dream of the South was destroyed. With the overthrow of the aristocratic principle in its final refuge the ground was cleared of the last vestiges of the eighteenth century. Thenceforth America was to become wholly middle class, and such romance as it might bring forth was to be of another sort.

The literature of this extraordinarily vigorous period we are now to deal with, not in the narrow field of *belles lettres* alone but in the outlying fields of social and political philosophies. The difficulties in the way are many. To endeavor to penetrate critically to the intellectual core of a period, to weigh this romance in realistic scales, to take off the outer wrappings and lay bare the inner truth, is no May-day undertaking. The critic finds himself at every turn confronted by reputations distorted by contemporary praise or censure. In the formal biographies written in that golden age of myth-making, criticism too often gave way to eulogy. Our fathers wrote like gentlemen, but unfortunately too often they believed that in preparing a biography a gentleman was under obligation to speak well of the dead. No blemishes were to be recognized, no disagreeable truths to find a place in their immaculate pages. In consequence scarcely a single commentary of the times is to be trusted, and the critic is reduced to patching together his account out of scanty odds and ends, or else settling down to do a series of full-length portraits, in which work, quite evidently, he will not get far. The inadequacies of the present study I am painfully conscious of: its omissions, its doubtful interpretations, its hasty generalizations, its downright guesses; but in the present lack of exact knowledge of the history of American letters, I do not see how such inadequacies can be avoided.

CONTENTS

Charleston, yet loyal to the Charleston parochialisms.
A realist hampered by the current romanticisms. The
most virile figure of the old South. A rich and generous
nature—likeness to Fielding. The picaresque note in his
work. Reasons for his exploitation of "blood-pudding."
Lieutenant Porgy. His two major themes: his special
frontier compared with Cooper's; his revolutionary tales.
His treatment of the Indian. *The Yemassee,* compared
with Cooper. Later life

PART III

THE ROMANCE OF THE WEST

I. New Worlds

II. Two Spokesmen of the West

III. The Frontier in Letters:

Book II: The Mind of the Middle East

Book III: The Mind of New England

The New England renaissance the last expression in America of eighteenth-century revolutionary thought. Given a native ethical bias. Twin tendencies of earlier New England. Static conditions of life—the renaissance a movement of liberalism, shaped by the Puritan strain $\qquad$ 261

PART I

THE TWILIGHT OF FEDERALISM

PART II

THE RISE OF LIBERALISM

PART III
THE TRANSCENDENTAL MIND

xxiii

character. An intellectual child of eighteenth-century romanticisms—influence of Goethe. Transcendentalism —Brook Farm. *Woman in the Nineteenth Century* and feminism. Work as a critic. Career in Europe. Influence of Jean Jacques. The price of her rebellions 418

PART IV

OTHER ASPECTS OF THE NEW ENGLAND MIND

I. THE REIGN OF THE GENTEEL

II. NATHANIEL HAWTHORNE—Skeptic:

III. THE AUTHENTIC BRAHMIN

reform. His escape to London—the final Lowell an
English liberal

BOOK ONE

The Mind of the South

To those who follow the main-traveled road of American experience, as we know it today, the mind of the old South seems curiously remote. It is so archaic, so wholly apart from all present-day ambitions, as to appear singular. Yet the continental highways we now travel so familiarly, it must be remembered, were not the highways of an earlier America. It is the North that has changed, and not the South, and the nationality that sits so easily upon us would have seemed ominous to the simpler world that determined the ideals of the Old Dominion. The southern mind has grown old-fashioned, but it is native and of long and honorable descent. It derived its singularity from the eighteenth century in which it took shape; and it retained the clear impress of its origins long after the eighteenth century had become an anachronism in America. It was primarily political, of the French rather than the English school; but it was economic also, out of Quesnay and Du Pont de Nemours rather than Adam Smith, with a frank bias towards the Physiocratic agrarianism that was so congenial to the needs and temper of a plantation society; and this political agrarianism, parochial in its outlook rather than national, suffices to explain the singularity of the southern mind in the eyes of a later industrialized America.

Simple and homogeneous in the early years of the nineteenth century, it nevertheless carried the seeds of disruption within it. Beneath the surface of this common political agrarianism disintegrating forces were at work, that were to produce broad cleavages of thought and lead to sharp differences of outlook and polity. An old South and a new South dwelt side by side, and to the West lay a frontier that took particular form as it came under the determining influence of one or the other. Virginia and South Carolina were the germinal centers of southern culture, from which issued the creative ideas that gave special forms

3

to the brood of frontier states. Kentucky and Tennessee were the intellectual heirs of Virginia; Alabama and Mississippi were the intellectual heirs of South Carolina. Of these two schools of thought that looked in different directions and sought different ends, Jefferson and Calhoun were the intellectual leaders; and the contrasts in their philosophies—the rejection by the latter of equalitarian idealism, and the substitution of economic realism—mark the diverse tendencies which in the end disrupted the South. Jackson and Lincoln were followers of the Jeffersonian school; Jefferson Davis finally went with Calhoun; and Henry Clay, lacking an adequate philosophy, wavered between them. The differences between these men were open and patent, and any analysis of the mind of the South, any attempt to understand the conflict of tendencies that marked the development of southern thought between 1800 and 1860, must give due weight to such differences. The problem, therefore, instead of being single is threefold, and involves an examination of the mind of Virginia, the mind of South Carolina, and the mind of the new West from the Ohio River to the Gulf.

PART ONE
THE VIRGINIA RENAISSANCE

CHAPTER I

The Old Dominion

The history of the Old Dominion is an easy chapter in the textbook of economic determinism. It is a modern instance that exemplifies the law of land distribution and political control as laid down by James Harrington; it is another Oceana seated by the James River, that would not suffer a king to rule because gentlemen held the land and acknowledged no feudal dues or royal prerogatives. On the surface its history seems little more than a bundle of paradoxes. From the raw materials of English middle-class stock it created a distinguished and capable aristocracy, that was restrained from feudal tyranny by a vigorous yeomanry that held its land in fee simple and stoutly maintained its rights. Established on a slave economy, it adopted an agrarian economy, espoused a republic, and accepted the doctrine of democratic equalitarianism. It was generous, humanitarian, independent; parochial in its jealousies, yet farsighted in outlook; tenacious of its authority and quick to defend it, yet never mean or grasping. During the noonday of its power its influence was always on the side of local democratic freedom and the common well-being. It opposed the encroachments of the centralizing state and the spirit of capitalistic exploitation; yet its domestic economy rested on the most primitive of all exploitation.

But these paradoxes disappear when the history of Virginia is interpreted in the light of its land economy. By force of circumstances the Old Dominion became broadly American in its social philosophy, the interpreter of America to herself. Native conditions created there a native psychology, and this native psychology spread widely through the frontier states where a like economics provided suitable breeding places. Virginia was the mother of the argarian West, as New York, Philadelphia, and Boston were the progenitors of the mercantile and industrial East; and in the frequent clashes between country and town, between agrarianism and capitalism, the ideas of Virginia have commonly opposed the ideas of the northern cities. Between the older colonial America and later industrial America, stand the ideals of the Old Dominion, more humane and generous than either, disseminating the principles of French romantic philosophy, and instilling into the provincial American mind, static and stagnant in the grip of English colonialism, the ideal of democratic equalitarianism and the hope of humane progress. The nineteenth century first entered America by way of the James River.

The renaissance in Virginia began with the transition from middle-class to plantation ideals that marked the last half of the eighteenth century; and it was given intellectual stimulus by the libertarian natural-rights philosophy that in England and France was undermining the old order. There were no cities either mercantile or social, in the Old Dominion, and no industrialism. Life everywhere centered in the plantation. The navigable rivers of the tide-water region were favorable to the development of a decentralized economics, and in spite of royal commands to create adequate seaports, and heavy taxes by the commonwealth, trading towns did not prosper. For two hundred years Virginia refused to create a native middleman group to handle its staples, but preferred to deal through British factors and ship directly, preferably in Dutch bottoms. Each planter insisted on putting his hogsheads of tobacco aboard ship at his own wharf, and receiving his merchandise direct from London. The system was wasteful, and Madison was active in an attempt to limit by law the ports of entry to two, in order to build up a middleman machinery; but the plan broke on the fixed prejudices of plantation masters who had come to share the old English dislike of tradesmen. Virginia stubbornly refused to adopt middle-class methods, even though refusal cost her dear. She preferred to be exploited by British factors rather than create a domestic class to devour her resources.

The system had grown up in earlier times when the merchant spirit was strong in Virginia. It is often assumed that the Virginia aristocracy was descended from emigrant

Cavaliers who fled from England during the commonwealth period; but the facts of history do not bear out such a theory. It was descended largely from vigorous middle-class stock—from men who had been merchants in England and in turning planters brought to the business qualities that had been developed in mercantile pursuits. In the seventeenth century Virginia society exhibited few of the usual charac teristics of the Cavalier. It was frankly *bourgeois*, pushing, avaricious, keen in driving hard bargains, with no high sense of honor, canny rather than impulsive, preferring the law to the duel, hating war and only half-hearted in defense against the Indians—a little world of London burgesses new seated on the banks of the James and the Rappahannock. "Beyond doubt," concludes a recent student, "the most numerous section of the Virginia aristocracy was derived from the English merchant class" (Thomas J. Wertenbaker, *Patrician and Plebeian in Virginia*, p. 28), pretty much the same class that settled Boston and Philadelphia. For a hundred and fifty years these merchant ideals characterized Virginia so- ciety. Speculation in land was universal; exploitation was open and shameless; the highest officials took advantage of their positions to loot the public domain, resorting to divers sharp practices from tax dodging to outright theft. One gentleman added a cipher to a grant for two thousand acres, and although the fraud was commonly known, so great was his influence that no one disputed his title to twenty thousand acres. While governor, Alexander Spots- wood issued patents for sixty thousand acres to dummy holders, who deeded the land to him after he had retired from office.[1]

In the third quarter of the eighteenth century such prac- tices came to an end. The merchant spirit died out among the Virginia planters, and the Cavalier spirit took its place. A high sense of personal and civic honor became the hall- mark of the landed aristocracy, and for upwards of a hundred years this common code gave to Virginia an enviable dis- tinction. Both in national and commonwealth politics her representatives were clean-handed and jealous to deserve the public faith reposed in them. Among the planters were good business men, of course, notably Washington, who under his stately manners concealed a capable mind for speculative affairs. He engaged in various enterprises; speculated heavily in western lands; was president of the Potomac Company,

[1] For these and other facts, see Wertenbaker's book (mentioned above), pp. 95–99.

7

organized to improve navigation and connect his holdings with salt water; and at his death was one of the wealthiest men in America. But such a career was very unusual in Virginia after the Revolutionary War. Washington, indeed, may properly be regarded as the last of the eighteenth-century gentlemen, who like Colonel William Byrd was interested in accumulating vast holdings as well as cultivating his plantation. Even more characteristic of an earlier day was John Marshall, the last of the great Virginia Federalists, who was nearer akin to Robert Morris, with whom he had business dealings, than with Jefferson or John Randolph of Roanoke.

The opportunity for such careers in Virginia was passing. Population was draining off into the West and few immigrants came to settle. With no rapidly growing cities the incentive to speculate in unearned increment was lacking and liquid capital was inadequate. The economics of plantation life developed agrarian rather than capitalistic interests. In the midst of a rapidly changing America, a world given over to exploitation, increasingly middle class and contemptuous of the older aristocratic order, the Old Dominion remained static and unchanging. The plantation aristocracy was marooned by the rising tide. It repudiated the ways of trade and industry and sharply criticised the North for its plebeian spirit. "Commerce is certainly beneficial to society in a secondary degree," said Governor Tyler in 1810, addressing the Virginia legislature, "but it produces also what is called citizens of the world—the worst citizens in the world" (quoted in Wertenbaker, *Patrician and Plebeian in Virginia*, p. 102). Enterprising young men who a generation before would have been strong Federalists and supported the new capitalism, found such an atmosphere stifling and migrated to the new South—to Kentucky, Tennessee, Mississippi, or farther West still, where greater opportunity awaited them. Virginia produced no more Washingtons or Marshalls, but turned whole-heartedly to the school of Jefferson, providing the leaders of states-rights agrarianism. She broke off all intellectual alliances with the mercantile and industrial North, and withdrew within her own plantation world.

Purged thus of its Federalist remnant Virginia became increasingly libertarian in its social and political philosophy. Its mind had taken form at the time when French humanitarianism was in the air, and it discovered much in the new philosophy that appealed to its romantic spirit. A quick and jealous concern for personal liberty and the rights of man was a common passion. The gentlemen of the Old Dominion were bound together by caste solidarity, but they remained strikingly individual, never amenable to group coercion, expressing their convictions freely and ready to uphold their views by the code of the duel. "No people ever lived," said Alexander H. Stephens in 1867, "more devoted to the principles of liberty, secured by free democratic institutions, than the people of the South" (*Constitutional View*, etc., Vol. I, p. 539). The right of dissent from majority opinion was the imprescriptible right of every gentleman. In no other part of America could the career of John Randolph be parallel—a free-lance critic of polticians and political measures, who turned his caustic wit against whom he would, an arch individualist in opinions as other Americans were in acquisitiveness. Politics was an absorbing game in Virginia. Debarred from commercial pursuits, ambitious young Virginians went in for law and politics, with an eye upon a congenial career at Washington. This serves to explain the long predominance of southern leadership in the national government. For two generations the South provided a surprising number of first-class men whose influence was commanding. Until the problem of slavery became acute, and leadership passed from moderate Virginians to Fire Eaters from further south, the influence of Virginia at Washington was thrown on the side of republican simplicity, low taxes and the decentralization of power. The armed clash over slavery very probably might have been averted if the spirit of the Old Dominion had prevailed.

CHAPTER II

The Heritage of Jeffersonianism

I

To the young Virginia Republicans of the year 1800, Jeffersonianism seemed to be a comprehensive social philosophy peculiarly adapted to their needs. It offered a practical and humane program of national development in harmony with existing fact and native genius. It had not yet been distorted by the caprice of circumstance into a somewhat nebulous idealism, nor confined within the narrower limits of political equalitarianism and states-rights theory. By later generations Jefferson has been interpreted too exclusively in terms of the Declaration of Independence, the glowing idealism of which has proved curiously elastic and has been stretched by later libertarian movements to meet their special and particular ends: by the Jacksonian democracy in their struggle for manhood suffrage; by the Abolitionists in their attack upon a slave-sanctioning Constitution; by other idealists in their various crusades. The great name of Jefferson, in consequence, has come to be commonly associated with the conception of democracy and the ideal of social justice. But to his young Virginia followers in the morning of the Republican movement, the perennial suggestiveness of their leader lay in the fact that he embodied for them the many-sided liberalism of French revolutionary thought, its economic and social idealisms equally with political. They interpreted him more adequately, for they understood, as later interpreters frequently have not, how deeply the roots of his natural-rights philosophy went down into current economics. Of the different French writers who gave shape and substance to his thinking, the strongest creative influence on the mature Jefferson came from the Physiocratic group, from Quesnay, Condorcet, Mirabeau, Du Pont de Nemours, the brilliant founders of an economy that was primarily social rather than narrowly industrial or financial. Historically the Physiocratic school is as sharply aligned with idealistic agrarianism as the Manchester school is aligned with capitalistic industrialism. The conception that agriculture is the single productive form of labor, that from it alone comes the *produit net* or ultimate net labor increment, and that bankers, manufacturers and middlemen belong to the class of sterile workers, profoundly impressed the Virginia mind, bred up in a plantation economy and concerned for the welfare and dignity of agriculture.

Franklin had first given currency to the Physiocratic theory in America a generation earlier, but it was Jefferson who spread it widely among the Virginia planters. He did more; he provided the new agrarianism with a politics and a sociology. From the wealth of French writers he formulated a complete libertarian philosophy. His receptive mind was saturated with romantic idealism which assumed native, congenial form in precipitation. From Rousseau, Godwin and Paine, as well as from Quesnay and Condorcet, came the idea of political justice and the conception of a minimized political state, assuming slightly different forms from filtering through different minds. The early doctrine of *laissez faire, laissez passer*—a phrase given currency by Gournay, the godfather of the Physiocratic school—proved to be curiously fruitful in the field of political speculation, as in economic. From it issued a sanction for natural rights, the theory of progress, the law of justice, and the principle of freedom. The right of coercion was restricted by it to the narrowest limits, and the political state was shorn of all arbitrary power. "Authority," the Physiocratic thinkers concluded, "should only employ the force of the community to compel madmen and depraved men to make their conduct conform to the principles of justice."

So far Jefferson went gladly with the Physiocrats, but in their acceptance of a benevolent despotism he discovered a denial of their first principles, and turned to the more congenial democratic group. With the political principles of Godwin and Paine he was in hearty accord. With them he accepted as an historical fact the principle that government is everywhere and always at war with natural freedom, and from this he deduced the characteristic doctrine that the lover of freedom will be jealous of delegated power, and will seek to hold the political state to strict account. From this same principle, following Paine, he deduced the doctrine of the terminable nature of compact, which he set over against the legal doctrine of inviolability. In this matter French liberalism and English legalism were at opposite poles. Replying to Burke's doctrine of irrevocable compact, Paine had written *The Rights of Man,* which Jefferson did much to popularize in America, and with the broad principles of which he was in complete accord. "The earth belongs in usufruct to the living," Paine had argued, and the dead possess no rights over it. Government from the grave is a negation of the inalienable rights of the newborn; hence social justice demands that a time limit should automatically revoke all compacts. Since no generation can rightly deed away the heritage of the unborn, the natural limit of every compact is the lifetime of the generation ratifying it. "No society," Jefferson said, "can make a perpetual Constitution, or even a perpetual law."

In this suggestive theory of the terminable nature of compact is to be found the philosophical origin of the later

11

doctrine of states rights. However deeply it might be covered over by constitutional lawyers and historians who defended the right of secession, the doctrine was there implicitly, and the southern cause would have been more effectively served if legal refinements had been subordinated to philosophical justification of this fundamental doctrine. With a frank contempt for all legalists Jefferson believed that social well-being was not to be bounded by constitutional limitations or statutory enactments; that political action should be governed by reason rather than by historical precedent. He had discovered that the political state does not remain static, but gathers power by the law of physical attraction; with increasing power it becomes increasingly dangerous to natural freedom; hence a long-established and venerable constitution may become, by reason of its hold upon the popular affection, the most useful of agencies to cloak aggressions on the rights of the people. The love of profits is always seeking to overthrow the rule of justice. Human selfishness persistently distorts civic conduct, warping it from ideal ends. But the shortcomings of existing political states cannot abrogate the law of justice or destroy the love of freedom. To safeguard freedom from encroachment by the political state, and to establish the rule of justice, were always the great and difficult ends that Jefferson aimed at, and as a follower of the Physiocratic school and a Virginia planter he turned naturally to a *laissez-faire* agrarianism in opposition to a centralizing capitalism.

But he was much too sound a political thinker and too sagacious a party leader to rest his case upon abstract theory. In all his later writings and counsels he kept his mind close to economic fact, and the Jeffersonian movement was a long and effective training school in the economic basis of politics. It habituated the motley rank and file of the electorate to think in economic terms and to regard political parties as the instruments of economic groups. This was in keeping with the soundest eighteenth-century tradition, before romantic dogma had divorced politics and realism; and in so far Jefferson agreed with his Federalist opponents, Hamilton and John Adams. A decade of acrimonious debate had made it plain to the common voter that the real struggle in America lay between the rival capitalist and agrarian interests, of which the Federalist and Republican parties were the political instruments. The Congressional enactments of the first twelve years had further clarified the issue. The funding plan had visibly increased the number and wealth of the rising capitalist group. The first banks were being erected and the complex machinery of modern credit—the hated "paper system" that had driven out the traditional metallic currency—was being rapidly built up. A small financial group in the northern cities was growing powerful from discounting and money-brokerage. The truth was slowly coming home to the farmers and small men that war is profitable to the few at the cost of the many; that from the egg of war-financing was hatched a brood of middlemen who exploited the postwar hardships and grew rich from the debts that impoverished the producing farmers. This ambitious class, hitherto negligible in America, was provided with the means to make a vigorous fight; it invoked the political state as an ally, and under Hamilton's leadership used the administration to serve its financial interests. It looked with open hostility upon every agrarian program, was cynical towards French romantic theories, and was restrained by no scruples. To loose the hands of this capable class from the helm of government, to keep America agricultural, and the Federal state secondary in all but necessary police powers to the several commonwealths, was the avowed and logical purpose of the Jeffersonian Republicans.[1]

The leaders of the movement were men who in capacity and training were worthy opponents of the capable Federalists. In surprising number they were from the Old Dominion, gentlemen of the best Virginia stock, who in the last decades of the eighteenth century engrafted upon a generous plantation tradition the Physiocratic doctrines of France. A finer race of gentlemen America has never produced, and it was fortunate for the Jacksonian movement, which produced no notable thinkers and contributed little to political and economic theory, that the preceding generation had given adequate form to the philosophy of agrarianism. That theory took definite shape between 1800 and 1820. In the days of Hamilton's control of the Treasury Department, the agrarian opposition was weakened by the lack of such a theory; but the necessities of the situation were a prod to the young Republicans, and the philosophy of agrarianism rapidly crystallized. In its final form it was an extraordinarily interesting and native expression of two hundred years' experience of a society founded on agriculture—a reasoned defense of an older America against the ambitions of a younger and more vigorous.

[1] See Charles A. Beard, *The Economic Origins of Jeffersonian Democracy,* Chapter XIII.

II
JOHN TAYLOR: *An Agrarian Economist*

The intellectual leader of the young Republicans in the great attack on the economics of Federalism was a thinker too little recognized by later Americans. His just fame has been obscured with the cause for which he labored, and his reputation lies buried with the old agrarian *régime*. Nevertheless John Taylor of Caroline County, Virginia, "the philosopher and statesman of agrarianism," was the most penetrating critic of Hamiltonian finance and the most original economist of his generation. Unambitious, simple, honest, calm and dignified in bearing, he embodied the heroic virtues of the great age of Virginia. In his *Thirty Years' View*, Thomas H. Benton describes him thus:

> I can hardly figure to myself the ideal of a republican statesman more perfect and complete than he was in reality:—plain and solid, a wise counsellor, a ready and vigorous debater, acute and comprehensive, ripe in all historical and political knowledge, innately republican—modest, courteous, benevolent, hospitable,—a skilful, practical farmer, giving his time to his farm and his books, when not called by an emergency to the public service—and returning to his books and his farm when the emergency was over. . . . He belonged to that constellation of great men which shone so brightly in Virginia in his day, and the light of which was not limited to Virginia, or our America, but spread through the bounds of the civilized world. (Chapter XVIII.)

Taylor was a member of Congress at the time of the funding operations and contributed two notable pamphlets to the public discussion: the first, issued in 1793, entitled *An Examination of the Late Proceedings in Congress Respecting the Official Conduct of the Secretary of the Treasury;* the second, issued the following year, entitled *An Inquiry into the Principles and Tendencies of Certain Public Measures.* Twenty years later, in 1814, he embodied his matured convictions in a stout volume, printed at Fredericksburg, entitled *An Inquiry into the Principles and Policy of the Government of the United States.* The work is tediously prolix— dressed, according to Benton, "in a quaint Sir Edward Coke style"—even more tediously moralistic; but in spite of very evident stylistic shortcomings, it deserves, in the opinion of Professor Beard, "to rank among the two or three really historic contributions to political science which have been produced in the United States" (*Economic Origins of Jeffersonian Democracy*, p. 323). It was the last of the eighteenth-

14

century works, solidly reasoned, keeping a main eye upon economics and refusing to wander off into the bog of constitutionalism, concerned rather with the springs and sources of political action and the objectives of political parties. It summed up adequately the agrarian argument against capitalism, analyzed the current tendencies, and provided a convenient handbook for the Jacksonian movement, from which the latter drew freely in the dispute over the Bank.

Like Jefferson's, the agrarianism of Taylor was founded in the Physiocratic economy. He was convinced that the tiller of the soil was the only true economist, and that if republican America were to retain its republican virtues it must guard against every system of exploitation, for in exploitation lay the origin of social caste. America had rid itself of the feudal principle of a landed aristocracy, which in the past had provided the machinery of exploitation, by the abolition of the law of primogeniture and entail, only to be confronted by a graver danger, the new aristocracy of liquid wealth. His main purpose, therefore, was an examination of the sources of power of the capitalistic order, and the successive steps by which it had risen to power. His analysis is acute and reveals a mind concerned with the realities that lie beneath outward appearances. It is the economics of history that concern him most, for as fully as John Adams he was convinced that economics determine the form of the political state. In his analysis of the origins of government, he discovers in every society a master class that becomes the beneficiary of sovereign power: the political state is first erected and thereafter used to safeguard the past acquisitions and to further the present ambitions of a dominant economic group which calls itself an aristorcracy; and such an aristocracy imposes its will upon the exploited mass, crudely by the sword and purse, and subtly by the skillful use of psychology. Once in control of the political state it intrenches itself behind certain fictions which profess to carry moral sanction. This political jugglery plays many tricks to catch the gullible; arrayed in the garb of patriotism, loyalty, obedience to authority, law and order, divine right, it carries a weighty appeal. When these moral fictions fail, the fictions of the law step in, and such doctrines as the sacredness of contract translate the stealings of the master class into vested interests which the state is bound to protect. There is a fine irony in Taylor's implied references to Burke's doctrine of a changeless constitution based on a nonrevocable compact, and Hamilton's doctrine of the public faith, which, he argues, were clearly designed to sacrifice the common good to the interests of a class:

Law enacted for the benefit of a nation, is repealable; but law enacted for the benefit of individuals, though oppressive to a nation, is a charter, and irrepealable. . . . Posterity, being bound by the contracts of its ancestry, in every case which diminishes its rights, man is daily growing less free by a doctrine which never increases them. A government intrusted with the administration of publick affairs for the good of a nation, has a right to deed away that nation for the good of itself or its partisans, by law charters for monopolies or sinecures; and posterity is bound by these deeds. But although an existing generation can never re-assume the liberty or property held by its ancestors, it may recompense itself by abridging, or abolishing the right of its descendants. (Page 61.)

The two theories to which he devotes chief attention are the natural aristocracy theory of John Adams, and the capitalistic aristocracy theory of Hamilton. The first of these takes its bias from stressing the inequality inherent in the nature of men; individuals are biologically unequal; and from this fact Adams deduces that the thrifty rise to opulence and the thriftless sink into poverty by reason of individual qualities. Society can neither keep a strong man down nor thrust a weak man up. Between the rich and the poor, the capable and incapable, a state of war exists, held in check by the strong hand in feudal and monarchical societies, but necessarily open and bitter in a democracy. Hence the inevitable failure of democracy wherever it is tried, and the necessity of nicely calculated checks in a republic to prevent the equal tyranny of an aristocracy and a mob. The second theory, the Hamiltonian, justifies itself by the same theory of human nature. It accepts the fact of social inequality as inherent in men, but it sees no reason to pursue Utopian dreams. Recognizing the universal fact of economic control, it erects the state upon exploitation as preferable to anarchy. This capitalistic state it defends before a gullible public by eloquent appeals to the national faith, the security of property, the fear of lawlessness.

Having thus analyzed the two theories Taylor seeks to cut the ground from under both by arguing that social classes cannot be historically explained by the fact of biological inequality amongst individuals, but rather by accidental opportunity, unscrupulousness, and brute force. All aristocracies, whether feudal, natural, or capitalistic, take their origin and uphold their dominion, not from superior excel-

16

lence or capacity, but from exploitation, that beginning in a small way grows by what it feeds on till it assumes the proportions of a colossus. Exploitation breeds a continually augmenting exploitation that conducts inevitably to caste regimentation. All aristocracies are founded in a social theft. They are not established in the morality of nature, but exist as parasites on the social wealth; they levy upon the producer; and the only preventive is to destroy the foundations on which they rest by taking from them the means of exploitation.

In conjuring up phantom dangers of feudal aristocracies, Taylor pointed out, John Adams was fighting dead issues. No feudal aristocracy could arise in America; land was too plentiful and the quick jealousy of the people would strike it down. The danger to republican institutions was closer at hand; it was the poison of the new capitalism that was spreading its virus through all the veins of the national life. And in order that the American people might know something of the history of this innovating force which they must reckon with, John Taylor proceeded to open to them a page in the economics of capitalism. The aristocracy of credit, founded on "monopoly and incorporation," he pointed out, had arisen first in England with the growing power of the middle class; it had gone forward swiftly in consequence of the Napoleonic wars, and through the agencies of the Bank of England and the Consolidated Debt, it had secured control of the public credit. It had arisen first in America in consequence of the financial disturbance resulting from the Revolutionary War, and had further strengthened its position by the War of 1812. Ambitious men had taken advantage of the national necessities to create an artificial paper system identical with that of England. They had profited immensely from the funding operations and the National Bank; they were setting up their private banks in every city and town, and through the manipulation of credit were taking heavy toll of the national production. A money monopoly was the most dangerous of all monopolies, and the master of all.

Taylor had grown up under the traditional domestic economy. He was habituated to think of production in terms of consumption, and of money as a stable measure of exchange. He could not adjust his mind to the theory of production for profit, of middleman speculation, as socially legitimate; and when that speculation extended to the national currency, and exacted its profits from the medium of exchange, he took

17

alarm. Gold and silver are fairly stable commodities that allow of no sudden increase or diminution, and in consequence a specie currency does not readily lend itself to speculative juggling. But a paper system has no natural limitations. Expanded and contracted at the will of speculators, it subjects the business of the country to the exploitation of money brokers. Vast sums had thus been taken from the people by the funding operations. Gold and silver had been driven out of circulation, and with their disappearance a riot of speculation had begun by which only the brokers had profited. Such was the origin of the new money aristocracy that had already taken possession of the state and was using it for the sole end of exploitation. America must make choice between agrarianism and capitalism; the two were incompatible, John Taylor was convinced, and unless the ambitions of the paper-money aristocracy were held in check, the American producer would come under the heel of middle-class exploitation.

So suggestive was the reasoning of Taylor, so interesting for the light it throws on the agrarian mind of the Virginia Republicans, that it will be well to set down his theses in compact form. As summarized admirably by Professor Beard, his argument runs thus:

1. The masses have always been exploited by ruling classes, royal, ecclesiastical, or feudal, which have been genuine economic castes sustaining their power by psychological devices such as "loyalty to the throne and altar."
2. Within recent times a new class, capitalistic in character, has sprung up, based on exploitation through inflated public paper, bank stock, and a protective tariff, likewise with its psychological devices, "public faith, national integrity, and sacred credit."
3. In the United States, this class was built up by Hamilton's fiscal system, the bank, and protective tariff, all of which are schemes designed to filch wealth from productive labor, particularly labor upon the land.
4. Thus was created a fundamental conflict between the capitalistic and agrarian interests which was the origin of parties in the United States.
5. Having no political principles, capitalism could fraternize with any party that promised protection, and in fact after the victory of the Republicans successfully entrenched itself in power under the new cover.
6. The only remedy is to follow the confiscatory examples of other classes and destroy special privilege without compensation. (*Economic Origins of Jeffersonian Democracy,* p. 351.)

In the great battle of ideas that followed the conflict of interests, the Virginia agrarians armed themselves with trenchant weapons. In intellectual equipment they were a match for the ablest of the Federalists; in social idealism, in generous concern for the *res publica,* or common public business, in sober and practical humanitarianism, they were far superior. Between John Taylor of Virginia, spokesman of planter agrarianism, and Fisher Ames of Massachusetts, spokesman of Boston Federalism, the contrast could scarcely be greater. It is a contrast in social culture, in humane ideals, in interpretations of the native genius of America; and in the comparison it is not the Virginia Republican who suffers.

CHAPTER III

John Marshall
Last of the Virginia Federalists

Unlike John Taylor of Caroline, whose fame lies buried with his cause, the reputation of John Marshall has taken on immense proportions with the later triumph of his principles. There is abundant reason for the veneration in which he has come to be held by present-day disciples of Hamilton. More than any other man he saved the future for Federalism. During the critical years of the Jeffersonian and Jacksonian assaults upon the outworks of nationalism, he held the inner keep of the law, and prepared for the larger victories that came long after he was in his grave. His strategic judicial decisions served as a causeway over which passed the eighteenth-century doctrine of the sovereignty of the law, to unite with the new philosophy of capitalistic exploitation. The turbid waters of frontier leveling and states-rights democracy washed fiercely about him, but he went on quietly with his self-appointed work. He was one man who would not bow his neck to the majority yoke, would not worship the democratic Baal. He profoundly distrusted the principle of confederation. Convinced that the "continental belt" must be buckled tightly, he gave unstinted service to the cause of consolidation. The imperative need of a sovereign political state to curb the disintegrating forces of America was axiomatic in his thinking. Looking upon all democratic aspirations as calculated to destroy federal sovereignty, and convinced that the principle of equalitarianism was a bow strung to wield against society, he stoutly upheld the principle of minority rule as the only practical agency of stable and orderly government. Holding such views it was a matter of high and patriotic duty with Marshall to use his official position to prevent the majority will from endangering interests which were far more sacred in his eyes than any natural rights propagated in the hothouse of French philosophy. He was the last of the old school of Federalists and the first of the new.

That John Marshall should have come out of Virginia is perhaps the most ironical fact in the political history of the Old Dominion. Quite unrepresentative of the dominant planter group that had gone over to Jefferson, bitterly hostile to the agrarian interests that spoke through John Taylor, he was the leader of a small remnant of Virginians who followed Washington through the fierce extremes of party conflict. He was the last and ablest representative of the older middle-class Virginia, given to speculation and intent on money-making, that was being superseded by a cavalier Virginia concerned about quite other things than financial interests. He belonged rather to Boston than to Richmond. His intense prejudices were primarily property prejudices. He was the Fisher Ames of the South, embodying every principle of the dogmatic tie-wig school of New England Federalists. Profoundly influenced by Hamilton and Robert Morris, he seems to have found the Boston group more congenial in temper and outlook. The explanation of his strong property-consciousness is to be discovered both in his material ambitions and his professional interests. He was a business man rather than a planter. He was heavily involved in land speculation and held stock in numerous corporations launched to exploit the resources of the state. Robert Morris, whose daughter married Marshall's younger brother, was his financial adviser and advanced money with which to purchase the Fairfax estate, an investment that cost the buyers the very considerable sum of fourteen thousand pounds and numerous lawsuits. He was a director in banks and a legal adviser in important cases involving property rights. His financial interests overran state boundaries and his political principles followed easily in their train, washing away all local and sectional loyalties.

Like his kinsman Jefferson, Marshall was bred on the Virginia frontier, and to the end of his life he retained the easy and careless democracy of dress and manners that marked his early environment. In his deportment he was far removed from the prim respectability of the Boston Federalists. A friendly, likable man, fond of pitching horseshoes and sitting in a game of cards, he was outwardly a genial member of the crude little Richmond world where politics and law and speculation engrossed the common attention. An easy-going nature, he was wholly wanting in intellectual interests. Strangely ill-read in the law, he was even more ignorant of history and economics and political theory. His mind took an early set, and hardened into rigidity during the reactionary years that lay between Shays's Rebellion and the rise of Napoleon. Of social and humanitarian interests he was utterly devoid. One might as well look for the sap of idealism in a last year's stump as in John Marshall. French romantic philosophy he regarded as the mother of all vicious leveling. There is no indication that he had ever heard of the Physiocratic school of economics, or had looked into the writings of Rousseau or Godwin or Paine. The blind sides of his mind were many; his intellectual contacts were few; yet what he saw and understood he grasped firmly. The narrowness of his outlook intensified the rigidity with which he held to his fixed opinions; and his extraordinary courage coupled with a dominant personality clothed his strategic position as Chief Justice with fateful influence on the later institutional development of America.

Although Marshall's later fame is the fame of a lawyer, he was in reality a politician whom fate in the person of John Adams placed on the Supreme Court bench at a critical moment, where his political opinions translated themselves into the organic law of the land, and shaped the constitution to special and particular ends. Masterful, tenacious, manipulating his fellow judges like putty, he was a judicial sovereign who for thirty-five years molded the plastic constitution to such form as pleased him, and when he died the work was so thoroughly done that later generations have not been able to undo it. His political opinions, therefore, become a matter of very great importance to the historian, for they help to explain the peculiar direction taken by our constitutional development. Materials for a just estimate of his remarkable career were long wanting, but with the appearance of Beveridge's able and explicit *Life of John Marshall* it is now possible to view him in exact historical perspective. Carefully documented, the work is a genial and readable interpretation that will go far to revivify the fame of the great Federalist. And yet in spite of its abundant documentation—drawn perhaps somewhat overmuch from Federalist sources—it is essentially a *biographie à thèse* that is careful to magnify the nationalism of its hero and to minify the property consciousness. It provides a picturesque setting, but it is a bit careless in its evaluation of the rival philosophies then struggling for supremacy. Concerning the economics of the great contest between Federalism and Republicanism it offers very inadequate information, with the result that Jefferson is reduced to the status of a master politician set over against the constructive statesman. The intellectual limitations of the lawyer have reacted in these pages upon his political enemy. Certain of the old Federalist prejudices have come to life again in these entertaining pages.

The two fixed conceptions which dominated Marshall throughout his long career on the bench were the sovereignty of the federal state and the sanctity of private property; and these found their justification in the virulence of his hatred of democracy. No man in America was less democratic in his political convictions. Underneath the free and easy exterior of the Chief Justice was as stalwart a reactionary as ever sat on the Supreme Court bench. He was utterly indifferent to popular views, and he calmly overturned the electoral verdicts of his fellow Americans with the deliberateness of a born autocrat. Not only were his important decisions political opinions, but they were Federalist opinions. America had made definite choice between the Federalist and Republican theories of government. It had repudiated the rule of "gentlemen of principle and property" and set up a very different rule. But to this mandate of the supposedly sovereign people Marshall declined to yield. Defeated at the polls, no longer in control of the executive and legislative branches of the government, Federalism found itself reintrenched in the prejudices of John Marshall. He boldly threw down the gage to the majority will, and when the long fierce struggle was over, he had effectively written into the fundamental law of the land the major tenets of the repudiated philosophy. "Judicial statesmanship," Mr. Beveridge calls these political decisions, and bids us admire statesmanship on the bench; yet the phrase runs so far as to merge the judge in the politican—an honest but somewhat indiscreet admission that the law may be twisted to partisan ends. The frankly political nature of Marshall's decisions was universally recognized at the time, and this explains the intense partisanship they evoked, the fury of the Republicans and the extravagant praise of the Federalists. The so-called Jeffersonian assault on the judiciary, of which so much has been made by the orthodox historians, and which came near to wrecking the system, was not primarily an attack upon the courts but upon political judges who used their places to serve party ends. It is a dangerous thing for the bench to twist the law to partisan or class purposes, yet to this very thing John Marshall was notoriously given.

As a judicial statesman, then, rather than a lawyer, Marshall is to be judged, and to such a business the political historian is more competent than the legalist. His important decisions fall into two main groups: those like Marbury *vs.* Madison that assert the supremacy of the judiciary over the legislature—that is, the power of the Supreme Court to nullify an act of Congress; and those like the Yazoo Fraud case and the Dartmouth College case, that assert the irrevocable nature of contracts. The first was an official pronouncement of the principle that Hamilton had elaborated in *The Federalist,* namely, that the constitution is a law and as such lies within the field of judicial interpretation. This was sound Federalist doctrine, and Marshall welcomed the opportunity to engraft it upon the fundamental law of the land, going far out of his way to bring it within the judicial purview.[1] It was a bold and skillful move, and as Beveridge remarks, it announced a principle that "is wholly and exclusively American. It is America's contribution to the science of the law" (Beveridge, *Life of John Marshall,* p. 142). A contribution, it should be added, which with the multiplying of republican constitutions in the later nineteenth century was pretty generally rejected.

Even more partisanly Federalist were the decisions touching the nature of contract. These reached to the heart of the bitter opposition of the commercial and financial interests to the legislative acts of populistic majorities. Suffering heavily from the post-war confusions, those majorities had struck blindly at the profiteers whose well-feathered nests were securely protected by the law. The revolt was natural and human; a rough sense of social justice lay behind it; but

[1] For an excellent discussion see Beveridge, *Life of John Marshall,* Vol. III, Chap. III.

because it struck at the most prosperous and capable members of society, who held the professional classes in retainer and dominated the agencies of publicity, it aroused an extraordinarily vindictive opposition. Dip into the literature of the seventeen-eighties and nineties anywhere, in the *Anarchiad* and the *Echo* of the Hartford Wits, or the private letters of indignant gentlemen, and the animus of the respectable classes is clamorously revealed. At bottom it was no other than this, that the law of business must be made the law of the land, and that any populistic tampering with such law was wicked and anarchistic. How determining was the spirit in the matter of the Constitutional Convention is sufficiently well known. In the new constitution certain practices of populistic majorities were estopped—the emission of bills of credit and paper money, and laws impairing the obligation of contracts; but such provisions, strictly interpreted, did not reach to all cases. There were still gaps in the law of business through which populistic majorities might force their bills. To stop those gaps and complete the great work of rendering business secure was the problem to which Marshall addressed himself; and in the Yazoo Fraud case and the Dartmouth College case, he brought the long Federalistic struggle to a triumphant issue.

An examination of the first of these two celebrated cases will suffice to reveal the spirit of his judicial statesmanship. The state of Georgia, through its Legislature, had contracted to sell thirty-five million acres of land—the great part of the territory now comprising the states of Alabama and Mississippi—to certain speculative companies "at less than one and one-half cents an acre." The passage of the bill was marked by more than the usual jobbery, so common with a generation fond of looting the public domain. The fraud was so gross that the state of Georgia was thrown into a fury that visited itself upon the corrupt legislators. A new legislature repealed the law and rescinded the contract; but some of the land had already been resold to investors in Boston and Philadelphia, who brought their claims before the Supreme Court. The state of mind in which the chief justice heard the argument is thus suggested by Beveridge: "Marshall was profoundly interested in the stability of contractual obligations. The repudiation of these by the legislature of Virginia had powerfully and permanently influenced his views upon this subject. Also Marshall's own title to part of the Fairfax estate had more than once been in jeopardy. At that very moment a suit affecting the title of his brother's to certain Fairfax lands was pending in Virginia courts" (Vol. III, p. 584). To suggest that a nicer judicial honor would have inhibited Marshall from sitting in the case is perhaps going too far if one accepts the principle of judicial statesmanship. Certainly Marshall discovered none of the scruples that must have troubled George Wythe. In awarding claims for compensation to the investors he held that the act of the Georgia legislature was a contract and as such was inviolable. The crux of the decision, however, lay in the pronouncement that the courts cannot examine the motives that induce legislators to enact a law, that the people are bound by their agents and must suffer the penalties of choosing unwise or corrupt agents. The upshot of the verdict, in plain language, was that a legislative contract is sacred no matter how corruptly got. A curious decision, surely, for one who professed to venerate the common law. A Virginian of the type of John Randolph would never have reasoned thus to a conclusion that laid open the public domain to the deals of clever lobbyists and encouraged the betrayal of official stewardship. He would scarcely have sacrificed the public interests to the law of business.

The bitter hostility which Marshall's decisions aroused in his native commonwealth reveals how far the Virginia of Jefferson had traveled from the Federalism of the commercial North. The states-rights philosophy and the philosophy of consolidation were at swords' points; the agrarian and capitalistic economies were engaged in a mortal duel; that it should have been a Virginian who saved the day for the Hamiltonians, erecting the old Federalism into the law of the land, and conducting by his decisions straight to an augmented, consolidated state, under the shadow of whose power the development of corporate finance might go forward without agrarian let or hindrance, was a bitter brew for the Jeffersonian planters to drink. As Marshall grew old he drew farther away from his fellow Virginians. In his last years he was perhaps the most reactionary man in America. "Should Jackson be elected," he wrote in 1828, "I shall look upon the government as virtually dissolved" (Beveridge, Vol. IV, p. 463). His last hatreds he divided between Old Hickory and the rising democratic movement. He bitterly resisted the spread of manhood suffrage; he would make no change even in the antiquated judicial system of Virginia; he would have no overturning of anything established. A stubborn autocrat he remained to the end, and there was a certain ironic fitness in his last encounter with the executive power. The autocratic lawyer met his match in the autocratic soldier who grimly remarked, "John Marshall has made his decision, now let him enforce it."

Nearly a century has passed since these happenings [concludes Beveridge] and Marshall's attitude now appears to have been that of cold reaction; but he was as honest as he was outspoken in his resistance to democratic reforms. He wanted good government, safe government. He was not in the least concerned in the rule of the people as such. Indeed, he believed that the more they directly controlled public affairs the worse the business of government would be conducted. He feared that sheer majorities would be unjust, intolerant, tyrannical, and he was certain that they would be untrustworthy and freakishly changeable. (Vol. IV, p. 507.)

A strong, resourceful, honest, capable man was John Marshall. In so far there is pretty common agreement. Beyond this, comes in the sundering blade of political theory. Concerning the wisdom of his judicial statesmanship it is idle to expect Federalist and Democrat to agree.

CHAPTER IV

The Older Plantation Mind

I
PLANTATION BACKGROUNDS

The literary renaissance of Virginia began in the late twenties when the English romantic movement reached the quiet plantations. Till then the Virginia mind had lingered pleasantly in the twilight of the liberal eighteenth century, following ways of thought it had learned of revolutionary France, and writing with a leisurely finish it had learned of Augustan England. In that older Virginia dignified sentiment was accepted as the hall-mark of breeding—a sentiment somewhat ornate and consciously elegant, that recognized its obligations to a strict morality, and laid its nosegay at the feet of the pure and beautiful and good. When the Virginian essayed somewhat infrequently to commit his thoughts to paper, he wrote as an old-fashioned gentleman, conscious of his social responsibility, consulting classic standards of taste, and embellishing his sentences with bits of choice Latin. But after the year 1830 sentiment gave place to romance, and dignity to exuberance of fancy. A new generation, trained in the school of Sir Walter Scott, fell to the pleasant task of portraying the familiar plantation life in glowing colors and investing it with romantic charm.

The plantation tradition, it will be remembered, first took shape in the Old Dominion and assumed its salient features at the hands of Virginia romantics. Its development was contemporary with the New England transcendental movement, and in origin and spirit it was as native to Virginia as the philosophy of idealism was native to Massachusetts. Inspired by an overseas romanticism, it accepted the materials it found at hand and transmuted the easy-going plantation life into enduring romance. The work was begun by Kennedy in his idyllic *Swallow Barn*. The picture thus slightly sketched was given stronger colors by Caruthers, and received completer form from John Esten Cooke. From their hands Thomas Nelson Page took his materials to refashion to suit the taste of a later day. No realism added its sobering touches to the romantic picture thus early drawn, and none has since been added. A golden light still lingers upon the old plantation. Memories are still too dear to the Virginian to suffer any lessening of the reputed splendors of *ante bellum* days. The tragedy of a lost cause has woven itself into the older romance and endowed the tradition with an added sanction. It has long since spread beyond the confines of Virginia and become a national possession. North as well as South is so firmly convinced of its authenticity that realism has never had the temerity to meddle with it.[1]

It was a romanticizing age, and in Virginia congenial materials were ready to hand. The distinction of a plantation aristocracy set in the midst of a bucolic republican society, with its genial hospitality, its individuality, its sharp contrasts of whites and blacks, its clutter of cabins for background to the pillared mansion, its wide neighborhood interests, its outdoor life, its patriarchal spirit, was a distinction that no romantic could overlook, the most individual and native picturesque in all America. Life on the planta-

[1] For an excellent study, see Francis Pendleton Gaines, *The Southern Plantation*, 1925.

tion was uncramped by the drab routine and skimpy meanness of the New England farm; it was unsoiled by the coarseness and vulgarity of the frontier; it had none of the sordidness of the middle-class town. It might be wasteful, but it was good material for literature; and hence the Virginia romantic had no need to seek the picturesque in England and Spain, as Irving had done. He had only to pick and choose from the familiar stuff lying all about him, emphasizing the agreeable, overlooking the unpleasant, fashioning his figures and action to suit the ideal of a golden age of plantation society. Yet the result, it must be confessed, is not wholly adequate. Virginia has suffered gravely from the want of a sober realism. It is not so much that the worst did not get into the romantic tradition—shortcomings in Virginia life which even Wirt hints at—as that the best did not get in. The plantation master of the romantics falls grossly short of the reality that Virginia provided. The simple dignity of John Taylor, the ingrained Puritanism of Lee and Jackson, the catholic culture and fine integrity of George Wythe, have been left out of the tradition. The Virginian created by the romantics is absurdly inferior to such men, who by any standard were as admirable a group of gentlemen as America has ever bred. A little honest realism would have corrected the picture, to the advantage of the Old Dominion.

At the time when the romantics were beginning their work of constructing the plantation tradition the intellectual renaissance of Virginia was passing. With the fading of the French influence after 1820 came increasing isolation and a conscious sectionalism. Intellectual discipline and catholic tastes became rarer. Virginia had no share in the revolutionary enthusiasms of the Utopian thirties and forties, when New England expected the Promised Land to appear at the next turn in the road; it received no stimulus from the expansive systems of thought that were setting all Europe in ferment. The new Germany seems to have made no impression on the Virginia mind, neither its philosophical idealism nor its provocative higher criticism. The new interest in social speculation and experiment that arose in Massachusetts with the beginnings of industrialism awakened no response in Virginia. Plantation society was static, and social speculation was unwelcome. The theories of Comte, of Fourier, of Owen were unknown; Utopian experiments were untried. If Virginia escaped the curse of industrialism it lacked the intellectual stimulus that came

28

to New England with the rise of the textile mills. Social unrest bred no protests against the plantation order. The revolutionary mood was gone, and after 1820 the stimulus to intellectual life grew weaker. English romanticism as exemplified in the work of Scott and Tom Moore was the single foreign influence that spread amongst the plantations, and the new literature accepted the cult of the picturesque romantic. With the passing of the great age of Virginia the tradition of her greatness remained to be gathered up and preserved.

II
WILLIAM WIRT

To Virginia gentlemen of the old school it must have seemed a bit ironical that William Wirt should have come to be accepted as the literary representative of the Old Dominion in the days of John Randolph of Roanoke. Born in Maryland in 1772 of Swiss parentage, Wirt belonged to Virginia only by adoption, and although on terms of intimacy with the plantation gentry he embodied few of the traits that went to the making of the plantation tradition. In temperament he was far removed from the easy-going planter. A certain canny thrift marked him, a pronounced desire to rise in the world and cut a distinguished figure. He was careful to make a good investment of his talents, attentive to profitable undertakings, whether in law or eloquence or speculation. His mature life ran a singularly prosperous and dignified course. He gathered property and reputation and office, and in every position he acquitted himself honorably. To do less than well in any undertaking he would have accounted a stain upon his reputation. In every company he made himself liked. There was none of the aggressive individualism of John Randolph, in wait for an opportunity to send home a shaft of rankling wit, but always a studious concern to please. He was troubled that anyone should think his criticism severe in *The British Spy,* and he hesitated long before publishing his *Patrick Henry* for fear offense would be taken at the few blemishes he discovered in his hero. An honest man and a capable, sterling after his kind but not notably intellectual, not creative, he owed his advancement to very practical qualities: an engaging personality and genial wit, a knack at formal oratory, a graceful pen, a persevering pursuit of his profession, the cultivation of desirable friendships. An excellent lawyer, he never turned aside from the law to meddle with politics; yet he was on good terms with the politicians, and he reached the top of his ambition by appointment to the Attorney-Generalship of the United States, a post which he held for upwards of twelve years.

In training and culture Wirt was of the sound eighteenth-century tradition. He was bred in the classics, English literature, and the common law. When he set up in his profession his library consisted of Blackstone, *Don Quixote,* and *Tristram Shandy.* His literary taste was formed by the later writers of the eighteenth century, by Gray, Hervey, Young, Ossian, Burke, Sterne, rather than by Pope and Dryden. In *The British Spy* he praises Bacon highly and lavishes commendation upon Addison, regretting that the *Spectator* "should be thrown by, and almost entirely forgotten, while the gilded blasphemies of infidels, and the 'noontide trances' of pernicious theorists, are hailed with rapture, and echoed around the world" (*Letter X*). Yet the determining influence in his own writings, it is clear, came from the sentimentalists and from Burke. From the former he caught the note of polite emotion and from the latter the strain of sonorous eloquence. His well-bred sensibilities were constantly in the service of his pen or tongue, to lend pathos to an affecting bit of description or to transport his hearers by a melting appeal. A look, a gesture, a pose, was nicely calculated to bring sympathetic tears to the eyes of his auditors. To touch the emotions he considered the triumph of art, and to conduct through the emotions to a sound morality, its sole justification.

As a member of the Virginia bar Wirt took pride in the tradition of sober culture that had grown up amongst its distinguished practitioners. The members of that bar were gentlemen as well as lawyers, who would rather go wrong in their legal authorities than in their classical embellishments; they were orators as well, careful of their diction and meticulous in rounding a period. In these excellent qualities Wirt early distinguished himself. He had read more than most, and apposite quotations from the classics came easily to his pen to grace the pellucid flow of his English. One of the signal triumphs of his life was when in an elaborate legal argument before the Supreme Court at Washington, he retorted a passage of the *Aeneid* upon his opponent, to provide a text for a burst of the exuberant rhetoric that so delighted his generation (*The British Spy,* 1855, pp. 88–90). His love of ornate speech seems to us curiously old-fashioned, yet it was the manner of the times, and he gave himself to it with enthusiasm—*vivo gurgite exundans,* as he would have chosen to say. The chief interest of his life was oratory, and how skillful a practitioner he was adjudged by his own generation is revealed in the comment of a contemporary who often admired "the blaze of his reasoning and declamation":

The march of his mind is direct to its object, the evolutions by which he attains it, are so new and beautiful, and apparently necessary to the occasion, that your admiration is kept alive, your fancy delighted, and your judgment convinced, through every stage of the process. . . . There is no weak point in his array, no chink in the whole line of his extended works. Then the sweet melody of voice, the beautiful decorations of fancy, the easy play of a powerful reason, by which all this is accomplished, amaze and delight. His pathos is natural and impressive; there is a pastoral simplicity and tenderness in his pictures of distress, when he describes female innocence, helplessness, and beauty, which the husband on whom she smiled should have guarded from even the winds of heaven which might visit it too roughly, "shivering at midnight on the winter banks of the Ohio, and mingling her tears with the torrent, which froze as they fell;" it is not a theatrical trick, to move a fleeting pity, but a deep and impressive appeal to the dignified charities of our nature. (*Ibid.,* pp. 84–85.)

Wirt's literary reputation rests chiefly upon *The British Spy* and *Sketches of the Life and Character of Patrick Henry,* both of which may be characterized in the admirable phrase above quoted, as studies in "the dignified charities of our nature." The former was done hastily at the age of thirty, the latter was toiled over for years and appeared when he was forty-five. They were received with vast approval and set him quite in the front rank of American literary fame. Yet the contemporary popularity of *The British Spy* is inexplicable to us today. It is astonishing that so slight a thing should have achieved so great a reputation, and it suggests the depths of literary poverty in which the Virginia of 1803 was sunk. The work is miscellany—hodgepodge perhaps is a juster term—of character sketches, geology, description, rhapsody, moralizing, with the faintest suggestion of criticism. The sketch which achieved the greatest celebrity, the description of the blind preacher (*Letter VII,* pp. 195–202), is elaborately artificial and sentimental, done from Sterne. The sketches of contemporary politicians, and in particular that of Jefferson, contributed much to current appeal, and the casual criticism aroused a mild remonstrance. There is a certain grace of style after the late eighteenth-century manner, abundant sentiment and little wit. Perhaps the happiest touch is the title; only a British spy could discover material for criticism in the excellent life and ideal institutions of Virginia, or insinuate that the commonwealth was lacking in public spirit—that its roads were as bad as its schools, and that the "one object throughout the state" was "to grow rich." But it was a very moral spy who was troubled that "the noxious weed of infidelity had struck a deep, a fatal root, and spread its pestilential branches far around"; and who lamented that "our eccentric and fanciful countryman, Godwin, had contributed not a little to water and cherish this pernicious exotic" (*Letter VII*, p. 203).

The demands made upon the dignified charities of our nature Wirt found more insistent when he came to write the life of Patrick Henry. He was troubled by his materials, as well as by the want of them. He complains repeatedly in his letters of the difficulties of the task. There were blemishes in the character of his god, spots that marred his divinity; yet how to clean them away and not spoil the natural appearance was a problem. He could not tell Virginians that Patrick Henry in his old age was grasping and vain, that he changed his politics as he grew rich. The idea was too repugnant to his own good nature, and to the taste of the times. The age was sentimental and romantic even in its eulogy. It took seriously the motto, *de mortuis nil nisi bonum;* it was patriotically engaged in making a myth out of the figures and events of the Revolution; and sober truth is not to be expected from the stately biographies that emerged from this period of excessive patriotism. The writers were too much in awe of their subjects, too much concerned to present them in full dress with wig and cloak and sword, and see to it that they acted a proper part. It was in this attitude that Wirt first approached his theme, but failing to achieve the desired result, he turned the work into eulogy of Henry's oratory. This was the most congenial of tasks to one so deeply interested in the art of the orator. The fragmentary records that had come down were a challenge to his inventiveness, and he set himself to re-create the lost speeches, from scanty notes. How admirably he succeeded is shown in the celebrated "give me liberty, or give me death" speech, that became at once an American classic. One could forgive him much for such a masterpiece.

The leaders of that older Virginia society were lawyers rather than planters, and Wirt's excursions into the field of *belles lettres* were only pleasant outings from the court-room. His intellectual interests were narrow. Though bred in an atmosphere of politics, he cared nothing for political theory, was wholly unread in the political classics, and untouched by the flood of social speculation that came with the French Revolution. He drifted politically with the stream of his generation, taking color from the changing waters. Brought up a Jeffersonian Republican, he remained curiously ignorant of the economic and political philosophy of agrarianism. He was little given to abstract speculation on the rights of man, and was never partisan to a cause. He was a genial embodiment of those colorless times when the enthusiasms of eighteenth-century liberalism were dead and the romanticisms of nineteenth-century exploitation were not yet risen, known in the history books as the era of good feeling. Fundamentally conservative and somewhat conventional, he would not look with approval upon the new men and new ways that came in with the western democracy. Upon the accession of Jackson he went over to the Whig party. He supported Clay, yet for some reason, perhaps a harmless vanity, he accepted a nomination for the presidency by the Anti-Masons in 1832 and went down before the hosts of the Jacksonians. Two years later his blameless life was brought to a close. A kindly and honorable gentleman of old-fashioned tastes, with a culture founded in Blackstone, embellished by Addison and Sterne, and given a classic dignity by Livy, he filled the measure of the excellencies as they were understood in the Old Dominion in the days before romance had created the plantation tradition.

III

NATHANIEL BEVERLEY TUCKER: *A Virginia Fire Eater*

In striking contrast to the amiable Attorney-General was another Virginia lawyer and judge who ventured into literature and whose one important novel created a mighty stir in its day. Beverley Tucker was twelve years younger than Wirt. Half brother of John Randolph of Roanoke, for some years on the bench in Missouri, and long professor of law at William and Mary College, he was a well-known figure in the Old Dominion, and his vigorous speech was much applauded at conventions where southern gentlemen met to talk over their grievances. In him were richly embodied all the picturesque parochialisms that plantation life encouraged. He was so completely and exclusively Virginian as to deserve the epithet "Virginianissimus." He never traveled, never compared diverse civilizations, never questioned the excellence of that in which he had been bred. His loyalty to his native commonwealth was a consuming jealousy for its honor, and he tucked the horizons of Virginia about him like a Hudson's Bay blanket and defied the cold winds of the North. Beyond Mason and Dixon's line lay a foreign country, and he judged all foreign countries by their size and color on his wall map. He was the arch-romantic of his generation and his *Partisan Leader* is the repository of the curious political and economic romanticisms of the ardent southern mind.

Over his after-dinner bottle of Madeira, Beverley Tucker may well have been the raciest and most delightful of companions. Like Samuel Johnson, he found his pleasure in a mind well stocked with robust prejudices and a wit to phrase them tellingly. He never spared his epithets nor hesitated to damn an opponent. Like Fisher Ames, he coddled an aggravated case of political spleen and luxuriated in a picturesque pessimism. The clouds hung low over his mind, and the future of Virginia appeared as black to him as the future of Massachusetts appeared desperate to the Boston Federalist. His pessimism no doubt was a solace to his old age and provided a sauce for his dinner. Temperamently he was curiously like the New England Jeremiah. He followed Calhoun with the unreasoning and passionate conviction with which Fisher Ames followed Hamilton. He foresaw a future laid waste by the ravenings of democracy, and like Ames he took pleasure in sketching the dark picture. It would be no fault of his if the easy-going planters remained indifferent to the political monster that in the guise of Jacksonian democracy had made his den at Washington and was preparing to devour the liberties of sovereign commonwealths. He would make haste, while the shadows of those liberties remained, to arouse Virginia to its peril before the jaws closed upon it.

It was to this end that he wrote *The Partisan Leader,* an obvious attempt to dramatize the political philosophy of Calhoun and breathe into it a war psychology. Its single purpose was to popularize the doctrine of secession and encourage Virginia to act upon it. The book was printed at Washington by the notorious Duff Green, who had quitted Jackson and gone over to Calhoun, and appeared under the pen name of Edward William Sidney. Written in the last years of Jackson's second term, it prophesied Van Buren's succession and his setting up a dictatorship. The beginning of the action is projected thirteen years into the future. Van Buren is assumed to be in his third term and is seeking election a fourth time. He is in secure and insolent possession of "the presidential throne." He has surrounded himself with a horde of democratic sycophants; his political machine is well oiled and the army and navy are at his bidding. Virginia has been split asunder by factions. Mercenaries in Van Buren's pay occupy the public stations, and supported by Federal bayonets they carry things with a high hand. The lower South, under the leadership of South Carolina, has already seceded, and freed from the exploitation of northern tariffs is economically rejuvenated. The Virginia patriots are biding their time, working under cover and making detailed plans to carry the commonwealth over to the new Confederacy when the hour shall strike. The hand of fate is no other than economic pressure. The free South has provided an eloquent object lesson to Virginia planters. By reason of a trade treaty with England, by the terms of which each country exports to the other its natural wares unvexed by artificial restrictions—an industrial economy and an agricultural mutually benefiting by the exchange —the cotton and tobacco growers to the south of Virginia are enjoying a prosperity unshared by the exploited planters of the Old Dominion. When economic depression shall have finally opened the eyes of Virginians to the folly of a federal union that sacrifices southern interests to fatten northern manufacturers, the commonwealth must drop into the lap of the Confederacy like a ripe persimmon. In the meantime a mysterious Mr. B.—presumably Calhoun—moves adroitly behind the scenes, shaping matters for the great event—a super-statesman, a man of godlike sagacity and divine benevolence, a heroic embodiment of all the magnanimous southern virtues, compared with whom Webster and Clay are common political mercenaries and Jackson a paltry charlatan.

It is a romantically extravagant book, quite the absurdest in the library of the old South. It possesses no savor of humor or pleasantry of satire. Tucker was too deadly in earnest to play with his theme. He had so long and bitterly brooded over the supposed wrongs of Virginia that he had lost all sense of proportion. He lacks a cool skill in dissection; he has not learned the gentlemanly art of flaying his victim; he defends Virginia with a matchlock instead of a rapier. Gilmore Simms credited him with one of the most finished prose styles of the day, and a very recent critic remarks that "no other American of the time wrote with such classical restraint and pride as Tucker" (*Cambridge History of American Literature,* Vol. I, p. 312). But there is little evidence of such mastery in *The Partisan Leader.* It is the work of an unpracticed writer, with a command of rhetoric to furnish forth a southern stump-speaker, but quite inadequate to the needs of a competent novelist. Compared with Simms or Kennedy he is a mere bungler. His characters are as wooden as Cooper's females, and his plot is grossly distorted by his polemics. The drama sags under the weight of the sacred cause. There is inadvertent comedy in the picture of Van Buren as the man on horseback—the sleek, well-groomed politician of history rises somewhat inadequately to the rôle. In comparison with Kennedy's *Quodlibet* his attack upon Jackson is only caricature. Beverley Tucker was a patriotic Virginian whose craftsmanship proved inadequate to the serious business in hand.

The backgrounds of his thought are clearly Jeffersonian. His prejudices run strongly for eighteenth-century *laissez faire.* He is a confirmed agrarian and his hatred of industrialism amounts to an obsession. He will have nothing to do with protective tariffs that lay a tax upon the planter to aid the manufacturer. In his advocacy of political decentralization he is a disciple of Calhoun, but more pessimistic than his master. Southern interests can be adequately protected, he is convinced, only by a jealous insistence on the sovereign powers of Virginia, and so long as Virginia remains within the centralizing federal Union those sovereign powers will suffer a subtle diminution. The simple-minded and magnanimous southern planter was no match in the political game with unscrupulous and ambitious Northerners. But in certain significant aspects of his political philosophy, Beverley Tucker broke with the Jeffersonian tradition. Two current developments had quite destroyed his faith in the democracy of Jefferson. The rise of Jacksonianism had seated the rabble in power, and the spread of Abolitionism was threatening to infect that triumphant rabble with its poison. The very life of Virginia was at the mercy of a hostile democracy, and to protect themselves and their slaves from the encroachments of a democratized federal government seemed to him the urgent business of the southern planters. Unless a move were made speedily it would be too late, for the power of the northern democracy was fast outstripping the confederate power of the South.

Tucker's intense prejudices color every judgment, and in consequence his misunderstanding of the North was colossal.

He imagined a profit-mongering clown whom he dubbed Yankee, and solemnly assured himself that it was an authentic likeness. The Abolitionist was a Yankee with an added Puritan malignancy. In his defense of slavery Tucker has corrected the sentimental mistake of Jefferson in assuming the extinction of slavery to be desirable, but he professes an equally humanitarian spirit. His benevolence toward the Negro is so warmly generous that one is ready to weep at the sad fate of the faithful slave who is in danger of being turned out into the cold world by the wicked Abolitionists. The loyal attachment between master and servant, he argues, is too finely generous to be understood by the mercenary North. The Yankees "have not the qualities which would enable them to comprehend the negro character. Their calculating selfishness can never understand his disinterested devotion. Their artificial benevolence is no interpreter of the unsophisticated heart. . . . They know no more of the feelings of our slaves, than their fathers could comprehend of the loyalty of the gallant cavaliers from whom we spring; and for the same reason. The generous and self-renouncing must ever be a riddle to the selfish" (p. 205, edition of 1861). Hence it is the clear duty of the magnanimous planter to keep his generous and self-renouncing slaves out of the clutches of the selfish Abolitionists.

Something of the ardency of Beverley Tucker's convictions is revealed in certain fragments of his letters to Gilmore Simms, to whom he poured out his heart in uncensored words, and whose magazine, *The Southern Quarterly Review,* he made use of to further the cause. In those letters he writes himself down a frank and whole-hearted Tory. There is an inveterate and ingrained aristocracy of temperament that will not mince words when it comes to dealing with democracy. In his comment on the growing democratic spirit he is virulent. He has lost all hope for Virginia in the year of grace 1851. "She is sunk in the slough of democracy, which has no sense of honor, no foresight, and is never valiant but against its own instruments" (W. P. Trent, *William Gilmore Simms,* p. 186). Georgia is in an even worse way. His spleen at the commonwealth of Stephens and Toombs—"filled as that State is with Yankee traders"—spits out venom: "She had been bought, and her price is in the pockets of those she trusted." He quotes sardonically the comment of a Georgia senator: "The State of Georgia is a damned rascal. I bought and sold her, and will buy her and sell her again when I please" (*ibid.,*

p. 182). His only hope is in South Carolina, and he pleads with Simms for decisive action. Calhoun's kingdom is singularly blessed, for no base democracy there sullies the purity of manly councils. As early as 1820 Tucker had come to realize that the Union was a curse to the South. "I vowed then, and I have repeated the vow, *de die in diem,* that I will never give rest to my eyes nor slumber to my eyelids until it is shattered into fragments. . . . Time was when I might have been less desperate, because I could have sought refuge under some emperor or king. But all such refuges are broken up, and there is now no escape from the many-headed despotism of numbers, but by a strong and bold stand on the banks of the Potomac. . . . If we will not *have* slaves, we must *be* slaves." He then makes his great appeal:

And what are our democracies but mobs? South Carolina alone can act, because she is the only State in which the gentleman retains his place and influence, and in which the statesman has not been degraded from his post. You are fast coming to that hopeless and irreclaimable condition; and then all hope of action is gone. Work now. . . . The twilight is already upon you, and hence I fear you will not act even *now.* And if not now—never, never, never! (*Ibid.,* p. 187.)

It was not granted to Beverley Tucker to know what harvests were to be gathered from his sowings. He did not live to see the fields of his beloved commonwealth drenched in the blood that he had done more than his share to let. In that bitter struggle it is certain that he would have borne his part valiantly. He had sown to the wind, and he would have welcomed the whirlwind. But the outcome must have broken his proud heart, and it is well that he was not spared to see his hopes turn to ashes in his mouth.

CHAPTER V

Adventures in Romance

I

WILLIAM ALEXANDER CARUTHERS: *A Virginia Liberal*

In the early thirties came the transition in Virginia from
the essay-sketch that had prevailed since the appearance
of *The British Spy*, to the full-blown romance of love and
adventure. The older type had been a blend of nature description, social observation, character sketches, with somewhat injudicious portions of sentiment and moralizing, and
with frequent resort to the old letter-form of fiction that
lingered out a surprising old age. Not only is the transition
revealed in the work of John P. Kennedy, whose *Swallow
Barn*, written in 1832. was followed in 1835 by *Horseshoe
Robinson*, but quite as strikingly in the work of Dr. William
Alexander Caruthers, whose *Kentuckian in New York, or,
the Adventures of Three Southerns*, published in 1834, was
followed at once by *The Cavaliers of Virginia*, 1834–35.

Dr. Caruthers was a genial and cultivated Virginian from
the Piedmont region, with a ready wit and a clever pen, who
had pretty well rid himself of the intense and narrow parochialisms that restricted the sympathies of Beverley Tucker.
He was a Virginia liberal of the older school, before the
renaissance of the slave cause transferred southern leadership to the South Carolina group, and he shared none of
Tucker's partisanship for Calhoun. He had traveled widely
both south and north, and had discovered that human nature
was much the same on both sides of Mason and Dixon's line.
This experience qualified him to become a shrewd and kindly
interpreter of both sections of the country, and his *Kentuckian in New York* was an excellent contribution to the
cause of intersectional good-will. He sends two young South
Carolinians just out of college on a trip north, who fall in
with a Kentuckian on the way, and together they enjoy life

in New York City, lose their hearts and meet with divers romantic and amusing adventures. A fourth character, a young Virginian, he sends to South Carolina, likewise to lose his heart and encounter adventures; and the copious letters that travel between them are filled with intelligent comment on unfamiliar ways. The writers are generous-minded young liberals with keen eyes, and their observations still make excellent reading after nearly a hundred years.

The South Carolinian who falls romantically in love with a New York girl is far from a Calhoun Fire Eater. He can see good even in the Yankee, whom he defends against the common southern prejudice by arguing that Yankee chicanery has resulted from a niggardly environment and the competition that comes with over-population, a competition that Virginia has been spared by the draining off of her population west; and as for the Yankee "canting and sniveling," "tell me," he remarks, "if you have not, in the very bosom of your great valley, as genuine Presbyterians and Round-heads as ever graced the Rump Parliament, or sung a psalm on horseback? And to give the devil his due, these same Presbyterians are no bad citizens of a popular government" (Vol. I, p. 72). Virginia has judged the North out of her prejudices rather than knowledge, and the advice Caruthers gives his Virginia neighbors, as an antidote to the suspicions of Beverley Tucker, is to travel beyond the boundaries of the Old Dominion.

Every southern should visit New-York. It would allay provincial prejudices, and calm his excitement against his northern country-men. The people here are warm-hearted, generous, and enthusiastic, in a degree scarcely inferior to our own southerns. . . . Many of these Yorkers are above local prejudices, and truly consider this as the commercial metropolis of the Union, and all the people of the land as their customers, friends, patrons, and countrymen. Nor is trade the only thing that flourishes. The arts of polished and refined life, refined literature, and the profounder studies of the schoolmen, all have here their distinguished vo-taries,—I say distinguished, with reference to the standard of science in our country. (Vol. I, p. 181.)

The material prosperity of the North contrasts painfully in his mind with the condition of his native Carolina, and there is a note of apprehension in his comment:

The more I see of these northern states, the more I am con-vinced that some great revolution awaits our own cherished com-munities. Revolutions, whether sudden or gradual, are fearful things; we learn to feel attachments to those things which they tear up, as a poor cripple feels attached to the mortified limb, that must be amputated to save his life. A line of demarkation in such a case is distinctly drawn between the diseased and the healthy flesh. Such a line is now drawing between the slave and free states, I fear. God send that the disease may be cured without amputation, and before mortification takes place. I know that this latter is your own belief. What think you now, since you have seen the greater extent of the disease? (Vol. I, p. 165.)

The question is addressed to another young man on his travels, a young Virginian who has gone south, and who is even more troubled at what he finds. He cannot bring himself to think well of the sacred institution as he sees it in South Carolina. There it is laid bare in all its naked exploitation. The humaner relations between the races that he has known in Virginia have been destroyed by the absentee system with its drivers and overseers—"to these animals," he says, "I have always had an utter aversion." The evils of the large-scale system have carried farther; slavery in the Carolinas has destroyed the middle class of yoemen, unduly exalted the aristocracy and utterly debased the poor white. The single spot he heartily approves in the two commonwealths is Salem, a Moravian settlement where no slavery exists, where all work, and where education is thought so well of that the daughters of the first southern families go there for their schooling. In Salem he found an answer to the southern problem far more competent than Nullification.

Here, then, is a triumphant answer—an answer in deeds, instead of words—in the happiness, and the substantial wealth of these simple and primitive Moravians. Here . . . is an industrious, intelligent, and healthy community, in the very heart of all the misery I have described. Let us then improve by the lesson, seek out the sources of their prosperity, find the point where their plans diverge from ours, and, my word for it . . . we become a great, a flourishing, and a happy people. (Vol. I, p. 80.)

To the problem of slavery he returns constantly, and his views may perhaps be sufficiently understood from the following passages:

The poor of a slave-country are the most miserable and the most wretched of all the human family. The grades of society in this state are even farther apart than in Virginia. Here, there is one immense chasm from the rich to the abject poor. In the valley of Virginia, or in the country where you are, there are regular gradations. The very happiest, most useful, and most industrious class of a well-regulated community, is here wanting. Their place

41

is filled up by negroes; in consequence of which, your aristocrats are more aristocratic, and your poor still poorer. The slaves create an immeasurable distance between these two classes, which can never be brought together until this separating cause be removed. You know I am no *abolitionist,* in the incendiary meaning of the term; yet I cannot deny from you and myself, that they are an incubus upon our prosperity. This we would boldly deny, if a Yankee uttered it in our hearing; but to ourselves, we must e'en confess it. If I am, therefore, an abolitionist, it is not for conscience-sake, but from policy and patriotism. (Vol. I, pp. 76–77.)

With us [in Virginia] slavery is tolerable, and has something soothing about it to the heart of the philanthropist; the slaves are more in the condition of tenants to their landlords—they are viewed as rational creatures, and with more kindly feelings. . . . *Here* slavery is intolerable; a single individual owning a hundred or more, and often not knowing them when he sees them. . . . The slaves here are plantation live-stock; not domestic and attached family servants, who have served around the person of the master from the childhood of both. . . . Here, besides your white overseers, you have your black *drivers;*—an odious animal, almost peculiar to the far south. It is horrible to see one slave following another at his work, with a cow-skin dangling at his arm, and occasionally tying him up and flogging him when he does not get through his two tasks a day. . . . I do not observe much difference between the North and South Carolinians, except in the case of those who inhabit the most southern portions of the latter state. There your rich are more princely and aristocratic, and your poor more wretched and degraded; but to tell you the plain truth, many of your little slaveholders are miserably poor and ignorant; and what must be the condition of that negro who is a slave to one of these miserable wretches? (Vol. II, pp. 115–119.)

To the solution of the difficult problem Caruthers offers no easy plan. He cannot go with the northern "enthusiasts" who propose immediate emancipation. They do not comprehend the complexity of the problem. "We cannot set slaves free among us. Such a course would dissolve the social compact. It would set at defiance all laws for the protection of life, liberty, and property, either among them or the whites." He foresaw clearly what happened during the unhappy days of reconstruction. "Would it be any reparation of an hereditary wrong, to plunge the subjects of that wrong, with ourselves, into irretrievable ruin, to attain nominal justice?" The free Negroes would constitute a menace more serious than the northern city mobs, which latter Caruthers had no liking for. "These city mobocracies, composed as they are, principally of wild Irish, are terrible things"; how much worse would be a Negro mobocracy? A confirmed agrarian, he finds his chief hope in a vigorous yeomanry, and until the South shall develop that, matters must go ill with it. In the midst of the Carolina system his thoughts return fondly to his native state. He is under no illusion in regard to the tide-water region of Virginia. It has lived a generous life, but spendthrift and wasteful, and has come to evil days. But in the West, beyond the mountains, a newer and more vigorous age is rising that "will sweep away the melancholy vestiges of a former and more chivalrous and generous age."

Poor, exhausted eastern Virginia! she is in her dotage. Her impassable roads protect her alike from the pity and contempt of foreign travellers; but with all her weakness, with all the imbecilities of premature age upon her, I love her still. (Vol. II, p. 194.)

Of this more vigorous age the prototype is the title-hero of the volume, the stalwart Kentuckian whose native intelligence and racy speech delight the Carolinian. This free son of the untamed West is portrayed with bold strokes, and if his talk leans somewhat heavily on the current convention of frontier humor, if Montgomery Damon in his picturesque exaggerations suggests Davy Crockett, the result is none the less salty. Caruthers does not descend to caricature, but writes with gusto, and the Kentuckian's single letter is a little masterpiece in the vein of the free frontier humor that was competing with the cavalier romantic for popular approval. His whimsicalities, Caruthers tells us, he hopes will encourage "a smile of good-humor" so that this maiden product of the author's pen may find its way into the good graces of the reader—a course reckoned "the more necessary by a southern aspirant, as there is evidently a current in American literature, the fountainhead of which lies north of the Potomac, and in which a southern is compelled to navigate up the stream if he jumps in too far south" (Vol. II, p. 218).

The Cavaliers of Virginia, or the Recluse of Jamestown, announced in the postcript to the *Kentuckian in New York,* and published soon afterwards, is a full-fledged historical romance, with Bacon's Rebellion for a background and a somewhat melodramatic figure of a recluse warrior for its romantic hero. There is brisk action, dramatic Indian fights, much ruffling of young cavaliers, and a fine aristocratic swagger, but Caruthers' sympathies seem to incline to the more democratic elements and in the end his rebellious hero proves himself a match for the brisk young blades. There is excellent reading in it, as there is in his last work, *The Knights of the Horse-Shoe; a Traditionary Tale of the Cocked Hat Gentry in the Old Dominion*, published in 1845, and reissued as late as 1909; a genial story of Governor Spotswood's time. Caruthers deserved a better fate than fell to his lot. In spite of his excellent work surprisingly little is known about him; even the spelling of his name and the date of his death are matters about which there is disagreement. From a slight sketch contributed to *The Knickerbocker Magazine* for July, 1838, *Climbing the Natural Bridge*, it is known that he was a student at Washington College, now Washington and Lee, at Lexington, Virginia, in the year 1818, and the signature affixed carries only one "r." He seems to have removed later to Savannah, Georgia, an enthusiastic description of which he gives in the *Kentuckian in New York*. No doubt he there practiced medicine and died in his prime, perhaps in the year 1846. Virginia historians have inconsiderately neglected a cultivated and open-minded writer who embodied the finer spirit of the Old Dominion and whose stories have contributed their portion to the plantation tradition.

II
JOHN PENDLETON KENNEDY: *A Southern Whig*

A far more prosperous course was run by John P. Kennedy, whose sympathies drew him north rather than south, and who early learned that it is better to serve a rising than a decaying order. Very like Caruthers in temperament and gifts, a liberal in all his sympathies, he found the ties that bound him to the Old Dominion more fragile, and the drift of circumstance carrying him with the stronger current. It was a kindly fate that took him in charge, bringing him abundant prosperity and contemporary fame.

One of the most attractive figures of his generation was this son of a Maryland father and a Virginia mother. A gentleman of much personal distinction, high-minded and of wide culture, endowed with a pleasant wit, easy manners and generous nature, he is an agreeable representative of the *ante bellum* Southerns, an American Victorian of the Cobden-Bright school, standing midway between the northern radical and the southern Fire Eater. Like Henry Clay, he was a Whig engrafted on a Jeffersonian root. Born and educated in Baltimore, he was a son of the borderland, with strong ties of kinship and love that drew him to the Old Dominion, and even stronger ties of intellectual, social and

44

financial interests that drew him towards Philadelphia and New York, Saratoga and Newport. As a young man he found his inspiration in the life of William Wirt, whose biography he afterwards wrote. Like Wirt, he dreamed of combining law and letters and adopting the life of a southern gentleman; but he discovered little that was congenial in the exactions of the law, and in spite of considerable success as attorney for certain Baltimore interests, he largely abandoned the profession. He loved his Chaucer and Shakespeare more than his Coke and Blackstone: he was more interested in Dickens and Thackeray and Carlyle and Irving and Scott than in John Marshall's decisions, and he followed the more congenial path. He tried his hand likewise at politics. He was a member of Congress for six years, was Secretary of the Navy during the last months of President Fillmore's administration, and was of service to the Whig party as spokesman on dignified occasions. But he was never a practical politician, and the rough and tumble of political life he found utterly distasteful. As he grew older he unconsciously drew further away from his southern antecedents. In his later years there was little to distinguish him from Irving and Robert C. Winthrop and other northern friends. He had left the world of Beverley Tucker far behind him. He had severed all ties with Virginia and South Carolina, and during the Civil War he was a militant Unionist, though it cost him much grief and the loss of old friendships.

Kennedy's life ran an unusually placid and prosperous course, greatly unlike that of Gilmore Simms. His father was a Scotch-Irish merchant of Baltimore who married Nancy Pendleton, daughter of an excellent Virginia family with many honorable connections. His early years were not unlike Irving's—a little Latin and Greek and much outdoor life, with a desultory education got from vagrant books. The course of study at the local college afforded far less intellectual stimulus than *Tristram Shandy*, over which he pored of evenings, dissecting the prose style to discover the secret of its charm, and filling his notebooks with elaborately colloquial sentences, highly seasoned with dashes and exclamation points. Graduating at eighteen, he enlisted in a Baltimore regiment to fight the British, who were preparing their raid on Washington. He went through the campaign as a summer lark, emerging unscathed from the single skirmish. The field was lost, but whether the honor of the crack Fifth was left on the battle ground may be judged from Kennedy's humorous comment. "Soon we had the famous 'trial of souls'

—the battle of Bladensburg. The drafted militia ran away at the first fire, and the Fifth Regiment was driven off the field with the bayonet. We made a fine scamper of it. I lost my musket in the mêlée while bearing off a comrade" (Tuckerman, *Life of Kennedy*, p. 79).

Throughout his twenties Kennedy was a studious dilettante in letters and politics and law. He married but lost his wife and son within the year; with his friend Peter Hoffman Cruse he published a series of Baltimore sketches in two volumes entitled *The Red Book;* and at the age of thirty-four married again. His second wife was the daughter of Edward Gray, a wealthy Baltimore cotton-spinner who at the age of eighteen had emigrated from northern Ireland to Philadelphia, became a bank clerk and a Federalist simultaneously, adopted Washington and Hamilton—whom he occasionally met in a professional way—as his particular heroes, prospered greatly, purchased the Ellicott Mills a few miles out of Baltimore, and set up a half feudal estate vastly attractive to discriminating visitors like Irving.

Kennedy's marriage to Elizabeth Gray in 1829 seems to have been the turning-point of his life. Before this he had been a disinterested liberal in his views, concerning himself in a political way with such humanitarian issues as the repeal of the brutal debtor laws. He had never been an avowed Jeffersonian like William Wirt and many of his Virginia connections, but the Jeffersonian idealism must have appealed to the generous sympathies of the young man. Immediately upon being taken into the Gray family he adopted its ample scale of living, its genial hospitality, its social and political philosophy. The influence of the masterful Edward Gray was thenceforth a dominant creative factor in Kennedy's life, and he followed faithfully in the footsteps of his father-in-law. The profits of the Ellicott Mills had been greatly increased by the tariff act of 1824. Naturally Edward Gray was an ardent protectionist, and Kennedy frankly espoused the same policy. He accepted Henry Clay as his political leader, was sent to Congress on a protectionist platform, lectured before Workingmen's Institutes on the advantages of industrial development, and gained a very considerable reputation as an expounder of the American Plan. After the war he became a Republican, voted for Grant, and adopted extreme nationalist views. That the family income was dependent on tariff favors is a detail which only a more realistic generation would suggest in explanation of his political course; the fact remains, nevertheless, that the youthful disciple of William

46

Wirt adopted the new philosophy of prosperity, became president of the board of directors of the Baltimore and Ohio Railway, invested in West Virginia coal lands, and was by way of becoming a captain of industry. The break with his southern antecedents was complete and final; he went with his native city in preferring the industrial to the plantation economy.

Baltimore in Kennedy's day was a thriving port with a growing trade to the West Indies and Europe. It had long been a convenient market for the tobacco of Virginia, and with the development of the clipper service its over-sea commerce expanded greatly. Unlike Charleston, the mercantile interests predominated over the planter. Middle-class ideals, to be sure, were still tempered by the dignified decorum that lingered on from the eighteenth century. Merchants still emulated the gentry and strove for personal distinction. They professed benevolent ideals and their talk was much of public spirit and the progress of the town. They adopted the romantic faith of their class in the beneficent processes of trade and industry in furthering social well-being, and they endowed Mechanics Institutes and founded public libraries and museums with all the ardor of converts. In this agreeable work of expounding the gospel of progress, Kennedy joined heartily. It satisfied the latent idealism of his nature and recompensed him for the loss of his Virginia heritage. Intellectually he was too honest to pervert the gospel of progress to selfish class interest and seek to hide the perversion behind sonorous platitudes, as his friend Robert C. Winthrop of Boston was guilty of doing. He had too much love for the English language to misuse it even in defense of the family income. He could not contract his mind to the compass of a Whig politician's. His defense of industrialism, in consequence, embodies the spirit of the best English liberalism as that liberalism was interpreted by Victorian Englishmen. He seems to have been honestly convinced that the future well-being of America was dependent upon the development of an industrialism to provide an economic balance between manufactures and agriculture.

Like his friend Irving, Kennedy was a devout romantic, with a love of the old-time picturesque; but as a consistent Whig he would spin and weave his romance out of domestic materials, refusing to import. He was a child of the effervescent days following 1812, when the static eighteenth century was breaking up and an ebullient romanticism was permeating the land. Of this youthful period his thought reveals the clear impress. Washington Irving from long pottering over the old-world picturesque had become English romantic, with an inveterate dislike of all innovation. The vulgar nineteenth century was destroying for him the charm of the eighteenth; he would have had the world remain as it was before the American and French revolutions had despoiled life of picturesque feudal ways. Whereas Kennedy, sharing in a romanticism that was economic and social—that was creating a wonderful America of the future out of the raw materials of life—was content to remain native, at home in the land of his birth. He might turn to the past for the figures and scenes of his stories, but he discovered in the activities of the present materials for romance quite as fascinating. He was wholly Victorian in his genial optimism. He was receptive to new ideas and promising ventures. He listened sympathetically to inventors and scientists and promoters. He was instrumental in securing Congressional aid to erect Morse's telegraph line between Washington and his native city. As Secretary of the Navy he provided for Commodore Perry's expedition to Japan, and the expedition to search for Dr. Kane in the Arctic regions. But unfortunately his economic romanticism gradually undermined his literary romanticism; he outgrew his earlier literary ambitions, and the romances of his later life never got written. In the end the gospel of progress was his undoing.

That the generous comfort in which he lived afforded him leisure, means of travel, contact with distinguished people, goes without saying; but that it was favorable to letters is far from clear. Divided interests consumed his energies and kept him an amateur to the last. His literary development was an evolution from a sketchy and humorous Addisonian, with its echoes of the eighteenth century, to the full Victorian romantic. The foreign elements from an earlier time slowly settled to the bottom of the vat and left the pure wine of romance. But it took time. Like other amateurs he was influenced by current literary successes, and was much given to following the changing fashions. His three best-known books, written between the ages of thirty-six and forty-five, are unlike enough to have been written by different men. *Swallow Barn*, like the youthful sketches of *The Red Book*, is Irvingesque, and the Irving influence crops out again in a late book *Quodlibet*; but *Horseshoe Robinson* is substantial Revolutionary romance, done in sober narrative with touches of realism; and *Rob of the Bowl* is light and whimsical cavalier romance, all atmosphere and small talk, utterly unlike Irving. It is in this latter book, perhaps, written in 1838 at the age of forty-two, that Kennedy really found himself; he seems to move through the scenes more easily and with greater delight than in any other of his pages.

That the leisurely sketches of *Swallow Barn* belong to the school of Irving is a fact as obvious as Kennedy's love for the idling plantation life. Quite too much, however, has been made of this imitativeness—it is an imitativeness rather of method than of theme or style. If it was not quite a pioneer work in the field of local description, it was amongst the earliest. Paulding had dealt with Dutch colonial life, and Timothy Flint and James Hall had begun the descriptive literature of the West; but little else had been done at the time *Swallow Barn* appeared. Longstreet's *Georgia Scenes* came out two years later. Intrinsically as well as historically the work is curiously suggestive. Nowhere else does the plantation life of the Old Dominion in the days before its decline appear so vividly as in these discursive pages: "the mellow, bland, and sunny luxuriance of her old-time society—its good fellowship, its hearty and constitutional *companionableness*, the thriftless gaiety of the people, their dogged but amiable invincibility of opinion, and that overflowing hospitality which knows no ebb."

Like Irving, Kennedy went back to the old home, but that old home was Virginia and not England; and there he found still lingering on the great plantations charmingly romantic anachronisms that had disappeared elsewhere—a spontaneous romanticism of temperament that gave color and zest to the daily routine. The aloofness of plantation life had bred in the Virginia gentry a piquant individuality, a distinction as of old morocco or calfskin. Philly Wart, the shrewdly humorous fox-hunting lawyer; old Mr. Tracy of The Brakes, "turning a little sour with age" and resembling "that waterish, gravelly soil that you see sometimes around a spring, where nothing grows but sheep-sorrel," who cherishes a hereditary boundary dispute, pursuing his hypothetical rights through all the law courts and discovering, when the matter has been amicably settled by arbitration, that much of the zest has gone out of his life; the heroine Bel Tracy, a frank wholesome girl with a dash of Di Vernon in her romantic affectations that lead her to play at hawking: such figures fit as naturally into the background as the pampered house servants, the horseback riding, the constant visiting, the abundant dinners. Especially the dinners, when the neighborhood is invited in. The table spread with opulent hos-

49

pitality and careless profusion—the baked ham at one end and the saddle of roast mutton at the other, with fried chicken, oysters, crabs, sweet potatoes, jellies, custards—a prodigal feast that only outdoor stomachs could manage, and all by way of preliminary to the dusty wine-bottles and easy stories that hold the men long after the ladies have withdrawn. Surely the romance of Old Virginia, preserved in these light-hearted discursive pages, is worth remembering by later generations who have forgotten how to live so genially.

In 1832 when *Swallow Barn* was written, the southern mind was just at the turn in its attitude towards slavery, and Frank Meriwether, a Virginian Sir Roger de Coverley, bred in the humanitarianism of the older liberals, accepts the institution as a present evil that is in a way of natural extinction. Slavery in *Swallow Barn* is kept in the background. There are slaves, of course, on the plantation, many of them; but they are in the tobacco fields or the quarters, far from the mansion; and not till near the end of the book does Kennedy's curiosity induce him to visit the cabins and draw out Frank Meriwether in talk on slavery. The result is what one could have foreseen. The plantation master was the victim of a benevolent romanticism that vaguely looks for a solution to colonization schemes that will return the Negro to Africa; but like other southern gentlemen he is somewhat testy at the suggestion of outside interference. Slavery he regards as an exclusive southern problem, to be solved by those who understand its complex domestic implications. It would be better for everybody if Abolition busybodies would mind their own affairs and cease stirring up feelings where no good can come of it. To prove that Virginia gentlemen are aware of their responsibility, Meriwether offers a half humorous suggestion that Negro emancipation might well follow the example of English villeinage, with a slow break-up of the system, the emancipated Negro to remain in a protective feudal relation to his master. It was an amiable notion to play with, and it fitted the feudal psychology of the plantation.

In these early sketches Kennedy revealed an easy knack at writing that gave promise of excellent work later. He has lightness, grace, refinement, an eye sensitive to picturesque effects, delight in line and texture and color, an agreeable wit and playful sentiment, a relish for English idiom and the literary colloquial. In *Horseshoe Robinson*, written three years later, he abandoned the essay-sketch and turned to the school of historical romance then in full swing. The story is done in the orthodox manner of the thirties; it is compounded of equal parts gentry and commoners, the former providing respectability and the latter dramatic interest, the whole garnished with a few historical figures. There is quite obvious concern for authentic reality. The title-hero, a shrewd homespun scout, is carefully drawn from life; the background of bushwhackings and forays and onsets, and the numerous company of blackguards and honest folk, are painted in skillfully; and the whole conducts to a dramatic finale in the battle of King's Mountain. It is an excellent tale, quite worth reading today, but scarcely comparable in vividness and brisk action—in picaresque realism which any true war story must embody—with *The Partisan* of Gilmore Simms, written in the same year of 1835. Realism was not Kennedy's forte and after *Horseshoe Robinson* he abandoned the field of the Revolution which offered so rich an opportunity for the robuster genius of the Charleston romancer.

In *Rob of the Bowl* Kennedy opened a promising vein that he never adequately explored—the vein of the cavalier romantic. Temperamentally he was ill fitted to deal with rollicking action or picaresque adventure; he preferred the leisurely, discursive romantic, subdued to gentle raillery or humorous tenderness. One trembles to think what Simms would have made of the materials that Kennedy brought together in this tale of old St. Mary's in the days of Charles II. Here is the raw stuff of a true bloody-bones thriller: a gentlemanly blackguard with the stumps of his legs bound in a huge rocking trencher and moving about with the help of crutches, who is deep in the contraband trade; a swaggering young pirate, a Brother of the Bloody Coast, who falls in love with the daughter of the Collector of the Port and kidnaps her from her father's house; a romantic lover, slender and clerky, but skillful with the rapier, who turns out to be the son of Rob; a haunted house that covers the smuggling operations of Rob and Captain Cocklescraft; and all this set against a background of partisan struggle between Roundhead and Cavalier, Protestant and Catholic, in the early days of the Maryland settlement.

But in the handling the story is far removed from a bloody-bones tale. The action is deliberately subdued to the humoresque; atmosphere is studiously created; adventure is held in strict subjection to the whimsical; and a mellow old-time flavor is imprisoned in the leisurely pages. Kennedy had

51

an appreciative eye for picturesque characters, and in *Rob of the Bowl* he has gathered a choice group, limned—as he would choose to say—with a partial hand. Garret Weasel, the garrulous pot-valiant innkeeper, and Dorothy his termagant spouse; Captain Jasper Dauntless, the cogging, wheedling swordsman who twists Dame Dorothy about his fingers and inveigles his host into undue commerce with his cups—these to be sure are stock characters, but they are done with excellent vivacity. Their abundant talk is well seasoned, and if the action sometimes drags, the company is good and the drinking is a sufficient end in itself. All the while he is writing Kennedy keeps half an eye on Elizabethan literature to assure himself of the exact turn of phrase. His vocabulary is saturated with the homely old speech, and his characters talk as if they had culled all the simples of English cottage gardens to garnish the staple of their wit. He has a keener delight than Simms in the picturesque archaic. He far surpasses Irving in easy mastery of the old-fashioned colloquial, as indeed he surpasses all our early novelists. He delights in the courtly wit of the Cavalier equally with the humors of Dogberry and Falstaff and Captain Bobadil, and he quite evidently is seeking to cross the sparkle of Congreve with the robustness of the Elizabethans. The result may sometimes appear a bit self-conscious; his phrases too often seem to be on dress parade; but he can plead his precedents in justification. In its fondness for the literary colloquial his prose style almost suggests Thackeray, and it is this suggestion, perhaps, that gave rise to the tradition that Kennedy wrote for the former a certain chapter of *The Virginians*. That he supplied Thackeray with materials for his Virginia backgrounds may be accepted as true, but the indebtedness probably went no further.

Rob of the Bowl is certainly Kennedy's best work, as it is one of the most finished and delightful of our earlier romances. Although it ran to six editions, the latest in 1907, it has scarcely received the recognition its lightness of touch deserves. But instead of opening the vein further he turned away to venture in new fields. *Quodlibet*, written in 1840,[1]

[1] The characteristic title is *Quodlibet: Containing some Annals thereof, with an Authentic Account of the Origin and Growth of the Borough and the Sayings and Doings of Sundry Townspeople: Interspersed with Sketches of the Most Remarkable and Distinguished Characters of that Place and its Vicinity. Edited by Solomon Secondthoughts, Schoolmaster, from original MSS. Indited by him, and now made Public at the Request and under the Patronage of the Great New Light Democratic Central Committee of Quodlibet.*

is a surprising successor to *Rob*—a satire on Jacksonian democracy, done with a light touch and great good humor. In those acrimonious days when Old Hickory's attack on the Bank so embittered its Whig partisans, Kennedy kept his temper, tipped his shafts with laughter and sent them neatly between the joints of the Democratic armor. Against such amusing satire fustian is helpless. The book is keen, vivacious, sparkling. The supposed follies of Jacksonianism —its deification of the majority vote, its cant of the sovereign people, its hatred of all aristocrats, its demagoguery and bluster and sheer buncombe—are hit off with exuberant raillery. The story professes to be an account of the rise to prosperity of the Borough of Quodlibet, under the beneficent smile of Democratic finance. Mean and insignificant before the coming of Jackson, with the removal of the "Deposites," "like Jeshurun, it waxed fat," with its rows of brick shops built on speculation and its Patriotic Copper-Plate Bank that issued an unlimited supply of beautifully engraved notes as a stimulus to enterprise. To be sure the bank broke and the cashier absconded with his family to Europe, but its untoward end was attributed by all Jacksonian New Lights to the vile machinations of the Whigs. It was certainly Nick Biddle and the Barings, with their hatred of Old Bullion Benton's democratic gold coinage, that were the devil in the pot to spill the people's porridge.

Yet even in its laughter Kennedy's political bias is sharply and narrowly partisan. The satire is a capitalistic counter to the agrarian attack on the rising money power, and it is colored by the chagrin of gentlemen who find themselves displaced by plebeians. Something of the old aristocratic contempt for the plain man functioning as a political animal lingers in its pages, which the bubbling humor does not wholly conceal. In Jackson's onslaught on the Bank, Kennedy discovers only an impudent demagoguery; it is selfish and stupid, turmoiling the country for partisan ends and seeking to cover its petty spite with the mantle of patriotism. The Old Hero cuts a sorry figure in these brisk pages, and Van Buren a still sorrier one. The satire sparkles amusingly, but it is drawn from the old Federalist vintage and it preserves the flavor of a time when gentlemen frankly resented the rule of the unwashed majority. For that very reason *Quodlibet* is an unusually interesting document. It is the most vivacious criticism of Jacksonianism in our political library, one of our few distinguished political satires, and it deserves a better fate than to gather dust on old shelves.

After *Quodlibet* Kennedy did little else. The last twenty years of his life were largely wasted. His dignified life of William Wirt, published in 1849, seems to have met with approval, for it ran to six editions. Our grandfathers liked stately narrative that portrayed their subjects in full dress; and Kennedy gave them an impeccably respectable work in which all the rugosities of character were ironed out neatly and a fine starchy effect achieved. It is hard to understand how a writer so keen to detect the whimsical should have drawn so lifeless a picture of the genial Attorney-General. Perhaps the memory of Wirt's reputed greatness rested too heavily upon him; or it may have been that a lawyer in old Virginia lived as colorless a life as the narrative suggests; at any rate the novelist who never had failed to breathe life into the characters of his fiction, somehow failed in depicting this excellent gentleman of the old school. During the Civil War Kennedy contributed to the northern cause his *Letters of Mr. Paul Ambrose on the Great Rebellion in the United States,* in which he again showed that he could keep his temper and argue calmly. It was a difficult theme for which he was inadequately equipped. His constitutional argument is not impressive and it makes an ill showing when set over against Alexander H. Stephens' *Constitutional View of the War between the States.* He was a man of letters rather than a lawyer, and if he had eschewed politics and law and stuck to his pen our literature would have been greatly in his debt. Few Americans of his day were so generously gifted; none possessed a lighter touch. He has been somewhat carelessly forgotten even by our literary historians who can plead no excuse for so grave a blunder.

III

EDGAR ALLAN POE: *Romantic*

It is from this slovenly background of aristocratic Virginia, with its liberalisms and conservatisms running at cross purposes, that the enigmatical figure of Poe emerged to vex the northern critics. In so far as any particular environment determined his highly individual and creative nature, it was the indolent life of the planter gentry, shot through with a pugnacious pride of locality, with a strong dislike of alien ways, with haughtiness, dissipation, wastefulness, chivalry. In his proud, irascible individualism that went out of its way to pick a quarrel, there is something of the spirit of John Randolph of Roanoke, but pied and streaked with unfortunate qualities that to many observers seemed the marks

54

of the mere charlatan. As a southern gentleman he imbibed the common dislike of New England, and this dislike was aggravated by its diverse conception of the functions of art, and by the misfortunes that attended his literary career An aesthete and a craftsman, the first American writer tc be concerned with beauty alone, his ideals ran counter tc every major interest of the New England renaissance: the mystical, optimistic element in transcendentalism; the social conscience that would make the world over in accordance with French idealism, and that meddled with its neighbor's affairs in applying its equalitarianism to the Negro; the pervasive moralism that would accept no other criteria by which to judge life and letters—these things could not fail to irritate a nature too easily ruffled. The Yankee parochialisms rubbed across his Virginia parochialisms; and when to these was added a Yankee preëmption of the field of literary criticism, when a little clique engaged in the business of mutual admiration puffed New England mediocrities at his expense, the provocation was enough to arouse in a sensitive southern mind an antagonism that rivaled Beverley Tucker's. In his unhappy pilgrimage through life Poe was his own worst enemy, but he took comfort in charging his ill fortune upon the malignancy of others.

Southern though he was in the deep prejudices of a suspicious nature, his aloofness from his own Virginia world was complete. Aside from his art he had no philosophy and no programs and no causes. He got from Virginia what was bad rather than good, and his alienation from the more generous southern ideals did him harm. It was perhaps harder to be an artist in that slack southern society than in New England—harder to be a romantic concerned only with twilight melancholy. It would have been hard enough anywhere in Jacksonian America. His romanticisms were of quite another kind than those his countrymen were pursuing; and the planter sympathized with them no more than did the New York literati, or the western men of letters. In a world given over to bumptious middle-class enthusiasms, there would be scant sympathy for the craftsman and dreamer. There was no unearned increment to be got from investments in "the misty mid-region of Weir," which Poe threw on the market. The technician concerned with the values of long and short syllables would find few congenial spirits in a world of more substantial things; and the purveyors of shoddy tales would not take it kindly if their shortcomings were pointed out and a more competent craftsmanship insisted upon. And so, like Herman Melville, Poe came to shipwreck on the reef of American materialisms. The day of the artist had not dawned in America.

So much only need be said. The problem of Poe, fascinating as it is, lies quite outside the main current of American thought, and it may be left with the psychologist and the belletrist with whom it belongs. It is for abnormal psychology to explain his "neural instability amounting almost to a dissociated or split personality," his irritable pride, his quarrelsomeness, his unhappy persecution complex, his absurd pretentions to a learning he did not possess, his deliberate fabrications about his life and methods of work, his oscillations between abstinence and dissipation, between the morbidly grotesque and the lucidly rational, his haunting fear of insanity that drove him to demonstrate his sanity by pursuing complex problems of ratiocination. Such problems are personal to Poe and do not concern us here. And it is for the belletrist to evaluate his theory and practice of art: his debt to Coleridge and Schlegel; the influence of the contemporary magazine on his conception of the length of a work of the imagination; the value of his theory of the tyrannizing unity of mood in the poem and short story; the provocation to the craftsman of the pretentiousness of contemporary American literature, jointed to a flabby and crude technique; the grossness of the popular taste and the validity of his critical judgments. Whatever may be the final verdict it is clear that as an aesthete and a craftsman he made a stir in the world that has not lessened in the years since his death, but has steadily widened. Others of greater repute in his day have fared less prosperously in later reputation. He was the first of our artists and the first of our critics; and the surprising thing is that such a man should have made his appearance in an America given over to hostile ideas. He suffered much from his aloofness, but he gained much also. In the midst of gross and tawdry romanticisms he refused to be swallowed up, but went his own way, a rebel in the cause of beauty, discovering in consequence a finer romanticism than was before known in America.

PART TWO
THE RENAISSANCE OF SLAVERY

CHAPTER 1

Southern Imperialism

I

By the year 1824 a change was becoming evident in the South that was to affect profoundly the course of southern thought in regard to her peculiar institution. The passing of the long Virginia hegemony was a sign that southern opinion was undergoing a revolutionary overturn, and that leadership henceforth would rest with men of a different philosophy. The humanitarian spirit that marked the thought of the preceding generation was dying out, to be replaced by a frank recognition of local economic interests. Expectation that slavery was on the way to natural extinction was yielding to the conviction that the system was too profitable to the South to permit its extinction, and this in turn bred an imperious desire to spread it westward to the Pacific. With this significant shift from apology to imperialism, it became clear to ardent pro-slavery men that lukewarm Virginians of the old tradition were not the spokesmen to entrust with the fortunes of the South, and leadership passed to the South Carolina school. In that momentous shift much was implied. It was more than a shift from Jefferson to Calhoun, from humanitarian idealism to economic realism. It marked the complete ascendancy of a small minority of gentleman planters over the inarticulate mass of southern yeomanry, and the assertion of the aristocratic ideal as the goal of southern society. It denied the principle of democracy as that principle was understood in the North and West, and it rejected the new humanitarian spirit of western civilization.

It abandoned the Jeffersonian equalitarianism that was so deeply rooted in the southern mind from Kentucky to Georgia; it cast aside the agrarianism of John Taylor and the older Virginians; and it set up in place of these congenial conceptions the alien ideal of a Greek democracy. Most momentous still, it threw down the gauntlet to the ideals of the middle class, then in the first flush of a triumphant career, and in the armed clash that eventually resulted, it was destroyed by that class.

The intellectual capital of southern imperialism was Charleston, but its numerical strength lay in the Black Belt, with South Carolina to the east and Texas to the west, a compact territory the heart of which was Georgia, Alabama, Mississippi and Louisiana. In this new South that was rapidly passing through its frontier development, the patriarchal system of Virginia gave way to a system of Negro exploitation, more naked as it passed further westward. It was here that the proportion of slaves to whites was greatest; it was here that slave labor was most profitable; and it was here in consequence that the slave economy was most militant. The Black Belt became the native habitat of the southern Fire Eater. In the late twenties and early thirties South Carolina provided the outstanding leaders of the new school; but the philosophy of imperialism spread rapidly and western men came more and more to the front. George McDuffie and Bob Toombs, perhaps the boldest of the loquacious tribe of Fire Eaters, came from Georgia; Alexander H. Stephens was bred in the same turbulent state; L. Q. C. Lamar and Jefferson Davis were from Mississippi. For the most part self-made, products of a frontier environment, these western extremists had got from Jefferson little more than an assertive individualism that easily espoused the states-rights philosophy and prompted them to defend their immediate interests. It was this vigorous group that largely created the new southern psychology and prodded the southern mind along the path marked out for it to travel. Democratic in their attitude towards the white voter, middle class in their love of exploitation, they retained little of the spirit of the Virginia school.

The expansion of the South to the Gulf region came a generation later than the settlement of the Ohio valley. The Creek Indians who clung tenaciously to the rich lands of Mississippi were long an obstacle to the white advance, and the settlers filtered in slowly. Moreover the slave economy was ill fitted to the business of pioneering. It was difficult to transport Negroes and establish great plantations in a wilderness; there was too little security in a region that offered every temptation to the slave to run away. The plantation system could prosper only after a considerable degree of development had been effected and sufficient Negroes provided. On the other hand, the rich soil, virgin and productive, offered every inducement for large-scale production of cotton, tobacco and sugar. Here the economics of slavery could be fairly tested, and if the system were found to be profitable it would spread of its own impulse beyond the Mississippi, becoming more imperialistic with every extension, ambitious to seize Texas with its filibusters, looking as far as California and the Oregon territory for future expansion. But while planning for such expansion it must secure its strategic front at Washington, making certain that no rival economy should control the central government to its disadvantage. It was an ambitious program, but it was all implicit in the evident fact that slavery in the Black Belt proved to be profitable.

The explanation of this sudden prosperity of the Black Belt is a matter of familiar knowledge. Coincident with the first westward expansion of slavery came a revolution in the technique of the English cotton industry that brought about corresponding changes in southern agriculture. The production of cotton textiles in England had long been held back by the difficulty of spinning a fine and even thread. When this problem was solved at the beginning of the century by the invention of new machines, the cotton industry at once developed amazingly, making heavy demands upon the supply of American raw materials. This supply in turn was greatly increased by the invention of the cotton gin, and the combined result of these inventions was an upheaval in southern agriculture. In the eighteenth century the southern staples were tobacco, rice and indigo; by 1825 the staples had become cotton, tobacco and sugar. Almost in a decade cotton had become king. In 1791, three years after Andrew Jackson settled in Nashville, the total export of cotton was only 200,000 pounds. In 1803 it had risen to 40,000,000 pounds, and by 1860 the export for the year was of the value of nearly two hundred millions of dollars. Such figures provide a sufficient explanation of the militant spirit of the slave economy after 1820. Here was an enormous vested interest, the economic life of the South, that could not suffer its present or future profits to be put in jeopardy by any political party on any pretext. Its well-being and its prestige

were both at stake. The peculiar institution, which a generation before was commonly believed to be in the way of
natural extinction, had the South by the throat.

It was the strategic weakness of the South that the spirit
of exploitation, which following the peace of 1783 had
spread through America like the itch, should there have
assumed its most hateful form, far more revolting to the
humanitarian sense and far less justifiable to uneasy consciences than wage slavery. With every extension the system
became necessarily more brutal in exploitation. As new
plantations were opened the natural increase of Negroes was
inadequate to meet the pressing demands for slaves. Since
the abolition of the traffic with Africa the occasional smuggling by venturesome runners—many of whom were respectable New England church members—had provided a
totally inadequate supply of raw material; the price of slaves
rose steadily, and this in turn led to increasing speculation
in Negroes. Buying and selling by middlemen went on
briskly, to the horror of northern humanitarians and the
concern of southern. So brutal and open was the exploitation
that Alexander H. Stephens—the kindest-hearted of men—
went so far as to advocate the reopening of the slave trade
with Africa, as the lesser of the two evils. The better South
hated what it could not help. Although the slave trader
remained a social pariah with whom no gentleman would
associate, his business was a necessary evil of the system
and could not be eradicated.

The reaction of the slave system upon the southern people,
both plantation masters and poor whites was wholly evil.
The generous culture of Virginia failed to take root in the
Black Belt. The development of the plantation system under
hired overseers infected the masters, few in numbers and absolute in power, with an exaggerated sense of their own
greatness. The aristocratic spirit of the Old Dominion had
been tempered by a feeling of patriarchal responsibility that
humanized the relations between master and slave, and more
generous social contacts had created an admirable republican squirearchy. But in the frontier Gulf states the rapid
expansion of the plantation system created an aristocracy
given to swaggering, bourgeois in spirit, arrogant in manners. Republican simplicity was losing vogue and there was
much loose talk about the superiority of the classes. It is
said that when Alexander H. Stephens was appointed a
delegate to the Confederate Convention at Montgomery, he
refused to attend till he was assured that the jingoes would

make no attempt to set up a monarchy. Gideon Welles is authority for the story that when news came to Washington of the secession of South Carolina, Mrs. Jefferson Davis was all aflutter: "She said she wanted to get rid of the old government; that they would have a monarchy South, and gentlemen to fill official positions" (*Diary*, Vol. II, p. 256). Such stories were probably the result of war hysteria; nevertheless they suggest a bias in the southern temper that reveals how far the new South had drifted from its Jeffersonian moorings.

Of this new South with its grandiose dreams of slave imperialism, fate selected Jefferson Davis to be the political leader and spokesman. The choice may have proved unfortunate, but it was logical. Much calumny has been heaped upon his name, but that is the common fate of partisans of lost causes. The real Jefferson Davis is to be sought in some mean between the extravagant adulation of his friends and the slanders of his enemies. Not a great man certainly; in no sense comparable to Lee or Stonewall Jackson or Alexander H. Stephens; he was very far from a petty or time-serving nature. As time softens the old animosities it reveals the features of a high-minded southern gentleman who possessed the virtues and the weaknesses of his race. Simple and austere in tastes, he was the product of a crossing of the southern Puritan with the aristocratic tradition of the Old Dominion. If he was not of the old cavalier stock he was a gentleman by instinct and training. His father was half Welsh, half English; his mother Scotch-Irish. He came of Revolutionary stock. After the war his father settled in Georgia and later removed to Kentucky, where the son was born in Todd County in 1808. While still a small child he was taken to Wilkinson County, Mississippi, where he was brought up on a plantation. Educated at Lexington, Kentucky, and at West Point, he proved a serious, capable student, who loved reading but possessed little intellectual curiosity. His ideas were few, but those he embraced he clung to with the tenacity of a strong nature. Resigning from the army after a few years of honorable service, he settled down as a plantation master. He was summoned from his isolation by the call for troops to serve in the Mexican campaign, went through several battles with unusual distinction, and proved himself an extremely able officer. With his military fame the path to political preferment was open and he demonstrated his ability in Congress. At the outbreak of the secession movement he was eager to receive the appointment as commander of the southern armies, but fate called him to the presidency of the Confederacy and he devoted his best strength unselfishly to the cause, only to find the accumulated bitterness of the North heaped upon his single head. It was an unhappy lot, but there was iron in him, and he bore it like a man.

Jefferson Davis was cut out of the same tough oak that fashioned John C. Calhoun. Hard and unyielding, tenacious of opinion, dictatorial, somewhat inclined to arrogance, he might break, but he would not bend. The Scotch-Irish stock was rarely genial or tolerant, and Davis possessed none of the seeming pliability of Lincoln that yielded the non-essentials to secure the essentials. Utterly lacking in humor and easy-going good nature, he offended by his very virtues. Profoundly Puritan, he was narrow and rigid, a legalist in temperament, proud and jealous of authority. Meticulously honest, he could not get on well with men; he quarreled with his generals and wore himself out trying to do everything himself. Politically he was a strict constructionist of the most rigid views. He refused to follow Calhoun into the camp of Nullification. His patriotism was extreme, and only a greater loyalty to his state made him an advocate of secession. At bottom he was a Jeffersonian and to the end of his life he was faithful to the principles of his party. Kindly and humane, he treated his dependents with singular consideration. He set up a curious little democracy amongst the slaves of his plantation, and his Negroes were devoted to him with rare loyalty. There was in his nature not the slightest trace of the exploiter; he was a patriarchal master after the old Virginia ideal, with no hint of the speculator or middleman. The background of his thought was agrarian and he shared with Jefferson a dislike for capitalistic industrialism. The President of the Confederacy may have been an unfortunate civil leader, but the slanders that so long clung to his name are only worthy of the gutter. The sin that he was led into was not counted a sin in his southern decalogue; it was the sin, not of secession, but of imperialism—a sin common to all America in those drunker times when the great West invited exploitation.

CHAPTER II

Winds of Political Doctrine

I

An economic revolution so widespread and profound could not fail to impress its ideals on current political thought. In the year 1825 three streams of tendency were flowing through the southern mind, rising from different sources, incompatible in spirit and purpose, strong in their diverse appeals; and in the end the major current was certain to engulf the lesser. The humanitarianism of Virginia, the individualism of the new West, and the imperialism of the Black Belt might seem to mingle their waters for a time, but there would be confusions of thought and diversity of counsels until one or another had worn a deeper channel through which the dominant opinion might run. There could be no more fascinating study in the economics of political theory than the changing mind of the South during the critical decades from 1820 to 1850, as it followed the course determined by its peculiar institution. Political thought passed under the jurisdiction of slavery, and every southern writer took his daily bearings from that polar fact. It is unintelligent to charge upon southern politicians a lack of consistency—to point out that after 1820 Calhoun reversed himself on every major political principle. It was true of Calhoun, as it was true of Webster and true of Clay. In a rapidly changing America, with economics in a state of flux, men were no longer free political agents, guiding themselves by the fixed stars of accepted theory; they were borne like corks on the current of the times, and their inconsistency is the surest evidence that they spoke for their constituents. The North and the South were at the parting of the ways, and if southern imperialism created for its needs a philosophy of particularism, it was met by a counter philosophy of nationalism created for its needs by northern capitalism, which likewise was following the path of its manifest destiny. The charge of innovation, indeed, lies more justly against northern theory than southern; it was Webster rather than Calhoun who ignored the teachings of the fathers.

Of these three streams of tendency it was the new imperialism of the Black Belt that wore the deepest channel, gathering its tributaries till it was swollen to an overwhelming flood that drew in every lesser current. Every other interest was eventually sacrificed to slavery, every ambition was laid upon that consuming altar. Southern political thought, in consequence, came to be an ingenious study in the strategy of defense. From the somewhat vague doctrine of states rights as struck off by the Virginia school was elaborated a complete philosophy of particularism with its principle of a protective state veto. Tremendous as was the stir created by the doctrine of Nullification, that doctrine was little more than a warning gesture, a militant expression of the southern temper. The time was not ripe for the critical issue, the philosophy of the new South was not yet clarified; the objective was clearly seen, but the defenses were incomplete, the line of campaign not yet laid down. That great work was in the skillful hands of Calhoun, and much was yet to be done. The deeper purpose that lay behind the gesture of Nullification was the purpose of erecting in the slave states a civilization founded on a landed aristocracy that should serve as a sufficient counterweight to the mercantile and industrial civilization of the North; and in the event that the institution of slavery were not assured of peaceful extension through the new West, to secede and establish a southern Confederacy wherein a generous civilization might develop, modeled after the Greek democracy. Such at least was the dream of the noblest minds of the South.

Thrown early upon the defensive, southern political thought found too little time to examine fundamental principles. The necessities of the situation entailed a meticulous constitutional debate, in which the terms of the Constitution were examined with microscopic care, and interpreted in the light of their historical origin. Something of the sterility of the lawyer's mind marked the long debate; and little of the suggestiveness of the philosopher's. Acute as was Calhoun's reasoning, it reveals the weakness of contemporary political thought, northern as well as southern. It concerned itself too exclusively with government under the Constitution—its origin, the just interpretation of the terms of the fundamental law, the potentialities of consolidation inherent in the principle of loose construction. To the broader problems of the nature and functions of the political state—questions that had so deeply interested the speculative minds of the French school—quite inadequate consideration was given. The drift of circumstance was in the way of creating a leviathan state. Southern orators railed at consolidation in abundant and florid language, but they concerned themselves little with the deeper problem of the relation of the political state to the well-being of the citizen. This common weakness is strikingly evident in the work of Calhoun's successor, Alexander H. Stephens, whose interest was so exclusively historical and constitutional as almost to exclude him from a place among political philosophers.

II
JOHN C. CALHOUN: *Realist*

The greatest figure in that long controversy was certainly John C. Calhoun, a man who set his face like flint against every northern middle-class ambition, and with his dream of a Greek democracy steered his beloved South upon the rocks. A truly notable figure was this ascetic Carolinian. In the passionate debates over slavery he daily matched powers with Webster and Clay and proved himself intellectually the greatest of the three. He is the one outstanding political thinker in a period singularly barren and uncreative. His influence was commanding. Tall, lean, eager, with no humor, no playfulness, lacking the magnetic personality of Clay and the ornate rhetoric of Webster, speaking plainly and following his logic tenaciously, this gaunt Scotch-Irishman became by virtue of intellect and character, driven by an apostolic zeal, the master political mind of the South, an uncrowned king who carried his native Carolina in his pocket like a rotten borough. Long before his death he had expanded a political philosophy into a school of thought. What he planned a hundred disciples hastened to execute. Like Jefferson he was a pervasive influence in shaping men's opinions. It was impossible to ignore him or to escape the admonitory finger that pointed at every weak and shuffling compromiser.

Whatever road one travels one comes at last upon the austere figure of Calhoun, commanding every highway of the southern mind. He subjected the philosophy of the fathers to critical analysis; pointed out wherein he conceived it to be faulty; cast aside some of its most sacred doctrines, provided another foundation for the democratic faith which he professed. And when he had finished the great work of reconstruction, the old Jeffersonianism that had satisfied the mind of Virginia was reduced to a thing of shreds and patches, acknowledged by his followers to have been a mistaken philosophy, blinded by romantic idealism and led astray by French humanitarianism. To substitute realism for idealism, to set class economics above abstract humanitarianism, was the mission to which Calhoun devoted himself. He undid for the plantation South the work of his old master. Speaking in the name of democracy, he attacked the foundations on which the democratic movement in America had rested, substituting for its libertarian and equalitarian doctrines conceptions wholly alien and antagonistic to western democracy, wholly Greek in their underlying spirit.

Calhoun's career was linked indissolubly with slavery. He was the advocate and philosopher of southern imperialism, and in defense of that imperialism he elaborated those particularist theories which prepared the way for the movement of secession. Born and bred in South Carolina, he was enveloped from infancy in the mesh of southern provincialisms. Except for two years at Yale, where he graduated in the class of 1804, and eighteen months reading law in Connecticut, his life was spent between Washington and his plantation. He was in temperament a Puritan, of that Scotch-Irish strain which, scattered along the wide American frontier, greatly modified the American character and gave to the South such different leaders as Stonewall Jackson and Jefferson Davis. It was a hard, stern race—that Scotch-Irish—little responsive to humanitarian appeal; and Calhoun was harder and sterner than most. He held his emotions in strict subjection to his reason. Intent on thinking every problem through from premise to conclusion, concerned always with fundamental principles, he would have become, in an environment congenial to humanistic thought, a distinguished intellectual. His mind would have lost its rigidity and become pliable from contact with diverse streams of theory, and his speculations would have found new horizons from more generous intellectual acquisitions. But unhappily there was nothing either at Washington or in South Carolina that tended to liberalize his thinking. He had not gone to school, as Jefferson had done, to the great thinkers of Europe; he had not found an intellectual stimulus in revolutionary systems of philosophy. He dwelt all his life in the arid world of politicians. His two years at Yale may even be accounted a calamity. Timothy Dwight and Calhoun were cut out of the same cloth. The South Carolina Puritan would only be confirmed in his dogmatisms by the most dogmatic of Yankee Puritans; and in consequence his career, like Jonathan Edwards', suffered from a narrow, ingrowing intellectualism. He was a potential intellectual whose mind was unfertilized by contact with a generous social culture.

Calhoun's public life covered the forty years from 1810 to 1850, from the first administration of Madison to that of Zachary Taylor. For nearly half of the total period, up to the year 1828, he was a politician of ability but without distinction. He entered Congress at a time when the young men from the South and West were becoming impatient with the cautious policy of the old Republicans led by Jefferson and Madison. The war psychology was mounting under British pin-pricks, and the young nationalists, forgetful that bayonets and cannon and ships are not easily defeated by rhetoric, were eager to teach the Mistress of the Seas some much-needed international manners. In those early years Calhoun joined with Clay in driving through Congress a war policy. In this he seems to have represented his constituents, whose patriotism was always somewhat bellicose. During the shameful war experience, the cool analytical Calhoun came near to exhibiting the tawdry marks of the jingo; and thereafter for years there was little to distinguish him from a Hamiltonian Federalist. He was a thoroughgoing nationalist of the school of loose construction. He advocated a protective tariff on the ground that "it would form a new and most powerful cement, far outweighing any political objections that might be urged against the system" (Gaillard Hunt, *John C. Calhoun*, p. 29). As yet he had discovered no constitutional scruples against the exercise of this or other implied powers. He was, he said, "no advocate for refined arguments on the Constitution. The instrument is not intended as a thesis for the logician to exercise his ingenuity on. It ought to be construed with plain, good sense; and what can be more express than the Constitution on this point?" (*ibid.*, p. 30). As Secretary for War in Monroe's cabinet he was an advocate of internal improvements, and he submitted to Congress an elaborate report on a proposed system of roads and canals. Until the critical year 1828 there was little in Calhoun's career to distinguish him from Clay. The tide of national expansion was running strong; the growth of exploitation was creating a middle-class psychology; and Calhoun in these earlier years was as unconsciously middle class as afterwards he became consciously aristocratic. He sprang from an acquisitive race, and to the end of his life some remnants of the old instincts clung to him despite his repudiation of the middle-class political philosophy.

The year 1828, marked by a fierce discussion in South Carolina of the Tariff of Abominations, proved the turning-point of his career. As Vice President he had been little more than a spectator of the growing discontent in his native state at the contrast between the industrial prosperity of New England and the agricultural depression of the South. But he could no longer remain an idle spectator. Pamphlets and newspaper articles were appearing that sharply challenged his position. Capitalistic Federalism and democratic equalitarianism were equally under fire. The celebrated Dr. Cooper, an Englishman long resident in South Carolina, who had suffered under the Alien and Sedition law, had vigorously attacked the natural-rights dogma, and was active in arousing the public mind against Calhoun's consolidationist tendencies.[1] The publication in 1821 of Yates's *Minutes of Debates of the Constitutional Convention* had awakened widespread interest in an historical interpretation of the Constitution, and the time was ripe for a new period of constitutional debate. The tariff act of 1828 provided the immediate occasion. It opened the flood gates, and the waters of states-rights doctrine that had long been gathering rushed forth in a torrent. Calhoun hesitated no longer. The problem and the solution had both clarified themselves in his mind, and he at once took the lead in directing the unrest to achieve a definite end.

Calhoun's contribution to political theory—a contribution that elevates him to a distinguished place among American political thinkers—was the child of necessity, and received its particularist bias from the exigencies of sectional partisanship. With the rapid expansion of the nation westward, and the consequent augmenting of a potentially hostile free-soil power, the South was doomed to become increasingly a minority voice in the councils of government; and if it were to preserve its peculiar institution it must find more adequate means of self-protection than it had enjoyed hitherto. The tendencies most to be feared, in his judgment, were

[1] See Merriam, *American Political Theories*, p. 231; Gaillard Hunt, *John C. Calhoun*, p. 64.

the spontaneous drift towards consolidation, and an uncritical faith in numerical majorities. He was convinced that America had too thoughtlessly accepted the principle of political democracy as a sufficient safeguard against the danger of arbitrary government. Soon or late it must discover, what the South already was discovering, that numerical democracy, unrestrained by constitutional limitations on its will, is no friend to political justice. The critical test of every government is the measure of protection afforded its weakest citizen; and judged by this test a democratic state, when power has come to be centralized in few hands, may prove to be no other than a tyrant. Irresponsible in its unrestraint, the majority vote may easily outdo an Oriental despot in arbitrary rule, and the more power it wields the more ruthless will be its disregard of minority opinion. The political philosopher who proposes to formulate an ideal democratic system of government, therefore, must deal critically with this fundamental problem of political justice, for upon the solution will turn the excellence and permanence of every democracy. It was to this baffling problem that Calhoun addressed himself.

In seeking a constitutional defense for the threatened southern interests, he drew from the two great reservoirs of American constitutional theory. From the Jeffersonian Republicans he derived his familiar doctrine of states rights in opposition to the consolidating principle; from the Federalists of the Montesquieu school he drew his theory of static government, resulting from exactly balanced powers; and from the amalgamation of these diverse theories he formulated a new principle. Both schools of earlier thought, he had come to believe, had been sound in their major premises, but both had gone astray in certain important deductions. The experience of forty years, with the democracy constantly augmenting its powers, had demonstrated to Calhoun's satisfaction both the grave danger that lay in the principle of consolidation, and the insufficiency of existing checks on the Federal government. The prime mistake of the Jeffersonians, he conceived, was their belief that the democratic majority will necessarily serve the cause of political justice; and the miscalculation of the Federalists resulted from the belief that the division of powers provided in the Constitution was adequate to prevent arbitrary government. He now proposed to correct these two mistakes by providing an additional check through the simple expedient—as logical as it was efficacious, granted his premises

—of recognizing the veto power of the individual common-wealth upon an act of the Federal government. Stripped of its states-rights limitation, this was in germ the principle of the referendum, modified, however, by certain suggestive provisions.

The veto power as a protective principle Calhoun regarded as the hallmark of constitutional government. Granted that sovereignty under the Constitution inheres in the people, and that all authority is delegated, it follows that government is no more than an agent with strictly defined fiduciary powers, all the acts of which are subject to review by the principal. Whether such review shall be immediate and plenary, or at more or less remove and limited, becomes therefore a fundamental question of constitutional polity. Unfortunately much confusion has resulted from an intentional vagueness, contributed by interested groups to further particular ends, in the common understanding of the terms, the people and government. The former is rarely, as is usually assumed, a homogeneous body with common interests, but a congeries of individuals and groups and classes with diverse and often antagonistic interests; and the latter—in a republic—is never a sacred entity, the residuary legatee of sovereignty, to criticize which is to commit the crime of *lèse-majesté*, but a group of officials invested with temporary authority and actuated by motives common to all men. A necessary preliminary, therefore, to an intelligent understanding of the principle of veto is a critical analysis of these much misunderstood terms.

Calhoun was far too honest a realist to be under any hallucinations in regard to political government. He estimated at its full significance "the never-ending audacity of elected persons." Power he knew to be the most insidious of poisons; every government is liable to the disease of auto-intoxication. Seated securely in office the agent assumes all the prerogatives of the principal and clothes his acts with the sanctity of sovereignty. Armed with the taxing power, he distributes penalties and benefits with partial hand, and unless an adequate defense protects the weaker interests they will suffer a legal exploitation. Every government justly rests under suspicion, and only the most critical scrutiny of its conduct can keep it decently honest. Popular government, from which the Republicans hoped too much, changes only the outward form of the selfish struggle for power by substituting party rule for class rule. With its disciplined party machine the lure of political spoil encourages the most shameless exploitation of the weaker groups, who have no recourse.[2] Hence, the more popular the government, the more ruthless becomes the majority rule; and any system of checks and balances that does not adequately restrain this inherent tendency of party rule must prove a failure. However carefully the political philosopher may provide for a division of powers among executive, legislature and judiciary, he must fail of his object, for a regnant majority will control all three branches of government, and thus intrenched will defy the protests of the minority. The Montesquieu theory had proved a failure in practice.

An even greater danger, in Calhoun's judgment, lay in the current misinterpretation of the term "the people," the result of which was the obscuring of the economic basis of society and the befuddling of the whole problem of government. To this disastrous result, he believed, both schools of political thought had contributed. The early Republicans had oversimplified the political problem by assuming a clear division between ruler and subject. The conception was a heritage from European experience, where it had taken form as a strategic move to align the unthinking mass against a despotic monarchy. The Jeffersonians had used it to like purpose in their struggle against consolidation, appealing to a common democracy against the aristocracy. The early Federalists were even more blameworthy, for, understanding clearly the economic origins of political power and the economic ends served by the political state, they made their knowledge serve their interests and concealed their designs by deceptive appeals to patriotism. Every realist knows that "the people" is a political fiction. Society is made up of individuals, each with his particular interest. The total interests of the subject-citizens are necessarily complex. Group and classify them as he may, the political philosopher can never merge the parts in a coalescing whole, but must recognize that the problem remains one of adjustments and compromises. It follows therefore that any facile assumption that government represents the people or rests on the will of the people is a disastrous fallacy. Popular government rests on the will of the majority; aristocratic government rests on the will of the aristocracy; and despotic government rests on the will of the despot. It is an axiom that the political state is partisan to those who administer it. The stakes of

[2] See "A Disquisition on Government" in Calhoun's *Works*, Vol. I, pp 41–42.

71

rulership are high; the game of politics never lacks its devotees; the business of deceiving the people in order to pluck the goose has long been one of the respectable professions.

The perennial problem of constitutional government, then, in Calhoun's philosophy, remains what it was seen to be by the Federalist followers of Montesquieu—the problem of restraining government by constitutional checks to the end that it be kept just. Existing machinery having demonstrated its inadequacy, it remained to provide more effective. Freedom Calhoun regarded as the crown jewel of civilization, hardly won, easily lost. But freedom was not to be measured by *habeas corpus* acts and similar legal restraints on tyranny; it was freedom from legal exploitation and statutory dictatorship. "The abuse of delegated power, and the tyranny of the stronger over the weaker interests, are the two dangers, and the only two to be guarded against; and if this be done effectually, liberty must be eternal. Of the two, the latter is the greater and most difficult to resist" (*Works,* Vol. VI, p. 32). In more definite terms the problem is thus stated:

Two powers are necessary to the existence and preservation of free States: a power on the part of the ruled to prevent rulers from abusing their authority, by compelling them to be faithful to their constituents, and which is effected through the right of suffrage; and a power to compel the parts of society to be just to one another, by compelling them to consult the interest of each other—which can only be effected . . . by requiring the concurring assent of all the great and distinct interests of the community to the measures of the Government. This result is the sum-total of all the contrivances adopted by free States to preserve their liberty, by preventing the conflicts between the several classes or parts of the community. (*Ibid.,* Vol. VI, pp. 189–190.)

In elaboration of the second phase of the problem Calhoun contributed the principle on which his reputation as a political thinker must rest—the doctrine of a concurrent majority. He found his solution in an expansion of the principle of democracy—recovering the true principle, he was fond of insisting—by superimposing upon the consolidated, indiscriminate numerical majority the will of a geographical majority; or in other words, by a special form of sectional referendum.

It results, from what has been said, that there are two different modes in which the sense of the community may be taken: one, simply, by the right of suffrage, unaided; the other, by the right through a proper organism. Each collects the sense of the majority. But one regards numbers only, and considers the whole community one unit, having but one common interest throughout; and collects the sense of the greater number of the whole, as that of the community. The other, on the contrary, regards interests as well as numbers;—considering the community as made up of different and conflicting interests as far as the action of the government is concerned; and takes the sense of each, through its majority or appropriate organ, and the united sense of all, as the sense of the entire community. The former of these I call the numerical, or absolute majority; and the latter, the concurrent, or constitutional majority. ("A Disquisition on Government," in *Works*, Vol. I, p. 28.)

In such speculation on the possibility of achieving political justice by the machinery of representation, Calhoun was face to face with a revolutionary conception—the conception of proportional economic representation. The idea was implicit in his assumption of an existing economic sectionalism that must find adequate expression through political agencies. He had come to understand the futility of a miscellaneous numerical majority; he had only to go back to eighteenth-century philosophy and substitute economic classes for economic sectionalism, finding his social cleavages in economic groups instead of geographical divisions, to have recast the whole theory of representation. Clearly, he had made enormous strides in his thinking. He had long since put behind him the philosophy of Jefferson. He had subjected the principle of democracy to critical scrutiny. But instead of rejecting it as an unworkable hypothesis, as the Hamiltonian Federalists had done, he proposed to establish it on a sound and permanent basis. The ideal of democracy he conceived to be the noblest in the whole field of political thought, but misunderstood and misapplied as it had been in America, it had become the mother of every mischief. This betrayal of democracy he laid at the door of the Jeffersonians. They had accepted too carelessly the romantic dogmas of the French school, and had come to believe that democracy was synonymous with political equalitarianism.

It was this false notion that had debased the noble ideal, and delivered it over to the hands of the mob. To assert that men are created free and equal is to fly in the face of every biological and social fact. The first business of the true democrat, therefore, was to reëxamine the nature of democracy and strip away the false assumptions and vicious conclusions that had done it incalculable injury. The Greeks, he pointed out, understood its essential nature better than the moderns. Democracy assumes a co-partnership among equals. Its only rational foundation is good will, and it can function only through compromise. From this it follows that in a society composed of high and low, capable and weak, worthy and unworthy—as every historical society has been composed—a universal democracy is impractical. The numerous body of social incompetents will suffer one of two fates: they will be exploited by the capable minority under the guise of free labor, or they will be accepted as the wards of society and protected by the free citizens—they must inevitably become either wage slaves or bond slaves, in either case incapable of maintaining the rights of free members of the commonwealth. Democracy is possible only in a society that recognizes inequality as a law of nature, but in which the virtuous and capable enter into a voluntary co-partnership for the common good, accepting wardship of the incompetent in the interests of society. This was the Greek ideal and this ideal had created Greek civilization.

Calhoun was thus brought face to face with the natural-rights theory, which the glowing rhetoric of the Declaration of Independence had disseminated throughout America, and which lay as a virus at the heart of Jacksonianism. To destroy that theory, he believed, was a necessary preliminary to any rational theory of democracy, and he turned to the business with characteristic frankness. Upon the venerable dogmas he threw the light of his realism, subjecting them to critical analysis. The origin of government in compact was only a myth. The amiable being known as man in a state of nature, whose portrait had been drawn by the French romantics, he discovered in neither social nor biological history. The true origin of government, he asserted in common with John Adams, is to be found in practical necessity; government arises, as Hobbes had pointed out, from the universal fact of human selfishness. It has always been found necessary to lodge coercive powers in certain hands as a social protection against individual aggression; and since all men are impelled by self-interest, political systems are determined in form and scope by this universal instinct. Without government there is anarchy; with government there is potential tyranny. The crucial problem to be solved by the political philosopher, hence, is to determine the just delimitation between sovereign power and individual liberty; the one protecting the rights of the whole, the other keeping open fresh opportunity to advance.

Having thus established government on the firm basis of

social necessity, he proceeded to examine the romantic dog mas of liberty and equality.

It follows, from what has been stated, that it is a great and dangerous error to suppose that all people are equally entitled to liberty. It is a reward to be earned, not a blessing to be gratuitously lavished on all alike;—a reward reserved for the intelligent, the patriotic, the virtuous and deserving;—and not a boon to be bestowed on a people too ignorant, degraded and vicious, to be capable either of appreciating or of enjoying it. Nor is it any disparagement to liberty, that such is, and ought to be the case. On the contrary its greatest praise,—its proudest distinction is, that an all-wise Providence has reserved it, as the noblest and highest reward for the development of our faculties, moral and intellectual. A reward more appropriate than liberty could not be conferred on the deserving;—nor a punishment inflicted on the undeserving more just, than to be subject to lawless and despotic rule. This dispensation seems to be the result of some fixed law;—and every effort to disturb or defeat it, by attempting to elevate a people in the scale of liberty, above the point to which they are entitled to rise, must ever prove abortive, and end in disappointment. . . .

There is another error, not less great and dangerous, usually associated with the one which has just been considered. I refer to the opinion, that liberty and equality are so intimately united, that liberty cannot be perfect without perfect equality. That they are united to a certain extent,—and that equality of citizens, in the eyes of the law, is essential to liberty in a popular government, is conceded. But to go further, and make equality of *condition* essential to liberty, would be to destroy both liberty and progress. The reason is, that inequality of condition, while it is a necessary consequence of liberty, is, at the same time, indispensable to progress. . . . It is, indeed, this inequality of condition between the front and rear ranks, in the march of progress, which gives so strong an impulse to the former to maintain their position, and to the latter to press forward into their files. This gives to progress its greatest impulse. To force the front rank back to the rear, or attempt to push forward the rear into line with the front, by the interposition of the government, would put an end to the impulse, and effectually arrest the march of progress. ("A Disquisition on Government," in *Works,* Vol. I, pp. 55–56.)

It was the persuasive ideal of a Greek democracy in the plantation states that lay back of Calhoun's defense of slavery—a defense that thrusts into sharp relief the change of southern attitude in the decade of the thirties. The earlier Jeffersonian attitude had been fairly expressed by a

Georgia representative in the debate on the Missouri question:

> Believe me, sir, I am not a panegyrist of slavery. It is an unnatural state; a dark cloud which obscures half the lustre of our free institutions! . . . Would it be fair; would it be manly; would it be generous; would it be just, to offer contumely and contempt to the unfortunate man who wears a cancer in his bosom, because he will not submit to cautery at the hazard of his existence? (Quoted in Hunt, *John C. Calhoun*, p. 53.)

But with slavery put upon its defense, the southern spokesmen passed from apology to praise. From the first, Calhoun accepted the system implicitly, but now he subjected it to critical analysis in the light of his theory of a Greek democracy. Over against it he set the northern system of wage labor, and he came to the conclusion that the latter was more brutal and inhumane than the former. He was convinced that heretofore the South had made a serious mistake in apologizing for its peculiar institution, and in expecting its eventual extinction. In this matter the fathers had been wrong. No serious-minded Southerner any longer believed that slavery was on the way to natural extinction. It was spreading daily and must be permitted to spread. The hopes of southern civilization were bound up with it. The North must be brought to recognize it as a beneficent institution, necessary to a free, cultivated democracy, the only alternative to those fierce conflicts between wage and capital which already in the manufacturing states were threatening the permanence of American institutions. In a speech delivered in 1838, Calhoun thus sketched the new southern conception:

> Many in the South once believed that it [slavery] was a moral and political evil. That folly and delusion are gone. We see it now in its true light, and regard it as the most safe and stable basis for free institutions in the world. It is impossible with us that the conflict can take place between labor and capital, which makes it so difficult to establish and maintain free institutions in all wealthy and highly civilized nations where such institutions as ours do not exist. The Southern States are an aggregate, in fact, of communities, not of individuals. Every plantation is a little community, with the master at its head, who concentrates in himself the united interests of capital and labor, of which he is the common representative. These small communities aggregated make the State in all, whose action, labor, and capital is equally represented and perfectly harmonized. Hence the harmony, the union, the stability of that section which is rarely disturbed, ex-

cept through the action of this Government. The blessing of this state of things extends beyond the limits of the South. It makes that section the balance of the system; the great conservative power, which prevents other portions, less fortunately constituted, from rushing into conflict. . . . Such are the institutions which these deluded madmen are stirring heaven and earth to destroy, and which we are called on to defend by the highest and most solemn obligations that can be imposed on us as men and patriots. ("Remarks on the State Rights Resolutions in Regard to Abolition. January 12, 1838," in *Works*, Vol. III, p. 180.)

Thus in the end the political philosopher turns partisan to a cause. His fruitful speculations on the theory of representation, his inquiry into the economic basis of politics, remained incomplete, the larger reaches only half explored. Espousing the ideal of democracy, he yielded to the seductions of a Greek republic. Beginning as a Jeffersonian, he ended as the philosopher of a slave aristocracy, from whose principles men like Governor McDuffie of South Carolina deduced the dictum that "the laboring population of no nation on earth are entitled to liberty, or capable of enjoying it." It was a curious dream, yet no more curious than his faith in an obsolete article in the Constitution to withstand the advance of a hostile economy. There is something almost tragic in the self-deception of this clear-minded realist in his appeal to a paper defense against economic forces. "The Constitution—no interference—no discrimination," he cried passionately in repudiating the right of Abolition petition. "These are the grounds on which the battle may be safely fought. . . . You must tell these deluded fanatics, you have no right to intermeddle in any form or shape. . . . Expediency, justice, plighted faith, and the Constitution: these, and these only, can be relied on to avert conflict" (*Works*, Vol. III, p. 190).

Lost faiths and repudiated prophets go down to a common grave. The living have little inclination to learn from the dead. The political principles of Calhoun have had scant justice done them by later generations who incline to accept the easy opinion that the cause which triumphs is altogether the better cause. What Calhoun so greatly feared has since come about. He erected a last barrier against the progress of middle-class ideals—consolidation in politics and standardization in society; against a universal cash-register evaluation of life: and the barrier was blown to pieces by the guns of the Civil War. Historically he was the last spokesman of the great school of the eighteenth century, the intellectual descendant of John Adams. The two men were much alike in the broad principles of their political philosophy, and identical necessities brought them to identical conclusions. They agreed in the fundamental principle that property will rule by reason of its inherent power, and that political justice is attainable only by a nicely calculated system of checks and balances, which provides each important group with a defensive veto. But in the social experience on which Adams founded his doctrine, political antagonism was potential in rival classes, and justified a division of powers on the model of the British constitution. In the intervening years, however, the economic alignment had become sectional, the rise of party government had created a new problem, and the earlier division of powers seemed to demand a supplementary veto if the nice balance contemplated in the Constitution were to be maintained. This was the kernel of the states-rights doctrine which Calhoun elaborated with such skill. That he should have associated the principle with a cause that was doomed was disastrous to the just fame of Calhoun. More, it was disastrous to the vital democratic principle of decentralized powers. In championing a Greek democracy Calhoun affronted the latent idealism of America, and the harm he did to agrarian democracy was incalculable.

III

ALEXANDER H. STEPHENS: *Constitutionalist*

Southern scholars are pretty well agreed that the ablest defender of the doctrine of secession was Alexander H. Stephens, the Georgia commoner. He was sprung from the plain people. Brought up in severe poverty, self-taught, the friend of the poor, he was no child of an exclusive planter aristocracy, and was never quite trusted by them. The victim of a slight, ramshackly physique, never weighing a hundred pounds, never knowing a well day, fearfully handicapped in the everyday matter of living, it is amazing that soul and body held together for seventy-one years and more amazing that he accomplished what he did. "Throughout life," says one of his biographers, "he was practically a brain without a body." Temperamentally despondent, he was driven into restless activity to forget self. His will was fine-tempered steel and ill health never broke his courage even when it laid him on his back. He feared nothing, but took a position and argued a cause without regard to personal consequences. He never flinched from the personal encounters which the

lawless code of Georgia politics invited. A morbid consciousness of his feeble physique sometimes drove him into trucu-
lence, and on one occasion he was stabbed eighteen times
by a certain ornament of the Georgia bench, and saved his
life only by grasping the blade that was driven at his throat.
But such encounters can be explained on the ground of over-
correction; the real Stephens was gentle, peace-loving, hating all swaggerers military or civilian, "a man of generous
sympathies, of broad humanity, a democrat of democrats, a
friend of all the world" (Pendleton, *Alexander H. Stephens,*
p. 253). The words *Non sibi sed aliis,* cut in his tombstone
at Crawfordville, come nearer the truth than epitaphs usually
do. He was never selfishly ambitious and he could justly say
after the fall of the Confederacy, "I am old and weak in
bodily infirmity, but I have done my duty to God and my
country, and I am ready for whatever fate may be assigned
me" (*ibid.,* p. 393).

Stephens was a lifelong student of politics, regarding it as
"one of the most intricate, as well as interesting subjects that
can engage the attention of reflecting minds." He was not a
political philosopher like Calhoun, concerned with principle
and theory, but a constitutional historian concerned to trace
the genesis and development of the fundamental law of the
land. He was probably more widely read in the early literature of the Constitution than any other man of his generation. He had thumbed and dog-eared Elliot's *Debates,* and
could cite dates and explain circumstances for the elucidation of doubtful points or the correcting of an unhistorical
interpretation. He knew the genesis of every article, of almost every word in the Constitution, and the reasons which
determined the special form which each assumed; and this
exact knowledge equipped him for the task of critical commentator on earlier commentators. Unfortunate was the theo-
rizer who fell into his hands. Federalist expositors like Story
and Motley, given to rash generalization from inadequate
data, suffered disaster under his critical inspection. With his
fund of historical knowledge he was amply prepared for the
labor of love to which he turned after the war, and in his
Constitutional View of the War between the States he produced one of the most notable studies in the origin of the
Constitution that we have.

Certain deep personal needs, taking form in passionate
conviction, determined the bias of Stephens' political philosophy, which was quite simple, consistent and inflexible, from
his first entry into public life until his death. There was no

subtlety in his intellectual processes, no balancing uncertainly between diverse appeals, but a clear faith which he expounded to the common voter in confident expectation that it would awaken sympathetic response. His extensive reading was not so much a disinterested search for light on the ideal relations of men in society, as for confirmation of certain prepossessions. That those prepossessions were shared by his fellow Georgians, that they were the natural product of existing social conditions, gave to them an added sanction. The creative source of his philosophy was a passionate love of freedom; and his meditations convinced him that the only freedom worth a tuppence is civil liberty under civil law—that the test of any civilization is the concern it manifests for the safeguarding of such liberty by exact and adequate constitutional provisions. His reverence for law was a religion with him, and his love of the Constitution as the fostering mother of the law was only this side idolatry. "No stronger or more ardent Union man ever lived than I was," he asserted late in life. Intense loyalty was almost commonplace amongst the people from whom he sprang. Love of the Union, and of the Constitution as a guarantee of that Union, was far stronger in the South before the Civil War than in the North. But it was the Constitution of the fathers, not a newfangled consolidating instrument that drew all power to Washington, that they loved. Pride of locality—naïve though it might be and provincial—the spontaneous pride of a simple untraveled people—was rooted in the southern heart. It was nourished by a deep love of homestead and neighborhood, natural to an agrarian society; and it came to political expression in the doctrine that the commonwealth must be free to manage its own affairs in its own way. The theory of states rights, amongst such a people, was not an abstract principle but an expression of the psychology of localism created by everyday habit. This explains the intensity of conviction which colors the thought of Stephens. The principle of local sovereignty was inbred. He rarely deigns to argue the question. He never concerned himself with abstract argument—as Jefferson had done—to prove the superior excellence of local home rule. This failure, indeed, may perhaps be accounted his greatest weakness as a political thinker. Rather he was concerned to prove that state sovereignty existed prior to the Union, that it was jealously guarded at the making of the Constitution, that it had never been surrendered, and hence was the constitutional order until destroyed by the Civil War. But if he refrained from abstract argument touching the desirability of localizing political power, he exhibited a Jeffersonian fear of unregulated power which consolidation makes possible.

This passionate love of freedom he exemplified in his own career. He followed his convictions and spoke his own mind, regardless of occasion or circumstance. He was no man's tool. He hated a demagogue and never curried favor with his constituents or calculated popular response. In his public life he considered himself a representative of the people of Georgia, and the one object of his labors was the preservation of that constitutional liberty in which they had grown up. In furtherance of this policy he found himself not infrequently at odds with other southern leaders. He vigorously opposed his party in its Mexican war policy, looking upon it as no other than imperialistic vandalism aimed at a weaker neighbor for the purpose of extending slave territory. There was no glamor for him in military victories; he would not concede that a republic might plead manifest destiny in extenuation of armed aggression, or that the ends of civilization may be furthered by war. In a speech opposing the policy of his fellow Whigs, he thus expressed his conception of national progress:

I am no enemy to the extension of our domain, or the enlargement of the boundaries of the republic. I trust the day is coming, and not far distant, when the whole continent will be ours; when our institutions shall be diffused and cherished, and republican government enjoyed, throughout the length and breadth of this land. . . . That this is our ultimate destiny, if wise counsels prevail, I confidently believe. But it is not to be accomplished by the sword. . . . Republics never spread by arms. We can properly enlarge only by voluntary accessions. . . .

There is much said in this country of the party of progress. I profess to be of that party; but I am far from advocating that kind of progress which many of those who seem anxious to appropriate the term exclusively to themselves are using their exertions to push forward. Theirs, in my opinion, is a downward progress. It is a progress of party, of excitement, of lust of power; a spirit of war, aggression, violence and licentiousness. It is a progress which, if indulged in, would soon sweep over all law, all order, and the Constitution itself. . . . It is to progress in *these* essential attributes of national greatness that I would look: the improvement of mind, the "increase and diffusion of knowledge among men," the erection of schools, colleges and temples of learning; the progress of intellect over matter; the triumph of mind over the animal propensities; the advancement of kind feeling and good will among the nations of the earth; the cultivation of virtue and the pursuits of industry; the bringing into subjection and subservience to the use of man of all the elements of nature around us; in a word, the progress of civilization, and everything that elevates and ennobles man. This . . . is not to be done by wars, whether foreign or domestic. Fields of blood and carnage may make men brave and heroic, but seldom tend to make nations either virtuous or great. (Quoted in Pendleton, *Alexander H. Stephens,* pp. 79–80.)

A man of peace, Stephens was greatly agitated over the movement of secession. He fought the Fire Eaters to the bitter end in his native state, but like other high-minded Southerners he went out with his commonwealth. Loyalty to Georgia was stronger than loyalty to the nation. But in the new order he preserved his old principles. The Jeffersonian democrat could not forget his teachings. When the Confederacy was discussing its proposed Constitution, he took alarm at some loose talk about the desirability of setting up a monarchy. His old friend Bob Toombs, one of the ablest of the southern leaders, quite frankly preferred the English system to the American.[3] There seems to have been considerable comment to like effect amongst the Tory hot-heads; but the wind was not blowing in that direction and such straws were only the stirrings of vagrant eddies. The Constitution as adopted was more democratic than the older instrument—an outcome to which Stephens contributed greatly.

As Vice President of the Confederacy he constituted himself the special guardian of constitutional liberty, and his jealous concern at what he regarded as administrative usurpations of power brought on grave differences with President Davis. Even in the urgent crises of war he would not sanction the use of extra-constitutional powers. He knew better than most that power grows by what it feeds on, that too often war destroys the liberty it professes to be serving. To win the war and lose the peace, to secede in defense of constitutional rights and then tamely yield them up, seemed to him a pitiful ending, and when President Davis suspended the right of *habeas corpus* and his generals proclaimed martial law, he took alarm. "All such orders," he said, "are palpable and dangerous usurpations, and if permitted to continue will end in military despotism. . . . Better in my judgment that Richmond should fall, and that the enemy's armies should sweep our whole country from the Potomac to the Gulf than that our people should submissively yield obedience to one of these edicts of our own generals" (Pendleton, *Alexander*

[3] See Pendleton, *Alexander H. Stephens,* p. 231, note.

H. Stephens, p. 292). Freedom of speech he would not have interfered with under any excuse. The suspension of civil law he considered a threat aimed at every citizen of the South. He had heard, he said, that one purpose of the act was "to control certain elections and certain expected assemblages in North Carolina"—where there was a good deal of disaffection—"to put a muzzle upon certain presses, and a bit in the mouth of certain speakers of that State. If this be so, I regard it as the more dangerous to public liberty" (*ibid.*, p. 313). To the question, "Can you not trust the President?" he replied in words that deserve to be remembered:

> To the question of whether I would not or cannot trust him with these high powers not conferred by the Constitution, my answer is: I am utterly opposed to everything looking to or tending toward dictatorship in this country. There is no man living and not one of the illustrious dead, whom, if now living, I would so trust. . . . I would not turn on my heel to choose between masters. I was not born to acknowledge a master from either the North or the South. I shall never choose between candidates for that office. I have no wish or desire to live after the degradation of my country, and have no intention to survive its liberties, if life be the necessary sacrifice of their maintenance to the utmost of my abilities. (*Ibid.*, pp. 313–314.)

No argument of expediency, no appeal to military necessity ever moved him from the belief that the sole justification of government is the maintenance of liberty, and that the sole guarantee of such liberty is the orderly process of civil law. He was harassed by the encroachment upon individual freedom demanded by war, north as well as south. "The North to-day," he said, "presents the spectacle of a free people having gone to war to make freemen of slaves, while all they have as yet attained is to make slaves of themselves" (*ibid.*, p. 293). Perhaps no other public man in America kept his head amidst the passions of the time so completely as Stephens. He was utterly beyond reach of jingo appeal, and he suffered what the individual must expect to suffer who pits his single conscience against the mass will. He was branded as a traitor, and only his extraordinary hold on the affections of the plain people of Georgia saved him from the bitterest experience.

During the black period following the southern collapse, when he was disfranchised, broken in health past mending, and hated by the followers of President Davis, Stephens sought distraction in writing American history. Three and a half years, from 1867 to 1870, he devoted to his *Constitutional*

View of the Late War between the States. The case for states rights has never been more convincingly put than in this monumental study. The first volume in particular, which deals with the history of the Constitution, is an acute and able work. The thesis on which it rests is the doctrine which Paine and Jefferson derived from the French school, namely, that a constitutional compact is terminable. Elaborated by Stephens and applied to the case in question, the doctrine becomes this: that the right of secession is a civil as well as a revolutionary right; that it is implied in the compact originally entered into by the several states; that any state may rightfully take back what it had peacefully granted, when such action shall seem to it desirable. The sovereign commonwealth has never abrogated its sovereignty; the Constitution is a Federal compact amongst equals; the United States is a federated Union, not an organic nation. To conceive of the organic law as a consolidating instrument binding the individual citizen immediately to the central government, as Webster and Judge Story had done, was not only unhistorical but contrary to every fact and every tradition. To arrive at the principle of consolidation, and hold that the right of secession is only a revolutionary right, one must deliberately shut one's eyes to the early history of the Constitution.

Not content to prove the original compact nature of the Constitution—an argument that runs through fourteen hundred pages, buttressed by a mass of citations from all sources and wholly convincing in its evidence—Stephens undertakes to prove the wisdom of the fathers in establishing the federal union in compact. In respecting existing loyalties to the several commonwealths, they not only preserved the local democracies—which, as a Jeffersonian, Stephens believed were the foundation of good government—but they established the federal state on a strong and enduring foundation. The Hamiltonian consolidationists had asserted that a strong state must rest on the principle of coercive sovereignty, that it can be held together only through the exercise of authority. Stephens replied by laying down the counter principle that the secret of a strong and enduring state is to be discovered in the spontaneous loyalty of its citizens, and that in consequence a democracy which rests on the good will of the people as a whole is the most enduring of all forms.

A Government, to be worth anything, . . . must be strong. Its parts and members must be held together by force of some sort This I cordially admit. We do not differ as to the force or its extent; we differ only as to its nature and character. Should it be a physical or moral force? In my judgment, the strongest force that can hold the parts or constituent elements of any Government together is the affection of the people towards it. (*Constitutional View, etc.*, Vol. I, p. 526.)

Affection, he reasoned, cannot be coerced. It must spring spontaneously from the recognition that government is useful, that it is just, that it treats all its parts and members equally, that it is an agency erected by a free people to serve the ends of freedom. Allegiance is an individual compact between the citizen and government. Destroy the principle of voluntary allegiance, seek to coerce the citizen, impose upon minorities the ruthless will of majorities, subjugate individual commonwealths, and the federal Union which Jefferson believed to be "the strongest Government on Earth," would indeed become what Hamilton in his blindness to the secret of power believed that it was—"a frail and worthless fabric." "But the indissoluble union between the several states of this Confederated Nation is, after all, not in the *right,* but in the *heart*" (*ibid.,* Vol. I, p. 527). So long as the rights of all are respected, the common interest and common loyalty will preserve the union. Injustice alone is to be feared, for no political bonds can long resist the action of this most potent of social dissolvents.

Modern as Stephens was in the assertion of the principle of good will as the source of sovereignty in democratic government, he belonged to his own generation in his blindness to economic motives. He thought exclusively in legal and constitutional terms; he remained wholly a lawyer. It is hard to understand how one so profoundly read in our political history should have failed to discover the workings of economic forces beneath the surface of politics. Calhoun, bred in the same Jeffersonian school, had found his way through the mist of equalitarianism to the solid realism of an earlier day; but to the last of his fourteen hundred pages of exposition Stephens retained the illusion that the political state is something apart from economics and superior to it. He conceived of government as an end in itself, and this lends an air of unreality to his thinking. An ardent Jeffersonian, he reduced the philosophy of his master to the compact theory of government. The economic basis of Jefferson's philosophy, his love of an agrarian order and hatred of capitalistic exploitation—motives which serve to explain and justify his theory of local self government—Stephens wholly ignores. The result is a grotesque perversion of a philosophy which John

Taylor had elaborated clearly. Jefferson was a much greater political thinker than Stephens conceived, although he called him the "greatest philosophical stateman" America has produced. In his estimate of Andrew Jackson he falls into the same mistake. He attempts to reduce the confused career of Jackson—half middle-class in his earlier years and later returning to agrarian principles—to the same narrow compass of the compact theory. Even Webster, for whom he entertained "the highest esteem and admiration," and in praise of whose moral qualities he is almost fulsome,[4] he quite failed to understand. Webster's theory of the Constitution, he clearly demonstrated, was utterly unhistorical; but Webster's economic alliances he ignored. What havoc was wrought in current politics by suffering political theory to obscure economic reality is suggested by the fact that Stephens, a Jeffersonian in every instinct, turned Whig and voted for Webster in 1852—after the latter's death. Politics makes strange bed-fellows, yet it must have been an ample bed that could sleep the spokesman of an agrarian economy and the spokesman of capitalism side by side.

In his attitude towards slavery Stephens was a product of his Georgia environment. His views were ready-made, out of the common southern storehouse. The economic determinism which he ignored in politics had its revenge, and the man who often differed with his constituents on political issues fell victim to the subtle power of economics. As the South Carolina philosophy took form, issuing finally in the romantic conception of a Greek democracy, it imposed itself imperiously on the southern mind, on the commoner equally with the aristocrat. It was impossible to escape, unless, like Moncure Conway, one were of an idealistic temper far different from the common run. For Stephens it proved impossible. In this matter of slavery he had no individual opinion; his mind was molded by the common psychology and became a repository of the common prejudice. He followed his fire-eating friend Bob Toombs into the camp of Calhoun, and talked about a Greek democracy in true Charleston style. In a speech delivered on March 21, 1861, shortly after he was chosen Vice President of the Confederacy, he gave expression to the new philosophy in these words:

The prevailing ideas entertained by . . . most of the leading statesmen at the time of the formation of the old Constitution

4 See A Constitutional View, etc., Vol. I, pp 406–408.

were that the enslavement of the African was in violation of the laws of nature; that it was wrong in principle, socially, morally, and politically. It was an evil they knew not well how to deal with, but the general opinion of the men of that day was that, somehow or other in the order of Providence, the institution would be evanescent and pass away. . . . Those ideas, however, were fundamentally wrong. They rested upon the assumption of the equality of races. This was an error. Our new government is founded upon exactly the opposite idea; its foundations are laid, its corner-stone rests upon the great truth that the negro is not equal to the white man; that slavery—subordination to the superior race—is his natural and normal condition . . . in conformity with the ordinance of the Creator. . . . Our Confederacy is founded upon principles in strict conformity with these [Divine] laws. This stone which was rejected by the first builders "is become the chief of the corner"—the real "corner-stone" in our new edifice. (Pendleton, *Alexander H. Stephens*, pp. 251–254.)

To the end of his life Stephens saw no reason to change his opinion on Negro slavery. He regarded it as more humane than wage slavery because of the patriarchal responsibility devolving upon the master. The institution was not founded, he said, on "the erroneous dogma of the greatest good to the greatest number," but on the broader principle of securing "the greatest good possible, morally, intellectually, and politically, to all classes of persons . . . without necessary wrong or detriment to any" (*Constitutional View, etc.*, Vol. I, pp. 539–542). In his relations with his own slaves he followed the best traditions of the South. His kindness won their loyalty and affection. "Ef he ain't in heaven," said a house servant after his death, " 'tain't no use for anybody else to try to git dere" (Pendleton, *Alexander H. Stephens*, p. 100). To the argument of Hinton Helper that the system was economically ruinous to the poor white, he seems to have given no consideration; but to the argument of the Abolitionist that it was immoral, he replied with deep conviction. On that point he would not yield an inch. After quoting a miscellany of Biblical texts from the earliest Hebraic times down to Paul, he comments naïvely:

To maintain that Slavery is *in itself sinful*, in the face of all that is said and written in the Bible upon the subject, with so many sanctions of the relation by the Deity himself, does seem to me to be little short of blasphemous! It is a direct imputation upon the wisdom and justice, as well as the declared ordinances of God, as they are written in the inspired oracles, to say nothing of their manifestation in the universe around us. (*Ibid.*, Vol. II, p. 83.)

It is doubtful wisdom for the layman to meddle with Scripture. Stephens was a sounder interpreter of the writings of the constitutional fathers than of the will of God.

A careful historian devoted to a single idea rather than a creative political thinker; a thorough democrat of the Jeffersonian school, humanitarian, liberty-loving, courageous; a man who devoted his life to the preservation of constitutional liberty as it had taken shape before the industrial revolution unsettled the basis of modern life, Alexander H. Stephens was an honest gentleman who bravely defended the traditions of the South in the face of a new order. He was of an earlier generation, instinctively hostile to all consolidation, which, under the impulse of economic evolution, was obliterating state lines, gathering financial power in great reservoirs, and creating a new alignment between labor and capital. With such evolution it was axiomatic that political practice should follow economic fact; that a consolidating wealth should create a consolidated political state. Great enterprises with ramifications in every section would not long tolerate a multitude of state sovereignties; sovereignty must be centralized at Washington where it could be guided and controlled. The war only hastened what in the nature of things was inevitable. Stephens rightly insisted that slavery was only the immediate *casus belli*. The deeper cause was the antagonistic conceptions of the theory and functions of the political state that emerged from antagonistic economic systems. That the principle of local self-government should have been committed to the cause of slavery, that it was loaded with an incubus certain to alienate the liberalism of the North, may be accounted one of the tragedies of American history. It was disastrous to American democracy, for it removed the last brake on the movement of consolidation, submerging the democratic individualism of the South in an unwieldy mass will, and surrendering the country to the principle of capitalistic exploitation. Stephens never seems to have realized this grave mistake in strategy. He never realized that the principle of democracy, in the cause of which he believed that he was faithful to the end, received a staggering blow from the enlistment of northern liberalism under the banners of a consolidating nationalism. He remained to the last an unreconstructed Jeffersonian, convinced that the lost cause was the cause of liberal democracy.

IV

FRANCIS LIEBER: *A New-Modeled Federalism*

To turn from Calhoun and Stephens to Francis Lieber is to
pass from the South to the North, from an obsolescent political theory to a prophetic conception, from the doctrine of
states rights to the principle of an evolving state that draws
all lesser sovereignties into its orbit by the law of attraction.
Joseph Story had educed the legal conception of the organic
nature of the federal union from the terms of the Constitution; Francis Lieber provided a philosophical background
that justified the same conclusion; and under the combined
legal and philosophical attack the compact theory found its
philosophical breastworks leveled, its natural-rights theory
undermined, and its commanding position effectively turned.

The figure of our first academic political philosopher appears oddly out of place in the midst of South Carolina politicians, yet fate set the studious German in the thick of the
Fire Eaters, to cogitate a philosophy of freedom in the land
of slavery, and to justify the spirit of nationalism amongst
the advocates of particularism. For twenty-one years he lived
quietly in his southern classroom and study, disregarding the
passions that buzzed about him, elaborating ideas that in
later years came to exercise a determining influence upon
our academic political thinkers, and publishing ponderous
volumes that marked the beginning of the swing away from
the natural-rights philosophy and towards the conception of
an engrossing political state. Applying German liberalism
to American constitutionalism, he succeeded in new-model-
ing the Federalism of Hamilton and sending it forth to meet
the needs of an imperializing generation. He agreed with
Calhoun in the latter's attack on French romantic theories;
he agreed with Webster in the conception of the organic
nature of the federal compact; but he went further and
elaborated a theory of the state as an historical development
that receives its form and spirit from the impress of social
needs. Building on a foundation provided by Montesquieu
and Burke, guided by Hamilton and Marshall, he set about
erecting a structure that in the hands of Theodore Woolsey
and John W. Burgess came to overtop all local and state
sovereignties—an imperial authority that, in the words of
Burgess, must become "the organ of interpretation in last
instance of the order of life for its subjects" (Merriam, *American Political Theories*, p. 299). In that subtle shift of vocabulary from citizen to subject appears the final result of

the speculations begun by Lieber, which in rejecting the natural-rights philosophy overthrew the defenses erected by the eighteenth century against an engrossing political state, and set the individual citizen at the mercy of a new divine-right sovereignty. "Really the state cannot be conceived," according to Burgess, "without sovereignty, *i.e.* without unlimited power over its subjects; that is its very essence" (Merriam, *American Political Ideas: 1865–1917*, p. 380).

Between the democratic Stephens and the imperializing Burgess stands the work of Francis Lieber. Born in Germany in the year 1800, son of a well-to-do Berlin family, Lieber's youth and young manhood fell in stirring times. When only fifteen he served in the Waterloo campaign under Blücher, was wounded, stricken with typhus, and nearly lost his life. From those perilous experiences he emerged a pronounced liberal. During the Metternich reaction he fell under suspicion, served a prison term for his political opinions, graduated from the University of Jena, and in 1822 went to Greece with a group of young German idealists to serve the cause of revolution. Disgusted with the Greek character he made his way to Italy, fell in with the historian Niebuhr, became tutor to the latter's son for a year, continued his university studies, was a second time imprisoned, and finally in 1826 quitted a hopelessly reactionary Germany, spent a year in England, and then emigrated to America, following the example of Prof. Charles Follen. In Boston he taught gymnastics for a time, edited the *Encyclopedia Americana*, and in 1835 was appointed to the professorship of history and political economy in South Carolina College. Here he remained till 1856, teaching, writing, and acquiring academic fame. In 1855 he aspired to the presidency of the college, a post then vacant, but his political theories were in disrepute with the legislature, and his views on slavery were under general suspicion. Becoming embroiled with the politicians, he lost the post, resigned his professorship, and went to New York City, and in 1857 he was called to the new chair of history and political science at Columbia, where he remained till his death in 1872.

The two books on which rests his reputation, *Political Ethics* (1838–1839) and *Civil Liberty and Self-Government* (1853), are substantial volumes quite lacking the genial note that marks his *Stranger in America* (1834), a series of sketchy letters that among other things contains an extraordinarily vivid account of his experiences at Waterloo (*Letters VI, VII*). To a casual reader these excursions into the philosophy of politics are as soberly respectable as a judge's wig, as studiously conventional as a professor's gown. He went about the business of blowing up the accepted Jeffersonian philosophy decently, in the name of the law and under the high sanction of liberty. There can be no doubt that this German liberal was a passionate lover of liberty, and no doubt of his conviction that freedom is possible only in a society under the reign of law. Like Hamilton, he had no local ties or state loyalties to circumscribe his political allegiance. It was natural for him to think in terms of nationality. His bitter experience in Germany had laid open to him the fatal weakness of petty states, and he was loath to see repeated in America the history of warning antagonisms that disrupted the German people. He was a profound admirer of the British constitution, more English than German in his conception of liberty.

The nationalism of Lieber was identical with that of John Adams. It was, in a phrase, government by law. But this government by law was both political and legal. The former, he believed, was admirably provided for by the federal Constitution; the latter was equally provided for by the body of the Common Law; with these twin safeguards, he was convinced, the liberty of the citizen Lieber was assured. In his interpretation of the Constitution Lieber added little that was new. He followed the older Federalists back to Montesquieu, and accepted the existing system of constitutional checks as the final word of political wisdom. In *Civil Liberty and Self-Government* he glorifies the federal system as the apotheosis of representative republicanism, quite unconcerned at its undemocratic features. The sufficiency of the Common Law to all social needs and the implicit sovereignty of the judiciary, he regards as equally axiomatic. "The law," he says, "must be the lord and our 'earthly god,' and not a man, a set of men, or the multitude" (*Civil Liberty and Self-Government*, p. 208). Yet with the common blindness of the legalist, he proceeds to erect a profession above society, and exalts a group of judges, appointive and not elective, preferably holding office for life, as the embodiment of impartial justice. That it is a presumption contrary to fact seems not to have entered his mind. That judicial interpretation implies judicial legislation, and that judicial legislation implies the sovereignty of lawyers, are logical deductions of which his philosophy made no account. Unfriendly to a democracy, he was content to yield authority into the hands of the judiciary.

But if in his exaltation of the Common Law he was as extreme a legalist as Hugh Legaré, in his doctrine of historical evolution he discovered the seeds of freedom in what he calls institutions. By these he means the organic expressions of daily life, or the customs of society which take spontaneous form from its needs. It is no other than the social fabric that Tom Paine was fond of contrasting, in its pervasive and beneficent coöperation, with the repressive tyrannies of the political state. Where liberty reposes thus in the social fabric, Lieber argues, the sovereign power is held in check; and where institutional freedom has not taken root, the political state will run into absolutism.

"Liberty," he argues, "is a thing that grows, and institutions are its very garden beds. There is no liberty which as a national blessing has leaped into existence in full armor like Minerva from the head of Jove. Liberty is crescive in its nature. It takes time, and is difficult, like all noble things. . . . It must be defended, developed, conquered, and bled for. It can never be added, like a mere capital on a column; it must pervade the whole body" (*Civil Liberty and Self-Government,* pp. 334–335, third edition). "Liberty stands in need of character," and this character is received from social institutions. He then proceeds:

. . . An institution is a system or body of usages, laws, or regulations of extensive and recurring operation, containing within itself an organism by which it effects its own independent action, continuance, and generally its own farther development. Its object is to generate, effect, regulate, or sanction a succession of acts, transactions, or productions of a peculiar class or kind. The idea of an institution implies a degree of self-government. Laws act through human agents, and these are, in the case of institutions, their officers or members. (*Ibid.,* p. 300.)

It was the deep-rooted *civisme anglais,* he believed, that had developed the orderly liberty of the English race; and it is this same institutional spirit that provides the surest check upon the augmenting power of the political state. There can be no tyranny where society is trained and disciplined in liberty.

The creative source and origin of this excellent *civisme anglais* Lieber discovered in the principle of local self-government; in the exercise of local control of local interests; the enjoyment of innumerable lesser sovereignties within the larger national organism. These lesser sovereignties are both civil and social, and the amount of liberty enjoyed in a given society is measured by the independent vigor with which they function. The exercise of definite rights by the several states is clearly one of the important institutional functions of self-government, but it is only one. The New England town-meeting, county and city governments, are even more important, while outside these civil organisms are innumerable social organisms, exercising their common right of establishing by-laws for their own governance, and spreading the spirit of liberty through all the practices of society.

According to the Anglican view, institutional self-government consists in the fact that all the elementary parts of the government, as well as the highest and most powerful branches, consist in real institutions . . . [but it] consists, farther, in the unstinted freedom and fair protection which are granted to institutions of all sorts, commercial, religious, cultural, scientific, charitable, and industrial, to germinate and to grow—provided they are moral and do not invade the equal rights of others. It receives its ailment from a pervading spirit of self-reliance and self-respect— the real afflatus of liberty. (*Ibid.*, p. 320.)

This, quite evidently, is the spirit of *laissez faire* applied to political philosophy. A people thus used to order their social affairs, as the English people have long done, will prove competent to manage their political affairs; and the widespread spirit of individual independence will prevent the drift towards unregulated centralism with its corollary of tyrannical power. The conception of institutional liberty embodies much of the spirit of Jeffersonianism, and it goes back in its origins as far as Roger Williams. The states-rights advocates, Lieber implies, were mistaken in seeking the principle of liberty through particularism. In magnifying the individual commonwealth they overlooked the more vital units of self-government. To erect the state above the nation was no lasting solution of the most difficult problem in political philosophy, namely, the coördination of sovereign power with individual liberty; it was only to substitute one sovereignty for another, whereas to encourage the spread of self-governing bodies through society was to provide the necessary countercheck to centralizing power and coördinate liberty and sovereignty under the reign of law.

A stimulating thinker was this German liberal with his historical method and his conception of an evolutionary freedom rooted in the institutions of the English people. He gave a new turn to speculation on the origin and nature of the political state, the immediate consequence of which was the repudiation of the compact theory and natural-rights philosophy by our academic political scientists. The organic conception of the political state fell in with the centralizing movement that followed the Civil War, a movement which the forces of institutional self-government have been powerless to prevent. On the whole the influence of Lieber has been rather against than for that liberty which was so dear to him, and the explanation is to be found in the tragic divorce, in his thinking, of politics and economics. His inveterate legalism and his failure to investigate the economics of politics proved in the end the undoing of his liberalism.

CHAPTER III

The Dream of a Greek Democracy

I

The pronounced drift of southern thought, in the years immediately preceding the Civil War, towards the ideal of the Greek democracy, has been too carelessly forgotten by later times. It was no vagrant eddy but a broadening current of tendency. In its blend of romanticism and realism it fitted exactly the temper of the plantation mind, imparting a fine idealism to shiftless realities and setting a generous goal to be achieved by somewhat inadequate agencies. A humane and cultivated democracy, set free from the narrow exactions of economics to engage in the higher work of civilization, was a conception worthy of the generous southern mind, a conception that does not suffer by contrast with the northern dream of an exploitative industrialism. That it was an impossible dream does not lessen its significance as an expression of the best southern aspiration in the days when slavery was on the defensive.

It is plain enough now that this drift of thought resulted from the need of clarifying the logic of the situation, by bringing into harmony two seemingly irreconcilable facts, the system of Negro slavery and the rising spirit of white democracy. The feudal principle, which lurks in the background of all slave systems and which was peculiarly congenial to the plantation temper, was confronted on every

94

side by the stubborn democracy of the yoemanry. A hundred miles beyond Charleston the feudal spirit encountered the leveling individualism of the frontier; and this passion for equality, that grew fiercer with every remove westward, was a stumbling-block in the way of the planter aristocracy. Caught thus between the two forces of a Jeffersonian democracy and a slave economy, southern thought found in the Greek ideal the most natural compromise. Since manual labor was black, a white skin was a guarantee against serfdom, and the common race prejudice was accounted sufficient to draw even the poor whites to the support of slavery. The sharp cleavage between the races provided the basis for conception of a common white democracy of the master ss, every member of which shared in the supremacy of the race and was free to enjoy the profits of Negro exploitation. The enterprising small farmer might rise to be a gentlemanly planter, providing his children with leisure to fit themselves for citizenship in the commonwealth and assist in the great work of creating a southern civilization. The Greek ideal, in short, met the double need of southern economics and southern prejudices, and made its appeal even to the frontier spirit of equalitarianism.

A native growth and rooted deep in southern realities, the new conception emerged in response to the changing times. It may be considered the plantation counterpart of northern industrialism, marking the reaction of the southern mind to the economic revolution in western civilization. With their diverse economics, North and South were facing in different directions, and the Greek ideal was as natural in Charleston as industrial feudalism was natural in Lowell. Created in part as an ingenious measure of defense, it provided an excellent counter offensive against alien critics by turning the light of inquiry upon the bases of capitalism and thrusting upon the attention of godly Puritans the dependence of culture upon exploitation. The new industrialism was creating a new philosophy of labor, and this philosophy the southern apologists seized upon and turned to their special ends. They accepted certain of the capitalistic premises, but they interpreted those premises in a spirit of drastic realism, deducing conclusions disconcerting to the apologists of industrialism. In defending the plantation system they attacked the factory system; in upholding black slavery they attacked wage slavery; and in this game of the pot and the kettle the exploitative root of both systems was nakedly exposed.

The major premise of the new southern philosophy was

identical with that of northern capitalism, namely, that every civilization rests on labor exploitation. However quaintly they might embroider this fact with romantic patterns, they saw it clearly and deduced from it the conclusion that the North was indulging in a vicious fallacy in confusing wage labor with free labor. In every industrialized society, they pointed out, free labor is an anachronism; where it exists it is a hold-over from a simpler social order. The development of industrialism tends to draw all labor into its capacious maw, and the labor surplus that results from evicting the peasant from the land creates a competitive labor market that speedily reduces the laborer to the status of a wage-slave. Since slavery, then, in some form is the inevitable counterpart of modern civilization, the question that presses on the conscience of every enlightened and generous observer is the question of the relative well-being of the slave under the different systems. Upon this question the southern apologists turned their shrewdest analysis. They examined the condition of the proletariat in the English mill towns; they commented on the callous exploitation of the textile workers in Massachusetts; they assessed the waste in the labor turnover under the factory system; they considered the seeds of class war sown by industrialism and pointed out the insecurity of society under a system of capitalistic irresponsibility. In their estimate of the social evils of industrialism they concurred in the findings of Carlyle and antedated much of the criticism of Ruskin. The huge mass of unpalatable fact which they uncovered was the same mass that inspired George Ripley and Albert Brisbane and Horace Greeley to seek a way out by the path of coöperative commonwealths.

But in the hands of these apologists the argument was turned to the narrower end of proving that the southern field-hand fared better than the northern mill-hand. They recognized both systems as capitalistic, established in labor exploitation; but they proved to their own satisfaction that the southern was far humaner, more truly social. In the South, they pointed out, there was no waste in the labor turnover, no ugly labor scrap-heap, no ruthless efficiency in using up the human material. The master was responsible to society for the treatment and conduct of his slaves, and the southern conscience was far tenderer in the matter than the northern. The workers were never troubled by uncertain means of subsistence. The young were free from care, the old and infirm were adequately provided for. Living conditions were commonly pleasant, and the personal relations between master and slave kindly and loyal. When every argument against slavery had been urged it still remained true that the patriarchal tie that existed on the plantation was more humane than the cash-nexus of capitalism. In this fundamental matter Carlyle was right; and right also in his insistence on the need of capable masters. The South was fortunate in its system. On the self-sufficient plantations there was many an Abbot Sampson directing his little world wisely and humanely; collectively these Abbot Sampsons formed a capable and socially responsible ruling class worthy of their trust. The economic returns of a wage-slave industrialism might be greater, but the returns in civilization were far less.[1]

Such, in brief, was the reaction of the southern mind in the early fifties to the challenge of an industrializing generation. It was not till the publication of *Uncle Tom's Cabin* in 1851 that southern apologists were fully aroused to the need of counter propaganda. They had been moving slowly towards the conception of a Greek democracy under the leadership of Calhoun, but now under the sharp prod of Abolitionism they turned militant. Facts were collected and arguments clarified, and the war was carried home to New England. In three years following *Uncle Tom*, according to a recent student, fourteen pro-slavery novels appeared together with other matter.[2] Much of the material made use of in these stories was conveniently assembled in a work entitled *Pro-Slavery Argument*, published in 1852, a collaboration by Professor Dew of William and Mary College, Chancellor Harper of the Supreme Court of South Carolina, Governor Hammond of South Carolina, and Gilmore Simms. The first reviewed the Scriptural authority for slavery; Chancellor Harper drew from Hobbes the familiar argument that "a state of nature is a state of war"; Simms elaborated the patriarchal theory; but Governor Hammond developed the more significant argument of the degradation of the wage-slave, an argument elaborated at considerable length in an-

[1] The same argument was made use of by northern supporters of slavery. Gordon Bennett's *New York Herald*, for example, "printed a description of slum life in Liverpool, remarking that compared with the English laborer, 'the slave lived like a prince.' He had his cabin, neat, clean, and weatherproof: he had his own garden patch, over which he was lord paramount; he was well fed, well lodged, well clothed, and rarely over-worked; sleek, happy, contented, enjoying his many holidays with gusto, he lived to a great age" (quoted in Allan Nevins, *The Evening Post: A Century of Journalism,* p. 271).

[2] See Jeannette Reid Tandy, "Pro-Slavery Propaganda in American Fiction in the Fifties," *South Atlantic Quarterly,* January–March, 1922. See also Francis Pendleton Gaines, *The Southern Plantation,* Chapter III.

other work entitled *Letters on Slavery,* in which he presented the results of his investigation of English factory conditions. The novels that Miss Tandy comments upon have been pretty much forgotten, but the titles of some of them sufficiently reveal the lines of attack. L. B. Chase's *English Serfdom and American Slavery* (1854), J. W. Page's *Uncle Robin in His Cabin in Virginia and Tom without One in Boston* (1855), and S. H. Elliott's *New England Chattels* (1858) quite evidently reflect the new southern philosophy. If the South were attacked, it was not without weapons to defend itself.

II

WILLIAM J. GRAYSON

Of this very considerable literature of defense, *The Hireling and the Slave* presents in convenient compass the most telling southern arguments, and reveals in its sharp contrast of realism and romanticism the common southern temper. Its author, William J. Grayson, was a cultivated South Carolinian who had served two terms in Congress and for years was collector of the Port of Charleston. He was widely read, was familiar with contemporary English writers on economics, and possessed a fluent pen. He had published "an elaborate heroic poem entitled *The Country,*" in which he had sung "the praises of rural life and agricultural pursuits" (Introduction to Grayson's *Life of James L. Petigru*), and a volume entitled *Chicora and other Poems,* the title work of which was a romantic poem celebrating the primitive virtues of the Indian. Politically he was affiliated with the anti-Calhoun party of Unionists. His closest friend was James L. Petigru, a sketch of whose life he wrote as a last labor of love, during the unhappy days of the Charleston siege. He did not go so far as Petigru in refusing to have any part in a war that he opposed, but the tragedy of it cut him to the quick. He was no Fire Eater, but a southern moderate—a gentleman of old-fashioned tastes whose views may be taken as those of the cultivated Charleston group to which he belonged, of Petigru, of Legaré, of Alfred Huger.

The Hireling and the Slave, published in 1856 when Grayson was sixty-eight and dedicated to Petigru, is a poem in heroic couplets of approximately 1600 lines, divided into two parts. The first part draws a realistic picture of the life of the wage-slave, the second paints an idyllic picture of the life of the bond-slave. In this second part the spirit of romance holds high carnival; the descriptions are done with gusto and the rural pleasures that fall to the lot of the Negro provide a striking contrast to the mean environment of the factory worker. About this contrast are grouped the lesser arguments: the hypocrisy of the Yankee Abolitionist, the sentimentalism of English humanitarians, the wisdom of providence in providing masters to protect the Negro from destruction by a superior race and train him through apprenticeship in slavery to carry the blessings of civilization to Africa. The heroic couplet was deliberately adopted to offer "some variety to the poetic forms that are almost universally prevalent." "The poetry of the day is, for the most part," Grayson remarked, "subtile and transcendental in its character"; yet "the school of Dryden and Pope is not entirely forgotten," and "the most fastidious appetite may tolerate an occasional change of diet, and exchange dainties now and then for plainer fare" (*The Hireling and the Slave,* Preface, pp. xiv–xv). The poem seems to have been popular in the South, and a southern reviewer declared that "it ought to be on every man's mantel" (*Life of James L. Petigru,* p. vii).

In the preface Grayson discusses the subject of slavery with a candor somewhat unusual, acknowledging its evils, yet discovering compensations. As an expression of intelligent southern opinion on a question in which the passions of the country were becoming deeply engaged, his views deserve quotation. Slavery, he says,

. . . is that system of labor which exchanges subsistence for work, which secures a life-maintenance from the master to the slave, and gives a life-labor from the slave to the master. The slave is an apprentice for life, and owes his labor to his master; the master owes support, during life, to the slave. Slavery is the Negro system of work. He is lazy and improvident. Slavery makes all work, and it insures homes, food, and clothing for all. It permits no idleness, and it provides for sickness, infancy, and old age. It allows no tramping or skulking, and it knows no pauperism.

This is the whole system substantially. All cruelty is an abuse; does not belong to the institution; is now punished, and may be in time prevented. The abuses of slavery are as open to all reforming influences as those of any civil, social, or political condition. The improvement in the treatment of the slave is as marked as in that of any other laboring class in the world. . . . If slavery is subject to abuses, it has its advantages also. It establishes more permanent, and, therefore, kinder relations between capital and labor. It removes what Stuart Mill calls 'the widening and imbittering feud between the class of labor and the class of capital.' It draws the relation closer between master and servant. It is not an engagement for days or weeks, but for life. There is no such thing with slavery as a laborer for whom nobody cares or provides. The most wretched feature in hireling labor is the isolated, miserable creature who has no home, no food, and in whom no one is particularly interested. *This is seen among hirelings only.* (*Ibid.,* Preface, pp. vii–viii.)

The principle on which Grayson bases his argument is the principle that civilization rests on labor exploitation, but as a good churchman he attributes the evil to God and discovers the children of Adam to be suffering from the primeval curse—"Slave, hireling, help—the curse pursues him still." More specifically the thesis which he defends is this, "The state of the hireling and the slave [is] the same substantially—the condition hard labor, the reward subsistence"; and the conclusion which he draws is that the slave obtains a larger return for his labor than the factory hand. The picture he paints of the condition of the wage slave of England is Hogarthian in its details:

> There, unconcerned, the philanthropic eye
> Beholds each phase of human misery;
> Sees the worn child compelled in mines to slave
> Through narrow seams of coal, a living grave,
> Driven from the breezy hill, the sunny glade,
> By ruthless hearts, the drudge of labor made,
> Unknown the boyish sport, the hours of play,
> Stripped of the common boon, the light of day,
> Harnessed like brutes, like brutes to tug, and strain,
> And drag, on hands and knees, the loaded wain:
> There crammed in huts, in reeking masses thrown,
> All moral sense and decency unknown,
> With no restraint but what the felon knows,
> With the sole joy that beer or gin bestows,
> To grow excess and brutalizing strife,
> The drunken hireling dedicates his life:
> Starved else, by infamy's sad wages fed,
> There women prostitute themselves for bread,
> And mothers, rioting with savage glee,
> For murder'd infants spend the funeral fee;
> Childhood bestows no childish sports or toys,
> Age neither reverence nor repose enjoys,
> Labor with hunger wages ceaseless strife,
> And want and suffering only end with life;
> In crowded huts contagious ills prevail,
> Dull typhus lurks, and deadlier plagues assail,
> Gaunt Famine prowls around his pauper prey,
> And daily sweeps his ghastly hosts away;
> Unburied corses taint the summer air,
> And crime and outrage revel with despair.
> (*Ibid.,* pp. 24–25.)

Grayson does not stint his facts but traces the wretchedness of the wage-slave through all the phases of his misery to provide a background for the happier lot of the bond-slave. It is an unlovely picture, done with considerable vigor, from which one turns gladly to contemplate life on the southern plantation.

> And yet the life, so unassailed by care,
> So blessed with moderate work, with ample fare,
> With all the good the starving pauper needs,
> The happier slave on each plantation leads;
> Safe from harassing doubts and annual fears,
> He dreads no famine in unfruitful years;
> If harvests fail from inauspicious skies,
> The master's providence his food supplies;
> No paupers perish here for want of bread,
> Or lingering live, by foreign bounty fed;
> No exiled trains of homeless peasants go,
> In distant climes, to tell their tales of woe:
> Far other fortune, free from care and strife,
> For work, or bread, attends the Negro's life,
> And Christian slaves may challenge as their own,
> The blessings claimed in fabled states alone—
> The cabin home, not comfortless, though rude,
> Light daily labor, and abundant food,
> The sturdy health that temperate habits yield,
> The cheerful song that rings in every field,
> The long, loud laugh, that freemen seldom share,
> Heaven's boon to bosoms unapproached by care,
> And boisterous jest and humor unrefined,
> That leave, though rough, no painful sting behind;
> While, nestling near, to bless their humble lot,
> Warm social joys surround the Negro's cot,
> The evening dance its merriment imparts,
> Love, with its rapture, fills their youthful hearts,
> And placid age, the task of labor done,
> Enjoys the summer shade, the winter sun,
> And, as through life no pauper want he knows,
> Laments no poor-house penance at its close.
>
> (*Ibid.*, pp. 50–51.)

Convinced of the righteousness and humanity of slavery Grayson turns with scorn upon the Abolitionists and their meddlesome interference with the beneficent ways of Providence. With a few dexterous turns of the spit he browns each one nicely like a roasted goose. His descriptions strip off the gay plumage and reveal the naked fowl. He makes a good job of it, as witness these bits:

There supple Sumner, with the Negro cause,
Plays the sly game for office and applause:
What boots it if the Negro sink or swim?
He wins the Senate—'tis enough for him. . . .
He heeds nor court's decree nor Gospel light,
What Sumner thinks is right alone is right. . . .

There Greeley, grieving at a brother's woe,
Spits with impartial spite on friend and foe. . . .
To each fanatical delusion prone,
He damns all creeds and parties but his own,
Brawls, with hot zeal, for every fool and knave,
The foreign felon and the skulking slaves; . . .
And faction's fiercest rabble always find
A kindred nature in the Tribune's mind;
Ready each furious impulse to obey,
He raves and ravens like a beast of prey. . . .

There Seward smiles the sweet perennial smile,
Skilled in the tricks of subtlety and guile;
The slyest schemer that the world e'er saw;
Peddler of sentiment and patent law;
Ready for fee or faction to display
His skill in either, if the practice pay. . . .
                                    (*Ibid.*, pp. 38–40.)

As he contemplates Mrs. Stowe his full wrath is stirred.
He does not spare her sex. Southern chivalry serves the pure
and good in lovely woman, not the malignant and selfish.
An unsexed woman is hateful to it, and after extolling the
true womanliness of Florence Nightingale, angel of mercy,
Grayson pays his compliments to the Yankee propagandist
thus:

Not such with Stowe, the wish or power to please,
She finds no joy in gentle deeds like these;
A moral scavenger, with greedy eye,
In social ills her coarser labors lie;
On fields where vice eludes the light of day,
She hunts up crimes as beagles hunt their prey;
Gleans every dirty nook—the felon's jail,
And hangman's mem'ry, for detraction's tale,
Snuffs up pollution with a pious air,
Collects a rumor here, a slander there;
With hatred's ardor gathers Newgate spoils,
And trades for gold the garbage of her toils.

In sink and sewer thus, with searching eye,
Through mud and slime unhappy wretches pry;
In fetid puddles dabble with delight,

Search every filthy gathering of the night;
Fish from its depths, and to the spacious bag
Convey with care the black, polluted rag;
With reeking waifs secure the nightly bed,
And turn their noisome stores to daily bread.

                                    (*Ibid.*, pp. 42–43.)

The Hireling and the Slave, is vigorous propaganda, carefully documented and pointed with modern instances, the
work of an intelligent and humane writer who might be
blind to certain evils in slavery but whose eyes were open
to the social ills that grew rankly in the muck of industrialism. Outside of the South few in America had as yet come
to understand so much—a handful of New England idealists,
Parker and William Henry Channing and Emerson and
Wendell Phillips, and Orestes Brownson, and a handful
of Utopians, Albert Brisbane and George Ripley and Horace
Greeley. The inadequacy of southern thought was identical
with that of northern: blinded by sectional economic interests, they saw only half the truth. They beheld the mote
in a brother's eye, but considered not the beam that was
in their own.

CHAPTER IV

Adventures in Belles Lettres

I

OLD CHARLESTON

In the year 1825 the little city of Charleston, with its fourteen thousand whites and more than fourteen thousand
blacks, was perhaps the most delightful spot in America.
The Mecca of plantation fashion and the capital of plantation politics, it prided itself on its genial and distinguished
society. It was the last stronghold in America of the older
pride of aristocracy. The tone of society still remained pretty
much what it had been before the schism of '76. Social lines
were rigid and an old-fashioned conservatism of temper

marked the upper class. Despite the large admixture of French Huguenot blood the manners and prejudices of the aristocracy retained the pronounced British cast that came down from pre-Revolutionary times, and if Dr. Johnson could have stepped from the Fleet Street of 1780 to the Charleston of 1825 he would have felt almost at home. "We are decidedly more English than any other city of the United States," said Hugh Legaré, whose love of the English character was second only to his love of Charleston. It was a gay world with its country squires and their horses and racing, its Madeira drinking, its promenades and dancing and assemblies; one to win the affection of all who liked lighthearted ways.

But underneath this gay life was a more serious Charleston, which in certain of its aspects was not unlike Boston. From both the Huguenot and Scotch-Irish strains came a sobering Puritanism that gave a serious cast to thoughtful natures and disciplined them in a strict morality. Calhoun was far more Puritan than Fisher Ames, and Hugh Legaré than Edward Everett. Life was likely to be a serious business to these southern Puritans, filled with weighty responsibilities, to be lived, like Milton's, as ever in the great Taskmaster's eye. Aristocrat though he was, young Hugh Legaré was no gay cavalier treading the primrose path, but as serious-minded as any Roundhead. Victorian in manners, he would have found the bluff speech of the old revolutionary, General Charles Cotesworth Pinckney—"more pregnant with meaning than prudish in dress"—somewhat too "salt" for refined ears. It was this note of Puritanism that marked the finest characters in Charleston and gave its tone to society; but it was a Puritanism of conduct rather than dogma. Charleston gentlemen were of the English church, and their Puritanism, unwarped by Calvinism, assumed a moral rather than a theological cast.

The lawyer came to assume the position of intellectual leadership taken by the minister in New England. A profound respect for law dominated the Charleston mind. Blackstone was the Charleston Bible, and the lawyer who was master of dignified oratory was looked upon with high regard. The aristocracy opened its doors to young James Louis Petigru, an Irish-Huguenot lawyer with his own way to make, but it closed them tightly against young Gilmore Simms, apprentice to an apothecary and unread in the classics. Ambitious youths therefore turned to the law as a congenial career, for there reputations lay, and political influence. A pronounced cult of the law, and regard for orderly procedure, went hand in hand with the old English respect for individual rights. Charleston gentlemen could not be coerced, even by their own politicians, and Legaré was bitter against the Nullifiers because the spirit of dictation was "alien to our old habitudes, to the gentle courage, the courteous hostility, the mind and merciful justice, the proud submission to *law* and respect for right, which once distinguished our low country society from and above all other American society" (*Writings*, Vol. I, p. 211).

Politically Charleston was of the old Federalist tradition, as that Federalism was embodied in the picturesque figure of General Pinckney. Outside the narrow circle of the aristocracy, Federalism had long since given way to a democratic faith with its background of states-rights Jeffersonianism; but it lingered amongst the gentry and provided the nucleus of the later Union party. Grayson tells a story of Petigru that suggests the bitterness of the back-country democracy towards the old Federalism. The latter one day was being abused by a swamp-sucker "who lavished on him all the foul epithets and appellations he could remember or invent, of which rogue and scoundrel were among the most moderate." At last he hit upon a term of reproach "which at that day comprised everything hateful—he called him a 'damned Federal,'" and was promptly knocked down for the insult (William J. Grayson, *James Louis Petigru*, pp. 83–84). But the Charleston vintage of Federalism was little more than a stout conservatism that idealized the Union and preached the sufficiency and sacredness of the law. It was social rather than political or economic—the assertion of the prescriptive right of gentlemen to govern the state. Jeffersonianism never took possession of the first circles of Charleston as it did in Virginia, and French revolutionary philosophy found there an uncongenial soil. The profound conservatism of the aristocracy is sufficiently expressed in a comment of Hugh Legaré—"The politics of the immortal Jefferson! Pish!" (*Writings*, Vol. I, p. 207). Physiocratic agrarianism found few advocates amongst Carolina gentlemen. The Charleston mind was political and legal rather than economic in its interests, and as a commercial port Charleston was more sympathetic with capitalism than with agrarianism. Its politics, in which it found much diversion, it preferred highly seasoned, and when Nullification divided the state into hostile camps, the Nullifiers and Unionists brought Charleston to the verge of civil war. Respect for law and the amenities vanished before the hot demands of partisanship.

The culture of Charleston was as conservatively old-fashioned as its politics. Such a renaissance as it enjoyed before the Civil War wrought its destruction was delayed by its rejection of French romantic thought until the beginning of the thirties, and synchronized with the renaissance of New England. When the romantic spirit appeared about 1825, it was primarily English, of the school of Tom Moore. There had never been any literature in Charleston worthy of the name, except such as had come from London, bound in calfskin and tooled morocco. Those who affected a love of letters were still enamored of the heroic couplet and the Addisonian essay. Not until he went to Brussels in 1832 did Legaré, the most brilliant southern linguist, take up the study of German. The classics still dominated education, and literary taste inclined to a mingling of wit and sentiment. Young and Ossian and Mrs. Radcliffe held honored places on Charleston bookshelves. The young poets were deep in Byron, and Sir Walter was in high repute. But Wordsworth and Shelley and Keats were scarcely mentioned, and Carlyle could not hope to gain a hearing. Nevertheless by the year 1828 the example of the *North American Review* proved so stimulating an incentive that the scholarship of Charleston collaborated to establish the *Southern Review,* which ran a sober course for four years, providing a medium for learned articles on law, letters and politics. It was a serious venture that concerned itself little with *belles lettres,* but the intellectual resources were inadequate, and on Legaré's departure for Europe *The Review* came to an end. Later, Gilmore Simms labored to the same purpose, but even his enormous energy was insufficient to sustain a magazine esteemed worthy of southern genius, and the work languished. Facile writers were fewer in Charleston than in Boston.

But despite any shortcomings in the way of letters, to members of its polite circles Charleston was the most delightful of American cities, and its society the most distinguished. "I have never, since I could form an opinion on such matters," wrote Legaré from Brussels, where he mingled with the most cultivated society, "doubted of the immense superiority of Carolina society over all others on that continent, and now feel it more than ever" (*Writings,* Vol. I, p. 218). It was a common opinion of southern gentlemen, who, with their English notions of a landed aristocracy, believed that "fixed landed property is of the essence of civil society, properly so called." It embodied the planter ideal of a social capital, uncorrupted by a vulgar plutocracy. Its highways ran out to the plantations; the free citizen of the Greek democracy drew his wealth from the soil; the slave labored while the master rode to and fro from the city. Law and politics were regarded as respectable vocations for sons of gentlemen, but the ideal life was acknowledged to be that of the planter, with his three thousand acres, his three hundred Negroes, his ricks of rice and bales of tobacco and cotton. The profits that came from the law were certain to be invested in land, and the young attorney dreamed of retiring in middle life to a well-stocked plantation. To become a member of the ruling squirarchy was an ambition that filled and satisfied the Charleston imagination.

II
WILLIAM CRAFTS: *Charleston Wit*

The slightness of literary achievement in the Charleston of 1825 is sufficiently attested by the considerable local fame that rewarded the efforts of the volatile William Crafts. Born in Charleston in 1789, the son of a well-to-do Yankee father and a southern mother, he was sent to Harvard to complete his education, distinguished himself in the classics and in declamation, achieved a gownsman's fame for the brisk informality of a Latin oration, and carried back to Charleston a great reputation as a wit and scholar. He went into the law but burnt too few candles at the shrine of Blackstone; was seized with political ambition and proposed to make a great name for himself as a statesman, but his politics were not agreeable to his constituents and his career failed to arrive. He was a graceful orator in the florid southern style, an agreeable fellow with a pleasant wit, who loved society, dabbled in prose and verse, but proved to be unstable. He spread too much canvas to the uncertain winds and his unballasted bark came to grief. He died at the age of thirty-seven, leaving his writings to be gathered up and published by his family—a miscellany that brought down upon it the severe judgment of Hugh Legaré.

William Crafts was a transplanted Bostonian who essayed to domesticate Harvard culture among the polite circles of Charleston. As an undergraduate he admired the graceful preaching of Buckminster and the acrid eloquence of Fisher Ames. The latter he seems to have adopted as his political godfather, and from him he accepted a decadent

Federalism that got him into trouble when later he entered politics. But the chief model on whom he shaped his life seems to have been Robert Treat Paine, in the declining sun of whose fame the young Harvard undergraduate warmed himself. With a less pregnant wit, a less trenchant prose style, a less masculine oratory, he succeeded in becoming a smaller edition of a petty master. The parallelism in the lives of the two apostles of wit is striking. They were both dabblers, but Crafts possessed less skill and dabbled less felicitously. They both broke with the rigid decorum of their circles, but Paine achieved a more tragic shipwreck. They both marked the last ebbing of the eighteenth century before the wit ideal was submerged by the incoming tide of romanticism, and the reputations of both have been forgotten.

In Crafts' case, certainly, no injustice has been done. Such literary wealth as he displayed would seem notable only in an indigent society. His prose is vapid and feeble in the essay, and stilted and artificial in the oration. His verse is insignificant in quantity—two formal poems and a handful of occasional pieces—and wanting in distinction of phrase or imagery. It is the work of a graceful imitator of doubtful models. He wrote at the moment when the long supremacy of Pope was yielding to the popularity of Moore, and his verse wavered between the old loyalty and the new love. *Sullivan's Island,* a carefully elaborated descriptive poem, applies the structure and method of *Windsor Forest* to a local theme, following the original so closely as to imitate the detail. His skill in the grand manner may be judged by a single passage that phrases feebly what Pope had done vigorously:

> When cooler gales foretell departing day,
> The plaintive curlew homeward wings his way—
> Now stoops, then soars, and fearing danger night,
> To guardian heaven pours forth its piteous cry.
> Alas! in vain. The fowler's fond reply,
> Still deemed its own, but tells it where to die.

The Raciad is less crudely imitative. It is a brisk and rather amusing account of the outpouring of Charleston society to the races, the great event of the year in the gay southern capital. It is done with some sprightliness, it is an amiable historical document, but it is not important. When Crafts died in 1826 Charleston had done little in the way of creative literature, but the stirring of the waters was beginning. The

108

following year a young apothecary just admitted to the bar published a volume entitled *Lyrical and Other Poems,* first fruits of the colossal labors of Gilmore Simms. In 1828 Hugh Legaré got *The Southern Review* on its feet, a substantial magazine that aspired to be the mouthpiece of southern culture. With the beginning of the thirties the Charleston renaissance was under way.

HUGH SWINTON LEGARÉ: *Charleston Intellectual*

A far solider nature than the ebullient Crafts was Hugh Swinton Legaré. Of distinguished social position, the most cultivated mind in the South before the Civil War, and one of the most cultivated in America, he was an embodiment of the serious Charleston that served as counterweight to the gayer. In Legaré the moral earnestness of the South came to its most attractive expression. The repository of two streams of ethical idealism, he was as Puritan as Calhoun. Natively aristocratic, with a high sense of personal integrity and civic responsibility, a profound student of law and letters, with the Charleston parochialism brushed away by wide travel and intimate acquaintance with old-world civilizations and classical cultures, he represented the excellent seriousness that came to flower on the Carolina plantation as well as in the New England meetinghouse. Southern Puritanism might be less ungainly than that of Massachusetts, but it was equally introspective, given to melancholy; and Hugh Legaré found his life as serious an affair, and as laborious, as any New England Calvinist discovered his to be. It is no holiday business to serve righteousness; wisdom does not flower in the primrose path of dalliance; and this Charleston gentleman emerged from a prolonged and arduous self-discipline as complete a Puritan as Theodore Parker.

Descended in the fifth generation from a Huguenot ancestor who settled in Charleston about 1695, he was French in name and by cherished family tradition, but in little else. Through successive intermarriages, the original French strain was pretty much diluted by the Scotch and English, and few Gallic traits came down to him. In temperament and sympathies he was the child of his mother, Mary Swinton, of Scotch Covenanter blood. The native seriousness that came to him by right of inheritance was intensified by fate. Inoculated for the smallpox in his fourth year, the poison lingered in his system, keeping him sickly for years and permanently stunting the lower half of his body. Thus set apart from active life, he turned to books and entered upon the career of a scholar. At the time of his death in 1842, at the age of forty-five, he was perhaps the best linguist and the most widely read man in America. A mature student of the classics, he was intimately acquainted with French, Spanish, Italian and German, and had added Romaic as a help to his Greek. This may seem a meager list in comparison with Theodore Parker's nineteen languages, but the substantial acquisitions he gathered from the several bodies of literature were far from meager.

Yet immense as were those acquisitions they were only supplementary to his professional studies. The Charleston Puritan gave to the study of law the same intensity that the Boston Puritan gave to theology. Not content with a three years' reading course in a law office, he went to Europe to pursue his studies more comprehensively. At the University of Edinburgh he plunged into an investigation of the Roman and Civil Law, which henceforth was to be his major intellectual interest. He found in the continental systems, he believed, a body of legal principles more comprehensive and philosophical than the English Common Law, and the ambition grew upon him to ingraft certain features of the Civil Law upon American practice. After two years' intense study he came home, engaged in active practice of his profession, and ten years later, at the age of thirty-five, was appointed *chargé d'affaires* at Brussels, where he spent four rich years. His diplomatic and social life was subordinated to his studies, into which he threw himself with the keenest zest, enlarging his knowledge of modern letters and adding to his encyclopedic knowledge of legal systems. In 1841 he was appointed Attorney-General of the United States in the cabinet of President Tyler, and upon Webster's retirement was given the additional portfolio of Secretary of State *ad interim*. While on a visit to Boston with President Tyler to assist in the Bunker Hill Monument celebration, he was taken suddenly ill and died at the home of his friend Professor Ticknor.

The man thus prematurely cut down was a nature of vast solidity. Profoundly serious, inclined to the blackest melancholy, as pessimistic as Fisher Ames, with no leaven of humor, no romance, no careless idling, he was a hard taskmaster to his days. He toiled prodigiously at his self-appointed tasks. His standards were severe, whether in letters or law or politics or morals. As a critic he dealt with substantial subjects: *The Constitutional History of Greece; The Origin, History and Influence of Roman Legislation; Early Spanish Ballads; Jeremy Bentham and the Utilitarians; Lord Byron's Character and Writings*—solid dissertations done with German thoroughness—reviews of huge compass that provided opportunity for independent treatises. As a lawyer he was rather a philosophical historian than a special pleader. He was far more given to exploring the labyrinths of ancient codes than to arguing cases. His legal erudition appalls the layman. He had sat at the feet of black-letter philosophers; he had been instructed by sages long since forgotten. His mind was an ample storehouse of archaic legal maxims. He delighted in the crabbed law Latin—its sententious phrases worn to the quick, the residuum and repository of the wisdom bequeathed by past generations. Richer in poetry than any verses of Byron were the Latin words *habeas corpus* to one who, like this scholar, understood how packed they were with English history, how rich in suggestion to all who love English freedom. From this immense erudition came his love for old books and venerable authorities. Blackstone he looked upon as a modern—"a gentleman's law book, clear, but not deep"; and the wisdom of my Lord Coke seemed to him not so mellow as that drawn from the more capacious vats of earlier days. He quoted Grotius and Vattel and Pufendorf and Bourlamaqui more readily than the South Carolina Digest, and the names of Papinian and Ulpian and Modestinus and Voet and Cujacius, of the *Corpus Alaricianum,* of the Justinian, Gregorian, Hermogenian, and Theodosian codes, slipped familiarily from his pen. How many outlandish authorities were contained in the huge inkwell on his desk it is idle to conjecture. Probably not three men in America comprehended the significance of half the references that he offered for the consideration of his fellow lawyers, or were competent to question his deductions. Even the learned Judge Story and Chancellor Kent seem mere dabblers in comparison with this philosophical historian.

Such learning must inevitably mold one's thinking in kindred fields, and he came naturally to espouse what for want of an exacter term may be called the Common Law theory of politics. It is a conception of law as an organic growth, the result of man's laborious search for a rational freedom in the social body, the single and avowed end of which is justice. It has taken form not by the decrees of legislatures, but by decisions of the judiciary, tested and reëxamined and reargued generation after generation; built up code by code through slow evolution, the wisdom of the past serving as counselor to the present; continuously expanding its jurisdiction from the community to the nation, and from the nation to a world society; the one guarantee of a sober and rational progress. Theorists and philosophers come and go; revolutions succeed and fail; foolish statutes and temporary constitutions have their day; but the organic body of the law survives all surface change, building into the fabric of society what experience proves to be good, sloughing off what experience has outgrown—the tempered rule of social justice; the exact measure of every civilization compared with which the majority will is a crude and inadequate makeshift.

From such a conception it follows that government is little more than ancillary to the law, and political principles are sound in the measure that they are founded on legal principles. Thus by following the musty path of jurisprudence Legaré arrived at the same goal that John Cotton had reached two hundred years before—the apotheosis of magistracy. With the older Puritan he could assert, *Scripturae plenitudinem adoro*. The sufficiency of the law to social justice was axiomatic in his thinking. But the scriptures which he adored were the words of the judges, whose decisions were above the authority of legislator or governor and little concerned with a transient majorty will. The old theocrat had set up his theocracy; the modern lexolater would set up his lexocracy; but the end was pretty much the same. Very likely Legaré, like the present-day lexolater, would deny the conclusion, yet it was implicit in his premises, and his scorn of political theory was sufficient proof. Practical politics he regarded as rather a trumpery business that achieves no solid results.[1] The political philosopher he was profoundly suspicious of. The flood of speculation let loose upon the world by the revolutions of the seventeenth and eighteenth centuries seemed to him to have invited disaster, and the political classics of those revolutions he cared little for. He distrusted the "era of illumination" that sacrificed use and wont to abstract theory. "We have not too much faith in the 'march of intellect,'" he remarked dryly, "and would not . . . pitch our anticipations in too high a key" (*ibid.*, Vol. II, p. 264). But his greatest contempt he reserved for the intellectual revolutionaries—"hair-brained

[1] See *Writings*, Vol. II, p. 104.

metaphysicians and empirical demagogues" (*ibid.*, Vol. I, p. 216), who would upset the nice balance of the law. To this matter he returned again and again, with the scorn of the legal mind for ambitious political systems. "Innovators or Revolutionists, who go only for an imaginary abstract rectitude and symmetry of government," he said, "are always dangerous, and sometimes the greatest curse with which heaven in its wrath can visit an offending people" (*ibid.*, Vol. II, p. 286).

I have no faith at all in speculative politics. A theorist in government is as dangerous as a theorist in medicine, or in agriculture, and for precisely the same reasons—the subjects are too complicated and too obscure for simple and decisive experiments. I go for undisputed results in the long run. (*Ibid.*, Vol. I, p. 303.)

Man begins a revolution, but its issues are with God alone. The voluntary revolutions of man have always been abrupt, violent and for the worse: so that the wisdom of antiquity laid it down, as a maxim, that every fundamental change in the State must needs be bloody and deadly. (*Ibid.*, Vol. II, p. 297.)

This inherent conservatism of the legal mind explains Legaré's intellectual sympathy with Federalism and his contempt for Jefferson. The latter to him was the prince of demagogues, and his ink was vitriol when he wrote of him, as thus in one of his letters: "The immortal sayings and doings of the holy father in democracy—the servant of the servants of Demos (whose nose of wax he knew better than anybody how to shape to his own convenience,)—the infallible, though ever-changing, St. Thomas of *Canting*-bury. And here, you may be sure, I *cross* myself devoutly and cry out, with an all-fervent benediction to that canonized worthy, *pax tecum* (pronounced, you know, *Scottice, pox tacum*)" (*Writings*, Vol. I, p. 208). Modern political theories seemed to him mere upstart doctrines compared with the venerable principles of the law, and he came to look with suspicion on all political liberalism not sponsored by lawyers and supported by briefs. A passionate lover of liberty, he was as distrustful of democracy as John Adams, and his condemnation was as frank—"that scene of wild impulse, and tyrannical misrule—a pure democracy" (*ibid.*, Vol. II, p. 271). No state, Beverley Tucker pointed out, was so little democratic as South Carolina, and Legaré shared the common Charleston distrust of it. As he watched England and France during the tumultuous thirties, and saw the struggle over Nullification at home, his concern for the future became acute and his pessimism as black as Fisher Ames'. In a letter from Brussels, in the year 1833, shortly after the passage of the English Reform Bill, he wrote:

Mankind have too little sense to maintain, for any length of time, a well-tempered democracy, and a great deal too much to bear an unlimited one—the most dreadful form of "State sovereignty," beyond all doubt, in which the descendants of the father of the first murderer have ever given loose to their ruffian instinct of violence and oppression. If they have a moderate policy of the kind, which happens (as all complicated machines will) to be occasionally a little out of order, their only idea of a remedy is to pull it down, and along with it every thing that makes a civil society worthy of its name. Who could ever have dreamed that the law of brute force which now crushes Europe . . . should be deliberately adopted in America, instead of the really sublime institutions of a federal jurisdiction, (fallible, of course, but generally right) and that this relapse into downright barbarism should be vaunted, by the most enlightened men in the Southern States, as a *grand* improvement and the only thing wanting to make our government as perfect as we have been swearing it was all along. (*Ibid.*, Vol. I, p. 210.)

Back of this ingrained conservatism was a tender Puritan conscience that must twist his legal studies to ideal ends. After all it was no other than a juridical romanticism that Hugh Legaré discovered in the bottom of his scholar's cup. As medieval as Sir Walter, he sought his romance in old law-courts rather than in feudal castles, in black-robed advocates rather than in knights and ladies; and he persuaded himself that those old litigations, preserved in scraps of Latin and law French, were dramatic episodes in the ceaseless battle for human rights, whereof the single objective was justice. Slowly, stone upon stone, the lawyers were erecting an impregnable citadel, within which justice kept her inviolable court. It is a pleasant fiction still believed in by lawyers of the old school, and to Legaré in his study it bore the very semblance of truth. He had read too many law books; he had speculated too little on politics; immersed in his codes, he had forgotten to inquire into the hidden springs of sovereignty. In his contempt for practical politics he had neglected to study even the primer of economic determinism. To the economic historian, Legaré's boundless faith in the sufficiency of legal processes is incomprehensible. A few lessons from the wiser Jefferson would have taught him much that he needed to know concerning the economic sources of power. In his attitude towards the law Jefferson was a suspicious realist. He had no faith in legal codes that had grown up under monarchical and aristocratic systems, and he put no trust in government by lawyers. He could not understand how the Common Law, interpreted by the Tory Blackstone, and applied by Federalist lawyers, should serve the needs of a democracy. Democratic America, he was convinced, must create a new democratic law, and hold its judiciary in strict subjection to its will; to surrender sovereignty to an aristocracy of the bench would mean the abdication of democracy. But Legaré refused to go to school to Jefferson. He clung to his romantic conception of the law with the same passionate conviction that Calhoun clung to his romantic dream of a Greek democracy; and with the ebbing of the romantic tide they were both left stranded.

But if Legaré was unsympathetic towards the new political theory that came from the French intellectuals, and frankly hostile to the new political practice that came in with the Jacksonians, he warmly approved the new economics that came with the Industrial Revolution. In his whole-hearted acceptance of Adam Smith he seems not a Carolinian at all, but an English liberal of the Cobden-Bright school. He adopted the principle of *laissez faire*, the gospel of progress, the attitude of optimism. He accepted the theory of the beneficence of commerce as a universal civilizing agency, and he looked forward confidently to an eventual parliament of man, a future federation of the world. Commerce in the end must outlaw war, and peace with freedom would spread the blessings of civilization to the ends of the earth.[2]

A convincing object-lesson in the sufficiency of the principle of *laissez faire*, he discovered in the amazing progress of America. The mainspring of that progress he found in economic freedom—freedom "from those undue restraints and that impertinent interference of government in the interests properly belonging to individuals." "I know," he said, "that the cardinal spring and source of our success is freedom—freedom of thought, freedom of speech, freedom of action, freedom of commerce" (*Writings*, Vol. I, p. 306). The greatest of these was free trade between the states. His travels in England and the contrast between English progress and continental backwardness confirmed him in this belief. "The doctrine of Free Trade," he asserted, "is a great fundamental doctrine of civilization. The world must

<hr />

[2] See "The Arbitrament of National Disputes," in *Writings*, Vol. I, pp. 355–357.

come to it at last, if the visions of improvement in which we love to indulge are ever to be realized" (*ibid.*, Vol. I, p. 272). He went further and accepted the Industrial Revolution with its division of labor as a necessary agency of social amelioration. "It is evidently in the order of nature, and we must take it with all its good and all its evils together." In forecasting the effect of that revolution he was troubled by no fears.

Sir, it is a favorite phrase of those who boast of what is called "the march of intellect," that things are thus changed because the "schoolmaster is abroad." But I tell you that something far more effective than the schoolmaster, a mightier than Solomon, is abroad. It is the STEAM-ENGINE—in its twofold capacity of a means of production and a means of transport—the most powerful instrument by far of pacification and commerce, and therefore of improvement and happiness that the world has ever seen; which, while it increases capital, and multiplies beyond all imagination the products of industry, brings the most distant people into contact with one another . . . effaces all peculiarities of national character, and promises, at no distant period, to make the whole Christian world, at least, one great family. . . .

A people well clad and well housed will be sure to provide themselves with all the other comforts of life; and it is the diffusion of these comforts, and the growing taste for them, among all classes of society in Europe—it is the desire of riches as it is commonly called, that is gradually putting an end to the destructive and bloody game of war, and reserving all the resources hitherto wasted by it, for enterprises of industry and commerce, prosecuted with the fiery spirit which once vented itself in scenes of peril and carnage. (*Ibid.*, Vol. I, pp. 285–286.)

Remembering how dependent were southern cotton interests on English industrialism and commerce, one can understand Legaré's acceptance of *laissez-faire* economics. His idealism, his local pride, his romanticism, were all enlisted in its behalf, and he painted in glowing colors. But his frank advocacy of capitalism is harder to understand, except perhaps on the ground that Charleston was a considerable shipping port and his clients were engaged in commerce. In the bitter dispute with Jackson over the Bank, Legaré adopted northern views on national finance. Although nominally a Democrat, he had never been an agrarian, and he went with Webster and Clay against the subtreasury scheme and a metallic currency. His thoughtful speech on *The Spirit of the Sub-Treasury*, delivered in 1837, was thoroughgoing Whig doctrine, asserting the excellence of the modern banking system and extolling the economic fruitfulness of credit.

He repudiated every principle of John Taylor; denied every dogma of agrarian economics; and eulogized the English financial system as the germinal source of English greatness. Applying the principle of credit to American conditions, he discovered the secret of American expansion in the principle of speculative borrowing, and expanded his doctrine of economic freedom by asserting that freedom to borrow was a necessary preliminary to freedom to work. "A people have been enriched by debt," he argued, overlooking the possible fallacy of a *post hoc ergo propter hoc,* "and 'by owing, owe not.' " As he contemplated the amazing progress of the nation, his lyric enthusiasm becomes prologue to a somewhat lame conclusion that enthrones the banker as the fairy godmother of the hardy pioneer.

There is a grandeur and a majesty in this irresistible onward march of a race, created, as I believe, and elected to possess and people a continent. . . . We may become so much accustomed to such things that they shall make as little impression upon our minds as the glories of the Heavens above us; but, looking on them, lately, as with the eyes of the stranger, I felt, what a recent English traveller is said to have remarked, that far from being without poetry, as some have vainly alleged, our whole country is one great poem. Sir, it is so; and if there be a man that can think of what is doing, in all parts of this most blessed of all lands, to embellish and advance it, who can contemplate that living mass of intelligence, activity and improvement as it rolls on, in its sure and steady progress, to the uttermost extremities of the west; who can see scenes of savage desolation transformed, almost with the suddenness of enchantment, into those of fruitfulness and beauty; crowned with flourishing cities, filled with the noblest of all populations; if there be a man, I say, that can witness all this passing under his very eyes, without feeling his heart beat high, and his imagination warmed and transported by it, be sure, sir, that the raptures of song exist not for him. . . .

But of this rational, diffusive liberty, among a people so intelligent as ours, the credit system is the natural fruit, the inseparable companion, the necessary means and instrument. It is part and parcel of our existence. Who ever heard of CREDIT in a despotism, or an anarchy? It implies *confidence*—confidence in yourself, confidence in your neighbor, confidence in your government, confidence in the administration of the laws, confidence, in a word, in your destiny, and your fortune, in the destinies and the fortunes of the country to which you belong; as, for instance, in the case of a great national debt. It is the fruit, I say, of all that is most precious in civilized life, and to quarrel with it is to be ungrateful to God for some of the greatest blessings he has vouchsafed to man. (*Writings,* Vol. I, pp. 306–307.)

Such ebullient rhetoric fits the mouth of the politician rather than the scholar, and such careless logic comes oddly from a southern intellectual. In his ignorance of the economics of John Taylor, Legaré was unprovided with principles to reply to his own arguments, and unaware of the lameness of his confident conclusions. But though he might glow with optimism as he contemplated the westward expansion, for the future of the South and of his own beloved state he was deep in pessimism. From the first he had dissented vigorously from the program of Nullification. An ardent Union man, he believed with his friend James Petigru that secession meant ruin for South Carolina. Calhoun seemed to him a monomaniac, consumed by a single idea. He feared the hot passion of the states-rights party and he was troubled over slavery. His travels abroad had acquainted him with European views on the subject; he watched the spread of English humanitarianism and he had come to recognize the institution as an anachronism. It seemed to him impossible for the South to withstand much longer the augmenting pressure of civilized opinion. He could justify slavery in his own eyes both by ancient law—*servitus est constitutio juris gentium*—and by comparison of the condition of the Negro with that of the English wage worker. The ideal of a Greek democracy was vastly congenial to his aristocratic temperament, but he knew that it was a romantic dream, and he was oppressed by the shadow of impending ruin. Writing from Brussels on April 8, 1833, he concluded an anxious letter thus:

It ends in my not knowing what to think, except that dangers are around and above and below and within our poor little State, —which may God preserve us from! I ask of heaven only that the little circle I am intimate with in Charleston should be kept together while I live,—in health, harmony and competence; and that, on my return, I may myself be enabled to enjoy the same happiness, in my intercourse with it, with which I have been hitherto blessed. *We* are (I am quite sure) the *last* of the *race* of South-Carolina; I see nothing before us but decay and downfall,—but on that very account, I cherish its precious relics the more. . . . Yet my heart sinks within me often when I think of what may too soon be, and I say, in those touching words, "Why should not my countenance be sad, when the city, the place of my fathers' sepulchres, lieth waste, and her gates are burnt with fire." (*Writings*, Vol. I, p. 215.)

Thus like old John Winthrop two hundred years before, this descendant of southern Pilgrims, this Charleston lawyer and intellectual, found the words of the Hebrew Scriptures rising to his lips in moments of deep emotion. In spite of travel and many books and ripe culture and catholic sympathies, Hugh Legaré remained Puritan at heart, sorely puzzled with life, the burden of his days heavy upon him, walking soberly in the way of duty. North or south, the Puritan was still Puritan, whether he were Theodore Parker, the Boston radical, or Hugh Swinton Legaré, the Charleston conservative.

IV

WILLIAM GILMORE SIMMS: Charleston Romancer

From the background of old Charleston emerged, about the year 1825, the figure of Gilmore Simms, lately a drug clerk but now come to the dignity of admission to the bar; a tall, vigorous young fellow, with little formal schooling, no Latin or Greek, without land or slaves, but heavily involved in Byronic odes and like unprofitable investments; a social nobody soon to be married at the age of twenty to a girl of no better station than his own, who offered himself as candidate for the poet laureateship of the South. A somewhat presumptuous proceeding on the part of a plebeian quite outside the cultivated circle of the Petigrus and Grimkés and Hugers and Legarés, who were the accepted custodians of Charleston culture and who did not take kindly to ambitious newcomers. They regarded literature as a polite art that could flourish only in polite circles, and they turned a cold shoulder upon a young man whose ways suggested the Carolina buckra.

After all these years one may well cherish a grudge against the amiable little city for its shabby treatment of Gilmore Simms. The most richly endowed of any son she ever gave birth to, he was snubbed for years by the social oligarchy and suffered keenly from the ostracism. His extreme parochialism made him the more sensitive to the slight. An ardent Southerner, loyal to all the Carolinian totems and taboos, he accepted the Charleston judgment in literature and politics as the very law and the prophets. He loved the soil of South Carolina, he loved the people and the way of life, and he was steeped as no other Carolinian in local history and tradition. He could perceive no shortcomings in a society he warmly admired, and he accepted the Charleston provincialisms as the lover accepts the mole on his mistress's cheek. The more Charleston snubbed him, the more admirable he professed to believe was an aristocracy that so jealously guarded its fine exclusiveness. His life-long ambition was to receive recognition from his native city, and when after the death of his first wife and his marriage to the daughter of a prosperous planter, he gained admission into the ranks of the lesser gentry, he eagerly made common cause with them. He accepted the Carolinian standards and conventions; he advocated social caste; he honored the southern gentleman as God's best handiwork; he unconsciously reflected an aristocratic arrogance towards all social inferiors. He abandoned the Jeffersonian philosophy of his youth and adopted the revised gospel of Calhoun. He became, in short, a Carolina Fire Eater. He set up as a militant defender of slavery and collaborated with other eminent Carolinians to develop the pro-slavery argument.[3] He could have escaped the subtle compulsions of the southern system only by emptying his mind of his dearest prejudices, and this he had neither the will nor the wish to do. And so in spite of the fact that his every instinct was democratic, and every natural impulse generous and manly, he fought the battles of the peculiar institution as stoutly as if he had been born to his three hundred slaves; and he suffered in consequence the loss of pretty nearly everything, including his art. After his death, his friend Paul Hayne wrote of him: "Simms's genius *never had fair play!* Circumstances hampered him!" The judgment is just. Parochial Charleston brought about his literary undoing.

In taste and temperament Simms was a pronounced realist, but his career took shape from a generation given to every romantic excess. His genius, in consequence, was always at cross purposes with the popular taste. His realism turned naturally to low-life adventure; his upper-class romance became stilted and posturing, and his love of action degenerated into swashbuckling. That he survived such mishaps at all, suggests the enormous vitality of the man. If there had only been a little more of the intellectual in him, if he could have detached himself as an artist from the immediate and present, he might have risen superior to his unfortunate environment. But he was constitutionally incapable of aloofness, and hence incapable of criticism. To analyze, compare and judge was impossible to so ardent a nature. He must be partisan to a people and a cause, rather than to his art. The South that he loved was romantic, and he would appeal to the world as a Southerner. He wore his sectional prejudices as the southern politician wears his

[3] See above, page 97.

rumpled Prince Albert coat, broad-brimmed hat and black string tie. He never realized what a clutter of useless luggage he carried into his study. It is a pity that he constructed himself to the shell of an outworn order, instead of realizing that social orders and institutions are significant to the novelist only as he stands apart from them, observing their ways and considering their interplay in the lives of men and women. It was a major loss to American letters that he should not have striven to be an artist first, and a southern romantic only at a later and more convenient season. If he had served his art more jealously, if he had learned from Poe to refuse the demands of inconsequential things, he would have viewed his beloved Charleston with keener eyes and portrayed it more adequately.

But he would not serve his art alone. Unhappily he conceived that he owed an imperative duty to his native commonwealth, and in fulfillment of that duty he frittered away his enormous vitality in delivering patriotic orations and occasional addresses, serving in the Legislature, pottering over politics, lecturing upon literature, founding and editing magazines and essaying to bring culture to Charleston by fiery impetuosity of appeal. He struggled as few other Americans have done to further the cause of letters in a desperate environment; but creative literature could neither be cajoled nor coerced to take up an abode in the indolent little city, and Simms wore himself out in a fruitless undertaking. Our literature has suffered few greater losses than this wasting of the genius of Gilmore Simms in trumpery fields that belong to the literary dray horse. It was the inevitable outcome of the conflict between the creative artist and the citizen of South Carolina.

Little as he is known to later readers Simms is by far the most virile and interesting figure of the Old South. He was built on a generous plan. He was endowed with a rich and prodigal nature, vigorous, spontaneous, creative. There was in him much of Whitman's largeness and coarseness, much of his delight in the good things of earth. He wrote with extraordinary gusto, and his fine strong face suggests that he lived with equal gusto. As a professional man of letters he turned out an incredible amount of work, by ordinary two tales a year—solid works of five hundred pages each —together with poems and plays and pot-boiling stuff to tax the capacity of two or three hack writers. He poured out his material copiously, lavishly, with overrunning measure. His stories flow as generously as his Jamaica rum.

He is a veritable geyser of invention, an abundant sea of salty speech. He has no sense of restraint; he does not stop to prune the tangle of his imagination; he refuses to strip the plot of extraneous incident to hasten its action. He is as episodic as Dickens at his worst, piling up action and multiplying threads till the story bogs down. The major plot is always struggling from hummock to hummock in the endless swamp where his characters slip in and out, rarely getting to firm ground, yet never quite submerged. Prodigal of adventure and loving action, clumsy as the natural man when confronted with sentiment, he is an American Fielding with a dash of Smollett. He is at ease only out of doors, in the fields and swamps and highways; there his speech becomes racy, and there the rich poetry of his nature, which somehow rarely got into his verse, comes to abundant and spontaneous expression. When he enters the drawing-room his stilted language betrays his lack of ease. He writes with his pen and not with his heart. The plantation tradition has him in its grip and his fine ladies and gentlemen are done up with much literary starch. But let him come upon a happy-go-lucky blackguard and he loves him as Fielding would have loved him. The amusing scene in which Lieutenant Porgy heaves a pot of hot hominy in the face of a Scotch dragoon is quite evidently reminiscent of Parson Adams' recourse to a dish of hog's blood in a certain tavern brawl.[4] Like Fielding also is his criterion of morality. A frank and generous nature is his infallible test of worth, and if his patriotism led him to bestow a large share of generosity on the patriots, and a correspondingly meager share on the Loyalists and British, he was but exercising an ancient prerogative of the romancer.

Contemporary romanticism engrafted on a nature fundamentally realistic developed a pronounced strain in his work, which, for lack of an exacter word, we may call picaresque. This comes out at its worst in the crude border tales of *Richard Hurdis* and *Border Beagles*, stories marked by the coarseness of the eighteenth century, backwoods versions of *Jonathan Wild*. At its best it created a goodly company of blackguards that are an asset to American literature. Simms dearly loved a rogue, and the more picturesque the latter's knavery the more he loved him. A gentleman villain turns to a thing of wood in his hands, but a low-born rascal he creates out of living flesh and blood. A surprising number of low figures, both rogues and honest men, enliven his cluttered

[4] See *Katherine Walton*, Chapter XLI.

pages, individual, racy, often poetic. Realistic in speech and action, they are men of special gifts, nimble of wit and rich in imagination, sometimes fallen to base uses and sometimes ennobled by affection for their superiors. Thumbscrew, Supple Jack Bannister, and Joe Ballou, the partisan scouts; Isaac Muggs, mine host of the Black Riders; Goggle the half-breed; Hell Fire Dick of Tophet, the blackguard converted by *Pilgrim's Progress;* Sam Bostwick the Squatter—these are admirable figures, done with inimitable spirit, the choicest collection of homespun in American literature. They impart life and drama to Simms's tales. Remove them, and his romances are only a welter of stilted language and starchy situations. The scene, for example, between Jack Bannister and Isaac Muggs, in which the latter is converted to true republican principles by appeal to a backwoods ordeal by battle, is magnificent in its broad humor, and it is a pity that Simms did not give freer rein to his genius for such work. It is incomprehensible that a man who could put into the mouth of Thumbscrew such language as the following could have stooped to scribble the love scenes between Ernest Mellichampe and Janet Berkeley:

When it so happens that the things a man's got to love gits fewer and smaller, they gits more valuable, Airnest, in his sight; for he knows mighty well, if he loses them, that he's jist like an old bird that comes back to the tree when the blossoms and the flowers have all dropped off, and are rotting under it. It's mighty nigh to winter in his heart then, Airnest—mighty nigh—and the sooner he begins to look out a place to sleep in, the wiser man you may take him to be. (*Mellichampe,* Chapter IX.)

But Simms was too inveterately episodical to construct a pretty plot, and too careless in his generous southern hospitality to discriminate between guests at his board. He throws a huge miscellany on the table from which each may choose what pleases his taste.

Here again romanticism did him an evil turn. Southern taste was too aristocratic to like coarse fare. Gentlemen must dine like gentlemen even though black rascals served as waiters. Common fellows were well enough in the background, but they must not presume to crowd their betters from the table. In such matters Simms was constrained to follow the orthodox literary tradition. From Shakespeare to Scott the notion prevailed that legitimate romance must be conceived of as a flitch of bacon, the lean of vulgarity alternating with the fat of gentility. Hence Simms was forced to keep a weather eye on the popular taste lest it be offended by too free an offering of the low. His Negroes, such as Scipio and Bram and Benny Bowlegs, are more worth while than their masters, and his swamp-suckers are done with more gusto than the officers; but when the plot demands the appearance of the gentry he sends his black-bottle rapscallions about their business. Except in occasional instances, as in the case of old Colonel Sinclair, the Carolinian baron —a testy old gentleman done in the best gouty manner— Simms does the "quality" badly and the canny reader soon learns to skip the genteel passages in order to visit with Lieutenant Porgy or follow the adventures of Hell Fire Dick or Supple Jack Bannister. There is ample fare at his generous board, but one must pick and choose.

The critics have made quite too much of the Gothic extravagancies that mar so many of his pages. It is true that Simms was a generous purveyor of "blood-pudding" romance with its gory exploitation of crime and mystery. Nothing can excuse or extenuate such folly in the abstract; but it is easily comprehensible. It was a part of the price which the professional man of letters had to pay as caterer to a provincial reading public. After the surprising success of *Guy Rivers*, Simms deliberately tested the taste of his readers by sending forth *Richard Hurdis* under a pen name; and the equal success of the latter convinced him that American readers liked such fare. He had a living to make; the market was limited, and he resolved to give the public what it wanted. This accounts for his major sins. An enormous number of chapters, together with whole volumes such as *Charlemont* and *Beauchampe*—preposterous accounts of a notorious murder case in Kentucky—deserve no better fate than the rubbish heap. They are in no sense literature; yet unfortunately the very great powers of Simms are too commonly measured by such trash, instead of by his Revolutionary tales.

Simms was a loving student of older English literature and drew much of his water from excellent wells. A happy instinct led him back to the robust time of Elizabeth and those masculine playwrights whose ample natures were so like his own. Shakespeare may be reckoned his particular master —especially the prose of Shakespeare with its Cheapside colloquialisms and racy idiomatic rhythms. No better training school could be desired, and his loving apprenticeship to the older vernacular serves to explain the source of Simms's greatest literary virtue. From long familiarity with the Elizabethans he derived his mastery of English idiom that sets him widely apart from most other contemporary Americans. In easy outpouring of picturesque speech, of the lithe and muscular idiom of the old literature, he was without a rival in his generation. Many an old Elizabethan phrase lingered in the southern backwoods, and many an indigenous turn of speech had sprung from homely new-world experience. All such Simms seized upon with the relish of a gourmand, stirring them into the great pot from which he ladled such generous spoonfuls. Later critics have been singularly obtuse in their failure to do justice to his rich linguistic equipment. Quite too much comment has been devoted to his careless slips in rhetorical construction, and quite too little to his command of masculine English prose. It is absurd to couple him with Cooper in sinning against good writing. They are as unlike as two men could well be. Simms is incomparably the greater master of racy prose, as he is much the richer nature. The only contemporary indeed who approaches him is Melville in *Moby Dick*. He is careless and slovenly enough in all conscience; when he goes on a rampage he mouths his lines like any town crier. But though he keeps a sharp eye on the groundlings, though he is often preposterous, he is rarely wooden, never feeble.

The Elizabethan influence comes out strikingly in the character of Lieutenant Porgy, the spoilt child of his imagination, who runs through the Revolutionary romances as a sort of comic chorus. Despite Professor Trent's opinion to the contrary, Porgy is a South Carolinian Falstaff, quite evidently done with a close eye to the original. He is a very mountain of a fellow, with huge paunch and spindling shanks from too much sitting at the table and in the saddle—the most amusing and substantial comic character in our early fiction. As a South Carolina gentleman, Porgy of course was no liar or coward or woman cheater. In battle he is an avalanche of patriotic valor, and in his deference to the weak and dependent, in his free-handed generosity that encumbers him with penniless hangers-on, he is model of southern chivalry. But in the far greater matters of the belly, he is strikingly Falstaffian. He is not so much a valiant trencherman, as an artist in food and drink. He lived to eat and he ate to speculate on the virtues of a good dinner. "He took philosophy with him to the table, and grew wise over his wine" (*Woodcraft*, Chapter XVIII). He is an epicure in words, a gourmand of wit. The copious stream of his speech runs on in an endless flow, sometimes roily but never stagnant. A pat aphorism or a picturesque phrase is as succulent to him as Carolina terrapin. When philosophy fails he stoops to horseplay, but his practical jokes are carried off with theatrical splendor, with colossal assurance. Like Falstaff he is fond of practicing his wit on his followers. His Bardolph is a certain Geordie Dennison, the swamp poet of the troop; and Porgy honors him as one artist honors the craft of another.

But the most satisfying comradeship lies between Porgy and Black Tom, fellow practitioners of the gentle art of cookery, sworn liegemen to roasts and soups and stews. Together they make the swamp commissariat bloom like a Covent Garden market. They are master foragers untroubled by an overnice conscience. "Do as much stealing in an honest way as you can," the lieutenant remarks to Tom. "D—n the patriotism that can't eat stolen fruit!" At a pinch the native resources of the swamp are boldly commandeered. The creative masterpiece of the valiant Porgy was a notable banquet which he proffered General Greene and his staff in their swamp quarters. His infinite resourcefulness in this great affair, his huge inventiveness, elevate the dinner to the rank of a culinary epic. The swamp frogs that he speared by moonlight, and the young alligators that he took by subtle stratagem, were transmogrified into delectable dishes served to his guests under the alluring names of *alerta* and *lagarta*.[5] The scene is done with a gusto that only the worshiper of fleshpots could achieve. Simms delighted in Porgy because he was himself something of a Porgy. There is good fare for those who sit at table with the fat humorist of *The Forayers;* the ready talk does not lack the salt of wit. The later Porgy of *Woodcraft* scarcely comes up to the earlier. His debts weigh too heavily on his spirits for the easy play of his fancy; he is less redoubtable as a wooer than as a warrior; nevertheless there is excellent humor to be enjoyed at Glen Eberle, and some extraordinary pranks.

The two major themes with which his romances deal, as has been often pointed out, are the frontier and the Revolution; but the intimate connection between them has not been so commonly remarked. In much of his better work the two themes blend into one. The conditions of civil war in the South thrust into sharp relief the cultural and psychological frontier that clung to the outskirts of the plantations—the ragged edges of a society that kept the poor whites submerged and bred a numerous progeny of coarse and primitive creatures, little better than social outcasts. Not the least of the curses of slavery—as Helper pointed out—was its

[5] See *The Forayers*, Chapters XLIII–XLVI.

blighting effect on the less prosperous whites who environed every plantation with its special frontier. With his strong bias towards realism Simms refused to romanticize what was inherently unlovely. Like Baldwin in his *Flush Times of Mississippi and Alabama*, he discovered an ample supply of blackguards and sharpers in the no man's land beyond the settlements. The log cabins of the swamp country harbored their motley crew in no wise different from their fellows of the farther frontier along the Mississippi; and these precious rascals he drags from their lurking-places to exhibit in the light of day. The frontier in consequence is rarely absent from his stories, and it is this picaresque interpretation that sets him so sharply off from Cooper. A recent student, in commenting on the contrast between the frontier of Cooper and Simms, suggests that "perhaps the earlier frontier had been intrinsically more dignified than that which Simms had observed; perhaps the difference is that Cooper's had lain deeper under the softening shadow of the past" (Van Doren, *The American Novel*, p. 65). But this is quite to miss the point, both of Cooper and Simms. The real explanation is to be sought in the different interpretations of the romantic and the realist. Cooper's frontier existed only in his imagination. When he came face to face with the reality, as in the case of old Aaron Thousandacres and his lawless brood, he hated it too frankly to portray it justly. The stern Puritan squatter and his fiercer wife are magnificent caricatures, drawn to serve a partisan purpose. They provide a romantic contrast to the honest Chainbearer, spokesman of the psychology of the settlements; but set beside Simon Suggs, master of the frontier technic of easy money, as depicted by Joseph Baldwin, they are as romantic as Cooper's Indians.

The picaresque note is frankly emphasized in Simms's Revolutionary tales. All the swamp-suckers and rapscallions found their heaven-sent opportunity in the disorders of civil war. No realist could write about the Revolution in South Carolina without noting the flocks of buzzards gathering to fall upon the carrion. War is not a heroic thing in these stirring pages. It invites debauchery and encourages brutality. Blackguards put a black stain on military glory. In the preface to *The Scout*, Simms remarks:

> To burn and slay were not the simple performances of this reckless period and ravaged country. To burn in wantonness and to murder in cold blood, and by the cruellest tortures, were the familiar achievements of the time: . . . The face of the country was overrun by outlaws Detached bands of ruffians, formed upon

the frontiers of Georgia, and in the wilds of Florida—refugees from all the colonies—availed themselves of the absence of civil authority to effect a lodgment in the swamps, the forests, and the mountains. These, mounted on swift horses, traversed the state with the wind; now here, now there; one moment operating on the Savannah, the next on the Peedee; sometimes descending within sight of the smokes of the metropolis; and anon, building their own fires on the lofty summits of the Appalachian ridge.

Now and then in his pages war flashes out in romantic or heroic episodes, but for the most part it is mean and degrading, a thing to be hated. Simms loved action too keenly not to make the most of the countless onsets and forays, the ambushing of Hessians and the cutting off of wagon trains; he found in them material for many a brisk page and stirring adventure; but in the end it is the brutality of it all, the unhappy loosing of evil passions, that gives him most concern. It was a hard world, and the soft-hearted Jack Bannister, speaking with the tongue of Simms, could find comfort only in stoicism. "A man ought not to be too soft about the heart, in a world like this, so full of rascals that need the knockings of a hard and heavy hand."

It is this strong seasoning of the picaresque, perhaps, that accounts for the neglect that has befallen the work of Simms. Many blackguards and generous potations of Jamaica rum consorted ill with the genteel tradition in letters that grew up in the days following the Civil War; and romantic memories of a lost cause threw an idyllic haze over earlier times. The Revolutionary War lay too far in the past for a generation suffering from a great tragedy to concern itself with, and the vivid and vital work of Simms scarcely outlived its creator. The Revolutionary tales have been largely forgotten, and from his abundant work only *The Yemassee* has survived in popular affection, and this partly from the vogue of Cooper. The winnowing has been severe and scarcely just. The best of Simms is not in *The Yemassee*, but in those stirring tales of Marion's men who carried on a bushwhacking campaign under the hot sun of the dog days. *The Partisan* and *The Forayers* and *Woodcraft* deserve a better fate than has befallen them. The ghost of Cooper does not haunt their pages to challenge comparison, as it does *The Yemassee*, and bring into question their relative merits. There Simms is at home, in the swamps and fields and villages, with men whose ways he knew and loved, and his generous nature followed its own impulses.

But in dealing with the Indians he entered a domain preempted by the romantic, and his picaresque realism suffered a disastrous rivalry. Like Robert Montgomery Bird's *Nick of the Woods*, *The Yemassee* is heavily marked by the frontier psychology. It was unfortunate, perhaps, that Simms did not follow Cooper's example and plunge into the wilderness, leaving behind him the squatter and settler with their sordid prose. Instead, his Indians are encompassed by a dark background of civilization, and their tragic destiny is poignantly dramatized in the fate of young Occonestoga, besotted with the white man's rum, and doomed to a destruction far less poetic than befalls Uncas fighting his hereditary foes. Nevertheless a wealth of romantic material is crowded into the volume, enough to serve Cooper for half a dozen tales. In simplifying his plots to the uncomplicated problem of flight and pursuit, the latter gains in dramatic swiftness of movement, but he loses in abundance of accompanying action—the sense of cross purposes and many-sided activities, which *The Yemassee* so richly suggests. The latter is an elaborately carved and heavily freighted Spanish bark that is left far astern by the trim Yankee clipper ship; yet its cargo of the gold of the Indies is far richer. It is the familiar story of southern prodigality and wastefulness—an exuberant nature pouring out its wealth in spendthrift fashion, and failing to achieve the greater results attained by a simpler nature held in closer restraint. After all it is idle to compare Cooper and Simms, and even more futile to catalogue the latter as a disciple of the Cooper school. Simms was far too rich in his own right to live as a dependent on anyone, and certainly far too original to be an imitator. Nature was lavish in her gifts to him, and as if his fame as a story-teller is less than Cooper's, the debit must be charged against his unfortunate environment.

The later years of Simms were utterly devastated by the unhappy war, in which, as was to be expected, he was a stalwart and uncompromising partisan. His native commonwealth that had long treated him shabbily, sacrificed him in the end to her folly. It was his own fault of course, but how could one warped by the pervasive southern provincialism hope to escape? Scratch a Carolinian of the Calhoun school and you find a Fire Eater. In this respect Simms was not different from the McDuffies and Hamiltons from whom he took his cue—gentlemen whom, because they were politically prominent, he regarded as socially intelligent. That a man of such native powers as Simms should have taken seriously the Charleston politicians—blown up like a pig's bladder after butchering; that he should himself have aspired to become another such bladder—these are sobering facts to remind us that the man of letters is very likely to be a child outside his study walls. What was wrong with Simms that he read the signs of the times so badly? This, that he lived in a world of unreality, of social and economic romanticism, that was forever benumbing his strong instinct for reality. His father-in-law owned seventy slaves; his neighbors and acquaintances owned slaves; all South Carolina gentlemen owned slaves; and in judging this matter of slavery Gilmore Simms went unquestioningly with his little world. He who had drunk of the rich wine of Elizabethan culture came at last to drink himself under the table with his drafts of Charleston Jamaica. The dream of a Greek civilization based on black slavery was discovered in the bottom of the cup of southern romanticism. And Simms emptied his bottle with the rest. Charleston, no doubt, has paid a sufficiently heavy price for her too copious potations, but she can never atone for the undoing of her greatest son—for the foolish intoxication that befuddled the generous mind of Gilmore Simms. The loss is not Charleston's alone; it is a loss to our common American literature. There is food for thought in the words of the epitaph which he composed for himself: "Here lies one who, after a reasonably long life, distinguished chiefly by unceasing labors, has left all his better works undone." Juster words could not have been written, nor more tragic.

CHAPTER I

New Worlds

I

While Calhoun was instructing the South in the theory of a Greek democracy, other sons of the South were learning, in the new world to which they had removed, the ways of a very different democracy—a democracy native to the frontier and quite unconcerned with Greek ideals. In the Ohio valley was gathering a multitude of rough libertarians who had exchanged the restrictions of the old settlements for the freedom of the new. To these bumptious levelers rulership by established authorities made no appeal. They attached no respect to broadcloth, but preferred to manage their affairs in their own way by appeal to the majority. Taught by experience the worth of certain Jeffersonian principles, they took seriously the doctrine of equality and proposed to put it into practice. They were coonskin apostles of liberty and equality—if not of fraternity—backwoods democrats who by virtue of numbers established in common practice the principle of the sovereignty of the popular will. Springing up naturally on the frontier, the practice of democracy received from it a new validity and became the determining factor in the nationalism that America was creating in the early years of the nineteenth century. That it was a crude and often shoddy democracy, that it never justified its pretentions in the eyes of a critical realism, did not lessen the zeal with which men clung to it or weaken their loyalty. Democracy became the common faith of the West, and in becoming the common faith of the West it was put in the way of becoming the common faith of America.

If the romantic temper is a spontaneous by-product of social change, that temper found in the upheaval attending the western migration a plentiful aliment that had been wanting in the static eighteenth century. In that older world men had been held fast in the grip of the customary and familiar; but in the free West all was new and strange. The crossing of the Appalachian barrier that had long held back the settlements was an adventurous undertaking that fired the imagination. Romantic in spirit and scope, it was meanly picaresque in a thousand unlovely details. Plain men engaged in it, provident and improvident, hard-working and shiftless; heroes had a share in it, but blackguards and outlaws and broken men—the lees and settlings thrown off from the older communities—had a share as well. The world that provided a stage for the courage of Daniel Boone and the fighting qualities of George Rogers Clark bred also the Davy Crocketts and Mike Finks and Col. William Suggses, who discovered there opportunities for the development of less admirable qualities; and it engulfed in its depths a host of nameless adventurers who drifted into the wilderness settlements, drank and quarreled and begot children, suffered from the chills and ague, spread a drab poverty along the frontier, and were put away under ground and forgotten by the more fortunate who salvaged prosperity from the abundant wreckage.

From this crude society emerged the new states with governments designed to serve simple ends. Jealousy for his sovereign right to do as he pleased was the chief concern of the free western voter; as a sovereign citizen he refused to be subject to the creature commonwealth. If governors and legislators and judges got uppish he would throw them out of office and put in others who better understood the rights of free Americans. It was this rude equalitarianism that marked the early stage of western commonwealth building. Naïve Jeffersonians, these frontier citizens had not learned from Hamilton how useful the political state may become to those who know how to control its policies to their particular ends; but that lesson they were soon to learn. The citizens of Georgia received excellent instruction from no less a man than Chief Justice Marshall in the matter of the Yazoo frauds; and as such lessons sank into their minds their political philosophy underwent a silent change. The coonskin individualism that created Jacksonian democracy was gradually undermined by a middle-class individualism that inclined to the Whiggery of Henry Clay. The former was a spontaneous expression of the frontier spirit, the latter a calculating expression of the maturing settlement. The one discovered its native habitat on the backwoods farm, the other in the county seat town. The one was agrarian *laissez faire,* the other was exploitative paternalistic. The followers of Jackson wanted the state kept simple and frugal, the followers of Clay wanted it to engage in ambitious programs of internal improvement; and from these antagonistic principles emerged a bitter feud between Democracy and Whiggery that in western townships revived the old alignment of agrarian and Federalist of earlier times.

In such a contest the principle of Whiggery must eventually triumph. It was an expression of "the genius of the times." Economics and psychology were daily arguing in its behalf. From the first early settlements of the Ohio valley, it must be remembered, circumstances were creating a new middle class that was to stamp itself indelibly on western life and institutions. The spirit of speculation had entered the wilderness with the early surveyors. With its vast resources the Inland Empire offered the first opportunity to exercise the newly won right to exploit the western hinterland, and it was seized upon greedily. Agriculture was still the common business and land hunger the common passion. The irruption of the land-hungry hordes upon the fertile Ohio valley, it will be recalled, synchronized with the speculative debauch that followed the conclusion of the peace of 1783, and this in turn was a by-product of the sudden expansion of the new capitalistic finance. Speculation had suddenly become every man's business, and wild lands and wild-cat banks, joining fortunes for better or worse, brought forth a characteristic progeny. The new gospel of progress found more willing hearers than the old gospel of righteousness. Every adventurer into the Ohio valley was a potential speculator, and every settler was eager to sell out to a later comer at an advance. The real-estate agent followed close on the footsteps of Daniel Boone, quick to profit from the explorations. Land was the staple commodity and such a turnover had never before been known in America. Every clearing in the woods was speedily capitalized, and every townsite was reckoned rich in potential values. The new cities were founded in unearned increment and prospered with its increase. With European peasants flocking to the West from their poverty-stricken countries, and the exploited of the East seeking new openings there, it was an unlucky speculator who could not exchange his paper values for substantial

equivalents. Law, religion, education, culture, were pressed
into the service of speculation. How widely the spirit permeated the West is suggested in the experience of Timothy
Flint, frontier missionary. Writing from Saint Charles, Missouri, in 1818, he commented somewhat bitterly:

> Religion, when I came here was considered contemptible. The
> phalanx of opposition was in array from one end of the street to
> the other. Why did they invite me here? On speculation. A min-
> ister—a church—a school—are words to flourish in an advertise-
> ment to sell lots. (John Ervin Kirkpatrick, *Timothy Flint, etc.,*
> Appendix B, p. 293.)

From the determining factors, then, of abundant wild
lands, rapid increase in population, and an elastic credit,
operating on a vast scale, came the optimistic, speculative
psychology of the new West. It is the common disease of
every period of unstable economics. It had traveled west
with every extension of the frontier; and it became acute
in the Ohio valley in the romantic days following the War
of 1812. In colonial times before the upheaval of the Revolution, prices of land and commodities had been stable. The
basic silver currency varied little in quantity or value; coin
was scarce, but the occasional emission of paper money produced little disturbance, for the reason that the farmer ha-
bitually reckoned his income in the produce of his farm and
fireside. But with the unsettling of exchange values by the
wide use of bank notes, prices at once shifted to a speculative
basis. The familiar commodities ceased to have a fixed use
value, and a cash psychology superseded the traditional commodity value. The old stability was gone. The familiar domestic economy that functioned primarily in terms of consumption rather than profit disintegrated under the workings
of a paper system and gave place to a speculative economy

It was this revolution that set apart the new West from
the older traditional America and made it the special repository of the new middle-class spirit of progress. The change
had been long preparing. Writing from Boonesborough in
January, 1776, the agent of the Transylvania Land Company
pointed out that the western country "abounded with land
mongers," and that his company had already issued nine
hundred patents.[1] These adventurous spirits were only pioneers pointing the way for later hordes that after 1815
pushed eagerly onward. "Old America seems to be breaking up, and moving westward," commented a traveler in

[1] See James Hall, *Romance of American History,* Appendix.

1817 as he watched the long line of Conestoga wagons moving towards Pittsburgh; and in the fall of the same year Timothy Flint said of Saint Charles, Missouri, that "there was an average of one hundred people every day coming to the town, or passing to near-by points. Nearly all were poor and not one family in fifty had a Bible" (Kirkpatrick, *Timothy Flint, etc.*, p. 102). "This western fever has seized old and young," remarks a character in Cooper's *Home as Found,* "and it has carried off many active families from our parts of the world. . . . Most of the counties adjoining our own have lost a considerable portion of their population." One reason for this vast exodus from the East is suggested by a recent student who remarks: "A considerable part of the significance of the frontier lies behind the frontier. In one sense, the westward expansion of the American people was a flight from the new industrialism" (Norman Ware, *The Industrial Worker,* p. xx). To these adventurers from the East was added an increasing immigration. During the period from the close of the Revolution to the War of 1812, the annual immigration averaged no more than four or five thousand. In the year 1817 it rose to 22,000, and thereafter an augmenting stream poured into America and filtered westward. They were natural prey to shrewd promoters, and in *Martin Chuzzlewit* Dickens has drawn a picture—not wholly caricature— of what befell some of them. But whatever might be their individual fate, they provided fuel to the fire that was consuming the old agrarianism and clearing the ground for the western middle class.

II

With land as its staple commodity the West naturally interpreted progress in terms of increasing land values; and these in turn were dependent on better markets, better roads, and a freely flowing tide of immigration. In a country of such vast distances internal improvements were an everyday necessity. With every mile that a turnpike was driven into the wilderness new opportunities were opened up. Monies paid for wild land went into the Federal treasury; it was only just, according to the western view, that such monies should return to the West in the form of public improvements, for with such improvements tax values were increased, prices of all commodities rose, and progress was furthered. The Federal government could not fairly leave its offspring to shift for themselves, but must consider itself *in loco parentis* to the rising commonwealth. It was a persuasive argument, appealing alike to farmer and speculator, to town and country, but it played havoc with the older Jeffersonianism. Jefferson thought always in terms of the agrarian producer functioning in a stable economic world; speculation was not in his philosophy; unearned increment was a crop he never calculated on; and in sympathy with an older liberalism he would reduce the state to the narrow rôle of policeman. But the new West, thinking in terms of its immediate needs, desired a broad and benevolent paternalism. It wanted the Federal government to butter its bread regardless of the ultimate cost of the butter.

The complete embodiment of this spirit of paternalistic progress was the master politician of the times, whose dramatic career, beginning as a Jeffersonian and ending as a Hamiltonian, suggests the confusions of a world in transition. Henry Clay was the hero of the new West, the spokesman of the new ambitions. A man of great personal charm, engaging manners, buoyant temperament, exuberant patriotism, and persuasive tongue, he migrated in 1797 at the age of twenty-one from Richmond, Virginia, to Lexington, Kentucky, then a booming county-seat town only twenty-two years removed from the building of its first blockhouse. The population of the state had more than doubled in seven years, and by 1797 it had risen above 180,000. Of this aggressive little world Clay soon became the accredited representative at Washington. He had been brought up under the old domestic economy and carefully tutored in the Jeffersonian philosophy. For four years he had been private secretary to George Wythe, a distinguished Virginian of the older generation, a profound lawyer and teacher, a scholarly political thinker, a humanitarian, and a confirmed agrarian. When Clay left Virginia he carried with him the Jeffersonianism of Wythe; but he was wanting in the trained intellect of his preceptor and his views were inadequately grounded. His subsequent career revealed him as an impressionable nature modifying his convictions with his environment. In Kentucky the spirit of speculative expansion seized him and inoculated his mind with the new gospel of progress. He early convinced himself that government was not doing its full duty unless it helped its citizens to make money, and he persistently pressed on Congress the need of federal aid to develop the West. In 1812 he fell victim to the war psychology, turned jingo, and substituted an ardent patriotism for sober reason. Thereafter he became increasingly nationalistic, demanding a strong army and navy, pleading for a loose construction of the constitution, arguing for paternalism. His Jeffersonianism was quietly put away like a garment out of style. Grossly ignorant of the schools of economic thought, he was an opportunist who shifted from the older domestic economy to the later capitalistic, without comprehending the significance of the change. Unread in history and political theory, he trusted his fluency to get him out of any inconsistencies he might blunder into. In the course of his long career he found himself at different times on both sides of every important question; yet gravitating to the middle-class position, the exponent of exploitation in the name of progress, spokesman of the commercial, financial and manufacturing interests, a new-model Federalist passionately defending the new money economy—a curious ending for one who began as a pupil of George Wythe.

And yet not curious when one considers the ambitions of the world that molded him. Clay was a born politician who rarely came to grips with reality. Devoted to the principles of republican liberty as he found them in the Constitution, he professed to believe that government could be trusted to distribute favors with impartial hand. Personally honest, he never realized how often he allowed himself to become the unconscious tool of powerful economic interests. With his desire to please everybody he was an easy prey for skillful lobbyists. He had been at one time attorney for the Bank, yet he denied vehemently that his defense of the institution had been influenced by such connection. He had become a Hamiltonian without gaining Hamilton's clear understanding of the economic basis of politics. A brilliant opportunist, he was guided by no fixed political principles but tacked with the shifting winds. A brilliant romantic, he was the persuasive prophet of an age that was dreaming of a prosperity that should gather in certain favored reservoirs through the agency of subsidies and taxes, and trickle thence through all the land to water the roots of industry. It was fitting that such a man should be the father of Whiggery, and fitting also that he should stand as the embodiment of the spirit of compromise. One great lesson, at least, he had learned, that greater men too often do not learn, the lesson that republican government rests on good will and that such good will demands a policy of give and take among rival interests. Compromise may be displeasing to earnest souls, but it is implied in any workable system of democratic rule.

Like Calhoun and Webster, Clay was a victim of changing times. If he had lived a generation later, when the middle-class revolution had been accomplished and the principle of capitalism was in undisputed control, he would have achieved a far greater personal success. But capitalism was not yet strong enough to uphold him against rival economies, and he failed of his lifelong ambition to be President. He was broken by the Jacksonian revolution, in spite of the fact that no other American politician has been so loved by a hero-worshiping electorate—and it should be added, has been so lovable.

CHAPTER II

Two Spokesmen of the West

1

ANDREW JACKSON: Agrarian Liberal

Clay's pleasant dream of a paternalistic prosperity for America got its first rude awakening from General Jackson and his motley following of western equalitarians and eastern proletarians. Gentlemen were suddenly reminded that the plain people had been overlooked in the distribution of benefits. The waters of prosperity, it would seem, had been trickling somewhat too scantily to them from the great reservoirs where they were impounded; and as they saw the wealth pouring into private ponds through governmental pipe lines, a natural human envy took possession of them. In theory the pipe lines belonged to them, and the impounded waters were to be used for common irrigation; but in practice the mains seemed to conduct only to Lowell industrialists and Philadelphia and New York capitalists, and the waters turned out to be privately owned. As the recognition of this fact came home to the producing mass it provided a rallying point for an anti-monopolist movement and determined the great objective of the Jacksonian attack, the assault on the Bank.

The driving force of the new Democracy was the same class-feeling that had done service a generation before, the will to destroy the aristocratic principle in government. This conscious class-feeling had been strengthened by the spread of the dogma of equalitarianism through the frontier, and this in turn had brought about an extension of manhood suffrage which enfranchised a numerous body of voters who turned against an aristocracy that had long resisted their demands for the vote. The spirit of 1798 was rising afresh, and the re-alignment assumed the form of a democratic-aristocratic struggle, which for the moment obscured the more significant fact of an emerging middle class. The battle seemed to lie between homespun and broadcloth for control of government, and this serves to explain the odium that quickly attached to Jacksonian Democracy in polite circles. In drawing together mechanics and frontiersmen, the new party inevitably became a lower-class instrument, offensive to gentlemen of the old school of politics. The records of the times carry abundant evidence, often amusing, of this aristocratic contempt. In the early forties a girl of seventeen living on a Mississippi plantation, describing Jefferson Davis —whose wife she afterwards became—was surprised at the contrast between his politics and his manners. "Would you believe it," she wrote, "he is refined and cultivated, and yet he is a Democrat!" (*Jefferson Davis, A Memoir by his Wife,* Vol. I, p. 192.)

There were quite evident reasons for this aristocratic contempt. The new Democracy was heavily weighted with what gentlemen were pleased to call the rabble. Fresh Democratic recruits had been gathering since Jefferson molded the first party of protest. Industrialism was creating a city proletariat, and the frontier was producing the coonskin voter; neither as yet possessed any adequate political philosophy, but they needed no philosophy to enlist against the traditional privileges and perquisites of broadcloth. They had had their fill of such rule. The stake-in-society theory was worn threadbare, and other philosophies were preparing. Meanwhile in the person of Old Hickory they saw the visible embodiment of their vague aspirations, and they turned to him with an unquestioning loyalty that nothing could weaken. He was our first great popular leader, our first man of the people. If he aroused a wild enthusiasm in breasts covered by linsey-woolsey, it was because he believed that linsey-woolsey had its stake-in-society equally with broadcloth. He was one of our few Presidents whose heart and sympathy were with the plain people, and who clung to the simple faith that government must deal as justly with the poor as with the rich. Believing so, he could not be turned aside from his course by paid clamor, but with a courage rare in the White House he dared make a frontal attack on the citadel of exploitation in the face of an army of mercenaries.

The dramatic career of Andrew Jackson, so unlike that of Jefferson, which was determined by a speculative temperament and founded on a critical examination of diverse systems of society and politics, was shaped in large measure by prejudice and circumstance. A man of iron will and inflexible purpose, he was almost wholly lacking in political and social philosophy. His conclusions were the reactions of a simple nature of complete integrity, in contact with plain fact. Fundamentally realistic, he cherished few romanticisms. There was no subtlety in his mental processes and this lack kept him free from the temptation to follow devious paths beloved of politicians. He must take the shortest way to his objective, crashing through such obstacles as lay in his path. He was never a bookish man. He was surprisingly ill read, and his grammar and spelling were those of the plain people. He loved horse racing and was a master of profanity; yet in spite of characteristics that link him with Davy Crockett, he possessed an innate dignity and chivalry that set him far above the wag of the canebrakes. He was a born leader whose headlong onslaughts and rash mistakes might imperil the cause but could not shake the confidence of his followers. All who knew a man when they saw one respected Andrew Jackson. Imperious and dictatorial, he knew how to command but not to obey; he took orders from no one, not even his superiors, unless such orders fell in with his own plans. In short General Jackson represented the best which the new West could breed in the way of capable and self-reliant individualism, and the backwoodsmen loved him for the enemies he made, and backed him loudly in his fight against the aristocratic East.

When Jackson settled in Nashville in 1788, at the age of twenty-one, the Cumberland valley had somewhat under five thousand inhabitants scattered a distance of eighty-five miles along the river. The first settlements had been made only nine years before, and Nashville was a frontier post with frontier manners. Into this rough society the young Scotch-Irishman fitted easily. His smattering of the law sufficed to gain him clients and he soon became a local political leader. When he was only twenty-nine he was sent to Philadelphia as the first Congressman from the state of Tennessee, where he came in contact with the "aristocratic Neebobs" of the government and heartily disliked them. The next year he was sent to the Senate, but a single session satisfied him and he resigned to accept a judgeship in the state Supreme Court, which post he held for six years. During these early years he was unconsciously following the path that con ducted straight to a middle-class philosophy. He threw himself into speculation, bought and sold land in great blocks, traded in horses and slaves, set up a general store, and was well on the road to wealth when the panic of 1795 caught him unprepared. He lost most of his extensive holdings, including his homestead and many of his slaves, and removed to a six hundred and forty acre tract eight miles from Nashville—the Hermitage—which was to become one of the famous places of America. With this removal his middle-class ambitions fell away and he became a planter with a simple agrarian point of view; and this old-fashioned agrarianism became in later years the determining force in all his political thinking.

He was fifty-eight when he emerged as a potential candidate for the Presidency in 1822, and for years his sole interests, other than those of his plantation, had been military. He was singularly wanting in any formulated political philosophy, and his reëlection to the Senate two years later did little to supply the lack. He had picked up some shreds of the protectionist theory and in a letter written in 1824 he went so far as to declare for a "judicious" protective tariff, basing his view on the grounds of the country's economic unpreparedness at the time of the War of 1812, on the lack of markets for the produce of western farms, and on the desirability of drawing labor from the farm to the factory. But he added a significant passage that reveals the agrarian bias of his mind. To the end of his life he insisted that he was an old Republican of 1798, and this comment of 1824 suffices to connect his later attack on the Bank with Jefferson's attack on Hamilton's fiscal policy.

Beyond this, I look at the Tariff with an eye to the proper distribution of labor and revenue; and with a view to discharge our national debt. I am one of those who do not believe that a national debt is a national blessing, but rather a curse to a republic; inasmuch as it is calculated to raise around the administration a moneyed aristocracy dangerous to the liberties of the country. (Quoted in Bassett, *Life of Andrew Jackson*, Vol. I, p. 346.)

The tariff was the only question on which he was receptive to Whiggish arguments, and although he never openly repudiated a protectionist policy he soon grew lukewarm in its support. Such other fragments of Whiggery as found accidental lodgment in his mind were swept away in the fierce struggles that marked his years in the White House. During those eight years Jackson found himself, and the man who emerged from the struggle was an agrarian of the old Virginian school. As he came to understand the significance of the principle of exploitation he learned to interpret social classes in terms of economics. He instinctively hated all aristocrats, extending his dislike to the circle that pretended to social preëminence in Tennessee, speaking of them contemptuously as the "aristocrats of Nashville." But in these later years a change in his vocabulary appeared; his favorite phrases became "the monied capitalists" and the "hydra of corruption." He had come to associate aristocracy with the control of the economics of society. He was learning how aristocracies are built up through the instrumentality of the state; and as that lesson sank into his mind his opposition to such class favoritism hardened into adamant. He would put a stop to such practices, cost what it might. His attack on the Bank was perhaps the most courageous act in our political history; he knew how fiercely it would be defended; yet he was amazed at the number of hornets that issued from the shaken nest. "Such has been the scenes of corruption in our last congress," he wrote in 1833, "that I loath the corruption of human nature and long for retirement, and repose on the Hermitage. But until I can strangle this hydra of corruption, the Bank, I will not shrink from my duty." And a little later, "I want relaxation from business and rest, but where can I get rest; I fear not on this earth" (Bassett, *Life of Andrew Jackson*, Vol. II, pp. 635, 637).

As his policy unfolded it became clear that Jackson had not changed with the changing times. He remained to the last the product of an earlier domestic economy, with an old-fashioned horror of debt. He was too generous to be frugal, too kind-hearted to be thrifty, too honest to live above his means. He desired a simple independence for himself and for his country. He believed that the government should pay its debt, reduce its revenues, and live simply. In his austere personal rectitude he exhibited a Puritan conviction of the sacredness of stewardship; he must return to the common people, who had put their trust in him, an honest reckoning of that trust. It was not in his nature to betray their faith. He would have nothing to do with the new theory that government is an agency to help business. To take profits from an instrument erected supposedly for the common good was abhorrent to his old-fashioned views; it was impossible for him to lend the sanction of his office to particular or special interests; and when circumstances made the Bank the central vexing problem of his administration, his position was predetermined by every conviction of his mind. While he was President he would not allow the government to be used for business ends; he would not permit its funds or credit to be turned to private profits; he would not tolerate a money monopoly, no matter how conventionally correct its operations might be proved to be, that challenged the sovereignty of the national government. The twin powers of the purse and sword—to recall Clay's famous phrase that every Whig orator used on the stump—were in Jackson's opinion the ultimate tests of sovereignty; and to turn over the money of the government to private hands for private use, he believed, was as grave an abrogation of sovereign rights as would be the use of the army and navy by private interests for private ends.

In the judgment of many critics Jackson, in his ignorance of the intricacies of capitalistic finance, wantonly destroyed a necessary credit system, thereby bringing a devastating panic on the country. Whether or not that judgment is true is of little importance today. More interesting historically is the fact that in his attitude towards the Bank, as in his attitude towards internal improvements, Jackson returned to the agrarian position of Jefferson and John Taylor, nullifying for a time the victories gained by the middle class during the boom period of nationalism. The more he learned about the methods of capitalistic finance, the more he distrusted it. His prejudices were his strength. He disliked speculation and he could see nothing permanently wise or sound in a speculative economy that put American industry at the mercy of bankers to expand or contract credit. With an old-fashioned love of a stable currency he gave his warm support to the project to return the country to a specie basis. "The great desideratum, in modern times," he said in his message to the twenty-fourth Congress, "is an efficient check upon the power of banks, preventing that excessive issue of paper whence arise those fluctuations in the standard of value which render uncertain the rewards of labor." The establishment of additional mints to provide an adequate coinage of gold or silver became therefore a natural corollary of his attack upon bank currency. It was John Taylor's economics written into the law of the land.

In his attitude towards the state Jackson followed the nationalistic tendencies of the West. He was as patriotic as

Clay, and in spite of strong states-rights sympathies he contemptuously rejected Calhoun's theory of nullification. But he had no love for an omnicompetent state. More and more he drifted back to the Jeffersonian position in his conception of the powers and duties of the federal government. Replying to the vote of censure of 1834, he stated his ideal of government in words that would have become Jefferson's first inaugural speech. He had been charged with being ambitious, to which he replied:

The ambition which leads me on, is an anxious desire and a fixed determination, to return to the people, unimpaired, the sacred trust they have confided to my charge—to heal the wounds of the constitution and preserve it from further violation; to persuade my countrymen, so far as I may, that it is not in a splendid government, supported by powerful monopolies and aristocratical establishments, that they will find happiness, or their liberties protected, but in a plain system, void of pomp—protecting all, and granting favors to none—dispensing its blessing like the dews of heaven, unseen and unfelt, save in the freshness and beauty they contribute to produce. It is such a government that the genius of our people requires—such a one only under which our States may remain for ages to come, united, prosperous, and free. (Benton, *Thirty Years' View*, Vol. I, p. 427.)

The evils entailed on America by the Jacksonian revolution were many, but they cannot properly be charged against Andrew Jackson. They came in spite of him, and they came as a result of the great object lesson in the manipulation of the majority will that his popularity had laid bare. His instincts and the main outline of his policy were Jeffersonian; but neither he nor any other man was strong enough to stop the current of middle-class individualism then running. The American people were wanting in an adequate democratic program suited to the changing times, as they were wanting in desire for a social democracy. And when his capable hands fell from the machine he had created, it was seized by the politicians and used for narrow partisan ends. Yet one far-reaching result survived the movement, the popularization of the name of democracy and the naïve acceptance of the belief that the genius of America was democratic. In choosing a party name the Jacksonians were shrewder politicians and better prophets than the Whigs. For better or worse the American masses, and in particular the nationalistic West, had espoused the principle of democracy, and interpreted it in terms of political equalitarianism—a principle that had inspired a fanatical hatred in the breasts of old Federalists. To gentlemen of that earlier school democracy had meant the right of the propertyless majority to plunder the minority in the name of the law. The later Whigs did not make so blundering a mistake. Instead of proclaiming democracy the mother of all mischiefs, they welcomed it as an effective aid in vote-getting. Learning their lesson from Jackson, the Whig politicians outdid him in democratic professions. They had discovered that business has little to fear from a skillfully guided electorate; that quite the safest way, indeed, to reach into the public purse is to do it in the sacred name of the majority will. Perhaps the rarest bit of irony in American history is the later custodianship of democracy by the middle class, who while perfecting their tariffs and subsidies, legislating from the bench, exploiting the state and outlawing all political theories but their own, denounce all class consciousness as unpatriotic and all agrarian or proletarian programs as undemocratic. But it was no fault of Andrew Jackson if the final outcome of the great movement of Jacksonian democracy was so untoward; it was rather the fault of the times that were not ripe for democracy.

II
LINCOLN: *Free-Soil Liberal*

The equalitarian West that bred Andrew Jackson bred Lincoln also, a man with the same homespun mind, the same sterling integrity of nature, the same instinctive democracy, but shaped by an environment in which the new philosophy of progress had displaced the older agrarianism. The road of middle-class ideals he traveled further than Jackson, but in the end he also turned back to pick up once more the democratic faith then being repudiated by the proponents of slavery, north as well as south. Long an ardent Whig of the Clay school, and thoroughly indoctrinated in a paternalistic nationalism, he was brought, as every thoughtful American of the times was brought, to weigh the program of slave imperialism in the scales with the Declaration of Independence. The doctrines of that great document lay before every man's feet in those uncertain days, to get over as one could. They could not easily be evaded or got round; they must be dealt with. Rufus Choate, representing Boston Toryism, had come upon them and dismissed them as "glittering and sounding generalities." Calhoun, representing southern imperialism, had come upon them and essayed to destroy them by a critical

145

realism. Lincoln, embodying the spontaneous liberalism of the West, came upon them and paused to take his bearings afresh. He could neither wave them aside nor destroy them. The deep-rooted equalitarianism of his simple social philosophy found in them an eloquent pronouncement of its democratic faith, that set him upon considering how such doctrine might be squared with the reality of slavery. The agrarianism of John Taylor and the Whiggery of Henry Clay could tell him nothing about that; he must seek elsewhere; and the solution he found in an amalgamation of equalitarianism and free-soilism, in an adaptation of western Whiggery to Jeffersonian principles.

Whatever party name he might call himself by, in his love of justice and his warm humanity Lincoln was essentially Jeffersonian. He respected property rights, but other rights he believed more sacred. And as he watched the emergence in the South of the ideal of a Greek democracy, as he considered how the party of Jackson had become the party of Calhoun and Douglas, bent solely on strengthening and spreading the institution of slavery, his equalitarianism took alarm. He could not sit quiet while the principles of the Declaration of Independence were being openly flouted; he must speak out; he must arouse the idealism of the people to deal with the iconoclasts. In an important pronouncement written in 1859, he set the problem before them thus:

Remembering . . . that the Jefferson party was formed upon its supposed superior devotion to the personal rights of men, holding the rights of property to be secondary only, and greatly inferior . . . it will be . . . interesting to note how completely the two [parties] have changed hands as to the principles upon which they were originally supposed to be divided. The Democracy of today hold the liberty of one man to be absolutely nothing, when in conflict with another's right of property; Republicans, on the contrary, are for both the man and the dollar, but in case of conflict the man before the dollar. . . . But, soberly, it is now no child's play to save the principles of Jefferson from total overthrow in this nation. . . . The principles of Jefferson are the principles and axioms of free society. And yet they are denied and evaded, with no small show of success. One dashingly calls them "glittering generalities." Another bluntly calls them "self-evident lies!" And others insidiously argue that they apply to "superior races." These expressions, differing in form, are identical in object and effect—the supplanting the principles of free government, and restoring those of classification, caste, and legitimacy. . . They are the vanguard, the miners and sappers

146

of returning despotism. We must repulse them, or they will subjugate us. (Letter to H. L. Prince and Others, April 6, 1859, in
Works, Vol. V, pp. 125–126.)

Two conceptions were here competing in Lincoln's mind,
the older equalitarianism that sprang from French humanitarianism and the newer economics that came from English
laissez faire; and the attempt to reconcile them suggests
how far he had traveled along the path of western Whiggery. With the spirit of enterprise he had no complaint; the
ideal of progress was associated in his mind with a fluid
economics that permitted the capable to rise through skillful exploitation. He had no love for the stable economics of
the eighteenth century that Jackson preferred; the profit
motive, functioning freely, he regarded as the legitimate
driving force of society; but he was concerned that competition should be open to all on equal terms. As he
watched the transition from an agrarian to an industrial
order, he found himself more in sympathy with the new
than the old. Accepting the principle of exploitation he
came to the position of the little capitalist who believed
that in America capitalism could be democratized by the
simple method of keeping the opportunities for exploitation
open to every citizen. It was common view of western
Whiggery, and in so far Lincoln remained a Whig, content
with a system which he accepted as peculiarly suited to the
genius of the American people. In a late speech he summed
it up thus:

What is the true condition of the laborer? I take it that it is best
to leave each man free to acquire property as fast as he can. Some
will get wealthy. I don't believe in a law to prevent a man from
getting rich; it would do more harm than good. So while we don't
propose any war upon capital, we do wish to allow the humblest
man an equal chance to get rich with anybody else. When one
starts poor, as most do in the race of life, free society is such that
he knows he can better his condition; he knows that there is no
fixed condition of labor for his whole life. . . . I want every man
to have a chance—and I believe a black man is entitled to it—in
which he can better his condition—when he may look forward
and hope to be a hired laborer this year and the next, work for
himself afterwards, and finally to hire men to work for him. That
is the true system. (Speech at New Haven, March 6, 1860, in
Works, Vol. V, pp. 360–361.)

But as a western man Lincoln was far more concerned
over the application of *laissez faire* to the problem of western lands, and as he contemplated the practical workings

of "squatter sovereignty" he learned how the free functioning of *laissez faire* may be interfered with by economic imperialisms. That lesson determined his final stand. The virgin prairies beyond the Mississippi were coveted equally by northern and southern exploiters; and who should finally possess them, whether the small freeholder or the slave-master, was a question that could not be put off forever. None knew this better than the small farmers who were already staking out homesteads there. If Congress yielded to the pro-slavery demands their economic future would be endangered. It was the free-soil West that sent the first anti-slavery men to Washington and provided the backbone of the new party. Not the respectable West, but the plain people, Whig as well as Democrat. "Much of the plain old Democracy is with us," said Lincoln in 1858, "while nearly all the old exclusive silk-stocking Whiggery is against us. I don't mean nearly all the old Whig party, but nearly all of the nice exclusive sort" (Letter to A. C. Henry, in *Works*, Vol. V, p. 95). It was no humanitarian regard for the rights of the Negro that welded them into a militant party. Racially and economically the free-soiler was hostile to the black, whether slave or free. The Topeka constitution adopted by the Kansas free-soilers barred all Negroes from the new state; Kansas was to be a white man's country. The free labor of the West wanted no competition with an alien race, and was prepared to fight both the white master and free black for exclusive possession of the national domain. There were few John Browns among these western homesteaders —uncompromising idealists who rebelled at the injustice done the Negro. The free-soiler hated slavery because it threatened his immediate interests; nevertheless as the great struggle developed, the moral injustice of slavery was thrust to the fore and imparted a humanitarian motive to the free-soil argument. This humanitarian motive Lincoln seized upon, wedded it to the ideal of national union, and thus doubly armed went forth to the fight.

To amalgamate idealism and economics is no easy task. "Public opinion," he said in a speech at Hartford, "is founded, to a great extent, on a property basis." But it is not the sole basis. The ideal of justice comes in to upset all purely economic calculations. "The property basis will have its weight. The love of property and a consciousness of right and wrong have conflicting places in our organization, which often make a man's course seem crooked, his conduct a riddle" (*Works*, Vol. V, p. 330). Beyond question it was his recognition of the perennial conflict between economics and justice, between realism and idealism, that explains the hesitancies and harassing doubts that marked Lincoln's development. To reconcile the principle of exploitation with the Declaration of Independence it was necessary to stick like a flea to *laissez faire*—to eliminate slave labor and accept only free labor. Lincoln was a slow man and cautious, and he pulled himself forward to such a position by main force. He was not a rare intellect like Thoreau, to think swiftly to a conclusion and abide the consequences. He was a political leader rather than an intellectual, and he could advance only a little ahead of the slow-moving mass he sought to draw after him. A hundred invisible ties held him back—his belief in the rights of local democracies, his respect for law and order, his devotion to the Constitution, his recognition of property interests in the slave, his understanding of the complexity of the problem, with the entire economy of the South resting on a slave basis. Here were difficulties enough to trouble an honest mind. His practical sense, which is only another name for political realism, restrained his idealism and made him of necessity an opportunist, willing to yield much if he might save the Union. A simple, tolerant, easy-going man, he was at bottom a realist who had come to understand what may be considered the greatest truth in political science, namely, that an enduring state must rest on willing allegiance. Force cannot compel loyalty; authority may put down revolt but it cannot destroy the seeds of discontent; for that only the sovereignty of good will is competent, and in free states the sovereignty of good will must rest upon compromise. Lincoln was a better democrat than Jackson, for he would rather persuade than drive. If Hamilton embodied the aristocratic principle of coercive government, Lincoln embodied the democratic principle of give and take, that prefers compromise to bayonets. With a cause resting on the common good will it might safely be trusted to muddle through.

Slowly pushed forward by his cautious realism, Lincoln was forty-nine before he reached the "divided house" position of the Douglas debates, that was to entail such consequences. It was a bold pronouncement to address to a generation desperately engaged in erecting sham defenses against reality, in fleeing from the truth that cried aloud to be heard. But he would not let men stop their ears longer; the truth must be spoken to their understanding.

In my opinion [he said] agitation will not cease until a crisis shall have been reached and passed. "A house divided against itself cannot stand." I believe this government cannot endure permanently half slave and half free. I do not expect the Union to be dissolved—I do not expect the house to fall—but I do expect it will cease to be divided. It will become all one thing, or all the other. Either the opponents of slavery will arrest the further spread of it, and place it where the public mind shall rest in the belief that it is in the course of ultimate extinction; or its advocates will push it forward till it shall become alike lawful in all the States, old as well as new. North as well as South. (Speech at Springfield, June 16, 1858.)

The situation could not have been put more neatly. It was an appeal of honest realism to put away all shoddy romanticisms, all mean evasions, and to face the situation fairly; and it cut across the murky clouds like a flash of lightning. Thenceforth there could be no longer a conspiracy of silence; the problem of slavery had been brought home to the common mind and common conscience, the question of its relation to our national unity and national well-being had been brought out into the realm of homely discussion. It is the democratic way, and as an honest democrat, Lincoln stripped away all the protective coloring of lies that politicians use and appealed to the honesty of plain men. The same method he applied to the Dred Scott decision. He proposed to bring to the bar of the majority opinion the stale legal romanticisms of the Supreme Court. He refused to accept the divine right of the courts to rulership, he denied the sovereignty of the judiciary, and proposed to make a political issue of the matter. He would have it settled in town-meetings and at the polls, by the plain people, and not by lawyers and judges. It was a reversion to Jeffersonian principles, to the simple democratic creed that fundamentals of public policy must be determined by the people themselves.

Lincoln had thought his way slowly to the "divided house" position, but he could not pause there. Those were hurrying times, and the liberalism of yesterday was inadequate for the liberalism of today. A weak man or a time-server would have gone upon the rocks, and a man of unyielding policy must have broken; to be certain of one's conclusions was possible only to one who saw less than the whole. Patience and an open mind alone could be relied on, an intelligent opportunism alone would serve during the months the country was fiercely debating with itself;

and the heart-breaking hesitation of Lincoln, the troublesome doubts and perplexed questionings, reveal as nothing else could the simple integrity of his nature. He must go forward, but he must carry the people with him, the North as a whole, the border states if possible, even with the rebellious South if charity might suffice. Though in arms, they were Americans, and their hearts must be brought to willing allegiance; how otherwise could a democratic people emerge from the bitterness of civil war? He was not made for a dictator, and blood and iron he accounted poor cement to mend the sundered democracies. He trusted the better impulses of men to prevail in the end, because with Jefferson he believed in the essential justice of the plain people. In this faith he exemplified his democracy. Not a great political thinker, he was a great leader because he never forgot that he was one with those he led.

The slow unfolding of Lincoln's mind is sufficiently revealed in the changing quality of his speeches. He was rarely eloquent—never after the ornate fashion of the time; and the bits of Hebraic poetry that have come to be associated with his name are singularly few and belong to the last years of his life. His usual style was plain homespun, clear and convincing, but bare of imagery and lacking distinction of phrase. The thought seems to break into speech hesitatingly, in the way of a man visibly seeking to adapt his words to his meaning. Matter he judged to be of greater significance than manner. Few men who have risen to enduring eloquence have been so little indebted to rhetoric. Very likely his plainness of style was the result of deliberate restraint, in keeping with the simplicity of his nature. When he let himself go he discovered a well of poetry in his heart. When he chose he could even play the rhetorician. In those rare moments when he put caution behind him, his words fell into a stately rhythm that suggests the orator. Witness such a passage as this:

In those days our Declaration of Independence was held sacred by all, and thought to include all; but now, to aid in making the bondage of the negro universal and eternal, it is assailed and sneered at and construed, and hawked at and torn, till, if its framers could rise from their graves, they could not at all recognize it. All the powers of earth seem rapidly combining against him. Mammon is after him, ambition follows, philosophy follows, and the theology of the day is fast joining the cry. They have him in his prison-house; they have searched his person, and left no prying instrument with him. One after another they have closed the heavy iron doors upon him; and now they have him, as it were, bolted in with a lock of a hundred keys, which can never be unlocked without the concurrence of every key—the keys in the hands of a hundred different men, and they scattered to a hundred different and distant places; and they stand musing as to what invention, in all the dominions of mind and matter, can be produced to make the impossibility of his escape more complete than it is. (Speech at Springfield, June 27, 1857, in *Works*, Vol. II, pp. 327–328.)

But he did not often let himself go. As one reads his speeches one feels that an English diffidence held him back —this and the strong prose of his environment. Like a true Anglo-Saxon he was reluctant to speak out, afraid to let his emotions seize upon his speech. Only at the last did that diffidence yield to complete unconsciousness. The Gettysburg speech and the Second Inaugural are marked by the sincerity and self-effacement that ennobled the words of John Brown in the Virginia court-room—it is the eloquence which rises from the heart when life has been felt in its tragic reality, an eloquence that Webster could not rise to. Such words come only to those who have been purified by fire; they are the distillation of bitter experience. But the mass of his speeches are in quite another manner—that of the simple, everyday world that bred him. He had none of the itch of publicity that afflicts the second-rate mind. Webster was a magnificent poseur; Edward Everett repeated the same academic oration a hundred times; but Lincoln was too modest to pose and too honest to turn parrot and speak by rote. He was a man who loved to talk with his neighbors in homely metaphor, and it was then that his thought clothed itself in whimsical humor. He did not wear his heart on his sleeve, but like Mark Twain he let it slip out in a witticism.

Even more than Washington has Lincoln suffered at the hands of the myth makers. Of late years he has come to be looked upon too often as the invaluable asset of the political party that he honored in its founding, and too rarely as the embodiment of the kindly, liberal soul of our native democracy in the simpler days of a fluid economics and an unsophisticated equalitarianism. With his instinctive kindliness, his abiding faith in the good will of men, his dislike of coercion, his readiness to compromise, he may seem old-fashioned to a generation that has grown intolerant—but that is a reflection on our own times rather than on Lincoln.

The real Lincoln can grow old-fashioned no more than Jefferson. As he went back in a day of sordid imperialisms to the earlier liberalism of the great Virginian, seeking to rescue the idealism of the Declaration of Independence from the desecration of the market place where it was openly flouted, so in a day of vaster imperialisms and greater complexity we may take counsel of his humanitarianism, his open-mindedness, his trust in tolerance and good will, his democratic faith that held firm in spite of disappointment. The market place is mighty now as it was then, and liberalism finds as few friends there: but when did its gods become immortal?

CHAPTER III

The Frontier in Letters

When the West began to appear in literature in the late twenties and early thirties, it was the Ohio valley that became the beneficiary of the new interest, and over the vast region through which flowed the Beautiful River—as far as the Mississippi and beyond—was thrown the romance of the settlement. It was a beguiling theme with its background of dark forests and bloody Indian fights, with its venturesome flatboats that drifted with the current, its picturesque rivermen, "half horse, half alligator," who towed their heavy crafts upstream, its rude miscellany of settlers who intrusted their families and goods and cattle to great rafts and set forth hopefully on waters that were to bear them presumably to the Promised Land—a theme to appeal to imaginations easily stirred to romance. There was a darker side to be sure; wrecks in plenty littered the shores, wrecks of fortune and character and life; outlaws and blackguards thronged the river and preyed on the adventurers; but in spite of such misadventures the great movement was invested with dramatic interest, and the Ohio valley became the particular repository of the romance of the frontier, a monopoly which later times never despoiled it of and which only the Golden Coast of California ever remotely rivaled. It was fortunate in that its early history was recorded by a romanticizing generation that wove its myths about the wilderness scouts, that delighted in the picturesque talk of river boatmen and discovered themes for epics in the founding of new commonwealths.

From the first, therefore, the literature of the new West fell naturally into the romantic note. The early writers who essayed to deal with frontier materials were eastern men who proposed to exploit the romance of the Inland Empire as frankly as their fellow adventurers were exploiting the material resources. Gradually in their work two main conceptions crystallized, which came to overshadow all lesser themes: one localized itself in Kentucky and took form in the poetic conceptions of the Dark and Bloody ground; the other associated itself first with the rivermen but quickly diffused its spirit through the backwoods and took form in the conception of western humor. The first was a heritage from the early days when the Indian tribes fought for their ancient hunting grounds and fell upon the isolated stations with knife and tomahawk; the second grew up with a later generation that had penetrated far into the wilderness, where, stimulated by much whisky, its rough vigor found issue in exaggerated boasting. Each created its legendary hero about whom popular imagination wove its myths: the figure of Daniel Boone came to symbolize the heroic qualities of a race of scouts and backwoodsmen who matched their wits in woodcraft with the Indians and proved the quality of their Kentucky rifles in many a brush with the warriors; and the figure of Davy Crockett came to embody in the popular mind the loquacious eccentricities and exaggerated wit that were already passing into a literary tradition. Many hands contributed to the common work: writers as different as James Kirke Paulding with his *Westward Ho!*, Robert Montgomery Bird with his *Nick of the Woods*, Nathaniel Beverley Tucker with his *George Balcombe*, Albert Pike with his *Prose Sketches and Poems*, Augustus Longstreet with his *Georgia Scenes*, and Joseph G. Baldwin with his *Flush Times of Alabama and Mississippi*—to name only a few. From such diverse elements was created the new literature of the West that was contemporary with the rise of Jacksonian democracy and that gave wide currency to certain romantic conceptions.

Of this very considerable group of writers the two who earliest wrote from immediate first-hand knowledge of frontier life were Timothy Flint, Harvard graduate and missionary, and Judge James Hall, Pennsylvania lawyer, both of whom spent a considerable portion of their mature lives in the West. Of Timothy Flint's restless wanderings and periodic settlements, at Saint Charles, Missouri, at New Orleans, at Alexandria on the Red River in Louisiana, at Cincinnati, with frequent returns to his native Massachusetts and a short editorial experience in New York City, it is impossible to speak in detail; they suggest, however, the breadth and intimacy of his knowledge of the West got from twenty-five years' experience there from 1815 to his death in 1840. Few men traveled so widely through the frontier, or carried with them such keenly observant eyes. He wrote much, conducted for several years a literary magazine in Cincinnati, was for a short time editor of *The Knickerbocker Magazine* on the withdrawal of Charles Fenno Hoffman, and established a considerable reputation as a representative of western letters. Much of his work was frankly casual, but his *Recollections of the Last Ten Years, Passed in Occasional Residencies and Journeyings in the Valley of the Mississippi*, published in 1826, and his four novels published between 1826 and 1830, make up the first important contribution to the new literature of the West.

In temperament Timothy Flint seems to have been something of a realist. In his daily life he was frankly outspoken and critical, often to his own hurt, and some of the many troubles he met with in his honest preaching to frontier heathen, resulted from this plain speaking. He refused to measure life and conduct by the crude western standards, and the enmities resulting from such refusal brought about a rupture with the home society that had supported his missionary undertaking. It was this intellectual honesty that filled his *Recollections* with an invaluable body of observation and criticism, and constituted it an important source-book for later historians. Paulding early made use of it writing his *Westward Ho!*—published in 1832—and in his introduction, after paying tribute to Flint's "picturesque description," he went on to say that the work "has not met its deserts, and he should be highly gratified if this passing notice served in any way to call public attention to its interesting details." Unfortunately the occasional realism of the *Recollections* gave place in his novels to romance saturated with sentiment and heavily coated with moralizing. With a fund of exact information at his disposal he chose to turn away from reality and project his stories into regions he had visited only in imagination. *Francis Berrian, or the Mexican Patriot,* deals with a Southwest far beyond his extremest journeyings; *The Life and Adventures of Arthur Clenning* is a romanticized version of Robinson Crusoe; and *The Shoshonee Valley* is a romance conceived out of tales told him by far western travelers, woven into an extravagantly romantic plot. The only one of his tales that makes use of familiar settings is *George Mason, the Young Backwoodsman; or "Don't Give up the Ship,"* in which he put some of the materials gathered in his journeyings up and down the Mississippi, but sentimentalized and moralized out of all realism. It is a pity that Flint should have fallen in with the extremest mode of the times, for in many essential respects he was the best qualified man of the West to write an honest account of a world just taking form.

The literary reputation of Timothy Flint soon came to be overshadowed by that of Judge Hall. "Among writers of short narratives, the most characteristically Western fiction of the time," remarks a recent student, "James Hall was clearly preëminent; and he became the central figure in a kind of school of experimenters in the materials of frontier life" (Ralph Leslie Rusk, *The Literature of the Middle Western Frontier,* Vol. I, p. 274). In the early twenties he had ridden the circuit in Illinois as a very young lawyer, when the settlements were scattered thinly through the southern portion of the state. At Vandalia he started the *Illinois Monthly Magazine,* which survived for two years, when he removed to Cincinnati and established *The Western Monthly Magazine,* which in the four years from 1832 to 1836 became one of the "most important of the pioneer period." "The purpose," says the student above quoted, "was not so much to introduce the East to the West as to make the West conscious of itself" (Rusk, *ibid.,* Vol. I, p. 173). To this end Hall was writing and publishing short tales and descriptions, and he had already collected a miscellany of prose and verse by several hands which he issued as an annual, *The Western Souvenir, a Christmas and New Year's Gift for 1829.* Thus launched on a literary career, he wrote in the next twenty years a very considerable amount, including tales, sketches of manners, history and casual comment.

His best-known story is probably *Harpe's Head,* which he later incorporated with other tales in a volume entitled *Legends of the West: Sketches Illustrative of the Habits, Occupations, Privations, Adventures and Sports of the Pioneers of the West,* and published in 1832. The work proved popular and passed through half a dozen editions. Sketchy and loose in construction, it belongs to the school that hovered between the essay and the romance, delighting in the picturesque, exuding sentiment, and going out of its way to exploit the pleasantly horrible. It is a mingling of Virginia chivalry and frontier bravery, woven about a central plot of a daughter of a Virginia house who removes to Kentucky under tragic circumstances, is abducted by a roving band of Indians, and subsequently rescued. Additional romantic interest is sought in the melodramatic deeds of the title hero—a well-known border ruffian with an insatiable blood-lust who murders his unsuspecting victims wherever he comes upon them—and in the curious exploits in rattlesnake killing of Hark Short, a waif from the Carolina swamps who lives like a fox in his den. The interest of the story today lies in the pleasantly idealized descriptions of such scenes as the barbecue and the camp meeting, rather than in the portrayal of backwoods characters. Although Hall frequently professed his devotion to realism, there is little evidence of it; occasional figures like Pete Featherton, whose rifle had been bewitched, and occasional indulgence in a conventionalized backwoods dialect, serve only to heighten the somewhat gaudy romance of the whole. Yet even such timid ventures brought on his head criticism from a Cincinnati editor "for tiring the reader with vulgar backwoods expressions" (Rusk, *ibid.,* Vol. I, p. 282).

That Hall's interest in backwoods eccentricities of speech and manner suffered a heavy handicap from the romantic taste of his readers may easily be believed. Matter excluded from his tales he sometimes put into his introductions. Thus in the third edition of *Harpe's Head* he analyzed at some length certain characteristics of the crude pioneers who were creating the psychology of the West—their fondness for drinking, betting, horse-trading, stump-speaking, swearing. Particularly it is the exuberance of their picturesque language that he emphasized, an exuberance that was already becoming a literary tradition and that flowered in the cento of western folk ways that were gathered into the Davy Crockett myth. A single passage will suffice to suggest some of the elements from which Davy was created:

> Though usually taciturn in the presence of strangers, [the frontiersman] is communicative to his friend or guest, has often strong colloquial powers, with quaint, singular, figurative, and even eloquent forms of expression. His language, which is commonly brief, sententious, and abrupt, becomes, when excited by the interest of the subject or by passion, highly expletive, and redundant with exaggerated forms and figures of comparison. When he swears—and he is probably not more given to this exceedingly vulgar vice than other men—but when he does swear in earnest, his philology becomes concentrated, and explodes with an appalling energy, which would have astonished even the celebrated army in Flanders. (*Ibid.*, Introduction, p. xii.)

In his last collection, *The Wilderness and the War Path,* published in 1846 and including some earlier tales, Hall contributed little that was new. There is the same heavy romance with touches of realism, and by way of reply to Bird's interpretation of the Indian character he exploits the romantic qualities of the red man; but his failures are commoner than his successes, and his work as a whole must be regarded as a sacrifice to the bad taste of his generation. From this judgment, perhaps, should be excepted his *Romance of American History,* which is still pleasantly readable.

II

THE REALISTIC FRONTIER

Far more vital than these literary tales with their heavy coating of romance are the few realistic sketches—only too rare in those exuberant days of the high-flown—that preserve the authentic ways of backwoods life in their rude vernacular. Of such sketches those that most faithfully reveal the impress of the frontier, preserving down to the present the note of verisimilitude, are *Georgia Scenes* by Augustus B. Longstreet, and the *Autobiography of Davy Crockett,* to which may be added, perhaps, Joseph G. Baldwin's *Flush Times of Alabama and Mississippi.*

1

AUGUSTUS LONGSTREET: *The Georgia Frontier*

For some reason no glamor has ever gathered about the Georgia frontier. It may be that fate conspired against it in bestowing no idealizing historian to throw a romantic haze over life in the pine woods. Or perhaps it was the Georgians themselves who did the commonwealth an evil turn. As a matter of sober fact what could even romance do with the raw materials that went to the making of this crude southern Yankee state? How could the most confirmed romantic discover rare graces in the indigenous Cracker, or weave poetry about the ubiquitous peddler with his pack of Yankee notions? Any honest historian could hardly avoid taking into account the ungainly throng that attended a gander pulling, or depict Ransy Sniffle as other than a pallid, pot-bellied, clay-eating grotesque. Crude, uncouth, drab, with primitive passions and unlovely manners, Georgia offered scanty materials for the most ardent eulogist. Frontier life there ran a petty round between fist fights and horse races, between politics and religion. These were the staples of everyday existence, as necessary to the natural man as whisky and salt pork; and the honest Georgian preferred his whisky straight and his politics and religion redhot. The Jeffersonian hated the Federalist vindictively; and Presbyterian, Baptist, and Methodist regarded each other malignantly, convinced that the devil was stoking his fires for the lost neighbor who persisted in sitting under the wrong preaching. Denominationalism on the Georgia frontier was as harsh and unforgiving as political partisanship. Alexander H. Stephens believed that the plain people of Georgia were the most democratic on the face of the earth, and the kindliest; yet the pugnacious little democrat was himself nearly butchered by a democratic neighbor. In depicting such a society realism was the only honest method; but to make it palatable it must be well seasoned with humor. If it were garnished with moralizing, so much the better. There must be no subtleties in the treatment, no literary touches. The humor must be in the backwoods vernacular, and the preaching open and aboveboard—frank pulpit-thumping lessons to awaken the surliest sinner.

For such business Gus Longstreet was ideally fitted. A true child of the Georgia border, he never quite outgrew his early environment. Born in Augusta in 1790 of New Jersey parents, Holland Dutch but with a large admixture of English blood,[1] he came of plain stock. A driving, robust, energetic fellow, never squeamish, with a ready wit, he was at home amongst the plain people, the greatest wag

[1] The family name of Langestraet was given in English form by his grandfather.

in every gathering. He could knock a man down or shoot out a squirrel's eye with any champion of them all; he could enter into a dance or a revival meeting with equal ardor, or take the stump against a seasoned campaigner. A fellow must be simple-minded who would expect to get the best of him in swapping horses, or in the way of a practical joke. It came hard for so vigorous a plebeian to settle down as a substantial citizen, and the dignified titles that he gathered in the course of a long and prosperous career—judge, doctor of laws, doctor of divinity—fitted him somewhat incongruously. On the whole one prefers the plain Gus Longstreet to Judge Longstreet, but his neighbors, who thought they knew a man when they saw one, thrust his titles upon him. Besides he had gone to college and was thereby lifted to a place of distinction which he could not avoid. The process of scraping off the bark of the frontier followed orthodox southern lines. A few years' schooling at Dr. Moses Waddell's celebrated Academy, where at different times Calhoun, Crawford, McDuffie, Petigru and Legaré prepared for college, and two years at Yale, provided him with a stock of rusty Latin to suffice a college president; and a winter or two at the law school in Litchfield, Connecticut, following Calhoun's high example, furnished him with enough Blackstone to meet the demands of Georgia law courts. Thus provided intellectually, he went forth boldly to cope with the Georgia world as he found it.

It was a plebeian world that approved his plebeian qualities. There was nothing of the southern patrician in Gus Longstreet, nothing of the ascetic Puritan that marked so deeply men like Calhoun, Legaré, and the Grimkés. In his strong instinct of acquisitiveness, his canny thrift that never failed to seize advantage by the forelock, his desire to get on in the world while serving God, he was a Georgia Yankee, with an emotional religion that took comfort in discovering that God was always on his side of any controversy. Yankee also was his knack of doing many things well enough to impress his less capable neighbors. He was a frontier jack-of-all-trades, passing easily from one profession to another, lawyer, newspaper editor, writer, minister, politician, teacher, and between times busying himself with all sorts of odd jobs, doing everything readily and nothing thoroughly well. A good talker, his chief interests were politics, religion, and moneymaking. He wrote much in careless haste, apologizing always for the lack of finish;

but except for the sketches which were gathered under the title of *Georgia Scenes,* he produced nothing that needs to be remembered. At the age of forty-eight he quitted the law for the Methodist ministry, proved to be a mediocre preacher, and was soon given the berth of president of Emory College, a denominational school then recently established at Oxford, for which his literary reputation and his reputed scholarship seemed to fit him. Later he was president for a few months of Centenary College, Louisiana, but found the place uncongenial, resigned, and was chosen president of the University of Mississippi, where he served seven years and made full use of the opportunity to speculate in real estate. At the age of sixty-six he was made president of the University of South Carolina, where he ruled patriarchally till the school was closed by the war.

How great a man he was judged to be by his fellow Georgians is hard for us to realize today. Throughout his later years he was regarded by his friends as the brightest ornament of Georgia society, a Christian gentleman who was a model to southern youth, a scholar who had brought honor to the commonwealth, an author who had silenced the reproach that the state had produced no literature. Yet it must be confessed that the Judge shrinks in compass when taken out of his native environment. Beside John P. Kennedy or Hugh Legaré, he lacks distinction either of mind or manner; compared with Gilmore Simms he is only an amateur in letters. His latest biographer[2] has sifted a mass of material to prove the solid and eminent worth of the man; yet no impression of intellectual vigor emerges from the analysis; one must take it on the authority of somewhat incompetent witnesses. The figure that emerges from the clutter of contemporary estimate is that of a capable, expansive, middle-class soul, disputatious in the lordly southern manner, genially domineering, magnificently superior to logic, given to erecting an imposing structure of convictions on the slightest of foundations, impatient of contradiction and inclined to lose his temper when the argument went against him—a witty, agreeable gentleman, at home amongst mediocre preachers, and an oracle to admiring friends. He was on terms of intimacy with not a single first-class mind. He had no intellectual curiosity and was incapable of rigorous intellectual processes. Yet good fortune had marked him for her own. A small investment in letters, made at odd moments between law cases and

[2] John Donald Wade, *Augustus Baldwin Longstreet.*

farming operations, returned him such dividends in the way of contemporary fame that for forty years thereafter he lived in the sunshine of a literary reputation. No other American, unless it were William Wirt, ever drew such ample revenues of popular praise from a casual investment, and certainly none ever expanded with greater self-satisfaction. To the end of his life he was the much-sought-after author of *Georgia Scenes,* and the most ambitious southern magazines were glad to publish his frequent effusions; in all of which the Judge delighted, for he was a simple soul and accounted himself an apostle of southern culture, a mentor of southern taste, and he loved to see his name in print.

As a man close to the people Longstreet reflected the current Georgia views on politics. He was an idolatrous admirer of Calhoun and George McDuffie. The former he rated "above William Pitt, or any other premier who ever lived before or since his day" (Wade, *Augustus Baldwin Longstreet,* p. 124) and the latter he regarded as "hardly inferior to him in anything." Calhoun's innate Hebraisms, so deeply imbued with a patriarchal spirit, fitted to a nicety his own Hebraized conception of a Jeffersonian order. Writing of Calhoun, in after years, Longstreet remarked with evident approval:

I believe that he regarded the government of the children of Israel in the wilderness, the most perfect that ever existed on earth. Be that as it may, he called my attention to it more than once as exactly the government ours ought to be, or was intended to be. "There," said he, "each tribe had its place on the march and in the camp, each managed its own concerns in its own way, neither interfered in the slightest degree, with the private affairs of another, nor did their common head interfere with any of them in any matters, save such as were of equal interest to all, but unmanageable by them as separate and distinct communities." (*Ibid.,* p. 60.)

The background of his political thought was Jeffersonian agrarian. He was always a countryman at heart, and his dearest interests were agricultural. But he seems to have been quite unread in political theory, and probably had never heard of John Taylor's economic principles. Suffering from an incurable political itch, he was one of the earliest and most ardent of states-rights advocates. He went for Nullification before either Calhoun or McDuffie had espoused it; and he followed his premises through to the logical end of secession. But with the growth of northern Abolitionism his Jeffersonianism began to disintegrate.

Garrison's appeal to equalitarianism and the rights of man aroused all his southern prejudices. A philosophy that could be turned against the sacred institution was no philosophy for a southern gentleman, and like Calhoun he repudiated the whole French liberal philosophy that he had imbibed in his youth. He even went so far as to play with Calhoun's doctrine of economic representation. Writing to President Lamar, of Texas, in the late thirties, he said, "A government should have a legislative assemblage to represent each of its large economic interests, one, say, agricultural, one manufacturing, one commercial. No bill not acceptable to all three of these assemblages should become a law" (*ibid.*, p. 138). But in defense of slavery he argued as a minister rather than an economist. He declined to consider it an economic question; he would not discuss it as a social question; political theories, he believed, had nothing to do with it. The right to hold slaves he regarded as a moral question to be determined exclusively by the authority of the Bible, and on such a question he professed to speak with assurance. He was vastly annoyed at the Abolitionists' unchristian appeal to the old doctrine of equalitarianism, and in 1845 he wrote angrily, "Will not some of you accept my ideas and then argue through the question on that basis, without taking recourse to the Declaration of Independence or throwing up a breastwork out of the long-forsaken rubbish of the Social Contract, or bewildering your pursuers in the mazes of metaphysical subtlety?" (*ibid.*, p. 282). His religion was deeply involved in the institution of slavery, and it seemed to him uncharitable for an intellectual like Theodore Parker to question the sufficiency of a southern minister's texts, or to drag him beyond his intellectual depths. So exasperated did he grow that finally he would have no fellowship with northern Methodists, and was a prime mover in the great schism that rent the church into sectional branches. Abolitionism seemed to him hypocrisy and blasphemy and as a minister of Christ he could not hold fellowship with those who rejected the Master's word. After the war, in reviewing the long controversy, his Christian pugnacity flared up anew, and he flung at the northern churches the accusation that they had been "the most man-astounding, God-offending foes that we had" (*ibid.*, p. 367).

There could be no more telling commentary on the literary poverty of *ante-bellum* Georgia than the extraordinary popularity of Longstreet's sketches. Written for the most part between the years 1832 and 1836, while he was publishing the *State Rights Sentinel,* they profess to be authentic documents of frontier life in Georgia in the early years of the century, and the deliberate note of realism contributes to the impression of authenticity. The love of the romantic that spread like the plague among southern men of letters during the long reign of Sir Walter, fortunately did not infect the robust nature of Longstreet. The best of the sketches are spun out of the vernacular; they are as objective as Longstreet could make them—conscious studies in the local, done with obvious delight in butternut ways and frontier dialect. The quality of the work improves as he draws nearer the backwoods, and comes upon the unregenerate Cracker in his native habitat. There his humor has free play, exuding in practical jokes and ready repartee, in boyish pranks and homely idiom. And there he finds characters to his liking and bits of realistic drama. If one were to single out the sketch that is most indigenous to the Georgia frontier, the truest local document, the choice might well fall on *The Fight,* an account of a bloody meeting between backwoods gladiators brought on by skillful diplomacy of Ransy Sniffle, a grotesque clay-eater and Longstreet's favorite character. Other excellent sketches are *The Gander Pulling, The Shooting Match, Georgia Theatrics, The Horse Swap, The Militia Company Drill*—stories that throw an unromantic light on the ways of the Georgia Cracker. Longstreet was as uncritical as his readers and his frequent failures are glaring in their badness. Perhaps the worst of the sketches are the absurd *The "Charming Creature" as a Wife,* a crude sermon on the folly of marrying a lazy woman; *The Song,* an overdone burlesque, and the puerile *The Debating Society,* a heavy practical joke which for some inexplicable reason Poe thought the best of the whole.

Slight though the sketches in *Georgia Scenes* are, they embody solid merits; they are not literary and they are quite unaffected by Irving and the exploitation of the picturesque. Realism was only too rare in those days of high-flown romance, and how honestly realistic was Longstreet's work is revealed by a comparison with James Hall's contemporary stories of the West, such as *Harpe's Head,* or even with Kennedy's *Swallow Barn.* After all Gus Longstreet was an original, and he set the style that was followed in a long series of frontier sketches, and established the tradition of frontier humor that flowered at last in Mark Twain.

THE DAVY CROCKETT MYTH

The Narrative of the Life of David Crockett of the State of Tennessee was woven from the same stuff that Longstreet made use of, but the fabric is of far better texture. It is the great classic of the southern frontier, far more significant than *Georgia Scenes*, far more human and vital. Realistic in method, it is romantic in spirit. In its backwoods vernacular it purveys the authentic atmosphere of the cabin and the canebrake; it exhibits the honesty, the wit, the resourcefulness, the manly independence of a coonskin hero; it reveals, in short, under the rough exterior of a shiftless squatter and bear-hunter, qualities that are sterling in every society where manhood is held in repute. It is an extraordinary document, done so skillfully from life that homespun becomes a noble fabric and the crudest materials achieve the dignity of an epic.

The thing had long been waiting to be done. The literary romantics had tried their hand at the frontier materials and had failed, and then came a realist of the Georgia school who used the stuff as he found it and created a lasting document. A practiced writer collaborated with a picturesque talker, and the fame of the Tennessee Congressman was made. Romantic America found a new hero and Davy Crockett reaped a surprising reward. He had the good fortune to preëmpt the romance of the backwoods, to file on an unsurveyed tract of western life, and when the lines were run it was found that his claim embraced all that was native and picturesque along the Mississippi frontier. Popular imagination seized upon him and endowed the mighty hunter of the canebrakes with the fugitive romance that had been gathering for years. He was erected into a mythical figure that drew to itself the unappropriated picturesque that sprang spontaneously from the crude western life. How this astonishing result came about, how good fortune came to single out Davy Crockett for her smiles, offers a somewhat amusing commentary on the ways of an unsophisticated generation.

That in its later development, if not in the beginning, the Davy Crockett myth was a deliberate fabrication scarcely admits of doubt, nor that its immediate purpose was frankly partisan. It did not spring from the soil of the Tennessee canebrakes; it was created at Washington. It was not the spontaneous product of popular imagination; it was the clever work of politicians. The successive stages through which it passed in its triumphant progress can be traced fairly accurately with the aid of a little historical imagination. Roughly they were three; the exploitation of Davy's canebrake waggery, the exploitation of his anti-Jackson spleen, and the exploitation of his dramatic death at the Alamo. The first phase is embodied in the *Sketches and Eccentricities of Col. David Crockett, of West Tennessee* (1833); the second, in *An Account of Col. Crockett's Tour to the North and Down East* (1835), and *The Life of Martin Van Buren* (1835); and the last, in *Col. Crockett's Exploits and Adventures in Texas* (1836). Midway between the first and second stages stands *A Narrative of the Life of David Crockett, of the State of Tennessee* (1834), which may be accepted in the main as authentic autobiography. None of the five was written by Crockett. He probably had a hand in the first in spite of his repudiation of the work, for most of the important facts of his life and the language of many of the picturesque episodes were taken from its pages to be reproduced in the *Narrative*. The *Tour* and *Martin Van Buren* were claimed by him and were certainly done under his eye and with his help, but the *Exploits* is quite as certainly sheer fabrication, done by a hack writer after Davy's death. It was the politicians who contributed most to the success of the myth. They exploited Davy as a convenient weapon against Jackson, saw their work prosper beyond all expectation, get out of their hands, enlarge itself to a cento of backwoods romance and pass into folklore. It was an unforeseen outcome that must have been vastly amusing to those who set the thing going.

The early thirties, it will be remembered, were robustious times when broadcloth in politics had suddenly gone out of style and homespun had come in. The new coonskin democracy had descended upon Washington, and picturesque figures provided with ample plugs of tobacco were making themselves free with Congressional perquisites. Nothing like it had been seen before in the city of dignified politicians, and the spectacle must have delighted the wags of the capital. But to the members of the overthrown dynasty the Jacksonian votes which these picturesque backwoodsmen represented were very far from amusing. The loss of desirable offices was a hard lesson that taught them the need of catering to this new element of the great American democracy. In their remunerative occupation as representatives of the prosperous and genteel constituencies of the East, the old-school politicians had too long overlooked the power of the plain voter which the progress of manhood suffrage was daily increasing. Hence began a desperate campaign to counteract the Jacksonian appeal. The coonskin vote could no longer be ignored and shrewd plans were laid to capture the backwoods for the new Whig party. The program of internal improvements was well enough in its way, and the old Revolutionary cry of the sword and the purse might prove useful; but the party needed a picturesque figure to draw the coonskin democracy to its standard. Men rather than principles appealed to the West, self-made men, speaking the western vernacular, imbibing western views with their whisky, uncorrupted by broadcloth. This explains the tremendous Whig hurrah over log cabins and hard cider that marked a later campaign; and this explains likewise the singular fate that overtook Davy Crockett, the bear-hunter from the canebrakes.

Davy had first come to Washington during Adams's administration, and in four years' loafing and boasting at the Congressional bar had achieved some distinction as a picturesque original with the tongue of a wag. He spoke rarely in the House and the few records in the *Congressional Debates* are sadly commonplace. Until after he broke with Jackson his political influence at Washington was negligible. But that fortunate break was the beginning of his fame. He had unwittingly made himself. He had become a valuable asset to the Whig party. To find a native Tennesseean, a real coonskin democrat, one who had served under Jackson and been sent to Congress as a Jacksonian, as authentic a Westerner as the General himself, at bitter personal odds with Old Hickory, ready to talk out in meeting and eager to repudiate the latter's attack upon the Bank, was a find indeed to the hard-pressed Whigs; and they would have been no politicians if they had not used what God sent. In consequence Davy soon found himself talked about. His picturesque eccentricities began to be exploited. His rugged western honesty was applauded; his shrewd backwoods intelligence was praised; his frontier humor was skillfully touched up; his characteristic motto, "go ahead," was seized upon as an expression of the progressive spirit of the lusty young Whig party. In short he was speedily turned into a myth by ways not unknown in our time, and sent forth as useful campaign material in the fight for political righteousness. Davy was vastly surprised at his sudden rise to fame. He had never realized how great a man he was; but he accepted it as an agreeable fact and went ahead.

The work had already begun with the publication of the *Sketches and Eccentricities of Col. David Crockett,* that came from the clever pen of some journalist with a liking for the new vein of backwoods humor. A Whig bias runs through the pages, but the book is more a character sketch than a political document. The first embroiderings laid upon the original homespun are seen in an extravagance of picturesque language—an extravagance quite lacking in the more realistic *Narrative.* A well-known passage professing to relate an occurrence on Davy's first trip to Washington will serve to reveal an early stage of the myth-making process—the fathering upon Davy of a type of humor then being exploited by clever young writers:

I was *rooting* my way to the fire, not in a good humour, when some fellow staggered towards me, and cried out, "Hurrah for Adams!" Said I, "Stranger, you had better hurrah for hell, and praise your own country." Said he, "And who are you?"
"I'm that same David Crockett, fresh from the backwoods, half-horse, half-alligator, a little touched with the snapping-turtle; can wade the Mississippi, leap the Ohio, ride upon a streak of lightning, and slip without a scratch down a honey locust; can whip my weight in wild-cats—and if any gentleman pleases, for a ten-dollar bill, he may throw in a panther—hug a bear too close for comfort, and eat any man opposed to Jackson." (*Ibid.,* Chapter XIII.)

The touching up of the picturesque in the *Sketches* seems to have been a little too much for Davy, who resented the note of clownishness; but he was not the man to permit undue modesty to blight so agreeable a myth in its tender stage. He loved to swagger in the public eye too much for that, and he joined heartily with his new political friends to clothe it in more dignified dress. His incredible egotism was aroused and he swallowed the Whig bait, hook, line and sinker. He began to take himself seriously and set about the business of propagating the myth. He conceived the plan of issuing in his own name books which he humorously claimed to have written in the same way that the President wrote his state papers. Some wag having suggested his name for the presidency to succeed Jackson, Davy was at great pains to advertise the fact to the world. To link himself with Jackson in the public eye and to contrast his own rugged honesty with the latter's reputed abandonment of democratic principles, was the single purpose of these Whig documents. The autobiography was quickly followed by the *Tour,* and this by the *Life of Martin Van Buren,* each more obvious propaganda than the last, and frankly designed to undermine the popularity of the President and his advisers with the coonskin democracy. Who the writer was that lent his pen to the work has never been determined. A recent student has adduced testimony to prove that it was Augustin S. Clayton, a Georgia Congressman, a ready talker and writer, a man of sound culture, a close friend of Longstreet and fond of the backwoods vernacular. The argument is plausible, but the case is not established.[3] In the *Life of Martin Van Buren* the mask is dropped and all the malicious gossip of the Congressional lobby is poured out on "little Van," the "heir-apparent to the 'government.'" The backwoods character is retained only in an occasional coarseness or deliberate lapse of grammar inserted in a text that is written with vigor and skill. The book is far less amusing than Kennedy's *Quodlibet.* Davy is pretty much lost out of its pages and its contribution to the myth was probably slight.

It is in the *Tour,* on the title page of which Davy formally accepts the brevet dignity of Colonel conferred upon him by the writer of the *Sketches,* that the myth expands more genially. A clever and amusing campaign document, it is a masterpiece of Whig strategy to gull the simple. The loquacious Davy joined heartily with his managers to cash in on his reputation. His egotism was played upon at every turn and he was quite unconscious that he had become a mere cat's-paw to pull Whig chestnuts out of the coals. He was paraded at meetings with Daniel Webster, given great dinners, applauded for his rustic wit and homespun honesty, presented with a fine rifle; and he seems never to have realized how grossly he was being exploited. His self-esteem was proof against dillusionment and he accepted the applause greedily. Wherever he went he was taken in charge by the young Whigs. Everything was carefully arranged beforehand. News was sent forward that he was coming; crowds were gathered to greet him; publicity was attended to; morning, noon, and night he was invited to speak, and the speeches were carefully reprinted—not

[3] See John Donald Wade, "The Authorship of David Crockett's *Autobiography,*" *Georgia Historical Quarterly,* September, 1922.

the authentic speeches, probably, but good campaign material nevertheless. It was a gratifying experience and Davy swelled up like a turkey cock.

As a result of his tour he was immensely strengthened in his new political faith and became a staunch nationalist. When he first went to Congress he was anti-tariff and had won his seat on that issue; but he was invited to Lowell, shown an idyllic picture of contented and prosperous mill-hands, dined, given a prepared table of statistics proving how industrialism "is calculated not only to give individual happiness and prosperity, but to add to our national wealth and prosperity," and bidden Godspeed in the work of spreading the true gospel among the honest, simple-minded and patriotic frontiersmen. After having been presented by Mr. Lawrence with a fine suit of domestic broadcloth, Davy would have been an ingrate not to vote for a protective tariff. But alas! the opportunity never came. A backwoods constituency that had never been dined by Lowell capitalists and had little use for fine broadcloth, a constituency that persisted in throwing up coonskin caps for Old Hickory in spite of Lowell statistics, resented his apostasy from the Democratic faith and at the next election invited him to stay in the cranebrakes. The gorgeous bubble was pricked. Davy had expanded under prosperity and could not now endure adversity. In a fit of anger he quitted his family and the state of Tennessee, went off on the mad chase to Texas and in March of the next year fell at the Alamo. Vain, ignorant Davy Crockett! A simple-minded frontiersman, he went down to Jericho and fell among thieves, and when they were done with him they left him despoiled politically but invested with a fame that has grown to this day. After his death other hands took up the work, wove around his name the humor and romance of the frontier, and made of him a legendary figure. It would have pleased Davy to know how the myth had prospered.

Yet from this crude romanticism, this picturesque propaganda of coonskin days, one solid contribution remains—the autobiography. It is a striking bit of realism, done after the manner of the Longstreet school. There is politics in it of course. Written just after Davy had gone through a bitter campaign from which he had emerged triumphant, it is a bold pronouncement that he wears no collar marked

---

[4] Among the miscellaneous material gathered together in the *Exploits and Adventures in Texas* and attributed to Davy is Longstreet's *Georgia Theatrics*, lifted verbatim from *Georgia Scenes*.

"My dog—Andrew Jackson." In the campaign of 1830 he had been defeated by the Jacksonians, but two years later he "made a mash" of his opponents, and the elation of that victory adds a certain cockiness to his habitual swagger. But it is much more than a political tract; it is a vital frontier document. The main facts of his biography, as set down there, may be accepted as true, and the general picture of backwoods existence in Tennessee; but the humor has been elaborated and the effect of the picturesque heightened by his collaborator. Such added touches were only natural. The real Davy was very far from romantic. An honest picture of the Tennessee democracy in its native habitat would reveal few idyllic features. It was a slovenly world and Davy was pretty much of a sloven. Crude and unlovely in its familiar details, with its primitive courtships and shiftless removals, its brutal Indian campaign and fierce hunting sprees, its rough equality, its unscrupulous politics, its elections carried by sheer impudence and whisky, the autobiography reveals the backwoods Anglo-Irishman as an uncivilized animal, responding to simple stimuli, yet with a certain rough vigor of character. Wastefulness was in the frontier blood, and Davy was a true frontier wastrel. In the course of successive removals he traversed the length of Tennessee, drinking, hunting, talking, speculating, begetting children, scratching a few acres of land to "make his crap," yet living for the most part off the country; and his last squatting place on the Obion River, seven miles from the nearest neighbor, was as primitive as the first. Willing to endure almost incredible hardships to obtain a keg of gunpowder to celebrate Christmas, risking his skin to kill a bear with a butcher knife, he was never much given to mending fences or enlarging his plow lands. He was a hunter rather than a farmer, and the lust of killing was in his blood. With his pack of hounds he slaughtered with amazing efficiency. A later generation would call him a game-hog. His family must have had Gargantuan appetites to have consumed one-tenth of the meat that fell before his beloved Betsy; the rest went to the dogs and hogs and buzzards. His hundred and five bears in a single season, his six deer shot in one day while pursuing other game—two of which were left hanging in the woods—serve to explain why the rich hunting grounds of the Indians were swept so quickly bare of game by the white invaders. Davy was but one of thousands who were wasting the resources of the Inland Empire, destroying forests, skinning the land,

171

slaughtering the deer and bear, the swarms of pigeons and turkey, the vast buffalo herds. Davy the politician is a huge western joke, but Davy the wastrel was a hard, unlovely fact.

Strip away the shoddy romance that has covered up the real man and the figure that emerges is one familiar to every backwoods gathering, an assertive, opinionated, likable fellow, ready to fight, drink, dance, shoot or brag, the biggest frog in a very small puddle, first among the Smart Alecks of the canebrakes. Davy was a good deal of a wag, and the best joke he ever played he played upon posterity that has swallowed the myth whole and persists in setting a romantic halo on his coonskin cap. Yet in spite of the romantic machinery the play turns out to be broad farce.

BOOK TWO

The Mind of the Middle East

The literature of the Middle East during the years of the romantic revolution, unlike contemporary letters north and south, revealed no coalescing unity of spirit and purpose; it was rather the casual and somewhat fortuitous expression of two cities, both of which were divided by language and custom into fairly equal groups, and neither of which had developed a homogeneous native culture. There were no intellectual hinterlands to Philadelphia and New York, as there were to Boston and Charleston and Richmond; no common ideals spread over broad areas, no dominant schools of thought, no branching roots by which a common literature might be nourished. In consequence it may, perhaps, be reckoned a misuse of terms to speak of the mind of the Middle East, as one may speak of the mind of New England or of the Old Dominion, where in spite of pronounced variations of individual temperament a common culture had set its mark on the literature. There were few common ties and few intellectual sympathies to bind together the men of letters of New York or Philadelphia. Certainly Irving and Paulding and Cooper and Melville and Whitman reveal none of that strong community of taste and purpose that marks the Concord group, or the Boston-Cambridge group, or even the Charleston group. They expressed no common culture, they had been disciplined in no common faith, and they were held together by no common economic or political or intellectual interests; as a result their writing is a frank expression of individual temperament and taste, unfettered by schools, drawing its nourishment from no common soil. They stand on their own feet, and to understand them requires no critical examination of a complex cultural background. And yet this very diversity may prove to be symptomatic of the hurrying changes that the rise of the middle class was bringing to America—to the city perhaps even more dramatically than to the country. The confusions and diversity of thought that mark the literature of Philadelphia and New York may, perhaps, most adequately suggest the mercurial temper of the revolutionary transition from the eighteenth century to the nineteenth, of which the romantic spirit was the natural expression.

CHAPTER I

The Old Capital

I

In the year 1800 one might well have expected Philadelphia to retain indefinitely its proud ascendency as the cultural capital of America. For decades no other colonial city had come near to rivaling it as a pleasant center of wealth and refinement. Its society was accounted the politest and most agreeable in America, and during the Revolutionary War young British officers had found its hospitable drawing-rooms an agreeable substitute for London clubs. It had long prided itself on its culture and it was on chatty terms with the fine arts, with books and music and painting, with actors and plays and playhouses. It was the recognized center of the publishing business, and its busy presses turned out books and magazines and newspapers for remote colonial readers. Ambitious young men were drawn to it as by a magnet, and Matthew Carey from Ireland and William Cobbett from England were outstanding figures amongst the many who found Philadelphia as attractive as Franklin had earlier found it. Certainly it was the least provincial spot in America in 1800, managing to keep abreast of the latest English fashions in letters as well as smallclothes; and when the supercilious Tom Moore favored the city with his presence in the summer of 1804, he found there the companionship which in some measure compensated for the meanness of the rest of America, where he professed to see:

> One dull chaos, one unfertile strife,
> Betwixt half-polish'd and half-barbarous life,
> Where every ill the ancient world can brew
> Is mixed with every grossness of the new.[1]

[1] Quoted in Oberholtzer, *Literary History of Philadelphia*, p. 178.

The pronounced intellectual stir expressed itself not only in *belles lettres,* and in the scientific experiments of Franklin and Rittenhouse, but more adequately still in politics. Political disputation would seem, indeed, to have been the common Philadelphia passion. Party forces were more equally divided than in Boston. From the beginnings of the Revolutionary disputes Philadelphia had produced notable disputants on both sides—pamphleteers like Joseph Galloway and John Dickinson, and satirists like Joseph Stansbury and Francis Hopkinson. In the succeeding decades partisan pens had augmented rather than abated their vigor. During Washington's administration the French Revolution shook Philadelphia as it shook no other American city, and the fierce battle between Federalist and Jacobin was waged with amazing fury and limitless invective. The deadly journalistic duel between Freneau and Fenno in their two *Gazettes* was reflected in the equally bitter duel of couplets between Matthew Carey and William Cobbett. If Philadelphia was not more catholic than Boston, it was at least better informed on party questions, for clever writers were daily flinging their arguments at its head. So long as the political capital of the nation remained in Philadelphia the city was clearly the place for the young American to sharpen his wits, inform his mind, and quicken his literary enthusiasm.

Economically the future of the city seemed equally bright. A younger generation of speculative merchants had taken the place of the older conservatives, and great fortunes were being made with a rapidity before unknown. When title to the western lands passed from the crown to the new republic, Philadelphia merchants took the lead in land speculation, and Robert Morris entered upon a spectacular career that profoundly impressed his generation. The city became the chief center of land speculation to which western and southern investors looked. Economic opportunities increased with the setting up of the new government, and the stir of national politics increased the general activity. With the establishment of the Bank, Philadelphia became the financial capital of the country, receiving and disbursing the monies of the government and attracting outside funds for investment. The decade of the nineties was its golden age. Then came the removal of the seat of the Federal government to Washington, and the gay little city underwent a swift eclipse. It was an unwilling victim to the topography of the North American continent. Between it and the Inland Empire, on which rested its future economic expansion, lay the Appalachian mountain range. To be sure, the opening of the Pittsburgh turnpike seemed to promise that Philadelphia should become the shipping port for the Ohio valley; but the law of gravity sent the produce of the back-country downstream to New Orleans, rather than upstream to the East. Mountains were a serious barrier then to cheap transportation, and in consequence the contributory hinterland to Philadelphia was narrowly restricted, and with the rise of the more fortunately situated New York her economic ascendency was lost past recovery.

A like unforeseen fate overtook the cultural aspirations of the ambitious little city. In the year 1799 Timothy Pickering, Secretary of State in Adams's cabinet, invited to Philadelphia as his secretary Joseph Dennie, a young Boston lawyer who had achieved a wide reputation as a writer of Addisonian essays; and with his coming the literary vigor of Philadelphia flared up in a last brilliant blaze. He established *The Port Folio,* gathered a club of congenial spirits, and gained an extraordinary reputation throughout the country at large. Dennie was a fierce Federalist who hated French Jacobinism with more than the ardor of his party, and he was encouraged by Tom Moore, who wrote,

> Long may you hate the Gallic dross that runs
> O'er your fair country and corrupts its sons.

But with the swift decay of Federalism Dennie's own fortunes fell into a like decay, and with the suspension of *The Port Folio* in 1809 the golden age of Philadelphia came to a definite end. Though it long retained its primacy as a publishing center, and though later *Godey's Lady's Book* became almost a national institution, its intellectual vigor lessened, and its literary leadership passed to other cities. It succumbed to the tastes of Victorianism and became the acknowledged home of "female genius" that for years fed the American reading public on cambric tea. It enjoyed no such renaissance as came to Boston and Charleston, and ambitious young writers abandoned it for more promising fields. While other cities were caught up in the swirl of romantic expansion that followed the War of 1812, Philadelphia remained content with the ways of the eighteenth century, immersed in an old-fashioned culture. With its geographical position disqualifying it to reap the harvest

of the westward movement, and with no Merrimac falls
to invite industrial development on a great scale, its fate
was sealed. It had been a delightful capital for an older
America, but it was too narrowly environed, too straitened
in potential resources for exploitation, to become the capital
of a more expansive and ambitious generation.

II

Yet it enjoyed a brief moment of literary creativeness before the hand of fate finally settled upon it. In the twilight
of the eighteenth century the new liberalisms that were
turmoiling Europe found their way to Philadelphia, and for
the moment it seemed as if the city were to lead the
thought of America in its venture into new fields. It was
a convenient port for the unloading of foreign romanticisms, and under the stimulus of national politics the demand for such commodities was greatly increased. Certainly
in no other American city did the French upheaval quicken
so sympathetic a ferment, and with this ferment came a
more romantic spirit in letters. The English pre-romantics
found there responsive readers. In the verse of young
Philadelphians began to appear a note of the vague, the
mysterious, the melancholy, echoes of Gray and Cowper
and Ossian, as a pleasant relief from vigorous satire as
practiced by the Hartford Wits. But it was in the field
of fiction that the new spirit most adequately revealed
itself, and particularly in the work of a young Philadelphian
who had broken wholly with the Federalism that immured
the sympathies of young poets like William Cliffton, and
welcomed the romantic philosophies then being formulated
by radical thinkers in France and England.

Brockden Brown was fortunately spared the fate that
might well have been his if circumstances had not determined otherwise. As a boy he had meditated epics on
romantic historical figures, inspired perhaps by Dwight
and Barlow; but from so profitless a career he was saved
by an early introduction to overseas fashions. By William
Godwin and Mary Wollstonecraft he was influenced as
profoundly as was young William Ellery Channing a few
years afterward, and with like results. Later generations
have too carelessly forgotten how persuasive to young
intellectuals, a century or more ago, was the philosophy
of Godwin. To generous minds there was something vastly
attractive in his confident appeal to reason and justice; and
to a new world and a new venture in government it came

with double appeal. How could the republican experiment better justify itself than by establishing justice in the new social order—justice for men and justice for women who had too long suffered under narrow handicaps? It was certainly an ideal worth serious consideration—particularly since the French school had suggested that the germinal source of social injustice must be sought in institutions rather than in the nature of man. It was natural enough for gentlemen who profited by social wrong to charge that injustice was inherent in human nature—that man's innate selfishness was to blame for the ills of society. But the new thinkers were of an inquiring turn of mind, and under their critical scrutiny the old conception was seen to rest on a perversion of fact. Gentlemen had got the cart before the horse. The crying evils of civilization, when analyzed, were traceable to vicious environment, to social and political maladjustments; not to human nature. The mind of the infant is plastic. Very well. If it is molded by social environment, why is it so often misshapen and perverted to base purposes, if institutions are not at fault? why may it not be molded to nobler ends under more beneficent institutions? Reason is a common possession; the ideal of justice is a common ideal. The evil genius that has hitherto thwarted their benevolent work is the overgrown political state, debased to selfish ends. Once let the beneficent sway of social instincts supersede the exploiting machinery of the political state, and reason must conduct to justice. The heart of man is sound. Let it be free to follow its natural promptings and war must give way to peace, the selfish struggle of classes disappear in a common brotherhood.

To an ardent young American like Brockden Brown, with the Hamiltonian struggle for power before his eyes, such a philosophy must have come with immense appeal. America confronted a future unmortgaged to the past; why should it repeat the old follies and mistakes that had reduced Europe to its present level? Here the pressure of vicious institutions was light as yet. Here the appeal to reason and justice was less hampered by selfish preëmptions. Let social commendation be bestowed on the uncorrupted heart, on generous impulses, on native integrity of character. Let education be a natural unfolding of humane instincts, not a sharpening of wits to overreach one's fellows. Let rewards go to frank, outspoken truth, rather than to chicanery and deceit. Inspired by such sentiments, Brockden Brown proposed to make fiction serve

social ends. He would spread the gospel of Mary Wollstonecraft and Godwin by means of popular tales. The views
of the former he elaborated in *Alcuin; A Dialogue*, which
in the year 1798 presented for the consideration of the
American people the Wollstonecraft feminism in such passages as this:

> Marriage is an union founded on free and mutual consent.
> It cannot exist without friendship. It cannot exist without personal
> fidelity. As soon as the union ceases to be spontaneous, it ceases
> to be just. This is the sum. If I were to talk for months I could
> add nothing to the completeness of the definition.

But it is in *Arthur Mervyn* that he gives his fullest pronouncement of what he conceives must be done in America.
He takes his hero fresh from the plowtail, one of nature's
noblemen, and traces his triumphant course through the
thick of sordid intrigue to a happy end. Generous in instincts, impulsive in sociability, responsive to suffering,
hating injustice, loving the pure and disinterested, Arthur
Mervyn is a Godwinian figure drawn to captivate the
imagination with the social ideal. It is not so much the
plot of the story that reveals the enormous influence of
Godwin—patent as the likeness is to *Caleb Williams,* but
rather the expansive nature of the title hero, whose instincts
bid him espouse justice, and whose life is an implied
criticism of all that is sordid and mean.

With the political romanticism of his work was joined a
literary romanticism that likewise came from England,
where it was muddying the stream of English fiction and
turning it aside from the vigorous realism of the middle
eighteenth century. The movement that Paulding dubbed
the "blood-pudding school" was one of the by-products
of the romantic development that ran a far more disastrous
course in America than in England, distorting the growth
of native fiction for half a century. It was perhaps unfortunate for the American novel that *Wieland* should have
been Brockden Brown's most finished work, for it contributed in consequence more powerfully to the spread
of the melodramatic. Lacking his strain of rationalism, other
writers reveled increasingly in the luridly picaresque, till
the popular taste was so debauched that Gilmore Simms
found it well-nigh impossible to struggle against it. For
this of course Brown was not to blame; yet his gross
romanticisms of manner persisted long after his Godwinian
romanticisms had faded out of the popular mind, if indeed
they ever found lodgment there.

Brockden Brown's career was in a sense symbolic of the fate of his native city—a few brilliant years and then a swift decline. Death cut him down before he fulfilled his promise. Something of a like fate befell his most brilliant successor, Robert Montgomery Bird, probably the ablest man of letters that Philadelphia produced. Caught up by the romantic movement at the beginning of his precocious career, he plunged into dramatic writing and from 1830 to 1834, between the ages of twenty-four and twenty-eight, he wrote four plays for Edwin Forrest, one of which, *The Gladiator*, met with extraordinary success, both in this country and in England; and another, *The Broker of Bogota*, kept the stage for years. At the age of thirty he gave over the writing of plays and turned to other fields. The explanation of so unusual a course, according to a recent historian, is not far to seek. He had been overreached by Forrest, and after parting with his manuscripts to the actor, the playwright found himself in the condition of the farmer who after shipping his potatoes to market discovers himself to be in debt to the commission merchant.[2] That he determined to try a different crop was natural enough, but unfortunate for the American drama.

Of his subsequent ventures into the field of romantic fiction, one at least was an extraordinary success, rivaling if not surpassing *The Gladiator* in popular favor. *Nick of the Woods, or the Jibbenainosay* still remains one of the few outstanding tales of the Kentucky settlement. Published in Philadelphia in 1837, it has been reissued in successive editions, more than twenty in all down to the present. It was translated into German in 1838, into Dutch in 1877, and into Polish in 1905. There is abundant reason for its popularity. It is a story of calculating revenge, done with extraordinary vividness and set against a romantic background. A frontier Quaker, trusting in the spirit of good will, finds his non-resistance futile; he is set upon by Indians, his family murdered before his eyes, and himself scalped and left for dead beside his burnt cabin. Recovering, he sets forth on a fierce career. Under the mask of a non-resistant, so effectively worn as to awaken the contempt of the frontier Indian-haters, he became a hunter of men, and his secret passages through the wilderness leave no other trail than the marked bodies of slaughtered warriors.

[2] See A. H. Quinn, *A History of the American Drama, etc.*, pp. 244–248.

The Jibbenainosay is an uncanny figure who strikes with appalling suddenness, a Nemesis that fills the hearts of border Indians with terror and turns their dreams to nightmares—one of the most striking and fearful figures in our early fiction. The Indians whom he pursues so remorselessly are depicted as thorough savages. In describing them Bird has put all his romanticisms aside. There is no sentimentalizing of the noble red man in the brisk pages of *Nick of the Woods;* the warriors are dirty drunken louts, filled with an unquenchable blood-lust, whom the frontiersman kills with as little compunction as he would kill a rattlesnake. The ugly feud that so long soiled the Border is depicted with almost startling frankness, and through its worst phases moves the figure of Bloody Nathan, professing to be a man of peace whilst cutting an appalling lot of notches in his gun, an epileptic who perhaps deceives even himself.

If one likes stirring action that is certain to end in blood-letting, there is good foraging in *Nick of the Woods,* despite its excesses of conventional romance. And there is much else as well. Bird had evidently studied his western materials with some care, and he did his part to popularize certain conceptions that literature had come to associate with the Ohio valley. The character of Ralph Stackpole is clearly suggestive of the wild antics supposed to be common to the river boatmen. "The history of this wild scape-gallows," says Bird, "his prowess in the pin-fold and the battle-field, his adventure on the beech-tree, and his escape from the meshes of the law, with other characteristic events not included in our relation, are recollections still cherished in some parts of Kentucky, and made the theme of many a gleesome story." But what seems more suggestive today is Bird's conscious attempt to reproduce the new type of western humor that found its expression in the Davy Crockett myth. Perhaps the wild extravagance of Ralph Stackpole's vocabulary goes back to Mike Fink, perhaps it derives from Davy himself; at any rate the mode had spread so widely by 1837 that this Philadelphia man of letters had come to believe that such was the indigenous form of humor in the new West of the Ohio valley, and he took particular pains to draw the irrepressible Ralph with vigorous touches. A pronounced romantic, Bird unconsciously contributed his mite to the myth of western humor.

CHAPTER II

The New Capital

I

Very different from the gay and cultivated Quaker City was the commercial port of Manhattan, with its Yankee energy ingrafted on the stolid Dutch stock, which fate seized upon and transformed into the greatest of our new cities, the favorite home of the genius of American enterprise. Never a cultural capital as Philadelphia had been, and as Charleston was becoming—a fact which Fenimore Cooper untactfully announced to the world—it was ambitious to acquire commercial and financial ascendency; and this ascendency of the economic over the cultural, this frank evaluation of progress in terms of exploitation, marks the definite transition from the eighteenth century to the nineteenth, the triumph of an aggressive middle class over the leisurely ways of an older landed aristocracy. The romance of expansion was creating there a new psychology, and this new psychology was preparing the city for leadership in the new age that was rising. Its strategic position brought to it the produce of the new settlements that were pushing west to the great lakes and beyond; its aggressive traders were reaching out for a share in the markets of the world; the plodding methods of money-getting that had satisfied an earlier generation no longer satisfied men who had discovered the richer possibilities of capitalistic manipulation. The potentialities that lay in the capitalistic system were shrewdly explored, and the necessary machinery of the new finance was devised. The acquisitive spirit of the city found itself in a position to profit from the rage of speculation that was running through the country, and it quickly outdistanced its rivals in the race for financial supremacy.

The changes that came to New York in the last years of the old century were enough to muddle a head stronger than Rip Van Winkle's. The quiet ways of colonial times were gone, and in their stead was a restless activity that had no leisure for its pipe and mug in the sleepy tavern. Business and politics could not wait on men who like Wouter Van Twiller pickled their dreams in tobacco smoke. The bewilderment of old Rip on his return from the hills was the bewilderment of the colonial mind in the presence of a new order. When Washington came to New York to assume the presidency, the town contained approximately 29,000 inhabitants, some two thousand of whom were slaves. Fifty years later the census of 1840 set down its population as 312,710. In 1789 Albany was a Dutch village of four or five thousand, and a few miles to the West lay an unbroken wilderness. Within the narrow zone of the quiet settlements old and new dwelt in close proximity. The most feudal of American aristocracies fringed the banks of the Hudson from Albany to Manhattan; and reaching out through the Mohawk valley that aristocracy was laying a network of speculative land-holdings through which a flood of Yankee pioneers was making its way from the long-settled lands of Connecticut and Massachusetts. The frontier was close at hand; the leveling spirit was near neighbor to the feudal; potential economic rivalries were becoming actual, and the days of a static, power-proud Dutch aristocracy were numbered. The spirit that had dominated the commonwealth from its founding was tenacious of life, but on January 26, 1839, died Stephen Van Rensselaer, last of the Patroons, courteous, dignified, a worthy embodiment of the old patriarchal virtues, who had outlived his age; and hard upon his death came the final break-up of the traditional order. The small men got the land they had long tilled and the influence of the Dutch gentry slowly disintegrated. A new order was rising that had discovered shorter roads to wealth than feudal rents. While the more energetic of the old order, men like Gouverneur Morris and Judge William Cooper, were deep in land speculation, in Manhattan a new aristocracy of capitalism was rising. Wall Street was losing the distinction of housing the most exclusive of the landed gentry, to gain a greater distinction as the home of the new aristocracy of credit. By 1825 the rise of industrialism, the development of banking, the completion of the Erie Canal, the influx of proletarian immigrants, and the drift of population to the towns had fixed the destiny of the city. In becoming the chief repository of the new capitalism New York had become the first and greatest of our middle-class capitals.

Of this new Manhattan the representative citizen was a man whose aggressive ambitions differentiated him sharply from Stephen Van Rensselaer, and whose dramatic career of exploitation seemed to Washington Irving to embody the romantic potentialities of America. John Jacob Astor was to the New York of 1825 what Robert Morris had been to Philadelphia a generation before—an evidence of the wealth that was to be got by those who would boldly exploit the vast resources of America. A German immigrant who landed in America with small funds, immediately following the Peace of Paris, Astor embarked in the fur trade, acquired a fortune which he invested in Manhattan land, and then laid his plans to engage in a great venture in imperialism. Stirred by the Lewis and Clarke expedition, he proposed to explore the virgin resources of the far Pacific Northwest. With the tacit approval of the government he undertook the hazardous project of the Astoria settlement, sent his agent to the Russian posts of Alaska, and by subsidizing an army of trappers proposed to gather the peltries of the entire Northwest for the rich Canton market. It was a grandiose conception worthy of a feudal baron of commerce. It was knit up with dreams of conquest; it necessarily entailed open warfare with the English companies whose ambitions were equally grandiose; it was certain to be attended by bitter hardships on the part of the venturesome agents to whom it was intrusted; and the outcome was uncertain as a gambler's chance. Irving has thrown over his narrative of the great venture a glamour of patriotism; to him it appeared as a plan of empire building; but whether patriotism or profit was the determining impulse in the mind of John Jacob Astor, the settlement of Astoria suggests the romantic aspirations that were making over the lethargic world of Dutch Manhattan, in the venturesome days of the new capitalism. Stephen Van Rensselaer and John Jacob Astor would have had difficulty in understanding each other.

II

In sharp contrast with Boston, New York was wanting in intellectual background and intellectual stimulus. It had never gone to school to dogmatic theology and neither clergy nor laity had been disciplined by a severe Puritan regimen. Gentlemen were little given to metaphysical speculation and the subtleties of creed never provided the staple of talk in the farmer's kitchen. The terrors of hell rarely troubled the sluggish imagination of the Dutch, and the extraordinary stimulus that came to the serious-minded New Englander from long contemplation of the ways of God, was lacking amongst a more prosaic people. No other stimulus supplied the want and in consequence ideas and books were held in low esteem and the things of the mind suffered. The English gentry commonly sent their sons to the English universities, but the Dutch by common report seem to have been indifferent to schooling and opportunities for education were sadly inadequate. The result was a low plane of intellectual life, which even in Cooper's time was remarked by him. There were brilliant and cultivated intellects, wits like Gouverneur Morris and statesmen like John Jay; yet even under the stimulus of Revolutionary and Constitutional controversy the contribution of New York to political theory was far slighter than that of New England or Virginia. *The Federalist* was its single notable production, and even in that the papers of Madison were no inconsiderable part. As a commercial port it attracted young men ambitious to rise in the world of affairs rather than in the world of letters. Unlike Philadelphia it had never been a cosmopolitan meeting ground for aspiring young intellectuals and purveyors of polite culture, nor an important center of printers, publishers and book dealers. Aside from Philip Freneau, who had long since established himself in New Jersey when he was not at sea, it had contributed little to pure literature, or even to the political satire that deluged Philadelphia. As a creative center it ranked far below Hartford, Connecticut, where in the seventeen-eighties and nineties wit had become a staple commodity for export. And yet despite its intellectual lethargy it was a pleasant little town, with a note of cosmopolitanism that rendered life amongst the upper classes genial and urbane. The spirit of aristocracy was as yet little weakened by alien newcomers from the more republican New England, and city and commonwealth were ruled by a little group of old-fashioned gentlemen who upheld the rigid Federalism of the tie-wig school.

In the year 1800 the political leaders of the state were men of long established reputations, Hamilton, Jay, Gouverneur Morris, Rufus King, with whom was closely associated the brilliant lawyer James Kent, afterward Chancellor. Only two of the five were of the older New York stock: Rufus King was from Maine, Hamilton from the West Indies, and Kent was of Yankee Presbyterian ancestry. Politics were already becoming turmoiled by faction, with bitter cleavages and vindictive struggles for the spoils of office that sadly confused the logic of the earlier alignment. The old Federalist party was led by the distinguished gentlemen named above; the Democratic party was led by the Livingstons and Clintons; and outside both was the ambitious Aaron Burr who played a lone hand against the field. After the death of Hamilton the disintegration of the old parties went forward rapidly. The Livingstons and Clintons broke, and a fierce political feud arose between them. The former were accounted the true Jeffersonians, but under the name of Lewisites they drifted towards the Federalist remnant; the Burrites went to pieces after the disgrace of their leader; and the Clintonians remained masters of the field, with a motley support drawn from Tammany Hall Irish, Wall Street bankers, and odds and ends of all factions. From this sordid situation, rendered conspicuous by the extension of suffrage under the new constitution, emerged two master politicians, adepts in all the arts of party manipulation, who exploited the prejudices of the voting masses in a way to justify the gloomy fear of demagoguery that haunted the minds of the old Federalists. Martin Van Buren and Thurlow Weed, Democrat and Whig, were finished products of the new school of practical politicians who held that office-holding was the great end of partisan struggle, and that principles must not stand in the way of success.

III

Through this fierce scramble of rival politicians moved a scholarly figure who preserved to the last the dignity and distinction of an earlier age. James Kent, whose long life and ripe legal learning were devoted to upholding what he conceived to be the ultimate principles of law and politics, was the chief political thinker of the transition days of New York. A disciple of Locke and Blackstone, remodeling seventeenth-century liberalism into eighteenth-century conservatism, he was concerned to erect the barriers of the Common Law about the unsurveyed frontiers of the American experiment, assigning exact metes and bounds beyond which it should not go. Like John Marshall

189

and Joseph Story he was expert in devising legal springes to catch unwary democrats, and while the Jeffersonians were shouting over their victories at the polls, he was engaged in the strategic work of placing the Constitution under the narrow custodianship of the English law. An ardent Federalist and later an equally ardent Whig, he reveals in his precise thinking the intimate relations that everywhere exist between economics, politics, and legal principles. With John Adams he accepted the dictum of Locke that "the great and chief end . . . of men's uniting into commonwealths, and putting themselves under government, is the preservation of their property"; and believing that the English Common Law was the securest of all agencies devised to safeguard the subject in the enjoyment of his property rights, he made no difficulty in imposing that law upon the Constitution, circumscribing the written document by Common Law fences. Government he conceived to be a patriarchal institution erected for the single purpose of coercing the vicious, and as such it must remain in the hands of the good, the wise and the wealthy. It did not need the authoritative pronouncement of his great master to convince him that the wealthy included the good and wise. Observation of the "barbarian Jackson" and his rude followers was enough to convince him of the truth of the fact. "All theories of government that suppose the mass of the people virtuous," he wrote to Webster, "and able and willing to act virtuously, are plainly utopian, and will remain so until the Saturnian age" (William Kent, *Memoirs and Letters of James Kent*, p. 207). Profoundly distrustful of democracy, he brought all his wide reading in the history of ancient and medieval republics to demonstrate the favorite Federalist conviction—a conviction that Paulding in his *Letters from the South* paid his respects to[1]—that democracy is only a euphemism for mob-rule and that it must speedily conduct to anarchy and despotism. All leveling principles he repudiated without waiting to hear cause. Until necessity counseled otherwise he looked with suspicion on the holders of liquid wealth, as likely to prove wanting in the wisdom and goodness that came naturally to the landed proprietor. He would have the many ruled by the few, but those few he would have owners of great estates.

After all, the learned Chancellor was only a transplanted Yankee of the Fisher Ames school, with something of the

[1] See *Letters*, etc., Vol. I, p. 207.

austerity and intellectual vigor of his two Puritan grand-fathers. An ardent admirer of Hamilton, he early broke with the more liberal faith of his family and joined himself to the extreme Federalists. He was advanced rapidly by Governor Jay, enjoyed for years both office and distinction, and ably defended the party of his choice. Fearful of agrarian laws and the sequestration of property by the enfranchised poor, he fought stubbornly every proposal for an extension of suffrage or a larger measure of self-government for the cities. Defeated in the great constitutional convention of 1821 he soon after lost his office and retired to write his *Commentaries on American Law,* a work that was to exercise a creative influence on the later development of our jurisprudence. That American law came to be deeply colored by Federalist political theory, that it upheld from the bench principles that had been repudiated at the polls, was due in no little measure to the legal scholarship of this last of the New York Federalists. What a recent historian has borrowed to describe another applies with equal felicity to Chancellor Kent—"his pigmy hope that life would some day become somewhat better, punily shivered by the side of his gigantic conviction that it might be infinitely worse" (Fox, *Decline of Aristocracy in New York Politics,* p. 243). As he contemplated the ways of the triumphant Jacksonians, he found such consolation as he could in turning back to an older century with its narrow outlook and sober culture. Writing to his brother in 1835, he said:

There never was such misrule. Our Tory rich men are becoming startled and alarmed at our downhill course. My opinion is that the admission of universal suffrage and a licentious press are incompatible with government and security to property, and that the government and character of this country are going to ruin. This suffrage is too great an excitement for any political machine. It racks it to pieces, and morals go with it. It is probable England is going the same way. We are becoming selfish, profligate, crazy. . . . Give me the writings of Addison and Locke, and the Presbyterianism of Dr. Ripley, Dr. Stiles, and old Dr. Rogers. (Kent, *Memoirs and Letters of James Kent,* pp. 218–219.)

IV

With the extraordinary upheaval in economics and politics New York unfortunately underwent no corresponding intellectual revolution. The renaissance that a generation earlier had created a new Virginia, and that was awakening in Massachusetts a many-sided intellectual activity, touched the mind of New York only lightly. The ground was unprepared for the new philosophies. To Virginia, French romantic theory had come with the appeal of a new gospel for the reason that plantation economics fell in with the major premises of Physiocratic liberalism, and the old-world dogmas seemed to find new-world justification. To New England, German idealism had come likewise with the appeal of a new gospel, after Unitarianism had broken the fetters of Calvinism and set free its traditional idealism. But among the young men of New York in 1825 neither France nor Germany was a determining influence. With an inadequate cultural background and no responsive economics, they were attracted only casually to the current European liberalisms. They were wanting in idealism and in consequence the major intellectual and social movements of the times influenced the form and content of the new Knickerbocker literature far less profoundly than was the case in New England. New York was as insular as Charleston. That the growing economic unrest would ultimately find expression in a controversial or Utopian literature, was a matter of course; and that the cosmopolitanism of the city should make for vigorous discussion, was equally a matter of course. Nevertheless Albert Brisbane, William Leggett, Parke Godwin and Horace Greeley were far less representative of the dominant literary spirit than Irving and Halleck and Willis of the earlier group, or Stedman and Stoddard later.

The Knickerbocker movement was inaugurated by four young men whose clever sketches caught the provincial ear of polite society and set the new fashion in prose and verse. Irving and Paulding in *Salmagundi,* and Halleck and Drake in the *Croaker Papers,* were lucky adventurers whose slight crafts made the most prosperous of voyages. Bright young fellows with a charming literary swagger, they aspired to be wits and exploit the amusing foibles of Broadway. Twelve years separated the two ventures, and in the interval Byron and Scott had been supplanting Moore and Campbell in the esteem of the Town, and the literary mode of New York was changing. From their gay provincialism, happily Irving and Paulding later freed themselves; Drake died at the age of twenty-five; but Halleck retained to the end of a leisurely life the mannerisms of the Croaker period—a crochety wit who affected persiflage, a brisk young buck who gently slid into a *blasé* old buck, a free lance in verse who lived in state on the income of a small literary investment made in his twenties.

The very considerable reputation of Fitz-Greene Halleck resulted in part from the literary sterility of New York in his early days, and in part from the personal popularity of the man. A Connecticut Yankee, descended on his mother's side from old John Eliot, he was drawn to the city as a promising field for an accountant, and eventually found his way into the office of John Jacob Astor by whom he was later pensioned. He accepted the views and shared the antipathies of his Wall Street associates, but with a certain affectation of individuality that took delight in shocking them by whimsical pronouncements in favor of the Catholic church and the monarchial system. There is perhaps a suggestion of seriousness in the remark that Bryant has preserved: "The ship of state," so he reports Halleck as saying, "must be governed and navigated like any other ship, without consulting the crew. What would become of the stanchest bark in a gale, if the captain were obliged to call all hands together and say: 'All you who are in favor of taking in sail, will please to say ay'" (*Orations and Addresses*, p. 186). His political affiliations were Federalist-Whig, and his satire exudes much of the old prejudice against the democratic mass. The pompous long-winded DeWitt Clinton was a fair mark for his shafts;[2] the demagoguery of office-seeking politicians was a fruitful theme for his wit;[3] and Halleck's satire plays upon them with good-natured raillery. But his gayety cannot hide a certain animus in dealing with the tousled-headed democracy. When the labor movement was painfully getting under way in New York Halleck contemplated the curious phenomenon with a tolerant contempt—in something of the spirit of a wit of pre-Revolutionary times who amused the Town with his couplet:

> Down at night a bricklayer or carpenter lies,
> Next sun a Lycurgus or Solon doth rise.

As an illustration of the attitude of polite society in New York a hundred years ago towards the aspirations of the proletariat, Halleck's forgotten *Epistle to Robert Hogbin, Esq., Chairman of the Committee of Working-Men, etc.*, deserves quotation:

[2] See *Governor Clinton's Speech.*
[3] See *The Recorder.*

Mr. Hogbin,—I work as a weaver—of rhyme—
  And therefore presume with a working-man's grace,
To address you as one I have liked for some time,
  Though I know not (no doubt it's a fine one) your face.

There is much in a name, and I'll lay you a wager
  (Two ale-jugs from Reynolds), that Nature designed,
When she formed you, that you should become the drum-major
  In that choice piece of music, the Grand March of Mind.

A Hogbin! a Hogbin! how cheering the shout
  Of all that keep step to that beautiful air,
Which leads, like the treadmill, about and about,
  And leaves us exactly, at last, where we were!

Yes, there's much in a name, and a Hogbin's so fit is
  For that great moral purpose whose impulse divine
Bids men leave their own workshops to work in committees,
  And their own wedded wives to protect yours and mine! . . .

When the moment arrives that we've won the good fight,
  And broken the chains of laws, churches, and marriages,
When no infants are born under six feet in height,
  And our chimney-sweeps mount up a flue in their carriages—

That glorious time when our daughters and sons
  Enjoy a *blue Monday* each day of the week,
And a clean shirt is classed with the mastodon's bones,
  Of a mummy from Thebes, an undoubted antique—·

Then, then, my dear Hogbin, your statue in straw,
  By some modern *Pig*malion delightfully wrought,
Shall embellish the Park, and our youths' only law
  Shall be to be Hogbins in feeling and thought.

In Halleck's better work there is sometimes evident a
certain critical detachment that permitted him to see both
sides of his theme. In the lines to his native Connecticut
he has taken pretty accurately the measure of the Puritan
and the Yankee. He rests under no awe in presence of the
old worthies, and he throws overboard the pious fairy-tales
of Cotton Mather—"that slanderer of the memory of our
fathers"—only to forgive the preacher who scolded his
friends "up from earth to heaven" because of the "sour
grapejuice in his disposition." Unfortunately little of his
work possesses the virility of *Connecticut*. His most ambitious poem, *Fanny*, is a feeble and discursive satire on the
social climber. It was a great favorite at the time and
passed through several editions, but the sparkle is gone
out of its affected jauntiness and little has been lost in its

being forgotten. Halleck's casual literary activity continued only for the brief period between the years 1819 and 1828; thereafter for close on forty years he was content to turn out an occasional *jeu d'esprit*, enjoy the deepening twilight of his reputation, and watch his fellow Yankee, Willis, invest his talents in the ephemeral. The day of the wit was past in New York.

CHAPTER III

Two Knickerbocker Romantics

I
WASHINGTON IRVING

Fortunately the stolid New York of earlier days was not to pass away without bequeathing to posterity some fragments of its chronicles. In the midst of a pleasant society of smallclothes and tie-wigs, of feudalism and Federalism, appeared young Washington Irving at the precise moment when Sansculottism was beginning to make a stir in the land, and gentlemen were putting away their knee-breeches to don a republican dress—a decline in taste to which he would not easily reconcile himself. A boyish wit from the eighteenth century, a genial loiterer in the twilight of the old, he found himself out of humor with the ambitions that were making over the little city he loved. The present seemed to him not so amusing as the past, nor so picturesque. That he had any business with the world of trade and speculation he could not believe. Its concerns were not his. Its new Wall Street counted for less in his eyes than the pipe of old Diedrich Knickerbocker. Its decadent Federalism that was clinging to the wreck of its hopes, and its roistering Democracy that wore greasy clothes, spoke with an Irish accent, and was marshaled to the polls by Tammany Hall, were of less consequence to him than the black bottle that brought such curious adventures to Rip Van Winkle. The wit and romance he took pleasure in were of another sort than the kind his generation was getting drunk on—more insubstantial, less heady, picturesque rather than profitable. So Irving gently detached himself from contemporary America, and detached he remained to the end of a loitering life, untroubled by material ambitions, enjoying the abundance of good things that fell in his way, mingling with prosperous folk and liking everybody—men as diverse as John Jacob Astor and Martin Van Buren and John P. Kennedy—and unconsciously taking the color of his environment, careful to turn into limpid prose such romantic tales as he came upon and achieving thereby both reputation and profit— a pleasant blameless way of living, certainly, yet curiously unrepresentative of the America in which chance had set him and which was to claim him as its first man of letters.

An incorrigible *flâneur,* Irving's business in life was to loaf and invite the picturesque. A confirmed rambler in pleasant places, in the many lands he visited he was a lover of the past rather than the present, seeking to re-create the golden days of the Alhambra or live over the adventurous mood of the fur trader. The immediate and the actual was an unsatisfying diet for his dreams. There was in him nothing of the calm aloofness of the intellectual that stands apart to clarify its critical estimate, and none of the reforming zeal of the Puritan that is at peace only in the thick of a moral crusade. The duty of saving the world was not laid on his untroubled soul. No man of his generation was less of a rebel than Irving, and he went his way unconcerned at things that quite upset Fenimore Cooper's peace of mind. In his early days, to be sure, he broke with the ambitious middle class—if gently drawing away can be called breaking—because he could not bring himself to like its ways and the devastation those ways were entailing on the leisurely world he loved. Revolutions seemed to him somewhat vulgar affairs. The French Revolution had brought destruction on too many lovely things, and the industrial revolution was taking too heavy a toll of the picturesque, to please him. He thought it a pity that steam should drive the clipper ship from the seas and put an end to snug posting in the tally-ho. Progress might be bought at too dear a price. The bluff squire with his hounds, the great hall with its ancient yuletide customs, the patriarchal relations between master and man, seemed to him more worth while than the things progress was substituting for them; so he turned away from the new and gently ingratiated himself into the past in order to gather up such fragments of the picturesque as progress had not yet destroyed.

But only for a time. His dislike of capitalism rested on no more substantial basis than its substitution of vulgar trousers for gentlemanly smallclothes. It was too new to have achieved dignity or the charm of assured position. When that time should come and masters of finance should stand before the world as generous dispensers of patronage, when the development of business should have produced its new barons, Irving's dislike would lessen and he would associate with the new capitalism on the same easy terms that he associated with the old feudalism. In the meantime he stood apart, unconcerned with praise or blame. The industrial revolution might work itself out as it would. The seventeen years he spent abroad on his great pilgrimage were black years for England. Wretchedness and poverty were all about him if he chose to see. The "condition of England" question was rising out of the factory smoke to challenge the conscience of England. But he did not choose to see and his conscience was untroubled. As he idled about the countryside or visited the hospitable manor houses, his eye was caught by the grace of medieval spires rising from parish churches rather than by the condition of the proletariat. He saw no children working in the coal-pits, for he did not choose to visit the collieries. He sympathized vaguely with the new social movements then getting under way, but it was not in his nature to be partisan to a cause. He may not have been a Tory but he had lived so long with Tories and enjoyed so frankly the charm of upper-class society, that his outlook was unconsciously determined by such intimate contacts. While Secretary to the Legation at London in the reform years from 1829 to 1831, he was aware of the tremendous stir all about him, but his infrequent references to the Reform Bill in his letters turned usually on its disastrous effects on the publishing business. Only once during his long residence abroad does he seem to have felt deeply the significance of the current revolutionary unrest, and the mood that swept him away from his habitual indifference bears the marks of a sudden awakening. Writing from London on March 1, 1831, he said:

We are in the beginning of an eventful week. . . . However, *the great cause of all the world* will go on. What a stirring moment it is to live in. I never took such intense interest in the newspapers. It seems to me as if life were breaking out anew with me, or that I were entering upon quite a new and almost unknown career of existence, and I rejoice to find my sensibilities, which were waning as to many objects of past interest, reviving with all their freshness and vivacity at the scenes and prospects opening around me. I trust, my dear Brevoort, we shall both be spared to see a great part of this grand though terrible drama that is about to be acted. There will doubtless be scenes of horror and suffering, but what splendid triumphs must take place over these vile systems of falsehood in every relation of human affairs, that have been woven over the human mind, and for so long a time have held it down in despicable thraldom. (Pierre M. Irving, *Life and Letters of Washington Irving*, Vol. II, p. 199.)

Irving lacked a month of being forty-nine when he wrote this confession of interest in matters political. It marks the first appearance of liberalism in his thinking, and the last —somewhat vague to be sure, unduly bottomed on romantic expectations, yet significant in so placid a life and explanatory of his course, when a year later he returned to America to knit up once more the raveled threads of his interests. It was as an incipient liberal that he came back to a land then in the first flush of the Jacksonian victory, eager to discover a romantic charm in the vast changes that had come during the seventeen years he had been abroad. He plunged into the business of re-discovery with enthusiasm. He was in want of new literary materials, and as he took his bearings, his creative interest was stirred to write on American themes. He went to Washington and for three months listened to the great debate on Nullification. He talked with business men and politicians, with those who were prosperous and prominent, and he drifted easily with the tide of liberalism. To be sure he could scarcely be called a Jacksonian. Parties and causes did not greatly interest him even then. An intelligent man, indeed, could hardly be less concerned about political principles. Thirty years before, as a clever young man about town, he had gone with the dominant Federalism of the times, and had amused himself with political ambitions. His brother Peter was editor of the Lewisite paper the *Chronicle*, but Josiah Ogden Hoffman, with whose firm Irving was connected during his desultory incursion into the law and to whose daughter Matilda he was be trothed, was an old Loyalist and ardent Hamiltonian. His wife, to whom Irving was warmly attached, was a daughter of John Fenno, Hamilton's editor. Under such tutelage it was natural for Irving to poke good-natured fun at President Jefferson's red velvet breeches in *Salmagundi;* but his venture into practical politics proving little to his taste, he quickly gave over such ambitions. In a letter to a clever young lady of Republican sympathies, he thus announced his abandonment of political hopes:

> I am as deep in mud and politics as ever a modern gentleman would wish to be; and I drank beer with the multitude; and I talked hand-bill fashion with the demagogues; and I shook hands with the mob, whom my heart abhorreth. . . . Truly this saving one's country is a nauseous piece of business, and if patriotism is such a dirty virtue,—prythee, no more of it. (*Life and Letters,* Vol. I, Chap. XI.)

Years now separated him from that youthful experience. His long absence from his native land had completely alienated him from the fierce partisanship of contemporary America and he could view matters political with calm detachment. Inclined to make the best of any government *de facto,* he found it easy on his return to accept Jacksonianism, and he soon discovered a genuine liking for Old Hickory. "The more I see of this old cock of the woods," he wrote from Washington, "the more I relish his game qualities" (*ibid.,* Vol. II, p. 255). No doubt his early friend Paulding had much to do with his ready acceptance of the new order, although he had come in close contact with Martin Van Buren at the London legation and was drawn to him. "He is one of the gentlest and most amiable men I have ever met with," he wrote to his brother, "with an affectionate disposition that attaches itself to those around him, and wins their kindness in return" (*ibid.,* Vol. II, p. 220). Although distrustful of some of the "elbow counsellors" of the Democracy he found little cause for criticism and soon came to be regarded as one with them. The Jacksonians were eager to make political capital out of his literary reputation, and he was urged by Tammany Hall to stand for Congress and later to accept a mayoralty candidacy. In 1837, probably through the intervention of Paulding, he was offered a post in Van Buren's cabinet. These partisan offers he had the good sense to decline, but when in 1842 he was tendered the post of Minister to Spain he gladly seized the opportunity to revisit a land he loved. His nephew is explicit in his statement that the offer came wholly unsolicited, but Fenimore Cooper was of another opinion.[1] Very likely Cooper was misinformed, but whatever the truth the appointment was a godsend to Irving. His affairs were in a bad way. The popularity of his writings was on the wane, the panic had caught him with much of his capital invested in unprofitable land speculations, and the "Roost" at Tarrytown was a heavy drain, although he wrote whimsically, "I beat all the gentlemen farmers in my neighborhood, for I can manage to raise my vegetables and fruits at very little more than twice the market price" (*Life and Letters*, Vol. II, p. 320). Only a severe nature like Cooper, sorely wounded by the angry reception of his own honest criticism, would cavil at an appointment so honorable to the government.

A friendly nature, Irving discovered friendliness wherever he went. His own generosity appealed to the generosity of others, and he found it easy in consequence to take a kindly view of men and parties. He was harassed by none of Cooper's quick suspicions and rigid principles, and it must be added he had none of Cooper's intuitive penetration into the secret springs of human action that made the latter so acute a critic of contemporary America. The sharp contrast in moods in which the two men returned to America from their travels, the one harshly critical of middle-class economics and frontier leveling, the other responding naïvely to the enthusiasm for speculative expansion and eager to exploit the romance of the westward movement, sufficiently reveals the difference between them. The one was a dogmatic Puritan with the dictatorial ways of the quarter-deck, the other was a play-boy of letters temperamentally incapable of critical analysis. There was not a grain of realism in Irving's nature. His cheerful optimism was little more than the optimism of the prosperous. Wholly ignorant of economics, he never comprehended the significance of the revolutions in process all about him, and this *naïveté* blinded him to the motive of John Jacob Astor in financing Astoria, as it blinded him to all the major forces of the times. He was easily brought to see the ro-

[1] Writing to his wife a month afterwards, Cooper said: "By the way, Mrs. Willing has let out the secret of Irving's appointment. He wrote to Webster to remember him *if any good thing offered*. So that instead of not asking for the office, he asked for anything that was good. There has been more humbug practised concerning this man than concerning any other now living" (Cooper, *Correspondence of James Fenimore-Cooper*, Vol. II, p. 469).

mance of the great struggle between rival companies for mastery of the fur trade, but he did not comprehend how the glamour he threw about the venture must inevitably strengthen his patron's investment in imperialism. Gullible as a child, he discovered nothing more significant in the great struggle between agrarianism and capitalism for control of government than the ungenerous suspicions and novel theories it bred. For the outstanding liberals of New York he had scant sympathy. William Leggett, Horace Greeley, Albert Brisbane, William Cullen Bryant, influenced his views far less than did the masters of Wall Street; and from the courageous movement of Locofocoism he drew back in distrust. The one letter in which he elaborated such political convictions as he had come to hold, is an interesting document that deserves quotation.

As far as I know my own mind, I am thoroughly a republican, and attached, from complete conviction, to the institutions of my country; but I am a republican without gall, and have no bitterness in my creed. I have no relish for puritans either in religion or politics, who are for pushing principles to an extreme, and for overturning everything that stands in the way of their own zealous career. I have, therefore, felt a strong distaste for some of those locofoco luminaries who of late have been urging strong and sweeping measures, subversive of the interests of great classes of the community. Their doctrines may be excellent in theory, but, if enforced in violent and uncompromising opposition to all our habitudes, may produce the most distressing effects. The best of remedies must be cautiously applied, and suited to the taste and constitution of the patient. . . . Ours is a government of compromise. We have several great and distinct interests bound up together, which, if not separately consulted and severally accommodated, may harass and impair each other. . . . I always distrust the soundness of political councils that are accompanied by acrimonious and disparaging attacks upon any great class of our fellow-citizens. Such are those urged to the disadvantage of the great trading and financial classes of our country. You yourself know . . . how important these classes are to the prosperous conduct of the complicated affairs of this immense empire. You yourself know, in spite of all the common-place cant and obloquy that has been cast upon them by political spouters and scribblers, what general good faith and fair dealing prevails throughout these classes. Knaves and swindlers there are doubtless among them, as there are among all great classes of men; but I declare that I looked with admiration at the manner in which the great body of our commercial and financial men have struggled on through the tremendous trials which have of late overwhelmed them, and have endeavored, at every pecuniary sacrifice, to fulfill their engagements. (*Life and Letters*, Vol. II, pp. 312–313.)

This persuasive presentation of the philosophy of compromise, with its implicit defense of capitalism, marks Irving's drift back to the middle class with which he had long before broken. In the six years since his return he had watched the country react to the great panic, and he went with it in its veering towards the Whiggery of Henry Clay. The fragile bonds of his attachment to the Democracy were becoming tenuous; other attachments were insensibly drawing him towards the more congenial representatives of wealth. He had all his life associated with the Tory classes and it was easy for him to transfer his loyalty to the American Tories. Under such influences began a slow *rapprochement cordial* towards the new philosophy of progress. He was seized with the common mania of speculation and made some unfortunate investments in wild lands and railways that seriously hampered him later, and he commercialized his literary reputation by such money-making ventures as *Astoria* and the *Adventures of Captain Bonneville*. He discovered a new romance in the great business of exploitation, and found the hand of God in the profits of unearned increment. In the letter above quoted from, he justified the ways of speculation thus:

There are moral as well as physical phenomena incident to every state of things, which may at first appear evils, but which are devised by an all-seeing Providence for some beneficent purpose. Such is the spirit of speculative enterprise which now and then rises to an extravagant height, and sweeps throughout the land. . . . The late land speculations, so much deprecated, though ruinous to many engaged in them, have forced agriculture and civilization into the depths of the wilderness; have laid open the recesses of primeval forests; made us acquainted with the most available points of our immense interior; have cast the germs of future towns and cities and busy marts in the heart of savage solitudes, and studded our vast rivers and internal seas with ports that will soon give activity to a vast internal commerce. Millions of acres which might otherwise have remained idle and impracticable wastes, have been brought under the dominion of the plough, and hundreds of thousands of industrious yeomen have been carried into the rich but remote depths of our immense empire, to multiply and spread out in every direction, and give solidity and strength to our confederacy. All this has in a great measure been effected by the extravagant schemes of land speculators. I am, therefore, inclined to look upon them with a more indulgent eye than they are considered by those violent politicians who are prescribing violent checks and counter measures, and seem to have something vindictive in their policy. (*Life and Letters,* Vol. II, p. 314.)

Thus did Irving become completely domesticated in the new world that Rip Van Winkle had found so disconcerting when he came upon it out of the quiet colonial past. The rediscovery of America proved to be an agreeable business, and profitable in a professional way. His enthusiasms, which in 1831 he felt were "waning as to many objects of past interest," were stimulated by the vast stir of the country, and the spirit of romance once more ran briskly in his veins. The better part of a year he rambled widely about the country, in order, as he said, to get at home "upon American themes." He visited Boston and the White Mountains, then West to Ohio and St. Louis, then with an Indian commissioner he penetrated the southwest prairies as far as the wild Pawnee country beyond the South Canadian River, then to New Orleans and Charleston, finally settling down in Washington to immerse himself in politics. From there he passed over the Potomac for an extended trip through the Old Dominion, returning to New York where he spent some time with Astor at Hell Gate, finally in 1835 settling at Tarrytown which was to be his home to the last. He had definitely determined on his new field of work. His imagination had been stirred by his visit to the prairies; the romance of the westward expansion was beginning to find expression in the works of Timothy Flint and James Hall; the public interest was ripe and John Jacob Astor was at hand to encourage him. Thus stimulated Irving proposed to make the field of western romance his own, with the result that he published in quick succession *A Tour of the Prairies, Astoria,* and *The Adventures of Captain Bonneville.*

On the whole the new venture did not prosper. The spirit of the West was not to be captured by one whose heart was in Spain. In *A Tour of the Prairies* there is a certain homely simplicity and straightforwardness that spring from a plain recital of undramatic experience; and in *Astoria* there is an unembellished narrative of appalling hardship and heroic endurance, with none of the tawdry romantics that mar the work of Flint and Hall. Yet neither is creatively imaginative, neither stirs one with a sense of high drama. The atmosphere of Snake River could not be created in the quiet study at the "Roost"; it needed the pen of a realist to capture the romance of those bitter wanderings in mountain and sagebrush. It is journeyman work, and on every page one is conscious of the professional man of letters faithfully doing this day's allotment. It is much the same with his *Life of Washington.* In this last great undertaking

Irving no longer writes with gusto. The golden days of Diedrich Knickerbocker and Rip Van Winkle are long since gone; the magic is departed from his pen; and a somewhat tired old gentleman is struggling to fulfill his contract with his publisher. It was a mistake to venture on the work, despite the fact that he had long been planning it. His historical equipment was inadequate. He might make a pretty story out of Washington's early life and his days with the army, but he was far too ignorant of politics, too credulous in judging his materials, to interpret justly the fierce party struggles that seethed about the President. Quite unconsciously in this last work he returned to the political prejudices of his youth, and wrote an account of Washington's administrations deeply colored by his Federalist sources.

The most distinguished of our early romantics, Irving in the end was immolated on the altar of romanticism. The pursuit of the picturesque lured him away into sterile wastes, and when the will-o'-the-wisp was gone he was left empty. A born humorist, the gayety of whose spirits overflowed the brim, he was lacking in a brooding intellectuality, and instead of coming upon irony at the bottom of the cup—as the greater humorists have come upon it after life has had its way with them—he found there only sentiment and the dreamy poetic. As the purple haze on the horizon of his mind was dissipated by a sobering experience, he tried to substitute an adventitious glamour; as romance faded, sentiment supplied its place. So long as youth and high spirits endured, his inkwell was a never-failing source of gayety, but as the sparkle subsided he over-sweetened his wine. This suffices to account for the fact that all his better work was done early; and this explains why the Knickerbocker *History* remains the most genial and vital of his volumes. The gayety of youth bubbles and effervesces in those magic pages, defying time to do its worst. The critic may charge the later Irving with many and heavy shortcomings, but the romantic smoke-clouds that ascend from Wouter Van Twiller's pipe cannot be dissipated by the winds of criticism.

II

JAMES KIRKE PAULDING

Far more native to the limitations and hardships of American life and far more loyal to its homely aspirations was James Kirke Paulding, whose literary reputation came to be so deeply overshadowed by that of his early friend. Sprung from plain stock—whether English or Dutch his son remained in doubt, although inclining to believe the former —and cradled in the fierce partisanship of the Revolutionary struggle, he never abandoned his inherited liberalism or found his love of country growing less. To the end of his life he remained a primitive American of an earlier generation, somewhat puzzled by the ways of another age that speculated in prosperity by running in debt, and measured a man's wealth by the amount he owed. His father had been an active Whig in a Tory neighborhood who did not stint his service to the Revolutionary cause. He was a member of the local Committee of Safety, and acted as State Commissary to the Revolutionary forces, a post which in the end brought him to ruin. In the dark days of the struggle he pledged his private credit for supplies, and was never reimbursed by a negligent commonwealth. The outcome was financial disaster. The father was imprisoned for debt and his courage broken, and the family long suffered from want. "We were not only poor," the son wrote later, "but steeped in poverty." But there was excellent stuff in the awkward, dreamy country boy. He was "built of stubborn oak," he remarked whimsically, "seasoned in the school of poverty, like an old chimney-piece in a log cabin." When at the age of nineteen he was suddenly plunged into the world of New York City, he was shy, uncouth, self-educated, and felt himself an alien in Wall Street and Broadway. For the Federalist upper class he seems to have felt the instinctive hostility of the outsider; but through the agency of the Irvings—an elder sister having married William Irving—he was brought into the companionship of a group of clever young men, and under the stimulus of high talk and exuberant pranks, the latent idealism of his nature expanded freely. This was his university, and while it left something to be desired in the way of discipline, suffering too free a rein to his discursive fancy, it quickened his native wit, awakened his creative imagination, and put him to school to the pleasant craft of writing. The *Salmagundi Papers* were the first fruits of the literary apprenticeship of the group, and although Irving has come to receive the chief credit for them, the wit of Paulding seems quite as sprightly, and his gayety as fresh.

That his later career in letters was less notable resulted in part from the fact that he was an inveterate rambler by nature, and partly from the fact that writing with him was occasional, a pleasant relief from humdrum duties, and he did not choose to lay a curb on his vagrant ways. In letters as in life he was always discursive, forgetful of his objective in his delight at the beauty of the countryside, loading his pages down with nature descriptions and clogging the action of his tales with somewhat tedious homilies. After forty years of writing he remained still an amateur, incapable of pruning the wilful tangle of his fancy—an essayist of the leisurely school who ventured incautiously into the realms of verse and fiction without mastering the technic of the business. There was perhaps too much of the homespun in him to permit him to become an artist. The experience of his youth marked him too deeply, and all his life he remained as conscious a son of the people as Hamlin Garland was later, delighting to chronicle the ways of the obscure, somewhat militant in proclaiming the excellence of homely virtues. Formed in an environment that bred a spontaneous democracy, he was a confirmed equalitarian, untroubled by the itch to rise in the world or exploit his fellows. Alone among the Knickerbocker group, he was a Jeffersonian in the fundamentals of his social creed; not in the lesser matters of Kentucky Resolutions and the like, but in his Physiocratic leanings, in his profound distrust of all middle-class programs and his preference for the simple country ways over the city economy; and it was this deep-rooted agrarianism that set him against capitalism and made him a later Jacksonian. In him there spoke out the authentic New York, not of Broadway merchants or Wall Street bankers, but of the plain rank and file of the people. Untouched by foreign travel but widely acquainted with his native America, he was fashioned out of the wool from the fireside loom and domestic dye-pot.

A writer so consciously and completely American would find abundant occasion to put his pen to the service of his country at a time when every English traveler turned critic and on his return home published a volume of truculent disparagement of ways and things American. For the most part those volumes were a defense of Toryism by the easy method of attacking democracy, and they annoyed Paulding beyond measure. He would not let them go unanswered, and from *The Diverting History of John Bull and Brother Jonathan* (1812) to *John Bull in America* (1825), he published five different replies, varying his attack from argument to burlesque. Something more than loyalty to his country seems to have spurred him on. His dislike of England was inveterate, partly because of the old Revolutionary feud, partly because of later antagonisms. Almost at the hour of his birth the Paulding family had been forced to quit their home for fear of the British and Tories who daily threatened them; and a deep hatred of the British Tory he drew in with his mother's milk. To him England was a Tory country, reeking with social injustice, the home of ancient abuses, and necessarily the implacable enemy of democratic America. He was convinced that want and tyranny and subserviency dogged the daily life of the English common people; and the English Reviews that attacked the ways of democracy with caustic British superiority, filled his honest republican heart with wrath, and he jabbed his quill into the tough skin of John Bull with patriotic vigor. The shame of the burning of the capitol rankled in the American heart, and Paulding discovered fresh grievances in remembering that from England had come the banking system and the "shin-plaster dynasty" that would breed in the new country the evils of the old if they were not looked to. He was convinced that the mother country wished ill to her offspring, and he thanked God in successive volumes that democratic America was not what Tory England was.

For despite the English travelers—Weld, Parkinson, Ashe, Bradbury, Hall, Trollope, and all the rest of the loquacious tribe—Paulding was persuaded that America constituted the hope of the future. Here in this land he believed that men should eventually achieve a measure of well-being undreamed of in the old world; already the old tyrannies had been destroyed, the ancient poverty abated. From this stubborn idealism nothing could turn him aside. It finds expression in an early poem, and it provides the theme for his last novel. *The Backwoodsman*, published in 1818, is a rambling and somewhat plethoric idyll of the West, the hero of which is an archetype of the oppressed and exploited, who finds a generous asylum in the free land beyond the Alleghenies, and like Crèvecœur's Andrew the Hebridean, expands the horizons of his mind under the beneficent touch of freedom. *The Puritan and His Daughter*, written over thirty years later, deals with a different phase of the same general theme. It is a vivid picture of the strife engendered in America by immigrant families who bring hither their old-world feuds and animosities, and the curative influence of the free environment that, in discovering the good rather than the bad in neighbors, draws together the younger generation despite the jealous parental authority that would keep them apart. The bigoted fathers make trouble enough—the fanatical Puritan who fought with Cromwell and the headstrong Cavalier who defended divine right—wilful men whom even the common frontier perils cannot reconcile or make tolerant; but they are powerless to thwart the ways of nature. The son of the Cavalier discovers an attractive woman in the daughter of the Puritan, and when love walks in the twilight what matters theology or politics. Youth has its own notions of divine right; in its creed the dogmas of John Calvin and Robert Filmer have no place; and if the lovers are more tolerant than the fathers it only proves that a freer environment will manage to soften the traditional animosities and beget a kindlier race from the merging of classes. Such at least is the characteristic thesis that Paulding elaborates through two volumes of discursive narrative interspersed with bits of vigorous action.

Of this kindly melting pot Paulding himself was a product. He had rid himself wholly of all ties that would bind him to Europe. He was partisan to no cause or party, literary or political, of the old world. He was content to be American and suffer his native land to bound his loyalties. In his own literary practice he refused to imitate the current English fashions and he spoke his mind freely to the American reading public for its greedy swallowing of cheap imported food. He did not take kindly to the English romantic writers, and went often out of his way to have a dig at his two pet aversions, Scott and Byron.[2] His amusing tale of *Koningsmarke, the Long Finne,* is a good-natured burlesque of certain romantic mannerisms of the Waverley novels, and a defense of Cooper's *Pioneers* for its homely realism. Paulding's dislike of the "blood-pudding" fiction that had come over from England, and that proved so disastrous to the genius of Gilmore Simms, was inveterate, and in his whimsical dedication of *The Puritan and His Daughter* to the sovereign people he comments on the public taste thus:

I am not ignorant of your preference for high-seasoned dishes of foreign cookery, most especially blood-puddings, plentifully spiced and sauced with adultery, seduction, poisoning, stabbing, suicide, and all other sublime excesses of genius. I am aware also that Your Majesty, being yourself able to perform impossibilities,

[2] See *Letters from the South,* Vol. I, *Letter XXII.*

believed nothing impossible. Possessing this clew to Your Majesty's royal approbation, I solemnly assure you I have gone as far as I could to secure it, with a safe conscience. I have laid about me pretty handsomely, and sprinkled a good number of pages with blood enough, I hope, to make a pudding. If I have any apology to make to Your Majesty, it is for permitting some of my people to die a natural death, a thing so unnatural that it has been banished from all works of fiction aiming at the least semblance to truth. . . . But, may it please Your Majesty, I am troubled with weak nerves, and my great grandfather was a Quaker. I am, therefore, naturally averse to bloodshed, and have more than once nearly fallen into convulsions over the pages of Monsieur Alexandre Dumas, whom I consider a perfect Guillotine among authors. In short, may it please Your Majesty, I abjure poisoning, or smothering with charcoal, and confess myself deplorably behind the spirit of this luminous age, which is as much in advance of all others, as the forewheel of a wagon is ahead of the hind ones.

In his politics—and as a good American of the times he took his politics seriously—Paulding found in the popular drift towards Jacksonian democracy an expression of his deepest convictions. It was moving in the direction he had long faced, and he went with it whole-heartedly, enjoyed some of the emoluments of office, and eventually served as Secretary to the Navy in the cabinet of Van Buren. With Jackson's attack on the Bank he must have been in deep sympathy, for his dislike of the new financial system was of long standing. His father had suffered heavily from a depreciated Continental currency, and he early came to distrust all banks and banking. His political views, indeed, were pretty much determined by the Physiocratic convictions that underlay his thinking. He had been a Jeffersonian long before the rise of Jacksonianism. Portions of his *Letters from the South,* published in 1817, seem like excerpts from the agrarian writings of John Taylor of Caroline. There is the same contemptuous analysis of the "shin-plaster dynasty," the same concern at the growth of trading towns, the same conviction that cities and poverty and low morals go hand in hand, the same trust in the perennial wholesomeness of country life. Such a passage as this will suffice to reveal his leanings towards a Physiocratic economy:

I was saying, that we have too many people living in cities, in proportion to our farmers, who, after all, are the backbone of every country, whence originates its riches and its solid strength. . . . Yet our people cling to the towns and cities, attracted by the hope of sudden wealth, and despising the slow, yet sure, rewards of agriculture, which, without leading a man to inordinate riches, secure him for ever from the chances of sinking into beggary or want. The race of paupers receives no recruits from them; for in all my sojournings, I may say with truth, that I never saw an industrious farmer forsaken, "or his seed begging bread." One great cause of the disproportion of numbers . . . between the agricultural and other classes of the community, is the great system of paper money, which has struck at the root of regular, persevering industry, whose rewards, though slow, are always certain. For some years back, hardly a tradesman in our cities, and of late in our little towns (each of which, however insignificant, has now its snug little bank) thinks of growing rich by his industry. No; he must get accommodations at some bank, and plunge into speculations: nor can you now go into a cobbler's stall without seeing a bank notice, or perhaps two or three, stuck up with an awl at the chimney-piece, to remind the honest gentleman that he owes a great deal more than he can pay. Thus is the axe laid to the very root of national morals, and consequently national prosperity, and the whole American people, farmers excepted, sunk into an abject subjection to banks and their directors. (*Letters from the South,* Vol. I, pp. 100–102.)

So confirmed an agrarian would easily arrive at agrarian conclusions in his meditations on the nature and functions of the political state. Unlike Irving, who, having no political convictions, was equally pleased with Whig or Democrat if he happened to be a gentleman, Paulding was something of a political philosopher with clear-cut doctrines. He was too shrewd an observer of ways political to be caught by party cries, or to ignore the class selfishness that would make government a party to its ends. As a Jeffersonian he retained an old-fashioned distrust of the political state. As an eighteenth-century liberal he would keep the state within narrow bounds. Jealous for a freedom worthy of free citizens, he wanted government to keep hands off what did not concern it. He would not have the state used as a cat's-paw to pull anybody's chestnuts out of the fire, whether in the form of Clay's American System, or what not. For protective tariffs and internal improvements—those grandiose schemes for hastening prosperity—he felt an old-fashioned repugnance that found issue in amusing caricature. In *Westward Ho!* he introduces a French publican of a Mississippi River village who does not care for Yankee improvements and describes them thus:

Diable! monsieur, another improvement; last year they assess me for one grand public improvement! one road to go somewhere,

I don't know. Eh bien! I pay the money. Well, this year they assess me for one other grand public improvement—very grand —voilà, monsieur, one other road, right alongside the other, both going to the same place. Diable! I no want to travel on two turnpike roads. Ah! monsieur le colonel, I shall be very rich, O! very rich indeed, by these grand improvements. They take away all my land to make room for the grand improvement; they take away all my money to pay for him, and then they tell me my land worth four, six time so much as before. Peste! what that to me when my land all gone to the dem public improvement, hey? I shall be very rich then. Diable! I wish myself gone to some country where everything was go backwards—what you call tail foremost, instead of forwards, for the dem march of improvement shall ruin me at last. (Vol. II, Chapter XVI.)

Satire aimed at the new gospel of progress is not infrequent in Paulding. In *Koningsmarke* he drew the picture of a politician that was perhaps intended for a burlesque of Henry Clay. The worthy Wolfgang Langfanger, member of the council of Elsingburgh, having "brought his private affairs into great confusion, by devoting too much time to the public good," began "to think it high time the public good should repay some part of its weighty obligations. He had accordingly invented, and persuaded the Heer Piper to put into practice, a system of internal improvement, which has been imitated, from time to time, in this country ever since with great success. The essence of his plan consisted in running in debt for the present, and living afterwards upon the anticipation of future wealth" (Book Second, Chapter VI). Big with his wonderful idea the busy councilor projected great docks and wharves for the commerce that was to be invited to come, a fine canal that would cut off a full six miles for barges that were not yet on the stocks, and a magnificent plan of new streets that led through houses that must be pulled down and fields that must forego their usual harvests. Such goodly improvements naturally cost money, and to maintain the public credit taxes were levied, and still more taxes, until, like the French tavern-keeper, the good people of Elsingburgh were brought to doubt the wisdom of investing in future prosperity at so high a present cost.

But the masterpiece of Langfanger's policy was that of pulling down an old market, and building a new one in another part of the village, in the management of which business he is supposed to have laid down the first principles of the great and thriving science of political economy, or picking people's pockets on a grand scale. He caused the people living near the old market to pay roundly for its removal as a nuisance; and then he caused the people that lived about where the new one was to be built, to pay roundly for the vast pleasure and advantage of its neighbourhood. Thus he pinched them through both ears, and got the reputation of a great financier. (Book Seventh, Chapter III.)

Koningsmarke is Paulding's most interesting work, and the utter neglect that has overtaken it is far from deserved. It is native and original, full of shrewd comment and sly satire, and it embodies most of Paulding's pet theories and aversions. Few books of the time are more amusing than this tale of the Long Finne who moves in a dark cloud of mystery woven by Bombie of the Frizzled Head, barks his sturdy shins on many a blood-curdling adventure, proves a true knight to his lady, and in the end turns out to be a very ordinary fellow who has been blown up to heroic size by the black art of romance. Paulding must have had great fun writing it, for his wit still preserves its freshness after a hundred years. It is a whimsical satire on the ways of the hour, literary and other, set against the background of an old Swedish settlement on the banks of the Delaware; but the chief purpose of its quizzical pages is the pouring of a broadside into the picturesque hull of contemporary fiction. It is an attack on the abundant extravagance of current romance that had been inflated by "Monk" Lewis and Sir Walter. Paulding cleverly hits off the high-flown and ghostly, the love of blood pudding, the snobbish contempt for the homely and native. Written in 1823, the year of Cooper's *Pioneers,* it defends the realism of characters and setting in that work against the charge of vulgarity and commonplace, but it takes pains to satirize Cooper's noble red man of the forest. Paulding's Indians are more like Bird's than Cooper's, material for burlesque rather than romance, but as he runs over the names of the warriors— "the Big Buffalo, the Little Duck-Legs, the Sharp-Faced Bear, the Walking Shadow, the Iron Cloud, the Jumping Sturgeon, the Belly Ache, and the Doctor, all legitimate sovereigns, with copper rings in their noses, blanket robes of state, and painted faces"—amusement at their childishness is tempered by the recognition that they have been overreached and dispossessed by the grasping white men.

In some of his later work the line between burlesque and serious is not so clearly marked, and one hesitates to pronounce whether *Westward Ho!* is a sober attempt at popular romance or a *reductio ad absurdum* of the current romantic flummery. Certainly it is a preposterous story with its melancholy hero driven mad by fear of madness and indulging in gibberish that comes straight out of Shakespeare, and with its ample crop of stock characters —Master Zeno Paddock and Mrs. Judith Paddock with their prying inquisitiveness, Colonel Dangerfield the easy-going Virginia gentleman who in staking his estate on a horse race embodies the plantation tradition, and Bushfield the backwoodsman who cannot live in a world that has left off its moccasins, and removes to a place where there are no laws and no lawyers and where constables do not visit a man who has thrashed his neighbor. *Westward Ho!* is not an amusing book; it is quite lacking in local color, and its casual bits of realism and occasional satire are too inconsequential to signify. *The Dutchman's Fireside,* written at about the same time, is far more successful. It purports to be an account of the Knickerbocker society in the days of the Old French war, and it contains some lovely pictures of old times that one reads with pleasure; but it indulges somewhat freely in adventure amongst the Indians and in the war, and its love story is needlessly romantic. Although Paulding still protests against a blood-pudding diet, he indulges occasionally in the high-flown, to the detriment of the idyllic note. Romance was all about him and he could not wholly escape its compulsions. Too casual in his work, too undisciplined in the craft of writing, he remained to the end an amusing amateur, a homespun man of letters who never took the trouble to master his technic. There was excellent stuff in him, solider perhaps than in Irving, but his failure suggests the difference between the journeyman and the artist.

CHAPTER IV

James Fenimore Cooper: Critic

Fenimore Cooper is one of the puzzling figures of his generation. In his substantial character was embodied what
may well appear no more than a bundle of contradictions.
Romancer and social critic, feudal-minded yet espousing a
republican faith, he pretty much baffled his own generation in its testy attempts to understand him, as he has
pretty much baffled later times. No other major writer, unless it be Whitman, has been so misunderstood, and no
other offers a knottier problem to the student of American
letters. The stubborn clay of his nature was molded to a
pattern unlike that of his fellows, and the difference was
long accounted to him as a grave shortcoming. His outspoken individualism was a constant irritant to a sensitive
majority, and his aloofness from the common enthusiasms
was reckoned no better than treason to his native land. The
right of the individual to question the herd pronouncements was a right not acknowledged by the herd, and the
more it tried to silence Cooper's tongue the more caustic
and loquacious it became. He refused to be silenced though
it should come to open warfare. His later years in consequence were rendered unhappy by a thousand petty vexa-
tions, and his creative work was brought only this side
of shipwreck.

How and why so great a misadventure befell him are
questions of prime importance to which little attention has
been given. That his tactlessness was at fault is commonly
believed—his tactlessness and a certain pugnacious virtue
that would inculcate righteousness by means of a broken
head. But such an explanation, true enough so far as it
goes, does not go far enough. The trouble lay deeper than
that; it lay in the mind of Cooper himself, in the doubts
and uncertainties that dwelt side by side with stubborn

dogmatisms, troubling his speculations and perplexing his plainest counsels. And that trouble must be traced to an underlying conflict between the man and his age, between the ideal and the real, between high loyalties and petty fact. Fenimore Cooper was the barometer of a gusty generation, sensitive to every storm on the far horizon. No other observer of that changing generation suffered so keenly in mind and conscience from the loosening of ancient ties, and none labored so hard to keep his countrymen to the strait path of an old-fashioned rectitude. His busy life covered the middle years of the great shift from an aristocratic order to a capitalistic order, and this revolutionary change provided him ample materials for brooding speculation. At every turn in the road fresh doubts assailed him. The perplexities and dogmatisms that clutter so many of his later pages, playing havoc with his romantic art, are a testimony to the confusions of a generation in the midst of epic changes. As honest a man as ever spoke his mind frankly, he endeavored to reconcile the irreconcilable, and establish sure standards amid the wreck of all standards. He could not drift. He must discover some working agreement between the old America and the new, between the reputed excellencies of the traditional aristocratic order, and the reputed justice of the democratic ideal. But unfortunately for this difficult business he was temperamentally ill-equipped. He was always at war with himself. His loyalties and his conscience ran at cross-purposes. His mind was packed with prejudices as an egg with meat. He was too partisan to compromise, and too honest to be content with the shoddy. His instinctive romanticisms were always being buffeted by fact, and his troubled mind in consequence was forever constructing laborious defense-mechanisms.

For those deep confusions that marred his later work and brought such bitter misunderstanding upon him, his heritage was much to blame. A romantic at heart, he was out of sympathy with the dominant romanticisms of his generation. Certain hold-overs from the past held him back from hearty participation in the present. He loved the world that was falling into decay too much to put away its virtues with its smallclothes; he would preserve what was excellent in the old to enrich and dignify what was excellent in the new; he would have the young democracy learn the decorum of a staid aristocracy. It is this fond lingering between worlds that sets Cooper apart from his fellows. He was an English squire of the old school turned republican, who did not quite like the company he found himself in He was equally puzzled at the bumptious leveling of the coonskin democracy, and the exploitative spirit of Wall Street Whiggery. But though he railed at the newfangled ways with the testiness of a squire, he was too confirmed a republican, too deeply concerned that the great venture in republicanism should demonstrate its wisdom, to overlook its shortcomings. He would have it be so true to its ideal that the world would acknowledge its excellence. He could not circumscribe his duties to election-day hurrahs; he must ferret out treason in the market place; he must be faithful in counsel though he utter unwelcome truths. It was the very faithfulness of Cooper to his conception of an ideal republic that brought him into collision with his fellows and filled his later days with bitterness.

It is easy to see where Cooper got those stubborn notions that marked him as the last of our eighteenth-century squires and left him obsolete after the adoption of the Constitution of 1821. From his father, from the Tory rector of St. Peter's, Albany, who first schooled him, from the Loyalist family of De Lancey into which he married, from Governor Jay and the old gentry with whom he was brought up, he imbibed certain stalwart conservatisms—political, religious, social, economic—that mingled in his blood and nourished the tissues of caste prejudice from which his maturer social philosophy struggled in vain to escape. In spite of his deliberate acceptance of the democratic principle, as he understood that principle, he remained at heart as sturdily eighteenth-century as any fox-hunting master of English acres. He had early been bred in the old traditions at Otsego Hall where he spent his boyhood. His father, Judge William Cooper, "a testy and choleric gentleman easily wrought into passion,"—whom he idealized as Judge Temple in *The Pioneers*—was an old-school politician of high Federalist persuasion, a vigorous, not to say truculent, embodiment of the stake-in-society principle of statecraft. Smitten with the common itch for large land holdings, he had got his hands on a huge virgin tract which he managed in the old baronial fashion. He was a real lord of the manor and late in life he recalled that "there were 40,000 souls holding land, directly or indirectly, under me"; and in the year 1800 "he set up a claim to having placed the plough upon more acres than any other man in America" (quoted in D. R. Fox, *The Decline of Aristocracy in the Politics of New York*, p. 136).

Otsego Hall in Cooperstown was a frontier citadel of Federalism defending the western marches against Jeffersonian democracy, and Judge Cooper used his economic power over tenants with telling effect. He "rode far and wide in the cause of Jay and later Aaron Burr, always preaching the musty doctrine that government had better be left to gentlemen, and that simple folk should vote as they were told" (*ibid.*, pp. 136–137). When persuasion failed he resorted to threats, and in 1792 he was before the legislature on impeachment charges. From the testimony it appears that the patriarchal Judge used direct methods with tenants in arrears; he "had been round to the people and told them they owed him, and that unless they voted for Mr. Jay, he would ruin them" (*ibid.*, p. 140). By such arguments it was thought some seven hundred votes had been brought into the Federalist column by this exemplar of the old virtues.

But Cooper had drifted with his age far from such old-fashioned methods of class domination. In spite of his great love for his father he seems never to have espoused the latter's political creed. With the disintegration of Federalism the young man went with the country in its turning towards French romanticism. When and why he adopted the democratic faith is not apparent, but until middle life it would seem that he concerned himself little with political theory. He remained a provincial American with an intense pride of patriotism. But his long stay in Europe, lasting from June, 1826, to November, 1833, and the Jacksonian revolution that took place during his absence, put him upon an anxious examination of first principles, and thereafter to the end of his life the social and political problems of America were a burden on his conscience. He arrived late at a reasoned political faith, as he arrived late at his literary art, and it is impossible to trace the steps of his intellectual development; yet confused though his thinking was, and shot through with narrowing prejudices, he persistently sought for the light; and the germinal source of his dissatisfactions was the deepening conviction that, in Franklin's phrase, the affairs of this world are preposterously managed. From this conviction Cooper never swerved. The contrast everywhere between the real and the ideal took hold of his mind as an obsession, and put an end to his contentment. His romantic art suffered from the intrusion of realism; the romancer was constantly impelled to turn critic. It was his travels more than anything else that destroyed his provincial contentment. The perturbing influence of that experience abroad has never perhaps been adequately considered by his critics. No other American was so unsettled by contact with European civilization. It was a Europe in the throes of revolution and Cooper threw himself with enthusiasm into French politics, hoping for a wise republican issue from the overturn. But it was a Europe also of dignified and generous culture that was a challenge to his Americanism. It made a critic of him and turned his mind to political and social problems. Europe appealed to his native aristocratic prejudices, but repelled his democratic; Jacksonian America appealed to his democratic prejudices, but rode roughshod over his aristocratic. He found himself nowhere at home. Puzzled and perturbed, he leveled his shafts at both worlds and sought a haven of refuge in vicarious existence, at times in the wilderness beyond the soil and smutch of the Jacksonian frontier, at times in the Utopian world of *The Crater* where an honest man could find free play for his creative energy, until the trouble makers came upon him.

In temperament and outlook this later Cooper was another John Adams modified by changing times. A realist in his long brooding over social and political evils, he was at heart an idealist greatly concerned with justice amongst men, with a romantic fondness for dwelling on the virtues of earlier days. Like Adams he understood very well that equality is a Utopian dream; that social classes exist in every society that has accumulated property, and that sovereignty in the long run will fall into the hands that control the social economics.[1] The problem he set himself to consider was the problem of reconciling this universal fact with his own predilection in favor of democracy. That he regarded himself as a democrat his emphatic assertions suffice to prove; but no more than Emerson was he deceived by the spurious democracy of the times. "The writer believes himself to be as good a democrat as there is in America," he said in the Introduction to *The American Democrat*. "But his democracy is not of the impracticable school. He prefers a democracy to any other system, on account of its comparative advantages, but not on account of its perfection. He knows it has evils; great and increasing evils, and evils peculiar to itself; but he believes that monarchy and aristocracy have more. It will be very apparent to all who read this book, that he is not a believer in

[1] See the Preface to *The Redskins*.

the scheme of raising men very far above their natural propensities." He would lift his voice in no hurrah for the majority, for he knew that the majority was very likely to be the tool of the demagogue. He saw no peculiar virtue or special intelligence in a coonskin cap, and he discovered no advantage in log cabins and hard cider as a training school for statesmen. He had watched the disgraceful campaign of 1840 with concern that gentlemen should stoop to the demagoguery that marked that electoral debauch; and it confirmed him in the conviction that "old-fashioned, high principled gentlemen" of an earlier age would never have been guilty of such traffic in votes—men like Chancellor Livingston who devoted his later years to raising Merino sheep, or John Jay who after filling with dignity many high offices retired to his estate to concern himself with new varieties of melons.

Hating all humbug, Cooper made it his business to free his mind from the several varieties of cant that were overrunning America like pigweed. "Had a suitable compound offered," he said of *The American Democrat,* "the title of this book would have been something like 'Anti-cant.'" Roughly, the history of his essays in criticism falls into two broad phases: the struggle to pull himself out of the bog of eighteenth-century caste philosophy—from that stake-in-society theory which his father upheld; and the struggle to escape the fallacies of the nineteenth-century philosophy rising about him—from the rude equalitarianism of Jacksonian democracy, and the materialism of capitalistic exploitation. His abandonment of the principle of gentleman-rule marks his definite break with the philosophy of Federalism and the substitution of democracy. It cost him a prolonged struggle, for the social-stake theory ran with many of his oldest predilections, and the evidence of that struggle is scattered broadly through the pages written in the late thirties; but having convinced himself of the social wrong involved in the principle, he was tireless in refutation. In *The American Democrat* he laid down the principle that "A government founded on the representation of property, however direct or indirect, is radically vicious. . . . It is the proper business of government to resist the corruptions of money, and not to depend on them" (*On Property,* p. 141). But it is *The Monikins,* a strange book much laughed at by the critics, rarely read and little understood, that concerns itself most largely with the theory. Sadly bungled though the satire quite obviously is, it is nevertheless a spirited attack on the social-stake principle that reveals how far Cooper had traveled from the doctrines of Hamilton and Webster, of Federalist and Whig. Both England and America—Leaphigh and Leaplow—show meanly under his caustic analysis, the former perhaps more meanly than the latter; their institutions, societies, politics, manners, are an unlovely compound of cant and hypocrisy; and the root of the common meanness he discovers in human selfishness. He conceives of man as a queer mixture of good and evil from whom much is not to be expected; something nearer to Swift's conception than William Ellery Channing's; with too much of the Monikin in him to pass for a child of God; prone to error even under a republican system; insolent, tyrannical, loving fetishes, given to brag, too poor-spirited to be free, gilding his fetters and belying Locke's saying that chains are an ill wearing. There are depths of bitterness in *The Monikins* that startle the reader. It is a tale of doubt and disillusion, Gulliver-like in its fierceness of attack, that strikes through all the shoddy romanticisms of the times and reduces the current democracy to humbug. Subjected to such analysis the old Federalist shibboleth of men of principle and property is no more than the East wind in empty bellies. The possession of money does not change human nature; rich as well as poor are driven by selfish interest, and to give a loose to property power is to invite political disaster.

Your social-stake system supposes that he who has what is termed a distinct and prominent interest in society, will be the most likely to conduct its affairs wisely, justly, and disinterestedly. This would be true, if those great principles which lie at the root of all happiness were respected; but unluckily, the stake in question, instead of being a stake in justice and virtue, is usually reduced to be merely a stake in property. . . . Now, all experience shows that the great property-incentives are to increase property, to protect property, and to buy with property those advantages which ought to be independent of property, viz., honors, dignities, power and immunities. I cannot say how it is with men, but our [Monikin] histories are eloquent on this head. We have had the property-principle carried out thoroughly in our practice, and the result has shown that its chief operation is to render property as intact as possible, and the bones, and sinews, and marrow of all who do not possess it, its slaves." (*The Monikins,* Chapter XXVII.)

But though Cooper might deny the validity of the eighteenth-century social-stake theory, he saw no valid reason to abandon his eighteenth-century economics. In his preference for a social order founded on agriculture he was as confirmed a Physiocrat as Franklin or Jefferson; and this preference determined his judgment on the economic revolution under way in America. A people living close to the soil was living more wholesomely, he believed, than a city people immersed in trade and manufacture. For the capitalistic expansion that followed the new fiscal system of the seventeen-nineties, he felt an instinctive repugnance. Banking and the manipulation of credit seemed to him mean and sordid, and the spirit of speculation that was overrunning the land he believed was destructive of common morality. The activities of Wall Street he looked upon with the eyes of an English squire. To expect any sane progress from such worship of money, to assume that a high and excellent civilization could result from such worship, seemed to him plain madness. "God protect the country that has nothing but commercial towns for capitals," he wrote his wife in 1839 (Cooper, *Correspondence of James Fenimore Cooper*, Vol. II, p. 404), and the comment found amplification in many a caustic passage in his novels of criticism. A materialistic middle class with its gospel of progress interpreted in terms of wasteful exploitation seemed to him the hateful progeny of a period of "moral occultation"; and against this "Yankee" philosophy he waged an unrelenting warfare. In *The Monikins* he drew a gloomy picture of the America of the thirties when the land had come under a great moral eclipse; and in *Home as Found* and *The Redskins* he commented bitterly on the universal restlessness that was driving thousands to the new West to seek their fortunes. The settlement of the Inland Empire was no romance for him. The Great Migration seemed to imply the break-up of the older America he loved; and the impact of the frontier spirit upon the country seemed likely to destroy the last excellence of an earlier age. It marked for Cooper the final triumph of the acquisitive Yankee spirit, grasping and lawless in its crude leveling.

From these germinal sources—his love of the dignified ways of the old manorial families, his contempt for the middle class, his dislike of a bumptious leveling, his hatred of brag and cant and enterprise—came those sharp contrasts in his pictures that set the vulgar present over against the dignified past. His criticism was in no small part the reaction of a romantic to the unlovely works of an economic revolution. From his loyalty to the old came that subtle romanticizing of the eighteenth century that lends a charm to his tales, and from it came also that vindictive hatred of the frontier that spurred him to ill-balanced criticism. He could not like the new that was destroying the old. Like Emerson he was a man without a party, but unlike him he sought consolation in the past rather than the future. The excellence he yearned for he found in that older world whose stable ways were as yet unsettled by the romantic revolution, and from the meanness of the present he stole away to find consolation in the dignity and worth of honester times. The late eighteenth century became, therefore, his romantic haven and City of Refuge to which he returned gladly. He was always seeking to revitalize the old in an environment where, as he lamented, "the eighteenth century may be set down as a very dark antiquity."

That Cooper unconsciously romanticized the past is only too evident. Too often he accepted its self-proclaimed virtues as sober fact and created a race of squires that never existed outside his pages. Realist though he was in certain moods, he abandoned his realism in the presence of the tie-wig gentry. His father was as graspingly eighteenth century as Gouverneur Morris and saw to it that his own nest was well feathered; yet the son failed to perceive that the dignified professions of those old gentlemen were little more than splendid gestures. He made the mistake of taking them at their face value. Honest himself, he attributed an equal honesty to the older generation, and he watched with unfeigned regret the disintegration of an order that seemed to him the repository of much that was excellent. Fragments of its ideals he clung to; its dignity, its concern for breeding and manners, its fine distinction. Fragments also of its political convictions: its concern for law and order, its belief that all just law is founded in morality, its insistence that American government is one of principles and not of men. He put his finger shrewdly on certain fallacies of eighteenth-century theory, but he took too many of its values at par. The twilight is a mighty sorcerer and Cooper was bewitched by the half light that lingered softly on the familiar past.

This suffices to explain the grounds of the charge of aristocratic leanings that Cooper was persistently brought under. His bold defense of the landed gentry gave mortal enmity to the Jacksonians, and the tactlessness with which he pointed out the crude provincialisms of America—the bumptious plebeians he set over against the priggish gentlemen—was rubbing salt on open sores. *Home as Found* and *The Redskins* were onslaughts on the ways of the sacred majority that America could not forgive him for. Yet no counter criticism ever moved Cooper from his conviction that gentlemen of an earlier generation possessed dignity, principles, character, far beyond the speculators and politicians and "small-potato lawyers" of the present time of "moral occultation"; and the difference in favor of the old he traced to the economic basis of the tie-wig gentry. Believing with John Adams that an aristocracy is implicit in every established society, he frankly preferred a landed to a capitalistic aristocracy. Gentlemen of the old school were neighborhood patriarchs. Secure in position and possessions they disdained to keep an ear to the ground or court a silly popularity. They were squires with a high sense of responsibility to themselves and society. Their stake in the land was a stabilizing influence in their lives; and their ample way of living, their well-bred leisure, their courteous bearing learned from a cosmopolitan experience, seemed to Cooper a desirable influence in a society lacking refinement and exact standards. To supplant them with the new gentry of Wall Street seemed to him plain folly, and he watched the decay of the old families with a pathetic concern. The Anti-Rent novels are a long defense of a thesis that comes to final expression in such a passage as this from *The Redskins*:

I say that, in a country like this, in which land is so abundant as to render the evils of a general monopoly impossible, a landed gentry is precisely what is most needed for the higher order of civilization, including manners, tastes, and the minor principles, and is the very class which, if reasonably maintained and properly regarded, would do the most good at the least risk of any social caste known. (Chapter XXVI.)

It is not hard, indeed, to understand Cooper's preference for Stephen Van Rensselaer the Patroon, to John Jacob Astor the fur trader, or Commodore Vanderbilt the ferryman; yet such preference was charged against him as un-American.

It was this revulsion from the meanness of the present that sent Cooper into the wilderness or out on the high seas, to seek adventure in the company of nature's noblemen, and forget the sordidness of the real. Here again the French school prompted his thinking, if only to supplement the romance of his boyish recollections. Natty Bumppo is quite evidently man as he came from the hand of nature, uncorrupted by the vices of the settlements; indeed one might question whether the back-to-nature literature can show another figure so enduringly vital as the Leatherstocking. From this same material is fashioned Uncas and the younger Chingachgook and still other lovable figures of his romances. They belong to the free wilderness beyond the settlements, where the dramatic flight and pursuit go on unchecked by impertinent fences. Here their native virtues expand and their generous gifts find ample play. They shunned the settlements as Cooper shunned them. On the frontier, the middle ground between nature and civilization, Cooper's spirits flagged. He had no love for the stumpy clearings, the slovenly cabins, the shiftless squatters; the raw devastation of the ax grieved him and he breathes contentedly only after he has left the scars behind and is in the deep woods beyond the smell of rum. Such a man obviously was unfitted to write a just account of the frontier as it straggled westward. He hated its ways too fiercely to do justice to it, and when he comes upon it in his tales, when he introduces a frontier figure such as Ishmael Bush in *The Prairie* or old Aaron Thousandacres in *The Chainbearer*, it is to depict the unhappy state of society where the virtues of nature are gone and the refinements of civilization not yet come. No writer has set down a more sweeping indictment of the frontier than Cooper, and he set it down because the frontier seemed to him the muddy source of the vulgar leveling he hated so heartily. A gentleman, whether Indian or squire or scout, Cooper loved to be with; but a vulgarian he could not endure, and a rascal stirred his Puritan wrath. In consequence there runs through his work little of the amusing picturesque strain that the heartier nature of Gilmore Simms delighted in, and that made him a truer chronicler of frontier ways.

Democrat though he professed to be, Cooper shrank from the logical application of the democratic principle. The adoption of manhood suffrage in New York brought in its train a sorry scramble of demagogues to sway the popular will, a debasement of the press, and a vulgarizing of political life that proved a sore trial to Cooper's faith. He was too severely moralist to enjoy the little weaknesses of human nature, but must set himself up as custodian of public morals. Affronted by a bumptious vulgarity, he became the assailant rather than the critic of Jacksonian ways. The land to which he returned in 1833 was a broad target for his shafts and he sent them into the white. The America of log cabins and hard cider seemed to him to have repudiated the traditional standards, moral as well as cultural, and he attributed the disintegration to the corruption that came from the extension of the suffrage to classes unprepared to use it wisely. It was this that embittered his criticism in the caustic pages of *Homeward Bound* and *Home as Found*. He was startled and resentful at the changes. "You have been dreaming abroad," remarked one of the characters in the former, "while your country has retrograded, in all that is respectable and good, a century in a dozen years" (*Homeward Bound*, Chapter XVII). The colossal brag, the meaningless unrest, the abysmal provincialism, he marked as the natural by-products of the mob mind. In throwing off its old restraints America was coming to deny all standards of decency and excellence. "What then do you deem our greatest error— our weakest point?" asks one of his characters, and the reply is explicit:

Provincialisms, with their train of narrow prejudices, and a disposition to set up mediocrity as perfection, under the double influence of an ignorance that unavoidably arises from a want of models, and of the irresistible tendency to mediocrity in a nation where the common mind so imperiously rules. (*Home as Found*, Chapter XXV.)

It was during the bustling decade of the forties, when the agrarian unrest in York State was putting in jeopardy the old manorial system, that Cooper's antagonism to the spirit of leveling became bitterest; and it was in defense of the old system that he wrote the Anti-Rent trilogy that should always be set over against the Leatherstocking tales. Taken together the two series contain pretty much the whole of Cooper, his sea tales excepted; either alone gives an inadequate and partial view. The one is a social study, the other a romantic epic. The one gives a picture of the changes the years have brought to a given region, the other follows the retreating wilderness as the frontier moved westward. The Anti-Rent novels present the reverse of the romantic picture of the Leatherstocking tales. Their central figure is Aaron Thousandacres the squatter, who has come out of Connecticut to possess what pleases him, regardless of legal rights. Offspring of generations of covetous, psalm-singing Puritans, he has no difficulty in justifying his lawlessness by Yankee logic. The devil can quote Scripture, and in this respect old Thousand-acres is the devil's own son. When Scripture fails the easy gospel of natural rights comes to his aid; the written law may be on the side of the title-holder, but natural law is on the side of the squatter.

"There's two rights to all the land on 'arth, and the whull world over," the squatter replied to Chainbearer's legal argument. "One of these rights is what I call a king's right, or that which depends on writin's, and laws, and sich like contrivances; and the other depends on possession. It stands to reason, that fact is better than any writin' about it can be." (*The Chainbearer,* Chapter XXV.)

Such lax doctrine, to Cooper, was the evil fruit of the spirit of lawlessness that was laying a blight upon America. A retributive bullet ends the fierce career of old Thousand-acres, but his tigress wife, his rough sons and slattern daughters are driven from their home to plunge deeper into the wilderness, there to beget other generations of squatters whose vicious doctrines return to plague society. No romance blends with the tale of their lives; no sympathy softens the picture of the stern old Yankee. He has set himself against law and order and must yield or be destroyed. It is the old story of the struggle for land, a struggle that went on for generations between speculator and squatter, between rich and poor, with much wrong and much right on both sides; yet Cooper's sympathies are cold to the squatter's plea and he enlists God, morality, and the law, in defense of a title to forty thousand acres wheedled from the Indians for ninety-six pounds, York currency, spent in trinkets. Righteousness without a sense of humor is not easy to live with.

In much of his later work Cooper's romantic impulses are held in check by a growing tendency towards realism. It was there from the first but as he grew more critical it spread over more of his pages. He tried to hold the scales of his judgment even, but his realism was marred and distorted by his vehement nature. A mind exuding prejudice is ill equipped to deal objectively with material, and Cooper was too inveterate a moralist to accept the principle of impersonal detachment. He prided himself on facing fact, but he loved to preach; and having pointed out the wrong-fulness of vicious morals he must follow it with a vigorous homily on right conduct. And yet despite his gross short-

226

comings there is a deal of realism scattered through his volumes. He consciously tried to be a chronicler of manners, to depict America truly, to recreate fairly present and past, red man and white, Dutch and Yankee. His prejudices certainly got the better of him in dealing with New England, and his romance certainly got the better of him in describing the Mohicans. Yet though he might romanticize Uncas he did not romanticize Saucy Nick in *Wyandotté*, but drew an excellent picture of the struggle between the drunkard and the warrior in the heart of the Tuscarora that reveals much of the Indian nature—an analysis that holds the scales more evenly than they are held in *The Last of the Mohicans* or in Bird's *Nick of the Woods*. The book as a whole, indeed, is an excellent example of Cooper's desire to substitute a critical for a romantic treatment of materials. In his discriminating analysis of the motives separating families in the Revolutionary war, there is no glorification of partisanship, no prejudiced espousal of a sacred cause, no division of sheep and goats. Cooper will have none of the cheap romance of patriotism, but probes skillfully into the motives and impulses that divided honest men amid the difficulties of civil war. More than that, he makes his villain one of the patriot party who uses the unsettlement of the times to cover his dirty tracks. It is a characteristic document that deserves to stand beside *Satanstoe* as an example of his later work.

Politics was all about Cooper while he was writing these tales, and his sporadic incursions into criticism led him into the field of political theory. So doughty a warrior must break a lance when all America was engaged in a great political tourney. While Whig and Democrat were loudly professing allegiance to the new doctrine of a majority rule, Cooper was making his way back to the principles of the eighteenth century and discovering the essence of good government in self-restraint. The mistake of the new school, he was convinced, lay in confusing the present will of the majority with the rule of the people; the mistake of the old school lay in confusing the will of the minority with the rule of the people. Above and beyond both majority and minority is the eternal principle of justice, and any government that flouts that principle is bad government, no matter how sanctioned. In a republic which foolishly believes that the voice of the people is the sole criterion of right, the problem of justice is peculiarly difficult, for what remedies are available in cases "in which the people themselves happen to go astray, *en masse*"? It is the problem that attends every ethical interpretation of sovereignty, and it awakened acute concern in Cooper's mind. He could find no solution except in the good sense of the people, and with a vicious press and persuasive demagogues doing their best to befuddle the public mind, the outlook seemed dark. It was not the people he distrusted, but the self-seekers who set up to be leaders of the people. All the noise was made by demagogues who proclaimed their own mouthings to be authentic public opinion. How ineffectively Cooper struggled with the problem is written down in many a passage in his critical novels.

God help the nation [he said in *The Redskins*] where self-government, in its literal sense, exists. . . . When a people that has been properly educated by experience calmly selects its agents, and coolly sets to work to adopt a set of principles to form its fundamental law or constitution, the machine is on the right track, and will work well enough so long as it is kept there; but this running off and altering the fundamental principles every time a political faction has need of recruits, is introducing tyranny in its worst form—a tyranny that is just as dangerous to real liberty as hypocrisy is to religion. (Chapter XII.)

Some observers pretend that . . . respect for law is gradually decreasing among us [he argued in *The Chainbearer*] and that in its place is sensibly growing up a disposition to substitute the opinions, wishes, and interests of local majorities, making the country subject to men instead of principles. The last are eternal and immutable; and coming of God, men, however unanimous in sentiment, have no more right to attempt to change them, than to blaspheme His holy name. All that the most exalted and largest political liberty can ever beneficially effect is to apply these principles to the good of the human race, in the management of their daily affairs; but when they attempt to substitute for these pure and just rules of right, laws conceived in selfishness and executed by the power of numbers, they merely exhibit tyranny in its popular form, instead of in its old aspect of kingly and aristocratic abuses. It is a fatal mistake to fancy that freedom is gained by the mere achievement of a right to govern, unless the manner in which that right is to be both understood and practised is closely incorporated with all popular notions of what has been obtained. The right to govern means no more than the right of the people to avail themselves of the power thus acquired to apply the great principles of justice to their own benefit, and from the possession of which they had hitherto been excluded. It confers no power to do that which is inherently wrong, under any pretense whatever. (Chapter XXVIII.)

228

Like Hugh Henry Brackenridge before him, Cooper was a democrat who criticized the ways of a reputed democracy because of his love for an ideal republic. Too few of his kind have arisen in America; too few who dare to speak their minds unterrified by public opinion. An individualist of the old English breed, he could not be intimidated or coerced in the matter of his rights by any clamor, whether of newspapers or mobs. He had his shortcomings in plenty, both as romancer and critic. Testy, opinionated, tactless, forever lugging in disagreeable truths by the ears, he said many wise things so blunderingly as to make truth doubly offensive, and he hewed at his art so awkwardly as well-nigh to destroy the beauty of his romance. Yet the more intimately one comes to know him, the more one comes to respect his honest, manly nature that loved justice and decency more than popularity. His daily life became a long warfare with his fellows, who exacted of him a great price for his idealism; but later generations should love him none the less for the battles he fought. That America has been so tardy in coming to know him as a man and a democrat, as well as a romancer, is a reflection upon its critical acumen.

CHAPTER V

Some Contributions of New England

It was the good fortune of New York to draw to the bustling city some of the best and most vigorous minds of New England. If the sons of Yankees flocked thither, the sons of Puritans came likewise, and the contributions of these latter to the idealism of a society rather too fond of material progress must not be overlooked. The literature of New York in particular was heavily indebted to New England. One need only run over a list of writers who came from New England to realize how great was its total contribution to the production of the New York group. Bryant and Halleck and Willis and Greeley and Beecher and Curtis and Tuckerman and Parke Benjamin and Stedman and Stoddard and even, in a sense, Melville, were products of that more serious-minded world that was to create transcendentalism and issue in strange projects of social reform; they were men who would easily share the ethical enthusiasm of their Puritan fellows, and create a literature concerned with other than aesthetic values. Not all of them were Puritan in ideals; Halleck and Willis quite evidently not; nevertheless the severe idealism of their work sets it apart from the productions of the Knicker-bocker school. Perhaps not above, but certainly apart; and this unlikeness calls for some special consideration. Over against Irving and Paulding and Cooper may be set Bryant and Greeley and Melville, and the sharp contrast between them will serve to differentiate the native mind of New York from that of New England.

I

WILLIAM CULLEN BRYANT: *Puritan Liberal*

For upwards of half a century now too much of Bryant has been obscured by the brightness of his early fame. Since his death a serious injustice has been done him by the critics, who have dwelt too exclusively on his work in the field of verse to the neglect of other work in fields perhaps quite as significant. The journalist has been for-gotten in the poet, the later democrat who spoke for American liberalism has been displaced by the youthful versifier who described American scenery. For this our bellettristic historians, who are impatient of any incursions into matter of fact, are to blame. Yet to ignore so much of Bryant results in underestimating him, and this serves to explain the thin and shadowy quality of his present reputation. He was a much larger man and more significant than the critics have made him out to be. His active and many-sided life is very inadequately expressed in the slen-der volume of his verse, excellent as much of that is. The journalist and critic who for fifty years sat in judgment on matters political and economic as well as cultural, who reflected in the *Evening Post* a refinement of taste and dignity of character before unequaled in American journal-ism, was of service to America quite apart from his contri-bution to our incipient poetry. He was the father of nineteenth-century American journalism as well as the father of nineteenth-century American poetry. In the columns of the *Evening Post* the best liberalism of the times found a place, inspired and guided by Bryant's clear intelligence. The lucidity of his comment and the keenness of his humanitarian criticism set the editor apart from shriller contemporaries, and made him a power for sanity in a scurrilous generation. But with his death the evanescent character of even the highest journalism asserted itself, and with the fading of his journalistic reputation the earlier Bryant of *Thanatopsis* shouldered aside the Bryant of the *Evening Post*, and an unconscious distortion of his career began, a distortion made easier by the fact that no outstanding work of the later period remained to restore the balance. In this he is like Jefferson. He is scattered piecemeal through his occasional writings as the latter through his letters, and the task of piecing him together and visualizing his work as a whole has not yet been done.

It will not prove an easy task. The narrow but real genius of Bryant is peculiarly elusive. His was essentially a self-pollenizing nature that needed few contacts with other minds. He lived within himself, little swayed by modes of thought, slowly maturing the native fruit of his speculation. The very tenacity and persistence of his intellectual life, the rigid integrity of his thinking, suggest the confidence of one who drew his nourishment from within, whose life was an organic growth. It is impossible to mistake his origins. The roots go down to deep substrata of Puritan seriousness and Puritan austerity, and the fruits which they nourish—somewhat scanty it may be but of firm texture and good keeping qualities—possess the slightly acrid flavor of old Puritan orchards where the care of the husbandman is pitted against harsh seasons and a meager soil. There is no pagan luxuriance, no riot of color or scent. The ethical idealism of New England is given stately form if not rendered altogether lovely; the passion for righteousness is held in restraint but it retains much of its tempered acidity. Happily there was little of the schools in Bryant, and nothing of the intellectual play-boy. His early life in the Berkshire hills, on his father's farm, as student at Williams College for a few months, and as a country lawyer, threw him upon his own intellectual resources and made possible a normal unfolding of his mind. He was fortunately spared a much-coveted life at Yale, where the narrow classicism and ungenerous dogmatisms could have done him little good. From Timothy Dwight the young Bryant could have got little to enrich his mind, and he might have got some disastrous checks. Left to himself he appropriated such nourishment as fell in his way and went forward on the path of a sober liberalism.

That he went forward at all is sufficient testimony to his native integrity of character. In 1825 when he removed to New York, the intellectual renaissance of Boston was just at the beginning, and in his new environment he never quite kept pace with the transcendental enthusiasms that so stimulated the New England radicals. At Great Barrington where he had been growing more discontented with his "shabby" profession of the law, he discovered little to encourage an independent liberalism. Bred up in an environment of intolerant Federalism and an equally intolerant Calvinism, he had much to outgrow and little to feed on. Few innovating ideas penetrated to the Berkshire hills where he was brooding on life and poetry, and the training of his youth was strong upon him. As a mere boy he had expostulated with President Jefferson in shrill heroic couplets, declaiming on the latter's reputed moral lapses and inviting him to resign his high office. He had summoned Napoleon to the bar of Cummington respectability and adjudged him guilty of high crimes against humanity; but such rhetorical outbursts were only echoes of a narrow world he was soon to outgrow. The blight of the tie-wig school of Fisher Ames did not fasten itself deeply on him, and by the time he had reached his twenties he was moving towards the twin goals towards which liberal New England was moving—the Unitarianism of Channing and the democracy of Jefferson. It was far more difficult for a Berkshire man to think his way through to such revolutionary goals than for a Concord; yet the unschooled Bryant who had never visited Boston till he went there in his twenty-seventh year to read a poem before the Phi Beta Kappa society at Harvard had already outstripped the Cambridge scholastics in the great work of setting his mind free. The stages through which he passed cannot easily be traced, but the fact of his decisive break with the dogmas of his youthful world is plain enough. During the last years at Great Barrington he put himself upon a course of reading and thinking, and from that provocative experience emerged the Bryant that we know. Calvinism and Federalism he put away, and he went up to New York completely new-outfitted in a fashion he never afterwards saw reason to change. In politics and religion, as in poetry, he was a man of few ideas, but those ideas were creative, and determined all his thinking.

For this change that was unconsciously preparing him for his later work on the *Evening Post*, Bryant owed something to his father, who had turned moderate Unitarian, but very much more to the Berkshire family of Sedgwicks, one of whom, Catherine M. Sedgwick, was just beginning her modest career as a "lady novelist"; another, Henry M. Sedgwick, was at the head of the New York bar, wealthy and liberal-minded; and a third, Theodore Sedgwick, Jr., was a trusted adviser on legal and economic matters, on whose pen Bryant came to rely in a difficult situation. Theodore Sedgwick seems to have been a liberal of the English school of Bright and Cobden, a confirmed free trader, and he induced Bryant to undertake a course of reading in political economy. During the years 1822 to 1824 the young man turned away from poetry and law to study Adam Smith, Thornton, and Ricardo, together with a number of pamphlets that issued from the Parliamentary debates over free trade in 1820. The adventure proved stimulating and definitely determined his attitude towards men and measures at a moment when American ideas were in a state of flux. It was therefore as an English liberal that he judged Jackson and Clay and Webster, and as an English liberal that he weighed the Utopian programs of Greeley and Brisbane and Ripley. There is no evidence that he read the works of the French romantics, although the major ideas of Rousseau came to him in the guise of Unitarianism; and this aloofness from the social enthusiasm of French thought, this failure to sympathize with the idealism of the new sociology, may perhaps be accounted his greatest intellectual shortcoming. Rousseau and Godwin and Mary Wollstonecraft could have taught him much that he needed to know, could have warmed his cool blood and awakened his Puritan sense of justice to the wrongs of an exploitative order. A dash of Utopian enthusiasm would have made him a better poet and a better editor; but lacking that he found himself sometimes out of sympathy with men and women whom he should have understood better. A liberal might smile at the measureless zeal of Fanny Wright and Robert D. Owen; might dislike the militancy of the Abolitionists; he might well counsel moderation; but he should not add his shaft to the flight sent against them. But unfortunately Bryant too often distrusted those who outran him, and would rather attack than restrain them.[1]

As an English liberal it was inevitable that Bryant should turn Democrat and support Jackson against Clay and Adams; and an ardent Democrat he remained till the realignment over the slavery question turned him into a free-soiler. He early supported Lincoln for the Republican nomination—the more easily because members of his family had removed to Illinois and there followed the career of Lincoln sympathetically—and he accepted the Republican faith till the open alliance of the party with post-war capitalism aroused his opposition and weakened his allegiance. Democrat though he was in conviction and sympathy, Bryant was never a Jeffersonian, perhaps not even a Jacksonian, but rather an anti-Whig, who measured the new America of the industrial revolution and capitalistic finance by the yardstick of eighteenth-century liberalism. As a disciple of Adam Smith, believing in the sufficiency of *laissez faire*, he looked askance at an engrossing political state that enlisted its sovereign powers on the side of the longest purses, and he viewed with scorn the mercenaries of the bench and Senate who defended the new citadels of capitalism. In spite of his augmenting wealth he remained a simple countryman at heart, never a city man, never liking the ways of Wall Street, concerned with other things than moneymaking. If he had supplemented Adam Smith with Du Pont de Nemours he might easily have followed Jefferson into a Physiocratic agrarianism; if he had been bred in the frontier West he might have discovered more sympathy for a coonskin equalitarianism with its engrossing majority will. As it was, he occupied a middle ground between Jefferson and Jackson, an economic individualist who refused to conceive of the political state as a fat cow to be milked by whoever could lay hands on her. He wanted no share of the milk for himself and he saw no reason why others should have any. He turned his back on all middle-class temptations, refusing to speculate, not grasping at unearned increment, believing that America had a nobler destiny in store than could be measured by exploitation. An old-fashioned liberal, he set himself resolutely against the exploitative spirit that was clamoring for internal improvements, a protective tariff, speculative profits. The

[1] See his satire on Fanny Wright in *The Evening Post*, January 29, 1829, quoted by Allan Nevins, *The Evening Post, etc.*, pp. 126–127.

bitter struggle over the Bank and the American System, in which he was drawn to Jackson by principle as well as by admiration for his courage, laid the emphasis in his mind on financial and industrial problems and made him the outstanding journalistic opponent of Henry Clay. From first to last Bryant was anti-Whig.

There were times, to be sure, when he went further than that; times when his ingrained liberalism threw off its cool restraint and flamed up in dangerously disturbant fashion. In the depths of his Puritan nature was a quick sense of justice that might uncover strange potentialities; and associated as he was in the intimacies of daily work with two of the most radical spirits in New York, William Leggett and Parke Godwin, he could not remain untouched by their social enthusiasms. The former was a man of immense vitality and boundless sympathies, to whom social justice was a religion. A left-wing equalitarian democrat, Leggett hated all tariffs, subsidies, monopolies, credit manipulation, everything that the new capitalism represented. His sympathies were enlisted on the side of the new proletarian movement, and with the zeal of a knight-errant he greeted every opportunity to do battle for the cause. A home-made radical, created out of the native economics of the industrial revolution, he has been called by a late historical writer "one of the most sincere and brilliant apostles of democracy that America has ever known." His political leaders in the *Evening Post* aroused the admiration of such different men as Whittier and Walt Whitman, and were "perhaps the most potent force in shaping the ideas of democracy" held by the latter (Allan Nevins, *The Evening Post, etc.*, p. 141). His son-in-law, Godwin, on the other hand, was a radical of the imported school, an ardent disciple of Fourier, deeply concerned with communistic experiments at Brook Farm and elsewhere, and an assistant editor of *The Harbinger*, the mouthpiece of Brook Farm after it passed from transcendental to Fourierist control. His *Democracy, Pacific and Constructive*, was accounted by Horace Greeley the best of the contemporary studies of collectivism. Less militant than Leggett, his radicalism ebbed with the years and growing prosperity, but it sufficed to instruct Bryant in the elements of the current Utopian philosophies.

With such associates the older man was led somewhat unwillingly into the thick of social struggle and his mind shifted unconsciously to the left. The movement of Locofocoism in particular absorbed Leggett and drew Bryant after him. Set on foot by a combination of reforming economists opposed to banks, paper money, and monopolies, and the rising proletarian movement then beginning its long struggle to unionize the city workers, Locofocoism represented the extreme left wing of democratic equalitarianism, the avowed objective of which was to take government out of the hands of bankers and lodge it in the hands of the producers. It was one of the first native attempts at conscious class alignment between capital and labor. "What distinguishes the present form from every other struggle in which the human race has been engaged," wrote Fanny Wright, "is that the present is evidently, openly and acknowledgedly a war of class. . . . It is the ridden people of the earth who are struggling to overthrow the 'booted and spurred riders' whose legitimate title to work and starve will no longer pass current" (quoted by Fox, *Aristocracy in the Politics of New York*, p. 396). How the democratic radicalism of Leggett was received by conservative New York is thus described by the historian of the *Evening Post*:

He was charged [says Nevins] with Utopianism, agrarianism, Fanny-Wrightism, Jacobinism, and Jack Cade-ism. His writings were said to set class against class, and to threaten the nation with anarchy. Gov. William M. Marcy called Leggett a "knave." The advance of the Locofoco movement was likened to the great fire and the great cholera plague of these years. When Chief Justice Marshall died in the summer of 1835, Leggett unsparingly assailed him and Hamilton as men who had tried "to change the character of the government from popular to monarchical," and to destroy "the great principle of human liberty." . . . Ex-Mayor Philip Hone was handed that editorial on the Albany steamboat by Charles King, and dropped the journal with the vehement ejaculation, "Infamous!" "This is absolutely a species of impiety for which I want words to express my abhorrence," he entered in his diary. (Allan Nevins, *The Evening Post, etc.*, p. 152.)

The enthusiasm of Leggett sometimes carried further than the more tempered liberalism of Bryant could follow. He shared Leggett's distrust of Marshall and Hamilton, but he seems to have been only a moderate supporter of Locofoco principles. The paper had been brought close upon financial breakers by its attack on the money-interests. The working classes read it eagerly, but their indorsement could not make good the loss of advertising and patronage by the wealthy; yet even in such straits Bryant remained true to his liberalism and joined his associates in upholding the proletarian cause. The labor union movement had aroused the wrath of the employers and the courts were appealed to to suppress it. In May, 1836, "twenty-one journeymen tailors who had formed a union were indicted for a conspiracy injurious to trade and commerce," and after a trial the presiding judge charged the jury to bring in a verdict of guilty. Bryant at once attacked the judge in the *Evening Post:*

We do not admit, until we have further examined the question, that the law is as laid down by the Judge; but if it be, the sooner such a tyrannical and wicked law is abrogated the better. . . . The idea that arrangements and combinations for certain rates of wages are injurious to trade and commerce, is as absurd as the idea that the current prices of the markets, which are always the the result of understandings and combinations, are injurious. (*Ibid.*, pp. 164–165.)

When the tailors were heavily fined by the court Bryant returned to the attack. He again pointed out the fatuousness of the legal logic by showing how the very price current was a similar evidence of conspiracy, and then appealed to a sense of common fairness:

Can anything be imagined more abhorrent to every sentiment of generosity and justice, than the law which arms the rich with the legal right to fix, by assize, the wages of the poor? If this is not slavery, we have forgotten its definition. Strike the right of associating for the sale of labor from the privileges of a freeman, and you may as well bind him to a master, or ascribe him to the soil. (*Ibid.*, p. 165.)

From defending the rights of free labor to defending the rights of free speech was an easy step. When James G. Birney's Abolitionist press was suppressed by a Cincinnati mob, Bryant spoke out vigorously. "So far as we are concerned, we are resolved that this despotism shall neither be submitted to nor encouraged. . . . We are resolved that the subject of slavery shall be, as it ever has been, as free a subject for discussion, and argument, and declamation, as the difference between whiggism and democracy, or the difference between Arminians and Calvinists" (*ibid.*, p. 171). And when Elijah P. Lovejoy was murdered and his press thrown into the river, Bryant replied to those who believed that the Abolitionists had got their deserts: "Whether they erred or not in their opinions, they did not err in the conviction of their right, as citizens of a democratic State, to express them; nor did they err in defending their rights with an obstinacy that yielded only to death" (*ibid.*, pp. 171–172). From the defense of free speech Bryant went forward to the defense of free soil, and in 1848 he bolted Lewis Cass, the Democratic nominee, and joined the "Barnburner" movement that nominated Martin Van Buren. The terse pronouncement of the convention, indeed, might well be taken as an epitome and summary of Bryant's lifelong liberalism—"We inscribe on our banner Free Soil, Free Speech, Free Labor, and Free Men."

A trenchant critic of the rising capitalism, delighting in exposing the fallacies of the new economics and in pricking the bladders of political reputations—suggesting, for example, that it was scarcely god-like of the great Webster to accept a purse of $65,000 from his high tariff friends—Bryant was perhaps the most distinguished of the liberals created by the revolutions that were enthroning the middle class in power. The simplicity of his *laissez-faire* philosophy, like his admiration for "Old Bullion" Benton—whom he rated one of the greatest statesmen of the times—may seem somewhat old-fashioned today; but his ingrained democracy, his sturdy defense of the rights of free men, his championship of unpopular causes, his tolerance and fairness and keen sense of justice, ought not to seem old-fashioned. He may not have been a great poet, but he was a great American.

II

HORACE GREELEY: *Yankee Radical*

Horace Greeley has suffered far more disastrously than Bryant the common fate of journalists, yet his place in nineteenth-century America was too important and his influence on current democratic ideals too great, to be carelessly ignored. A Yankee radical transported to New York, he was the spokesman of the common sense and practical intelligence of the plain people of the North, seeking to understand the revolutionary upheaval then going forward, and bring it if possible to some issue in elementary justice. Far from being the visionary he was so often accounted, he was the most practical of men, accepting fact and seeking to square theory with reality; as ready to adopt new social machinery as the mill-owner to adopt a new invention. If there were social maladjustments, why should they not be set right? The patent confusions of the times seemed to him a challenge to the common intelligence. If civilization meant anything it ought to mean a generous life for the producing mass, and with the abundant resources of America the common well-being would never lie in jeopardy if simple justice prevailed. America had not yet fulfilled its promise; it had not yet become the haven for the poor and outcast its potential means allowed; nor with its growing cities where poverty found a congenial home, and its patrimony of raw lands flung to speculators, was it likely to become so unless greater ingenuity were applied to the problem. The industrial revolution was driving western civilization into unchartered seas; clearly, it was only common sense to take bearings and lay as fair a course as possible. To accomplish this Greeley was ready to entertain any promising suggestion. Intellectually curious, he had the wit to understand that the older agrarian America was being destroyed by forces that could not be stopped; they could only be guided. His eyes were wide open to what was taking place. He foresaw certain consequences implicit in the industrial revolution that his fellows were blind to. If it brought material advancement and the multiplication of conveniences—things excellent in themselves —it brought as well a sinister exploitation of the producers, as England with her Manchester slums had learned to her sorrow. If America were driving straight toward such deadseas of wretchedness, surely only a conscienceless fool would refuse to help trim the sails.

No more admirable Yankee than Horace Greeley ever went West to make his fortune. With his Yankee capacity for hard work, his daring enterprise, his vigorous independence, he embodied an extremely sensitive social conscience, keen sympathy for those who do the work of the world, and a transparent honesty of mind and purpose. Bred up in the narrow poverty of the Vermont hills, remote from the culture of Boston and Cambridge, he retained the angularities that marked his frontier origin. His ungainly and shabby exterior was the outward, visible sign of a niggardly youth; yet underneath the uncouth exterior was as warm a heart as ever beat in Yankee bosom. His early life was a bitter struggle, aggravated by the succession of economic depressions that from 1819 to 1838 repeatedly brought hardship upon the country. Cradled thus in the anxieties attending the transition from an agrarian to a capitalistic order, nurtured in the harassing uncertainties that followed the break-up of the old static economy, he longed for a more rational social system, unsoiled by the heart-breaking wreckages that drifted into the new slums, unembittered by the lonely tragedies that laid a blight on the frontier. He believed that the honest worker, whether in the factory or on the farm, deserved a better fate than commonly fell to his lot. It was a scandal that poverty should dog his footsteps in a land potentially so rich as America; that those who did the necessary work of society should find themselves reduced to the status of the slave, whether black or white; and he early determined to explore the reasons why the workingman received so small an increment of the augmenting wealth of the industrial revolution. His struggles to gain a foothold in New York set him upon thinking, and before he was thirty he began those speculations on ways and means of returning to the producer a fair reward for his work, that were to occupy his mind to the last. The farmer and the wage-earner he took to his heart, and the furtherance of their well-being—despite the persistent and vindictive opposition he encountered—became a major objective of *The Tribune*.

Greeley's mind was as homespun as his clothes, and he never quite outgrew certain Vermont parochialisms that retarded his intellectual development. The environment in which he was bred was staunchly Federalist-Whig, marked by the exuberantly nationalistic spirit that sprang from the War of 1812; and the seeds of his national economy were sown in those years when to become nationally self-sufficient was the great ideal of America. It was natural for him to accept the leadership of Clay, whom he idolized, and to look to the Federal government for an adequate policy of internal improvements and national development. "We Vermonters were all Protectionists," he said in his *Recollections*. In 1828 the village of Poultney, where he was serving his apprenticeship, gave 334 votes for John Quincy Adams and only four for Jackson. Starting with this back-country faith in a benevolent paternalism, Greeley early began his speculations on an ideal national economy; and the conclusion to which he came, and which he never saw reason to question later, was that government must impose an intelligent wardship upon economic forces, that, left to themselves, tend always to the anarchy of individualism. He had suffered in his own person from the inadequacy and uncertainty of the financial and industrial machinery of the times; he was impatient of all purposeless floundering; the more he read the more rational it seemed that statesmanship must be judged by its intelligent concern to lessen the social waste and reduce the social friction. *Laissez faire* he pronounced a "suicidal" policy; it was an invitation to anarchy; it had impoverished India, and must impoverish America. From a critical study of the teachings of the Manchester school he came to two major conclusions: that agriculture and manufacturing are complementary industries, and the closer they are drawn together the better for the nation; and that a wide national economy can result only from investing the state with adequate regulatory powers. Hence his approval of Clay's American System. The judicious intervention of government by means of a protective tariff to foster the "infant industries" would secure them a domestic market that would—he allowed himself to hope—be regulated by domestic competition, would do away with the waste represented by transportation charges, and would return to the farmer an increase in price represented by those charges. In his opinion, however, protection was a temporary expedient, necessary only until American industries should get on their legs. "Protection is the shortest way to get free trade," he said in 1851 (*The Tribune*, January 23).

Greeley was never the tool of capitalistic interests that such an argument might seem to imply. All his mature life he persistently fought the aggressions of capitalism; yet in this crucial matter of protection his influence was thrown powerfully on its side, and the ingenious argument he expounded was at once taken over by the industrialists and used with telling effect. What particular turn he gave to the older Whig statement, adapting it to the prejudices of a more democratic electorate, a present-day economist has thus summarized:

The protective tariff, favored by the Whigs, was something different in his hands. The tariff arguments of his boyhood had been capitalistic arguments. Protect capital, their spokesman said, because wages are too high in this country. Eventually wages will come towards the European level and we shall not need protection. Greeley revised this plea; protect the wage earner, he said, in order that he may rise from this present condition of slavery. The only way to protect him against the foreign pauper is to protect the price of his product. But since capital owns and sells his product, we must needs protect capital. We know right well, he says, that a protective tariff cannot redress all wrongs. . . . The extent of its power to benefit the laborer is limited by the force and pressure of domestic competition, for which Political Economy has as yet devised no remedy. (John R. Commons,

"Horace Greeley and the Working Class Origins of the Republican Party," *Political Science Quarterly*, Vol. XXIV, pp. 468–488.)

The argument for protection has been little improved since it came from Greeley's hands in the late forties and early fifties.[2] Nor, it must be added, has political economy devised the remedy for the evils of competition, that Greeley was concerned about, unless monopolistic control be regarded as such. Considering his extraordinary influence with the mass of farmers north and west, it must be accounted a calamity to agrarian prospects that *The Tribune*—a paper that Professor Commons characterized as "the first and only great vehicle this country has known for the ideas and experiments of constructive democracy" —should have thrown its influence on the side of artificial industrial expansion. That the mind of the northern farmer became so deeply inoculated with protectionist views, and has since persistently remained so. was due to Horace Greeley far more than to any other man.

The irony of it becomes apparent when the deeper spirit of Greeley's life is probed. Though he called himself a Whig, he was in all fundamental interests and conceptions a Jeffersonian, seeking in the spirit of the great Virginian to fashion a new philosophy to suit the new times, more like him in free speculation than any other northern thinker of the day. It needed years for him to throw off the Federalist-Whig prepossessions of his youth, and work back to Jeffersonian fundamentals; but in the end he did work back, and in the end—always excepting this one matter of protection with its corollary of state paternalism—he came by his own path to the major conclusions Jefferson had reached a half century before. He was a spokesman of the older America seeking a way out of the confusions the middle class was bringing on the later America. In his social-mindedness that set justice above exploitation; in his readiness to change existing institutions in order to achieve justice; in his strong preference for an agrarian order as more wholesome than an industrial; in his trust in the good will of the plain people and faith in the local democracies; in his acceptance of the principle of states rights that during the struggle over slavery led him to advocate that the South be suffered to depart in peace:—in such conceptions he was a Neo-Jeffersonian, seeking to adapt the old principles to the needs of a different order. Greeley had never

[2] For his statement, see "Labor's Political Economy," in *Hints toward Reforms.*

read the works of the French Physiocrats; he was unacquainted with their doctrine of the *produit net;* very likely he would not have accepted their teachings to the extent that Jefferson did. Nevertheless from his own experience he had come to agree with them in the exaltation of agriculture over other forms of labor, as he had come to agree with them in their social-mindedness. Greeley may be accounted a stepson, at least, of the old French school.

That for so long a time he should have turned aside from the path of Jeffersonianism to immerse himself in Utopian speculations and adventures may appear strange; and yet for so eager and hopeful a temperament it was the most natural thing in the world. It marked a step in the speculations through which he passed in pursuit of that remedy for domestic competition which the political economists had not provided. He was twenty-nine when Albert Brisbane's *The Social Destiny of Mankind* appeared in 1840, and on October 21, 1841, the first comment on Fourier socialism was printed in *The Tribune,* then only six months old. Thereafter for years *The Tribune* was the chief organ for the spread of collectivistic principles in the United States, Brisbane expounding Fourierism in the fifties, and Karl Marx contributing a weekly letter on European movements in the sixties, while lesser men contributed freely according to their special Utopian lights. With all this Greeley was in profound sympathy. Much of the theory he did not agree with; many of the plans and specifications seemed to him ill conceived; but convinced of the gross evils of civilization he welcomed free speculation as promising the only hope for their cure. Like Jefferson and William Ellery Channing, he put his trust in the unshackled mind, for like them he believed in the essential excellence of human nature when unperverted by vicious institutions.

It was this romantic faith that induced him to invest heavily in time, thought and money, in the Fourieristic foundations of the forties, the North American Phalanx in particular offering an opportunity for experiment on a considerable scale. In his deep concern over the selfishness of the competitive struggle, he was willing to turn from the bankrupt political economists to consider the plans of the "social architects." From Plato down those architects had been engaged on plans of ideal commonwealths, wherein the principle of brotherhood should supersede the principle of competition, and he believed the time had come when the great experiment might be tried with some reasonable hope of success. If the principle of collectivism could be successfully substituted for a chaotic individualism, the solution of the ancient problem of social injustice might be in a way to be achieved. This in itself, he believed, "would do for domestic competition what protection would do for foreign competition" (John R. Commons, *Horace Greeley, etc.*). When associationism failed, Greeley turned his thoughts eagerly to coöperation as a promising means of eliminating the waste of the middleman and destroying the wage system.[3] Somehow the middleman must be got rid of, he believed, if labor were to reap an adequate reward from its work. If one method did not achieve the result, another must be tried. To leave off seeking a solution was to acknowledge that society must remain a pigsty, with the strongest hogs appropriating the swill.

Such persistent venturing into Utopian experiment made Greeley the laughing-stock of more practical men who accepted the acquisitive instinct as the voice of God and were busily engaged in exploitation for their individual advantage; more important, it reveals how tenuous were the ties that held him to the Whiggery he still professed. Stalwart Whigs of the Webster school, middle-class bankers and industrialists, grew impatient with such pestilent heresies as exuded from *The Tribune,* and denied that Greeley was a Whig. In 1847 *The Courier and Enquirer* angrily protested:

There can be no peace in the Whig ranks while the old New York Tribune is continued to be called Whig. . . . The *principles* of the Whig party are well defined; they are *conservative* and inculcate a regard for the laws and support of all established institutions of the country. They eschew *radicalism* in every form; they sustain the constitution and the laws; they foster a spirit of *patriotism.* . . . The better way for the Tribune would be at once to admit that it is only Whig on the subject of the Tariff . . . and then devote itself to the advocacy of Anti-Rent, Abolition, Fourierite, and Vote Yourself a Farm doctrines. (*The Weekly Tribune,* August 21, 1847; quoted in Commons, *Horace Greeley, etc.,* p. 473.)

The real animus of the middle-class dislike of Greeley is to be sought in his active championship of the great exploited classes, the farmer and wage-earner. He was always sowing the seeds of discontent amongst them The

[3] See "The Organization of Labor," in *Hints toward Reforms.*

betterment of their condition, he believed, was fundamental to any sound social progress. He was convinced that their well-being was interrelated; that whatever affected the one must affect the other. If the city proletariat were prosperous, the farmer's produce sold at better prices; and if the farmers were prosperous, the country would draw off the surplus labor from the towns and thereby sustain the wage scale. The key to the situation, he came to believe, lay in the land situation. The application of science to farm processes was a necessary preliminary to agrarian improvement, and he put the great influence of *The Tribune* behind the movement for scientific instruction in crop handling. But far more fundamental and immediate was the need of a drastic change in the Federal laws governing land sales. Believing that the wild lands of the West were a natural refuge for those who fled from the exploitation of the factory, he was concerned that those lands should be made available to the poorest settler. Greeley very well knew that the ruthless exploitation of the English proletariat was an inevitable consequence of the enclosure movement. Dispossessed of their land and lacking means to emigrate, the peasant had been thrown like sheep to the industrial wolves. Sunk in a hopeless wage-slavery, the Manchester factory-hand was an object-lesson in the fate that awaits the landless, too striking for a shrewd observer like Greeley to miss; and his agrarian program was proof that he had taken Goldsmith's warning to heart:

> Ill fares the land, to hastening ills a prey,
> Where wealth accumulates and men decay.

The freeholder, whatever the hardships of his lot, was still a free man and a free citizen, no fodder to fling to a huge-bellied industrialism.

To keep him thus free and independent, Greeley put himself vigorously into the great agrarian movement of the forties and fifties—the movement to democratize the national land policy that eventuated in the Homestead Act of 1862. The conception of the strategic usefulness of the western lands as a refuge for the city proletariat he derived from George Henry Evans, who in 1828 had established *The Working Man's Advocate,* was active in organization work with the mechanics of New York City, and contributed to the cause numerous pamphlets, one of which, issued in 1844, was entitled *Vote Yourself a Farm.* The pioneer work had been well done when, in 1845, Greeley joined the movement, accepted the arguments, and thenceforth was tireless in spreading the doctrine. The principle on which he should work he laid down in *The Tribune:*

The freedom of the public lands to actual settlers and the limitation of future acquisitions of land to some reasonable amount, are . . . measures which seem to us vitally necessary to the ultimate emancipation from thraldom and misery. What is mainly wanted is that each man should have an assured chance to earn and then an assurance of the just fruits of his labors. (Quoted in Commons, *Horace Greeley, etc.*, p. 482.)

To accomplish this result Greeley introduced into Congress the first Homestead bill, according to the proposed terms of which any *bona fide* settler might file on one hundred and sixty acres of public land, to be paid for within seven years at the rate of $1.25 an acre; all public lands not thus filed on by actual settlers were to be listed at $5.00 an acre.[4] Greeley's bill was aimed directly at the old scandal of favoring wealthy speculators at the expense of the small man, a scandal that ran far back into the past. The traditional argument had been that the government could not go into the retail land business, but should sell in great blocks to responsible men who should in turn put settlers on the land. The policy had bred huge corruption, it had aroused bitter opposition, and had roiled the politics of more than one state holding western lands. In the early years of the century the province of Maine had repudiated Massachusetts Federalism and turned to the Republican party by reason of discontent with the old system[5] and the fierce Anti-Rent riots in New York State were of recent occurrence. It was against this policy of favoritism that Greeley protested, thereby bringing on his head sharp criticism from the respectable class, who declaimed bitterly against the demagoguery of a man who openly advocated a "vote yourself a farm" policy. To pay a middleman's price for public land, after that land had been wheedled from Congress in the dark of the moon, seemed to many gentlemen the only honest and patriotic way; but Greeley was unconvinced by such reasoning, and his concern over the problem became acute when the railroads began to appropriate huge tracts of the public domain. The policy of subsidizing them thus seemed to him wasteful and vicious; it ran directly counter to his fundamental principle

[4] See Charles Sotheran, *Horace Greeley*, p. 255.
[5] See William A. Robinson, *Jeffersonian Democracy in New England*, pp. 43–45.

of limitation of land holdings; it was repeating on a vast scale the ominous landlordism of the past.

Man has a *natural right* to produce and acquire property [he wrote], and therefore, I condemn a system of Land Monopoly, which robs the producer of one-half to seven-eighths of the fruits of his toil; and often dooms him to absolute starvation on the soil which he has faithfully and effectively tilled! The right of owning land is one thing: the right to own thousands and even millions of acres of land is another. The problem is learning to distinguish the one from the other. (*The Tribune*, April 24, 1849.)

"Settle the lands compactly and railroads will be constructed through them rapidly and abundantly," he said later. "The grants do essentially interfere with the true policy of granting lands in limited allotment to actual settlers" (*ibid.*, March 16, 1852). His proposed policy was far-sighted and socially just, but it was repudiated by a speculative middle class that would not have its unearned increment curtailed by visionaries.

Thoughtful as was Greeley's concern for the farmer, his concern for the city worker was even greater. The wretchedness of the New York slums was daily under his eye, and his honest heart was troubled at what he saw. That he should have sympathized with the emerging labor movement was inevitable; his conscience dictated his stand, but his eager mind drove him to intelligent inquiry and vigorous support. He was the first American of wide reputation and influence to give serious consideration to the effects on the working class of the industrial revolution with its gospel of exploitation. The exploitation of natural resources was well enough; but the exploitation of human life was a different matter. A material prosperity based on social injustice, a civilization founded on slavery, he would have none of. That this great matter of slavery was inadequately understood and too narrowly interpreted by the Abolitionists, he was early convinced. He agreed with William Grayson and the southern apologists, that slavery existed in New York as well as in Charleston. "The worker of the Nineteenth Century," he said in *The Emancipation of Labor*, "stands a sad and care-worn man"; in America as well as in Europe he is falling into "that train of thought which is beginning to encircle the globe, and of which the burden may be freely rendered thus—'*Why should those by whose toil ALL comforts and luxuries are produced or made available enjoy so scanty a share of them?*'" If Theodore Parker could have lived a few years longer he must have shared Greeley's concern; but amongst the Abolitionists only Wendell Phillips joined with him in espousing the cause of the working class. Others held aloof. When appealed to in the middle-seventies to aid the labor movement, William Lloyd Garrison denied the existence of wage-slavery in America, and indignantly declined to take part in the proletarian agitation.[6]

Greeley's views would be reckoned advanced even today; before the Civil War they were regarded as incendiary, calculated to awaken class prejudice in a country where, as all patriotic Americans knew, classes did not exist. What, for example, could simple-minded Abolitionists make of a letter he wrote declining to attend an anti-slavery convention in Cincinnati in 1845?

You will readily understand that, if I regard your enterprise with less absorbing interest than you do, it is not that I deem Slavery a less but a greater evil. If I am less troubled concerning the Slavery prevalent in Charleston and New-Orleans, it is because I see so much Slavery in New-York, which appears to claim my first efforts. . . . [I would not] undertake to say that the Slavery of the South is not more hideous in kind and degree than that which prevails at the North. The fact that it is more flagrant and palpable renders opposition to it comparatively easy and its speedy downfall certain. But how can I devote myself to a crusade against distant servitude, when I discern its essence pervading my immediate community and neighborhood?

I understand by Slavery, that condition in which one human being exists mainly as a convenience for other human beings— in which the time, the exertions, the faculties of a part of the Human Family are made to subserve, not their own development, physical, intellectual, and moral, but the comfort, advantage, or caprices of others. . . . In short, wherever service is rendered from one human being to another . . . where the relation . . . is one not of affection and reciprocal good offices, but of authority, social ascendency and power over subsistence on the one hand, and of necessity, servility, and degradation on the other—there, in my view, is Slavery. ("Slavery at Home," in *Hints toward Reforms*.)

Here is a definition that may well be considered Utopian; but however transcendental his general conception, Greeley was far too practical to pursue abstractions. Having diagnosed the common disease that infects all modern civilization, he was willing to use remedies that came to hand. Before 1845 he opposed labor legislation, on the ground

[6] Garrison, *Life of Garrison*, Vol. IV, p. 248.

that the evil was social; but later he supported the movement to limit the legal working day by statute. More and more, however, he came to believe that any lasting betterment must come from effective organization of the workers; that the salvation of labor lay in its own hands; and the great end towards which he looked was coöperation. The stumbling-block that stood in the way of coöperative effort was the common distrust and suspicion that poisoned the minds of working men; until they emptied their hearts of that evil, the path that labor must follow would be flinty and its life meager and hard.

An incorrigible idealist, clearly, was this Yankee plebeian whom Cooper believed a vulgarian, Godkin held in contempt, and Bryant turned his back on and would not speak to—a strange, child-like figure, with his round moon-face, eyes blinking through spectacles and a fringe of whiskers that invited the pencil of the cartoonist—yet carrying the sorrows of the world in his heart and vexing his soul with all the problems of society; an idealist who in the most sordid place in America, and after years of fruitless experiment, could still stand before his fellow Americans and thus sum up his social philosophy—"the avocations of Life, and the usages and structure of Society, the relations of Power to Humility, of Wealth to Poverty, of served to servant, must all be fused in the crucible of Human Brotherhood, and whatever abides not the test, rejected" (*Hints toward Reforms*, p. 400). In this faith— foolish it may be accounted by practical men, and futile, but certainly not mean, not ignoble—Horace Greeley lived and worked; to it he gave such strength and powers as were his, and he died at sixty-one of a broken heart. He foolishly wished to be President, but the American electorate that read his paper refused its votes, and his hopes were destroyed by the careless many who were untroubled about industrial pigstys.

III
HERMAN MELVILLE: *Pessimist*

Set down beside the austere Bryant and the plebeian Greeley, Herman Melville seems grotesquely out of company; and yet such proximities may suggest, better perhaps than words, an explanation of the futility of his dreams and the irony of the bitter penance of his days. Lifelong he was lacerated by the coldly moral in his environment, and harassed by the crudely practical; and without forcing the comparison, one may feel that Bryant and Greeley embodied in nobler form the twin forces that seized upon his bold and rich nature, and bound it to the rocks to be fed on by eagles. Like Jacob he wrestled all night with an angel, yet got no blessing from the touched thigh. Instead, his free spirit was tormented and his adventurous heart seared with fire. Far more truly than of DeQuincey might one say of Melville: *Eccovi*, this little child has been in hell! All the powers of darkness fought over him, all the devils plagued him. They drove him down into the gloom of his tormented soul, and if they did not conquer, they left him maimed and stricken. The golden dreams of transcendental faith, that buoyed up Emerson and gave hope to Thoreau, turned to ashes in his mouth; the white gleams of mysticism that now and then lighted up his path died out and left him in darkness. Life could not meet the demands he made on it, certainly not life in America in the eighteen-fifties; the malady lay deeper than Greeley thought —it lay in the futility of life itself; and so after pursuing his vain dreams to the ends of the seas, the rebellious transcendentalist withdrew within himself while awaiting annihilation. There is no other tragedy in American letters comparable to the tragedy of Herman Melville. Bryant's melancholy is only the gentle pensiveness of twilight compared to the midnight of his pessimism. Hawthorne's gloom is no more than the skeptical questioning of life by a nature that knew no fierce storms; Poe's is only the atrabilious wretchedness of a dipsomaniac.

In the presence of a nature so tempestuous and fiercely honest, it is a rash critic who will dogmatize. There is no simple clue to his mystery, no common pass-key to unlock his mind. Raymond Weaver in his brilliantly creative study has perhaps done all that the critic can to light up the darkness, and later commentators can only follow in his footsteps. In so far as a simple explanation may suffice, the biographer finds it in certain frustrations that curdled the milk of his romance and turned it sour. Like Mark Twain in later years, he recoiled savagely from the smug conventions of society; but when he spoke out his views— instead of discreetly locking them up in his safe—and found himself fiercely assailed for unorthodoxy, he bade the world go to the devil and would have nothing more to do with its praise or blame. A proud sensitive nature, he took the world's contumely *au tragique*, and suffered it to mortify him. Or perhaps he was more like James Branch Cabell than Mark Twain. An arch romantic, he vainly sought to erect his romantic dreams as a defense against reality, and suffered disaster. In love with the ideal, and pursuing it in a wild adventure into the South Seas—his magic realm of Poictesme—yet "not so much bound to any haven ahead as rushing from all havens astern," he found there only disenchantment. Seeking his satisfactions in love of mother and wife, he came upon utter disillusion. The austerely prim and coldly correct Maria Gansevoort, to whom his boyish heart yielded itself passionately, was clearly no woman to satisfy his need of intelligent sympathy, and he fled moodily from the pale negations of a stifling environment. Even the finely loyal Elizabeth Shaw whom he married seems only to have completed his disillusion, and he withdrew into his study, and falling into "Plato's honied head," like Tashtego into the whale's head, "sweetly," or wretchedly, "perished there." It is the plague of the idealizing mind that is forever comparing a wife in her morning kimono with the Helen of his dreams. It is the curse of possession that plays havoc with romance; and because Melville's dreams were passionately beautiful, because he made heavy demands on life, his disillusion was bitter. And so like Felix Kennaston in Cabell's *Cream of the Jest,* and like Shelley in *Epipsychidion,* Melville fashioned his dream-figure to love. The elusive figure of Yillah in *Mardi,* whom he loves and loses and seeks, in a madly grotesque and satirical pursuit through all the civilizations of his land of Poictesme, is so suggestive of Cabell's *Domnei,* that it perhaps may be accounted the latter's prototype.

Remembering the mingled strains of Melville's ancestry, the critic is tempted to discover in his New England blood the source of his transcendental visions. Yet the influence is not easy to trace. Half Dutch and half Yankee, he certainly got his vigorous physique and hot temper from the former. His maternal grandfather, Major General Peter Gansevoort, was a huge bulk of a man who achieved high distinction in the Revolutionary War, and whose traditional prowess filled the boy's heart with pride. His mother, Maria Gansevoort, whom the son closely resembled in physique, was crossed in blood with that of the Van Rensselaers, the Ten Broecks, the Van Schaicks—the proudest families of the old Dutch *régime*—and was deeply imbued with the distinction of her patroon ancestry—"a cold, proud woman, arrogant in the sense of her name, her blood, and the affluence of her forebears" (Weaver,

Herman Melville, p. 34). His debt to the New England strain is not so easily appraised. His paternal grandfather, Major Thomas Melville of Boston, a graduate of Princeton and wealthy in his own name and through his wife Priscilla Scollay, was not without his flashes of enthusiasm in early life, taking part with Joseph Story's father in the Boston Tea Party. But his incipient radicalism was soon washed out of him; he turned rigidly conservative, and to his death in 1832 he lingered in the twilight of the eighteenth century. As Federal naval officer of the port of Boston, he was a familiar figure in his cocked hat and knee breeches; and it was of him that Holmes wrote the verses, *The Last Leaf*.

He was of Scotch descent, and Melville's father traced the family line back to the thirteenth century, Herman Melville being twentieth in direct descent from Sir Richard Melvill, who in 1296 was forced to swear allegiance to Edward I of England. The blood seems to have run somewhat thin in Allan Melville, a conventional, pragmatic soul, who after making five trips to Europe, at the age of thirty-two, having carefully weighed the advantages, fixed his affections on Maria Gansevoort whom he met at Albany, and wooed with more propriety than passion. He entered business in New York City as an importer of French goods; but hard times descended on "the greatest universal mart in the world," and in 1832, when Herman was thirteen, Allan Melville died leaving Maria Gansevoort and her eight children pretty nearly penniless. The struggle with poverty set its mark on the cold, proud woman whose ambitions centered about the success of affluence; and it left a mark of quite another sort on the son who was soon to measure her ideals with devastatingly critical eyes. The ways of mother and son were at the parting.

The volcanic passions pent up in Herman Melville's heart, the ardent imagination that sent him forth on long quests and brought him home empty-handed, can scarcely be traced to any source in Maria Gansevoort or Allan Melville. A strange, incomprehensible child he seemed to his mother, and strange and incomprehensible he remained in the eyes of the family—an ugly duckling of another breed than theirs. A bitter sense of aloofness and alienation from the intimacies of family sympathy seems early to have taken possession of him, and he felt himself quietly thrust out of the circle of respectable contacts. Melville's writings are filled with thinly veiled autobiography, and it is a careless reader who does not see in *Pierre* and *Moby Dick* confessions as frank as Rousseau's. "Call me Ishmael," is the opening injunction of the latter, and the book closes with a glimpse of "the devious cruising *Rachel*, that in retracing search after her missing children, only found another orphan" (Weaver, *Herman Melville*, p. 62). An Ishmael Melville unhappily conceived himself to be, an outcast and wanderer on the earth because man is an outcast and wanderer, to whom Nirvana is the only comfort and hope; and when he returned disillusioned from the South Seas, when he found no home by his own fireside, when he discovered his transcendental craftsmanship driving on the rocks of economic necessity, when the public rejected his mystical dreams and he was inexorably "damned by dollars," he perforce turned in upon his own broodings and sought solace in Plato. Driven by need from his hill farm in the Berkshires, he buried himself in the "Babylonish brick-kiln of New York," to pass long years pottering about the customhouse. It was the vast futility of life as he experienced it, that sent him to his study to find there such compensation as he might.

The stages in Melville's progress towards Nirvana are sufficiently marked by the four books, *Typee, Mardi, Moby Dick,* and *Pierre*. The first is his answer to the French romantic Utopia of man in a state of nature. That the rankling wounds in man's heart are poisoned, if not originally inflicted, by social institutions, he was partly convinced, and he felt a lively concern lest western civilization should bring its futile restlessness to the simple island people. The kindliness and simplicity of life in the valley of Typee, the compensating virtues of the unsophisticated primitive, he found lovable; but as the unhappy heir of centuries of Christian conscience, as a child of Hebraic ideals of righteousness, he could not eradicate the deep roots of ethical unrest. With Fayaway it was different. "Civilization had given her no veils; Christianity had given her no compunctions. She was neither a mystery nor a sin" (*ibid.*, p. 260). But he could not become a simple child of nature had he wanted to. He could never find his Nirvana in mere sensuousness; he could not sink into the mud of animal existence. Even while he bathed in the languorous calm of Typee, floating idly with Fayaway on the stream of being, his heart was beyond the narrow hills, and a cosmic nostalgia seized upon him. That chapter of his life ended in futility, and so he made his way back once more to the familiar places, with expectation still undaunted. Certain of his experiences on that return journey he has recorded in *White Jacket,* the story of his cruise on a man-of-war; and how near it brought him to oblivion is told in the episode of the threatened flogging before the mast, when fate intervened to save Melville from flinging himself overboard, carrying with him the brutal captain of the *Neversink.*

Amidst the constrictions of the old world to which he had come back, a fresh vision of happiness opened to him in his love for Elizabeth Shaw, and he made a desperate plunge into marriage. The post-thalamion of that thwarted romance was *Mardi*—a far-ranging "pilgrimage for a lost glamour," "a quest after some total and undivined possession of that holy and mysterious joy that touched Melville during the period of his courtship" (*ibid.,* p. 279). *Mardi* is a vast welter of satire and idealism, formless and wild, which in turn was no more than prologue to *Moby Dick.* This colossal book, fierce as *Gulliver,* broad as Rabelais, with its *saeva indignatio* that laughs as it rends life, is the great confession of his defeat. "It is good to laugh," he says in *Mardi,* "though the laugh be hollow. Women sob, and are rid of their grief; men laugh and retain it. Ha! ha! how demoniacs shout; how all skeletons grin; we all die with a rattle. Humor, thy laugh is divine." And the conclusion to which the philosopher comes is this: "Beatitude there is none. And your only Mardian happiness is but exemption from great woes—no more. Great Love is sad; and heaven is Love. Sadness makes the silence throughout the realms of space; sadness is universal and eternal" (*ibid.,* p. 279).

After *Moby Dick,* what remained but to put the external world of experience aside and turn in upon his own thwarted hopes to analyze them? *Pierre, or the Ambiguities* is his spiritual autobiography, the confession of a stricken soul. In the inconsequential matter of plot, a story of incest and murder and suicide, in its deeper purpose, it is a wild fierce tale of mortal passions, that traces the *élan* of mystical idealism to the buried depths of procreative instinct. It is the last bewildering attempt to understand the sources of the dream that had ridden him, and it is discovered in the passionate struggles of Enceladus, titanic offspring of the incestuous union between Heaven and Earth, to regain the kingdom from which he has been thrust. In *Mardi* the search for Yillah had been carried on under the watchful eye of Hautia, the temptress, whom "his whole heart abhorred," yet to whom at last he went in her bower of Flozella-a-Nina—"The Last-Verse-of-the-Song"; for in "some mysterious way seemed Hautia and Yillah connected." In *Pierre* Hautia reappears as Isabel, likewise a child of Heaven and Earth, who is set over against Lucy—the pure daughter of Heaven alone; and this dark Isabel robed in the midnight of her hair, by appealing unconsciously to Pierre's noblest impulses, draws him from the safe orbit of the Gansevoort moralities, and makes of him "the fool of Truth, the fool of Virtue, the fool of Fate." Isabel is wild, unquestioning, mysterious passion, untouched by any Hebraisms; and this half-sister of his blood, this lovely embodiment of his star-crossed dreams, drives him unwittingly to destruction. Pierre learns at last that the vision brings poison in its kisses, for the divine in the heart of Enceladus is mingled with the clay of earth. The dream is man's final ironical curse; Yillah and Hautia and Lucy and Isabel—changing embodiments of the same mystical idealism—bring death to their lovers —this is the conclusion of *Pierre*, a conclusion that Mr. Cabell would not take kindly to. It was a black and bitter book, like *Moby Dick* "broiled in hell-fire," to fling at an easy-going public that cherished its Gansevoort conventions. With its fierce disillusions *Pierre* is the apogee and Nirvana of the spiritual romanticisms of the day.

That Melville was the spiritual child of Jean Jacques, that the consuming nostalgia he suffered from was mortal, the most casual acquaintance with his passionate rebellions should make clear; and that his pessimism was a natural end and outcome of his transcendental speculations, once those speculations had come to intimate contact with life, is perhaps equally clear. Transcendentalism in Concord village and at Walden pond was one thing. Emerson's infrequent anger at the folly of men was soothed by the perfect art with which he phrased it, and never seriously ruffled his temperamental placidity. Thoreau's mystical communings were with the young god Pan; he was too wise to seek to domesticate a woodland nymph, and he was fortunate in escaping the dun twilight that gathers about the slow years of physical decay. But transcendentalism in the forecastle of the whaler *Acushnet*, transcendentalism that drove fiercely into the blood-red sunsets of dwarfing seas, transcendentalism in the hot and passionate heart of a man whose vast dreams outran his feet—this was something very different from the gentle mysticism of cooler natures and unembittered hearts where no Promethean fires were raging.

For Herman Melville, amidst the nameless obscenities of an alien environment, to keep his faith in the goodness of life strong and sweet, would have needed the boundless charity and simple paganism of Walt Whitman. But unfortunately for his peace of mind, though he might immerse himself in Plato, Melville was no Greek; he was Hebraic rather, out of Ecclesiastes, and Solomon and Jesus. "Away," he cries in *Pierre*, "ye chattering apes of a sophomorean Spinoza and Plato, who once did all but delude me that the night was day, and pain only a tickle. Explain this darkness, exorcise this devil, ye cannot. Tell me not, thou inconceivable coxcomb of a Goethe, that the universe cannot spare thee and thy immortality. . . . Already the universe gets on without thee. . . . Thou wert but the pretentious, heartless part of a man. Lo! I hold thee in this hand, and thou art crushed in it like an egg from which the meat hath been sucked" (Chapter XXII —3). From the lips of the ancient Preacher he had learned that all is vanity—even Pan. "The truest of men was the Man of Sorrows," he says, "and the truest of all books is Solomon's, and Ecclesiastes is the fine hammered steel of woe. All is vanity. ALL. . . . He who . . . calls Cowper, Young, Pascal, Rousseau, poor devils all of sick men; and throughout a care-free lifetime swears by Rabelais as passing wise, and therefore jolly;—not that man is fitted to sit down on tombstones, and break the green damp mould with unfathomably wondrous Solomon" (Weaver, *Herman Melville*, pp. 151–152). After *Pierre* came *Clarel*—years later —in which the theological doubts and religious unrest that mark the poetry of Arnold and Clough in England came to expression in a world that was untouched by them.[7] The abyss that lay between Melville and America had become deeper and wider.

Like all the transcendentalists Melville was a democrat, but his democracy sprang rather from his sympathies than from his philosophy. It was a democracy learned rather from Ecclesiastes than from Emerson; it sprang from his pessimism rather than from any transcendental faith in the divinity of man. He knew only too well how weak and foolish are the children of Adam; but in presence of the common fate to which the indifferent years hurry us, how stupid and callous are the social distinctions that society

[7] See Weaver, p. 365.

erects! Why should not life be a leveler, as well as death? His experience before the mast had taught him sympathy for the common man; he regarded quizzically the ways of the exploiting few and the sufferings of the exploited many; and he smiled ironically at the neat little classification that divides the human animal into sinners and saints. He was as comprehensive a democrat as Whitman, of the same all-embracing school that denied the common social and ethical categories of excellence; but alienated from his fellows, not drawn to them as Whitman was. It was not a sense of social aloofness that held him apart, but the isolation of loneliness. "When you see or hear of my ruthless democracy on all sides," he wrote to Hawthorne, "you may possibly feel a touch of a shrink, or something of that sort. It is but nature to be shy of a mortal who boldly declares that a thief in jail is as honorable a personage as Gen. George Washington. . . . It seems an inconsistency to assert unconditioned democracy in all things, and yet confess a dislike to all mankind—in the mass. But not so" (*ibid.*, pp. 320–321). He then goes on: "But truth is the silliest thing under the sun," and does not deign to explain. "Believe me," he says of *Pierre*, "you will pronounce Pierre a thorough-going Democrat in time; perhaps a little too Radical altogether to your fancy" (*ibid.*, p. 37).

Such a man would not so much turn critic as embody criticism. His life—even more than Emerson's—laid upon America was a yardstick to measure the shortcomings of a professed civilization. Cooper was a critic whom America could understand, and America hated him for his unpleasant frankness. Melville it could not understand, and it turned away and ignored him. Perhaps it was well enough that his generation could not comprehend his devastating speculations, and called him mad; or it would have cried out to crucify this maligner of all the tribal fetishes. He would level every barrier against the unpleasant that his age was erecting. He outran Thoreau in contempt for current material ideals. To turn scornfully away from the triumphs of his fellows—from the fruits of the industrial revolution and the romantic gospel of progress—this was incomprehensible blasphemy! Yet what had Herman Melville in common with middle-class America? Its hopes and fears were not his. He was troubled about life, and not about things. He was not concerned about politics or the political state. He was not concerned with trade, or money-getting, or romantic imperialisms. He was not even greatly concerned with political democracy, although in his time he had been as hot a republican as the best of them. The shoddy democracy of his time made his gorge rise; and to this shoddy democracy that shrilly proclaimed its excellence he paid his respects in words that suggest Lowell's *Cathedral*, but with a depth of significance that Lowell was incapable of. In the poem *Clarel*, into which Melville crowded so much of his later speculations, he comments thus:

> This world clean fails me: still I yearn. . . .

> This side the dark and hollow bound
> Lies there no unexplored rich ground?
> *Some other world:* well, there's the New—
> Ah, joyless and ironic too!

> Ay, Democracy
> Lops, lops; and where's her planted bed?
> The future, what is that to her
> Who vaunts she's no inheritor?
> 'Tis in her mouth, not in her heart.
> The past she spurns, though 'tis the past
> From which she gets her saving part—
> That Good which lets her evil last.

> Behold her whom the panders crown,
> Harlot on horseback, riding down
> The very Ephesians who acclaim
> This great Diana of ill fame!
> Arch strumpet of an impious age,
> Upstart from ranker villeinage:
> Asia shall stop her at the least
> That old inertness of the East. . . .

> But in the New World things make haste:
> Not only things, the *state* lives fast—
> Fast breed the pregnant eggs and shells,
> The slumberous combustibles,
> Sure to explode. 'Twill come, 'twill come!
> One demagogue can trouble much:
> How of a hundred thousand such? . . .

> Indeed, those germs one now may view:
> Myriads playing pigmy parts—
> Debased into equality:
> Dead level of rank commonplace:
> An Anglo-Saxon China, see,
> May on your vast plains shame the race
> In the Dark Ages of Democracy. . . .

Your arts advance in faith's decay:
You are but drilling the new Hun
Whose growl even now can some dismay;
Vindictive in his heart of hearts.
He schools him in your mines and marts
A skilled destroyer. . . .

Old ballads sing
Fair Christian children crucified
By impious Jews: you've heard the thing:
Yes, fable; but there's truth hard by:
How many Hughs of Lincoln, say,
Does Mammon, in his mills, to-day,
Crook, if he does not crucify?

The impieties of 'Progress' speak;
What say *these,* in effect to God?
'How profits it? And who art Thou
That we should serve Thee? Of Thy ways
No knowledge we desire; *new* ways
We have found out, and better. Go—
Depart from us!' And if He do?
Is aught betwixt us and the hells? . . .

For Herman Melville, at least, the barriers betwixt him
and the hells had long been gone, and only Nirvana
awaited him.

BOOK THREE

The Mind of New England

The New England renaissance was tardy in appearing and of brief duration, yet in the few years of its extraordinary vigor it imparted a stimulus to American life that its historians have not greatly exaggerated. We are now far enough from it to see that it was the last flowering of a tree that was dying at the roots, but in the tumultuous thirties it seemed to be a new birth of the native New England mind, opening on new worlds and great adventures. Though its prophecies might be little heeded at its own fireside, and unheard in the vast stretches of the West where men were clearing and building after quite different plans than the Concord architects were drawing, its significance in the development of American idealism—the ethical imprint it stamped on American culture—endured long after it had spent its force. It was the last and in certain aspects the most brilliant of the several attempts to domesticate in America the romantic thought of revolutionary Europe; and with its passing, civilization in this western world fell into the hands of another breed of men to fashion as they saw fit.

The revolutions in thought that lie between the eighteenth century with its aristocratic rationalism that conceived of human nature as evil, and the nineteenth century with its middle-class economics that conceived of human nature as acquisitive, are more clearly defined in New England and more sharply differentiated, than elsewhere in America. The flood of romantic speculation with its humanitarian emphasis on the potential excellence of man and the equality of human rights, that in Europe had diffused itself widely, in Massachusetts flowed into narrow channels prepared by Puritan discipline, and swept away habits of thought that had dominated New England for two hundred years. The intensity of the Puritan nature, once it embraced the new conceptions, imparted to them an intellectual and emotional unity that serves to explain the creativeness of the New England renaissance, as it serves to explain its failure to spread widely beyond the confines of Massachusetts. Appearing a generation later than in Virginia, it drew its inspiration more largely from Germany than from France; it was intellectual and ethical rather than political and economic; and in consequence it held little in common with the Physiocratic agrarianism of Jefferson. The latter was sufficiently native to American economics to appeal to the common man from Maine to Georgia; the former was native only to New England Puritanism. Its idealism appealed only to rare souls, disciplined by speculation and trained in ethical values, men of strong character and fine distinction who counted for much more than numbers.

After all it is the ethical note that marks the Puritan. That New England has run so different a course from other parts of America has been due chiefly to its desire to serve God even though it might be serving self. Its material life has always been plentifully seasoned with the salt of religion. It sat under the teachings of an austere ethics, as it lived under the compulsions of a narrow economics; and the result was the development of a middle class distinct from that of the West where the desire to get on was less hampered by the desire to get to heaven. The outstanding social figures in early New England were the minister and the merchant; and these twin authorities—joined after the Revolution by the rising profession of the law—ruled in patriarchal fashion the inarticulate mass of the yeomanry. From these traditional leaders the policy of New England received a twofold bent: a bent to the ethical and a bent to the practical. The two have rarely fused in a harmonious and fruitful life, but for the most part have dwelt side by side under a covenant of noninterference, the character of current social ideals taking its impress from one or the other as it gained a temporary ascendency. In the three hundred years of New England history the minister has enjoyed two periods of intellectual ascendency: the first during the early days of the theocracy, when the commonwealth was ruled by the laws of God and John Calvin; and the second, between the years 1830 and 1850, when John Calvin was finally put aside and New England was in the way of being remodeled in accordance with the plans of God alone. Between these brief periods of ethical enthusiasm lies the main history of New England, a history that counts for little in our intellectual and aesthetic development, but that meant much and ill to the cramped minds of her sons.

This long stretch, arid and unlovely, was dominated wholly by the merchant. Its parsimonious thrift, relieved by few generous impulses, was hostile to all change and to the romance that is bred of change. There was no rapid inflow of settlers to bring fresh energy and expansion. The exuberant growth of other parts of America was never shared by rural New England, and in consequence the harvest of unearned increment was rarely reaped from her sterile acres. Except in the shipping towns there was little economic development. On its secluded little farms New England was living a narrow parochial life, cooping up its mind in a rigid theological system and disciplining its character by a self-denying ordinance. Public affairs were managed by the squire, for the minister was too busy defending John Calvin against the Arminians to have a care for much except morality and dogma. The renaissance became of necessity, therefore, a movement of liberalism—a vehement protest against the torpor of the dogmatist whose mind was shut up in a dead system. It was a sudden reawakening of the ethical passion of Puritanism that had slept for two centuries; a vision of a new heaven and a new earth that it proposed to take by storm. It proposed to rid the mind of New England of its decadent loyalties—the nightmare dreams of Calvinism that debased human nature, and the counting-house dreams of Federalism that conceived of man as an exploitative animal. It had discovered anew the beauty of righteousness, and in the name of righteousness it proposed to throw off the old tyrannies and create a society wherein the mind should be free and the soul enjoy its religion. The battle against Calvinism was only preliminary to greater battles which constituted the intellectual revolution that marked the renaissance.

It was the New England minister, and the spiritual heirs of the minister—a group of intellectuals and reformers more notable than New England had before bred—that gave to the movement its pronounced ethical quality. It was freedom for individual righteousness that they sought; not freedom for intellectual epicureanism, for romance, for aesthetic or pagan beauty. The transcendentalists and reformers had little time to amuse themselves with such things. They were too eager for the coming of the kingdom to dawdle over fiction or patronize the playhouse. They had been bred from their youth up on printer's ink; they came of a race that had long respected the printed page. Literary men by inheritance, they esteemed themselves stewards of a great cause. In rejecting their fathers' hell they became the more zealous to make a heaven of this world; and although the more practical Yankee was skeptical of their plans and would not suffer them to turn Boston into a transcendental Utopia, they succeeded in making such a stir as New England had never before known. For a brief time, at least, liberal ideas found a welcome in homes where they had hitherto been strangers; for a brief time the intellectual and not the merchant dominated New England.

PART ONE
THE TWILIGHT OF FEDERALISM

CHAPTER I

The Passing of the Tie-Wig School

I

OLD BOSTON

The year 1815, that brought to a close the unfortunate American venture into the maelstrom of the Napoleonic wars, may be conveniently taken to mark for New England the transition to the nineteenth century. With the rise of Unitarianism and the development of the new industrialism, a ruder and more vigorous age entered Boston. It met with a somewhat chilly reception. The patriarchal eighteenth century still clung to its warm chimney corner, not liking to be dispossessed by heirs of whom it testily disapproved. The old order stood on its dignity, tenacious of its habitual authority. It lived quietly in an aristocratic past, unregardful of the vigorous commonwealths rising beyond the Appalachian mountains, and contemptuous of the new political philosophy that preached the rights of man. A persistent continuity of temper marked the ruling class, a continuity little disturbed by the tumultuous revolutions of the past two generations. Although nearly half the voters of Massachusetts, in the year 1800, were Jeffersonian republicans, the knowledge of that fact only stiffened the backbones of the regnant caste. It colored their minds with a virtuous pessimism, but it edged their temper with the zeal of righteousness. The Boston mobsters, it would appear, were republican, and when the present custodians of the ark of decency were gathered to their fathers, very likely evil days would come upon the land; but while the righteous lived they would be faithful to their stewardship. Their own households, at least, they would keep clean of all democratic pollution; and so Boston and New Haven and Hartford—the capitals of New England culture—drew about them the garments of Federalist righteousness. Since the Revolution of '76 a new authority had risen on the ruins of the old Tory authority, but in spite of the change of personnel and outward political forms, the spirit of respectable New England remained pretty much what it had always been. John Quincy Adams and Fisher Ames and Josiah Quincy were little different in character and aims from Thomas Hutchinson and Joseph Sewall and Daniel Leonard—they were common chips from the tough old New England oak. High-minded yet narrow; devout yet not emotionally religious; thrifty yet generous in approved causes; engaged in overseas commerce yet oddly parochial —they were men fashioned by a rugged environment into vigorous stock, that would hold tenaciously to what they had got and would tolerate no insubordination on the part of their social inferiors.

With its twenty-five thousand inhabitants Boston ranked fourth in size among American cities. Philadelphia, the social capital of America, was nearly three times as large; New York nearly two and a half times; and even Baltimore had lately come to exceed her in population. The economic forces that make for liberalism had become largely impotent. Free land had long since been exhausted in Massachusetts and social lines were fixed. The northern frontier of Maine and New Hampshire was rugged and uninviting, and York State lay to the West. Except in the Connecticut valley the soil was thin and farming unproductive, and in consequence the more ambitious turned to commerce and manufacture which the physical conditions of the country invited. The dominant interest of Boston was commercial, and the ruling coterie of merchants and lawyers was narrowly Whiggish. They had modified their pre-Revolutionary political philosophy no further than to substitute the word republican for monarchical. The aristocratic temper dominated the town meetings, and the principle of property rule was commonly accepted as the essence of political wisdom. In substituting Federalism for Toryism there was no easing of the restrictions on rebellious plebeians. Quite repudiated were the rude leveling ways of the great Revolutionary adventure. Boston gentlemen had come to understand too well the danger of encouraging the mob, for as Fisher Ames pointed out in 1787, "The people have turned against their teachers the doctrines, which were inculcated to effect the late revolution" (*Works*, p. 11). Boston had had enough of revolutions since Daniel Shays had got up one of his own aimed at the Boston purse, and French Jacobins had let loose their devastating ideas upon a gullible world. Revolutions that were not made in Boston, by Boston gentlemen, were quite certain to be wicked and seditious; and Boston had definitely gone out of the revolution business. It wanted above all things to undo the mischief that had already been done, and take back into safe hands the political power which in the days of revolutionary enthusiasm had been seized by the agrarian democracy.

In the last decade of the eighteenth century the intellectual isolation of New England was sharply accentuated and the consequent intellectual stagnation became more disastrous. In other portions of America French revolutionary theories of man and society were spreading widely and shouldering aside the outworn past. A romantic equalitarianism, based on the doctrine of human perfectibility, was displacing the traditional economic realism, established on the dogma of total depravity. The leveling movement, in consequence, was provided with a persuasive idealism that awakened troublesome aspirations in the disfranchised majority and gave a strong impetus to the democratic movement. But New England leaders stood resolutely apart, accounting all equalitarianism sheer romantic folly. The old stubborn realism held its ground, interpreting political principles in terms of economics, and dogmatically maintaining the sacred rights of property. Boston Federalism refused to have anything to do with "atheistic France," the fruitful mother of Jacobin follies. Pollution, it was convinced, must result from any commerce with infidel and innovating ideas. Gunpowder that was played with might explode, and New England wanted no blowing up of her excellent society. Virginia had lent credulous ears to the voice of France, and the result was the atheist Jefferson and the rabble of his licentious followers. Massachusetts was not gullible and it would tolerate no Jeffersonian atheisms. And so instead of adapting French romantic philosophy to new world needs, seizing upon its social idealism to leaven the crude American lump—as Jefferson and Colonel Mason and John Taylor and many another Virginia gentleman had done—Boston Federalism rejected French ideas in the mass, dubbed French idealism Jacobinism, and turned back upon a stubborn reaction.

The disastrous consequences of that rejection upon the mind of New England cannot easily be measured. It is clear enough, nevertheless, that the renaissance was delayed a full generation, and when it came it assumed certain provincialisms that greatly lessened its permanent influence upon the rest of America. The impress of its contribution upon our national thought has been far less permanent than that of Virginia, that came a generation earlier and was primarily economic and political. It is a suggestive fact that in the work of adapting the new Federal Constitution to democratic ends, New England contributed no creative leader, none in any way comparable to Jefferson; but on the contrary her most representative leaders—and in particular Webster—followed the eighteenth-century tradition in combating the equalitarian advance in the interest of economic groups. Some explanation of this fact may be found, perhaps, in the selfish isolation of New England Federalism, that closed the door on the liberal thought of France.

In consequence of such isolation Boston became the recognized home of the philosophy of a stake-in-society. If it clung tenaciously to an old-fashioned Federalism after it had been abandoned elsewhere, it was because Boston was more middle-class than Charleston, and had not learned from experience with Jacksonianism how easily the majority will may be shaped and controlled to particular ends. It inherited the old Tory contempt for democracy and relied on the old stock arguments to combat it. Its habitual tone was one of virtuous arrogance. The one great and ever-present fear that haunted the pillows of worthy Boston merchants and turned their dreams to nightmares was fear of the mob getting out of hand; and democracy, for them, was only a euphemism for the mob—the ever-present menace to sober and decent government. In the judgment of Theodore Dwight, brother of Timothy, "there could be nothing more dreadful this side of hell." Nowhere else in America did the reaction against the democratic ideal carry so far as in Boston. The church and the merchant associations joined with polite society to cry it down, and upon the head of the democrat fell the most extravagant vituperation. For a generation few respectable New Englanders raised their voices in defense of democracy, but gentlemen of principle and property followed the lead of the little clique that was driving straight towards the Hartford Convention—blind sailors navigating the Dead Sea of Federalist pessimism.

All this was before the reputed time of plain living and high thinking. Intellectual Boston was as parochial as political Boston. The lights whom Bostonians regarded as the torch-bearers of New England culture have long since been extinguished and their names forgotten even in Beacon Street. Amongst the literati of the little Boston of 1800 the historian need concern himself with no more than two or three: Fisher Ames (1758–1808), the Federalist lawyer-wit, and Robert Treat Paine (1773–1811), esteemed the ninth wonder of the Boston world. Other figures there were, of course, in addition to the literati: Harrison Gray Otis, the eloquent voice of Faneuil Hall, and Josiah Quincy, whom Lowell likened to an old Roman of the elder virtuous days, and who during a long life of ninety-two years was an example of stalwart and antiquated Federalism. Old Boston bred dignified figures in plenty, men admirably equipped to be college presidents, ambassadors, orators on formal occasions, purveyors of cultivated inutilities and polished commonplace—men like Edward Everett, whom all Boston praised while they lived and forgot when they were dead; but it bred no thinkers or men of letters who count in the larger history of America. Boston was still parochial, content with little things.

II

FISHER AMES: *The Oracle of the Tie-Wig School*

Of this testy little world that clung to its smallclothes and tie-wig, refusing to adopt the Jacobin innovation in dress and manners and politics, declining to temper its prejudices to the gusty whims of a leveling age, Fisher Ames was the universal counselor and oracle. A vivacious little gentleman to whom politics was the breath of life, he achieved so tremendous a reputation in his short lifetime that all New England looked to him for leadership and Harvard College wanted to make him its president. He came of vigorous stock, prone to consult its own will and speak its opinions with no squeamish concern for a neighbor's views. His brother, Dr. Nathaniel Ames, was as violent a Republican as Fisher was a Federalist, a hater of all lawyers whom he accounted the "pettifogging interest"; and when the two members of the family came together at dinner the talk must have been worth hearing. Diverse worlds and hostile philosophies faced each other over the roast, and the sauce no doubt was well spiced. Dr. Nathaniel had a pretty gift himself in the way of pungent speech, and Fisher's wit was the admiration of all New England. When Gouverneur Morris—reputed the greatest wit in America—visited Massachusetts, Fisher Ames was pitted against him, and Boston believed that the honor of the Bay State was worthily upheld. His pet hobby was the inherent tyranny of all democracies, and when he once got astride his wooden horse and dug in the spurs, the onset was tremendous. The letters that have come down to us are a gold mine of picturesque vituperation, from which one may dig a wallet of choice nuggets. The vivacity of his anathemas is delightful, and one would give much to have heard Dr. Nathaniel's retort militant.

There are the solidest grounds for regarding Fisher Ames as the representative citizen of Boston in the year 1800. He was the cleverest and most intelligent spokesman of a social and political circle quite untouched by the new French liberalisms, content with the habitual and familiar, and mightily concerned that the future should be as like the past as one generation of oysters is like another. A lawyer who shared the strong property consciousness of the Boston merchant, and a churchman who accepted the moral leadership of the Calvinist clergy, he offered stout and uncompromising resistance to innovation. "A change, though for the better, is always to be deplored by the generation in which it is effected," he said. "Much is lost and more is hazarded" (*Works,* p. 15, edition of 1809). The new gospel of progress that came in with French romanticisms, he would have none of. In the face of a noisy Jacobinism that threatened to carry all before it, he fought a spirited fight, turning pamphleteer when his broken health removed him from Congress, counseling and scolding his fellow Federalists with his last breath. Others might truckle and compromise, but not Fisher Ames. His faith was founded on the solid granite of Yankee prejudice.

The very solidity of that prejudice made him the trenchant spokesman of the older Boston conservatisms—that and the vivacity of his prose style which is approved Augustan, uncorrupted by what he dubbed "pompous Johnsonian affectation." His contemporary reputation was enormous. Accounted a great orator, he was accounted an even greater political philosopher, and his pamphlets were appraised by President Kirkland of Harvard as "the light of genius and wisdom darted athwart the gloom of our political chaos." "In the character of Mr. Ames," said the Harvard president, "the circle of the virtues seemed to be complete, and each virtue in its proper place" (*Works,* Introduction, p. xxviii). Yet in spite of so authoritative a pronouncement, Fisher Ames does not seem today so great a man as he seemed to his own generation. From the data collected in a stout volume published soon after his death as "a voice of instruction and warning to his country," and from the letters published by his son in 1854, it is plain enough that this "powerful and original genius" was a retailer of somewhat shopworn goods, a complete Federalist Tory after the current Boston fashion. To Fisher Ames Federalism, as understood in New England, was a religion. He defended it with the ardor of the moralist, convinced that it included all the political virtues, and that whoever rejected it was a child of the devil. Whenever he considered the unpromising state of the country—which luxury he often indulged—whether in the midst of Shays's Rebellion or of the Jeffersonian revolution, he fell into black pessimism. He grew hot from fires of his own kindling, and the gloomier he became the more vigorously he blew the bellows.

To the sinful publican self-conscious virtue is peculiarly irritating, and since Fisher Ames accounted most of his generation political publicans, he was at odds with all but a scant remnant of Federalist saints. From this isolation, from the defeat that overwhelmed his party in the great election of 1800, and from aggravating ill health, which beginning when he was thirty-seven incapacitated him three years later for public life, he fell into a state of chronic political despondency that extracted a grim pleasure from the contemplation of democratic follies and the anarchy towards which the country was hastening. During his last years his wit became acid; his letters are filled with caustic comment to sharpen the temper of those on the fighting line. Of these racy comments, so characteristic of Federalist spleen, a few examples must serve to convey the spirit: "Our country is too big for union, too sordid for patriotism, too democratic for liberty." "We are in the hands of the philosophers of Lilliput." "I have as loyal and respectful an opinion as possible of the sincerity in folly of our rulers." "As to liberty, we are to have none—democracy will kindle its own hell, and consume in it." "Democracy is a troubled spirit, fated never to rest, and whose dreams, if it sleeps, present only visions of hell." In his last years Fisher Ames had become a shrill Jeremiah crying in the gates of an Israel that mocked the old prophets.

His political philosophy was simple, yet so native to Calvinist-Yankee New England, and historically so characteristic, that it provides a useful candle to throw light into the old New England garrets. In certain aspects it is close kin to the Whiggery of Locke and Pitt, particularly in its concern for the sacred right of property rule—a principle that he casually recognizes in his frequent assertion that "the mass of the federalists are the owners of the commercial and monied wealth of the nation" (*Works,* p. 426). But in post-Revolutionary Boston, suffering from the acute fright inflicted by Daniel Shays, this English Whiggery had come to assume a particular native form that differentiated it from its original. In the primitive Calvinist-Yankee world political theory had been shaped by the theocratic conception of stewardship, by which was meant an authoritative leadership reposing in the best and wisest, yet subject to the will of God as revealed in the Bible. Minister and magistrate, therefore, professed to justify their acts, not by expediency or interest, but by absolute ethical standards. From this early practice developed the pronounced ethical temper of New England political thought that set it apart from the Virginia school, a temper that persisted after the transfer of authority from Puritan minister and magistrate to Tory merchant and lawyer. With the growth of the aristocratic spirit in the middle eighteenth century, the squirearchy assumed unchallenged political leadership, and it was from the remnant of the old gentry remaining after the expulsion of the Loyalists, strengthened by a new generation of merchants and lawyers, that Boston Federalism drew its personnel. It professed republicanism, but it was instinctively aristocratic. It was true to its Puritan origins in expounding its political philosophy in terms of an absolute morality, and true to its aristocratic origins in assuming to be the special custodians of law and order. It no more questioned its special right to rulership in the state than it questioned its social position; and in both politics and society it professed the ancient doctrine of stewardship.

The kinship between the political philosophy of Fisher Ames and John Adams is quite evident. They are cut out of the same Puritan-Yankee cloth, but the former is a more careless tailor. Founded on less adequate analysis and lacking the wide historical appeal of Adams, assuming rather than proving the fact of a universal property aristocracy, and the economic origins of political power, the philosophy of Ames postulates the same ideal of justice as the end of government, discovers in faction the dragon to be slain, and concludes that only a static division of powers can insure political stability. Nevertheless the difference between the two men is enormous. John Adams was a philosopher, and Fisher Ames was only a lawyer-politician. The ideal of justice which the former postulated was fundamentally noble, whereas the ideal of justice which the latter assumed was narrowly legal. Both accepted the Puritan doctrine of human wickedness—a doctrine derived from medieval Toryism—and from it deduced the necessity of a coercive sovereignty; but Fisher Ames went further and assumed that the Puritan doctrine of the elect and the Yankee doctrine of the successful were one and the same, and that God's remnant in Israel was no other than the prosperous merchants and lawyers of Boston. All the great multitude of the unprosperous, by the same doctrine, were the mass of the unregenerate, condemned for the good of society to be ruled by a rod of iron.

The noble doctrine of justice, therefore, became for Fisher Ames little more than the divine right of the minority to coerce the majority, in the name and through the agency of laws and statutes. In his view justice was little more than a drab realist in a lawyer's wig, adjudicating title deeds, and delivering its findings out of law books. Its one concern was to safeguard what had been got, rather than to secure just and equal rights. It dreaded all rude and tumultuary innovation, and would tolerate no change that was not implicit in legal principles. Its golden rule was due process of law. Love of one's neighbors was, no doubt, an excellent private virtue, but it was impractical, if not immoral, in the state. Concern for the improvident sinners must not influence government to impair the rights of the thrifty saints; for government was instituted and exists to safeguard established things. "The chief duty and care of all governments," he argued, "is to protect the rights of property and the tranquillity of society" (*Works*, p. 125). Hence to Fisher Ames government was the common policeman and judge, whose function was to arrest the turbulent and bring them to the bar of the Common Law. Its beginning and end was the Tory principle of coercion. Its sovereignty was arrogant and domineering, taking no account of the democratic principle of good will. "The motives to refuse obedience to government are many and strong," he explained; "impunity will multiply and enforce them. Many men would rebel, rather than be ruined; but they would rather not rebel, than be hanged" (*Works*, "Lucius Junius Brutus"). With government thus conceived of, naturally he desired that it should be strong; that it should impose its will ruthlessly upon the rebellious. Naturally also he regarded every idealist, the Rousseaus and Paines and Jeffersons—all the mischievous hosts of "democratick babblers"—as a dangerous enemy of law and order, desperately bent on overturning the rights of vested interests and the tranquillity of society. This is sufficient to explain the vindictiveness of his assault upon Shays and his followers, as "bankrupts and sots, who have gambled or slept away their estates"—while in the Revolutionary army —and were now engaged in the business of treason against the commonwealth, and the characteristic conclusion that he draws—"the certainty of punishment is the truest security against crimes" (*Works*, "Lucius Junius Brutus," p. 3). To Fisher Ames and Daniel Shays, justice seems to have had very different aspects.

To the uncritical there is a certain persuasive dignity in the philosophy of Boston Federalism. Gentlemen like Fisher Ames were careful to appear well in public; they liked to be regarded as faithful stewards of the common weal. Concern for the *res publica* they professed so heartily that it seems ungracious to question their motives. How excellently they could make out a case for themselves will appear from the following exposition of Fisher Ames's philosophy, as it was understood by a Harvard president:

Mr. Ames was emphatically a republican. He saw that many persons confounded a republick with a democracy. He considered them as essentially distinct and really opposite. According to his creed, a republick is that structure of an elective government, in which the administration necessarily prescribe to themselves the general good as the object of all their measures; a democracy is that, in which the present popular passions, independent of the publick good, become a guide to the rulers. In the first, the reason and interests of the society govern; in the second, their prejudices and passions. The frame of the American constitution supposes the dangers of democracy. . . . [The constitutional checks] are contrivances and devices voluntarily adopted by the people to restrain themselves from obstructing, by their own mistakes or perversity, the attainment of the publick welfare. They are professed means of insuring to the nation rulers, who will prefer the durable good of the whole to the transient advantage of the whole or a part. When these provisions become ineffectual, and the legislator, the executive magistrate, and the judge become the instruments of the passions of a people, or of the governing majority, the government, whatever may be its form, is a democracy, and the public liberty is no longer safe. True republican rulers are bound to act, not simply as those who appoint them *would,* but, as they *ought;* democratick leaders will act in subordination to those very passions which it is the object of government to control. . . . Then it is, that men, not laws, govern. (*Works,* Introduction, pp. xxiv–xxv.)

"The durable good of the whole" is an excellent phrase; but when the skeptical critic asks for more exact plans and specifications, the only answer is a request for a vote of confidence. The representative is presumed to be wiser and more patriotic than his constituents—quite above passion or interest—and may safely be intrusted with "the publick good." "The love of country," Fisher Ames was fond of insisting, "is the morality of politics," and the Federal Constitution he believed to be so happily balanced that partisan selfishness must transmute itself into patriotism. But when we dismiss these amiable generalities—which reveal to what straits gentlemen were reduced in their contest with democracy—and examine the political principles that lie behind them, they do not appear so amiable. They imply as necessary corollaries a continuous aggrandizement of the political state, the principle of coercion, and the psychology of fear. It is no other than the old Tory arrogance, new-modeled to suit republican taste. Fisher Ames seems to have had no faith in the principle of good will or the expediency of compromise; his contempt for the opposition was as frank as Hamilton's.

Government does not subsist by making proselytes to sound reasons or by compromise and arbitration with its members; but by the power of the community compelling the obedience of individuals. If that is not done, who will seek its protection, or fear its vengeance. (*Works,* "Lucius Junius Brutus," p. 5.)

For let it be remarked, that a feeble government produces more factions than an oppressive one; the want of power first makes individuals legislators, and then rebels. Where parents want authority, children are wanting in duty. It is not possible to advance further in the same path; the one will conduct us first to anarchy, and next to foreign or domestick tyranny; the other, by the wise and vigorous exertion of lawful authority, will lead to permanent power, and general prosperity. I am no advocate for despotism; but I believe the probability to be much less of its being introduced by the corruption of our rulers, than by the delusion of the people. (*Works,* "Camillus," p. 17.)

A weak government, Ames argues insistently, is no other than a hotbed of faction, and faction is the fruitful mother of democratic anarchy. Again and again he returns to an exposition of the familiar eighteenth-century dogma that found its classic exposition in the tenth number of *The Federalist;* and his argument takes on darker colors from the Calvinist background of his mind. To those who have been reared on the sour doctrines of reprobation and election, the children of Adam become a major political concern. If God has cast off and denied the mass of the unregenerate, how shall the political philosopher hope to redeem them? If divine wisdom has granted them no part in the congregation of the righteous, what rights have they in the republic of the patriotic? To Fisher Ames town and village and farm showed plentiful examples of those whom the devil had marked for his own, and if they were gathered into a numerical democracy with the saints, how should the minority of the latter safeguard the Ark of the Sanctuary? How should the durable good of the whole be provided for? Thrift and godliness were not exactly synonymous terms to the Calvinist-Yankee, but it was clear that the godly will practice thrift, and those who have thriven, have *ipso facto* made out a case for their godliness. In this uncertain world two things seemed reasonably clear: that the poor are in a more doubtful state than the rich; and that in a moral world only the elect may be expected to serve the cause of morality. The wicked incline to democratic faction, but the prosperous serve the durable good of the whole.

To one cradled in such prejudices, the current phrase, "gentlemen of principle and property"—a phrase that provides the chorus to his thought—lacked the savor of cynicism that it suggests to modern ears. It was compounded of the ideals of Puritan and Yankee, and Fisher Ames seems never to have questioned its adequacy, or doubted its finality. To gentlemen of principle and property he looked to provide a bulwark against the immoral multitude; they were the stewards of society, on whom devolved the duty of protecting the whole from democratic faction. They had erected the Federal Constitution, which Jacobins were seeking to destroy; and in defense of that Constitution he brought forth his heaviest artillery. He contributed nothing new to the discussion; but he repeated the familiar arguments with the gusto of a dogmatist. "Simple governments," he asserted, "are despotisms; and of all despotisms, a democracy, though the least durable, is the most violent" (*Works*, "American Liberty," p. 382). The mortal weakness of all democracies he discovered in their immorality. A democracy will make every people "thoroughly licentious and corrupt." "The known propensity of a democracy is to licentiousness, which the ambitious call, and the ignorant believe to be liberty."

> The great object, then, of political wisdom in framing our constitution, was to guard against licentiousness, that inbred malady of democracies, that deforms their infancy with grey hairs and decrepitude. (*Ibid.*, p. 384.)

> There is universally a presumption in democracy that promises everything; and at the same time an imbecility that can accomplish nothing, not even preserve itself. (*Works*, "Falkland," p. 151.)

"Politics should have no passions," this caustic old Federalist professed to believe, yet his bitterness against the Jeffersonians who threatened to overturn the funding law, the national bank, the midnight judicial appointments, and other measures of the best Federalist minds, was almost unseemly. It would appear that "the durable good of the whole" flew out at the window, when danger to commercial interests came in at the door. To erect a strong government and then lose control of it was a disaster indeed. With the political state in the hands of atheistic democrats, Fisher Ames was prepared to welcome the coming of anarchy, and his pessimism throve on the prospect. But that no warning might be lacking he laid down the whole theory of government in plain terms, that even Jefferson might understand:

> But the essence, and almost the quintessence, of good government is, to protect property and its rights. When these are protected, there is scarcely any booty left for oppression to seize; the objects and the motives to usurpation and tyranny are removed. By securing property, life and liberty can scarcely fail of being secured: where property is safe by rules and principles, there is liberty. (*Works*, "Phocion," p. 181.)

This is pure Federalism, stripped of all cant, speaking out frankly. It is the philosophy of John Locke brought in to serve the rising capitalism of New England, threatened by a Physiocratic agrarianism. The dogma of political morality has yielded to economic realism. The stake-in-society principle is the reply of the Puritan-Yankee to the democratic romanticism of Jefferson and Madison—a principle which, fortunately, 'these apostles from the race-ground and the cock-pit" paid little heed to.

To a sophisticated generation, long familiar with the political ways of gentlemen of principle and property, Fisher Ames appears as a caustic little gentleman, vivacious and intolerant, who nodded his tie-wig dogmatically, and spoke his opinions oracularly. He quite evidently relished his ample store of old-fashioned prejudices, cherished them carefully, and prided himself on the wit with which he set them forth. If he was not the repository of all political wisdom that he believed himself to be, he was at least no demagogue, and in honoring him the Boston of the year 1800 was but painting its own portrait. It would be ungracious, perhaps, to add that Fisher Ames and Boston Federalism, defeated in their cherished projects, were both suffering from an extraordinarily aggravated case of the political spleen.

III

ROBERT TREAT PAINE, JR.: Wit

Young Tom Paine, who took his brother's and his father's name—partly because a certain other Tom Paine had achieved a fame that Boston did not regard as enviable—shared with Fisher Ames the literary renown of the New England capital, a renown so great that Boston paid him quite astonishing sums for such couplets as his indolence suffered him to turn off. The popularity of his wares was a notable instance of the working of the law of supply and demand. The patriotism of Boston preferred domestic to imported goods, and he offered his verses to a public not very critical of quality. Boston had never had a poet of her own, while Connecticut with her Hartford Wits was the envy of all New England. Certain poetesses to be sure, had tried with "hallowed hands" to "attune Columbia's lyre"—to quote Paine's eulogy of Mrs. Sarah Wentworth Morton, "blest Philenia, noblest of the choir" (*Works,* "Menander to Philenia," p. 129)—but their sentimentality was a bit cloying, and when genius appeared in the person of a Harvard graduate, graced with wit and adorned with all the learning of the schools, Boston was quick to acclaim him as her own.

The young man thus seized upon, and as it were raped by fame, was the last of the eighteenth-century wits, the most dashing product of a generation that patched its verse with tags of the classics and called it lisping in numbers. In temper and manners he belonged wholly to the tie-wig school that swaggered till the War of 1812 and then became obsolete overnight. As a young man about town he displayed the latest London clothes and set himself up as the very glass of fashion. Although he wore his own hair, he clung to smallclothes and like an honest Federalist refused to adopt Jacobin trousers. He was indisputably clever and he cultivated a pretty wit as assiduously as any Augustan. He talked in epigrams, and a convivial evening—of which he was quite too fond for his own good—was a failure that did not produce a *bon mot* to run through the town. His biographer has preserved a number of such for the amusement of posterity, and one at least deserves to be remembered by our younger critics. When the prohibition against the theater was repealed in 1793, he remarked, "The Vandal spirit of puritanism is prostrate in New-England." In cleaving to wit and abandoning Puritanism, Paine broke with sober Boston convention, and soon all respectable folk began to shake their heads. A thriftless fellow, he played with the devil openly in the eyes of all Boston. He drank too much, he gambled, he haunted the theater and was a favorite of the greenroom, he became the first dramatic critic born and bred in New England, and when he married the daughter of an English actor, his father disowned him. Quite naturally he came to poverty, dissipated his strength, suffered many a humiliation, and died at the age of thirty-seven, leaving his widow and young children to be provided for by a public benefit at his beloved Federal Street theater.

Little of his wit, unfortunately, found its way into his verse, which, modeled ostensibly on Dryden and Pope, lacks their vigorous common sense, and laboring to be sublime succeeds in being heavy. His couplets swell sonorously, but his thought does not keep pace with his rhetoric. He follows his recipe carefully; adjectives duly support the nouns; the caesuras are justly spaced and the balance of the parts is as nice as if weighed in an apothecary's scales. He seasons the whole with the staples of personification and poetic diction; everything has been provided for, and yet the cake is fallen that he takes from the oven. Something is lacking to lighten the sodden mass. A contem-

281

porary critic, viewing the finished product, expressed his judgment thus:

> Of Mr. Paine, as an author, we cannot speak in terms of unmingled praise. His verse, indeed, seldom loiters into prose; but it must be confessed, that his prose is here and there "tricked and frounced, till it out-mantles all the pride of verse." His numbers are, perhaps, never feeble or faultering, but a wild and frolic imagination, occasionally, wantons through his periods, and sometimes displays itself in contemning the chaster elegancies, and sometimes in neglecting the severer decencies of thought and diction. (*Works,* Introduction, p. lxxviii.)

It is certainly a partial eye that discovers a wild and frolic imagination in these lumbering imitations of Pope, or in the occasional excursions into the languorous fields of Della Cruscan sentiment. When Paine ceases to be a wit he becomes an offense. To his admiring contemporaries his poetry seemed to be pure metal, but to later generations it is only plate, with the brass showing through the worn spots. *The Ruling Passion,* delivered before the Phi Beta Kappa Society in 1797, is perhaps the first poem of Paine's that is much more than vacuous and turgid rhetoric; and this is redeemed, in spite of liberal helpings from Pope, by a certain vivacity of satire, phrased with Augustan smartness. Such couplets as these still preserve a jaunty literary swagger for later ears; how they tickled the more susceptible ears of our grandfathers must be imagined:

> Where you send genius, send a fortune too;
> Dunces by instinct thrive, as oysters woo!
> For ne'er were veins of ore by chymist found,
> Except, like Hebrew roots, in barren ground!

Paine early grew old, and before he had reached his thirties his mind had taken a rigid conservative bent. His affections were fixed upon a past that was visibly falling into decay, and its ways were endeared to him in the measure that they decayed. It was a matter of personal pride with him to embody in his own manners the aristocratic bearing of pre-Revolutionary times.

> Mr. Paine [says his biographer] attached great consequence to *manners.* . . . He was modelled upon the *old school.* Without being familiar, he was easy among friends, and courtly to strangers. In colloquial discussions, he rigidly adhered to the law of politeness; and in mixed society, he neither courted the *high,* nor avoided the *low.* . . . He frequently deplored a supposed decay of *manners.* With concern, he used to inquire "*In manners, where*

is the successor of Gen. Knox to be found?" It was with him a constant topick of complaint, that *"The old, genteel, town families, had been elbowed out of house and home, by newcomers:"* that *"instead of the polished manners of a city, we should soon exhibit that growth of gentility, which is produced by ingrafting dollars upon village habits and low employments."* (*Works*, Introduction, p. lxix.)

Affecting an aristocratic bearing, Paine was as complete a Tory as the republican environment permitted. If he despised the new, pushing middle class that had risen since the Revolution, he held in contempt the numerous company of those he dubbed the yokel, the peasant, the hind, or the plow-tail. Under the circumstances the best that he could do politically was to turn Federalist, and he embraced the principles of Fisher Ames with genteel conviction. "In politics," says his biographer, "Mr. Paine was a disciple of the old federal school. He understood the constitution, as Washington administered, and as Hamilton had expounded it" (*ibid.*, p. lxxvii). During his undergraduate days he had dabbled in French revolutionary philosophy, and "the fanatic Atheism of France, decorated in all the meretricious charms of eloquence and philosophy, took a transient possession of his mind" (*ibid.*, p. lxxviii). At graduation in 1792, he read a poem entitled *The Nature and Progress of Liberty*, in which he eulogized "liberal thought," proposed to follow "Reason," declared that "the rights of man" are a gift from heaven, proffered the hand of fellowship to France—

> May struggling France her ancient freedom gain,
> May Europe's sword oppose her rights in vain—

and launched a devastating couplet at the great English opponent of the Revolution—

> The fame of Burke, in dark oblivion rust,
> His pen a meteor—and his page the dust.

Three years later, on proceeding Master of Arts, he presented a poem in very different vein. Three years were a generation in those stirring times, and by 1795 the penetrating vision of this genius of twenty-two had discovered the atheist poison in the cup of French democracy. *The Invention of Letters* rises to a climax in a satirical elaboration of a line from the poem of 1792—"Licentious morals breed disease of state." Having learned his lesson from Fisher Ames, the sapient young Federalist announces that

283

democracy is the mother of faction, and faction leads on to anarchy. In this poem for the first time Paine's wit runs freely, and certain lines are as jaunty as he ever penned.

> For place or power, while demagogues contend,
> Whirled in their vortex, sinks each humbler friend.
> See Crispin quit his stall, in Faction's cause,
> To cobble government, and soal the laws!
> See Frisseur scent his dust, his razor set,
> To shave the treaty, or to puff Genet!
> In doubtful mood, see Mulciber debate,
> To mend a horse-shoe, or to weld the state!
> The whip's bold knight, in barn, his truck is laid,
> To spout in favour of the carrying trade!
> While Staytape runs, from hissing goose, too hot,
> To measure Congress for another coat,
> And still, by rule of shop, intent on pelf,
> Eyes the spare cloth, to cabbage for himself!
>
> Envy, that fiend, who haunts the great and good,
> Not Cato shunned, nor Hercules subdued.
> On Fame's wide field, where'er a covert lies,
> The rustling serpent to the thicket flies;
> The foe of Glory, Merit is her prey;
> The dunce she leaves, to plod his drowsy way.
> Of birth amphibious, and of Protean skill,
> This green-eyed monster changes shape at will;
> Like snakes of smaller breed, she sheds her skin;
> Strips off the serpent, and turns—Jacobin.

In view of the fact that Governor Samuel Adams, chief of the New England Jacobins, was to occupy the stage, President Willard had diplomatically struck from the manuscript the ten lines last quoted; but Paine had the audacity to re-insert them in speaking, and the tumultuous applause was sufficient proof that it was not from a Harvard audience that Sam Adams got the votes that annually returned him governor.

Verse imposed some slight restraint on Paine's rhetoric, but in prose when he was in full career—as in the grotesque eulogy of Washington which stirred the patriotism of Boston Federalists—the reins are on the neck of his eloquence, and he takes all barriers with fiery abandon. Fact troubles his wild and frolic imagination not at all, but like any plebeian demagogue—whose factional appeals he so furiously condemned—he blew the bellows of Federalist partisanship with extraordinary vigor, stoking his fire with rumor and misrepresentation and party spleen. No slander was too gross, no lie too palpable to serve his end. He baited the democrats quite shamelessly, and aroused the mob of Boston gentlemen like a true Tory. One of his political orations has been preserved by his editor in the collected edition of his works, for the enlightenment of posterity—an oration delivered in 1799, "at the request of the young men of Boston," on the theme of France and democracy. In this extraordinary composition Paine seems to have been quite ravished by his own rhetoric, that flashes in many a feint and parry before it impales its victim. It is a Federalist philippic, designed to destroy the good name of all who have quitted the sacred Federalist tribe. Words could hardly go further; disregard for truth could scarcely be more brazen. Paine's delight in clever antitheses overweighs any scruples in regard to just statement. "The French Republick," he asserted, "has exhibited all the vices of civilization, without one of the virtues of barbarism." One or two bits from this tremendous oration, that in "the glow of feeling, the swell of language, and the brilliancy of sentiments" has "very seldom been surpassed," and that was "received with rapturous and enthusiastic applause," must suffice to illustrate the justice of the Federalist claim to the custodianship of political good manners. "Politics should have no passions," Fisher Ames asserted—which excellent principle young Robert Treat Paine exemplified thus:

Political Empiricism has never attained, in any age or nation, so universal an ascendency, as at the present day in the "Illuminated Republick." Unfettered by the fear of innovation, and unshackled by the prejudice of ages, the modern Frenchman is educated in a system of moral and religious chimeras, which dazzle by their novelty those volatile intellects, which prescriptive wisdom could never impress with veneration. Every Frenchman, who has read a little is a pedant; and the whole race of these hornbook Philosophers is content with the atheism of Mirabeau . . . the absurd philanthropy of Condorcet, and the visionary politics of Rousseau. These are the boundaries of their literary ambition, of their political science. Hence it is, that they pretend to be too enlightened for belief, too virtuous for government.

The feculence of party is not yet drained of its rankest sediment. The worshippers of democracy, though their altars are thrown down, are not yet converted from their devotions. The frozen snake has still some sparks of animation; and, if placed by compassion near your hospitable fires, he will revive with exasperated venom, and sting the hardy fool that fostered him. Deal therefore with these ferocious demoralizers, as our crafty mariners

trade with the savages of the Indian ocean—with your men at
their posts, your guns loaded, and your slow matches burning.
(*Works,* p. 319.)

For all democrats Paine had the hearty contempt of an
honest man for a rogue, but for the intellectuals who expounded the new romantic philosophy his indignation was
measureless. "The legitimate plebeian democrat," he asserted, is "an enemy to all government, under which he
holds no office"; but fling him a bone from the public table
and "he becomes the very scavenger of administration."
The "Illuminated Jacobin," on the other hand, "never
changes his principles."

His whole science is directed to unhinge society, his whole
ambition to plunder it. He is too ravenous to be content with a
system of order himself; and too selfish to permit its enjoyment by
others. Like a hog in a flower-garden, he sets no value on the
variegated foliage he destroys, and seems only desirous to root
out every twig of vegetation, that can satiate his voracity. (*Ibid.,*
p. 321.)

To such fustian was he reduced when his wit left him.
That a gentleman could talk like that, and other gentlemen
applaud, is a sad commentary on the intellectual honesty
of partisanship, even amongst decent Federalists. Fustian
was the order of the day, and Paine was merely baying
with his pack. If only he had not professed such virtues
his extravagance might be forgiven; but extravagance ill
becomes a distinguished repository of political wisdom.
Once, indeed, his vivacity got him into a nasty mess. While
editor of *The Federal Orrery,* he accepted in 1795 a political poem entitled *The Jacobiniad,* the satire of which
Paine "new-pointed and new-edged" before printing. The
democrats, at whom it was directed, were vastly incensed,
and a mob gathered before his lodging but was dispersed.
Later the son of one of the victims challenged him to a
duel. Paine declined but armed himself with an unloaded
pistol. Accidentally meeting his challenger in the street, he
drew his weapon, but the young fellow, standing in no
awe of a favorite of the muses, struck the pistol down and
proceeded to give Paine a sound drubbing. To such base
treatment may genius come, when wit forgets that a sally
of the tongue may invite a counter sally of the fists. And
so we leave him in the dust of the street, ignobly laid low
by the strength of that vulgar democracy which was to
bring down so many things held dear by Boston Tories. His

was, very largely, a wasted life—wasted by sheer indolence and feeble will. He was a fellow of some parts, and a sentence from one of his dramatic criticisms may not inaptly apply to him: "The character is not a sot, but his humor has a mellower tilth for having been husbanded and manured by 'the excellent endeavor of drinking.'"

CHAPTER II

Winds of Political Doctrine

I

Into the complacent little Boston of Fisher Ames and Robert Treat Paine came the Embargo, the War of 1812, and the industrial revolution to upset its static order and destroy its snug provincialism. The old Federalism with its Hartford Convention and plans for New England secession went the way of mortality, carrying with it to the grave the old pessimism and the old spleen. The jealous isolationist policy was quietly forgotten in Boston; the gospel of secession was preached no more; George Cabot and Timothy Pickering gave way to other leaders; and provincial Boston joined with Kentucky and Tennessee in extolling a romantic nationalism. It sent to Washington a new spokesman, who joined with Henry Clay in a paternalistic program of national expansion, and took command of the forces combating the rising separatism of the South Carolina school. By the year 1830 Boston had traveled far from the times of the Hartford Convention.

The sufficient explanation of so striking a change is to be found, of course, in the changing economics of Massachusetts. The Embargo had proved a major disaster to New England shipping; and the Boston merchants, counting their losses from idle and dismasted ships, water-logging at the wharves, found just cause for hating the policy of the administration. But if the shipping business was brought face to face with tragedy, the manufacturing interests stumbled upon unexpected prosperity. With British imports cut off, the home market offered a tempting opportunity to Yankee enterprise. The familiar story of the swift rise of New England industrialism need not be recounted here. It is enough to remark that with the growth of domestic manufactures a new group of economic leaders appeared, and the policy of New England shifted from pro-mercantilism to pro-industrialism. It was a difficult choice at first between the antagonistic claims of the Boston merchant and the Lowell manufacturer; between the carriers of foreign goods who demanded free trade, and the makers of domestic goods who demanded a protective tariff. The traditional view of New England was strongly for free trade. In 1807 a Federalist lawyer asserted it to be "an unalienable right," and in 1820 Judge Story asked, "Why should the laboring classes be taxed for the necessaries of life?" [1] The tariff bill of 1824 got only one vote from Massachusetts; but in the four years between the passage of that act and the "Tariff of Abominations" of 1828, Massachusetts went over definitely to industrialism. Thenceforth she was to be the leader in the movement looking to governmental paternalism, substituting the expansive Federalism of Hamilton for the restrictive Federalism of Fisher Ames, and becoming in consequence whole-heartedly nationalistic.

Equally significant, though less observed, was the changed attitude of Massachusetts towards the great republican experiment. Gone was the older generation, with its face turned to the past and its heart bound up with the patriarchal ideals of a decadent squirearchy. Gone also were the disturbant fears of democracy. The menace of Daniel Shays, that had put the old Federalists in a rage at democracy, was long since forgotten; and the nervous panic over French Jacobinism, that had upset New England for a decade, had subsided. In the light of longer experience with its ways democracy was seen to be far from terrifying. The hobgoblin of faction that had benightmared the dreams of Fisher Ames was discovered to be only a bogey to frighten naughty boys. Massachusetts had kept off the agrarian reef, despite war and economic unrest, and with her new constitution of 1820 property interests were as secure as any old Federalist could have wished. Gentlemen of principle and property were still in control of the state; and if less emphasis was laid on principle and more

---

[1] Quoted in Theodore Parker, *Daniel Webster: Additional Speeches*, Vol. I, p. 195. Considerable information will be found in this excellent study.

on property—if less regard seemed to be paid to gentle-men of breeding and manners, and more to assertive self-seeking—business was no less secure than in the good old days, and its profits were greater. And so, master of its looms and a growing home market, New England indus-trialism regarded genially the great western movement, fostered by a benevolent paternalism, confident of extend-ing its markets with every mile of westward expansion. To encourage the development of the West and South by a Federal policy of internal improvement became, therefore, common business foresight, provided of course that the Constitution should follow population and safeguard busi-ness interests against local agrarianism and the menace of particularism.

By the year 1830 both dangers lay black against the political horizon. The triumph of Jackson had enthroned the agrarian menace at Washington and produced such a scrambling of frightened interests—such a rattling among the old bones of Federalism and scurrying among the young limbs of industrialism—as the country had not seen for many a year. Henry Clay appealed to his followers in the West, and Webster marshaled his adherents of the East, and from the coalescing of these incongruous elements emerged the Whig party to do battle with Old Hickory. It was a patchwork army at best. In the hour of peril, princi-ples go by the board. The Whig party was lineal heir of the old Federalism, but it denied its philosophical patri-mony. It substituted expediency for the old economic real-ism, and began and ended intellectually bankrupt. Its bitter and unseemly squabbles over the Bank and tariff, its platitudes of patriotism and its pose of disinterestedness, the venom of its personal attack upon Jackson, were the earmarks of a policy of shallow opportunism that failed to make use of such victories as fell to its lot, for the simple reason that it could never agree on what to do. Such cohesive power as held it together—aside from petty antagonism to Jackson—was the vague assumption that the well-being of the American people was dependent on gov-ernmental patronage; the belief that each economic group and section must receive its special favor, and that through tariffs and bonuses and internal improvements the country as a whole must prosper. Of this principle of special favors —a return to the seventeenth century from which eight-eenth-century liberalism was a reaction—the American System of Henry Clay was the chief expression, and it remains the most significant bequest of the Whig party to our political history.

The Whig party was the first attempt of our rising middle class to erect a political platform in accordance with middle-class ideals, and its failure was due to the fact that the time was not ripe for undisputed middle-class control. The merchant aristocracy of the North was overthrown, but the planter aristocracy of the South was still to be reckoned with; and its particularistic ambitions in the end wrecked the Whig coalition of the West and East. By 1820 a revolutionary change had taken place in the political philosophy of the plantation school. From an ardent nationalism Calhoun was leading his followers back to the earlier doctrine of states rights; and New England in dustrialism found itself confronted with the doctrine which the Hartford junto had played with, but now with far more drive behind it. The slave economy was entertaining imperialistic dreams, and to effect its ends was building up a new constitutional philosophy. Southern writers had long been at work, and the weight of their authority was behind the new particularism. *Rawle on the Constitution,* a states-rights exposition, was the official textbook on civics at the United States Military Academy, and from it, while a student at West Point, Jefferson Davis declared that he first imbibed states-rights principles. Other authoritative southern works that were widely read were John Taylor's two studies: *Construction Construed and Constitutions Vindicated* (1820), and *New Views of the Constitution of the United States* (1823); some years later came Henry St. George Tucker's *Lectures on Constitutional Law* (1843); and these were only preliminary to Calhoun's searching exposition in his *Disquisition on Government* and *An Inquiry into the Nature of the Constitution of the United States.*

To meet this theory of particularism there was need of a resurgent Federalism, with a new nationalistic interpretation of the Constitution. The compact theory of the Federal state must be refuted by the organic theory; the conception of federated commonwealths must yield to the conception of a coalescing sovereignty. The old battle must be fought over again with fresh arguments. The sanctity of the Constitution must be asserted, but that sanctity must be thrown over a nationalistic rather than a particularistic interpretation. It must be shown that despite the vehement protestations of southern loyalty, a particularistic Constitution was a denial of loyalty and must end in the destruction of the national union. For this difficult business New England was as yet unprepared. The old Federalist arguments were obsolete, and many of those Federalists had been deep in the Hartford Convention. The new industrialism must provide its own theory, and it was fortunate in discovering two men whose combined learning and eloquence proved equal to the task.

II

The name of Webster has been so closely associated with the movement of constitutional nationalism as to overshadow the just fame of one who has many claims to be regarded as the intellectual leader of the school. Joseph Story was a Salem lawyer whose reputation, considerable as it is, is scarcely commensurate with his influence on our later constitutional development. Of the same Harvard class with William Ellery Channing, he dabbled in polite letters as a young man, but went into the law, entered politics, became Associate Justice of the Supreme Court, and for a time was Dane professor of law at Harvard. He came of radical stock. His father, a physician at Boston till he removed to Marblehead, was a militant Revolutionary Whig, one of the score or so of Indians who made up the Boston Tea Party, and a leader amongst the group of Sons of Liberty who seized and gagged the sentinels and carried off two brass fieldpieces from the Common where the British commander had posted them to overawe the town. The son grew up an ardent republican. As a very young man he became an outstanding leader of the unfashionable party, then in the minority, and suffered certain humiliations on account of his political opinions; on one occasion, according to Theodore Parker, being "knocked down in the street, beaten, and forced to take shelter in the house of a friend, whither he fled, bleeding, and covered with the mud of the street" (*Additional Speeches*, Vol. I, p. 178). Of these youthful heresies few indications appeared in his later life. Republican though he might be, he was utterly devoid of any radical tendencies, and when he took his seat on the Supreme Court bench he was speedily drawn into the powerful orbit of John Marshall, shared the latter's views on all major constitutional questions, and turned Whig. He became a close friend of Webster and from 1816 to 1842 he was his chief adviser on knotty legal, constitutional, and international questions. "From that deep and copious well of legal knowledge," Parker asserts, Webster drew freely "whenever his own bucket was dry" (*ibid.*, p. 170).

This shift from Republican to Whig came about quite naturally. New England liberalism, it must be remembered, produced no intellectual leaders till late, and no clear-cut political philosophy. Though it nominally accepted the leadership of Jefferson it never was won over to the Physiocratic economics or states-rights principles of the Virginia school. Story was at no time a Jeffersonian, but rather an eager and avowed disciple of Washington, "little infected with Virginia notions, as to men or measures." In his *Autobiography* he wrote:

> The republican party then and at all other times embraced men of very different views on many subjects. Nay, a Virginia republican of that day, was very different from a Massachusetts republican, and the anti-federal doctrines of the former state then had and still have very little support or influence in the latter state, notwithstanding a concurrence in political action upon general subjects. I was at all times a firm believer in the doctrines of General Washington, and an admirer of his conduct, measurers and principles. . . . I read and examined his principles, and have made them in a great measure the rule and guide of my life. I was and always have been a lover, devoted lover, of the constitution of the United States, and a friend to the union of the states. I never wished to bring the government to a mere confederacy of states; but to preserve the power of the general government given by all the states, in full exercise and sovereignty for the protection and preservation of all the states. (Story, *Life and Letters of Joseph Story,* Vol. I, p. 128.)

That he had as little sympathy with the Physiocratic economics of Jefferson is apparent from his early activities in furthering the new paper system. While a member of the Massachusetts legislature, as a young man, he was active in pressing for bank franchises, and upon the establishment of the Merchants' Bank of Salem he became its president. Like Washington and Marshall he espoused the new gospel of capitalism, with none of the agrarian prejudices of the landed gentry to hold him back. He was the political twin of the great Chief Justice, and a Whig in spirit long before Webster. "I seem to myself," he remarked late in life, "simply to have stood still in my political belief, while parties revolved about me; so that, although of the same opinions now as ever, I find my name changed from Democrat to Whig, but I know not how or why" (*ibid.*, Vol. I, p. 546). Though somewhat naïve the comment is just. Anti-federalism in Massachusetts would seem to have been largely a capitalistic protest against the narrow tie-wig Federalism; and while Joseph Story sat upon the Supreme Court bench, adapting legal principles to the new needs of business, the country was moving forward to the middle-class philosophy that he had early come to hold.

In the year 1833 he published his *Commentaries on the Constitution*, the fruit of long labors, which was at once accepted throughout the North as a classical authority, and which has held its ground pretty well since. In method and temper, as well as objective, the exposition of Story stands in sharp contrast to that of the southern school. In its particularism the latter appealed to the history of the Constitution in the making, and to French romantic philosophy; whereas the former followed English constitutional theories to nationalistic ends. Story was steeped in the Common Law and his thinking reveals the strong influence of Blackstone. In passing through the mind of the great Tory commentator, English constitutional theory had received a pronounced Tory bias, and something of this remains after filtering through the mind of Story. The ideal of a strong and efficient political state, with its corollaries of a coercive sovereignty, of the duties of a subject rather than the rights of a citizen, of loyalty to government rather than concern for political justice, derives immediately from English theory and practice. Much likewise he took from the older Federalists: their fear of an encroaching legislative power; their concern at faction; their faith in checks and balances to restrain the majority will. But his chief inspiration came from the spirit of the Common Law—that subtle influence that Jefferson so greatly feared. His legalism was inveterate; the final, authoritative answer to all questions he discovered in the decision of the courts. Against such a mind, deeply read in the law and with scanty knowledge of economics and political theory, the waves of liberal and romantic thought broke impotently. His reasoning may be convincing to a lawyer, but to the historian his exposition is often weak, his data inadequate, and his conclusions not infrequently contrary to fact.

In building his argument Story drew his materials freely from *The Federalist*, from the writings and decisions of Marshall, and from Blackstone. The backbone of the work is Hamilton and Marshall, from whom he quotes constantly, supplemented by a host of decisions by Federalist judges. With its pronounced bias *The Commentaries* must be regarded as a partisan document, which like *The Federalist* has grown in authoritativeness with the triumph of its party principles. Its surprising weakness on the historical side has come to be overlooked since the downfall of southern particularism, but during the debates that preceded the Civil War the work was sharply handled by southern historians, and in his *Constitutional View of the War between the States* Stephens quite demolished Story's feeble attempt at an historical justification of the anti-compact theory. The weight of historical evidence, to present-day students, would seem to be on the side of the states-rights argument, although in certain aspects both sides were innovators: Story in overleaping the period of French ascendency when the Constitution took shape, and going back to the older English tradition; and the compact school in reasserting the compact theory at a time when the spirit of nationalism was undermining it. Story seems to have been conscious of his weakness, for he expressly repudiates the method of interpreting the work in the light of contemporary testimony at the time of its formulation. In so doing he not only violates the principle that a document is to be construed in the light of the common understanding when it was drawn; but with naïve inconsistency, he constantly appeals to *The Federalist*, pretty much ignoring the opposition pamphlets, and interprets the Constitution in accord with its commentary. But for the most part he clings to the strict letter of the document. He lightly brushes aside the whole compact argument by asserting dogmatically that the phrase, "We the people of the United States," must be understood in its simple literal sense, and that thus interpreted, the Constitution is seen to derive immediately from the individual citizens acting in their sovereign capacity without the intermediation of the state governments. The dispute long waged furiously about this point and Story's analysis touches only the fringe of the argument.

Very likely it is presumptuous for one who is not a lawyer to express an opinion, yet these celebrated *Commentaries* seem today very little more than a new-modeled Federalism, adapted to changing conditions. Underneath the somewhat crabbed and narrow legalism is a common-sense realistic political philosophy, an embodiment of English constitutional tradition as it grew up under a Tory régime, that reveals scant sympathy with French romantic theories. The work is an unconscious testimony to the tenacious hold of the English Common Law on the legal mind of America, as well as to the rising spirit of nationalism. It did much to strengthen both. It was a triumph of the lawyer over the historian and political philosopher, and it marks the beginning of the lawyer's custodianship of the fundamental law. In spite of its somewhat petty legalism and prosaic common sense, a note of veneration for the great document runs through the tedious pages, constituting the work at once both a commentary and a eulogy.

III

DANIEL WEBSTER: *Realist and Constitutionalist*

A far solider mind, strongly realistic and broadly philosophical, acute in analysis and with great powers of imagination, was the mind of the distinguished leader of the New England Whigs. Not the equal of Story as a lawyer, he was far superior as a political thinker. No man more richly endowed in mind and person has played a part on the stage of our public life, and in spite of gross shortcomings in character and the betrayal of his own promise, Webster retains an aura of the heroic about him. He was a great man, built on a great pattern, who never quite achieved a great life.

In Emerson and Webster were completely embodied the diverse New England tendencies that derived from the Puritan and the Yankee: the idealistic and the practical; the ethical and the rationalistic; the intellectual revolutionary, ready to turn the world upside down in theory, planting at the base of the established order the dynamite of ideas, and the soberly conservative, understanding the economic springs of political action, inclined to pessimism, neither wishing for Utopian change nor expecting it. The physical contrast was as striking as the mental. The child of the Puritan was slender, nervous, with a lambent energy that played freely in a rarefied atmosphere; the child of the Yankee was massive, solid, somnolently heavy till an idea awakened his faculties, a lover of the fleshpots, careless of conventional morals, rankly physical, and yet with an assured stateliness of manner, a slow imagination that expanded majestically and a rich eloquence that moved forward by regular stages to a great objective. Emerson was the child of a long line of ministers, and ministerial in his unworldliness; Webster was a Yankee squire, the descendant of some fox-hunting master of broad English acres, who by a freak of fortune had got born into the family of a New Hampshire yeoman. No Englishman was ever more English than he. He loved the substantial things of life: his Marshfield farm; his cattle and horses and crops; his rides afield and the return to good dinners and rich wines. Nothing is more characteristic or more likable— more redolent of the natural Webster—than his concern for agricultural improvements. His homely talk on *The Agriculture of England,* filled with facts that had come under his observant eye, reveals a side that is too little known. It is an English country squire talking to his neighbors about the homely things they all care for; and when after long years and disappointed ambition and utter weariness, he returned to his Marshfield farm to die, it was his cattle and his fields that offered a last solace to the broken man.

Webster's intellectual development falls into distinct and rather sharply defined periods. Before 1825 his mental processes were still under the dominion of the solid, rationalist eighteenth century, with its realistic politics and its *laissez-faire* economics. With the emergence of the constitutional disputes at the end of the twenties, when the lawyers and historians were busy at their commentaries, he came increasingly to take a legalistic view of government. During the acrimonious forties, with slavery dividing the country into hostile camps, he was bitten deeply by presidential ambitions, and thenceforth to the end of his life he was little more than a politician—a rôle for which he was singularly ill-fitted, and which brought bitterness and disillusion to his last days. Since his death both earlier and later phases of his career have fallen into the background, and the middle period of constitutional interpretation has stamped itself indelibly upon his fame. Yet in many respects the solid reasoning of the political philosopher is more valuable than the stately but somewhat ill-grounded declamation of the defender of the Constitution; and his just fame is increased rather than lessened by recalling his earlier contribution to our institutional development.

Webster was a sound political scholar, if not an outstanding creative thinker. He was of the distinguished line of political realists, from Harrington through Locke and Burke, to Hamilton, Madison and John Adams. He derived equally from seventeenth-century liberalism and eighteenth-century Federalism. He was widely read in the political classics, and his vigorous mind laid hold upon major principles and examined them closely. His intellectual master was the acute thinker of the English Commonwealth period, James Harrington, whom he pronounces "one of the most ingenious of political writers," and to whose suggestive doctrine of economic determinism he returns persistently. That Harrington was not the originator of the doctrine he was well enough read to have discovered; but he pays him high tribute as the thinker who gave the doctrine form and currency. It is the substantial realism of the *Oceana* that appealed to a mind thoroughly indoctrinated with political realism, before the rise of manhood suffrage and the spread of equalitarianism had brought a change in American political theory. Both his major premises and his mode of reasoning bear the impress of the classic English school. In the year 1820, within a single week, he made two speeches, which as expositions of his political philosophy are the most illuminating he ever uttered, and which should stand side by side: the *Basis of the Senate*, delivered before the Massachusetts Constitutional Convention, and the Plymouth speech on *The First Settlement of New England*. They supplement each other and together give an admirable elucidation of the stake-in-society principle that embodied a conviction he never abandoned. They are compact of Harrington, Montesquieu and John Adams—the last authentic expression of the old Federalism, before the democratic storms had driven it into new roadsteads and whipped its flag from the halyards where it had long waved.

In his admirable argument Webster accepts as axiomatic the theory of division of powers, with the attendant machinery of checks and balances. He accepts equally the familiar view of eighteenth-century liberalism, that the legislature as the self-conscious custodian of the popular will is certain to prove the engrossing member of government whose ambition is most to be feared. To expect a stable balance between Senate and House when their characters are undifferentiated by diverse modes of selection—a result that must follow from choosing both on the numerical majority principle—seems to him the judgment of political inexperience. The wiser method, he believed, was to seek counsel of the philosophers and the clear teachings of history. The first, Webster insisted, have rightly laid down the principle of a stake-in-society as the true measure of political justice:

I take the *principle* to be well established, by writers of the greatest authority. In the first place, those who have treated of natural law have maintained, as a principle of law, that, as far

297

as the object of society is the protection of something in which the members possess unequal shares, it is just that the weight of each person in the common councils should bear a relation and proportion to his interest. Such is the sentiment of Grotius, and he refers, in support of it, to several institutions among the lesser states. ("The Basis of the Senate," in *Works*, Vol. III, pp. 13–14.)

At the basis of the stake-in-society principle is the doctrine of economic power as the controlling factor in determining the form and scope of the political state. In support of this doctrine of determinism Webster appeals to Harrington:

It is his leading object, in his *Oceana*, to prove, that power *naturally* and *necessarily* follows property. He maintains that a government founded on property is legitimately founded; and that a government founded on the disregard of property is founded in injustice, and can only be maintained by military force. "If one man," says he, "be sole landlord, like the Grand Seignior, his empire is absolute. If a few possess the land, this makes the Gothic or feudal constitution. If the *whole people* be landlords, then it is a commonwealth." "It is strange," says an ingenious person in the last century, "that Harrington should be the first man to find out so evident and demonstrable a truth as that property being the true basis and *measure* of power." In truth, he was not the first. The idea is as old as political science itself. It may be found in Aristotle, Lord Bacon, Sir Walter Raleigh, and other writers. Harrington seems, however, to be the first writer who has illustrated and expanded the principle, and given to it the effect and prominence which justly belong to it. To this sentiment, Sir, I entirely agree. It seems to me to be plain, that, in the absence of military force, political power naturally and necessarily goes into the hands which hold the property. In my judgment, therefore, a republican form of government rests, not more on political constitutions, than on those laws which regulate the descent and transmission of property. . . .

The English Revolution of 1688 was a revolution in favor of property, as well as of other rights. It was brought about by men of property for their security; and our own immortal Revolution was undertaken, not to shake or plunder property, but to protect it. The acts which the country complained of were such as violated the rights of property. An immense majority of all those who had an interest in the soil were in favor of the Revolution; and they carried it through, looking to its results for the security of their possessions. ("The Basis of the Senate," in *Works*, Vol. III, pp. 14–16.)

Harrington's principle that "if the *whole people* be landlords, then it is a commonwealth," Webster justified by appeal to American history. The spontaneous birth of republican institutions out of colonial experience he attributed to the wide diffusion of property. The land tenure of primitive New England was the creative source of her popular government.

Their situation demanded a parcelling out and division of the lands, and it may be fairly said, that this necessary act *fixed the future frame and form of their government.* The character of their political institutions was determined by the fundamental laws respecting property. . . . The property was all freehold . . . alienation of the land was every way facilitated even to the subjecting of it to every species of debt. The establishment of public registries, and the simplicity of our forms of conveyance, have greatly facilitated the change of real estate from one proprietor to another. The consequence of all these causes has been, a great subdivision of the soil, and a great equality of condition; the true basis, most certainly, of a popular government. "If the people," says Harrington, "hold three parts in four of the territory, it is plain there can neither be any single person nor nobility able to dispute the government with them; in this case, therefore, *except force be interposed,* they govern themselves." ("The First Settlement of New England," in *Works,* Vol. I, pp. 35–36.)

Wholly English then, after the soundest English liberal tradition, was Webster's political philosophy in the year 1820, compact of sober eighteenth-century realism, quite unaffected by French romantic equalitarianism. The great principle to which he adhered was the principle that government to be stable must be founded in men's interests; thus founded no cause is given for revolutionary upheavals. "The disastrous revolutions which the world has witnessed, those political thunder-storms and earthquakes which have shaken the pillars of society to their very deepest foundations, have been revolutions against property." Such were Webster's convictions on the eve of those two great upheavals, the rise of Jacksonian democracy and the rejuvenation of the slave economy, that unseated the authority of the old school of political realism, and turned him aside from the plain path to lose himself in a tangle of constitutional legalism.

English also was his economic theory, to which, like Franklin before him, he gave close thought. In the year 1820 he was a frank disciple of Adam Smith and the *laissez-faire* school. Mercantilism he derided as exploded;[2] and Physiocratic agrarianism seemed to him unduly hostile to commerce. He never concerned himself, like Franklin,

[2] See "The Tariff," in *Works,* Vol. III, pp. 118–122.

with humanitarian ends. His sympathies went strongly for free trade, individual initiative, and a competitive order— sympathies which to the end of his life he never wholly outgrew. In those early days the mercantile interests commanded his loyalty far more readily than the manufacturing interests. Next to his Marshfield farm he loved a full-rigged ship, and the thought of Yankee skippers plowing the seven seas in well-freighted bottoms fired his imagination and kindled his patriotism. But if in the background of his thought he remained *laissez faire,* with the necessary implications of a diminished political state and reliance upon the law of supply and demand above tariffs, bounties, and political regulations, unfortunately in the foreground of expediency were the loud demands of his constituents for protective tariffs, internal improvements, and a policy of governmental paternalism. His economics came into collision with politics, and under the drive of necessity he went reluctantly along the path which Hamilton had marked out a generation before.

The change came between the years 1824 and 1825. In the earlier year he aroused himself to a strong defense of *laissez-faire* economics in opposition to Clay's clever campaign cry, the American System; in the later year he endeavored half-heartedly to defend New England interests in the game of subsidies. He was honestly ashamed of the whole mess; to Webster any tariff was a "tariff of abominations"; but his mouth was stopped by the clamor of the Lowell textile masters.[3] But having chosen his side, thereafter he defended his course vigorously, and joined forces with Clay in extolling the principle of protection. The same dubious shift is revealed in his changing attitude towards public finance. In 1815 he was an old-fashioned Federalist in his preference for a metallic currency and his belief that the public credit must rest on the public income; bank paper, stocks, bonds, and other agencies of the new finance he distrusted as likely to encourage speculation.[4] Twenty years later he was the outstanding champion of the Bank in its mortal quarrel with Jackson. In defending his public career before his constituents in Faneuil Hall in 1842, he said: "The subject of currency has been the study of my life, in preference to all other public topics"; and the result of those studies had made him a confirmed bullionist. Nevertheless when "Old Bullion

[3] See his "Apology and Defense," in *Works,* Vol. V, pp. 146, 240.
[4] See "The Bank of the United States," *Works,* Vol. III, p. 35.

Benton" proposed to restore a metallic currency, Webster derided the plan on the ground that bank money was necessary; and when the subtreasury system was established he denounced it bitterly.[5] He was a partisan to the cause of the Bank, and as its attorney he defended its case before the American public, as he defended its cases before the Supreme Court. He was no longer a free man but was deep in the subsidies of financial interests; nevertheless his old realism convinced him—as it had convinced Hamilton—of the necessity of shaping the public policy to the desires of the bankers. He justified it not only on the grounds of economic determinism, but by professing to discover in business the strong friend of national unity. The planters and farmers were local and sectional in outlook, but the "mercantile classes, the great commercial masses of the country, whose affairs connect them strongly with every State in the Union and with all the nations of the earth, whose business and profession give a sort of nationality to their character"—these men, he argued, gave solidity and stability to government—they were the cohesive force that bound the whole together.[6] In serving such clients he was but serving a greater cause.

After 1824 the earlier Webster with his solid understanding, his frank realism, his honest exposition of fundamental principles, slowly gave way to the lawyer, the politician, the opportunist of the unhappy later years. With the change the last authentic voice of the eighteenth century was silenced; the break with the old English tradition was complete. Immediate, domestic issues muddied his thought, and Webster and America plunged into a bitter partisanship produced by the new alignments of an equalitarian agrarianism, a capitalistic industrialism, and a feudal slavocracy. Federalism was dead and in its stead was the Whig party, patched together of odds and ends, devoid of principles, seeking only expediency; and of this party Webster became an outstanding spokesman. It was an ignoble time, and his great abilities were not substantia! enough to save him from the common meanness. Whoever wishes to understand how great was his fall need only compare the speech of 1820 on "The Basis of the Senate" with the "Declaration of Whig Principles and Purposes" of 1840 (*Works*, Vol. II, p. 41).

To his contemporaries, however, his position was secure.

[5] See "Speech in Wall Street," in *Works*, Vol. II, p. 55.
[6] See "The Landing at Plymouth," in *Works*, Vol. II, pp. 204–205.

His reputation was extraordinary, and he seemed as fixed and brilliant as the north star. After the reply to Hayne, his fame as the defender of the Constitution was in every mouth. That celebrated speech, perhaps the most celebrated in our congressional history, was delivered on January 26, 1830, and awakened an amazing response. Men were moved to tears by its eloquence, and its circulation in pamphlet form exceeded that of any other pamphlet since the founding of the government. It is not a great constitutional argument, but it better served the purpose of inspiring in the public a grandiose conception of national unity under the organic law, than any reasoned statement could have done. For political purposes rhetoric was more effective than historical argument, and its sonorous sentences, and in particular the stately conclusion, vastly appealed to the taste of the generation. Three years later Webster applied himself more closely to the subtleties of the question. Calhoun's masterly argument with its exposition of the theory of concurrent majorities could not be answered by rhetoric, and on February 16, 1833, Webster spoke on "The Constitution not a Compact between Sovereign States" (*Works*, Vol. III, p. 449). His argument is strictly legal and rests on four theses: that sovereignty inheres in the people; that as individuals acting collectively in their sovereign capacity, they ordained and established the Constitution; that the Constitution thus established is the supreme law of the land, acting immediately upon the individual citizen and recognizing no intermediary sovereign state; and that as an "executed contract" it is irrevocable and final, with the necessary functions to construe its powers and execute its will.

Of these four theses, two may be regarded as Webster's chief contribution to the great debate: the doctrine of immediacy, and the doctrine of an executed contract. The latter, quite obviously, is no more than Burke's theory of the British constitution as founded on a compact entered into following the Revolution of 1688, and as such, by analogy from the Common Law, inviolable without the consent of both parties to the instrument. As developed by Burke the theory is somewhat tenuous, but as applied by Webster to the interpretation of a written document it is extraordinarily plausible to the legal mind. The doctrine of immediacy, on the other hand, would seem to have been derived from Judge Story. The argument of Webster in expounding the principle of immediate contact between the individual citizen and the Constitution follows the argument of Story's *Commentaries* too closely to escape comment. Theodore Parker explicitly states that Webster got his argument from Story, and circumstances bear out his assertion. The two men had long been close friends. Webster's speech was delivered a month after the *Commentaries* was finished. In his earlier speeches such principle found no place, and it is reasonable to suppose that, confronted by the Calhoun resolutions Webster should have turned to the materials gathered by his learned friend and frequent adviser. Here was his reply ready to hand, a mass of legal fact and constitutional exposition, together with a clear and simple theory. Nearly a month elapsed before Webster rose to speak, and then he threw *Story on the Constitution* at Calhoun's theory of compact. Whether such an interpretation is reasonable or not, the speech added greatly to Webster's reputation as an expounder of the Constitution.

In 1833 he stood at the meridian of his renown; thereafter the westering sun of his fame went slowly down. He had come to evil times when opportunism and compromise—so imperative if the country were to hold together at all—seemed immoral to men who insisted that righteousness be legislated upon America, and weakness to men who demanded their pound of flesh. The black shadow of slavery fell across his path, and despite his wish to avoid all controversy on the subject, he could not evade the issue. It drove him into a corner, and the sword of the Constitution that he sought to defend himself with was turned in the end against him. Webster's antipathy to slavery was of long standing and he gave frank expression to it in his speeches. The position which he finally came to assume, in face of the growing abolition sentiment in Massachusetts, was taken deliberately and was worthy of a lawyer. He would oppose the extension of slave territory, but he would not interfere with slavery in the old slave states. The Constitution, he argued, recognized slavery as existing in certain commonwealths by virtue of state laws, but those laws did not run beyond the confines of the state. The territories were under federal law, and no injunction was laid upon Congress to extend the laws or institutions of any state or group of states over the territorial domain. In his speech on "Exclusion of Slavery from the Territories," on August 12, 1848, he stated his position thus:

It will not be contended that this sort of slavery exists by general law. It exists only by local law. I do not mean to deny the validity of that local law where it is established; but I say it is, after all, local law. It is nothing more. And wherever that local law does not extend, property in persons does not exist. Well, Sir, what is now the demand on the part of our Southern friends? They say, "We will carry our local laws with us wherever we go. We insist that Congress does us injustice unless it establishes in the territory in which we wish to go our own local law." This demand I for one resist, and shall resist. It goes upon the idea that there is an inequality, unless persons under this local law, and holding property by authority of that law, can go into new territory and there establish that local law, to the exclusion of the general law. (*Works,* Vol. V, p. 309.)

It was the unfortunate Seventh of March Speech that proved Webster's undoing—this and the Fugitive Slave Bill in which he was deeply implicated. The situation was desperately critical, Webster was pessimistic, and this was a last gesture of reconciliation with the South. Presidential ambitions and runaway slaves were stewing in a common political pot with Abolition societies and northern mercantile interests. Webster was puzzled, hesitated, emptied another glass of the wine of the Constitution, and went for the Fugitive Slave Bill. It was a tragic political mistake. To be sure a tremendous address was presented to him, signed by the most respectable persons in Boston and Cambridge, but it was an empty honor. Webster's influence was gone, never to be regained. There is something pathetic in his futile attempt to stifle the New England conscience by ramming the Constitution down its throat:

Sir, the principle of the restitution of runaway slaves is not objectionable, unless the Constitution is objectionable. If the Constitution is right in that respect, the principle is right, and the law providing for carrying it into effect is right. If that be so, and if there is no abuse of the right under any law of Congress, or any other law, then what there is to complain of? ("Speech on the Compromise Measures," in *Works,* Vol. V, p. 433.)

And there is something pathetic also in the hurt vanity of the old man that his judgment should be questioned. His self-pride was offended when the Abolitionists rejected his legal dogmatisms, and set up their own dogmatisms. He regarded them as mischief-makers. "I am against agitators, north and south," he exclaimed petulantly. He recognized no higher law than the Constitution and Blackstone, and he would suffer no popular interference with Congress.

Then, Sir, there are the Abolition societies, of which I am
unwilling to speak, but in regard to which I have very clear
notions and opinions. I do not think them useful. I think their
operations for the last twenty years have produced nothing good
or valuable. . . . They have excited feelings. . . . I cannot but
see what mischiefs their interference with the South has produced . . . everything that these agitating people have done
has been, not to enlarge, but to restrain, not to set free, but
to bind faster, the slave population of the South. ("Seventh of
March Speech," in *Works,* Vol. V, p. 357.)

I desire to call the attention of all sober-minded men at the
North, of all conscientious men, of all men who are not carried
away by some fanatical idea or some false impression, to their constitutional obligations. I put it to all the sober and sound minds
at the North as a question of morals and a question of conscience. What right have they, in their legislative capacity or
any other capacity, to endeavour to get around this Constitution,
or to embarrass the free exercise of the rights secured by the
Constitution to the persons whose slaves escape from them?
None at all; none at all. Neither in the forum of conscience,
nor before the face of the Constitution, are they, in my opinion,
justified in such attempt. (*Ibid.,* p. 355.)

If the later Webster had no message for the conscience
of New England, neither had he any for the intelligence
of New England. The realistic Federalism that had listened
to him in 1820 was gone, submerged by the flood waters
of the renaissance; and the current transcendentalism
seemed to him insubstantial and dangerous. The rising
liberalism of the forties left him wholly untouched; it
could not leaven the heavy materialism of his nature. He
was quite unacquainted with the new Massachusetts that
was coming to expression; he had lived too long with "the
lawyers, the politicians, and rich merchants and manufacturers," to understand the greater world of Concord.
While he had been living on the subsidies of State Street,
and contracting his mind to the compass of a banker's,
the intellect of Massachusetts had become liberal. And in
becoming liberal it aroused him from indifference to hostility. Writing to a friend in explanation of his refusal to
visit Concord in his later years, he said:

Many of those whom I so highly regarded in your beautiful
and quiet village have become a good deal estranged, to my
great grief, by abolitionism, free-soilism, transcendentalism, and
other notions which I cannot but regard as so many vagaries of
the imagination. (Quoted in Sanborn, *Life of Thoreau.*)

But if he was scarcely acquainted with the little group of thinkers and liberals—Emerson, Thoreau, Channing, Parker, Garrison, Phillips, Edmund Quincy, Whittier, Lowell, Higginson, Harriet Beecher Stowe, Margaret Fuller—they were well acquainted with him and took his measure exactly. The intellect of Massachusetts—so long ignored by Webster—had its revenge. Its voice carried farther than his, and it painted his portrait in no flattering strokes. The fierce storm that suddenly beat upon him broke the old man's spirit. He had fed too long on adulation to endure censure. No doubt that censure was severe, but it was far juster than the earlier adulation had been. Whittier's *Ichabod* is familiar to every American schoolboy. Lowell, then in his liberal mood, characterized him as "a statesman who had communicated no impulse to any of the great ideas of the century, as a statesman whose soul had been absorbed in tariff, banks, and the Constitution, instead of devoting himself to the freedom of the future." Emerson, who had long studied him critically, gave an extraordinarily just analysis of his character:

Mr. Webster is a man who lives by his memory, a man of the past, not a man of faith or of hope. He obeys his powerful animal nature;—and his finely developed understanding only works freely and with all its force, when it stands for animal good; that is, for property. He believes, in so many words, that government exists for the protection of property. He looks to the Union as an estate, a large farm, and is excellent in the completeness of his defence of it so far. He adheres to the letter. . . . What he finds already written, he will defend. Lucky that so much had got well written when he came. For he has no faith in the power of self-government. Not the smallest municipal provision, if it were new, would receive his sanction. In Massachusetts, in 1776, he would, beyond all question, have been a refugee. He praises Adams and Jefferson, but it is a past Adams and Jefferson, that his mind can entertain. A present Adams and Jefferson he would denounce. So with the eulogies of liberty in his writings,—they are sentimentalism and youthful rhetoric. He can celebrate it, but it means as much from him as from Metternich or Talleyrand. This is all inevitable from his constitution. All the drops of his blood have eyes that look downward. ("The Fugitive Slave Law.")

To the transcendental mind Webster's economic realism was peculiarly repugnant, and it was this which inspired Theodore Parker's critical analysis of Webster's career—the most scathing and explicit of all contemporary estimates. What Parker discovers most hateful in Webster's career was his adherence to the principles of Federalism, from the "Basis of the Senate" speech in 1820, to the New York speech on November 18, 1850. The persistence of his economic realism was an affront to the liberals of the humanitarian school that had moved far from the position of Fisher Ames. Webster might do lip service to humanitarian ideals, Parker asserted, but always he came back in the end to his polar conception—"The great object of government is the protection of property at home, and respect and renown abroad" (*Works: Additional Speeches*, Vol. I, p. 220).

It was this same persistent realism that made Webster so useful to the rising capitalism. His work in the Senate was supplemented by his work in the court room. He was the greatest corporation lawyer of the day, certain to be found defending vested interests, never on the side of the leaner purse. Probably more than any other man except John Marshall, he contributed to the work of bringing the Constitution under the sovereignty of the judiciary. His most significant contribution, certainly, was his argument in the celebrated Dartmouth College case, delivered before the Supreme Court in 1818, which resulted in one of the foundation decisions on which later has been erected the solid structure of our corporation law.[7] By engrafting upon the Constitution the principle that a contract lies beyond the reach of legislative power to annul, the decision assured greater security for private property than exists under any other judicial system in the world. Alexander Hamilton could not have asked for more.

It was the singular ill fortune of Webster to have been born too late to profit from the old mercantile Federalism to which his affections were always attached, and too early to profit by the industrial Federalism that came to greatness after the Civil War. If fate had been kinder to him, and he had appeared on the political horizon a generation earlier or a generation later, he would have reaped in far greater abundance those high civic honors he so foolishly coveted. The economic groups whom he served would have been in position to reward a servant so conspicuously

---

[7] Theodore Parker denied Webster credit for the argument, pointing out that "the facts, the law, the precedents, the ideas, and the conclusions of that argument, had almost all of them been presented by Messrs. Mason and Smith in the previous trial of the case" (*Additional Speeches*, Vol. I, p. 171). The statement is confirmed by Beveridge.

able and useful. As a contemporary of John Adams he might have become a notable political philosopher—provided always that he had not turned Tory as Emerson suggested. But unhappily for his fame he was launched between tides on a stormy sea and his stately bark foundered in the squall of Abolitionism.

CHAPTER I

The Renaissance

> To write a history of Massachusetts, I confess, is not inviting
> to an expansive thinker. . . . From 1790 to 1820 there was not
> a book, a speech, a conversation, or a thought in the State.
> About 1820, the Channing, Webster, and Everett era begun,
> and we have been bookish and poetical and cogitative since.
> (Emerson, *Journals,* Vol. VIII, p. 339.)

In such summary fashion in the year 1852, Emerson recorded his judgment on half a century of intellectual life
in Massachusetts. It was the comment of an exacting critic.
In its characterization of the extraordinary ferment of
thought that marked the decades of the thirties and forties, it is quite inadequate; but in its contemptuous dis-
missal of the age of Fisher Ames and Robert Treat Paine
it was scarcely unjust. The utter sterility of those old times
Emerson understood only too well. It was the world of
his own youth, whose pale negations he had come to hate.
The creative impulse was stifled, the mind had grown stale
from tedious iteration. But at last the old barriers gave way,
and into this narrow illiberal world, that had long fed on
the crusts of English rationalism and Edwardean dogmatism—dry as remainder biscuit after voyage—broke the
floods that had been gathering in Europe for years, the waters of all the streams of revolution that were running
there bank-full. Before this inundation the old provincialisms were swept away, and for the first time in its history,
and the last, the mind of New England gave itself over
to a great adventure in liberalism.

Quite evidently the renaissance resulted from the impact of the romantic revolution upon the Puritan mind, and it issued in a form native to New England experience. Animated by the common spirit of Utopianism, its dreams were unlike those of Virginia or the West, founded on a different economics and seeking different ends. Massachusetts had discovered a particular road leading to Utopia by way of the industrial revolution, and the textile mills on the Merrimac began weaving a new pattern of life for New England. The old static agricultural order was broken in upon, and with the social disruption came naturally an intellectual disruption. The mind of that older New England had been held in the close keeping of the church, and the movement of intellectual emancipation became therefore at the outset a movement leveled at theological conservatism; it was concerned first to rid New England of the incubus of Calvinistic dogma. The Calvinists were of tough fiber and tenacious of opinion, and to turn their flank was no summer campaign. The result was a long battle of ideas, a fierce struggle between the old deterministic theology and the new romantic philosophy, with victory slowly inclining to the latter. This major struggle gave to the renaissance its profoundly ethical spirit that set it off sharply from the earlier renaissance of Virginia; and not the least important of the results of the movement was the liberation of the New England conscience from its long bondage to dogma, setting it free to engage in a larger work in the world. What that conscience accomplished in the brief period of its freedom; what causes it espoused and what reforms it carried through—how it quickened a humanitarian zeal in New England and imparted a militant spirit to its culture—these are phases of the total movement not to be neglected by the historian.

In the realm of ideas the renaissance was largely dominated by old-world thought. From the abundant stores of European revolutionary doctrine the New England liberals drew freely—more freely perhaps from German idealism than from French Utopianism. Germany meant much to the awakening mind of New England, by reason of its spiritual and intellectual kinship. Plato was their common father, a transcendental mysticism their common experience. Philosophical idealism with its indwelling Godhood that exalted man to the divine and transformed a mechanical universe into the dwelling place of divine love—this was a dynamic faith, appealing to men long nurtured in faith, more seductive to the children of Puritanism than any political or economic romanticisms. It opened to them new heavens when the old were closed and encouraged them to go forth on great ventures.

But the renaissance was very much more than a transplanting of German idealism. France had a shaping hand in it, and England. Jean Jacques came before Hegel, and Unitarianism before transcendentalism. It was social and literary as well as philosophical. In so far as that which was essentially one may be divided, the movement involved three major strands: the social Utopianism that came from revolutionary France; the idealistic metaphysics that emerged from revolutionary Germany; and the new culture that spread with the development of literary romanticism. To distinguish these three strands is one thing; to endeavor to separate them is quite another. They interweave and blend in varying patterns; they are but different, new-world phases of a comprehensive European movement that runs far back into the preceding century— a movement that in transferring economic and political mastery from the aristocracy to the middle class, in destroying the worm-eaten feudal order and clearing the way for the new capitalistic order, laid open a broad path into the nineteenth century. The extraordinary appeal of this vast movement to the liberal mind of America resulted from the fact that an identical revolution was under way here. In New England, perhaps more dramatically than elsewhere in America, the day of the middle class was dawning, aristocratic ideals were disintegrating, and the hopes of men were running high. To humanize this emerging society, to awaken it to a nobler faith in human destiny, to further the cause of social justice, to create a democracy of the spirit—this was the deeper romantic purpose, however vaguely comprehended, that was fermenting in the New England renaissance, and it was this that gave to it a spirit so warmly ethical.

Now quite evidently a movement so extraordinarily complex would appeal diversely to different minds, and in its development it drew to itself a singularly various following. To the sons of respectable Federalism it was the new romantic culture that appealed; to the militant conscience of Puritanism it was the inspiration of social Utopianism; to the emancipated intellectuals it was the metaphysical idealism. Its many-sidedness was both confusing and stimulating. How shall we explain a movement that embraced such different men as Everett and Channing and Parkei and Garrison and Whittier and Emerson and Longfellow and Holmes; men often mutually repellent, sometimes sharply critical of each other? No single mind sums up the whole—the theological, humanitarian, mystical, critical, and cultural aspirations of the awakening—as perhaps Goethe may be said to have done for Germany. Emerson, Thoreau and Parker possibly embodied it most adequately; they were transcendental individualists, intellectual revolutionaries, contemptuous of all meanly material standards. But quite evidently Everett would not travel far along the transcendental path they pointed out, nor Holmes, nor Longfellow. These latter expected no romantic Utopias, wanted no such Utopias. Cambridge and Boston satisfied their hopes; they found the world not such a bad place for those who knew how to meet it on its own terms. Yet they too were children of the awakening, and in following their individual paths they contributed in their own way to the disintegration of the old authoritarian order that had long held the mind of New England in subjection. Each in some measure and after his own fashion was a rebel, and their total rebellions made up the sum of New England's bequest to a more liberal America. Yet in this eager and somewhat vague liberalism to which the renaissance was dedicated in spirit, the note that runs through the several programs is a note of reaction from the aspirations of the middle class. It was an ethical protest against the harsh and unjust realities of the industrial revolution that was so ruthlessly transforming the old order of life in New England; and it took the form of a return to a simpler life. To struggle free from the chains of the eighteenth century, only to be bound in new chains, was an ignoble ending to the emancipation that free men could not envisage with satisfaction.

CHAPTER II

Liberalism and Calvinism

I

The first stirrings of new life were felt within the church, the repository of such learning as Harvard College disseminated through the Massachusetts villages. For two hundred years the dogmas of Calvin had lain as a heavy weight on the mind of New England. Revolutions had taken place in English and continental theology, but New England Calvinism had kept closely within the narrow confines of its creed, annually turning over the exhausted soil and reaping an ever scantier harvest. Since the days of Edwards there had been abundant speculation and much exercise in syllogisms, but no scrutiny of major premises. Such an examination was long overdue, with the romantic revolution under way in France, and new theories of human nature and the relation of man to society and the state, spreading widely. But unfortunately the odium which New England conservatism quickly fastened upon the French school frightened the orthodox. The stigma of atheism was put upon every harmless bantling of the numerous French brood, and in the terror of reaction the pulpit, following the lead of the reactionary pew, aroused itself to cleanse the church of every innovation. English Arianism, even worse things, it was discovered, had stolen into Congregational pulpits during the relaxed period of the Revolution; a dangerous spirit of liberalism had spread silently through the tidewater churches, capturing the strongholds of Boston orthodoxy.

By the year 1800 it was high time for the old Congregationalism of Jonathan Edwards to take counsel with itself. "Let us guard against the insidious encroachments of *innovation*—that evil and beguiling spirit which is now stalking to and fro in the earth, seeking whom it may devour," exclaimed Jedidiah Morse, the arch reactionary, in the days when French ideas were knocking at the doors of New England. And by innovation the doughty Jedidiah meant any idea that had been stumbled on, new since the days of the great Edwards. To go back to the pure Edwardean doctrine, to purge the church of incipient Arminianism and Arianism and Socianism—together with such other innovations as might show their faces anywhere—became thenceforth the chief business of the devout New England of 1800. To timid souls the ideas of their grandfathers seemed far safer than the ideas of their fathers; and so theology followed politics in turning its back upon the freer, more generous world that beckoned.

Nevertheless French liberalism slowly won its victories. It needs high walls to keep out ideas. Excluded from the drawing-rooms and counting-houses, ostracized in society and politics, romantic philosophy slipped quietly into Boston by the door of theology, and took lodgings in the homes of the first families. To those who enjoy the little ironies of history, the easy subjugation of respectable Boston by that very Jacobinical heresy against which Boston was so bitter is too amusing to be overlooked. Changing its name and arraying itself in garments cut after the best Yankee fashion, the gospel of Jean Jacques presently walked the streets of Boston and spoke from its most respectable pulpits, under the guise of Unitarianism. The heretical doctrines of the excellence of human nature and the perfectibility of man were preached to Federalist congregations so persuasively that instead of repudiating them and asserting the total depravity of their neighbors, simple-minded merchants approved the doctrines and cheerfully paid their pew-rent. It was a respectable and bloodless revolution. Under its discreet disguise Unitarianism accomplished for New England what Jeffersonianism had accomplished for the South and West—the wide dissemination of eighteenth-century French liberalism. It opened the New England mind to fresh ideas. Out of Unitarianism was to come the intellectual renaissance, with its transcendental philosophies and social reforms, its enlarged conception of democracy and its Utopian dreams, which made New England count so effectively in the developments of the half century.

The twenty-five years between 1790 and 1815 were the nascent period of Unitarianism, when it was reëxamining the old Calvinist dogmas in the light of the new liberalism, weighing the doctrines of election and reprobation in the scale with the doctrines of God's beneficence and man's excellence, and coming definitely to reject them as blasphemy against God and defamation of human nature. And it was during these critical years that the upholders of the traditional orthodoxy were most actively concerned to provide a defense for the sacred dogmas of their grandfathers. The liberal advance produced a conservative reaction, and the lines of battle were sharply drawn. The capture of Harvard College by the Unitarians in 1805, and the founding of Andover Theological Seminary by the Calvinists in 1808, were dramatic events in a long intellectual and legal struggle that aroused much bitterness and bequeathed to the churches a rich legacy of unchristian animosities. Good men on both sides—to recall a contemporary witticism—were quite too ready "to fight for the glory of God as if the very devil were in them."

The traditional Calvinism defended itself with spirit, asserting so vehemently that it was still a living faith, that the corpse was not yet an authentic corpse, that it succeeded at least in postponing its own burial. It was deeply entrenched in the inertia of custom, but intellectually it was in really desperate straits. It was slowly disintegrating from dry-rot with which both minister and theology were stricken. With its major premises tacitly denied by Yankee experience, it was unfortunate in being defended by as humorless and ungainly a breed of theologians as ever quarreled over the loving-kindness of God. Clinging to the defenses which Jonathan Edwards had erected against the incursion of old-world ideas, it declaimed its dogmas and damned the human race with tedious iteration. Overthreshed straw makes poor fodder, and after a two-hour battle with potential infidelities, many a good minister descended from his pulpit lamenting that his exhortations had been wasted on "a sermon-proof, gospel-glutted generation." Yet he went faithfully back to his study to consume the day in argument with a suppositious Arminian, and in spinning cobweb systems between the worm-eaten rafters, quite oblivious to the common-sense world without his walls. The difficulties in which those old Calvinists found themselves very likely seemed tragic to them; but to later generations, endowed with some saving grace of humor, the situation was not without its spice. The good men were undeniably caught in a distressing dilemma. They were laboring prodigiously both to sit tight in the old dogma of determinism and yet wriggle out; to maintain election and reprobation and yet insert somehow the thin edge of personal responsibility; to prove to the satisfaction of the pew that man is both bound and free. It was a hard necessity to be under, to damn man by predestination, and "yet worry out enough freedom for him to be decently damned on," as a late critic has remarked;[1] to send him to hell by divine decree, yet prove that he went of his own accord. Yet they must do that impossible thing if they were to justify their theology to commonsense congregations that were drifting into indifference.

The whole thing was monstrously unreal and it resulted in hatching such a brood of tenuous subtleties as we have difficulty in comprehending today. Theological fame in Massachusetts came to be measured by the skill with which the logician made out to stand on both sides of the fence at the same time. Had it not been for Jonathan Edwards New England Congregationalism would have drifted comfortably with the tide of liberalism; but his uncompromising spirit held it anchored. This masterly spinner of theological systems bequeathed to his successors an unfinished work; but he had clearly envisaged the problem and suggested a line of attack. In his great inquiry into the nature of will he had hoped to provide an infallible means of reconciling the irreconcilable by arguing that the will is dependent on desire. The natural man, according to the Edwardean logic, is free to serve God as the highest good if he desires, but he lacks the desire unless God reveals himself as that highest good, and such revelation rests with God's pleasure. "Moral responsibility lies in the choice, not in the cause of the choice." [2] With this distinction suggested between natural and moral freedom, Calvinistic speculation went on hopefully till it attained its culminating triumph in Nathaniel Walker's ingenious doctrine of certainty with power to the contrary. Walker was a pupil of Timothy Dwight's, and one of the foundation professors of the new Yale Divinity School, established to combat Unitarian heresies. A tremendous rattling of the bones of the Connecticut churches followed his pronouncement that man's acts are not necessitated by a rigid law of cause and effect, but that his choices are so connected with antecedent conditions of soul and environment, that

[1] See Fenn, *Religious History of New England; King's Chapel Lectures,* p. 130.

[2] See Williston Walker, *A History of the Congregational Churches in the United States,* p. 283.

to God's perception it is certain what they will be, although he possesses full power of contrary choice.[3]

As we contemplate those old theological abstractions, dead now as Lot's wife, the universe of our fathers shrinks to a petty compass, not much larger than the snug little state of Connecticut, curiously egocentric, curiously anthropomorphic. Obviously such grotesqueries could not endure indefinitely. Presently there must appear the common-sense housewife with her broom, and the dusty cobwebs would disappear. English Arianism, emerging out of English Presbyterianism, and long under suspicion of the New England fathers, first opened the windows and let a little fresh air into the New England churches. But back of Arianism was the total body of eighteenth-century rationalism, with its theology rooted in new political and social philosophies, and its doctrines derived from conceptions of God and man hostile to Calvinistic determinism. There could be no reconciling them. Calvinism must extirpate English rationalism or be disintegrated by it.

But rationalism refused to be extirpated. Here and there in Massachusetts pulpits appeared a new order of preachers, young men who had broken with the old dogmas and were plainly bitten with the English distemper. Of these the most notable was Jonathan Mayhew, from 1747 to 1766 pastor of the West Church, and the freest-spoken minister in Boston. Mayhew was a throughgoing liberal, not to say radical, an intimate friend of Otis and John Adams, and chief clerical leader of the opposition to the English ministry. He had broken through the narrow parochialism of Boston; he corresponded with the intellectual leaders of English dissent, and while still a young man was on the highroad to Arianism. He seems to have been a brilliant fellow, bold and frank in speech, with great and popular powers as a preacher, and his early death alone prevented him from anticipating some of the work of Channing.[4] A like fate abruptly terminated the work of another able young man, Lemuel Briant, pastor of the Braintree church from 1745 to his death in 1753. Briant was John Adams's pastor and, like Mayhew, an Arian, with a ready wit that his adversaries must have found disconcerting. "I have always tho't," he remarked apropos of the familiar dilemma, "that so far as any Man is pure (let it be in a greater or lesser Degree) he is not

[3] *Ibid.*, p. 356.
[4] *Ibid.*, pp. 276–277.

filthy." [5] But the coming on of the Revolutionary disputes and the disturbance of war put a stop to the normal development of the movement; and the general reaction following the treaty of peace gave encouragement to the Calvinistic reaction and temporarily strengthened the Edwardean school. Nevertheless the liberal doctrines of Mayhew and Briant, falling in with the French philosophy, prepared the way for the conscious Unitarian revolt at the end of the century.

That revolt was fundamentally ethical rather than theological, and the name Unitarian, which the liberal movement accepted somewhat reluctantly from its opponents, very inadequately describes its special genius. The term derives from the middle eighteenth century, before religious thought had come under the influence of the new social philosophy; and it suggests a primary theological bias in a movement that was far more significantly ethical and social. The early liberals, forerunners of Unitarianism, were theologians given to probing in rationalistic spirit, the mystery of the Godhood. Now, denial of the Trinity has been common to all Unitarians, although individually they might profess an Arian or a Socinian interpretation of the nature and rôle of Jesus; but what is more important, they have been from the first close Scripturists, disliking exact theological systems and setting biblical authority above human. By the time the name had come to be generally accepted—about the year 1815—it had already lost much of its earlier significance, for emphasis had shifted from the mystery of the Godhood to the problem of the relations existing between the children and the Father. On the one hand supernaturalism tended to disappear in morality, and on the other religion tended to seek an authoritative basis in idealistic philosophy and justify itself by intuitionism. "The soul," argued Channing, in his exposition of a later Unitarian theology, "is the spring of our knowledge of God." "Here is our primitive teacher and light." "The only God, whom our thoughts can rest on, and our hearts can cling to, is the God whose image dwells in our own Souls" (*Works*, Vol. VI, Introductory Remarks, p. 21). Unitarianism, in other words, reversed the thought process of Calvinism. Instead of debasing man to a mean creature, subject to a God of wrath, it professed to discover a loving Father in the human heart of love. Here was a revolution indeed, a revolution in which

[5] *Ibid.*, p. 272.

were the seeds of transcendentalism, of social Utopias, of pretty much the entire intellectual awakening of New England. The old Calvinism had no weapons to meet such an attack; the new creed lay outside its realm of thought. What that creed finally came to be, under Channing's influence, is thus stated by a recent historian:

Man is God's child, made in His image and object of His love; his reason and conscience are divine witnesses to truth and light, and when governed by them he walks in the ways of God, safe in his Father's love and care. The God in whom their opponents believed—a God of election and reprobation, capable of dooming an entire race because its ancestors disobeyed a God of arbitrary will and discriminating grace—seemed to them simply an immoral being and they frankly said so. (Fenn, *Religious History of New England, etc.*, p. 125.)

In its noblest expression Unitarianism became essentially a humanistic religion, rational, ethical, individual, yet with deep and warm social sympathies. In Channing's excellent phrase, it discovered the apotheosis of religion in "the adoration of goodness." It issued in conduct because it developed character. The highest testimony to the excellence of the faith is the noble company of men and women who subscribed to its creed. And yet after all, Unitarianism was rather an attitude of mind than a creed. It was the recovery of the original principle of New England Separatism, lost during the long years of orthodox conformity—the principle of the open mind and free inquiry. Let each devout soul, each group of fellow believers, Unitarianism announced, seek the truth where it may be found; let each give to it such outward form as best reveals its divine nature; not seeking to impose a particular interpretation upon others, but each taking upon himself full responsibility for his spiritual welfare. Authority it regarded as the prop of the weak; dogma, as the body of a faith that is dead. As free souls, mature and self-reliant, the Unitarians would be their own authority, would fashion their own creed. The Scriptures lie open and the heedful eye will discover God's revelation in their pages. The deeper spirit of Unitarianism is not inadequately embodied in the text, "Search the Scriptures, for they are they which testify of me." No abler or more devout Scripturists ever preached in America than the Unitarian ministers, and if bolder souls like Theodore Parker went further than others, if their free handling of old interpretations gave offense to the timid, that fact provided no sanction to coerce or stifle free inquiry. Toleration of differences, respect for devout free thought—this return to the position of Roger Williams two centuries before was the vital principle of Unitarianism. Like him, the Unitarian was a seeker, open-minded and free. Others might be intolerant, others might regard themselves as the sole custodians of truth, but not he.

But if the Unitarians who followed Channing were liberals in religion, they were conservatives in well-nigh everything else. Amongst the laity the adoration of goodness was sufficiently tempered by Yankee thrift to keep it from interfering seriously with the practical business of getting on in the world; and in consequence the new faith gathered its supporters from amongst the prosperous rather than the needy, from Federalists rather than Democrats. The commercial dominated the intellectual and emotional in their prim and somewhat cold congregations. "The Unitarians," it was commonly said, "were the cult of the arrived." As successful men, these Boston merchants and manufacturers did not believe that they were the sons of Adam, children of iniquity. They thought better of themselves and of God than Calvinism permitted them to think; "one who was born in Boston," the current jest put it, "had no need to be born again." Generous in all approved philanthropies these Unitarian laymen might be, but emotionally religious they were temperamentally incapable of being. Until the infusion of the rich sap of transcendentalism, that gave it new life and brought it to bloom, Unitarianism was in grave danger of dying at the root. But with the spread of the philosophy of intuitionalism, the negative individualism of Unitarianism became positive, broke with the respectable conservatism of commercial congregations, and overflowed in a rich and generous faith. Authority, dogma, creed, were swept away by this new faith in an indwelling divinity, with its intuitive sanctions, and Unitarianism merged in the larger movement of the renaissance.

II
WILLIAM ELLERY CHANNING

To the austerely spiritual Channing the guiding principle of Unitarianism was identical with the spirit of primitive New England separatism—the principle of freedom in religious matters, the individual speaking his mind frankly, shepherd and flock feeding as they would, without fear and without coercion. The soul is responsible to itself and its own conscience; there are no orthodoxies and no heterodoxies, but a duty is laid upon the individual to seek truth with an open mind and be steadfast in its service. It was this spirit of open-minded liberalism that led him along the path of unmilitant individualism, seeking freedom only to the end of righteousness, and counting righteousness the fine flower of freedom; desiring peace and universal fellowship; loath to found a sect; yet driven by those who denied freedom to themselves as well as others to become the champion and leader of a great schism that sundered the traditional unity of Congregationalism, and erected a new faith on the altars of the old.

Channing's heritage was drawn from the deepest wells of New England idealism; and filtered through his finely ethical mind it emerged pure and limpid, the living waters of the new faith. His noble preëminence was due to the simple spirituality of his nature. Intellectually, he was neither great nor original. In scholarship he was distinctly inferior to academic theologians like Andrews Norton and to omnivorous students like Theodore Parker. Almost wholly introspective he was influenced slowly by world-currents of thought, and such alien ideas as found lodgment in his mind took on a native form and color from his own convictions. Nevertheless though his meditations revolved about the pole-star of his own experience, his theology cautiously took shape under the pressure of two ideas that came to him from the latter years of the eighteenth century—the ideas of God's beneficence and of man's excellence. Once lodged in his mind, those ideas led to quite revolutionary consequences, not only in their disintegrating effect upon the Calvinistic dogmas in which he had been reared, but in the generous romanticism which they bequeathed to Unitarian theology. His intellectual development was late and halting, yet that he liberated himself at all was remarkable considering the world that bred him —Newport, frequented by wealthy planters and enriched by the slave trade, Cambridge and Boston then in the stagnancy of Federalist complacency. Of the same generation with Robert Treat Paine and Josiah Quincy, only a few years older than Rufus Choate and Edward Everett, as a boy sitting under the preaching of Samuel Hopkins— the rugged expounder of the Hopkinsian doctrine of willing to be damned for the glory of God, a doctrine so repugnant to the major tenets of Channing's theology—he belonged by temperament and training to the parochial world that accounted Fisher Ames a great orator, and looked with suspicion on the new century that was crowding in on its comfortable preserves.

From the deep New England ruts Channing pulled himself with incredible difficulty. His frequent reactions almost kept pace with his progress. For years he oscillated between freedom and dogma, now dominated by the Hopkinsian influence and thrown back upon a morbid Calvinism by ill health; then resolutely casting off the evil spell; until the year 1815, when the conservative wing declaring war upon the liberals, he was drawn into the controversy and took upon himself the burden of defending the liberal cause. He was then thirty-five, but it was not till four years later, in the celebrated Baltimore sermon at the ordination of Jared Sparks, that he offered a definitive statement of the new theology. The sermon brought him wide fame and fastened upon him the leadership of the Unitarian movement. Comment upon the new doctrines was widespread, and the circulation of the sermon in pamphlet form, according to a late biographer, "was not exceeded by any American publication until in 1830 Webster made his memorable reply to Hayne" (John White Chadwick, *William Ellery Channing*, p. 147). The creative influence of that sermon in clarifying certain doctrines of Unitarianism and integrating the society should not blind us to the fact that it embodies only a portion of Channing's theology—the idea of God's beneficence. It is a reasoned attack upon Trinitarian Calvinism, upon those dogmas which reveal—in Channing's expressive phrase—"how mournfully the human mind may misrepresent the Deity"; but it takes no account of the idea which later he came to place first—the idea of man's excellence.

Finer than the Baltimore sermon in its restrained eloquence—an eloquence that burns with an intensity rare in Channing—and in its dramatic exposition of the doctrine of the atonement, is the sermon entitled *Unitarian Christianity most Favorable to Piety,* delivered in 1826 at the dedication of the second Unitarian church in New York City. In this sermon Channing made use of a daring comparison which startled his friends and gave mortal offense to orthodox Calvinists. It is probably the most dramatic passage to be found in his writings, and it so well exemplifies the temper of the controversy that it deserves quotation. After discussing the Edwardean philosophy of infinite punishment and the nature of atonement, he proceeded:

Let me, then, set it before you, in new terms, and by a new illustration; and if in so doing, I may wound the feelings of some who hear me, I beg them to believe, that I do it with pain, and from no impulse but a desire to serve the cause of truth.—Suppose, then, that a teacher should come among you, and should tell you, that the Creator, in order to pardon his own children, had erected a gallows in the centre of the universe, and had publicly executed upon it, in room of the offenders, an Infinite Being, the partaker of his own Supreme Divinity; suppose him to declare, that this execution was appointed, as a most conspicuous and terrible manifestation of God's justice, and of the infinite woe denounced by his law; and suppose him to add, that all beings in heaven and earth are required to fix their eyes on this fearful sight, as the most powerful enforcement of obedience and virtue. Would you not tell him, that he calumniated his Maker? Would you not say to him, that this central gallows threw gloom over the universe; that the spirit of a government, whose very acts of pardon were written in such blood, was terror, not paternal love; and that the obedience which needed to be upheld by this horrid spectacle, was nothing worth? Would you not say to him, that even you, in this infancy and imperfection of your being, were capable of being wrought upon by nobler motives, and of hating sin through more generous views; and that much more the angels, those pure flames of love, need not the gallows and an executed God to confirm their loyalty? You would all so feel, at such teaching as I have supposed; and yet how does this differ from the popular doctrine of atonement? (*Works,* Vol. III, pp. 197–198.)

In seeking an explanation of Channing's break with New England orthodoxy—a breach that widened greatly with years, coming to embrace politics and economics as well as theology, alienating many of his own congregation and bringing acute grief to him—one can scarcely over-emphasize the influence of his Virginia experience. During the twenty-one months that he spent on the southern plantation, painfully isolated and lonely, he grappled seriously with a body of thought from which the environment of his youth had pretty much shut him away. Virginia in 1798 was ardently Jeffersonian, and French romantic philosophy was a commonplace in Virginia libraries. While Channing never went over wholly to Jeffersonianism, but retained certain Federalist prejudices after the old foundations had turned to quicksand under his feet, he there began a long process of speculative brooding that was to carry him far from the political principles of Boston. French revolutionary thought provided his chief intellectual stimulus during the critical Virginia period. Rousseau he read with profound interest, together with Godwin's *Political Justice* and Mary Wollstonecraft's *Rights of Woman*. The Physiocratic economics that sanctioned the agrarian bias of Jeffersonian democracy seems to have made no appeal to a mind primarily ethical in outlook, yet he went so far as to dabble in communistic theory, and for a time contemplated joining a communistic community. From France, moreover, he derived the idea of the excellence of human nature and the perfectibility of man, ideas which became the mainspring of his later thinking, creatively determining both his theology and his social philosophy, and transforming his whole intellectual world.

In July, 1800, eight months before it took formal possession of the White House, "French infidel philosophy" made its appearance in New England in the person of a slight, health-broken youth, who returned to his quiet theological studies, quite unmindful of the gunpowder he had brought back in his intellectual luggage. It was long before a spark was to strike home, but the powder was there and would do its work eventually. In passing through Channing's mind, the contributions of French romanticism merged with the native heritage of New England idealism, and supplemented by contributions from English Arian thought, slowly assumed definite form that came to issue in three dominating ideas, namely: God is love, man is potentially noble, religion is an excellent life. Enveloping these master ideas, in which they were carried as in a medium, was a pervasive ethical spirit that colored all his thinking and eventually took form in that striking phrase into which all of Channing is compressed, "the adoration of goodness—this is religion." This constituted his reply to the Edwardean theology that debased man to the sole end of exalting a monstrous God —the doctrine of "sweetness and light" was set over against the dogmas of reprobation and election.

With his profound sense of justice, Channing could not follow "the adoration of goodness" into an aloof and mystical pietism. The temptation was strong, for his finely aristocratic and hesitant nature prompted him to stand apart from all turmoil and partisan struggle. He disliked controversy and distrusted all dogmatists. The world of economics and politics was exceedingly distasteful to him; he would gladly stop his ears against the clamor of organized groups and strident parties. The Abolitionists, with whose purpose he deeply sympathized, seemed to him intolerant and their tactics vulgar. There is a measure of justice in Garrison's comment after Channing's death: "His nerves were delicately strung. The sound of a ram's horn was painfully distressing to him. He was firmly persuaded that nothing but a silver trumpet was needed to cause the walls of Jericho to fall; and he did his best upon his own." [6] And yet, however unwillingly, he was drawn inevitably into an agitation that touched both his religion and his humanity; and between 1835 and 1837 he issued three notable contributions to the controversy: *Slavery*, a reply to the Southern apologists; *The Abolitionists*, an open letter to James Birney, whose Abolition press had been wrecked by an Ohio mob; and a noble appeal to Henry Clay against the annexation of Texas. In the latter year he spoke in Faneuil Hall at a turbulent meeting called to protest against the murder of Lovejoy, the meeting at which Wendell Phillips made his dramatic first appearance on the Abolition platform.

The point of view from which Channing approached the problem of slavery is clearly set forth in his *Introductory Remarks*, written in 1841 for a collected edition of his works, and which constitutes his *apologia pro vita sua*.[7] In this extraordinarily lucid and just statement he reduces the master passions of his life to two—respect for human nature, and reverence for human liberty—passions which were inseparable in all his thinking. Of the first he says, "The following writings will be found to be distinguished by nothing more than by the high estimate which they express of human nature. A respect for the human soul breathes through them." This attitude he elaborates at length:

An enlightened, disinterested human being, morally strong, and exerting a wide influence by the power of virtue, is the clearest reflection of the divine splendour on earth. . . . The glory of the Maker lies in his work. . . . Those men glorify God most, who look with keen eye and loving heart on his works, who catch in all some glimpses of beauty and power, who have a spiritual sense for good in its dimmest manifestations, and who can so interpret the world, that it becomes a bright witness to the Divinity.

[6] Compare a fuller estimate in Garrison, *William Lloyd Garrison*, Vol. III, pp. 239–242.

[7] In the Glasgow edition of 1844 it prefaces the sixth volume.

I have also felt and continually insisted, that a new reverence for man was essential to the cause of social reform. . . . There can be no spirit of brotherhood, no true peace, any farther than men come to understand their affinity with and relation to God and the infinite purpose for which he gave them life. As yet these ideas are treated as a kind of spiritual romance. . . . The reception of this plainest truth of Christianity would revolutionize society, and create relations among men not dreamed of at the present day. . . . Men would know the import of the word Brother, as yet nothing but a word to multitudes. None of us can conceive the change of manners, the new courtesy and sweetness, the mutual kindness, deference and sympathy, the life and efforts for social melioration, which are to spring up, in proportion as man shall penetrate beneath the body to the spirit, and shall learn what the lowest human being is.

Out of this reverence for human nature flowed his "reverence for Liberty, for human rights; a sentiment which has grown with my growth, which is striking deeper root in my age, which seems to me a chief element of true love for mankind, and which alone fits a man for intercourse with his fellow-creatures."

It is because I have learned the essential equality of men before the common Father, that I cannot endure to see one man establishing his arbitrary will over another by fraud, or force, or wealth, or rank, or superstitious claims. It is because the human being has moral powers, because he carries a law in his own breast and was made to govern himself, that I cannot endure to see him taken out of his own hands and fashioned into a tool by another's avarice or pride. It is because I see in him a great nature, the divine image, and vast capacities, that I demand for him means of self-development, spheres for free action —that I call society not to fetter, but to aid his growth.

In such humanitarian idealism did French romantic philosophy come to flower in the generous mind of this son of New England. He was no longer narrowly Unitarian; he had become a social revolutionary with Utopian dreams. The minister's wealthy parishioners might worship the common Father complacently under the shadow of slavery, black or white, but the minister could not; he had caught a glimpse of the Promised Land and would lead his flock towards it. Unhappily, the vast abyss of Negro slavery lay between, and Channing considered it with growing concern. In his examination of the problem he was broadly philosophical rather than narrowly partisan. He rested his case against slavery on an ethical adaptation of the natural-rights theory.[8] Since man is both rational and moral, he argued, he cannot be deprived by law or custom of the essential prerogatives of personality. The inalienable rights of man are in essence no other than the rights of personality —the right to exercise his reason, to seek light of his conscience, to enjoy the fruits of his labor, to enter into domestic relations, in short to be free to live as a man in a state of civilization. To treat man as property is the grossest denial and violation of that which by its nature is inviolable and inalienable. Channing pushed his argument further and asserted that the institution of slavery was not only irrational and immoral, but a fundamental denial of democracy. It must end in perverting the political state to its own evil. The southern conception of a Greek democracy resting on black slavery he looked upon as the final prostitution of the democratic ideal. "Those who tell us that slavery is a necessary condition of a republic, do not justify the former, but pronounce a sentence of reprobation on the latter." For those text-mongerers who professed to justify slavery by Scripture, he had only scorn. By such methods polygamy might as readily be justified.

Inquiry into the nature and scope of individual rights brought Channing face to face with the problem of the political state and the duties of citizenship. Here his break with Boston Federalism was final and complete. He judged men and institutions by ethical standards; State Street judged them by economic standards. By his own path he went back to the eighteenth century, and interpreting the functions and province of government in the light of Godwin's *Political Justice,* he arrived at the conception of a constantly diminishing political state that should eventually disappear. The dogma of political sovereignty he denied: "The state is equally restrained with individuals by the Moral Law" ("Slavery," in *Works,* Vol. II, p. 37). The expediency of some restraint upon individual action he accepted, but with the proviso that it be exercised only to the end of the common well-being. "The authority of the state to impose laws on its members I cheerfully allow; but this has limits, which are found to be more and more narrow in proportion to the progress of moral science" (*ibid.,* p. 38). "That government is most perfect, in which Policy is most entirely subjected to Justice, or in which the supreme and constant aim is to secure the rights of every

---

[8] For a brief discussion, see Merriam, *American Political Theories,* pp. 217-221.

human being" (*ibid.*, p. 38). To such a government loyalty will be given gladly; but in the event that expediency should prevail over justice, and the state should prostitute its power by exploiting one class for the benefit of another, then must loyalty be transferred from the state to the higher law. "Justice is a greater good than property, not greater in degree, but in kind." "The good of the individual is more important than the outward prosperity of the State" (*ibid.*, pp. 40, 44). In such doctrines Channing paid his respects to the political philosophy of Webster.

The final outcome of his political thinking was a close approximation to the position of Jefferson. His distrust of power grew more apprehensive as he reflected on the common abuse of power, and the cheap and paltry appeals by which the unthinking are swayed. Before the organized power of the mass, the individual is helpless. In the *Introductory Remarks* he went further than he had done in earlier writings in analysis of the state, and such a passage as this might have been penned by John Taylor of Caroline County. It is pure Jeffersonianism.

So fearful is the principle of which I have spoken, that I have thought it right to recommend restrictions on power and a simplicity in government beyond what most approve. Power, I apprehend, should not be suffered to run into great masses. No more of it should be confided to rulers than is absolutely necessary to repress crime and preserve public order. A purer age may warrant larger trusts; but the less of government now the better, if society be kept in peace. There should exist, if possible, no office to madden ambition. . . . One of the tremendous evils of the world, is the monstrous accumulation of power in a few hands. . . . Is any man pure enough to be trusted with it? Ought such a prize as this to be held out to ambition? Can we wonder at the shameless profligacy, intrigue, and the base sacrifices of public interests by which it is sought, and, when gained, held fast? Undoubtedly, great social changes are required to heal this evil, to diminish this accumulation of power. National spirit, which is virtual hostility to all countries but our own, must yield to a growing humanity, to a new knowledge of the spirit of Christ. Another important step is, a better comprehension by communities that government is at best a rude machinery, which can accomplish but very limited good, and which, when strained to accomplish what individuals should do for themselves, is sure to be perverted by selfishness to narrow purposes, or to defeat through ignorance its own ends. Man is too ignorant to govern much, to form vast plans for states and empires. Human policy has almost always been in conflict with the great laws of social well-being, and the less we rely on it the better. The less of power given to man over man the better. (*Works,* Vol. VI, pp. 26–27.)

Channing had evidently read his *Political Justice* to good effect, for the spirit of eighteenth-century liberalism had passed into his thought and given shape to his political philosophy. In his hatred of war, his pacifism, his humanitarian concern, his social-mindedness, his repudiation of all coercive centralizing power, he proved himself a child of Godwin. He would have no tyranny, whether by the organized state or by the unorganized mass. He extended to all men the right of free thought and free speech. In no other cause did he speak more vehemently than in defense of this democratic right. When the Abolitionists were mobbed and their presses broken he rejoiced in their refusal to be silenced. "From my heart I thank them," he wrote. "I am myself their debtor. I am not sure, that I should this moment write in safety, had they shrunk from the conflict, had they shut their lips, imposed silence on their presses, and hid themselves before their ferocious assailants. . . . I thank the Abolitionists, that in this evil day, they were true to the rights which the multitude were ready to betray." Then follows a passage that is perennially true, considering how hardly won and easily lost is the right of free speech:

Of all powers, the last to be entrusted to the multitude of men, is that of determining what questions shall be discussed. The greatest truths are often the most unpopular and exasperating; and were they to be denied discussion, till the many should be ready to accept them, they would never establish themselves in the general mind. The progress of society depends on nothing more, than on the exposure of time-honored abuses, which cannot be touched without offending multitudes, than on the promulgation of principles, which are in advance of public sentiment and practice, and which are constantly at war with the habits, prejudices, and immediate interests of large classes of the community. Of consequence, the multitude, if once allowed to dictate or proscribe subjects of discussion, would strike society with spiritual blindness, and death. The world is to be carried forward by truth, which at first offends, which wins its way by degrees, which the many hate and would rejoice to crush. The right of free discussion is therefore to be guarded by the friends of mankind, with peculiar jealousy. It is at once the most sacred, and the most endangered of all our rights. He who would rob his neighbor of it, should have a mark set on him as the worst enemy of freedom. ("The Abolitionists," in *Works,* Vol. II, p. 161.)

High-minded and generous was this child of Puritan idealism who had gone to school to French infidel philosophy—never untrue to the principle of free inquiry which in demanding for himself he willingly granted others. He calmly accepted the fact of disintegration which is implicit in all liberalism—the denial of traditional authority and ancient custom—partly because he believed the old ways were bad, but in part also because he held strongly to his faith in human nature. Despite failure and discouragement he clung to his cardinal belief—"My one sublime idea, which has given me unity of mind, the greatness, the divinity of the soul." He broke the more willingly with an ungenerous past because he envisaged a nobler future. An intuitive individualist, he was a forerunner of transcendental individualism, and he found himself in hearty accord with Emerson's doctrines in the Divinity School address. With the later rationalistic phase of Unitarianism which began with Theodore Parker's memorable South Boston sermon *On the Transient and Permanent in Christianity*, in May, 1841, he found himself only partly in intellectual sympathy. He remained a supernaturalist after the younger generation had rejected supernaturalism; but his sturdy adherence to the principle of liberalism would not suffer him to join in the Unitarian hue and cry raised against the young radical. Unitarianism turned orthodox, and bent on erecting new dogmas, seemed to him treasonable to every liberal hope. "As to Mr. Parker," he wrote, "I wish him to preach what he thoroughly believes and feels. I trust the account you received of attempts to *put him down* was in the main a fiction. Let the full heart pour itself forth!" (John White Chadwick, *William Ellery Channing*, p. 357.) Sixteen months after he penned those words Channing was dead, but the spirit of his life was embodied in the great ferment that was rising about him when he died. "Let the full heart pour itself forth"—to many sober Bostonians it seemed that New England had taken that injunction quite too literally and was pouring forth disturbant and gusty heresies, but Channing would scarcely have disapproved.

CHAPTER III

Liberalism and the Social Conscience

I
THE SOCIAL MIND

Unitarianism was generous in its bequests to New England, and amongst its contributions to a nobler life not the least valuable was its warm social sympathy. Channing's tender social conscience sprang directly from his humanitarian religion. Not from the hard old Calvinism did he get this fine flower of a humane life, but from the new French philosophy. Not from bounding his ethics by the Decalogue, or hating sin more than he loved generosity, did he break the hard shell of Puritan righteousness; but by metamorphosing the sinner into a child of God and sharing with him the divine promise. Other-mindedness came naturally to a religion established in a God of love. The social conscience could not remain indifferent to injustice visited upon the children of a common Father. Yet other-mindedness was a virtue practiced too little in Calvinist New England. That old world had been more concerned with hopes of individual salvation, with propitiating an angry God, than with its present obligations to its neighbors. Hard doctrine —which the old Puritan loved—was likely to make hard characters, and an ascetic society was likely to breed close-fisted natures. The conscience was tender in New England, but it was tender chiefly as the guardian and monitor of the Ten Commandments; it gave itself too little concern about the new commandment which Jesus laid upon his disciples. It disciplined men and women in personal righteousness, it created self-reliant characters, it scrutinized narrowly the neighborhood conduct; but its social issues were likely to be mean and petty. The righteousness of which it professed to be guardian and monitor too often fell far short of generous manly stature.

From this hardness of the old religion came the hardness of the social conscience. When the Yankee was driven by brutal fact to admit that he was his brother's keeper, he usually took care to get a few honest pennies out of his brother's board and lodging. The village poor were provided for by farming out, as the taxes were farmed out. The town meeting haggled narrowly over the terms, and substantial deacons underbid each other. Though the price might be low, some profit might still be got from the pauper's keep. It was a cold, hard, unsympathetic world for the social unfortunate, whether pauper, debtor, or idiot; and it was harsh as well to the children of all but the wealthy. The hours of toil were long, and the public schools about which the historians have bragged rather too loudly, were poor affairs, starved by the common niggardliness, ill taught and ill provided. The academies and colleges that professed to keep the torch of learning aflame were largely perquisites of the gentry. It is beside the point to assert that public schools existed in New England long before Virginia had any, and that poor boys stinted and starved their way through Harvard and Yale. Well known as such facts are, they do not testify to a high social sense in a people supposed to have been tender of conscience. The Calvinist was taught to fear God rather than to love him. It was a strong man's business to save one's soul and make a decent living; and in the social code of New England the weakling must take his chance.

There was helpful neighborliness of course in old New England, and much honest kindliness. Some of the hardest of dogmatic Calvinists were the most considerate and gentlest of men. Old Samuel Hopkins of slave-running Newport was a generous soul who preached the gospel of love to one's fellows, and practiced the virtues of apostleship to the poor and outcast. He denounced the slave trade to parishioners who knew all the inlets of the West African coast, and got himself well disliked. His congregation preferred his hard theology to his inconvenient humanitarianism, and kept him poor all his days. The dogmatic Timothy Dwight scathingly attacked slavery in his *Greenfield Hill*, denounced the injustice done the Negro, and even protested against the extension of capital punishment. Yet for all such protests the common conscience was untouched. The Yankee was always standing in the way of the Puritan's righteousness. Respectability was founded on property, and respectability was mightier in New England than even

John Calvin. It was the brutal debtor laws that brought on Shays's Rebellion, which Federalist church members put down and denied the grievances. It was no tender conscience that extinguished slavery in Massachusetts, for long after it became unprofitable there the Yankee skipper was still in the slave trade. Dignified Tory Row on what is now Brattle Street, Cambridge, was built by gentlemen who drew their wealth from West Indian slave plantations.[1] William Lloyd Garrison's offense in Baltimore, for which he was thrown into jail, lay in publishing the name of a Massachusetts shipmaster from Newburyport—Garrison's native town—who was engaged in the coastwise slave traffic.[2] In the year 1830 there were somewhat more than a hundred Abolition Societies in the United States, not one of which was in New England; and in the first number of the *Liberator* Garrison wrote, probably without exaggeration, that he found "contempt more bitter, opposition more active, detraction more relentless, prejudice more stubborn, and apathy more frozen," in New England, "than among slave owners themselves."[3] The old Puritan conscience might be tender, but it refused pretty steadily to take on any larger job than Sabbath-keeping and dogma-saving. It was inquisitorial rather than humanitarian, and the sins which it hunted down were theological rather than social.

The bridge between this older world and the later was thrown across by Unitarianism. With its shift of emphasis from a God of wrath to a God of love came the entering wedge that was to split away the egoism of the old theology—its thralldom to the conception of personal sin—and lay bare an inner core of altruism. It was another sort of conscience that Unitarianism discovered, a conscience that welcomed the new social thought of romantic Europe, and applying it to the facts of life in America created the new humanitarianism which bit so deeply into the New England of the forties. From this movement the intractable nature of the Yankee held him back, but the Puritan speedily transformed the hard theological conscience into a tender social conscience, that bewildered the conventional morality with its sweeping program of reform.

The awakening of the new spirit may perhaps be held to date from the growing opposition to war that was an

[1] See T. W. Higginson, *Old Cambridge*, p. 149.
[2] See Garrison, *William Lloyd Garrison*, Vol. I, Chapter VI. The court held that it was libelous to seek to bring into disrepute an action that was legal.
[3] Quoted by S. E. Morison in *Harrison Grey Otis*, Vol. II, p. 263.

aftermath of the Napoleonic period with its huge debts and vast social suffering. The inhumanity of war profoundly impressed thoughtful minds that had come under the influence of the sociological movement, and when Channing in 1812 preached his first anti-war sermon the new humanitarian spirit found expression. In his espousal of pacifism Channing was following in the footsteps of the social revolutionaries of the preceding century. He fell short of Tom Paine in analysis of the economic and dynastic sources of war, and in appreciation of its social consequences; nevertheless his denunciation was significant of a changing social attitude. From this early attack to the rise of the Garrisonian Non-Resistance Society of the late thirties and early forties, the spread of the pacifist movement was rapid. Transcendentalism was eloquently anti-militaristic, and Emerson, Alcott and Parker were outspoken in denunciation of the war spirit. To the war against war soon was added the war against drink, and with the establishment in Boston in 1826 of the *National Philanthropist,* under the patronage of the "Massachusetts Society for the Suppression of Intemperance"—a paper of which Garrison was editor for a few months—began the long agitation for the suppression of the liquor traffic. From such feeble beginnings the ardor of reform grew and spread swiftly, enlarging its program to embrace anti-slavery, woman's rights,[4] prison reform, repeal of the harsh debtor laws, vegetarianism, associationism, until it caught the contagion of the perfectionist and transcendental movements and issued in a comprehensive program of universal reform. The golden age of New England was quite as much the golden age of the New England conscience as of the New England mind.

II

The fame of transcendentalism has too much obscured the contemporary movement of perfectionism, a movement which marked the extreme expression of the new conscience, the most revolutionary of its aspirations, the apotheosis of ethical radicalism. Its want of literary skill narrowed its appeal and the archaic quality of its enthusiasm lessened its following; yet in spirit it was native to Puritan idealism,

---

[4] This was an outgrowth of the anti-slavery movement and emerged from the conservative opposition to women's appearing on the abolition platform. The reply of the Quakeress, Angelina Grimké, to Elizabeth Beecher's *Essay on Slavery and Abolitionism, with reference to the Duty of American Females,* in 1837, marks the definite beginning of the movement. See Garrison, *William Lloyd Garrison,* Vol. II, pp. 133–134.

and it enlisted the active sympathy of many of the finer souls of New England. How greatly reform was furthered by the movement of perfectionism is not easily determined, but it is clear that its influence permeated much of the revolutionary activity of the times. Scratch an ardent Abolitionist and you were likely to find a potential perfectionist.

The doctrine was first elaborated by John Humphrey Noyes, a young Vermont mystic, who, under the influence of the revivalist excitement of the early thirties, elaborated a social creed that re-embodied much of the teaching of the extreme left wing of English Commonwealth thought. Noyes was a primitive religious nature, with the tenderest of consciences, vastly troubled over current materialisms; and his speculations reveal a curious throw-back to early English Puritanism. He was a Yankee Fifth Monarchy man. Two hundred years of Yankee experience slipped from his mind, and he walked and talked with the old millennial spirits, the Diggers and Levelers of Commonwealth times. A devout Scripturist, he took literally the injunction of Matthew, "Be ye therefore perfect, even as your Father which is in Heaven is perfect." A primitive Christian, he proposed to re-order society with the naïve simplicity of the apostle Eliot. In his mystical speculations, social, political, and religious radicalisms were stirred in a common pot and simmered down to what may be called spiritual anarchism. Noyes was a Yankee "root and branch" man, a single-minded apostle of "thorough." He would not strain at gnats and swallow camels, but he rejected the camels first and then proposed to get rid of the gnats. In 1834 he established a small monthly paper called the *Perfectionist,* which was very probably as revolutionary a sheet as was ever printed in America. He made converts, including Garrison, Edmund Quincy, son of Josiah Quincy, the Grimké sisters, Henry C. Wright and other Abolitionists, and made an increasing stir in the world, to the great concern of respectable folk who swallowed their camels without a grimace.

Some notion of the main doctrines of this seventeenth-century creed may be gained from a letter of Noyes to Garrison, written in 1837, from which the following is taken:

I have subscribed my name to an instrument similar to the Declaration of '76, renouncing all allegiance to the government of the United States, and asserting the title of Jesus Christ to the throne of the World. . . . When I wish to form a conception of the government of the United States . . . I picture to myself a bloated, swaggering libertine, trampling on the Bible—its own Constitution—its treaties with the Indians—the petitions of its citizens. . . . I have renounced active co-operation with the oppressor on whose territories I live; now I would find a way to put an end to his oppression. But he is manifestly a reprobate: reproof and instruction only aggravate his sins. I cannot attempt to reform him, because I am forbidden to "cast pearls before swine." I must therefore either consent to remain a slave till God removes the tyrant, or I must commence war upon him, by a declaration of independence and other weapons suitable to the character of a son of God.

He then lays down seven reasons for choosing to make war upon the state, amongst which are the following:

1. As a believer in the Bible I know that the territory of the United States belongs to God, and is promised . . . to Jesus Christ and his followers. . . .

6. The Son of God has manifestly, to me, chosen this country for the theatre of such an assault—a country which, by its boasting hypocrisy, has become the laughing-stock of the world, and by its lawlessness has fully proved the incapacity of man for self-government. *My hope of the millennium begins where Dr. Beecher's expires*—viz., AT THE OVERTHROW OF THIS NATION.

I have stated to you only . . . the principal things which God has urged upon me by his Spirit, and by which he has moved me to nominate Jesus Christ for the Presidency, not only of the United States, but of the world. Is it not high time for abolitionists to abandon a government whose President has declared war upon them? I cannot but think that many of them hear the same great voice out of heaven which has waked me, saying, "Come out of her, my people, that ye be not partakers of her sins and of her plagues." . . . Allow me to suggest that you will set Anti-slavery in the sunshine only by making it tributary to Holiness; and you will most assuredly throw it into the shade . . . if you suffer it to occupy the ground, in your mind or in others, which ought to be occupied by UNIVERSAL EMANCIPATION FROM SIN. All the abhorrence which now falls upon slavery, intemperance, lewdness, and every other specific vice, will in due time he gathered into one volume of victorious wrath against *unbelief*. I wait for that time as for the day of battle . . . I counsel you, and the people that are with you, if you love the post of honour—the forefront of the hottest battle of righteousness—to set your face towards *perfect* holiness. (Garrison, *William Lloyd Garrison*, Vol. II, pp. 145–148.)

This curious appeal brought forth its fruit in a Peace Convention, held in 1838, which published a Declaration of Sentiments[5] that was quite as extraordinary a pronouncement—one that serves to explain the utter bewilderment of prosaic souls at the strange progeny of the times. It was only one of many strange conventions, marked by an ebullient faith of which Emerson remarked, "The core of the comet did not seem to be much, but the whole air was full of splendors" (*Journals*, Vol. VII, p. 5), and on which Josiah Quincy commented, "Such a mass of free mind as was brought together I have never seen before in any one assembly. . . . There was much talent and a great deal of *soul*." Men who take their Biblical teachings literally are likely to be curious fellows. Righteousness may prove a potent drink for them that love it, begetting its own particular intemperance; and a conscience that has slipped its leash of the practical will run many a mad chase. If it followed its logic this perfectionism must make short shrift of political parties, of loyalty to government, of the political state itself, and set up instead a social order in which familiar things would be topsy-turvy, with the just sitting in high places and the rich and great of earth brought low; and this is precisely what Noyes did in the Oneida Community—the most successful of the contemporary ventures in communism—of which he was the founder. In spite of his taste for the wine of new vintages Emerson was somewhat taken aback at certain of its ebullitions, and when the sabbatarian Charndon Street Convention in 1840 gathered together the choicest repositories of New England holiness, he shook his head dubiously. His humorous catalogue of the miscellaneous enthusiasts suggests more than a spice of criticism.

Madmen, madwomen, men with beards, Dunkers, Muggletonians, Come-outers, Groaners, Agarians, Seventh-Day Baptists, Quakers, Abolitionists, Calvinists, Unitarians, and Philosophers, —all came successively to the top, and seized their moment, if not their hour, wherein to chide, or pray, or preach, or protest. ("The Chardon Street Convention," in *Works*, Vol. X, p. 374.)

And even the catholic-minded Edmund Quincy, who was one of the callers of the Convention, confessed that "It was the most singular collection of strange specimens of humanity that was ever assembled." The wine of perfectionism was in high ferment in New England in 1840.

It was a curious anachronism in the midst of the indus-

[5] Written by Garrison; see *ibid.*, Vol. II, pp. 230–234.

trial revolution—this revival of the religious Utopianism of 1650, this April renaissance of the faith of a dead *saeculum theologicum*. It was in no sense a by-product of transcendentalism—no lunacy fringe of metaphysical speculation. It owed nothing to French romanticism or German idealism, not in origin at least. It was far more primitive and native, and its affinities run back to Roger Williams and the Fifth Monarchy millennialism, rather than to Rousseau and Kant and Jacobi. It was a breaking through of the submerged New England spirituality, a volcanic release from sterile conformity; and it summoned the awakening soul to go forth and conquer the world for righteousness. Millennialism is the prophetic hope of a primitive faith. To its disciples it is certain of fulfillment because God's promises are certain; but to practical minds, unconvinced that Biblical phrases are authentic divine contracts, any expectation of the speedy coming of the Kingdom of God seems grotesque. The millennial enthusiast is a fair butt of ridicule, and the perfectionists came in for a large share. It was Lowell who leveled at the militant godliness of the new sects the wittiest attack. Forgetting his English history he found himself puzzled, and being puzzled he allowed himself to become ill-natured. His clever sentences explode smartly about his subject, but there is no light in them.[6]

III

Upon another venture in Utopianism, and one far better known, the years have laid a pleasant, idyllic haze, softening the prosaic outlines and clothing them with romance. Brook Farm has been singularly fortunate in the posthumous fame that has dealt with it so tenderly as to transmute it into poetry. By virtue of the light reflected upon it by the transcendental illumination and the literary skill it commanded, the little communal settlement at West Roxbury has come to be regarded as a homely Yankee pastoral, a sort of May Day adventure in brown holland tunics, an inspiring quest of the ideal amongst furrows and manures. It is a social poem fashioned out of Yankee homespun. No hint of rude social leveling is associated with its aims; even its communism suggests no stigma. Of the dozens of communistic experiments which marked the first half of the nineteenth century in America, few were native in origin or ventured upon in New England. They were mostly undertaken by old-world groups, chiefly German, who sought

[6] See the essay on Thoreau.

cheap land and a free environment for primitive religious experiments. But Brook Farm was true Yankee, using the familiar dialect to clothe its unfamiliar thoughts, and escaping the prejudice that confronts the uncouth and alien; and in consequence the vagaries that all New England once laughed at have become enshrined as a cherished New England possession.

Perfectionism and Brook Farm embodied diverse phases of the renaissance and made appeal to different temperaments. Fellowship founded on common ownership and communal labor was an ideal that left the religious mystic cold, whereas the anarchistic holiness of perfectionism seemed to the Brook Farmers grotesque. Present economic maladjustment appeared to the latter the fundamental problem of the times. They were deeply concerned for the future that must emerge from the chaotic individualism of the present. Unless society were brought back to a wiser understanding of values, they foresaw only chaos; and so in a small way they set about a great experiment. Brook Farm grew out of the impact of the industrial revolution upon the social conscience of New England. Industrialism and social speculation were contemporary developments. The first cotton mill in New England was established at Lawrence in 1822, and the following year the Merrimac Mills were established in the newly founded city of Lowell. By absorbing the vast Irish immigration the factory system brought increasing wealth to Beacon Street homes, but it brought other consequences in its train which Beacon Street carelessly overlooked. How those consequences affected more sensitive and intelligent minds—men like William Henry Channing, Theodore Parker and George Ripley—is suggested by their eager talk of mutualism, association, co-operation, as potential cures for the growing evils of competition, discussions never before heard in New England. Describing the state of mind of the Boston group of social thinkers, John Weiss offers the following explanation:

A mutualism to secure culture and material welfare was consistently desired by those who believed in a community of the sources of moral and spiritual welfare. The social evils which result from the struggles of competitive labour seemed to outweigh all its benefits. Modern civilization was thought to be the culmination of isolated selfishness, madly struggling from bread to luxury and refined delights, which the strongest and least scrupulous only could acquire. Prisons and punishments were the defences of this artificial system, to repress instincts that were moral till they become illegal. Hospitals and benevolent institutions were also mere defences to absorb as much misery as possible ere it became malicious, to get the social gangrene reduced to limits. The providential impulses of the human being were forced to act in subversive ways and directions, when they might all be harmonized by their own inherent laws, and the blessing of mutualism succeed to the bane of antagonism. Each man ought to be the guarantee to all men against disorder; the carefully adjusted elements of a selfishness which threatens continually to blow the social fabric to atoms, would become not only innoxious but salutary in its proper combination; and a new civilization might arise in fair proportion from the serial development and movement of all possible human tendencies. Then all men and women might labor and be happy; all might earn with a minimum of toil a competence of culture. Property would be the ally of the whole instead of the oppressor of the many; and crime would disappear, because the instincts would no longer have motives to be criminal. (*Life and Correspondence of Theodore Parker,* Vol. I, pp. 106–107.)

The transcendental basis of such social speculation is evident enough. The new social thought was transcendental thought. A common belief in the excellence of human instincts drew these idealists together; but when it came to the vexing problem of reconciling individualism and mutualism, creating an economic fellowship out of electric personalities, the more ardent transcendentalists took fright and prudently kept without the gates of Brook Farm. Organization seemed to them the fatal poison in the bottom of the cup. When a community was planned in Massachusetts in 1841, by liberal Christians of the Universalist sect, a writer in the *Dial* subjected the proposal to sharp criticism:

A true community can be founded on nothing short of faith in the universal man, as he comes from the hands of the Creator, with no law over his liberty but the eternal ideas that lie at the foundation of his being. . . . The final cause of human society is the unfolding of the individual man, into every form of perfection, without let or hindrance, according to the inward nature of each. (Quoted by Frothingham in *Transcendentalism, etc.,* p. 157.)

Such a view is anarchistic rather than collectivistic, and as embodied in Alcott's Fruitlands, it may be regarded as the transcendental type of Utopia. Towards all systems of socialism the transcendentalists were instinctively hostile, as implying an industrial regimentation; and in planning

Brook Farm, Ripley rejected industrialism and reduced regimentation to a minimum. With the agrarian background of Brook Farm the transcendentalists were in hearty sympathy, quite oblivious of the fact that agrarianism could offer no solution for industrialism; but they balked at the principle of task allotment as a hindrance to the unfolding of individual differences. Upon the later introduction of the Fourier Phalanx their doubts grew into certainty, and they lost their faith in the experiment. Of all the transcendentalists William Henry Channing was clearly the most confirmed associationist, except perhaps Ripley; to the end of his life he remained a socialist, active in collectivistic movements and clinging fondly to his memory of Brook Farm as a "great college of social students." But few of his fellow transcendentalists shared his faith.

This growing skepticism of organization is clearly shown in the comments of Emerson's *Journals*. In October, 1840, he set down his first reaction to the plan as follows:

Yesterday George and Sophia Ripley, Margaret Fuller and Alcott discussed here the Social Plans. I wish to be conceived, to be thawed, to be made nobly mad by the kindlings before my eye of a new dawn of human piety. But this scheme was arithmetic and comfort; this was a hint borrowed from the Tremont House and United States Hotel; a rage in our poverty and politics to live rich and gentlemanlike, an anchor to leeward against a change of weather; a prudent forecast on the probable issue of the great questions of Pauperism and Poverty. And not once could I be inflamed, but sat aloof and thoughtless; my voice faltered and fell. It was not the cave of persecution which is the palace of spiritual power, but only a room in the Astor House hired for the Transcendentalists. I do not wish to remove from my present prison to a prison a little larger. I wish to break all prisons. I have not yet conquered my own house. It irks and repents me. Shall I raise the siege of this hencoop, and march baffled away to a pretended siege of Babylon? It seems to me that so to do were to dodge the problem I am set to solve, and to hide my impotency in the thick of a crowd. (*Journals,* Vol. V, pp. 473–474.)

In January, 1844, noting the spontaneity of life at Brook Farm, he drew the conclusion "that in the arrangements at Brook Farm, as out of them, it is the person, not the communist, that avails" (*ibid.,* Vol. VI, p. 492). With the introduction of Fourierist organization he became sharply critical. Neither in Fourier nor in Owen did he see any hope.

Fourier learned from him [Owen] all the truth he had, and the rest of his system was imagination, and the imagination of a banker. The Owen and Fourier plans bring no *a priori* convictions. They are come at merely by counting and arithmetic. All the fine *aperçus* are for individualism. The Spartan broth, the hermit's cell, the lonely farmer's life are poetic; but the Phalanstery, the "Self-supporting Village," are culinary and mean. (*Ibid.*, Vol. VIII, pp. 134, 135.)

And a few days later he gave his final judgment, "Dear heart, take it sadly home to thee, that there will and can be no coöperation"—a judgment that explains the clever phrase with which he demolished Brook Farm, "It is the Age of Reason in a patty-pan."

The transcendentalist with his Puritan conscience could understand and sympathize with the perfectionist zeal for universal righteousness; but collectivistic systems of economy seemed alien and a community of goods uncongenial to his Yankee individualism. Albert Brisbane, the American apostle of Fourierism, might bring George Ripley, the least individualistic and most prosaic of the transcendental group, to his views of organization; but he got on badly with the others who were quite too fluid to take a mechanical set. In consequence it was not at Brook Farm but at the North American Phalanx that the French system found its fairest experiment and met with its solidest success.

IV

With the awakening interest in social problems the conscience of New England could not longer remain indifferent to slavery. The incoming of French humanitarianism, the spread of idealistic sociology under the teachings of Unitarianism, above all the stimulus of English Abolitionism that provided argument and example in the freeing of slaves in the British West Indies, wore away the indifferentism that had calloused the mind of New England; and with the decay of her provincial particularism the conscience of New England slowly roused itself. The arrogance of the slave party nowhere else stirred such deep resentment. Southern steel, striking the flinty Yankee character, threw off sparks that would fire whatever combustible stuff lay near; and such combustible stuff was provided in plenty by the Utopian enthusiasts who gathered in conventions, each with a plan of universal reform in his waistcoat pocket. Little conflagrations were started in many an obscure Yankee soul, and the noise of the crackling spread over New

England, to the anger of the South and the vast concern of respectable Boston merchants. Sooner or later Abolition sentiment was bound to make a tremendous stir amongst the children of Puritanism; and when that time came it was bound to arouse tremendous antagonism amongst the sons of Yankees. The dominant commercial group would not tolerate a movement that was certain to alienate its southern customers. A mighty collision between the conscience and the self-interest of New England was inevitable; and in that collision of flinty characters, arguments were likely to be countered with blows.

The New England Abolitionists, men and women, were an extraordinarily interesting group. They were good fighters, outspoken and tenacious of opinion, unsparing in attack, refusing to be browbeaten, resilient and tough as seasoned hickory. In them the Yankee Tory met his match; against them coercion and intimidation, all the usual Tory weapons, failed as earlier they had failed with the primitive Quakers. They were daily charged with being social incendiaries. The commercial newspapers thundered against them as atheists, Sabbath-breakers, socialists, anarchists; the absurdest myths were given circulation; the public mind was skillfully poisoned against them. Yet as a matter of sober historical fact, they were the kindliest of men, with generous sympathies and disinterested motives. No blackguard was ever an Abolitionist—no ward-heeler, or mob-inciter, or purse-patriot; all such convenient tools of power were found amongst the baiters and mobsters in the commercial opposition. John Brown was the only direct-action Abolitionist and what befell him is well known among men. There was no money to be made, no place of honor or power to be got by espousing Abolitionism, but only self-sacrifice and social ostracism. Ambitious men, self-seekers, went with the dispensers of social favors. It was the remnant in Israel that gathered to the cause, few in numbers but the best New England had. And what an excellent company they were: Garrison, Samuel J. May, Edmund Quincy, Jonathan Sewall, Theodore Parker, Lydia Maria Child, Mrs. Chapman, Wendell Phillips, Thomas Wentworth Higginson, Whittier, Henry Ward Beecher, Sumner, Maria White and the young Lowell—such a fighting phalanx as the New England conscience had never before mustered, nor has since. To them were gathered heroic souls from other states: Arthur and Lewis Tappan and Gerrit Smith from New York, James Birney from Kentucky, Lucretia Mott from Philadelphia, the Grimké sisters from South Carolina. Harriet Martineau, who knew the group intimately, has left on record her judgment of them: "A just survey of the whole world can leave little doubt," she wrote in 1838, "that the abolitionists of the United States are the greatest people now living and moving in it" (Carpenter, *John Greenleaf Whittier*, p. 107). They gave New England and the country no peace. From their persistent agitation came the Emigrant Aid Society, Sharp's rifles, and the bloody struggle in Kansas; and from it came the temporary overwhelming of the Tory minority in Massachusetts. For a few brief years New England threw off the stifling grip of the commercial mind and was the home of American humanitarianism.

CHAPTER IV

Certain Militants

I

WILLIAM LLOYD GARRISON

The flintiest character amongst the New England militants, curiously enough, was the son of an immigrant family, brought to Newburyport and abandoned by a shiftless father. William Lloyd Garrison was not an offspring of generations of New England Puritanism, but a waif thrown by chance on the bleak shores of Massachusetts, and left to shift pretty much for himself. Born in Newburyport, half English and half Irish, with a heritage that promised ill, he was disciplined in the sternest of schools. His capable Irish mother had a bitter time providing for her three fatherless children, and the son suffered the privation and found the help that were the mixed portion of the destitute of old New England. Like Horace Greeley he ate the bread of poverty and grew strong on it. There was iron in his nature, and the narrow means that drove his father to drink and desertion, that sent his brother adrift, that broke

344

his mother and killed his sister, only strengthened his will and toughened his fiber. As a lad he was put to the cobbler's bench to learn the trade that Whittier was learning at Haverhill; later he was apprenticed to a carpenter and cabinet-maker. In both trades he was unhappy, and it was not till a freak of fate turned him over to a friendly printer that he found himself. For seven years he stuck to his case, and at the end of the apprenticeship he was not only a first-rate practical printer, but with some little knowledge of books and master of a vigorous and serviceable prose style. With the amazing capacity for self-training so characteristic of the Yankee, he had picked up a sort of education and was ready to do whatever work in the world should come to hand.

Chance threw in his way the job of village editor, and inclination plunged him into politics. His political opinions, which he embraced more ardently than intelligently, were faithful reflections of current Massachusetts partisanship. He was quite ignorant of political principles and the economics that determined political parties, and with unconscious naïveté he espoused the cause of Boston commercialism. He was a dogmatic, unquestioning Whig. Clay was his idol, General Jackson his abomination; and his first political speech was in support of Harrison Gray Otis, the discredited boss of the old Federalist machine. But this was only a vagary of youthful hero worship. Enthusiasm for reform was already setting up a ferment in his ardent soul and preparing him for quite other alliances. The unhappy fate of his father was a lesson that he took home, and he interested himself in the temperance movement then just getting under way, serving for a time as editor of a small temperance paper. Shortly thereafter he stumbled upon his life work. Benjamin Lundy, a homespun hero of the Society of Friends, had long been publishing intermittently his *Genius of Universal Emancipation*, and in the itinerant work of begging support he fell in with Garrison. The two discovered kindred interests and they entered into a compact to go forth together to fight the dragon of slavery. They sought out the den of the beast in Baltimore and delivered their blows lustily; with the result that Garrison was indicted by the grand jury for printing the name of a Newburyport merchant who was picking up some honest dollars in the coastwise slave traffic, and spent seven weeks in jail. On his release he returned to Boston to replenish a lean purse, and January 1, 1831, he issued the first number of *The Liberator,* a little paper that was to make a mighty stir in the world during a long period of hand-to-mouth existence.

Never was there a more foolhardy venture, judged by the wisdom of this world. With no following, no weapon but a borrowed font of type in a mean little print-shop, no money or credit, he flung his defiance at the entrenched enemy with the courage of uncalculating youth. A prospectus issued in the fall of 1830 thus set forth the purpose of the venture:

I shall assume, as self-evident truths, that the liberty of a people is a gift of God and nature:—That liberty consists in an independency upon the will of another:—That by the name of slave we understand a man who can neither dispose of his person or goods, but enjoys all at the will of his master:— That no man can have a right over others, unless it be by them granted to him. . . . That that which is not just is not law; and that which is not law, ought not to be in force:— That he who oppugns the public liberty, overthrows his own. . . . That there is no safety where there is no strength, no strength without union, no union without justice, no justice where faith and truth are wanting:—That the right to be free is a truth planted in the hearts of men, and acknowledged so to be by all that have hearkened to the voice of nature. . . . *Vide Algernon Sidney's Discourses on Government—the Declaration of American Independence—the Constitutions and Bills of Rights of the several States, etc., etc. (Life of William Lloyd Garrison, by his Children.* Vol. I, p. 200.)

This pronouncement was amplified in the salutatory address in the first number, as follows:

Assenting to the "self-evident truth" maintained in the American Declaration of Independence, "that all men are created equal, and endowed by their Creator with certain inalienable rights—among which are life, liberty, and the pursuit of happiness," I shall strenuously contend for the immediate enfranchisement of our slave population. . . . I am aware that many object to the severity of my language; but is there not cause for severity? I *will* be as harsh as truth, and as uncompromising as justice. On this subject, I do not wish to think, or speak, or write, with moderation . . . urge me not to use moderation in a cause like the present. I am in earnest— I will not equivocate—I will not excuse—I will not retreat a single inch—AND I WILL BE HEARD. (*Ibid.,* Vol. I, pp. 224–225.)

The young man just turned twenty-six who thus marked out the path he was to follow for thirty-five years was an extraordinarily single-minded and rugged character. His like has too rarely appeared in America. Arrogant, dictatorial, intolerant, he might be, as his warmest friends admitted; but it is a foolish judgment that will dismiss him thus. Unyielding as granite, sheer Yankee will driven by a passionate energy, he was born for hazardous leadership. He was a man utterly unacquainted with fear. Lied about daily, threatened, bullied, charged with every sin in the Decalogue and every crime on the statute-book, he could not be coerced nor intimidated nor turned aside from his purpose. An ascetic who cared nothing for ease or preferment; a pacifist who fought only with the sword of the spirit; a stern moralist prophesying wrath upon a nation of mockers, and pronouncing doom upon a people that had forgotten God, he was an agitator fashioned after the ancient Hebraic pattern. The stature of such a man cannot be measured by conventional standards. Outwardly a somewhat prosaic Baptist, deeply religious and in his younger days bigotedly orthodox, he was in reality a spiritual child of the Old Testament, a modern Puritan on whom had fallen the mantle of the Prophets. New England Calvinism never bred so Puritan a soul. Hebraism was in his marrow —its noble austerity, its consuming passion. He daily walked with righteousness and communed with conscience. He carried God's scales into the market place. He would not accept his law of men. Constitutions and statutes were vain and foolish pronouncements to him if he judged them to be contrary to the divine enactments. He counted property in Negroes and cotton as nothing when weighed in the balance of justice. A human soul, whether in black skin or white, was of far greater worth in his eyes than all the warring kingdoms of this world. As fully as John Humphrey Noyes he reëmbodied the root-and-branch righteousness of English Commonwealth times. Others might lash the sins of his generation with whips; he would scourge them with nettles and scorpions. He would raise such a clamor about men's ears that the drowsiest must awake. He would light such a fire in the slave market of America that the evil thing should be consumed as stubble in the white flame of righteousness.

Such primitive Hebraism, quite evidently, is calculated to make troublesome citizens who are certain to get themselves heartily disliked by those who approve of the world as it is. Any invasion of the devil's realms will create an uproar, for the devil is prompt to defend his own. Right-

eousness may prophesy in the gates, but the buying and selling of the poor goes on as usual. Amongst comfortable folk
conscience is rarely at home when justice knocks at the
door; it is gone a-visiting, or is busy, or is waiting upon
Caesar, or is gone forth to pray. Comfortable folk do not
like clamor, even from the prophets, and are content to
leave justice to God with the hope that He will not disturb
business. If the tithes are duly paid, it is a mean and
censorious God that will ask how the money was got.
Hence comfortable folk, north as well as south, did not
like Garrison; and not liking him they were zealous to damn
him. He was made out to be a bogy man, busily engaged
in stirring up Nat Turner insurrections, inciting peaceful
and contented slaves to discontent, flouting the Constitution
and seeking to disrupt the Union. His righteousness was so
great a stumbling-block that he was held to be an atheist
by eminent formalists who knew of righteousness only by
hearsay, and learned of God only from report. It was reckoned to him a major sin that he forgot his manners, for
must not the Lord's work be carried on in seemly fashion,
and the money-changers be scourged from the temple
politely? "The first movement here at the North, was a
rank onset and explosion," said the eminent Dr. Bushnell.
"The first sin of this organization was a sin of ill manners.
They did not go to work like Christian gentlemen. . . .
The great convention which met at Philadelphia drew up
a declaration of their sentiments . . . by which they will-
fully and boorishly cast off the whole South from them"
(Garrison, *William Lloyd Garrison*, Vol. II, p. 132, Note).
What could be done with a fellow who insisted that the
devil is rarely put in a quake by courteous treatment, and
who had never learned that the Hebrew prophets bore
themselves like Christian gentlemen? That he spoke with
plebeian directness was unquestionably true.

These are your men of "caution," and "prudence," and
"judiciousness" [he exclaimed in a speech at Philadelphia, May
14, 1838]. Sir, I have learned to hate those words. Whenever
we attempt to imitate our great Exemplar, and press the truth
of God, in all its plainness, upon the conscience, why, we are
very imprudent; because, forsooth, a great excitement will en-
sue. Sir, slavery will not be overthrown without excitement,
a most tremendous excitement. (*Ibid.*, Vol. II, p. 215. Note.)

If clerical gentlemen disliked Garrison, gentlemen of
State Street disliked him much more heartily, and being the

responsible custodians of law and order, they upheld existing institutions in their own way. Your Tory is always a Fascist at heart, and the Boston Tories naturally adopted the principle of direct action. Unpleasant things happened to Garrison in consequence. He was denounced at a most respectable meeting in Faneuil Hall, "at which Washington was cheered for being a slave-holder." He was mobbed in his print-shop by "gentlemen of property and standing from all parts of the city," and was thrown into jail by a timid mayor to save his life. Not since the days of Tom Paine had such unmeasured vituperation been poured out on the head of an American. It would seem that it was a perilous business to defend the downtrodden or to remind church-members of the injunction "to undo the heavy burdens and let the oppressed go free." When conscience throws down the gauntlet to economics it is certain to get some hard knocks. It is ill-trained for a rough and tumble contest; its scruples will not permit it to hit below the belt. But the Tory suffers no handicap of scruple and plants his blows where he can. On the occasion of an Abolition convention announced to be held within the shadows of Wall Street, Bennett's *New York Herald* exemplified the sweetness and light of the commercial mind in such pronouncements as this:

What business have all the religious lunatics of the free states to gather in this commercial city for purposes which, if carried into effect, would ruin and destroy its prosperity? . . . Public opinion should be regulated. These abolitionists should not be allowed to misrepresent New York. . . . When free discussion does not promote the public good, it has no more right to exist than a bad government that is dangerous and oppressive to the common weal. It should be overthrown. On the question of the usefulness to the public of the packed, organized meetings of these abolitionists, socialists, Sabbath-breakers, and anarchists, there can be but one result arrived at by prudence and patriotism. They are dangerous assemblies—calculated for mischief, and reasonable in their character and purposes. . . . That half-a-dozen madmen should manufacture opinion for the whole community, is not to be tolerated. (*Ibid.*, Vol. III, pp. 283–284.)

In consequence of which appeals to "prudence and patriotism" the meeting was broken up, public opinion was judiciously regulated, and the Bible and Constitution vindicated by a Bowery mob under the leadership of a ward-heeler. It was from the impact of such ruthless opposition that Garrison's strategy took form; and it was direct and uncompromising and outspoken—as sternly logical as Calhoun's. There were no shades in his thinking but only black and white, righteousness and sin. Expediency was not in his vocabulary. He was as narrow as he was intense. The catholic intellectual interests of the times touched him but little. Transcendentalism lay quite outside his world of thought. He was a religious soul rather than a speculative intellect, and he measured all things by the principles of primitive Christianity. As a young man he preferred the Calvinism of Lyman Beecher to the Unitarianism of Channing, but later he came to perceive the intimate relation between the major premises of Unitarianism and his social ideals. It is idle to seek a political philosopher in a Hebrew moralist. His somewhat naïve political conceptions were an amalgam of French equalitarianism and Yankee perfectionism. The Declaration of Independence was his one political textbook, in the light of which he judged Congressional enactments and interpreted the Constitution. With Channing he assumed an ethical sanction for natural rights, and this assumption conducted straight to the doctrine of the higher law. As early as 1830 his conscience was prepared to appeal from laws and statutes to ethics, on the principle that "that which is not just is not law." By 1837 he had accepted the philosophy of spiritual anarchism as set forth in the new gospel of perfectionism, and from this flowed naturally the doctrines of Nullification and disunion.

With amazing frankness Garrison published his views to friends and enemies, bringing all the hornets of conservatism about his ears. A furious discussion arose within the Abolition ranks on the question of loyalty to the political state, and the scandal of Garrison's Fifth Monarchy doctrine spread far. What that doctrine was he was at great pains to make clear. Writing to Henry C. Wright on the Quaker doctrine of non-resistance, he insisted on the sinfulness of all force whether in a private or public capacity, and then asserted:

Human governments will remain in violent existence as long as men are resolved not to bear the cross of Christ, and to be crucified unto the world. But in the Kingdom of God's dear Son, holiness and love are the only magistracy. It has no swords, for they are beaten into ploughshares—no spears, for they are changed into pruning hooks—no military academy, for the saints cannot learn war any more—no gibbet, for life is regarded as inviolate—no chains, for all are free. And that kingdom is to be established upon the earth, for the time is predicted when the kingdoms of this world will become the kingdoms of our Lord and of his Christ. (Garrison, *William Lloyd Garrison*, Vol. II, p. 149.)

From such premises he deduced the conclusion that government is a cross that God permits men to endure as punishment for their sins. When they shall voluntarily quit their sins political government will cease.

Human governments "are the results of human disobedience to the requirements of heaven; and they are better than anarchy just as a hailstorm is preferable to an earthquake, or the small-pox to the Asiatic cholera." From the silence of the Bible as to the *form* of such governments, he inferred not that each might claim a divine sanction, "but that the kingdom which Christ has established on earth is ultimately to swallow up or radically to subvert all other kingdoms." . . . "Shall we, *as Christians,* applaud and do homage to human government? or shall we not rather lay the axe at the root of the tree, and attempt to destroy both cause and effect together?" Foolish are the speculations about the best form of human government: "What is government but the express image of the moral character of a people?" (*Ibid.,* Vol. II, pp. 150–151.)

This is of course undiluted perfectionism, in which Garrison was the most ardent of believers. Prosaic political theory had lost all significance for him; he had got himself drunk on the new wine and was in no mood to listen to the counsels of expediency. Like John Humphrey Noyes he declared war upon the existing political state. He voluntarily disfranchised himself. He raised the banner of "disloyalty" in the *Liberator,* and summoned the Abolitionists to separate themselves from the unclean government that protected the sin of slavery. That the Constitution recognized the hateful system was sufficient proof to Garrison that the Constitution itself was unclean. Let it be consumed by its own iniquity. In 1843 he began an uncompromising attack upon it by nailing to the masthead of the *Liberator* his famous phrase, "A Covenant with Death and an Agreement with Hell," to which he soon added the words, "No Union with Slaveholders." He broke with many of his oldest friends, with Whittier and Gerrit Smith and James Birney, assailing them bitterly for meddling with third-party movements in the hope of curing the evil by political action. There followed, in consequence, a whirlwind and tempest of debate that brought a disastrous schism upon the Abolition movement. Cries of disloyalty and sedition filled all ears; but Garrison was indifferent to the storms that gathered about his head. He would go forward though he went alone. With every advance of the slave power his hatred of the Constitution, under cover of which its advances were made, grew more bitter. He outran southern fire eaters in advocacy of Nullification and secession. It became his daily work to undo the labors of Webster and bring the fundamental law into common contempt. The doctrine of no compromise with sin made no account of the complexities of social problems—the immediate, root-and-branch eradication of slavery or immediate dissolution of the Union, were his alternatives. "We dissolved the Union by a handsome vote, after a warm debate," wrote Edmund Quincy in 1843; "the question was . . . wrapped up by Garrison in some of his favorite Old Testament Hebraisms by way of vehicle, as the apothecaries say" (*ibid.*, Vol. III, p. 88).

It was at a Fourth of July meeting, following the Anthony Burns affair of 1854, that Garrison made use of the striking appeal that attests his extraordinary boldness and skill as an agitator. After contrasting the principles of the Declaration of Independence and the present state of the Republic, he went on:

He should now proceed to perform an action which would be the testimony of his own soul, to all present, of the estimation in which he held the pro-slavery laws and deeds of the nation. Producing a copy of the *Fugitive Slave Law*, he set fire to it, and burnt it to ashes. Using an old and well-known phrase, he said, "And let all the people say, Amen"; and a unanimous cheer and shout of "Amen" burst from the vast audience. In like manner Mr. Garrison burned the decision of Edward G. Loring in the case of Anthony Burns . . . the multitude ratifying the fiery immolation with shouts of applause. Then, holding up the U. S. Constitution, he branded it as the source and parent of all the other atrocities,—"a covenant with death and agreement with hell"—and consumed it to ashes on the pot, exclaiming, "So perish all compromises with tyranny! and let all the people say, Amen!" A tremendous shout of "Amen" went up to heaven in ratification of the deed, mingled with a few hisses and wrathful exclamations from some who were evidently in a rowdyish state of mind, but who were at once cowed by the popular feeling. (*Ibid.*, Vol. III, p. 412.)

In such fashion did this disciple of the gospel of peace carry the war into Macedonia. The law of conscience had come into collision with the law of the land, and he followed conscience. For Garrison majority votes held no mandate. He had come to regard the political state as the mother of all mischiefs; for behind this thing of shreds and patches he saw unscrupulous politicians whose profession was the deceiving of simple minds, befogging moral issues with their myths and cults—their appeals to patriotism and the Constitution—and bringing the law of God into contempt. It was the spiritual bondage of the North that held the Negro in slavery, Garrison had come to believe, and to free the conscience of the North was the great duty devolving upon the Abolitionists. With his intense single-mindedness he saw no other duty, and in doing that duty he would use no other weapon than the sword of the spirit. It is fortunate, perhaps, that the prophet knows so little of the resourcefulness of the market place on which he pronounces judgment, or his zeal might suffer abatement. Slavery was not destroyed by the conscience of Massachusetts, but by the economics of free labor. The free-soilers were more dangerous to it for they fought with material weapons; and old John Brown of Ossawatomie, more Hebraic even than Garrison, was a sterner realist, who took care to load his Sharp's rifle while girding on the sword of the spirit. From the prophet to the soldier is but a step, from the sword of the spirit to musket and ball, from conscience to the Emancipation Proclamation. Single-minded men—the Garrisons and John Browns—marshaling the discontent of their generation, sometimes do succeed in removing mountains; but unfortunately they leave a great scar, and the débris litters the whole countryside. Other mountains may even arise from the waste of the leveling. After the Emancipation Proclamation came the Fourteenth Amendment, and out of that came the triumphant gospel of "due process of law." The devil understands the ways of the world too well to become discouraged at a temporary set-back, for if righteousness succeed in breaking the bonds that bind a generation, he knows that the market place carries an ample stock of new cords to replace those that are broken.

II

JOHN G. WHITTIER: *Puritan Quaker*

If Garrison was the flintiest character amongst the militant Abolitionists, Whittier was certainly the gentlest. Among many lovable men he was perhaps the most lovable. Bred in a faith that had never been dominant in New England, he escaped the induration that was the price the New England conscience paid for its hard dogma. No thick shell of

353

Calvinism incrusted for him the soul of humanitarian religion. In the Society of Friends righteousness was not daily twisted into unloveliness, nor the beauty of holiness forgotten; and in consequence, it was easier for him than for his Calvinist neighbors to fashion his life upon the principles of the New Testament, and set Christ above the Prophets.

Whittier's family escaped many temptations by following quiet paths to their own ends. Prosperity had never wooed the Massachusetts Quakers away from the simple life, as it had done with so many Philadelphia Friends, but a narrow domestic economy and social non-conformity had nourished their religion of peace and good will. Long before Channing discovered the religion of love in the teachings of French humanitarianism, the early Quakers had found that primitive gospel in the byways of Carolinian England, and had brought it to the new world. There they had borne testimony in their daily lives to the excellence of Christian fellowship, and there they had suffered the reproaches and the blows of bigoted conformists. Their faith had been tried in the fires of persecution, and the Society of Friends had justified its use of that most excellent of sectarian names. In the sincerity of their equalitarian fellowship the Quakers were the friends of humanity, of the poor and the outcast of this world. Their religion was of the week-day as well as the Sabbath. With its mystical doctrine of the inner light—of the Holy Spirit that speaks directly to the soul without the intermediation of priest or church—it unconsciously spread the doctrine of democracy in an autocratic world. It interpreted literally the principle that members of the Christian fellowship are equals in the sight of God and in each other's eyes—that on earth there is neither high nor low but a common brotherhood in Christ. It quietly set aside the pretentions of priestly hierarchies, and substituted the principle that religion is a matter that lies with the individual and God. Naturally a "hireling ministry" could not look with favor on such doctrine, and the sharp hostility it aroused in theocratic New England sprang from the realization that the ideals of the Quaker fellowship were dangerous to the ideals of a priestly theocracy. The autocratic rulers of Massachusetts Bay could see little good in the democracy of the Friends.

As became a Quietist, the master passion of Whittier's life was ethical. He was neither a transcendental nor a Utopian visionary, but a primitive Christian, an apostle of good will and a friend of justice. Sprung from a long line of New England yeomen, wholly of the soil, simple in wants, quietly independent, he was the last lineal expression in our literature of the primitive faith, the last authentic echo of the spiritual democracy of the seventeenth century. A thorough Yankee in character, the Yankee never dominated him. As a young man, to be sure, he temporized with his Quakerism and dreamed fond dreams of worldly ambition. The stirrings of youthful romance awakened the desire to be a Byronic poet, and a Yankee knack with politics led him to meddle with the hope of representing his district in Congress. He was hand-in-glove with the time-serving Caleb Cushing, and the temptations of political intrigue almost led to his backsliding; but he soon put the devil behind him and gave security for his better behavior by coming out for the cause of Abolitionism. That was the end of his hopes of political preferment, and the more surely to burn his bridges he published in 1833, at his own cost, a little Abolition tract entitled *Justice and Expediency,* which was reissued by Lewis Tappan in a great edition and scattered broadcast. The same year he attended as delegate the National Anti-Slavery Convention at Philadelphia, and subscribed his name to its pronouncement. Thenceforth for over thirty years he gave his best strength to the cause, writing abundantly in prose and verse, serving as editor of Abolition publications, and suffering the unpleasant experiences common to the group, at one time being hunted by a mob and stoned.

This deliberate alignment with an unpopular cause, this calm response to the summons of conscience, was the fruit of his Quaker training. It was no new experience for the Quaker to dissent. The Whittier family had been Come-outers for generations, sacrificing material well-being for their faith, and he had grown up in dissent. The long struggle for democratic freedom in Massachusetts was a familiar story to him. The record had come down by word of mouth and stories of early persecutions were fireside tales in the Whittier household. His ancestors had lived in the hard old Puritan theocracy, and yet detached from it; and this detachment had rendered them shrewdly critical and sensitive to injustice. With their quiet dissent from what the Quaker conscience regarded as unrighteous, and their practical nullification of unjust authority, Whittier was in full sympathy. His intimate knowledge of early Massachusetts history had taught him certain things which official historians had overlooked, the chief of which was that dissent had been the ally and friend of freedom in New England. From his youth up he had been a loving student of the old annals, of those intimate narratives that preserve the voice and manner of the past; and as he discovered how often persecution had left its stain on the record, he was drawn to consider the superstitious aberrations of a people supposedly devout. In middle life he gathered up in *Leaves from Margaret Smith's Journal of Massachusetts Bay, 1678–79*, materials that he had long been collecting, and which, interpreted by a sympathetic imagination, provides a surprisingly vivid account of life in New England in the second generation.

All in all, it is Whittier's most notable achievement in prose. Pieced together out of old records, it is authentic as the yellow documents from which it was drawn. The soft light of romance lies upon its pages, sobered by historical fact and tempered by creative sympathy. Loving yet critical, quite devastating at times in its implications, it is an amazingly intimate narrative. The mind of Puritan New England is uncovered in these unpretentious pages, and it does not show to advantage. There was many a knot and seam in the old Puritan life, much that was mean and ugly woven into the honest web. The Puritan proneness to Quaker-baiting—aggravated to be sure by the ill manners of the Ranters; their vulgar credulity that encouraged witch-hunting; their callous treatment of the Indian and Negro; their hardness of nature that made them grasping and censorious: such knots and seams in the Puritan character did not escape Whittier's eye, but they appear in the sketches of avaricious deacons, sour women, intolerant magistrates—the Deacon Doles and Goody Lakes and Roger Endicotts, whose bigotry tyrannized over the better natures of the community. Whittier sifted his materials carefully to gather up what good wheat there might be, yet the showing it must be confessed is but paltry. Honest Robert Pine who will have none unjustly treated, good Mr. Russ who counsels moderation in dealing with the unhappy victims of mob suspicion, Captain Samuel Sewall who speaks up bravely for the outcast—these are the remnant in Israel, the generous minority that cannot leaven the dour and credulous mass. Yet even they are not heroic figures to Whittier. His heroes are the Come-outers, and in particular Peggy Brewster—reminiscent evidently of his great-grandmother, the Quakeress Mary Peaslee, who married

Robert Whittier in 1694—who is the good Samaritan of the Puritan neighborhood, and whose loving-kindness wins a reluctant good will that stops short of toleration of her non-conformity.

Such intimate studies in the psychology of persecution were a liberal education, and Whittier would have been no Quaker had he not learned his lesson. He was justified in not thinking well of the social conscience of respectable New England. Religious conformity, he had come to understand, had not kept alive the torch of freedom in Massachusetts, nor had Puritan righteousness befriended justice. Not the great of earth but the simple may be counted on to do God's work. So taking his lesson to heart he quietly put aside ambition, and like Peggy Brewster numbered himself among the remnant. Like her he would be a Comeouter and bear his testimony against the uncleanness of the American people in this matter of Negro slavery. Not with musket and ball would he fight, like old John Brown; but with the sword of the spirit. The solution must lie with the conscience of the American people. As a Friend, a man of peace, he would not deal harshly with the supporters of slavery; he would not counsel violence. But as a Yankee with a gift for politics, he would use political means to jog a slothful conscience and marshal its forces. And so Whittier became the politician amongst the Abolitionists. He proved himself a skillful lobbyist. He was active in getting up petitions to Congress. He supported John Quincy Adams and put pressure on the slippery Caleb Cushing. He advocated the policy of boring from within the old parties, but when such methods proved futile he became an active leader in the third party movement. He was an early supporter of the Liberal party—that in 1844 drew enough votes from Clay in New York to defeat him for the Presidency—of the Free-Soil party, and later of the Republican party.

It was this insistence upon the use of political methods that brought about the unhappy break with Garrison. Immediately it was no more than a difference over tactics, but it was embittered by a wide cleavage of political theory. With Garrison's conversion to spiritual anarchism the Abolition movement was sundered by a division between the perfectionists and the political actionists. The principle of non-voting and of refusing allegiance to the Constitution aroused strong opposition, and Whittier went with Birney and Gerrit Smith, with Jonathan Sewall, John Pierpont and

the Tappans in rejecting the perfectionist policy. His political common sense turned naturally to political agencies to
accomplish his ends. "Moral action apart from political"
seemed to him an "absurdity." But when he applied the
Quaker principle of Come-outism, and advocated separate
party alignment, Garrison attacked him with his habitual
intolerance. The latter feared a third party movement as
certain to provide a rallying cry for the commercial interest
to muster the mob to its support, and overwhelm the minority with the unthinking and selfish mass. "All political
minorities," he argued, "are more or less liberal," and by
throwing the Abolition strength to such organized minorities, the movement would be "feared and respected by all
political parties" (Garrison, *William Lloyd Garrison,* Vol.
II, pp. 310–311). The wisest strategy, he believed, was to
seek to hold the balance of power between the old parties
—rewarding friends and punishing enemies—while laboring to arouse the conscience of America, for ballots without
conscience were the enemies of justice.

Whittier was no such root-and-branch spirit as Garrison,
and in the political field he was a practical, somewhat prosaic Yankee, little given to abstract speculation, skillful in
minor strategical skirmishes, inclined to opportunism. He
belonged to no school of political thought. His equalitarianism came as a heritage from his Quaker religion rather than
from political theory. To prepare himself for his work he
read Milton and Burke. The pamphlets of the great Puritan
appealed to him as the voice of the moral fervor of a heroic
age, but Milton's aristocratic republicanism he seems to
have examined no more critically than Burke's Whiggish
legalism. Neither held anything in common with Quaker
equalitarianism. Rousseau and Tom Paine and Jefferson, with
whom he certainly would have sympathized, he seems not
to have been acquainted with. In Whittier's New England
they were in ill repute, and the young Whittier was as
naïvely provincial in his political partisanship as was Garrison. Economics had no part in his thought, and the economic interests that divided Federalism and Anti-Federalism he seems never to have understood. Though sprung
from six generations of farmers who tilled the same acres,
he reveals no sympathy with agrarianism. He swallowed
Clay and the American System without a qualm, and as a
young editor he wrote with pride of the developing industrialism of Massachusetts. Neither in politics nor in economics was he a rebellious soul. He was conscience rather

than intellect. He felt rather than thought. Only a moral issue could draw him into strife, and even in such contests he was ill equipped to lead the prosaic debates. His moral indignation found its natural expression in verse, and he early took his place as the poet of the Abolition movement, distilling into ready lyrics the emotion of the moment.

A great, even a noteworthy poet, Whittier certainly was not. Compared with Whitman he is only a minor figure. Among the better known American poets Bryant alone is so narrow in range and barren in suggestion. His austere and meager life bred too little sensuousness of nature and too few intellectual passions. An over-frugal watering of the wine of paganism had left the New England character thin. The sap of humor that ran so boisterously through the veins of the West, exuding a rough wit from Davy Crockett to Mark Twain, was quite gone out of the Yankee blood. His homely imagination was unquickened by a hearty village life as was the case with the English Bunyan and the Scotch Burns. He had become a bundle of Yankee nerves, responding only to moral stimuli. The comment of Whitman sums up the Quaker poet adequately:

Whittier's poetry stands for morality . . . as filtered through the positive Puritanical and Quaker filters; is very valuable as a genuine utterance. . . . Whittier is rather a grand figure— pretty lean and ascetic—no Greek—also not composite and universal enough (doesn't wish to be, doesn't try to be) for ideal Americanism. (Carpenter, *Life of Whitman*, p. 293.)

Never a great artist, rarely a competent craftsman, he wrote for the most part impassioned commonplace, with occasional flashes that are not commonplace.

The high-water mark of lyric indignation was reached in the lines to Webster. Written at white heat, they have the passionate directness of Thoreau's prose. Like other Abolitionists, Whittier had clung to his hopes of Webster in spite of frequent signs of the latter's backsliding. He did not sufficiently appreciate the economic alliances that tied Webster to State Street, and he underrated his presidential ambitions. But when the blow came with the Seventh of March Speech, it staggered him—not alone the defection of Webster, but the demonstrative approval of his wealthy constituents. For having "convinced the understanding and touched the conscience of a nation," Webster was formally thanked by some seven hundred addressers from the most respectable circles of Massachusetts—great men like Rufus

Choate, George Ticknor, W. H. Prescott, President Jared Sparks and Professor Felton of Harvard, Moses Stuart and Leonard Woods of Andover Theological Seminary. It was an hour of profound discouragement that laid bare what colossal difficulties stood in the way of Abolitionism. "The scandalous treachery of Webster and the *backing* he has received from Andover and Harvard," wrote Whittier to Garrison, "show that we have nothing to hope for from the great political parties and religious sects" (William Sloane Kennedy, *John G. Whittier,* p. 113).

The scathing lines of *Ichabod* were read throughout the North, and they must have rankled in Webster's heart. Even Whittier was troubled by their severity and thirty years later he wrote a second Webster poem which he set beside *Ichabod* in his collected works. *The Lost Occasion* is a testimony to the kindliness of Whittier's Quaker heart that did not love to offend; but no kindliness of memory would change or soften the just verdict of the lines:

> Of all we loved and honored, naught
> Save power remains;
> A fallen angel's pride of thought,
> Still strong in chains.

> All else is gone; from those great eyes
> The soul is fled:
> When faith is lost, when honor dies,
> The man is dead!

> Then, pay the reverence of old days
> To his dead fame;
> Walk backward, with averted gaze,
> And hide the shame!

If Whittier was ill acquainted with the Boston of State Street and the Back Bay, and the Cambridge of Harvard culture, he knew intimately the Massachusetts of the village and the farm, and the overwhelming repudiation of Webster and the Whig party, following the Seventh of March Speech, would seem to have justified his lyric confidence expressed in the vigorous heptameters of *Massachusetts to Virginia*. For those who lived in the social world of Commissioner Loring—professor of law at Harvard—and Rufus Choate, it was hard not to think that Massachusetts had come to degenerate days. The fine old-school Federalist, Josiah Quincy, commenting on the Boston that watched Sims returned to slavery, wrote:

When the [Fugitive Slave] law passed, I did think the moral sense of the community would not enforce it; I said that it never would be. But now I find that my fellow-citizens are not only *submissive* to, but that they are earnestly active for, its enforcement. The Boston of 1851 is not the Boston of 1775. Boston has now become a mere shop—a place for buying and selling goods; and I suppose, also, of *buying and selling men.* (Garrison, *William Lloyd Garrison,* Vol. III, p. 328.)

And Lowell, living in the same mean atmosphere, wrote:

> Massachusetts, God forgive her,
>   She's akneelin' with the rest,
> She, thet ough' to ha' clung ferever
>   In her grand old eagle-nest.
>   (*Biglow Papers,* Part I, 1.)

But Whittier professed to think better of the conscience of New England. A strong pride of the commonwealth runs through the lines that name over the towns of Massachusetts, from "free, broad Middlesex," westward and northward to the hills of Hampshire:

And sandy Barnstable rose up, wet with the salt sea spray;
And Bristol sent her answering shout down Narragansett Bay!
Along the broad Connecticut old Hampden felt the thrill,
And the cheer of Hampshire's woodmen swept down from
    Holyoke Hill.

The voice of Massachusetts! Of her free sons and daughters,
Deep calling unto deep aloud, the sound of many waters!
Against the burden of that voice what tyrant power shall stand?
No fetters in the Bay State! No slave upon her land!

When at last the long controversy was over and release from the struggle came to Whittier, his poetry grew richer and mellower. He was not made to be a fighter, and it was with a sigh of relief that he turned to the Elysian fields he had dreamed of, while he was turning with his plow the rough stubble of a cause. Looking back upon those arduous days, he sketched half whimsically his own portrait in *The Tent on the Beach.*

And one there was, a dreamer born,
  Who, with a mission to fulfill,
Had left the Muses' haunts to turn
  The crank of an opinion-mill,
Making his rustic reed of song
  A weapon in the war with wrong,
Yoking his fancy to the breaking-plough
That beam-deep turned the soil for truth to spring and grow.

Too quiet seemed the man to ride
    The wingéd Hippogriff Reform;
Was his a voice from side to side
    To pierce the tumult of the storm?
A silent, shy, peace-loving man,
He seemed no fiery partisan
To hold his way against the public frown,
The ban of Church and State, the fierce Mob's hounding down.

For while he wrought with strenuous will
    The work his hands had found to do,
He heard the fitful music still
    Of winds that out of deam-land blew.
The din about him could not drown
What the strange voices whispered down;
Along his task-field weird processions swept,
The visionary pomp of stately phantoms stepped.

The common air was thick with dreams,—
    He told them to the toiling crowd;
Such music as the woods and streams
    Sang in his ear he sang aloud;
In still, shut bays, on windy capes,
He heard the call of beckoning shapes,
And, as the gray old shadows prompted him,
To homely moulds of rhyme he shaped their legends grim.

Many excellent things he did in those quiet later years;
old time pictures like *Snowbound,* with its homely fireside
economy long since buried under the snows of forgotten
winters; vigorous tales like *Abraham Davenport;* ballads
like *Skipper Ireson's Ride,* that have something of the
spirit of the primitive. He had given thirty years of his
life to the cause of social justice, and surely none would
grudge him in old age his rambles in pleasanter fields. It
was well that he could turn to the past, for the America
of the new exploitative age, the New England of Lowell
and Lawrence, he never understood. Black slavery he understood, but wage slavery he comprehended no more than
did Garrison. To the end he remained a primitive soul,
ill equipped to understand a materialistic philosophy of
society. There is something pathetic in his *Songs of Labor.*
His economics, like his democracy, was of a bygone time,
having no kinship with a scrambling free-soilism or a
rapacious capitalism. There is scant room in this world
for the Friend with his unmilitant dream of the fellowship. With his passion for freedom, established in the gospel of righteousness, the Quaker Whittier was fast becoming

an anachronism in industrial New England that was concerned about very different things. How old-fashioned he had become is suggested by certain lines that phrase his greetings to later times. Spare, somewhat halting in rhythm, yet transparently sincere, they constitute an apologia that New England need feel no shame for.

> Yet here at least an earnest sense
> Of human right and weal is shown;
>   A hate of tyranny intense,
>   And hearty in its vehemence,
> As if my brother's pain and sorrow were my own.
>
>   O Freedom! if to me belong
> Nor mighty Milton's gift divine,
>   Nor Marvell's wit and graceful song,
>   Still with a love as deep and strong
> As theirs, I lay, like them, my best gifts on thy shrine!

III
HARRIET BEECHER STOWE: *A Daughter of Puritanism*

No more Puritan mind than Mrs. Stowe's ever contributed to the literature of New England. Her remarkable native gifts were unconsciously given specific shape by a rigid environment. For years the artist in her struggled to subdue the moralist, and never quite succeeded. Before she dipped her pen in ink her mind had taken its set. She could not hope to escape being a preacher. Daughter of a minister and wife of a minister, with brothers and sons ministers, she lived all her life in an atmosphere of religion. She was baptized in creeds and prattled the language of sermons as the vernacular of childhood. Born at a critical time for the old New England faith, her youth was passed amid the storm clouds of the Unitarian controversy, in an atmosphere charged with electricity. Connecticut was the very citadel of the Edwardean orthodoxy, and Litchfield was as rugged in its faith as the hills it nestled among; and when the old-school Calvinism of Boston was in danger of utter rout, it naturally turned to a Connecticut Daniel to save the venerable cause. Stout old Lyman Beecher was a host in himself. Son of a Connecticut blacksmith and himself brought up at the forge before he quitted it to seek learning at Yale College under Timothy Dwight, able, kindly, practical, with pronounced literary tastes and a capable pen, he was a stalwart Edwardean, militantly conservative, who damned our perverse human nature with incontrovertible logic. Harriet was eight years old when Channing preached his Baltimore sermon, and fourteen when her father was summoned to Hanover Street Church, Boston. Her childish heart had already been given to Baxter's *Saint's Rest,* and her imagination awakened by Cotton Mather's *Magnalia Christi Americana.* Theocratic New England lay enveloped for her in a haze of romance, more fascinating than any Sir Walter had woven about the Scottish Highlands; she had discovered there noble figures and heroic deeds to kindle an ardent hero worship. At fourteen she was converted—too easily it seems, for she could not demonstrate to the satisfaction of her spiritual counselors that she had been sufficiently under conviction of sin. Thereafter to the end of her life the greatest of all dramas for her was the drama of the soul concerned with the great business of salvation.

The surest clue to Mrs. Stowe's literary secret is to be found in her sympathetic understanding of the spiritual life of Puritan New England. She was a lifelong student of New England psychology, with its "profound, unutterable, and therefore unuttered melancholy" that resulted from open-eyed contemplation of grim fact. The past that lay bleak and stern behind the sober present she understood as few others did. Before her sympathetic eyes it fell into just proportions, and quite naturally she became the historian of her people. The autobiographical material that fills her later work—her husband's recollections in *Old-Town Folks,* and her own in *Poganuc People*—is much more than autobiography; it is intimate history of New England, written by one who in distilling her own experience was writing the chronicle of a race. In a brilliant chapter of the former work she gives a remarkable analysis of the intellectual development of Puritan New England, and provides the setting against which her own intellectual life should be placed. To overlook it is to miss the most suggestive commentary on her work that has ever been written.

This daughter of Puritanism traces her intellectual antecedents back to the long struggle of Puritan rationalism with feudal custom and medieval ideas. The old English Puritans, "by nature the most reverential and most loyal portion of the community," in destroying the divine-right sovereignty of King Charles, were impelled to transfer that sovereignty to a higher King. In pulling down the temporal, they erected a divine sovereignty; and their passionate attachment to the new Sovereign was the natural response to "the pleading and yearning within them of a faculty robbed of its appropriate object, and longing for support and expression." But the theologies to which they yielded intellectual allegiance were a "legacy from past monarchical and medieval ages." To free themselves from this unhappy legacy, and create a democratic theology, was an arduous work that needed two hundred years to accomplish; and not until the Revolution spread a new social philosophy through America, did the work go forward rapidly. Wanting such a democratic philosophy Puritan New England wandered in the old theological fogs. It was Jonathan Edwards who first turned the New England mind to rationalism, and began that long "controversy" that was to unsettle so much. But unhappily the rationalism of Edwards was turned aside to reactionary ends, and his *Treatise on True Virtue* was "one of the strongest attempts to back up by reasoning the old monarchical and aristocratic ideas of the supreme right of the king and upper classes." Nevertheless he set all New England to rationalizing, and it was this severe discipline that carried her people soberly through the Revolutionary War, and preserved them from the excesses which followed the Revolution in France. And it was this same discipline that prepared them for the eventual re-discovery of the humanity of Jesus and the democracy of his religion. New England had been struggling towards democracy through the bog of its feudal theology; it became consciously democratic with the appearance of the new theology (*Old-Town Folks,* Chapter XXIX).

This rationalistic bias of eighteenth-century New England suffices to explain for Mrs. Stowe the stern temper and angular individuality of the old Puritan Yankee. Her particular hero and saint was Jonathan Edwards, and her lesser hero and saint was Samuel Hopkins; and in both it was the courageous rationalism that appealed to her. In them, and more particularly in the former, she discovered the creative force that quickened a religion that was falling into dead formalism, that gave it fresh vitality and made it the central fact of everyday New England life. Across the world of her youth lay the shadow—or the light—of the great Edwards, and the great Hopkins was his intellectual heir. In another chapter of *Old-Town Folks* she sketches the Edwardean influence in bold outline.

The ministers of the early colonial days of New England, though well-read, scholarly men, were more statesmen than theologians. Their minds ran upon the actual arrangements of society, which were in great measure left in their hands, rather than on doctrinal and metaphysical subtleties. They took their confession of faith just as the great body of Protestant reformers left it, and acted upon it as a practical foundation, without much further discussion, until the time of President Edwards. He was the first man who began the disintegrating process of applying rationalistic methods to the accepted doctrines of religion, and he rationalized far more boldly and widely than any publishers of his biography have ever dared to let the world know. He sawed the great dam and let out the whole waters of discussion over all New England, and that free discussion led to all the shades of opinion of our modern days. Little as he thought of it, Waldo Emerson and Theodore Parker were the last results of the current set in motion by Jonathan Edwards. (Chapter XIX.)

In this flood let loose by the metaphysical saw of Jonathan Edwards, Mrs. Stowe found the material for her New England tales. In no other pages does one realize so fully the tremendous, vital significance of religion to the children of Puritanism, nor appreciate how narrow a course their lives ran between the farm and the meeting-house. A domestic economy and a parochial theology absorbed their energies, and they took on sharp and angular imprints from a severe routine. It was a school of discipline that created individual character, and Mrs. Stowe possessed a loving eye for the odd and original. She delighted in emphasizing the theological differences that ran through Yankee families, giving little twists to character, and rising to the tongue in scraps of confirmatory Scripture. Large-hearted, motherly Grandmother Badger, in *Old-Town Folks*, was a stern Calvinist who daily threw predestination in the face of her easy-going Arminian husband, and exchanged syllogisms in a Sabbath-day "battle of the Infinities" with her son from Yale. Theology provided the staple of talk in the farmer's kitchen; it was the axis on which turned the simple country life. *Old-Town Folks* and *Poganuc People* are cross sections of old New England, with its lingering prejudices in favor of rank,[1] its Arminian Parson Lothrop in wig and gold cane, and its Calvinist Dr.

[1] "It's a hard struggle for our human nature to give up titles and ranks, though," said Miss Mehitable. "For my part, I have a ridiculous kindness for them yet. I know it's all nonsense; but I can't help looking back to the court we used to have at the Government House in Boston." (*Old-Town Folks*, Chapter VI.)

Cushing hostile to all democratic Jacobinism, its country yokels, its stubborn yeomen who parade their independence by voting the democratic ticket openly in the face of gentlemanly Federalists, its sharp contrasts of a stately old order and a somewhat bumptious new, yet with the hard New England granite snugly laid up and bonded with the mortar of religion—a strange dead world that emerges distinctly through the haze of Victorian sentiment. For Mrs. Stowe was a child of her own romantic generation as well as a daughter of Puritanism, and it was easy for her to discover suggestions of Utopia in a world where minister and people mingled theology with their corn-huskings and apple-bees.

Between these sketches and the Abolition novels stands *The Minister's Wooing*, with its Puritan heroine bleached into pure holiness under the cold sunshine of Hopkinsian theology, and its unworldly minister who demonstrated the sincerity of his creed of disinterested benevolence—of willing to be damned for the glory of God—by voluntarily yielding his betrothed to an earlier lover. It is a love story without sex, as befits the wooing of a Puritan nun by her spiritual father, set against a Yankee background of capable housekeeping and dignified tea-drinking, subdued to proper decorum by religion, and touched with tragedy by the shadow of damnation that falls on the unregenerate—a world in which the beauty of holiness is somewhat pale and austere, and where disinterested benevolence finds a thin and obdurate soil to strike root in. Mrs. Stowe was drawn to the theme, very evidently, by the impulse of her two Utopian enthusiasms, her interest in Abolition and her affection for the ways of old New England. Such romance as blossomed under those bleak skies she loved to gather into a Yankee nosegay, and in her sympathetic hands the old slave-running Newport becomes almost lovable and human. She might find the theology hard, but she forgave the sermon out of love for the preacher. As the historian of the human side of Calvinism she tempered dogma with affection. In unsympathetic print those old sermons were almost unbelievably harsh and ungainly; as theologians those bewigged preachers were dry as the chips of last year's woodpile; but as husbands and fathers and neighbors, they were usually kind and unselfish and helpful. Her father Lyman Beecher was an arid dogmatist on the Lord's Day, but on week-days he fished and hunted rabbits and went nutting with his sons, made garden or smoked hams, or helped a neighbor with plowing or haying, and was an unusually capable and cheery member of a busy little world. In the light of such domestic exegesis the bleakness of his theology was softened, and the dogmatic theologian became a very human person.

Thus instructed Mrs. Stowe found no difficulty in discovering the human side of Dr. Samuel Hopkins, or understanding how the hard doctrine might cover the gentlest of souls—that the very intensity of devotion to the logic of a stern creed betokened a depth of religious sincerity that would find issue in generous deeds. A thinker who can dig from the harsh soil of Calvinism the doctrine of disinterested benevolence will discover a tender conscience in his own bosom. One might hazard a guess, indeed, that the story of Samuel Hopkins was an unconscious defense of the New England ministers against the sharp charges of the Abolitionists that the clergy were half-hearted in the cause or openly hostile. With her conviction of the unselfish nobility of their lives, Mrs. Stowe must have taken a secret pleasure in revealing the good Doctor as a forerunner of the Abolitionists, and in pointing out that the crabbed logician of the Edwardean school, the theologian immersed in the abstractions of a grotesque system, was nevertheless a light set upon a hill, a primitive Christian with heart overflowing with loving-kindness, who understood the iniquity of slavery and turned shepherd to the outcast to his own hurt. The figure of the unworldly minister is drawn with loving hand and his angularities made less rugged. His noble spirituality shrivels and consumes the mean excuses of his slave-running parishioner; it spreads quietly over the countryside, and his daily life is a sermon that quickens hearts that his theology leaves cold. There is preaching aplenty in the book—quite too much for later stomachs; but it scarcely detracts from the significance of the story as a document of Puritan New England, revealing how a tender conscience was stirring beneath the crabbed exterior of the old Calvinism.

In the light of such antecedents and such training Mrs. Stowe's passionate concern over slavery becomes easily comprehensible. Her Puritan conscience was quickened by her warm human sympathies. She had come close to the hateful thing during the years spent at Cincinnati, where the Abolition sentiment of the Lane Seminary students aroused such bitter opposition that President Lyman Beecher was forced to approve the decision of the trustees to forbid any discussion of slavery, with the result that so great a hegira of students took place from Lane to Oberlin that the seminary was forced to close. Only the fact that two miles of Ohio mud provided defensive outworks saved the building and the houses of the teachers from the hands of the Cincinnati mob. She had visited in Kentucky; she had been to the slave markets; she had seen her father and brother aid runaway slaves by means of the underground railway. A profound sense of the iniquity of the system oppressed her, and when the Fugitive Slave Bill came to fill up the measure of her wrath, she poured out her heart in *Uncle Tom's Cabin*. Despite its obvious blemishes of structure and sentimentalism it is a great human document that stripped away the protective atmosphere from the sacred institution, and laid bare its elementary injustice. It brought the system home to the common feeling and conscience. The strong religious coloring emphasized the Abolition argument that slavery trafficked in Christian souls, and rendered it hateful to every humanitarian instinct. It was noble propaganda, and the humor and pathos, the passion for social righteousness, still linger in its pages to make a later generation wonder that our fathers should so long have tolerated this evil thing.

Five years later she published *Dred, A Tale of the Great Dismal Swamp*, a thoughtfully elaborated statement of the complex problem, with a suggested solution that only thrust into relief the fact that it had indeed become an irrepressible conflict—the same solution that had been hinted at thirty years before in Kennedy's *Swallow Barn*, namely, a system of paternalistic emancipation, based on the historical analogy of the extinction of English villeinage, the slaves to be treated as wards by the masters and educated for gradual emancipation. It was a feudal solution of a feudal problem, but it took higher humanitarian ground than human nature can, and Mrs. Stowe recognized the complex of passion and interests in which the problem was involved, by removing her southern emancipationist to Canada to try his experiment. More striking, perhaps, is the shift from the Christian pacifism of *Uncle Tom's Cabin* to the economics of *Dred*. The former had made appeal to the humanitarianism of the North; the latter proposed to appeal to the self-interest of the South. The slave states, Mrs. Stowe's heroine argued, were being ruined by slavery, and if they were to expect a sane economic future, they must destroy the wasteful system. The contrast between Yankee thrift under free labor and plantation shiftlessness under slave labor had been pointed out by Whittier in his *Justice and Expediency* as early as 1833 and by Caruthers in his *Kentuckian in New York* in 1834—statements that perhaps drew Mrs. Stowe's attention to the economic phases involved; nevertheless the recognition of the complexity of the problem, and the attempt to deal with it adequately, lessened the popular appeal of *Dred*. The book is more skillfully done than *Uncle Tom*, it is far richer in background material—in vivid sketches of poor whites, of revivalist preachers, of plantation life—it provides in Old Tiff a delightful study of the Negro servant and it suggests the perennial fear of a Negro uprising; but it lacks the singleness of appeal that makes for telling propaganda. It was not its melodrama that hindered its success. The public had swallowed that in *Uncle Tom* with a hearty appetite. It was rather the dissipation of dramatic interest, the want of a striking figure to capture the imagination and sympathy. It is a better sociological study but a weaker story.

It was hard for the New England conscience to quit the pulpit and turn artist; and it was particularly hard for Mrs. Stowe with her ardent nature and multiplying domestic cares. She could bring her soul under discipline but not her art. She never trained herself in craftsmanship, never learned restraint, but suffered her pen to range freely as her emotions directed. The creative instinct was strong in her but the critical was wholly lacking. Richly endowed though she was her work has suffered the fate that pursues those who forget that beauty alone survives after emotion subsides.

CHAPTER I

The Genesis of Transcendentalism

From the doctrine of the open mind that was the core of Unitarianism, came the transcendental movement that marked the full flowering of the New England renaissance. It was the native response of the mind of New England to the summons of revolutionary romanticism, and its ardor was the greater for being so long delayed. Creatively influenced though it was by French Utopianism and German mysticism, its manners and mode of thought received a particular impress from an environment long preparing and that was natively congenial. "Practically," says its most penetrating historian, transcendentalism "was an assertion of the inalienable worth of man; theoretically it was an assertion of the immanence of divinity in instinct, the transference of supernatural attributes to the natural constitution of mankind." [1] It was the glowing expression of philosophic Utopianism, the flaring up of old fires of idealism, before the scientific and materialistic reactions destroyed its romantic dreams. It accepted kinship with the social idealism of the Declaration of Independence; it accepted the dynamic principle of equalitarianism; but it sought to go farther and provide a sure defense and justification of an idealism that it professed to find established in human nature, by establishing it in metaphysics.

The explanation of this curious throwback to earlier times in the mind of transcendental New England is clear enough to anyone acquainted with the history of Puritan

[1] See Frothingham, *Transcendentalism in New England*, Chapter VI.

thought struggling with the mystical element of Christian experience. Since the far-off days of Roger Williams—the seeker and mystic who was so great a puzzle to his realistic brethren—idealism had been starved in New England. Its mystical aspirations had been repressed by dogma, and its elusive dreams brought to nothing. Jonathan Edwards struggled life-long to hold his idealism in subjection to theology, and ended in abortive reaction; a potential Emerson, another Berkeley, he re-welded the bonds of dogma on the mind of New England, putting off for two generations the day of its release. Even in the freer minds idealism suffered from the repressions of the common rationalism; with Locke and Hume in the ascendancy the mystic found the times uncongenial to his needs. The dawn of a new day seemed to be breaking with the shift of interest from theology to politics, during the stirring days of the Revolution. The submerged idealism of New England came to expression in the dreams of homespun democrats like Sam Adams, and expanded in the sunshine of French Utopianism; but unfortunately Boston Federalism reasserted the old dogmatisms and put a speedy end to the movement. It shut the door upon all democratic aspiration and bade it go about its business. It was from such a narrow environment that the rising movement of Unitarianism received its impress. From a sterile rationalism, a respectable close-fisted conservatism, it could not escape; and in consequence the new movement of liberalism was taken over by Federalism and became a new orthodoxy. "The pale negations of Boston Unitarianism"—to use Emerson's well-known phrase—provided little nourishment for transcendental hopes.

Nevertheless Unitarianism carried within it the seeds of the new faith—in its intellectual attitude, if not in its philosophy. "The Unitarians as a class," remarks Frothingham, "belonged to the school of Locke, which discarded the doctrine of innate ideas, and its kindred beliefs. . . . Unitarianism . . . has rarely, if ever, been taught or held by any man of eminence in the church who was a Platonist" (*Transcendentalism in New England,* Chapter VI). But in spite of its eighteenth-century nurture—because of it, indeed—Unitarianism was a profoundly liberalizing movement. It was a narrow and local phase of a world-wide revolution; the special contribution of Boston to the great work of disintegrating the past to make ready for the future. It loosened the grip of dogma on the Puritan mind and widened the field of reading and thinking. But it did very much more—it recovered the original principle of Protestantism, the principle of individual responsibility, that had been tacitly denied by Calvinistic orthodoxy. It asserted the essential decency of human nature—men may not be the children of God but they are assuredly not children of the devil; and it summoned this decent human nature to live decently in accordance with its nature. It would not coop up the mind in dogma; it would not close all roads to heaven but one. The Unitarians might be instinctively conservative, as was natural to prosperous persons, but they at least acknowledged "themselves to be friends of free thought in religion." Their doctrine was not a creed but an attitude of mind. If they themselves were not Seekers, they professed a willingness for others to become Seekers. Very likely few of them measured up to the full stature of such liberalism; nevertheless they "honestly but incautiously professed a principle broader than they were able to stand by, and avowed the absolute freedom of the human mind as their characteristic faith" (*ibid.*, Chapter VI).

All this was excellent, but it was not enough. It remained to see what the free mind should discover in its venturesome quest into the unknown. Intellectually emancipated, with the bleak dogmas of election and reprobation put away, with the God of wrath dethroned and the God of love lifted up, and with the dynamic principle of freedom of inquiry in their possession, the younger generation of New England intellectuals naturally opened their eyes to discover what winds of new doctrine were blowing in the world. They were pretty much all Unitarians—the young transcendentalists—and largely clergymen; their primary interest was metaphysical and they had already abandoned Locke for Plato. The rationalistic eighteenth century was dead to them and they set forth to discover another age. Hints and suggestions of that better age had come to them from overseas—from Wordsworth and Shelley, from Cousin and Madame de Stael, from Coleridge and Carlyle; and the fresh beauty of that new poetry, the enormous stimulus of that new metaphysic, fired them with a desire to seek this inspiration at its source and drink from the living waters. And so they discovered romantic Germany where the new idealism had quite routed the philosophy of sensationalism, and a great school of transcendental thinkers was in triumphant possession of the field. It was a profoundly stimulating discovery, and from it dated the rise of New England transcendentalism.

The immediate creative influence of the new contact with Germany was to strengthen the incipient Platonism of the rebellious intellectuals, and provide it with an added sanction. Transcendentalism, it must always be remembered, was a faith rather than a philosophy; it was oracular rather than speculative, affirmative rather than questioning; and it went to Germany to find confirmation of its faith, not to reëxamine its foundations. Faith preceded metaphysics, and if the metaphysics had been lacking intuition would have supplied its place, poetic inspiration would have sufficed the needs of transcendental minds. They had found God for themselves before the philosophers justified them; they took to Germany what they sought there. Nevertheless it was a tremendous experience to come upon their own philosophy there, erected into a system, supported by a complete metaphysics; a philosophy that had put to rout the fashionable skepticism of Voltaire and Condillac, established on the sensationalism of Locke, and offering justification for faith in God and man—faith in a divinity indwelling in nature and the individual soul—by a masterly dialectics. That experience determined the development of New England transcendentalism. The metaphysic of Kant, the mysticism of Jacobi, the idealistic egoism of Fichte, the transcendentalism of Schleiermacher—the new gospel of the renascent German spirit—these were the living waters of truth to the thirsty minds of the New England intellectuals, from which they drank eagerly, never doubting their sufficiency. They were poets and prophets; they were young and strong in faith; others might concern themselves with the dialectics of idealism, they would apply it in their daily lives.

In essence this new transcendental faith was a glorification of consciousness and will. It rested on the rediscovery of the soul that had been dethroned by the old rationalism; and it eventuated in the creation of a mystical egocentric universe wherein the children of God might luxuriate in their divinity. The Unitarians had pronounced human nature to be excellent; the transcendentalists pronounced it divine. They endowed it with great potentialities; made of it a dwelling place of the Most High; discovered the secret voice of God in the buried life that men call instinct; refused to heed any other command save this inner voice of God. With ebbing faith men may deny their own

374

divine nature, but the divinity is not destroyed; the music of the indwelling Godhood murmurs in the shell till the tide returns to flood it again. The one great miracle is the daily rebirth of God in the individual soul; every day is a new day; every act is a fresh wonder; faith, hope, trust, accompany man in his adventurous journeyings. Why, therefore, demanded the transcendentalist, should he not trust himself? Why should he not walk confident in his own high purpose? Why should he doubt and question the buried compulsions that urge him forward? If he is indeed a child of God, let him live as unto God; and if it should turn out that there has been some mistake in the premises and he proves to be a child of the devil, then let him live as unto the devil. Better so than not to trust himself.

Quite obviously they were arch-romantics—these young poets of the new faith; children of an age given over to new hopes and disintegrating revolutions; inexperienced prophets of a world in flux, before the scientific spirit had stripped them of their wings. The fascinating book of nature and of man had been newly opened to them, and like Miranda they were ready to exclaim,

> O wonder!
> How many goodly creatures are there here!
> How beauteous mankind is! O brave new world,
> That has such people in 't!

They could see only God because in their thinking God had filled their minds. No evil lurked in the secret places of their hearts to whisper doubts concerning the goodness of life; no ominous clouds veiled the divine light that wrapped their universe about. After two hundred years of discipline in righteousness the old dogmatic pessimism was dissipated, leaving not a rack behind. The evil was gone and God remained; and in this new world the sons of God were to be henceforth heirs of the kingdom, free to fulfill that good which is the final reality. Arch-romantics, they were dreaming a transcendental dream, as other arch-romantics were dreaming their Jacksonian dream, their imperialistic dream, their Utopian dream. Romanticism comes to different issues in different men and different times: Emerson and Jefferson were unlike enough, as their worlds were unlike; but they were both romantics and their idealism was only a different expression of a common spirit.

Years after the transcendental ferment had subsided,

one of the lesser prophets of the movement offered a statement of the faith that deserves to be recalled:

Transcendentalism [he said] relies on those ideas in the mind which are laws in the life. Pantheism is said to sink man and nature in God; Materialism to sink God and man in nature; and Transcendentalism to sink God and nature in man. But the Transcendentalist at least is belied and put in jail by the definition which is so neat at the expense of truth. He made consciousness, not sense, the ground of truth. . . . Is the soul reared on the primitive rock? or is no rock primitive, but the deposit of spirit—therefore in its lowest form alive, and ever rising into organism to reach the top of the eternal circle again, as in the well one bucket goes down empty and the other rises full? The mistake is to make the everlasting things subjects of argument instead of sight. . . . Our soul is older than our organism. It precedes its clothing. It is the cause, not the consequence, of its material elements; else, as materialists understand, it does not exist. . . . What is it that accepts misery from the Most High, defends the Providence that inflicts its woes, espouses its chastiser's cause, purges itself in the pit of its misery of all contempt of His commands, and makes its agonies the beams and rafters of the triumph it builds? It is the immortal principle. It is an indestructible essence. It is part and parcel of the Divinity it adores. It can no more die than he can. It needs no more insurance of life than its author does. Prove its title? It is proof of all things else. It is substantive, and everything adjective beside. It is the kingdom all things will be added to. (C. A. Bartol, quoted by Frothingham in *Transcendentalism in New England,* Chapter XIV.)

This is sheer mysticism, and mystics in greater or less degree all the transcendentalists were—isolated and lonely in the midst of men, seeking always a larger fellowship, awaiting those fleeting moments of illumination that should light up the meaning of life. "Mine is a certain brief experience," says Emerson, "which surprised me in the highway or in the market, in some place, at some time,—whether in the body or out of the body, God knoweth,—and made me aware that I had played the fool with fools all this time, but that law existed for me and for all; that to me belong trust, a child's trust and obedience, and the worship of ideas, and I should never be fool more" (*The Transcendentalist*). Fleeting and incommunicable are such illuminations, yet like the clear sunlight to eyes that are open. "If you do not need to hear my thought, because you can read it in my face and behavior, then I will tell it you from sunrise to sunset. If you cannot divine it, you would not understand what I say" (*ibid.*). And because the realist found himself quite incapable of such understanding, the transcendentalist turned away from him to live by himself. "They feel that they are never so fit for friendship, as when they have quitted mankind, and taken themselves to friend."

Such an attitude of mind may easily become the father of criticism. Communing with the ideal rarely begets complacency; the actual seems poor and mean in comparison with the potential. Hence the transcendentalists, willingly or not, were searching critics of their generation. They were impatient of any falling short of the ideal, and their lives in consequence became an open indictment of a Yankee world given over to materialism. "By their unconcealed dissatisfaction," said Emerson, "they expose our poverty, and the insignificance of man to man." "Their quarrel with every man they meet, is not with his kind, but with his degree. There is not enough of him,—that is the only fault. . . . They make us feel the strange disappointment which overcasts every human youth. So many promising youths, and never a finished man!" (*The Transcendentalist.*)

As to the general course of living, and the daily employments of men, they cannot see much virtue in these, since they are parts of this vicious circle; and as no great ends are answered by the men, there is nothing noble in the arts by which they are maintained. Nay, they have made the experiment, and found that, from the liberal professions to the coarsest manual labor, and from the courtesies of the academy and the college to the conventions of the cotillion-room and the morning call, there is a spirit of cowardly compromise and seeming, which indicates a frightful skepticism, a life without love, and an activity without aim. (*Ibid.*)

Idealists though they were, they could not escape meddling with the real which encompassed them on all sides— with institutions, laws, society, with the state itself. They were far more interested in God than in Cæsar, and they found it impossible to divide loyalties that too often clashed. When Cæsar essayed to impose his will upon theirs, when he put their ideals in jeopardy by demanding allegiance to laws they did not approve, they quietly denied him sovereignty and followed their own paths. With such men nothing could be done; their very lives were a criticism and a judgment on New England and America. Transcendentalism may have run into its follies, but foolish in its critical judgment—blind to the gap between profession and reality—it was not. It might be severe, but it was honest and intelligent, and honest intelligent criticism America stood greatly in need of.

CHAPTER II

Ralph Waldo Emerson: Transcendental Critic

At the age of thirty-six the man who was to become the most searching critic of contemporary America expressed his conception of his mission in the following passage:

What shall be the substance of my shrift? Adam in the garden, I am to new-name all the beasts of the field and all the gods in the sky. I am to invite men drenched in Time to recover themselves and come out of time, and taste their native immortal air. I am to fire with what skill I can the artillery of sympathy and emotion. I am to indicate constantly, though all unworthy, the Ideal and Holy Life, the life within life, the Forgotten Good, the Unknown Cause in which we sprawl and sin. I am to try the magic of sincerity, that luxury permitted only to kings and poets. I am to celebrate the spiritual powers in their infinite contrast to the mechanical powers and the mechanical philosophy of this time. I am to console the brave sufferers under evils whose end they cannot see, by appeals to the great optimism, self-affirmed in all bosoms. (*Journals,* Vol. V, p. 288.)

Seven days before Emerson set down this transcendental pronouncement, he had written in his journal a different comment:

A question which well deserves examination now is the Dangers of Commerce. This invasion of Nature by Trade with its Money, its Credit, its Steam, its Railroad, threatens to upset the balance of man, and establish a new, universal Monarchy more tyrannical than Babylon or Rome. Very faint and few are the poets or men of God. Those who remain are so antagonistic to this tyranny that they appear mad or morbid, and are treated as such. Sensible of this extreme unfitness they suspect themselves. And all of us apologize when we ought not, and congratulate ourselves when we ought not. (*Ibid.,* Vol. V, pp. 285–286.)

In such comments and others scattered plentifully through his Journals, Emerson essayed to make clear to himself the function of transcendental criticism as he felt himself called to practice it. It was to be no trivial or easy duty. In the midst of a boastful materialism, shot through with cant and hypocrisy and every insincerity, fat and slothful in all higher things, the critic proposed to try the magic of sincerity, to apply the test of spiritual values to the material forces and mechanical philosophies of the times. His very life must embody criticism; his every act and word must pronounce judgment on the barren and flatulent gods served by his countrymen. He must be a thinker and as such he must summon to the bar of a nobler philosophy the current standards of value and conduct. Men of the greatest reputation must not be spared; he must "issue a *quo warranto* and revoke the characters of fame," overruling the verdict of newspaper editors and the acclaim of the electorate. Here was a revolutionary business indeed, that the critic was proposing to himself; and the calm serenity with which he set about it was disconcerting. A thinker loose in the America of Daniel Webster, a thinker who proposed to test men and measures by the magic of sincerity, was likely to prove an unpleasantly disturbant factor in a world of pretense. Measured by such standards the current philosophies must bate and dwindle, and the common ideals shrink to the mean and paltry. The life of an honest thinker laid on the America of 1840 would reveal how far short it came from the stature of intellectual manhood.

Emerson the critic has been too much obscured to common view by Emerson the brilliant dispenser of transcendental aphorisms. The oracular *Essays* with their confident wisdom—the sententious expression of the middle period of a life that came to late maturity—interpose themselves between the young priest whose intellectual interests quietly detached themselves from Unitarian orthodoxy, and the mature critic whose loyalties quietly detached themselves from the gods of his generation. The very brilliancy of the *Essays* conceals the laborious processes by which their abundant wisdom was distilled. One must go to the *Journals* for that—to those intimate records that reveal how patiently he sought for truth and how honestly he followed it. Wisdom did not come to him of its own accord; it was painfully groped for. As an introspective Puritan youth he began early to keep a diary of his intellectual life, gathering into successive journals the savings from his discursive readings. For years as a quiet student he lived in a world of moral aphorisms, a cold, thin atmosphere where gnomic phrases bloomed and ancient oracles uttered judgment. This was the seedtime of his mind. He was making acquaintance with the noble dead, gathering their utterances to make for himself a new testament. "No man could be better occupied," he said later, "than in making his own bible by harkening to all those sentences which now here, now there, now in nursery rhymes, now in Hebrew, now in English bards, thrill him like the sound of a trumpet." As a young man he made this his chief concern. His early journals are an ample nursery where cuttings from all philosophies are set out, there to grow into such plants as circumstance should permit. The ancestral cult of the book was in his blood, and living as he did under the threat of ill health, none too confident that the years would lengthen out before him, he forced himself to a severe intellectual regimen. To invest his days wisely was his single purpose. He wanted only the best securities for his investments, and what he got he carefully deposited, together with the increments of his own thought, to draw upon at later need. There were no wastrel forays in his intellectual life, no unpruned riot of growth, but the very odds and ends of his meditation were carefully treasured to be used when other materials were lacking. Fortunately the stuff was of good quality that outlasted many makings-over, till finally he got the cut to his liking. From this discipline of years came his superlative mastery of the sententious sentence; his brilliant utterances are rich with the thought he has crammed into them.

The cheerful serenity that never deserted him was a triumph of will over circumstance. It was a singularly cheerless world that bred him, subsisting by sheer will power, eating its heart out with heroic ambitions, too grimly earnest to enjoy what it got so laboriously—the lean aftermath of two centuries of asceticism. The business of plain living and high thinking was a joyless manner of life, and the young Emerson got little pleasure from it. A nature less insulated must have broken under the strain. It was a world stricken with tuberculosis. Of the five brothers one was mentally defective, another burnt up his vitality and went to the West Indies to die, a third of brilliant powers succumbed to consumption, his first wife died of the same scourge, his second wife and Emerson himself were long affected with incipient tuberculosis. To ease such anxious lives there was need of a great solace, and that solace was sought in religion. The ascetic youth ran as naturally to religious meditation as a normal child to play. No call to conversion ever came to him; the natural man postulated in Calvinistic dogma was washed out of him before he was born. The earlier jottings in the journals, before philosophy came to soften the inherited asceticism, and a transcendental revulsion from the common pessimism had turned him into a serene optimist, often are as bleak and austerely introspective as those morbid human documents that fill the old libraries of Puritanism. Such meditations are thin gruel for the nourishment of a vigorous life, and Emerson must have suffered from innutrition if he had not come upon more substantial food.

Fortunately the old Puritan anchors were already dragging, and Emerson was pretty well adrift when the romantic surge caught him and sent him far along new courses. The Puritan moralizer became the transcendental seeker; the curious-minded loiterer in the gates of the temple, who had studied the moral winds by watching the tiny straws of circumstance—erecting unconsidered trifles into ethical signposts—calmly quitted the church and set forth on his intellectual quest. The ties had long been loosening, but it was his year abroad where he discovered ways of thinking unknown to Concord and Boston, that effectively liberalized his mind and released him from the narrow Yankee provincialisms. On that momentous trip Goethe, Landor, Coleridge, Wordsworth, Carlyle, set him speculating on new themes, stimulating afresh the love of Plato, in whom he had long found inspiration. Continental idealism with its transcendental metaphysics refashioned Emerson and put him upon his life-work.

Speaking of the intellectual revival of New England later in life, he remarked that "Goethe was the cow from whom their milk was drawn"; but it would seem that the influence of Wordsworth proved more immediately stimulating, for on his return home Emerson set about the systematic contemplation of nature which left so considerable a deposit in his mind. Before this he had been too intent on his soul to consider the sunshine on the fields, but thereafter he made his pilgrimages into the country with the seriousnes of one conducting a novel experiment. In this new concern for nature there was a deliberate self-consciousness. In temperament he was a bookish recluse, in love with the printed page. He was not a Thoreau to love his Walden Pond for its own sake, and it needed an effort of the will to send him as far as Auburn wood, to lie on his back and translate nature into metaphysic. But he had come to the point where his developing philosophy must send him into the fields. He had looked within himself and discovered the divinity of the individual soul; but he had not probed the non-self, the great encompassing universe of matter by which the individual is circumscribed and of which he is a part. To discover there the diffused presence of God, to feel his kinship with man, to understand that the soul is a microcosm, were necessary preliminaries to the unfolding of his transcendental philosophy, and he went about the work with painstaking thoroughness. From this creative contact with nature emerged the Emerson we know, radiant with idealism, glad of life; and this radiant gladness he put into his maiden essay, *Nature*.

This was in 1836 when Emerson was thirty-three years of age. In the next two years he published *The American Scholar*, quintessence of transcendental individualism, and the *Divinity School Address*, the bible of transcendental religion. With the appearance of the second series of *Essays*, six years later, the major ideas of his philosophy were fully elaborated. Stripped of its idealistic phraseology, of its beauty and fervor, the master idea of the Emersonian philosophy is the divine sufficiency of the individual. In accepting himself he accepted his fellows, and he accepted God. The universe he conceived of as a divine whole, whereof each man is his own center from whom flows the life that has flowed in upon him, perennially fresh, perennially a new creation. The law for things is not the law for mind; man is unkinged in acknowledging any lesser sovereignty than the sovereignty of self. Statutes, constitutions, governments, schools, churches, banks, trade—the coercing sum of institutions and customs—these things do not signify; they are only idols with clay feet that blind men worship. The true divinity dwells elsewhere, in the soul of man; and that divinity must rule the world and not be ruled by it. The apotheosis of individualism—such in briefest terms was the gospel of Emerson; new only in its radiant dress and idealistic sanctions, the final transcendental form of a doctrine spread widely by the French romantic school. It was the same revolutionary conception that Channing had come upon, that Jefferson had come upon, that Rousseau had come upon—the idea which in the guise of political romanticism had disintegrated the *ancien régime,* and in the form of philosophical romanticism had disintegrated eighteenth-century rationalism— the idea that was providing Utopian dreams for an ebullient democratic faith.

Thus equipped with a philosophy Emerson was prepared to begin his work as a critic. The ideal he had drunk of was a perennial condemnation of the material. The mean and ignoble ends pursued by a mean and ignoble society were a challenge to the serenity of his faith, and he must set himself to analyze the causes of the low estate to which the potential sons of God had fallen. Lesser revolutions in thought were implicit in this greater one, revolutions which Emerson was bound to go through with. Despite the jaunty optimism of which he was often accused, his eyes were never blind to reality; to see, and measure, and judge, was to become his life business. He did not shrink from the ugliest fact, and the unhappy condition he discovered men to be in would have discouraged a less robust faith. At times even he doubted. At times he seems half persuaded, with Cotton Mather, that the potential children of light are "strangely and fiercely possessed of the devil." "Human nature is as bad as it dares to be," he commented in his journal; and at another time, "If it were possible to repair the rottenness of human nature . . . it were well" (*Journals,* Vol. VIII, p. 259).

In seeking an explanation of the tragic gap between the real and the ideal, he came to attribute a large measure of the cause, like the eighteenth-century romantics, to pernicious social institutions which stifle the nobler impulses and encourage the baser; and he became convinced likewise that the work to which the critic was called was the work of liberation, setting the mind free from false and ignoble loyalties that it might serve the true. He prepared therefore to lay his transcendental yardstick on the little world of Yankee reality and judge how far short it came of its potential divinity. New England had never been scrutinized so searchingly, measured so justly. Serene, imperturbable, he set the ideal in one pan of the scales, and all the New England realities in the other, and bade his neighbors see how the balance tipped. For a generation he was the conscience of America, a pricker of inflated balloons, a gauger of the national brag and cant and humbug. With keen insight he put his finger on the mean and selfish and the great and generous. He surveyed his world with the detachment of posterity and anticipated the slower judgment of time. His penetration was uncanny and few of his judgments on men and measures have suffered reversal in the court of final jurisdiction.

So shrewd a critic must concern himself greatly with the Jacksonian revolution that was hurrying America towards the acceptance of political equalitarianism. By every compulsion of his transcendental philosophy Emerson was driven to accept the abstract principle of democracy. He understood well what hopes for human betterment were awakened by the principle of majority rule, and as he followed the noise and tumult of the political campaigns he was driven to definition. In 1834 he commented in his journal:

> The root and seed of democracy is the doctrine, Judge for yourself. Reverence thyself. It is the inevitable effect of the doctrine, where it has any effect (which is rare), to insulate the partisan, to make each man a state. At the same time it replaces the dead with a living check in a true, delicate reverence for superior, congenial minds. "How is the King greater than I, if he is not more just?" (*Journals,* Vol. III, p. 369.)

Somewhat later in the same year he suggested:

> Democracy, Freedom, has its root in the sacred truth that every man hath in him the divine Reason, or that, though few men since the creation of the world live according to the dictates of Reason, yet all men are created capable of so doing. That is the equality and the only equality of all men. To this truth we look when we say, Reverence thyself; Be true to thyself. (*Ibid.,* Vol. III, p. 390.)

> When I . . . speak of the democratic element, I do not mean that ill thing, vain and loud, which writes lying newspapers, spouts at caucuses, and sells its lies for gold; but that spirit of love for the general good whose name this assumes. There is nothing of the true democratic element in what is called Democracy; it must fall, being wholly commercial. I beg I may not be understood to praise anything which the soul in you does not honor, however grateful may be names to your ear and your pocket. (*Ibid.,* Vol. IV, p. 95.)

His deepening concern over the state of politics in America—the property-mindedness of the Whigs and the mob-mindedness of the Democrats—drew him into an analysis of political parties and the nature of the political state. He was little read in the political classics, and although he professed a mild approval of Montesquieu and was never tired of praising Burke, he was little influenced by either. The latter's political theory, indeed, was so fundamentally hostile to Emerson's major convictions—so legalistic in its reverence for government from the grave, so explicit in denial of new-born rights—that it is a fair assumption that Emerson never took the trouble to understand him but was content to enjoy his glowing rhetoric. Later commentators are too much given to glossing over Emerson's political theory, not approving its implications; or explaining it away by appeal to certain comments jotted down when his nerves were tried by enthusiasts;[1] but there is no explaining away a theory that was the logical expression of his transcendental philosophy, unless his whole philosophy be explained away. Emerson knew very well where his political theory led, and he had no timid compunction about following it through.

In his speculations on the nature and functions of the ideal republic—a theme that was much in his mind—he elaborated what we may call the transcendental theory of politics, a theory closely akin to philosophical anarchism. All the elaborate machinery devised by political thinkers like Montesquieu and John Adams, with their schemes of checks and balances to preserve the *status quo*, he calmly throws overboard; constitutions he is not interested in, nor the complicated props of coercive sovereignty. The single, vital, principle on which the true republic must found itself, he insists, is the principle of good-will. Since "governments have their origin in the moral identity of men," the recognition of a common human nature with common interests must induce rational men to enter a common political brotherhood; and until men become wise enough voluntarily to coöperate to the common well-being, no good government is possible. The history of governments hitherto is a history of the tragic failure of men to achieve a rational political state. "The idea, after which each community is aiming to make and mend its law," he suggests in the *Essay on Politics,* following Carlyle, "is the will of the wise man. The wise man, it cannot find in nature, and it makes awkward but earnest efforts to secure government by

[1] See, for example, *Journals,* Vol. VII. p. 221.

contrivance." But he does not push his "wise man" theory to the patriarchal absolutism of Carlyle; with Channing he postulates an ethical sovereignty above the instrument. "Absolute right is the first governor; or, every government is an impure theocracy."

The doctrine of good-will establishes government in "moral identity"; it "separates the individual from all party, and unites him at the same time to the race"; and in so doing it accepts the sovereignty of the ethical absolute. This major conception of Channing's Emerson took over and made his own. He is explicit in his assertion of the need of a moral interpretation of the doctrine of natural rights. The doctrine of an ethical sovereignty, he asserts,

. . . promises a recognition of higher rights than those of personal freedom, or the security of property. A man has a right to be employed, to be trusted, to be loved, to be revered. The power of love, as the basis of a State, has never been tried. . . . There will always be a government of force when men are selfish; and when they are pure enough to abjure the code of force they will be wise enough to see how these public ends of the post-office, of the highway, of commerce and the exchange of property, of museums and libraries, of institutions of art and science can be answered.

Every man's nature is a sufficient advertisement to him of the character of his fellows. My right and my wrong is their right and their wrong. Whilst I do what is fit for men, and abstain from what is unfit, my neighbor and I shall often agree in our means, and work together for a time to one end. But whenever I find my dominion over myself not sufficient for me, and undertake the direction of him also, I overstep the truth, and come into false relations to him. I may have so much more skill or strength than he that he cannot express adequately his sense of wrong, but it is a lie, and hurts like a lie both him and me. Love and nature cannot maintain the assumption; it must be executed by a practical lie, namely by force. This undertaking for another is the blunder which stands in colossal ugliness in the governments of the world. . . . For any laws but those which men make for themselves are laughable. . . . This is the history of government,—one man does something which is to bind another. . . . Hence the less government we have the better,—the fewer laws, and the less confided power. The antidote to this abuse of formal government is the influence of private character, the growth of the individual . . . the appearance of the wise man; of whom the existing government, is, it must be owned, but a shabby imitation. . . . To educate the wise man the State exists, and with the appearance of the wise man the State expires. The appearance of character makes the State unnecessary. The wise man is the State. (*Essay on Politics.*)

Thus in transcendental fashion does Emerson range himself on the side of Jefferson, in opposition to a coercive sovereignty. A strong and energetic government he feared as an efficient instrument of tyranny; and of the several contrivances by which it enforced its will, he considered the police power the stupidest. As a sensible man he bore with the state; he would pay his taxes; he would not strain at gnats; but as a free man he would not suffer the state to coerce him; he would destroy it first. There is a passage in his journal, written at the time of the declaration of war against Mexico—when Alcott and Thoreau refused to pay their taxes—that states his position with whimsical directness:

The State is a poor, good beast who means the best: it means friendly. A poor cow who does well by you,—do not grudge it its hay. It cannot eat bread, as you can; let it have without grudge a little grass for its four stomachs. It will not stint to yield you milk from its teat. You, who are a man walking cleanly on two feet, will not pick a quarrel with a poor cow. Take this handful of clover and welcome. But if you go to hook me when I walk in the fields, then, poor cow, I will cut your throat. (*Journals*, Vol. VII, p. 220.)

With equal emphasis he rejected the economic interpretation of politics. As a child of the romantic revolution he understood quite clearly how the waves of humanitarian aspiration broke on the reefs of property rights, how economic forces were in league against the ideal republic. There could be no true democracy till this matter of economics was put in subordination to higher values. Both the political parties, the respectable Whigs and the voluble Democrats, he was convinced, were debauched by it; the one served property openly, the other secretly. "From neither party, when in power, has the world any benefit to expect in science, art, or humanity, at all commensurate with the resources of the nation." Emerson did not deny the fact of the universal appeal of economics. He could not, of course, accept the theory of economic determinism; but he was convinced that the whole matter must be probed deeply:

The philosophy of property, if explored in its foundations, would open new mines of practical wisdom, which would in the event change the face of the world; would destroy the whole magazine of dissimulation, for so many ages reckoned the Capital art of Government. It would purge that rottenness which has defamed the whole Science until *politic* has come to mean cunning. . . . It would go deep into ethics and touch all the relations of men. (*The Present Age.*)

Pending such exploration it was clear to Emerson that the Federalist-Whig theory of a stake-in-society, or rulership by persons of principle and property, was wholly vicious:

> The theory of politics which has possessed the minds of men, and which they have expressed the best they could in their laws and in their revolutions, considers persons and property as the two objects for whose protection government exists. Of persons, all have equal rights, in virtue of being identical in nature. This interest of course with its whole power demands a democracy. Whilst the rights of all as persons are equal, in virtue of their access to reason, their rights in property are very unequal. . . . Personal rights, universally the same, demand a government framed on the ratio of the census; property demands a government framed on the ratio of owners and owning. . . That principle no longer looks so self-evident as it appeared in former times, partly because doubts have arisen whether too much weight had not been allowed in laws to property, and such a structure given to our usages as allowed the rich to encroach upon the poor, and keep them poor; but mainly because there is an instinctive sense, however obscure and yet inarticulate, that the whole constitution of property, on its present tenures, is injurious, and its influence on persons deteriorating and degrading; that property will always follow persons; that the highest end of government is the culture of men. (*Essay on Politics.*)

In such suggestions as he offered touching the form of the ideal republic, where "every child that is born must have a just chance for his bread," Emerson reveals a pronounced bias in favor of the Physiocratic theory of society. He was at one with Jefferson in preferring an agrarian to an industrial order. Manchester economics—the doctrine of the economic man, of the iron law of wages, and other obscenities of the school—he quite frankly loathed. He did not, he said, "look with sour aspect at the industrious manufacturing village, or mart of commerce"; but he would not glorify the machine, nor reduce man to a factory hand. He questioned the sufficiency or finality of the division of labor. There is more than a suggestion of William Morris in the doctrine elaborated in *Man the Reformer;* that the industrial revolution with its factory system, must be judged in the light of its effect upon the workingman, that the true function of work must be explored and every man ply his tool to his own good. The suggestion that "a man should have a farm or mechanical craft for his culture" was an implicit denial of industrialism in the days of its first triumphs—a denial that Morris would have indorsed.

We must have a basis for our higher accomplishments, our delicate entertainments of poetry and philosophy, in the work of our hands. We must have an antagonism in the tough world for all the variety of our spiritual faculties, or they will not be born. Manual labor is the study of the external world. The advantages of riches remains with him who produces them, not with the heir.

I should not be pained at a change which threatened a loss of some of the luxuries or conveniences of society, if it proceeded from a preference of the agricultural life out of the belief, that our primary duties as men could be better discharged in that calling. . . . But the doctrine of the Farm is merely this, that every man ought to stand in primary relations with the work of the world, ought to do it himself, and not to suffer the accident of his having a purse in his pocket, or his having been bred to some dishonorable and injurious craft, to sever him from those duties; and for this reason, that labor is God's education; that he only is a sincere learner, he only can become a master, who learns the secret of labor, and who by real cunning extorts from nature its sceptre. (*Man the Reformer.*)

In all this—in the doctrine of the minimized state, of the sacred rights of the individual, of the wholesomeness of an agricultural life; in his concern for social justice and his tenderness for the poor and exploited among men—Emerson proved himself a child of the romantic eighteenth century, who by his own transcendental path had come upon the Utopia that an earlier generation had dreamed of, and which he sketched in the lovely poem prefacing the *Essay on Politics*. Much of Emerson is compressed in these lines:

> Fear, Craft, and Avarice,
> Cannot rear a State,
> Out of dust to build
> What is more than dust. . . .
> When the Muses nine
> With the Virtues meet,
> Find to their design
> An Atlantic seat,
> By green orchard boughs
> Fended from the heat,
> Where the statesman ploughs
> Furrow for the wheat;
> When the Church is social worth,
> When the state-house is the hearth,
> Then the perfect State is come,
> The republican at home.

The contrast between such Utopian conceptions and the realities of America in the forties was calculated to edge the critical judgment with a certain asperity. The older agrarian simplicity of New England was being submerged by the industrial revolution, and in the midst of the change Emerson quietly pronounced judgment upon the new idols of his generation, upon State Street and Beacon Street, upon Webster and Clay and Douglas, upon Everett and Choate, upon black slavery and white, upon the Mexican War and the Fugitive Slave Bill, upon the stolid poor and the callous rich. His judgment was severe but it was never unjust. His later journals are a rich storehouse of critical comment, keen, illuminating, disastrous in its analysis of all cant and humbug. At times—in his comment on Webster, in his hatred of State Street, in his criticism of the common materialism—he is almost savage; at other times he is consumed with a vast sympathy for the long-suffering, exploited mass of the people. "Alas, for the majority," he exclaimed, "that old, inevitable dupe and victim. What a dreary Iliad of woes it goes wailing and mad withal. Some dog of a Cleon or Robespierre or Douglas is always riding it to ruin" (*Journals*, Vol. VIII, p. 449). When the Fugitive Slave Bill passed he wrote: "This filthy enactment was made in the nineteenth century, by people who could read and write. I will not obey it, by God" (*ibid.*, Vol. VIII, p. 236). In smug and prosperous Boston he found no comfort —the Boston that applauded when "Thank-God Choate thanked God five times" in denouncing "the trashy sentimentalism of our lutestring enthusiasts." Emerson would have none of Boston:

In Boston is no company for a fine wit. There is a certain *poor-smell* in all the streets, in Beacon Street and Mount Vernon, as well as in the lawyers' offices, and the wharves, and the same meanness and sterility, and leave-all-hope-behind, as one finds in a boot manufacturer's premises. (*Ibid.*, Vol. VIII, p. 363.)

With Theodore Parker he judged Boston to be the home of Hunkers, of that "cotton aristocracy" that Webster served. It groveled servilely before State Street; how should the homely moralities get a hearing in such a place? Even Harvard College he charged with being a tool of the Boston counting-houses.[2]

[2] "Harvard College has no voice in Harvard College, but State Street votes it down on every ballot. Everything will be permitted there which goes to adorn Boston whiggism; . . . but that which it exists for,—to be a fountain of novelties out of heaven, a Delphi uttering warning and

It was the crass materialism of America, of the Democrats equally with the Whigs, of the northern capitalists equally with the southern planters, that drove him to exasperation, and tempered his optimism. There is no jaunty optimism in a passage written during the panic days of '37:

. . . Society has played out its last stake; it is checkmated. Young men have no hope. Adults stand like day-laborers idle in the streets. None calleth us to labor. The old wear no crown of warm life on their gray hairs. The present generation is bankrupt of principles and hope, as of property. I see man is not what man should be. He is a treadle of a wheel. He is the tassel at the apron-string of society. He is a money-chest. He is the servant of his belly. This is the causal bankruptcy, this the cruel oppression, that the ideal should serve the actual, that the head should serve the feet. . . . Pride, and Thrift, and Expediency, who jeered and chirped and were so well pleased with themselves, and made merry with the dream, as they termed it, of Philosophy and Love,—behold they are all flat, and here is the Soul erect and unconquered still. What answer is it now to say, It has always been so? I acknowledge that, as far back as I can see the widening procession of humanity, the marchers are lame and blind and deaf; but to the soul that whole past is but one finite series in its infinite scope. Deteriorating ever and now desperate. Let me begin anew; let me teach the finite to know its master. (*Journals*, Vol. IV, p. 242.)

To be a critic rather than a fighter, and a critic because he was a poet and philosopher—this was the duty laid upon Emerson; and yet he was sorely troubled when men from the skirmish line of social conflict reported to him the need of leaders. Why should he be privileged to remain in his study when slaves were abducted on the streets of Boston and John Brown was fighting at Harper's Ferry? With the extremest reluctance he was drawn into the struggle— it was not his fight.

I waked at night [he recorded in his journal] and bemoaned myself, because I had not thrown myself into this deplorable question of Slavery, which seems to want nothing so much as a few assured voices. But then, in hours of sanity, I recover myself, and say, "God must govern his own world, and knows his own way out of this pit, without my desertion of my post, which has none to guard it but me. I have quite other slaves to free than those negroes, to wit, imprisoned spirits, imprisoned thoughts, far back in the brain of man,—far retired in the heaven of

ravishing oracles to elevate and lead mankind,—*that* it shall not be permitted to do or to think of. On the contrary, every generosity of thought is *suspected*, and gets a bad name." (*Ibid.*, Vol. IX, p. 215.)

invention, and which, important to the republic of Man, have no other watchman, or lover, or defender, but I." (*Ibid.*, Vol. VIII, p. 316.)

But always in the end he was drawn in, and none spoke wiser or braver words to a careless generation. He never faltered, never compromised; the prophet of the ideal faced the real and told the truth about it, serenely and with clear insight. His heroes were not the heroes of State Street; Horace Greeley, Theodore Parker, Horace Mann, Henry Ward Beecher, he accounted the great Americans of his day, and not Everett and Webster and Clay and Calhoun. A friend of civilization, he was partisan only to the ideal; to justice, truth, righteousness. A Yankee of the Yankees, a Puritan of the Puritans, he had emancipated himself from all that was mean and ungenerous in the one and harsh and illiberal in the other. A free soul, he was the flowering of two centuries of spiritual aspiration—Roger Williams and Jonathan Edwards come to more perfect fruition.

CHAPTER III

Henry Thoreau: Transcendental Economist

"Wisdom crieth in the streets and no man regardeth her"; yet "she teacheth temperance and forethought, justice and fortitude; than which men can have in their life nothing more profitable."

The single business of Henry Thoreau, during forty-odd years of eager activity, was to discover an economy calculated to provide a satisfying life. His one concern, that gave to his ramblings in Concord fields a value as of high adventure, was to explore the true meaning of wealth. Honest, fearless, curiously inquisitive—a masterless man who would give no hostages to fortune—he proved his right to be called a philosopher by seeking wisdom as a daily counselor and friend, and following such paths only as wisdom suggested. Out of his own experience, tested in the clear light of the Greeks, he wrote a transcendental declaration of independence that may be taken as the final word of the Concord school touching the great issues of practical living. *Walden* is the handbook of an economy that endeavors to refute Adam Smith and transform the round of daily life into something nobler than a mean gospel of plus and minus.

It was the common opinion of his neighbors that Henry Thoreau was a queer fellow who had somehow got all his values topsy-turvy. And yet the more thoughtfully one considers him, the more doubtful it appears whether the queerness lay with him or with his critics. Unfortunately a wholly honest and original man is so rare as to fall under common suspicion. To the inmates of Bedlam a sane man will appear queer. In a society of serfs a masterless man will be accounted an outlaw. To the Concord farmers Thoreau appeared strange only because he applied in his daily life a truth they assented to on the Sabbath. The principle that life is more than the meat and the body than raiment was familiar enough to the Sunday doctrines of Concord; but that a man should seriously apply it on week-days; that he should propose to regulate his mid-week activities by the economy of the Sermon on the Mount, passed the comprehension of practical Yankees who followed quite another economy. It was Thoreau's conduct that perplexed them, rather than his philosophy.

From first to last that conduct was serenely logical. To this disciple of the ancient wisdom, Sabbath and week-day were one, and in seeking to square his daily life with the ancient precept, Thoreau became the arch-rebel of his group, the most individual amongst the "lunatic fringe" of the transcendental movement, the one who escapes elusively from the grip of an adjective. He slips out of all phrases devised to imprison him. "A bachelor of nature," Emerson, with his gift for cryptic phrase, called him; "poet-naturalist," Ellery Channing, who knew him intimately, chose to call him. "I am a poet, a mystic, and a transcendentalist," Thoreau said of himself, disregarding his nature writings. Yet none of these phrases, true as they are, quite adequately sums him up. At the risk of committing a fresh futility, one may perhaps suggest that he was a Greek turned transcendental economist. His life seems to have been a persistent experiment in values. A philosopher of the open air who kept his mind clear and his nerves robust by daily contact with wind and weather; a mystic who pried curiously into the meaning of nature and was familiar with Hellenic and Oriental systems of thought; a Yankee, skilled in various homely crafts, yet rather interested in proving for himself what things were excellent and taking nothing on hearsay —Thoreau's chief business would seem to have been with life itself, and how it might best be lived by Henry Thoreau; how a rational being, in short, might enjoy the faculties God has given him, following the higher economy and not enslaving himself to the lower, so that when he came to die he might honestly say, I have lived.

Amongst the members of the transcendental school Thoreau was the one Concord man, born and bred there, literally of the soil and loving the things of the soil. His tireless rovings were commonly bounded by the familiar Concord horizons. His life had taken deep root in the Concord fields, and he refused to join the restless multitude of the *déracinés,* who seek novel experiences in a succession of transplantings. No English peasant ever clung to the home-acres with more loving tenacity. He was a countryman in instinct, distrusting the great city twenty miles away that disseminated its virus through the outlying villages and farms. The city was wedded to the economy of industrialism and exploitation. But as a child of Jean Jacques, Thoreau chose to believe that the road to heaven ran through the fields and not over the cobblestones of Boston; he discovered an honest integrity of character oftener in the country than in Lowell mills, yet none too often there. It was easier to be free there, yet even in Concord village the herd mind was always laying springes to catch the unwary; and Thoreau would not be caught. He was poet and philosopher as well as countryman, and he weighed his own life and the life of his neighbors in the scales of Hellenic thought. He was surveyor of broader fields than his neighbor's wood-lot; was acquainted with other mysteries than the mystery of pencil-making. He desired other ends than those his shopkeeping, farm-tending neighbors served; he would not be encumbered as they were. He could not carry such gross impedimenta in his pack and be a free man; the pack was too heavy; and he proceeded to lighten it with a thoroughness that startled Concord. He "signed off" from Dr. Ripley's church; with Alcott, he refused to pay his poll tax: he severed his allegiance to the Commonwealth of Massachusetts and the Federal government; he rid himself of all concern at what Concord thought of his ways; he spoke out his honest con-

victions in the village Lyceum—convictions about John
Brown and slavery and Massachusetts' part in sending
Negroes back to their masters—quite careless of the dis-
approval of Judge Hoar and other Concord dignitaries. Such
a man had never before walked the village streets, and the
spectacle filled his neighbors with amazement.

With so much useless luggage got rid of, Thoreau was
ready to set about the high business of living. To outward
appearance a somewhat angular Yankee, practical and capable, he was at heart a Greek, with the delight in the
simple round of the seasons and a responsiveness to natural
beauty that belonged to the older civilization. Brought up
under the "pale negations" of Dr. Ripley's theology, he
emerged a pagan. He was the most widely read in Greek
literature of the Concord transcendentalists; had translated
Prometheus Bound, and much of Pindar; and was completely at home in the clear Greek atmosphere. Who but
a Hellenist could utter such words as these which serve as
his apology for the Walden experiment?

I went to the woods because I wished to live deliberately, to
front only the essential facts of life, and to see if I could learn
what it had to teach, and not, when I came to die, discover that
I had not lived. I did not wish to live what was not life, living
is so dear; nor did I wish to practice resignation, unless it was
quite necessary. I wanted to live deep and suck out all the marrow of life, to live so sturdily and Spartan-like as to put to rout
all that was not life, to cut a broad swath and shave close, to
drive life into a corner, and reduce it to its lowest terms, and, if
it proved to be mean, why then to get the whole and genuine
meanness of it, and publish its meanness to the world; or if it
were sublime, to know it by experience, and be able to give a
true account of it in my next excursion. (*Walden,* "What I Lived
For.")

To seek Pan in a tired world and recover joys that have
long been forgotten is a business that only a romantic will
engage in; yet Thoreau set out on the quest with a clear-
eyed purpose:

. . . My Good Genius seemed to say,—Go fish and hunt far
and wide day by day,—farther and wider,—and rest thee by
many brooks and hearth-sides without misgiving. Remember thy
Creator in the days of thy youth. Rise free from care before the
dawn, and seek adventures. Let the noon find thee by other
lakes, and the night over-take thee everywhere at home. There
are no larger fields than these, no worthier games than may here
be played. Grow wild according to thy nature, like those sedges

395

and brakes, which will never become English hay. Let the thunder rumble; what if it threaten ruin to farmer's crops? that is not its errand to thee. Take shelter under the cloud, while they flee to carts and sheds. Let not to get a living by thy trade, but thy sport. Enjoy the land, but own it not. Through want of enterprise and faith men are where they are, buying and selling, and spending their lives like serfs. (*Ibid.*, "Baker Farm.")

If the day and the night are such that you greet them with joy, and life emits a fragrance like flowers and sweet-scented herbs, is more elastic, more starry, more immortal,—that is your success. All nature is your congratulation, and you have cause momentarily to bless yourself. . . . The true harvest of my daily life is somewhat as intangible and indiscernible as the tints of morning or evening. It is a little star-dust caught, a segment of the rainbow which I have clutched. (*Ibid.*, "Higher Laws.")

To save one's soul has always been accounted in New England a matter worthy of a man's best effort, and Thoreau's days were given over to it with a single-heartedness without parallel even in New England. The Puritan, he believed, had suffered his high spiritual mission to be sacrificed to the economic; he would recover that mission by sacrificing the economic to the spiritual; but he would interpret the spiritual as a Hellenist rather than a Hebraist. The Christian other-worldliness seemed to him unduly regardless of the loveliness of this world. "Christianity," he says in the *Week*, "only hopes. It has hung its harp on the willows, and cannot sing a song in a strange land. It has dreamed a sad dream, and does not yet welcome the morning with joy."

I am not sure but I should betake myself in extremities to the liberal divinities of Greece, rather than to my country's God. . . . In my Pantheon, Pan still reigns in his pristine glory, with his ruddy face, his flowing beard, and his shaggy body, his pipe and his crook, his nymph Echo, and his chosen daughter Iambe; for the great God Pan is not dead, as was rumored. Perhaps of all the gods of New England and of ancient Greece, I am most constant at his shrine. (*The Week*, "Sunday.")

His extraordinarily frank evaluation of the New Testament, and of Calvinistic New England that had too long chewed the cud of conscience—"they did not know when to swallow their cud, and their lives of course yielded no milk"—is the work of a pagan from whom all creeds slip easily. Few more searching sermons have been preached in Massachusetts than the sermon that composed itself as Thoreau's boat floated down the Concord River, past the

Billerica meeting-house where the honest villagers were worshiping the God of New England—a sermon that with fine irony summons minister and congregation to consider the deeper teachings of their sacred book.

I know of no book that has so few readers. There is none so truly strange, and heretical, and unpopular. To Christians, no less than Greeks and Jews, it is foolishness and a stumbling-block. There are, indeed, severe things in it which no man should read aloud but once. "Seek first the kingdom of heaven."—"Lay not up for yourself treasures on earth."—"If thou wilt be perfect, go and sell that thou hast, and give to the poor, and thou shalt have treasure in heaven."—"For what is a man profited, if he shall gain the whole world, and lose his own soul? or what shall a man give in exchange for his soul?"—Think of this, Yankees! . . . . Think of repeating these things to a New England audience! thirdly, fourthly, fifteenthly, till there are three barrels of sermons! Who, without cant, can read them aloud? Who, without cant, can hear them, and not go out of the meeting-house? They never *were* read, they never *were* heard. Let but one of these sentences be rightly read from any pulpit in the land, and there would not be left one stone of that meeting-house upon another.

. . . When one enters a village, the church, not only really but from association, is the ugliest-looking building in it, because it is the one in which human nature stoops the lowest and is most disgraced. Certainly, such temples as these shall ere long cease to deform the landscape. . . . Really, there is no infidelity, now-a-days, so great as that which prays, and keeps the Sabbath, and rebuilds the churches. (*The Week,* "Sunday.")

As Thoreau understood the problem of economics there were three possible solutions open to him: to exploit himself, to exploit his fellows, or to reduce the problem to its lowest denominator. The first was quite impossible—to imprison oneself in a treadmill when the morning called to great adventure, to burden oneself with useless fardels when the pack must be kept light, was the folly of a slave mind. He had observed his neighbors closely and found little good in their way of self-exploitation.

I have travelled a good deal in Concord; and everywhere, in shops, and offices, and field, the inhabitants have appeared to me to be doing penance in a thousand remarkable ways. . . . How many a poor immortal soul have I met well-nigh crushed and smothered under its load, creeping down the road of life, pushing before it a barn seventy-five feet by forty, its Augean stables never cleansed, and one hundred acres of land, tillage, mowing, pasture and wood-lot. . . . The better part of the man is soon ploughed into the soil for compost. (*Walden,* "Economy.")

To exploit one's fellows seemed to Thoreau's sensitive social conscience an even grosser infidelity. The leisure of a slave driver, got by imprisoning his fellows in a treadmill, was an ignoble leisure from which came the empty vulgarity of modern life. "If I devote myself to other pursuits and contemplations," he said, "I must first see, at least, that I do not pursue them sitting upon another man's shoulders. I must get off him first, that he may pursue his contemplations, too." Freedom with abstinence seemed to him better than serfdom with material well-being, for he was only giving up the lesser to enjoy the greater, as was the privilege of the philosopher.

To be a philosopher is not merely to have subtle thoughts, nor even to found a school, but so to love wisdom as to live according to its dictates, a life of simplicity, independence, magnanimity, and trust. It is to solve some of the problems of life, not only theoretically, but practically. . . . When he has obtained those things which are necessary to life, there is another alternative than to obtain the superfluities; and that is, to adventure on life now, his vacation from humbler toil having commenced. (*Walden*, "Economy.")

It was the reply of the arch-individualist to the tyrannous complexities of society, and it set him apart even in the world of transcendentalism. Other members of the group professed to have found a better way out of the dilemma—the way of Brook Farm and Fruitland; a richer life was to be achieved not by espousing poverty but by coöperation. But Thoreau could not adopt the coöperative solution; he must either accept society as it was or remove. Convinced that it was not worth accepting—that one made a foolish bargain in selling oneself to it—he was content to remove to Walden Pond. "I came into this world," he said, "not chiefly to make this a good place to live in, but to live in it, be it good or bad." "I desire to speak impartially on this point, and as one not interested in the success or failure of the present economical and social arrangement." He did not advocate that other men should build cabins and live isolated. He had no wish to dogmatize concerning the best mode of living—each must settle that matter for himself. But that a satisfying life should be lived, that the fox should somehow get free even though he left his tail in the trap, he was vitally concerned about. "The youth may build or plant or sail, only let him not be hindered from doing that which he tells me he would like to do." Let him at least rid himself of the false gospel of creature comforts, which men pay too high a price for.

The story of Thoreau's emancipation from the lower economics is the one romance of his life, and *Walden* is his great book. More restrained than the *Week* and lacking the exuberant beauty of the latter—its noble talk and scathing criticism—it is "informed by a more explicit unifying philosophy." It is a book in praise of life rather than of Nature, a record of calculating economies that studied saving in order to spend more largely. But it is a book of social criticism as well, in spite of its explicit denial of such a purpose, and in its speculations much of Carlyle and Ruskin and William Morris crops out. In considering the true nature of economy he concluded, with Ruskin, that "the cost of a thing is the amount of what I will call life which is required to be exchanged for it, immediately or in the long run." Conceive of life as cheap, a poor thing to be exploited, and the factory system becomes the logical economic order; but conceive of it as dear, and the common happiness the great objective of society, and quite another sort of industrialism will emerge. Thoreau did not look with approval on the rising city of Lowell, with its multiplying spindles and increasing proletariat, and he did not understand why Americans should boast of a system that provided vulgar leisure for the masters at the cost of serfdom for the workers.

Where is this division of labor to end? [he asks] and what object does it finally serve? I cannot believe that our factory system is the best mode by which men may get clothing. The condition of the operatives is becoming every day more like that of the English; and it cannot be wondered at, since, as far as I have heard or observed, the principal object is, not that mankind may be well and honestly clad, but, unquestionably, that the corporations may be enriched. (*Walden,* "Economy.")

The whole middle-class philosophy of exploitation was hateful to him, the middleman equally with the manufacturer. "Trade curses everything it touches; and though you trade in messages from heaven, the whole curse of trade attaches to the business." Men have been deceived by a false economy—lured by the bog lights away from the open fields to flounder in the miasmic marshes. While Ruskin was still pottering over Turner, Thoreau was elaborating in *Walden* the text: The only wealth is life.

In other bits *Walden* is curiously like *Hopes and Fears*

for Art, and the drift of the whole is one with the revolutionary teachings of Morris, that the abiding satisfactions are those which spring from free creative work. This Yankee Greek had learned that it is a beautiful life back of the tool that creates beauty, and that if the work of our hands is ugly, it is because our lives are mean and sordid, affording no outlet for the free creative spirit. In New England, Puritan and Yankee alike had conspired against beauty, and the gods had taken revenge by clothing life in drab.

Before we can adorn our houses with beautiful objects the walls must be stripped, and beautiful housekeeping and beautiful living be laid for a foundation: now, a taste for the beautiful is most cultivated out of doors, where there is no house and no housekeeping.

What of architectural beauty I now see, I know has gradually grown from within outward, out of the necessities and character of the indweller, who is the only builder,—out of some unconscious truthfulness, and nobleness, without ever a thought for the appearance; and whatever additional beauty of this kind is destined to be produced will be preceded by a like unconscious beauty of life. The most interesting dwellings in this country, as the painter knows, are the most unpretending, humble log huts and cottages of the poor commonly; it is the life of the inhabitants whose shells they are, and not any peculiarity in their surfaces merely, which makes them *picturesque;* and equally interesting will be the citizen's suburban box, when his life shall be as simple and as agreeable to the imagination, and there is no straining after effect in the style of his dwelling. (*Walden,* "Economy.")

Thoreau needed only to have lived in a world that honored craftsmanship to have opened fully the vein of gold that Morris dug his philosophy from; he had the instinct of the craftsman but not his training. His turning from the workshop to the fields, hearing no call in the humdrum village economy to develop a beautiful craftsmanship, was an implied criticism of the common sterility of labor in everyday Concord; yet the honest sincerity of his nature led him to the conclusion that lies at the heart of the philosophy of the great English craftsman:

None have so pleasant a time as they who in earnest seek to earn their bread. It is true actually as it is true really; it is true materially as it is true spiritually, that they who seek honestly and sincerely, with all their hearts and lives and strength, to earn their bread, do earn it, and it is sure to be very sweet to them.

In short, I am convinced, both by faith and experience, that to maintain one's self on this earth is not a hardship but a pastime, if we will live simply and wisely; as the pursuits of the simpler nations are still the sports of the more artificial. It is not necessary that a man should earn his living by the sweat of his brow, unless he sweats easier than I do. (*Walden*, "Economy.")

At Walden Pond and on the Merrimac River Thoreau's mind was serene as the open spaces; but this Greek serenity was rudely disturbed when he returned to Concord village and found his neighbors drilling for the Mexican War, and when authority in the person of the constable came to him with the demand that he pay a due share to the public funds. The war to him was a hateful thing, stupid and unjust, waged for the extension of the obscene system of Negro slavery; and Thoreau was brought sharply to consider his relations to the political state that presumed to demand his allegiance, willing or unwilling, to its acts. Under the stress of such an emergency the transcendentalist was driven to examine the whole theory of the relation of the individual to the state. He was not political-minded; he had concerned himself little with political theory; he would gladly let the government alone if government would let him alone; he was even prepared to make excuses for government. But he would not compromise with his conscience; and when the state applied the principle of coercion, he applied the counter principle of passive resistance. It was while he was domiciled in Walden cabin that the hand of the law seized him and thrust him into Concord jail. He went with the constable quietly, but there was a dangerous contempt in his heart. It seemed absurd that a man could not go to the cobbler's for a pair of mended boots, but he must be interfered with by a neighbor playing the rôle of constable. Constable, jailer, the magistrate on the bench, all the elaborate machinery of the law, Thoreau contemplated quizzically and judged his neighbors fools to have exchanged their freedom for such masquerades. Those who got anything from such instruments—lawyers and propertied men—might think well of them, but they were a mere impertinence to Thoreau who wanted to go huckleberrying. When they let him out he went quietly after his berries, and discovered there was "no state in sight among the berry bushes." "I saw," he remarked casually, "that the state was half-witted, that it was as timid as a lone woman with her silver spoons, and that it did not know its

401

friends from its foes, and I lost all my remaining respect for it and pitied it."

But Thoreau was not done with the comedy. It set him upon thinking, and the result was the essay, *Civil Disobedience*. Taken by itself alone, it is a somewhat astonishing performance. This Yankee transcendentalist quite evidently has turned philosophical anarchist. But read in the light of Emerson's *Journals*, or in the light of Godwin's *Political Justice*, it is easily comprehensible. It is no more than transcendental individualism translated into politics, with all comfortable compromises swept away. Its sources run straight back to eighteenth-century liberalism with its doctrine of the minimized state—a state that must lose its coercive sovereignty in the measure that the laws of society function freely. Very likely Thoreau had never read Godwin, yet his political philosophy was implicit in *Political Justice*. In Godwin's thinking the problem of man in society is the problem of a voluntary adjustment of the individual to the state; and it is only by establishing economics and politics on morality, that political justice is possible. The moral law is the fundamental law, superior to statutes and constitutions; and to it the citizen is bound to render allegiance. "The object of the present state of society is to multiply labor," asserted Godwin; "in another state it will be to simplify it." "The only adequate apology of government is necessity." "Government however reformed" is "little capable of affording solid benefit to mankind." "Give us equality and justice but no constitution. Suffer us to follow without restraint the dictates of our own judgment, and to change our forms of social order as fast as we improve the dictates of our own judgment." "The pretense of collective wisdom is the most palpable of all impostures." "The true reason why the mass of mankind has so often been the dupe of knaves, has been the mysterious and complicated nature of the social system. Once annihilate the quackery of government, and the most homespun understanding will be prepared to scorn the artifices of the state juggler that would mislead him."

By his own path Thoreau came to identical conclusions. There is little in *Civil Disobedience* that is not in *Political Justice*. To neither thinker is there an abstract state, society or nation—only individuals; and to both, the fundamental law is the law of morality. Political expediency and the law of morality frequently clash, and in such event it is the duty of the individual citizen to follow the higher law.

Thoreau went even further, and asserted the doctrine of individual compact, which in turn implied the doctrine of individual nullification; no government, he said, can have any "pure right over my person or property but what I concede to it."

I heartily accept the motto,—"That government is best which governs least"; and I should like to see it acted up to more rapidly and systematically. Carried out, it finally amounts to this, which also I believe,—"That government is best which governs not at all"; and when men are prepared for it, that will be the kind of government which they will have. Government is at best but an expedient; but most governments are usually, and all governments are sometimes, inexpedient.

A government in which the majority rule in all cases cannot be based on justice. . . . We should be men first and subjects afterwards. It is not desirable to cultivate a respect for the law, so much as for the right. . . . How does it become a man to behave toward this American government today? I answer, that he cannot without disgrace be associated with it. I cannot for an instant recognize that political organization as *my* government which is the *slave's* government also. . . . There is but little virtue in the action of masses of men. . . . It is not a man's duty, as a matter of course, to devote himself to the eradication of any, even the most enormous wrong; he may still properly have other concerns to engage him; but it is his duty, at least, to wash his hands of it, and, if he gives it no thought longer, not to give it practically his support. If I devote myself to other pursuits and contemplations, I must first see, at least, that I do not pursue them sitting upon another man's shoulders. I must get off him first, that he may pursue his contemplations too. . . . If the law is of such a nature that it requires you to be an agent of injustice to another, then, I say, break the law. Let your life be a counter friction to stop the machine. . . . As for adopting the ways which the state has provided for remedying the evil, I know not of such ways. They take too much time, and a man's life will be gone. . . . Some are petitioning the State to dissolve the Union. . . . Why do they not dissolve it themselves,—the union between themselves and the state,—and refuse to pay their quota into its treasury? [1] (*Works*, Vol. X, pp. 131–170.)

[1] Compare the following entry in his *Journal* under date of March 26, 1842: "I must confess I have felt mean enough when asked how I was to act on society, what errand I had to mankind. Undoubtedly I did not feel mean without a reason, and yet my loitering is not without defense. I would fain communicate the wealth of my life to men, would really give them what is most precious in my gift. . . . I know no riches I would keep back. I have no private good unless it be my peculiar ability to serve the public. . . . This is the only individual property. . . . It is hard to be a good citizen of the world in any great sense, but if we do render no interest or increase to mankind out of that talent God gave us, we can at least preserve the principal unimpaired."

"Let your life be a counter friction to stop the machine" —in this doctrine of individual syndicalism Thoreau's conception of the relation of the citizen to the state is tersely summed up. In so far as he was a democrat it was of the transcendental school, rather than the Jacksonian. He would be governed by the majority no more than by the minority. The scorn of a fine ethical mind for practical government by politicians could scarcely be more tellingly phrased than in the bit of verse he tucks into *Civil Disobedience:*

A drab of state, a cloth-o'-silver slut,
To have her train borne up, and her soul trail in the dirt.

Such a man quite evidently would go for Nullification as fiercely as Garrison. Even though he might wash his hands of society, the cries of those who suffered injustice followed him, and when the Fugitive Slave Law passed, it robbed him of his peace, destroying his pleasure in wonted things. The slave hunters were in Boston streets, and justice in the person of Commissioner Loring was sending Anthony Burns back to slavery. As he contemplated the spectacle his wrath against a coercive government flamed up. "My thoughts are murder to the state," he complained bitterly, "and involuntarily go plotting against her."

I would remind my countrymen that they are to be men first, and Americans only at a late and convenient hour. . . . I hear a good deal said about trampling this law under foot. Why, one need not go out of his way to do that. This law rises not to the level of the head or the reason; its natural habitat is in the dirt. It was born and bred, and has its life, only in the dust and mire, on a level with the feet; and he who walks with freedom, and does not with Hindoo mercy avoid treading on every venomous reptile, will inevitably tread on it, and so trample it under foot, —and Webster, its maker, like the dirt-bug and its ball. ("Slavery in Massachusetts," in *Works,* Vol. X.)

The law will never make men free; it is men who have got to make the law free. They are the lovers of law and order who observe the law when the government breaks it.

Thoreau was a stern judge, and he held his age in low esteem. His Concord neighbors seemed to him poor fellows with too little spirit to be free men; they were the raw material of standing armies, militia, jailors, constables, and the *posse comitatus.* And then one day into the field of his vision came a plain Yankee, primitive and heroic, John Brown of Ossawatomie. In the contemplation of his life and death Thoreau felt a shock of new faith run like an electric current through his veins. The age was no longer dead to him, for it had bred a man. "I rejoice that I live in this age," he exclaimed, "that I am his contemporary." He had found his hero—not in past times as Carlyle and Emerson had done, but in the present and among his own Yankee kind. He had talked with John Brown in Concord and recognized him as a primitive idealist of rugged mold, a stern moralist who set justice above the law. That this man should be so grossly misunderstood by lesser men, so foully slandered, filled him with sorrow and with wrath also. "When a noble deed is done, who is likely to appreciate it? They who are noble themselves. I was not surprised that certain of my neighbors spoke of John Brown as an ordinary felon, for who are they? They have either much flesh, or much office, or much coarseness of some kind" ("The Last Days of John Brown," in *Works*, Vol. X, p. 241). His trial and conviction Thoreau regarded as a judgment, not on John Brown, but upon America; the lawyers and editors and politicians who judged him were only convicting themselves.

His company was small indeed, because few could be found worthy to pass muster. Each one who there laid down his life for the poor and oppressed was a picked man, culled out of many thousands, if not millions; apparently a man of principle, of rare courage, and devoted humanity; ready to sacrifice his life at any moment for the benefit of his fellow-man. It may be doubted if there were so many more their equals in these respects in all the country,—I speak of his followers only,—for their leader, no doubt, scoured the land far and wide, seeking to swell his troop. These alone were ready to step between the oppressor and the oppressed. Surely they were the very best men you could select to be hung. That was the best compliment this country could pay them. They were ripe for her gallows. She has tried a long time, she has hung a good many, but never found the right one before.

I do not believe in lawyers, in that mode of attacking or defending a man, because you descend to meet the judge on his own ground, and, in cases of the highest importance, it is of no consequence whether a man breaks a human law or not. Let lawyers decide trivial cases. Business men may arrange that among themselves. If they were the interpreters of the everlasting laws which rightfully bind man, that would be another thing. A counterfeiting law-factory, standing half in a slave land and half in a free! What kind of laws for free men can you expect from that? ("A Plea for Captain John Brown," in *Works*, Vol. X, p. 197.)

In Thoreau the eighteenth-century philosophy of individualism, the potent liberalisms let loose on the world by

Jean Jacques, came to fullest expression in New England He was the completest embodiment of the *laissez-faire* reaction against a regimented social order, the severest critic of the lower economics that frustrate the dreams of human freedom. He was fortunate in dying before the age of exploitation had choked his river with its weeds; fortunate in not foreseeing how remote is that future of free men on which his hopes were fixed:

> The life in us is like the water in the river. It may rise this year higher than man has ever known it, and flood the parched uplands; even this may be the eventful year, which will drown out all the muskrats . . . such is the character of that morrow which mere lapse of time can never make to dawn. The light which puts out our eyes is darkness to us. There is more day to dawn. The sun is but a morning-star. (*Walden.*)

With the dawning of that day perhaps men will sit once more at the feet of the ancient wisdom and fashion their lives upon the principle that the soul is more than the meat and the body than raiment. Perhaps they may even shape for themselves new heroes—"above and after all, the Man of the Age, come to be called workingman." He and his deeds are looked down upon in our time—"It is obvious that none yet speaks to his condition, for the speaker is not yet in his condition." "Literature speaks how much still to the past, how little to the future; how much to the East, how little to the West" ("Thomas Carlyle and his Works," in *Works,* Vol. X, p. 118). One of the great names in American literature is the name of Henry Thoreau. Yet only after sixty years is he slowly coming into his own.

CHAPTER IV

Theodore Parker: Transcendental Minister

Theodore Parker was described by one of his biographers as "the best working-plan of an American yet produced," and by a fellow minister as "a conscience since Luther unsurpassed." The two comments suggest still another, that he was completely and adequately New England. Yankee and Puritan contributed equally to his making. His rich and plastic mind was two-sided: one-half was wholly English, practical, logical, concrete, lucid; loving fact and tireless in its acquisition; master of everyday affairs and competent in dealing with this world; the other was emotional, mystical, idealistic, deeply and spontaneously religious, living daily with God as a son with the Father, carrying the sorrows of men in his heart and the wrongs of the world on his conscience. One of the greatest of New England ministers, he was shepherd as well as counselor, pastor as well as teacher. "I wish to stand on the earth," he said with true critical insight, "though I would look beyond the stars. I would live *with men,* but think with philosophers" (Weiss, *Life and Correspondence of Theodore Parker,* Vol. I, p. 115). The generous amplitude of his nature was too large for the narrow walls of a church; he took all Boston for his parish, all New England for his congregation. Amazingly active and vital, he consumed whole libraries in his pursuit of knowledge. "His mind," says Weiss, "was like the republican idea itself; it could afford to be hospitable, but could not afford to be exclusive" (*ibid.,* Vol. I, p. 178). Conversant with many fields of knowledge, with a memory extraordinarily retentive, he was master of many languages —nineteen or twenty, according to Thomas Wentworth Higginson—and at home in the most abstruse subjects. He spent his vast energy with the prodigality of Cotton Mather, and he achieved what Cotton Mather with his in- bred parochialism could not achieve, an intellectual cosmopolitanism that judged Boston by broader standards than it could gauge.

A first-class fighting-man was this child of yeoman New England—none braver, not even Garrison, none more effective; and yet tender-hearted, sympathetic, with the shrewd common sense of his homespun forebears. The son of a Lexington farmer and mechanic, self-trained, endowed with indomitable will, he came of the soundest stock in Massachusetts. His grandfather was captain of the Minute Men who faced the British troops on Lexington Common in April, 1775; and a conscious pride of ancestry broke out frequently in his speech. The words uttered before the Ministerial Conference in May, 1851, in justification of his repudiation of the Fugitive Slave Law, were characteristic: "I am not afraid of men, I can offend them. I care nothing for their hate, or their esteem. I am not very careful of my reputation." He then goes on:

I have had to arm myself. I have written my sermons with a pistol in my desk,—loaded, a cap on the nipple, and ready for action. Yea, with a drawn sword within reach of my right hand. This I have done in Boston; in the midst of the nineteenth century; been obliged to do it to defend the (innocent) members of my church, women as well as men! You know that I do not like fighting. . . . But what could I do? I was born in the little town where the first bloodshed of the Revolution began. The bones of men who first fell in that war are covered by the monument at Lexington, it is "sacred to Liberty and the Rights of mankind"; those men fell "in the sacred cause of God and their country." This is the first inscription that I ever read. These men were my kindred. My grandfather drew the first sword in the Revolution; my fathers fired the first shot; the blood which flowed there was kindred to this which courses in my veins today. Besides that, when I write in my library at home, on the one side of me is the Bible which my fathers prayed over, their morning and evening prayer, for nearly a hundred years. On the other side there hangs the firelock my grandfather fought with in the old French war, which he carried at the taking of Quebec, which he zealously used at the battle of Lexington, and beside it is another, a trophy of that war, the first gun taken in the Revolution, taken also by my grandfather. With these things before me, these symbols; with these memories in me, when a parishioner, a fugitive from slavery, a woman, pursued by the kidnappers, came to my house, what could I do less than take her in and defend her to the last? (*Additional Speeches,* Vol. I, pp. 13–15.)

With his sensitive conscience visited by such memories— a child of '76 living in the evil days of the Fugitive Slave Law, a devout freethinker borne on the crest of transcendental thought—Theodore Parker became the embodiment and epitome of the New England renaissance. More completely perhaps than any other representative, he gathered up and expressed the major revolutionary impulses of his time and world: the idealistic theism implicit in the Unitarian reaction from Calvinism; the transcendental individualism latent in the doctrine of divine immanence; and the passion for righteousness, to make the will of God prevail in a world where the devil quite openly kept his ledgers. He was an eager and thorough iconoclast, impatient to break the false images—the God of John Calvin with its slanders of human nature, and the god of State Street with its contempt for justice—which New England, he believed, had worshiped too long, forgetting the ideals of the Revolutionary fathers. The mind and conscience of Boston seemed to him stifled by the strait-jacket of respectability. Righteousness like a fugitive slave, was driven into hiding, or must walk the open streets with a Derringer in its pocket. As a free soul loving freedom, and a righteous man loving righteousness, he believed a duty was laid on him to cut away the strait-jacket, to shame the Boston that sold the poor in the gates for a pair of shoes. He must labor to set free the mind and conscience of Boston that they might go forth purified to work a beneficent work in a world that is God's and not the devil's. His attack was keen and unsparing; he laid on with gusto; he used homely words; he was just rather than polite. Impatient of humbug and self-seeking he dealt in searching criticism rather than conventional eulogy. At his touch distinguished reputations shrank to the mean and commonplace, and inflated dignitaries collapsed like a pricked balloon. Intellectually honest, he spoke the truth he had been at immense pains to gather, and in consequence those who suffered the sting of his attack—ministers and lawyers and merchants and politicians, men in high position, distinguished leaders of Boston society—were not slack in crying out against him as a demagogue and agitator. Next to Garrison he became the most hated man in New England; and something of that contemporary hatred, fierce and unforgiving, clings to his name still, coloring later estimates of his worth, hinting that his manners were not on a level with his morals.[1] An extraordinarily vital and interesting person, in short, was this Yankee preacher with his Puritan conscience—this transcendental critic with his quiver full of facts; one not to be ignored in casting up the accounts of the New England renaissance.

With his memorable sermon *On the Transient and Permanent in Christianity*, preached in May, 1841—a sermon that ranks in the history of Unitarianism with Channing's Baltimore sermon—the Unitarian movement entered upon its second broad phase. It abandoned supernaturalism established on the sufficient authority of the Scriptures, and adopted the conception of an evolutionary theism, of God progressively revealing himself to the developing faculties of men and speaking through the conscience. Under Channing's guidance Unitarianism had abandoned the major dogmas of Calvinism—total depravity, predestination, a

[1] See Wendell, *Literary History of America*, p. 348.

God of wrath; it had shifted the emphasis from stable will to boundless love; and by such teachings it had captured the greater churches of Boston. By 1830 it had become securely established as the religion of Boston respectability, with implied bounds set to its intellectual liberalism. As the first ardor abated it fell to defining the new orthodoxy, resting content with what already had been won. It was against this new orthodoxy that held fast to the old supernaturalism that Theodore Parker protested. "The defect of the Unitarians was a profound one," he pointed out; "ceasing to fear 'the great and dreadful God' of the Old Testament, they had not quite learned to love the all-beautiful and altogether lovely [God] of the universe." [2] He would have no pausing of the movement of adventurous thought, no settling back into the ruts of dogmatism; and so he threw himself with immense energy into the work of liberating Unitarianism from a premature orthodoxy.

For this work he was admirably equipped. The greatest scholar of his generation of New England ministers, deep in German theology and philosophy, with the latest results of higher criticism on his study table, he was critically trained to separate historical fact from ecclesiastical tradition, and establish his theology on a basis of naturalism. He was at once scientific and transcendental. He had translated DeWette's *Introduction to the Old Testament* and was intimately acquainted with Strauss's *Leben Jesu*. He knew the oriental backgrounds of Hebraic thought, had studied comparative religion with its suggestive record of taboos and fetishism, and was gathering materials for a comprehensive history of religion from primitive times. Intellectually acquisitive and curious, he far outran the less informed and courageous of his Unitarian brethren. But he was far more than a critic, he may well be accounted a religious genius. A convinced intuitionist, he tested every authority by appeal to transcendental experience. He frankly abandoned faith in the supernatural, with its corollaries of miracles and its "fetishism of the Bible," and was far advanced in a theism that compensated for the supernatural by a passionate love of God. Thus established in personal experience his religion issued in conduct. Love of God was more to him than historical faith embodied in

[2] See "Letter to the Members of the Twenty-Eighth Congregational Society of Boston," in Weiss, *Life and Correspondence of Theodore Parker*, Vol. II, Appendix II, p. 482. This account of his "Experience as a Minister" constitutes a brief intellectual autobiography, of first importance to the student of Parker.

an historical church; love to his fellow men was more appealing than dogma. Hence the profoundly ethical quality of his religion, warm, palpitating, generous, that set it apart from the colder and austerer ethicism of the conventional Unitarians. The spirituality of Channing was enriched in Parker by the ardency of his loving nature.

The three major doctrines of his theism, as elaborated in his "Letter to the Members of the Twenty-Eighth Congregational Society," were the infinite perfection of God, the adequacy of man to all his functions, and the sufficiency of absolute, natural religion. In his elaboration of these doctrines the controlling influence of transcendental thought is everywhere apparent. A metaphysical optimism throws a golden light on all his thinking. The trinitarian Godhead, equally with the devil, vanishes in "the infinitely perfect God," "immanent in the world of matter, and in the world of spirit, the two hemispheres which to us make up the universe"—a universe created "from a perfect motive, for a perfect purpose, of perfect substance, and as a perfect means." Hence it follows in Parker's logic, that

there must be a complete solidarity between God and the twofold universe which He creates. The perfect Creator is thus also a perfect providence; indeed, creation and providence are not objective accidents of Deity, nor subjective caprices, but the development of the perfect motive to its perfect purpose, love becoming a universe of perfect welfare. I have called God Father, but also Mother . . . to express more sensibility, the quality of tender and unselfish love, which mankind associates with Mother more than aught else beside. ("Letter," etc., in Weiss, Vol. II, pp. 470-471.)

The doctrine of the adequacy of man flows logically from the doctrine of the immanence of God, but Parker was not content to rest it on such basis alone. The conception of human perfectibility, as it filtered down to him through different strata of thought, romantic and idealistic, found a high sanction in his transcendentalism; but his practical nature demanded that it be established if possible on a scientific foundation. Anthropology must substantiate philosophy. Parker was not convinced that it could be thus adequately established; nevertheless he would travel the objective path as far as it might lead. Darwin's *Origin of Species* was published after Parker was seized with his fatal illness, yet in much of the latter's thinking he was groping his way toward some similar conception of "the unity of life of the human race," with its "progressive development" from "the state of ignorance, poverty, and utter nakedness of soul and sense, the necessary primitive conditions of the race, up to the present civilization." In the deep-buried scattered records of the past, slowly being gathered together and interpreted by science, he found "proof of time immense, wherein man, this spiritual Cosmos, has been assuming his present condition, individual, domestic, social, and national, and accumulating that wealth of things and thoughts which is the mark of civilization." The doctrine of human perfectibility might not be capable of scientific proof, but it was more than a reasonable hope; it was implicit in all the past.

But this progressive development does not end with us; we have seen only the beginning; the future triumphs of the race must be vastly greater than all accomplished yet. In the primal instincts and automatic desires of man, I have found a prophecy that what he wants is possible, and shall one day be actual. . . . What good is not with us is before, to be attained by toil and thought, and religious life. (*Ibid.*, Vol. II, pp. 471–472.)

Of this slowly and painfully evolving man with his expanding ideals, religion Parker believed to be the highest ultimate expression; and religion, as the eyes of men slowly open to larger truths, will be seen to be answerable to the needs of daily life, to embody the highest ideal of social excellence. The noblest religion he believed was not supernatural, but natural. "The absolute religion which belongs to man's nature, and is gradually unfolded thence," "is the idea of humanity, dimly seen but clearly felt, which has flitted before the pious eyes of men in all lands and many an age, and been prayed for as the 'Kingdom of Heaven.'" It is forever refashioning its ideal, re-embodying its vision, in every devout soul, in every creative age. "The religious history of the race is the record of man's continual but unconscious efforts to attain this 'desire of all nations'" (*ibid.*, Vol. II, p. 473). But unhappily every new advance soon crystallizes in dogmas and institutions; taboos and fetishisms are quick to re-imprison the mind that struggles to be free. Old forms, therefore, must be daily broken to make room for evolving experience. Religion must be free; it must rise spontaneously from the depths of life. Christianity has suffered grievously from a fetishism of the Bible, from its worship of the supernatural, from an ungenerous sectarianism beloved of "ecclesiastic skeptics," who believe "there is no place for the Christian Church or the

Bible till they have nullified the faculties which created both, and rendered Bible-makers and Church-founders impossible." Every age must write a new Bible out of its God-given instincts, permeated with the divine love that is slowly shaping society to the divine purpose.

No more is the atheistic mocker or the ecclesiastic bigot commissioned to stop the human race with his cry, "Cease there, mankind, thy religious search! for, thousand-million-headed as thou art, thou canst know nought directly of thy God, thy duty, or thyself. Pause, and accept my authenticated word; stop, and despair!" (*Ibid.,* Vol. II, p. 475.)

It was this ethical quality of his religion that kept Theodore Parker so sensitive to wrongs and so generous in response to the call of social justice. His religion quickened his social conscience and summoned him to serve the plentiful reform movements of the day. With Garrison and Wendell Phillips he organized the militants of Boston radicalism. His political principles were simple and uncompromising, woven from the strands of English and French libertarianism of the seventeenth and eighteenth centuries —from Sidney, Locke, Rousseau, the great leaders of the natural-rights school. One who accepted as axiomatic the nobility of human nature and the perfectibility of man, might be a political romantic, but he was certain to be a liberal. Parker was a primitive democrat, whose democracy was bone of his bone and flesh of his flesh. But the democracy that answered the needs of his dream of the kingdom was, like Emerson's and Channing's, ethical rather than political or economic—it was "the enactment of God's justice into human laws" ("The Nebraska Question," in *Additional Speeches,* Vol. I, p. 327). "The democratic idea has had but a slow and gradual growth even in New England," he pointed out; nevertheless he was convinced that it was spreading, and "government becomes more and more of all, by all and for all" [3] (*ibid.,* p. 33). He hated Federalism with an intensity equaling Jefferson's, and ecclesiastical Federalism that twisted the authority of the church to the side of wealthy pewholders, using Scripture as a sanction for exploitation, he denounced as scathingly as Garrison. The power of the political state he feared, because he discovered the political state to be the friend of the rich rather than the poor, of selfish advantage rather than of God's justice. With other Abolitionists he distrusted the

---

[3] This phrase of Parker's was probably the source of Lincoln's phrase.

machinery of centralization that was being skillfully erected at Washington. "Opposition to centralization of authority is very old in America," he remarked; "I hope it will be always young" (*ibid.,* Vol. II, p. 29). But he was no partisan to the rule of the majority, if it determined contrary to his conscience. A transcendental individualist, he went for the nullification of an immoral statute in the name of the Higher Law.[4]

Parker was never blind to the economic basis of politics. He saw so clearly, indeed, the close alliance between group interests and governmental statutes, that his political activities were almost wholly determined by that recognition. As a political critic he was the shrewdest realist of his generation. He was one constituent whom politicians talking for Buncombe could not befuddle. He was too deeply read in American history, gifted with too keen historical insight, to be impressed by the glittering rhetoric of the Rufus Choates. He had his own views of the American government, and majestic appeals to the Constitution left him cold. The Constitution, he asserted, "is a provisional compromise between the ideal political principles of the Declaration, and the actual selfishness of the people North and South." America was not a democracy. It had thrown off theocracy, aristocracy, and monarchy, only to set in their places the "institution of money—the master of all the rest." The economic basis of society in America he considered to be open and patent. In church and state, money "is this day the strongest power of the nation." He declined to be deceived by party cries and platforms, either Whig or Democratic; both parties served economics rather than justice.

So there is a party organization about the dollar as its central nucleus and idea. The dollar is the germinal dot of the Whig party; its motive is pecuniary. . . . It sneers at the poor; at the many; has a contempt for the people. It legislates against the poor, and for the rich . . . the few who are born with the desire, the talent, and the conventional position to become rich. "Take care of the rich, and they will take care of the poor," is its secret maxim. Everything must yield to money. . . . With this party there is no Absolute Right, no Absolute Wrong. . . . There is Expediency and Inexpediency. . . . Accordingly a millionaire is reckoned by this party as the highest production of Society. He is the Whig ideal; he alone has attained "the measure of the stature of a perfect man."

[4] See "The Law of God and the Statutes of Men," in *Additional Speeches,* Vol. II, p. 181.

The Democratic party appeals to the brute will of the majority, right or wrong; it knows no Higher Law. . . . There is . . . no vital difference between the Whig party and the Democratic party; no difference in moral principle. The Whig inaugurates the Money got; the Democrat inaugurates the Desire to get money. That is all the odds. . . . There is only a hand rail between the two, which breaks down if you lean on it, and the parties mix . . . a Democrat is but a Whig on time; a Whig is a Democrat arrived at maturity; his time has come. A Democrat is a young Whig who will legislate for money as soon as he has got it; the Whig is an old Democrat who once hurrahed for the majority—"Down with money! there is a despot! and up with the desire for it! Down with the rich, and up with the poor!" The young man, poor, obscure, and covetous, in 1812 was a Democrat, went a-privateering against England; rich, and accordingly "one of our eminent citizens," in 1851 he was a Whig, and went a-kidnapping against Ellen Crafts and Thomas Sims. ("The Nebraska Question," in *Additional Speeches*, Vol. I, pp. 331–335.)

The America of Parker's day was fast becoming middle class and Parker knew it, and like Lincoln he did not disapprove. Honest thrift he found wholly desirable, and wealth if it were honestly got. But speculation dissociated from creative work he regarded with old-fashioned distrust. "If a man fully pay in efficient, productive toil and thought, he is entitled to all he gets, one dollar or many million dollars . . . and if his estate be but what he has thus actually and honestly paid for with service given, equivalent to the service received, what he can virtuously keep or humanely apply and expend, then it will never be too large." [5] But he believed there were other gods, and greater, than the god of getting on; social justice was more desirable than unearned increment; and he set his face like flint against the common materialism of America. "I come to build up piety and morality; to pull down only what cumbers the ground," he said; but he had learned that the temples of State Street were not easily leveled; that they would not fall without a mighty crash. A less courageous man would have hesitated, but Parker was utterly fearless. Boston he knew "was a Tory town." "The Mother city of the Puritans is now the metropolis of the Hunkers" (*Additional Speeches*, Vol. I, p. 111). But the spirit of '76 was strong in him and he would "appeal from Boston drunk with gold, and briefly mad with hate, to sober Boston in her hour to come." He would appeal from

[5] Quoted in Weiss, Vol. II, p. 488.

Whiggish Boston to Revolutionary Boston; from State Street to Lexington common; from the Faneuil Hall of Rufus Choate to the Faneuil Hall of Sam Adams. He would awaken the ancestral idealism of Boston that slept uneasily under the spell of middle-class ambitions—that had sold its Puritan heritage for southern trade profits. Such an appeal Boston had never before listened to, ardent, unsparing, the Hebraic and the Yankee vernacular curiously mingled; and Boston writhed uncomfortably and pronounced the prophet ill-mannered.

When the Fugitive Slave Bill passed, the six New England states lay fast asleep: Massachusetts slept soundly, her head pillowed on her unsold bales of Cotton and of woolen goods, dreaming of "orders from the South." Justice came to waken her . . and she started in her sleep, and being frightened, swore a prayer or two, then slept again. But Boston woke,—sleeping, in her shop, with ears open, and her eye on the market, her hand on her purse, dreaming of goods for sale,—Boston woke broadly up, and fired a hundred guns for joy. O Boston, Boston! if thou couldst have known, in that thine hour, the things which belong unto thy peace! But no: they were hidden from her eyes. She had prayed to her god, to Money; he granted her the request, but sent leanness into her soul. ("The Boston Kidnapping," in *Additional Speeches*, Vol. I, p. 89.)

But he offended the Boston code of good breeding even more seriously. He became personal. He named names. Before vast congregations, in printed books, he pronounced judgment on Bostonians respected in the Back Bay, mighty in State Street. Boston gentlemen had never before suffered such tongue-lashings. How mercilessly he excoriated Commissioner Loring, judge of probate and Harvard professor, for soiling his hands in the Anthony Burns case! How neatly he pricked the empty culture of Edward Everett for his pro-slavery ardor—"a Cambridge professor of Greek, he studied the original tongue of the Bible to learn that the Scripture says 'slaves,' where the English Bible says only 'servants'!" (*Additional Speeches*, Vol. II, p. 115.) What an utterly devastating attack he made on the great Webster for the latter's subserviency to local economic interests! Much honest realism underlies that criticism, and much honest American history. The "Nebraska Address" and the "Webster Address" are notable historical documents, incisive analyses—rare in those romantic days—done by one who has kept a shrewd eye on current politics, and understands the hidden springs of party policy. Into the Webster address he put his vast knowledge, his power of analysis, his frank idealism. It was "a sad and dreadful day" when duty bade Theodore Parker speak on the man whose uncommon powers he had long admired; but he did his work thoroughly, refusing to shut his eyes to ugly fact, refusing to indulge in commonplace eulogy. It was the eighteenth-century economic realism of Webster that stirred the wrath of the transcendentalist—that and the lapses from integrity. Parker's text was found in Webster's dictum that "the great object of government is the protection of property at home, and respect and renown abroad"; and how starkly it runs counter to his own ideal of government, "the enactment of God's justice into human laws," is laid bare in page after page of scathing commentary. To the exacting ethics of Parker, Webster was wanting in principles; he followed expediency rather than justice; and how surely expediency digs pitfalls for its own undoing he discovered tragic illustration of in the career of the great senator. It is a hard fate for a politician, accustomed to the cheap praise of the gullible public, to fall into the hands of a critic who is honest and searching; and Webster had too many weak points to emerge from such an analysis with credit. It is probably the most critical examination of Webster's career that has ever been made, and withal just.

Surprisingly modern, far more so than Channing, was this brilliant preacher—impulsive, colloquial, natural, whose every arrow was pointed with a fact and feather to fly true; concerned more with righteousness than with policy; hating the dull commonplace and empty dignity of Tory ways; careless of convention, somewhat spectacular, with a keen relish for combat—a vital, vivid man, the apostle of conscience, the advocate of every unpopular cause. He possessed an amazing gift of words, yet he was too impatient, too practical, to become an artist; preferring immediate ends to more lasting reputation, and spending himself with a free prodigality. He was always the speaker rather than the writer and his printed pages bear the unmistakable remarks of impetuous oral discourse. Emerson accounted him one of the four great men of the age. Whether or not that judgment holds, whether he was too eager a militant to become a great transcendental philosopher, the historian sees in Theodore Parker one of the greatest, if not the last, of the excellent line of Puritan preachers.

417

CHAPTER V

Margaret Fuller: Rebel

The fame of Margaret Fuller has waned greatly since her vivid personality was blotted out in the prime of her intellectual development. Misunderstood in her own time, caricatured by unfriendly critics, and with significant facts of her life suppressed by her friends out of a chivalrous sense of loyalty, the real woman has been lost in a Margaret Fuller myth and later generations have come to underestimate her powers and undervalue her work. Yet no other woman of her generation in America is so well worth recalling. She was the completest embodiment of the inchoate rebellions and grandiose aspirations of the age of transcendental ferment; for to the many grievances charged against the times by other New England liberals, she added the special grievance of the stupid inhibitions laid upon women. Transcendental radical and critic, like Emerson and Thoreau and Parker, she was feminist also; and to the difficult business of freeing her mind from the Cambridge orthodoxies, she added the greater difficulty of freeing her sex.

The written record that Margaret Fuller left is quite inadequate to explain her contemporary reputation. In no sense an artist, scarcely a competent craftsman, she wrote nothing that bears the mark of high distinction either in thought or style. Impatient of organization and inadequately disciplined, she threw off her work impulsively, not pausing to shape it to enduring form. Yet she was vastly talked about, and common report makes her out to have been an extraordinary woman who creatively influenced those with whom she came in contact. Like Alcott, her power lay in brilliant talk. Her quick mind seems to have been an electric current that stimulated other minds to activity, and created a vortex of speculation wherever she passed. Hungry for ideas, intellectually and emotionally vibrant, she caught her inspirations from obscure impulses of a nature thwarted and inhibited from normal unfolding; and in her sensitive oscillations she was often drawn away from polar principles to which she would later swing back. There was quite evidently a fundamental unrest within her, a conflict of impulses, that issued in dissatisfaction; and this contradiction was aggravated by intense emotions, which both quickened her mind and distorted it.

A product of Cambridge bookishness, Margaret Fuller was both a wonder and a riddle to a generation that made little account of the psychology of sex. She was commonly looked upon as an intellectual monstrosity, the most fearful of Yankee bluestockings, and a later Bostonian has gone so far as to suggest that she was "an unsexed version of Plato's Socrates" (Wendell, *Literary History of America*, p. 300). But to present-day psychology her character is an extraordinarily suggestive document, and a recent critic has read her seeming contradictions like an open book.[1] Before Miss Anthony's penetrating analysis the Margaret Fuller myth vanishes, and a very real, natural, and unfortunate woman takes its place. She came of vigorous stock, independent, outspoken, opinionated. Her grandfather was a clergyman who was unfrocked by his church for being lukewarm in the Revolutionary War. Her father, Timothy Fuller, and her four uncles, worked their way through Harvard. In Timothy Fuller there was a large measure of Puritan grimness and severity that locked the door on the passions of his heart, that none might know of them; yet there seems to have been a volcano in the man who held off the world so brusquely. The rebel was strong in him. The Fullers were not of Brahmin stock and had no wish to please their social superiors. While a Harvard undergraduate, Timothy Fuller turned Jeffersonian republican and lost his place as first honor man by joining in an undergraduate protest against certain hated regulations. As a lawyer and politician he repudiated respectable Federalism, and although he was representative in Congress for four terms and enjoyed certain other offices, his non-conformity in the end cost him dear. No doubt he had counted on that, for he was stubborn oak that might break but would not bend. The tragedy of Margaret Fuller's life seems to have been sketched before in the life of Timothy Fuller.

To an extraordinary degree the daughter was the child of the father, in ideas and sympathies as well as blood. Like

[1] See Katherine Anthony, *Margaret Fuller, A Psychological Biography*.

him she was a rebel, but for the daughter to turn rebel involved greater hazards than for the father. Her sex was a heavy handicap, for the experience of Fanny Wright and Lucretia Mott had revealed that American chivalry had definite bounds; it did not shield the woman who ventured beyond the pale. Yet considering her blood and training, how could she help thus venturing into freer fields without? From her earliest years her father treated her as a comrade and gave her the training of a boy. In her studies he dealt with her as James Mill dealt with his brilliant son. Perhaps it was a mistake to force her into the rigid groove of classical learning when she should have been playing with her dolls. From it she got very unusual acquisitions, but overstimulation broke her health, and isolation turned her mind in upon itself and made her the victim of somnambulism and freaks of imagination. The result was the development, on one side of her nature, of a female counterpart of Cotton Mather—precocious, domineering, moody, visionary, given to long hours of greedy reading, gorging herself on books and well-nigh ruining her intellectual digestion as well as her health. Against this unfortunate overstimulation her vigorous nature struggled for years, and never quite successfully. Her emotions were forever embroiling her intellect. To conceive of her as sexless is curiously to miss the point of her emotionalism. She was rather the victim of sex. Her ardent friendships with other women, her flashes of mystical experience, her fondness for children, her love of luxury and creature comforts, her eager love affair with James Nathan who unchivalrously found safety in flight, her friendship with Mazzini and her more intimate friendship with Count Ossoli, that ended in an unconventional marriage after her situation rendered it necessary—such reactions can be explained on no other hypothesis. Her ardent nature was the victim of disastrous frustrations, rendered the more acute by premature development. If she had married early, as Harriet Beecher did, and her excessive energy had been turned into domestic channels, her life must have been less tragic, whatever the effect might have been on her intellectual development.

The acutest contemporary analysis of her contradictory character is that given by her friend William Henry Channing, who found his clue in the clash between endowment and environment:

Here was one fond as a child of joy, eager as a native of the tropics for swift transition from luxurious rest to passionate excitement, prodigal to pour her mingled force of will, thought, sentiment, into the life of the moment, all radiant with imagination, longing for communion with artists of every age in their inspired hours, fitted by genius and culture to mingle as an equal in the most refined circles of Europe, and yet her youth and early womanhood had passed away amid the very decent, yet drudging, descendants of prim Puritans. Trained among those who could have discerned her peculiar power, and early fed with the fruits of beauty for which her spirits pined, she would have developed into one of the finest lyrists, romancers and critics, that the modern literary world has seen. This she knew; and this tantalization of her fate she keenly felt. (*Memoirs of Margaret Fuller Ossoli*, by R. W. Emerson, W. H. Channing, and J. F. Clarke, Vol. II, pp. 36–37.)

This disastrous clash between endowment and environment is strikingly exemplified in her delight in Europe when at thirty-four she found herself there—in her admiration for George Sand, and in particular the extravagance of her love for Rome, where her starved heart found satisfactions she had long dreamed of. "Italy receives me as a long-lost child, and I feel myself at home here," she wrote in 1847; and a few weeks later, "I find how true was the lure that always drew me towards Europe. It was no false instinct that said I might here find an atmosphere to develop me in ways I need. Had I only come ten years earlier! Now my life must be a failure, so much strength has been wasted on abstractions, which only came because I grew not in the right soil" (*ibid.*, Vol. II, p. 225). She was too eagerly pagan to be satisfied with either Puritan or Yankee Cambridge. The pale ethicism of New England was thin gruel for such an appetite for life. Even Emerson she found cold, and her stomach rebelled at the food he throve on. But this was only half the story; the other half was this:

But the tragedy of Margaret's history was deeper yet. Behind the poet was the woman,—fond and relying, the heroic and disinterested woman. The very glow of her poetic enthusiasm was but an outflush of trustful affection; the very restlessness of her intellect was the confession that her heart had found no home. A "book-worm," a "dilettante," a "pedant," I had heard her sneeringly called; but now it was evident that her seeming insensibility was virgin pride, and her absorption in studying the natural vent of emotions, which met no object of life-long attachment. At once, many of her peculiarities became intelligible. Fitfulness, unlooked-for changes of mood, misconceptions of words and actions, substitutions of fancy for fact . . . were now referred to the morbid influence of affections pent up to prey upon themselves. And, what was still more interesting, the clue was given to a singular credulousness, by which, in spite of her unusual penetration, Margaret might be led away blindfold. As this revelation of her ardent nature burst upon me, and . . . I saw how faithful she had kept to her life purposes,—how patient, gentle, and thoughtful of others, how active in self-improvement and usefulness, how wisely dignified she had been,—I could not but bow to her in reverence. (*Ibid.*, Vol. II, p. 37.)

The inchoate rebellions in her heart were stimulated and given form by her reading. From the English, French, and German romantics she drew much of her intellectual food. The long hours spent with her father over Jefferson's letters were the best of preparation for Rousseau and Mary Wollstonecraft, and French romanticism provided an excellent introduction to the German. Her emotions were in high ferment when she came upon the German school, and she yielded her heart to it without reserve. Novalis, Richter, above all Goethe, became a passion and swept her along the path that Hedge and James Freeman Clarke were following. For years she gathered materials for a life of Goethe, but a feeling of self-distrust held back the project. Her love for him was the great literary enthusiasm of her life. "It seems to me," she wrote in 1832, "as if the mind of Goethe had embraced the universe. . . . I am enchanted while I read. He comprehends every feeling I have ever had so perfectly, expresses it so beautifully; but when I shut the book, it seems as if I had lost my personal identity; all my feelings linked with such an immense variety that belongs to things I had thought so different" (*ibid.*, Vol. I, p. 119). Later, with more critical analysis of Goethe, she found her enthusiasm modifying; she was repelled by his calm, aloof intellectuality;[2] but she never wavered in loyal recognition of his commanding powers.

Her romantic idealism was in full career when the transcendental movement caught her up and put its stamp upon her. It came as an emotional appeal to the vague aspirations of a life inadequately motivated, and she threw herself eagerly into the new philosophy and became the most hectic of its expounders. The intellectual foundations of her transcendentalism were so slight in comparison with the equipment of Hedge and Parker as scarcely to justify her pretentions to their fellowship. But what she lacked in knowledge of Kant and Fichte she made up in enthusiasm, and none

[2] See *Life Without and Life Within*, pp. 23–60.

questioned her right to speak for the group. The editorship of the *Dial* provided a convenient safety valve for her energy, but it neither absorbed her nor sufficed to satisfy her limitless desires. She needed to espouse a cause more concrete and dramatic, personal in its demands, calling for high sacrifice. Abolitionism was at hand, but it repelled her by its narrow dogmatisms. Garrison was never a hero of hers. She regarded him with "high respect" for his "noble and generous" course; but "he has indulged in violent invective and denunciation till he has spoiled the temper of his mind" ("Frederick Douglass," in *Life Without and Life Within*, p. 122). Later, when she was in Europe, she looked back half regretfully at her indifference to the movement.

How it pleases me here to think of the Abolitionists! I could never endure to be with them at home; they were so tedious, often so narrow, always so rabid and exaggerated in their tone. But, after all, they had a high motive, something eternal in their desire and life. (*Memoirs*, Vol. II, p. 229.)

Even Brook Farm repelled her as much as it attracted her. Though she loved many of the members, bore her share in the discussions preliminary to its establishment, and often visited there, she would not join the venture. She had had enough of farm life at Groton. To open a road to Utopia with a common plow was, perhaps, too prosaic a business for her romantic nature, and when the Fourier Phalanx was introduced she grew skeptical. Fourierism seemed to her too mechanical a conception, in spite of her sympathy for the humanitarian spirit that lay behind it. As she looked back upon it from the vantage point of her French experience, she modified her judgment somewhat, although the old transcendental bias that Emerson had voiced still colored her views.

The more I see of the terrible ills which infest the body politic of Europe, the more indignation I feel at the selfishness or stupidity of those in my own country who oppose an examination of these subjects,—such as is animated by the hope of prevention. Educated in an age of gross materialism, Fourier is tainted by its faults; in attempts to reorganise society, he commits the error of making soul the result of health of body, instead of body the clothing of the soul; but his heart was that of a genuine lover of his kind, of a philanthropist in the sense of Jesus; his views are large and noble; his life was one of devout study on these subjects, and I should pity the person who, after the briefest sojourn in Manchester and Lyons, the most superficial acquaintance with the population of London or Paris, could seek to hinder a study of his thoughts, or be wanting in reverence for his purposes. (*Ibid.*, Vol. II, p. 206.)

It was in part from Fourier, certainly from the collectivistic theories discussed so generally by the transcendental group, that she received her equipment for the cause which, more than any other except the dramatic Roman revolution, appealed to the deeper rebellions of her soul. She had dealt much with the woman question in her "Conversations," and in 1844 she published *Woman in the Nineteenth Century*, a work that made a great stir in America. The "little book was the first considered statement of feminism in this country" (Katharine Anthony, *Margaret Fuller*, p. 80), and its novelty was emphasized by its boldness. The question of woman's place had emerged sharply from the Abolition movement, when the appearance of women on the platform had aroused opposition even from radical reformers, and Angelina Grimké had encountered insults when she spoke at Abolition meetings. But Margaret Fuller was the first since Mary Wollstonecraft, fifty years before, to undertake a reasoned defense of the claims of woman to emancipation from man-made custom. It was a somewhat shocking book to fling at respectable Boston bluestockings—male as well as female—for not only did she discuss equality of economic opportunity and equality of political rights for women, but she went further and spoke frankly about sex equality, marriage, prostitution, physical passions—pretty much everything that was taboo in Boston society. It was a bold thing to do, needing more courage even than to engage in a Fourieristic onslaught upon the conventions of private property. Only a first-class rebel would have had the temerity to offer such morsels to wagging tongues.

This was her parting shot at a world that had done its best to stifle her. Thenceforth her field was to broaden out immensely. In 1844 she went to New York to live in the family of Horace Greeley and write critical reviews for *The Tribune*—a shift that marked the beginning of her intellectual maturity, the end of her mystical sentimentalism. She was thirty-four years of age, and she plunged vigorously into the work of criticism, never perhaps very successfully, certainly never with high distinction. Her judgments were penetrating and individual, she awakened some Cambridge animosities by her comment on certain Cambridge poets, but she was not a notable critic A fine craftsmanship she

424

never attained. A light touch she could never command. Nevertheless the experience was sobering. Honest, practical Horace Greeley, with his pugnacious fondness for social reform, was an excellent antidote to Concord transcendentalism; and an awakening sociological interest discovered ample opportunities in New York for the expression of her mother-instinct. She took to her stormy bosom the inmates of Sing Sing prison, the poor and outcast of the city. At last she went to Europe, fell in with Mazzini, and found a cause dramatic enough and real enough to satisfy her rebellious instincts. She was profoundly stirred by the Roman revolution, took charge of one of the hospitals, and spent her strength freely. On the tragic failure of the revolt she started home with her husband and child, only to perish on the sandy shores of Fire Island—a fate she did not turn her finger to escape. Perhaps it was well. She had only too good reason to be fearful of her reception and of the future. Tongues that had wagged before would certainly have risen to a virtuous gabble over her misadventure in Italy. On the whole one must be glad that her friends refused to permit her good name to be thrown to the gossips. Why shouldn't gentlemen lie stoutly if by so doing they can cheat the salacious?

A sensitive emotional nature offers the best of social barometers, and Margaret Fuller's tragic life, despite its lack of solid accomplishment, was an epitome of the great revolt of the New England mind against Puritan asceticism and Yankee materialism. She was the emotional expression of a rebellious generation that had done with the past and was questioning the future. Not a scholar like Theodore Parker, not a thinker like Thoreau, not an artist like Emerson, she was a ferment of troubled aspiration, an enthusiasm for a more generous culture than New England had known—the logical outcome of the romantic revolution which, beginning with Channing's discovery of humanitarian France, and leading thence to idealistic Germany, was to break the indurated shell of life in New England, and release its conscience and its mind. She was the spiritual child of Jean Jacques even more than of Goethe—a fact that she eventually came to realize. Writing from Paris in 1847, she said:

To the . . . Chamber of Deputies, I was indebted for a sight of the manuscripts of Rousseau, treasured in their library. I saw them and touched them,—those manuscripts just as he has celebrated them, written on fine white paper, tied with ribbon. Yellow and faded age has made them, yet at their touch I seemed to feel the fire of youth, immortally glowing, more and more expansive, with which his soul has pervaded this century. He was the precursor of all we most prize. True, his blood was mixed with madness, and the course of his actual life made some *detours* through villainous places; but his spirit was intimate with the fundamental truths of human nature, and fraught with prophecy. There is none who has given birth to more life for this age; his gifts are yet untold; they are too present with us; but he who thinks really must often think with Rousseau, and learn him ever more and more. Such is the method of genius,—to ripen fruit for the crowd by those rays of whose heat they complain. (*Memoirs,* Vol. II, pp. 206–207.)

The rebel pays a heavy price for his rebellions, as Margaret learned to her cost. She suffered much in her daily life, but it was her art that suffered most. She was evidently a far richer nature than her printed works reveal. Intense in her extravagant demands upon life, a radical humanitarian in all her sympathies and instincts, generous in response to whatever was fine and high, living unduly an inner life as became a daughter of Puritanism—Margaret Fuller was too vivid a personality, too complete an embodiment of the rich ferment of the forties, to be carelessly forgotten. The deeper failure of her career—its vague aspirations and inadequate accomplishment—was a failure that may be justly charged against the narrow world that bred her. Perhaps no sharper criticism could be leveled at New England than that it could do no better with such material, lent it by the gods.

CHAPTER I

The Reign of the Genteel

I

The discussion of the New England mind hitherto has kept pretty much to the outskirts of Boston, to Concord and Roxbury and undistinguished precincts; it has not penetrated the Back Bay where dwelt the authentic representatives of Brahminism, nor has it concerned itself greatly with Cambridge that was a lesser Back Bay. Nevertheless there were other ideals than those of transcendentalism and social reform in the New England of the renaissance—ideals of culture, of scholarship, of *belles lettres*, to which the Brahmin mind contributed, and which after the subsidence of the ferment came to dominate genteel New England and for a generation largely influenced American letters. To the revolutionary aspirations of the forties the Back Bay contributed little. Brahmin Boston might turn Unitarian with Channing, but it was at heart neither French romantic nor German idealist; it desired rather culture for its own sake, and scholarship it regarded as the handmaid of culture. It hoped of course that righteousness and the will of God should ultimately prevail in human affairs, but it was not exigent in its demands. Occasion and means it willingly left to God, anticipating that the walls of Jericho must fall of their own weakness. It is surprising how little the greater issues of the time ruffled the serenity of the Brahmin mind, and how uncritical were its judgments on such issues as came under its review. Divided between State Street and the Back Bay, its life ran a smoothly agreeable course with no hint of potential antagonisms between exploitation and culture. It followed so strictly the injunction, let not thy left hand know what thy right hand doeth, that the two were almost total strangers to each other. Like Edith Wharton's contemporary Knickerbockers, the Brahmins conceived the great business of life to be the erection of barriers against the intrusion of the unpleasant. They took it ill when those barriers were assaulted by rude militants, and when indisputable Brahmins—men like Edmund Quincy and Wendell Phillips—took part in the assault, the Back Bay regarded them as more than a little queer.

The immediate consequence of this concern for defensive breastworks was the reign of the genteel in life and letters, a reign that set up a court of critical jurisdiction over the domain of American letters. The essence of the genteel tradition was a refined ethicism, that professed to discover the highest virtue in shutting one's eyes to disagreeable fact, and the highest law in the law of convention. Gone were the franker days of Robert Treat Paine when a wit might find his choicest *bons mots* in the bottom of his cups. Coarseness had given way to refinement. It was the romanticism of Brahmin culture, with all Falstaffian vulgarity deleted, and every smutch of the natural man bleached out in the pure sunshine of manners. It was Victorianism of a more maidenly purity than the English strain, so carefully filtered by passing through the close Puritan mesh that the smallest impurities were removed. The first of literary commandments was the commandment of reticence. Literature was conceived of as belonging to the library and the drawing-room, and it must observe the drawing-room amenities. Only a vulgarian would lug a spade there. Any venture into realism was likely to prove libidinous, and sure to be common. Certainly Margaret Fuller had overstepped the bounds of decency with her remarks about women of the streets. The Adamite school was the vulgar expression of the natural man, and Continental realism—the French and the Russian—was only bringing the gutter into the library. Literature must be fine and pure and noble, and as such it will serve decency and manners; what excuse is there for it otherwise? The case for the true church of literature, as against the Adamite and other heresies, was admirably stated by Lowell:

I have not seen Swinburne's new volume—but a poem or two from it which I have seen shocked me, and I am not squeamish.

. . . Why should a man by choice go down to live in his cellar, instead of mounting to those fair upper chambers which look towards the sunrise of that Easter which shall greet the resurrection of the soul from the body of this death? *Virginibus puerisque?* To be sure! let no man write a line that he would not have his daughter read. . . . But I have outlived many heresies, and shall outlive this new Adamite one of Swinburne. The true Church of poetry is founded on a rock, and I have no fear that these smutchy back-doors of hell shall prevail against her. (*Letters,* Vol. I, p. 377.)

II

Though it willingly recognized the superior claims of poetry and the essay, the Brahmin mind found a more congenial field for its literary ambitions in history; and the quiet scholarship that it pursued with exemplary diligence was likely to flower in substantial historical studies. Excellent work much of it is, brilliant in certain instances; yet it too is subtly marked by the psychology of the environment that produced it. The renaissance of Boston scholarship began with Everett and Ticknor, whose German training was imposed on natures instinctively aristocratic, swayed by the older Federalist prejudices. The latter applied himself to Spanish literature, but his colleague and fellow historian, Jared Sparks, proved that in the American field even painstaking scholarship could not subdue the temptation to improve upon reality. Sparks applied Boston ethics to biography and conceived that his mission in writing the life of a great American like Washington was to portray a national hero as a model to the youth of the land. In pursuance of this aim he studiously perfected nature by correcting all the little blemishes of manner and little weaknesses of character in order to produce an immaculate effect. He edited Washington's letters with a free hand, not only correcting the grammar and spelling, but silently deleting such passages as did not become the hero he had in mind. He did not of course go to the absurd lengths of Parson Weems in inventing episodes and effects, but he refused to deal with his materials realistically and the result was a falsifying of the total impression.

The greatest and in certain respects the most characteristic work of the period was George Bancroft's *History of the United States,* to which with single-minded purpose he devoted sixty laborious years. Trained in Göttingen, he gathered his materials with German thoroughness, but the underlying spirit and purpose of his exposition were native to the ardent nationalism of Jacksonian America. Bancroft was the only important member of the New England group of historians who was a militant Democrat, and he set out to justify to the world the ways of democratic America. It was a great undertaking and in the opinion of Ranke, the German historian, it justified itself. "Your history is the best book ever written from the democratic point of view," [1] he wrote Bancroft. The praise was perhaps not excessive. Conceived in the early days of the Jacksonian triumph, it reflects the grandiose conception of the future of America and the beneficent influence of republican institutions on western civilization, that were common in the golden days of equalitarianism and that even such a scholarly legalist as Hugh Legaré shared. But unfortunately, with his generation Bancroft had lost his economic bearings, and he drove forward somewhat too confidently into the new seas of political idealism trusting to the pole-star of emancipated human nature. As a democrat he was too easily persuaded that democratic America lay in the particular keeping of Providence, and he assumed too readily that the democratic development of American institutions was in response to the divine will. It reflects something of the partisanship of honest patriots who believe God is on their side; but it served to correct the teachings of Federalists like Richard Hildreth who insisted that God was on the side of Federalism. Till Bancroft took up his pen the bias of American chronicles had been anti-democratic. Every Federalist with leisure, a quill, and a smattering of historical knowledge, had added his mite to the Federalist myths that long constituted the body of our history. The democratic interpretation ran so counter to Boston tradition that Bancroft found little congeniality amongst his fellow historians, and he eventually quitted his native state and took up his home in Washington.

More representative of the Brahmin spirit was the work of William H. Prescott, John L. Motley, and Francis Parkman, who constitute what may be called the romantic school of Boston historians. They sought the romantic in theme and aspired to the romantic in treatment quite as consciously as did the contemporary novelists. Of excellent Brahmin strain, with leisure, wealth, opportunity, they were free to pick and choose as they would. Prescott and Motley turned away from the partisanships of America, and while Jacksonianism was in full swing the former wrote his *Ferdinand and Isa-*

[1] Quoted in Stanton, *Manual of American Literature*, p. 103.

bella, and while the country was wrangling over slavery the latter wrote his *Rise of the Dutch Republic.* Broad in conception and dramatic in treatment, they are admirable works, yet they suggest that aloofness from the sordid realities of America so characteristic of the Brahmin mind. Far more brilliant and significant was the work of Francis Parkman who turned his imagination to the far West over which the struggle for exploration and conquest had long persisted between the French and English. In his twenties he had made a venturesome trip to the great plains, and that experience gave life and vitality to his later historical writings, that were enriched by close research, a brilliant style, and a creative imagination. The theme he set himself was not alone a "history of the American forest," but a clash between civilizations—the "feudal, militant, and Catholic France in conflict with democratic, industrial, and Protestant England"; and with fine tenacity of purpose, in the teeth of ill health, he wrought at his project till the America of the old French War times was gathered into his pages. The Brahmin mind has contributed to American letters no more brilliant work than came from the pen of Francis Parkman.

III

If the highest aspirations of the Brahmin nature sought satisfaction in poetry, Longfellow may be reckoned its most characteristic product. In his work the romantic, the sentimental, and the moralistic, blended in such just proportions, and expressed themselves with such homely simplicity as to hit exactly the current taste and establish a reputation that later generations have difficulty in understanding. A gentle, lovable soul, widely read and in maturer years possessing a ripe literary scholarship, he was a skillful purveyor of gentle, lovable ideals. Although he drew his materials from Spain and Sweden and Italy, from primitive New England and aboriginal America, it was Germany that largely provided the staple of his romance. With Emerson and Margaret Fuller and Theodore Parker, he found Germany a singularly congenial land—not Königsberg with its transcendental metaphysics, nor Weimar with its pagan culture, nor Tübingen with its higher criticism. Such things, transcendental and critical, he was not concerned about; it was the minor romantics, Freiligrath rather than Heine, the gentle melancholy and pervasive *Sehnsucht* of the German folknature, that drew him irresistibly and quickened his sympathetic pen. There was little intellect in Longfellow, little creative originality. He was the poet of an uncritical and unsophisticated generation, as yet untroubled by science and industrialism, and his mind was detached from politics and his conscience rarely disturbed by social questions. He came of excellent Federalist stock, his father having been a delegate from Maine to the Hartford Convention; and with his courteous manners he fitted easily into the little world of Cambridge Brahmins. However one might question his poetry, none could question that he was a gentleman amongst gentlemen.

If he was never the omnivorous bookman that Lowell was, he was distinctly a poet of the library. His placid and singularly happy life was pretty much bounded by his library walls. One could scarcely have lived more detached from contemporary America, more effectively insulated against the electric currents of the times. Though Thoreau might flee to Walden he carried his questioning intellect with him; even the constable would not leave him alone there. But Longfellow's door shut securely against all intrusion. The winds of doctrine and policy might rage through the land, but they did not rattle the windows of his study to disturb his quiet poring over Dante. The translation of the *Divina Commedia* would go forward even while the country was being torn asunder. In a sense such work was his refuge against the storm and stress of malignant forces that troubled him. He did not like the tumult and the shouting, and much of Longfellow is compressed into the sonnets that preface the translation, much of the gentleness of his evasion, and much of the finer craftsmanship of his later years

> Oft have I seen at some cathedral door
>   A laborer, pausing in the dust and heat,
>   Lay down his burden, and with reverent feet
>   Enter, and cross himself, and on the floor
> Kneel to repeat his paternoster o'er;
>   Far off the noises of the world retreat;
>   The loud vociferations of the street
>   Become an undistinguishable roar.
> So, as I enter here from day to day,
>   And leave my burden at this minster gate,
>   Kneeling in prayer, and not ashamed to pray,
> The tumult of the time disconsolate
>   To inarticulate murmurs dies away,
>   While the eternal ages watch and wait.

How strange the sculptures that adorn these towers!
   This crowd of statues, in whose folded sleeves
   Birds build their nests; while canopied with leaves
   Parvis and portal bloom like trellised bowers,
And the vast minster seems a cross of flowers!
   But fiends and dragons on the gargoyled eaves
   Watch the dead Christ between the living thieves,
   And underneath, the traitor Judas lowers!
Ah! from what agonies of heart and brain,
   What exultations trampling on despair,
   What tenderness, what tears, what hate of wrong,
What passionate outcry of a soul in pain,
   Uprose this poem of the earth and air,
   This mediaeval miracle of song!

A single incursion Longfellow made into the field of Abolition controversy, prompted perhaps by Dickens, whose
"grand chapter on slavery" in *American Notes* he had read
in London. The seven poems were written to beguile the
tedium of a sea voyage. They are unreal enough to seem
quite harmless, yet they created a decided stir on their appearance. For a Harvard professor to express publicly even
a mild sympathy with the Abolition movement, may well
have been somewhat perilous, considering the fate of Professor Follen; and the sacred institution may have scented
a real danger in such romanticisms. Grotesque as these academic poems were, with their burnt-cork figures, they perhaps served to romanticize and sentimentalize the Negro for
northern minds, as *Uncle Tom's Cabin* did a decade later
with tremendous effect. Slavery had no weapon against such
an attack, and no doubt Longfellow's contributions proved
serviceable to the cause of Abolitionism. But this one venture satisfied him, and having got safely back to his library,
he shut the door on the whole vexatious question of slavery.
He was not made for battle, and causes commanded an unwilling allegiance. Little remained of his Puritanism save
conscience, a sense of struggle against somewhat vague and
indolent powers of evil, a pleasant melancholy that transmuted itself into pleasant verse. He lived vicariously the
lives of other poets, sharing their emotions, repeating their
thoughts, reproducing their pictures; yet adding some individual color from his own sincere nature. Not richly endowed, he was more than an echo. He marked the transition
from the nebulous ferment of the creative renaissance to the
scholarly culture of Brahmin Cambridge. After Longfellow
came Charles Eliot Norton in whose blameless life that culture flowered, and after that came sterility.

CHAPTER II

Nathaniel Hawthorne: Skeptic

After his immersion for some months in the Utopian dreams of Brook Farm, Miles Coverdale in *The Blithedale Romance* discovered that he had drifted far from reality. "No sagacious man," he remarked, "will long retain his sagacity, if he live exclusively among reformers and progressive people, without periodically returning into the settled system of things, to correct himself by a new observation from that old standpoint."

It was now time for me, therefore, to go and hold a little talk with the conservatives, the writers of the North American Review, the merchants, the politicians, the Cambridge men, and all those respectable blockheads who still, in this intangibility and mistiness of affairs, kept a death-grip on one or two ideas which had not come into vogue since yesterday morning.

In this suggestive pronouncement the intellectual position of Hawthorne is revealed. Cool, detached, rationalistic, curiously inquisitive, he looked out upon the ferment of the times, the clash of rival philosophies and rival interests, only to bring them into his study and turn upon them the light of his critical analysis. One after another he weighed the several faiths of New England, conservative and transcendental and radical, and ended skeptic. He was too much of a realist to change fashions in creeds. Time, experience—he is always remembering—have created men as we find them, and very likely only time and experience can make them over into something different. The conservatives would seem to have common sense on their side, for they are seeking to retain what has hitherto been won; but the reformers are not without justification as well, for impelled by an ardent faith they are seeking to win new conquests. But whether that which the conservatives defend so valiantly is worth defending, or whether the goal towards which the reformers drive so furiously is worth the trouble, are questions about which the rationalist may be permitted his doubts. The universe in which he found himself was a moral universe, Hawthorne on the whole believed; and if that were true then man's chief business and urgent problem was the matter of a sufficient morality.

Radical in his intellectual processes, he could never become greatly interested in specific radicalisms. He is often thought of as a transcendentalist, and his association with the Peabodys and his venture into Brook Farm might seem to lend color to such an interpretation. Yet nothing in his intellectual sympathies marks him as of the school. The polar conceptions of transcendentalism repelled rather than attracted him. Political and metaphysical speculation left him cold, and the twin revolutionary forces of the time, French romanticism and German idealism, never deeply affected his thinking. Amid all the flux he retained much of the older Calvinist view of life and human destiny. Though nominally a Unitarian he did not share Channing's faith in the perfectibility of man. The buried voice of God that the transcendentalists professed to have discovered in instinct, he greatly distrusted. Man seemed to him quite as likely to turn out to be a child of the devil as the first-born of God. Perhaps through a long and uncertain process he may grow into something nobler than he now is, but for the present the fact remains that the human heart, if not desperately wicked, is at least on familiar terms with evil; too often it is cold, selfish, malignant, and its secret promptings need watching. Doubting the indwelling presence of the divine Over-soul, he could find no justification for the transcendental faith in the excellence of the universe, out of which came the genial optimism of the Emersonians. Too pronounced a rationalist to comprehend the mysticism that lurked in the heart of the transcendental faith, he remained cold to the revolutionary criticism that was eager to pull down the old temples to make room for nobler. Eager souls, mystics and revolutionaries, may propose to refashion the world in accordance with their dreams; but evil remains, and so long as it lurks in the secret places of the heart, Utopia is only the shadow of a dream. And so while the Concord thinkers were proclaiming man to be the indubitable child of God, Hawthorne was critically examining the question of evil as it appeared in the light of his own experience. It was the central, fascinating problem of his intellectual life, and in pursuit of a solution he probed curiously into the hidden, furtive recesses of the soul.

The isolation in which he chose to brood over the problem, seeking to take the solution by surprise in unguarded moments, was the natural consequence of his temperament and his habits. He lived singularly remote from common interests, singularly self-sufficient. Both as thinker and artist he suffered from his self-imposed isolation. The twelve years of his apprenticeship, closely immured and given over to spinning cobwebs about the old Puritan rafters, drawing the stuff of his romance out of his own bowels, may have facilitated the development of technic, but it laid narrow limitations on the matter of his art. Intellectually unlocalized in his Yankee world, he was the romancer of a dead but unforgotten past, at home only where the New England conscience brooded over sin—subduing the old nightmares to less terrifying dreams, intruding his doubts into old dogmas yet never emerging from the old shadows. Although he was a child of the liberation and had broken the web that Calvinism had woven about the mind of New England, he did not choose to quit the world from whose bondage he had freed himself. He would examine the old problem in a new light. In rejecting Calvinism as a religion, he retained it as a background for his inquisitive probing. It appealed to his imagination after his reason had rejected its dogmas; it determined his art after it had ceased to command his loyalty. In consequence, all his life Hawthorne dwelt between worlds. Though at times he tried to establish contact with Yankee reality, though he essayed to establish an intellectual *rapport* with his generation, he never quite succeeded, but remained to the last isolated, a frequenter of the twilight.

Only in a narrow and very special sense was Hawthorne a romantic. With the romance of love and adventure he was never concerned; what interested him was the romance of ethics—the distortions of the soul under the tyranny of a diseased imagination. How little he shares in common with other romantics is revealed in his detachment from his native Salem. The place was not lacking in picturesque charm, present and past. During the long years he spent in his Salem study, the city was rising to the zenith of its brisk sea life, with its ships in the China trade, its venturesome fisheries, its echoes of the whaling industry at Nantucket. Materials for romance were lying all about the Salem wharves—such a show of canvas and spars and rigging, such briny smells, such suggestions of far voyages to outlandish places, such strange figures slipping in from the ends of the earth—such romantic promptings in short as would have intoxicated the imagination of Herman Melville, and that Joseph Hergesheimer wove into the rich tapestries of *Java Head*. A romantic could scarcely have found in America a setting better calculated to awaken a sense of brave adventure than in old Salem; yet for three years Hawthorne sat in the Custom House, with such materials all about him, and then turned away to the seventeenth century to write of Hester Prynne. For a man gifted with imagination to fail to lift his eyes to the horizon beyond which the hurrying ships were seeking strange markets, and instead to turn them in upon a shadowy world of half unreal characters; to overlook the motley picturesque in the foreground of the actual, in order to brood over an old adultery and twist it into theological sin, can be explained only on the ground that Hawthorne was concerned with ethical rather than romantic values, that he was interested rather in the problem of evil than in the trappings of romance. Aloofness of time and place served to isolate the problem, stripping away the wrappings of the physical, delocalizing it, transmuting the individual act into the universal. Thus isolated, Hester's sin becomes a symbol of that ancient evil which forever waylays human life and by strange perversions brings havoc to our hopes—the greatest havoc to him whose heart, like Chillingsworth's, is cold, selfish, malignant.

This temperamental aloofness from objective reality was both the strength and the weakness of Hawthorne's art. In choosing to follow the way of the inner life he was true to his Puritan breeding. The perpetual turning-in of the mind upon itself, the long introspective brooding over human motives, came naturally to one who lived in the shadow of a Puritan past. In their anxious concern over sin the Puritans had become in some measure psychologists; how else could the secret impulses of the soul be probed and its dark workings laid bare? Hawthorne was only doing what Jonathan Edwards before him had done in his psychological clinic of the Great Awakening—examining the reactions of sin on conscience and character. From this comes the simplicity of his theme and the compelling unity of his handling. To be sure it is pathological phenomena that he deals with, as the phenomena that Edwards dealt with in his *Narrative of the Surprizing Work of God*, were pathological; and like Edwards, Hawthorne is led into insubstantial and tenuous regions where he breathes with difficulty. The substantial world of Puritan reality that Samuel Sewall knew, Hawthorne seems scarcely to have been aware of; he created instead his own Puritanism, fantastic and unreal. He was forever dealing with shadows, and he knew that he was dealing with shadows, and this consciousness was a perennial source of doubt and uncertainty that bred self-distrust. In setting himself the task of dramatizing sin rather than sinners, of creating romance out of the problem of evil, he encountered difficulties that oppressed him. The well-springs of his imagination were constantly running dry and he must wait till they filled again slowly. Hence the "development of his art is towards ever greater elaboration of scantier and scantier materials, until the joy of the whole becomes lost at last in the milder pleasures of detail." [1]

From the grave difficulties inherent in his theme came the inveterate habit of sliding into symbolism and allegory —from this and from the narrowness of his emotional life and the restrictions of his sympathies. The cold thin atmosphere of his work, one comes increasingly to feel, was due not alone or chiefly to the severity of his artistic restraint that forbade all rioting of the sensuous imagination; it was due rather to a lack of nourishment, to a poverty of ideas and sensuous imagery. His inveterate skepticism robbed him of much, but his inhibitions robbed him of more. A romantic uninterested in adventure and afraid of sex is likely to become somewhat graveled for matter. Like the Pyncheon fowls, Hawthorne's imagination had suffered from too long inbreeding; it had grown anemic, and every grain of fancy is clucked over and picked at and made much of. Once an idea comes into his head he is loath to let it go, but he must turn it about curiously and examine it from every angle. The striking chapter in *The House of the Seven Gables,* where the death of Judge Pyncheon is played upon so persistently, is only an extreme example of his habitual method. The tongues that wagged over the minister's black veil were no more inquisitive and tireless than Hawthorne's when his imagination is fired by a vivid image. He will not let it go till it is sucked as dry as last year's cider cask. It is the way of one to whom ideas are few and precious. Knowing how little is in the bottle he will linger

[1] Amy Louise Reed, "Self-Portraiture in the Work of Nathaniel Hawthorne," *Studies in Philology,* Vol. XXIII, No. I.

out the flavor of every drop. Hence his fondness for symbolism, and hence his frequent lapse into allegory when imagination grows dull. Because Hawthorne was an artist he was saved from the shipwreck that such a method might seem to invite; yet perhaps it is not unreasonable to suggest that he was an artist for the reason that only through the mastery of a refined technic could his scanty stock of ideas make any show at all.

The intellectual poverty that resulted from his long immuring himself in a void is sufficiently revealed in his *American Note-Books.* In the somewhat tedious volume covering the eighteen years between 1835 and 1853—the most vigorous years of the renaissance—there is no suggestion of interest in the creative ideas of the time, in metaphysics or politics or economics or humanitarianism. It is the occasional record of one who lived an unintellectual life, and it makes but a paltry showing when set beside the journals of Emerson for the same years. Few books are referred to; systems of thought lie beyond his ken. Compared with the thinkers and scholars of the time he is only an idler lying in wait for such casual suggestions as he may turn into stories. Almost childish is his delight in marvels. There is something of the spirit of Cotton Mather in his persistent recording of the gruesome and fantastic, in the hope that they will open a quarry for his art. In the year that Emerson wrote *Nature,* Hawthorne set down the following amongst some dozens of similar suggestions: "A snake taken into a man's stomach and nourished there from fifteen to thirty-five years, tormenting him most horribly. A type of envy or some other evil passion." The *Note-Books,* of course, are very inadequate records of his life, and yet that a mind should lie in wait for such grotesqueries, and treasure them, offers food for speculation. After his marriage they are much less frequent and his jottings become more normal—a change which the Freudians, no doubt, would be ready enough to explain.

The one great adventure of Hawthorne's life was the plunge into Brook Farm Utopianism, a plunge that only proved the waters colder and less hospitable than he had hoped. It was a curious adventure for one of his temperament to engage in, and his eventual disillusion might have been foretold. Perhaps it may be explained as reaction from his long isolation. The glowing enthusiasms of the times must often have tempted him to leave his narrow walls, and share the intellectual and emotional stimulus that others professed to discover in the work of making society over. Whatever the explanation the venture turned out to be a failure. His skepticism followed him there and came to later expression in *The Blithedale Romance*, a work as thin and unreal as anything he ever did. It is worse. There is in its pages more than a hint of ill humor that colors his interpretation of the Fourieristic stage of the experiment, and slips out in his portraiture of the major characters. Hollingsworth both fascinates and repels him. A dramatization of the intransigent spirit of reform, his single-minded zeal for righteousness, is subtly fused with an intolerant egotism that destroys Zenobia, cows Priscilla, and wrecks the venture. Perhaps Albert Brisbane may have been in the background of Hawthorne's mind when he drew Hollingsworth, for it was Brisbane who influenced the change he seems to have resented; perhaps Garrison may have served to fill out the picture. Whoever it was, the figure of Hollingsworth is Hawthorne's reply to the summons of the social conscience of the times, done by a critic whose insistent skepticism will not shut its eyes, but discovers under a new masquerade the ancient evil of a cold imperious heart. Seventeen years before he wrote *The Blithedale Romance*, he had jotted down in his *Note-Book* the conception out of which came the later portrait:

A sketch to be given of a modern reformer,—a type of the extreme doctrines on the subject of slaves, cold water, and other such topics. He goes about the streets haranguing most eloquently, and is on the point of making many converts, when his labors are suddenly interrupted by the appearance of the keeper of a madhouse, whence he has escaped. Much may be made of the idea. (*American Note-Books*, pp. 20–21.)

Hawthorne's interpretation of Margaret Fuller is not so easily explained. Perhaps it came out of a subconscious personal spleen. Her rich paganism may well have disturbed a nature so reticent as his, so restrained by certain Puritan inhibitions. In an early sketch he commented on the unfitness of authorship for women, on the ground that "there is a delicacy . . . that perceives, or fancies, a sort of impropriety in the display of woman's natal mind to the gaze of the world, with indications by which its inmost secrets may be searched out" (quoted by Amy Louise Reed, "Self-Portraiture in the Work of Nathaniel Hawthorne"). Margaret's frankness in displaying her natal mind to the gaze of the world, her bold discussion of prohibited subjects

440

like prostitution, could not fail to rub across Hawthorne's deepest prejudices. She was too vigorous and outspoken, too consciously endowed with sex, too frankly feminist, not to have ruffled his instinctive squeamishness. It was not her radical feminism in the abstract that offended him, if he may be trusted; but certainly in the concrete. A sexless feminism would not greatly disturb a mind tolerantly familiar with the current radicalisms; but the frank avowal of sex touched a sensitive nerve. It offended certain latent Puritanisms in him. He was fascinated by Zenobia and yet afraid of her—or of himself; so his hero falls in love with the anemic and witless Priscilla. How characteristic of a mind long fed on symbols, to turn away from the wealth of reality and prefer a shadow!

After Brook Farm came no further experiments in the unsatisfactory business of a *rapprochement* with his generation. His marriage with Sophia Peabody brought with it the prosaic duties of providing for a family, and he had no leisure to play with social reform. Abolitionism he would have none of, nor perfectionism, nor Jacksonianism—the futility of such things became for him a fixed idea. That he once had the courage to make his plunge he seems to have rejoiced over: "Whatever else I may repent of," Miles Coverdale wrote, "let it be reckoned neither among my sins nor follies that I once had faith and force enough to form generous hopes of the world's destiny,—yes!—and to do what in me lay for their accomplishment." Yet the truer Hawthorne is to be found in the judgments set down in the *Note-Book:* "It is my opinion that a man's soul may be buried and perish under a dung-heap, or in a furrow of the field, just as well as under a pile of money." "Oh, labor is the curse of the world, and nobody can meddle with it without becoming proportionably brutified." The man who wrote that had much to learn about life and society, much that he might have learned from Thoreau. But Hawthorne never grappled with economics as Thoreau did, and he learned no more from him than from Melville, or from Emerson, or from any of the books he read by the wise of other days. Self-sufficient he remained to the last, hard-headed and practical, yet missing many a deeper truth that more receptive minds discover. He was traveling the path that leads to sterility, and the lifelong business of playing Paul Pry to the secrets of the conscience brought him at last to the comment, "Taking no root I soon weary of any soil in which I may be temporarily deposited. The same

441

impatience I sometimes feel, or conceive of, as regards this earthly life." He was the extreme and finest expression of the refined alienation from reality that in the end palsied the creative mind of New England. Having consumed his fancies, what remained to feed on?

CHAPTER III

The Authentic Brahmin

I

OLIVER WENDELL HOLMES: Beacon Street Wit

Since the death of Holmes in 1894, his reputation has shrunk and dwindled with that of his group. With the rise of other literary schools, New England standards have been submitted to a somewhat rude overhauling, and Brahmin ideals are no longer reckoned so authoritative as they were once believed to be, nor the supremacy of Boston genius so indisputable. Concord has risen as Cambridge and Beacon Street have declined, and in the shadow of Emerson and Thoreau, the wit of Back Bay is in danger of being obscured. Unsupported by his physical presence, his writings seem far less vital than they did when the echoes of his clever talk were still sounding through them. Certain intellectual shortcomings are more obvious when his works are brought together in a library edition: in the mass his prose seems far more discursive and his verse thinner and more jingly than when the several bits appeared singly, personally sponsored by the author in whose cleverness everybody delighted. Read with sprightly vivacity to a group of sympathetic listeners at the mellowest hour of the dinner, his occasional verse must have sparkled brightly and have gone off with such a crackle of laughter as to convince the Back Bay that the asthmatic little gentleman with bubbling spirits was a veritable poet, on the same friendly footing with the muse that he was with Beacon Street. So frequently on pleasant occasions did Holmes appear before his classmates and friends copy in hand, so often and so happily did he respond to the invitation to write something, that it would have been ungenerous of Boston—and Boston meant the Back Bay, the Saturday Club and Harvard College—not to have crowned him with a wreath of her own ivy.

For upwards of half a century, throughout the prime and on past the Indian Summer of the New England renaissance, Holmes was Boston's own wit, inexhaustible in clever sayings, bubbling over with satire and sentiment, the autocrat of her social gatherings, the acknowledged head of her mutual admiration society. Not since Robert Treat Paine had there been such a master of Yankee small talk. If he monopolized the conversation he dealt generously with his listeners. The stream was copious and the waters were never bitter or astringent, but with just enough effervescence to suit the Boston palate. As a young man the wit sparkled more brightly; as an old man the humor exuded more gently. At twenty-five he described William IV of England with republican irreverence: "The King blew his nose twice, and wiped the royal perspiration repeatedly from a face which is probably the largest uncivilized spot in England"; late in life he commented on his obvious fondness of praise: "I was always patient with those who thought well of me, and accepted all their tributes with something more than resignation." Taste had changed with the times in Boston. Wit was yielding place to humor; eighteenth-century frankness had given way to nineteenth-century refinement; Victorianism was in full and vigorous bloom in the Beacon Street of 1850, and so Holmes became a Yankee Victorian. The morals of an impeccable society required no castigation, and he was under no obligation to satirize vice. Audacious sallies would have been reckoned in bad taste. If the old-fashioned masculine wit of Robert Treat Paine, with its echoes of Charles Churchill, had presumed to intrude itself into the teacup society of Back Bay drawing-rooms, the indignant Doctor would have shown it the door, and the small talk would have flowed again, decorous and clean and amiable, far more refined than the wit that had delighted their fathers.

And yet, though a full-blown Victorian in manners and tastes, Holmes was something of a child of the eighteenth century at heart. The situation in which he found himself might have proved disconcerting if he had chosen to speculate upon it. By nature a thoroughgoing rationalist, he lived in a romantic age. A gentleman of "parts and learning," with a quick and lively fancy that blossomed in the pat phrase and neat couplet, he loved wit and hated dullness with true Augustan zeal. The great days of Queen Anne were a perennial inspiration to him. He clung to the heroic couplet through all the changes of romantic styles. He moralized in rime with the fluency if not the finish of Pope.[1] He satirized Calvinism with an honest wrath that he might have learned of Swift. He commented in his table-talk on the manners of the times with the chatty discursiveness of Addison. Like the earlier wits, he discovered a deep sympathy for the maturity and ripe wisdom of the classics. Writing to his friend John O. Sargent, he remarked:

> I wish I had become as familiar with some classic author as you are with Horace. There is nothing like one of those perennial old fellows for good old gentlemenly reading; and for wit and wisdom, what is there to compare with the writings of Horace? You make me envious,—I vow I shall have to get up Juvenal or Catullus, naughty but nice, or somebody that nobody else knows. . . . I get so tired of the damp sheets of all sorts of *literati* (worse than the "screeching women of Marblehead") and clamorous essayists, that I want something always by me, calm, settled beyond cavilling criticism,—a cool, clear draught of Falernian that has been somewhere near two thousand years in the cellar. (Morse, *Life and Letters*, Vol. II, p. 311.)

But unhappily what could he do? He was the most sociable of persons, and he lived and moved in an atmosphere surcharged with various and sundry romanticisms. How could he preserve the spirit of quiet rationalism, or assure himself gentlemanly leisure, with a host of "isms" clamoring in his ears? He was amongst them even if he was not of them. He strove to keep himself aloof, unfuddled by heady idealisms and untroubled by strident reforms, but he could not shut his study door against the infection. He could not deny his generation, and inevitably he suffered his thought to be streaked and pied with the current romanticism. He gave Lyceum lectures on Wordsworth and Keats and Shelley, and their influence seeped into his verse. The Longfellow fame was all about him, and he fell to composing ballads and idyls and tales, quite as if he did not know better. Romantic garments fitted him ill, yet he persisted in trying them on. He even got to like them, and came finally to prefer *The Chambered Nautilus* above his

[1] See *A Rhymed Lesson*.

other poems—a strange perversion of taste for a rationalist. *The One-Hoss Shay* is worth a volume of such pretty moralizing. *Parson Turell's Legacy* and *The Moral Bully* are in better vein—witty, lucid, critical—than any half-hearted ventures in romanticism. The eighteenth-century wit does not appear to advantage patched with Victorian sentiment, and he should have been rationalist enough to know it.

As a Beacon Street Victorian Holmes was as full of virtuous prejudices as an egg is full of meat; but as a rationalist, with a modest scientific equipment that came from his professional training, he kept the windows of his mind open to the winds of scientific inquiry that were blowing briskly to the concern of orthodox souls. Many a barnacled craft was foundering in those gales, and Holmes watched their going-down with visible satisfaction. He was perhaps the most militant Unitarian amongst Boston laymen. Hatred of Calvinistic dogma was an obsession with him; it dominated his thought and colored much of his work, *Elsie Venner* and his table-talk as frankly as *The One-Hoss Shay*. The criticism to which he subjected the old-school dogmas was always vehement, often vindictive. Long after the battle had been won he kept annoying the retreating enemy. His father, Abiel Holmes, was a rigorous follower of the Edwardean school, who after nearly forty years' service lost his pulpit for refusing to compromise with Unitarian liberalism that had gained the fortress of the near-by College Yard; and the stalwart among his congregation, having to yield the building, the endowment and the communion plate, were forced to establish themselves anew. In this unhappy schism that came about the time Oliver Wendell Holmes was graduating from Harvard in 1829, the latter went with the liberals. He had broken with the Calvinism of his father, and in the reaction he went further than most along the path of Unitarian rationalism—not the path of Channing that led to French romanticism and transcendentalism, but the path of Andrews Norton that led to a harder-headed rationalism. The reasons for this shift are sufficiently evident in his writings. At his father's table he had watched too many "whey-faced" brethren to like the breed—men with "a weedy flux of ill-conditioned hair," whose

> acrid words
> Turn the sweet milk of kindness into curds,
> Or with grim logic prove, beyond debate,
> That all we love is worthiest of hate,

As the scarred ruffian of the pirate's deck,
When his long swivel rakes the staggering wreck!
(*The Moral Bully.*)

The words are bitter, but they reveal the length of his
reaction from the Calvinism on which he had been over-
fed at home and at Phillips Andover Academy; and they
suggest also why, next to Theodore Parker, Holmes came
to be the best hated of Boston Unitarians amongst the
orthodox. On this one subject he was militantly radical,
never shirking debate, but whetting the edge of his satire
and impaling his victim neatly with his logic. He took sar-
donic delight in turning Calvinism against itself, in the
clever *reductio ad absurdum* of the Edwardean argument.
Perhaps this major intellectual interest appears most adequately in his picture of the Master, the autobiographical
rationalist whom he introduces into *The Poet of the Breakfast Table.* A dabbler in the law, theology and medicine,
a philosophic contemplator of the Order of Things, who
refused to permit "the territory of a man's mind" to be
"fenced in," who agreed with the Poet in thinking somewhat ill of the specialist who dedicated his life to the study
of beetles, preferring to range widely through time and
eternity, who followed Darwin and was deep in bacteri-
ology, trying "curious experiments in spontaneous generation"—this was Holmes on the intellectual side, a genial
disseminator of the latest scientific speculations, a tolerant
amateur of the things of the mind, a friendly dabbler in
absolute moralities, who hoped "to do some sound thinking
in heaven" if he ever got there, but who was too pleasantly
engaged with Beacon Street to settle things now.

In his own special way, then, as a Brahmin of the Brahmins, Holmes was a rebel, a puller-down of worm-eaten
structures, a freethinker rejoicing when free thought tossed
a cargo of obsolete dogma into Boston Bay, or drew out
a linchpin of some respectable social coach. He loved Boston the more because he believed that Boston was the
home of free thought and free speech, the capital of American brains, the intellectual rebel of the continent. He did
not agree with Emerson's strictures, or Parker's. He would
not concede that Boston was the "home of the Hunkers."
It was provincial; it had crooked little streets; but

I tell you Boston has opened, and kept open, more turnpikes that
lead straight to free thought and free speech and free deeds than
any other city of live men or dead men—I don't care how broad

their streets are, nor how high their steeples. (*The Professor at the Breakfast Table,* p. 4.)

When he contemplated the future of America, with Boston as its intellectual leader, he was carried on the crest of an exuberant optimism:

A new nursery, Sir, with Lake Superior and Huron and all the rest of 'em for washbasins! A new race, and a whole new world for the new-born human soul to work in! And Boston is the brain of it, and has been any time these hundred years! That's all I claim for Boston—that it is the thinking centre of the continent, and therefore of the planet. (*Ibid.,* p. 104.)

If the mind is free other things will take care of themselves—this pretty much sums up Holmes's social philosophy. Only, he would add, when the mind is used to its freedom, it will create a culture that is well-mannered, that does not run to extravagant agitation, that considers time, place, and outward circumstance in effecting needful changes—the quiet decency of Channing rather than the noisier way of Parker. The Brahmin way, after all, was the better way, Holmes believed; and Channing was a Brahmin:

Parson Channing put a little oil on one linchpin, and slipped it out so softly, the first thing they knew about it was the wheel of that side was down. T'other fellow's at work now; but he makes more noise about it. When the linchpin comes out on his side, there'll be a jerk, I tell you! Some think it will spoil the old cart, and they pretend to say that there are valuable things in it which may get hurt. Hope not—hope not. But this is the great macadamizing place—always cracking up something. (*Ibid.,* p. 19.)

Certainly not on the intellectual side could Holmes be set down as a conservative. He did not relish any such imputation and defended himself with vigor:

If to be a conservative is to let all the drains of thought choke up and keep the soul's windows down—to shut out the sun from the east and the wind from the west—to let the rats run free in the cellar, and the moths feed their fill in the chambers, and the spiders weave their lace before the mirrors, till the soul's typhus is bred out of our neglect, and we begin to snore in its coma or rave in its delirium—I, Sir, am a *bonnet-rouge,* a redcap of the barricades, my friends, rather than a conservative. (*Ibid.,* p. 18.)

It was this spirit of rationalism that made him—at some risk of unpopularity—an unsparing critic of romantic equalitarianism. Here again is an echo of the older century. Neither the Jacksonian nor the transcendental version of

447

the new gospel found favor in his eyes; both seemed to run
counter to the open facts of history. As a realist he discovered justification for John Adams's doctrine of economic
determinism: all society, he was convinced, tends to stratify
in lines of wealth distribution, in America as well as in
Europe, and no dogmas can prevent it. He went further
and insisted that the possession of wealth makes possible
comfort, ease, leisure, culture; that those lacking wealth
are necessarily unfree and their lives in consequence are
meaner and narrower. Much of his criticism of Yankee villagers and countrymen—and except Cooper, he was perhaps
the most critical commentator on Yankee provincialisms of
speech and manners—springs from the conviction that a
niggardly economics had created a niggardly society. He
desired more wealth to the end of more culture. He was
too completely Brahmin to set material well-being as the
ultimate goal of the competitive struggle; that seemed to
him the object of State Street and of the plutocracy he
frankly detested. In *The Poet at the Breakfast Table* he
apologizes for calling one of his characters a capitalist, on
the ground that "the word seems to be equivalent to highway robbery in the new gospel of Saint Petroleum." Wealth
as a means to power he would have none of; but wealth
as a means to leisure, and leisure as a means to cultivated
living, he was fond of extolling. The machinery of Brahmin
life must be well oiled, but the life is more than the machinery. Always he returned to the intellectual as the hall-
mark of every society that may be accounted excellent, and
his instinctive dislike of the middle class was founded on
its intellectual sterility. It lived opulently but meanly; its
rich dinners wanted the spice of wit, its ostentatious display lacked the salt of manners. It was vulgar at heart, and
Holmes hated vulgarity even more than he hated John
Calvin's dogmas.

Unfortunately his Brahminism sealed pretty tightly certain windows of his mind that might better have been kept
open. A radical in the field of theology where personal concern brought him to serious grappling with the problem,
a tolerant rationalist in the realm of the intellect, he remained a cheerfully contented conservative in other fields.
He was unconsciously insulated against the currents of social and political thought flowing all about him. Economic
inequality he accepted rather too complacently. His daily
life ran so easy and comfortable a course as never to prod
him into questioning how other lives might be running. By

instinct and traning he was an aristocrat, and he was never at pains to conceal his preference for the well born and well mannered. He professed a philanthropic sympathy for the cause of the slave, but he shared the Beacon Street dislike of agitation—it was not well bred and it might bring down more things than he cared to have brought down. The most completely class-conscious of the Boston writers, he deprecated all proletarian appeals. They were not, in his opinion, "wholesome moral entertainment for the dangerous classes. Boys must not touch off their squibs and crackers too near the powder-magazine." The less said about the wrongs of labor, the better—at least publicly. Social strata being determined by economics, the agitator is little better than a firebrand.

You can't keep a dead level long, if you burn everything down flat to make it. Why, bless your soul, if all the cities of the world were reduced to ashes, you'd have a new set of millionaires in a couple of years or so, out of the trade in potash. In the meantime, what is the use of setting the man with the silver watch against the man with the gold watch, and the man without any against them both? . . . Here we are travelling through the desert together like the children of Israel. Some pick up more manna and catch more quails than others, and ought to help their hungry neighbors more than they do; . . . but we don't want the incendiary's pillar of a cloud by day and a pillar of fire by night to lead us in the march to civilization, and we don't want a Moses who will smite the rock, not to bring out water for our thirst, but petroleum to burn us all up with. (*The Poet at the Breakfast Table*, pp. 5–6.)

In his attitude toward the present comfortable arrangement of society, Holmes was no rebel. He was not callous to the evils of society, but he was willing to take a longer time in the march towards civilization than more exigent souls wished; it was a pleasant march on the whole, and why quarrel over the difference in packs? If his attitude was not the indifferentism of the well-to-do, it was near kin to it. He reflected the negative qualities of Unitarianism, rather than the positive, the free mind rather than the tender conscience. His social bias is sufficiently revealed in the tributes of praise he bestowed so generously. Among those whom he delighted to honor, the names of Garrison, Phillips, Parker, Thoreau, Greeley, John Brown, do not appear; instead he offered his praises to Everett, Webster, Bryant, Whittier, Agassiz, Parkman, Wilkie Collins, the Grand Duke Alexis, and a host of lesser celebrities known

449

to the Back Bay. His heroes were respectable souls rather than militant. As a critic his vision seems to have been blurred by certain astigmatisms, and he discovered heroic qualities more readily in the militant dead than in the militant living. He delighted in the Boston of '76, but it is reasonably certain that if he had lived then he would have walked the streets of that older Boston as a genial Tory, and would have suffered the fate of other gentlemen who found it desirable to withdraw with Gage's Redcoats— unless, indeed, his love of the place had held him despite his politics.

In his literary work Holmes was always the talker rather than the writer. The charm of the vivid and racy colloquial marks every page. A clever aphorism or telling pun is the objective of every paragraph, and it explodes with a brilliant shower of sparks. But like every talker his discursiveness is inveterate; he wanders far in pursuit of his point and sometimes returns empty-handed. He was always an amateur; life was too agreeable for him to take the trouble to become an artist. The essay was his most congenial form —his novels are to be taken no more seriously than his occasional verse. *Elsie Venner* wraps up the familiar problem of moral determinism in pleasantly discursive chat of Yankee bumpkinism in contrast with Yankee Brahminism, and he returns his impeccable hero to Beacon Street, after his sojourn in the provinces, to reward him with the Brahmin rewards—a munificent practice, a charming wife, and an exalted social position. What richer reward could be desired by one who had tasted to the full the mellow flavor of that society? Staid, delightful, self-satisfied, righteous little Beacon Street! Last refuge and citadel of the old Brahmin respectability; basking in the afternoon sunshine of its culture, not realizing that its sun is already well past the meridian; in love with its own virtues and unaware that the morrow will see the invasion of the Huns and Vandals of plutocracy, to whose plethoric bank books Brahmin culture must eventually bow—who would not have liked it? It was something after all to have been its favorite wit, its ready oracle, its clever poet, who in praising his fellow Brahmins was well aware that he discreetly praised his own admirable qualities. Kindly, delightful, fortunate Dr. Holmes! chief citizen of the Hub of the Universe! He was born and lived with a silver spoon in his mouth, and if a grudging posterity inclines to rate him and his little world somewhat lower than he rated them, what difference can that make to him? Tolerant himself, we should perhaps emulate his example, and not insist too rudely that he is only a minor figure in American literature.

JAMES RUSSELL LOWELL: *Cambridge Brahmin*

Whatever the critics may eventually come to say about Lowell, he was certainly the ablest and most distinguished of the old Cambridge breed, in the days when the Brahmin caste was disintegrating and Brahmin ideals losing their hold on New England—a man of fine native abilities in whom Harvard culture did its best to strike fire and light and understanding to serve as a beacon to the rest of America. He was not of the Concord line of transcendental individualists, nor of the militant strain of reforming enthusiasts; but of the true Brahmin line of Josiah Quincy and Edward Everett and Oliver Wendell Holmes—men of sound culture who could serve God valiantly in the social station in which He had placed them, without wanting to pull down the old church to build a new. Like Charles Eliot Norton—*clarum et venerabile nomen*—he had no plans of a new building in his pocket, but was content to enlarge and embellish the old. He would serve culture rather than causes. His gifts were Brahmin gifts, his prejudices were Brahmin prejudices; and so in spite of a "certain sprightliness of brain" that tempted him to rebel at the aridity of the scholastic commons on which he fed, and in spite of certain youthful vagaries and incursions into indiscreet places, he remained at bottom a Harvard conservative, content with his birthright, hopeful that his ways were God's ways. This suffices to explain the extraordinary reputation of Lowell in Cambridge circles, and the difficulty with which it made headway elsewhere. Though he traveled much in his library—as Thoreau would say—his prejudices remained narrowly local. To the last he remained extraordinarily parochial.

Yet the culture he served so faithfully never fruited in wisdom. He was never quite certain of himself, of what he really believed. He was fond of standing off and studying himself quizzically, to learn what sort of person he was; yet he was swayed by so many impulses he was never quite sure what sort of legs were under him. He was hopelessly bewildered by his own vast disorder. His mind was as cluttered as a garret, filled with an endless miscellany of odds and ends. Life puzzled him, as it puzzles every serious mind; but he allowed himself to be too easily discouraged by his inveterate unwillingness to think. He never speculated widely or analyzed critically. Ideas, systems of thought, intellectual and social movements, he had no interest in; he was content to remain a bookish amateur in letters, loitering over old volumes for the pleasure of finding apt phrases and verbal curiosities. With all his reading, history remained a blank to him; and science he would have none of. "I hate it," he confessed late in life; "I hate it as a savage hates writing, because I fear it will hurt me somehow." A good many things hurt him in those later years, and it was characteristic of him to say, "I continue to shut my eyes resolutely in certain speculative directions." He defined culture as "intelligent purpose"; yet of such intelligent purpose his intellectual life revealed little. Naturally he did not relish the theological unsettlement that came with the advance of scientific inquiry. Leslie Stephen's rationalism troubled him, and after reading the former's *English Thought in the Eighteenth Century*, he wrote, "I am very much in the state of mind of the Bretons who revolted against the Revolutionary Government and wrote upon their banners, 'Give us back our God!'" (*Letters*, Vol. II, p. 168.) Neither did he relish the economic unsettlement the industrial revolution was bringing to Cambridge and America, but he looked back longingly to the quiet days "before our individuality had been trampled out of us by the Irish mob." Standing between the older America and the new, with the foundations disintegrating under his feet, he confused the disorder in his own mind with the disorder in the external world of society, and desperately sought to cling to his ancient hopes. A pathetic yearning for orderliness in an age that has grown heedless of it was natural enough in a mind that had come to expect little of life; but surely orderliness, like charity, should begin at home.

It was, perhaps, not altogether his fault. His impulses were liberal and his mind generous, but he was never strong enough to overcome the handicap of the Lowell ancestry and training. When he spoke of himself half whimsically as a natural Tory, he was putting his finger on the Brahmin strain. The sanctity of the Lowell blood is a commonplace in New England; but that it was Tory blood is less frequently remarked. His grandfather, John Lowell, to be sure, was visited by certain humanitarian compunctions, and in 1772 convinced himself that at Common Law slavery could not stand, and was eager to put it to the test in Massachusetts. But John Lowell was high in the councils of the Federalist party, and a judge, and it is a safe guess that his radicalism did not go deep. Certainly, the next generation was stalwartly conservative. The three brothers represented the three major professions of law, theology, and business, that constituted the New England hierarchy. His father, Charles Lowell, after traveling abroad, was settled as pastor of the West Church, Boston—Jonathan Mayhew's church—a post he held for fifty-six years. He was a stout Federalist, a good hater of Jefferson,[2] a pleasant, cautious gentleman who refused to be drawn into the bitter Unitarian-Trinitarian controversy of the day—as unlike the militant Mayhew as a conventional soul could well be.[3] His uncle, John Lowell, was a capable lawyer-politician, one of the directing minds of the Federalist machine, earnestly engaged in defending Massachusetts against the wicked Republicans. Another uncle, Francis Cabot Lowell, was an enterprising capitalist, founder of the city of Lowell, whose multiplying spindles, it was hoped, would turn the wives and daughters of Yankee farmers, and the poverty-stricken Irish immigrants, into efficient revenue-producers for State Street securities.

From this pleasant background of Brahmin conservatisms, Lowell went forth into a world given over to momentous changes, contemptuous of all Brahmin standards, to find his way as he might. An original mind would have marked out its own path, as Emerson did; a conventional mind would have gone with the better sort, as Josiah Quincy did; but Lowell was neither Emerson nor Quincy. Sensitive to change, he was rarely self-reliant; generous in sympathies, he was timid in convictions. He was no Come-outer to stand alone against the world, but unconsciously he took color from his environment and was always glad to find a staff to lean on. It was fortunate for his peace of mind that he never realized how frequently he was no more than an echo of other minds; yet the confusions and contradictions that mark off the several periods of his life can be explained in no other way. From Brahminism he drifted to radicalism, and from radicalism back to a modified Brahminism; and these changes resulted from no native intellectual unfolding, but from certain dominant personalities who drew him aside from his natural orbit. He quitted college as a pleas-

[2] See *Letters*, Vol. I, p. 82.
[3] See Hale, *James Russell Lowell and His Friends*, p. 10.

ant young Tory, who paused in his Commencement Poem to address some pointed remarks at Abner Kneeland—the last man imprisoned in Massachusetts for religious opinion —upon the wickedness of an atheism that denied the faith of Charles Lowell. But the ferment of the times was already working in him, and when he was nineteen he wrote with youthful fervor, "I am fast becoming ultra-democratic. . . . Liberty is now no longer a cant word in the mouths of knaves and fools" (*Letters*, Vol. I, p. 33). Within a year he had met Maria White, whose influence till her death in 1853 was the determining factor in his intellectual life. She was an ardent Abolitionist and reformer, and under her pleasant tutelage Lowell was indoctrinated in the current philosophy of radicalism. He spoke at Abolition meetings, and contributed to the Abolition press. More important, he conceived that he had come upon his true mission in letters. In an ode beginning "In the old days of awe and keen-eyed wonder," he put into verse his new creed, a prose statement of which he elaborated in a letter explaining his *Prometheus* in 1843, a year before his marriage to Miss White:

Although such great names as Goethe, Byron, and Shelley have all handled the subject in modern times, you will find that I have looked at it from a somewhat new point of view. I have made it *radical,* and I believe that no poet in this age can write much that is good unless he give himself up to this tendency. For radicalism has now for the first time taken a distinctive and acknowledged shape of its own. So much of its spirit as poets in former ages have attained (and from their purer organization they could not fail of some) was by instinct rather than by reason. It has never till now been seen to be one of the two great wings that upbear the universe. . . . The proof of poetry is, in my mind, that it reduces to the essence of a single line the vague philosophy which is floating in all men's minds, and so renders it portable and useful and ready to the hand. (*Letters,* Vol. I, p. 73.)

Six years later he asserted confidently, "I am the first poet who has endeavored to express the American Idea, and I shall be popular by and by." Yet within a few months he found the vein nearing exhaustion. In a survey of his course up to 1850, he remarked that he had served love and freedom hitherto, and he now proposed to serve beauty, adding the significant comment, "I find that Reform cannot take up the whole of me, and I am quite sure that eyes were given us to look about us sometimes, and not to be always looking forward. . . . I am tired of controversy" (*ibid.,* Vol. I,

p. 173). Between these several confessions lies the bulk of Lowell's contribution to the "causes" of the times, and how adequately he served them is revealed in the successive poems that came from his pen.[4] Their equal as a whole is not to be found in the work of other contemporary radicals. The better work is solidly vigorous, with competent iambs that often rise to the dignity of such lines as "Slowly the Bible of the race is writ." The eager rhetoric of *The Present Crisis* was the highwater mark of Abolition argument in verse; but its serviceableness for quotation cannot make it so good a poem as *Prometheus* with its muscular blank verse, or as *A Glance behind the Curtain* with its portrait of Cromwell, strong in his faith, ready for all needful iconoclasms.

> I have no dread of what
> Is called for by the instinct of mankind;
> Nor think I that God's world will fall apart
> Because we tear a parchment more or less."

This is frank transcendental radicalism, yet the truer Lowell of those days of youthful enthusiasm is found in the *Biglow Papers*, first written with spontaneous gusto out of his hatred of the imperialism of the Mexican war, and later carefully embedded in the heavy machinery of the prose setting. The native clutter of Lowell's mind is there laid bare—the grotesque mixture of homely satire, moral aphorisms, Yankee linguistics, literary criticism—an unwieldy mass that he could neither simplify nor reduce to order. The machinery spoils the propaganda and weighs down the satire; yet the verse has survived because for once Lowell let himself go and hit such heads as he had a mind to.

Lowell saw fit to retain most of his radical verse in the definitive edition of his works, but his radical prose he disowned, and it was left for pious hands to gather together long after his death. It was perhaps as well for his reputation that the ambassador at the Court of St. James's should not be plagued by his youthful indiscretions. In those prose writings were combustible materials. He went with the Abolitionists in their brisk assaults on law, order, and the Constitution. Whatever revolution was stirring anywhere found him sympathetic. He was strong for the workingman's revolution of 1848 in France; it was social injustice that was

---

[4] The more significant titles are: *Prometheus* and *A Glance behind the Curtain*, 1843; *Columbus* and *The Present Crisis*, 1844; *On the Capture of Fugitive Slaves near Washington*, 1845; *Biglow Papers*, begun in 1846; *The Pioneer*, 1847; *Bibliolâtres*, 1849; *Anti-Apis*, 1851.

to blame for mob violence, and the fetish of *laissez faire* was a sorry enough god to worship.

> The great problem of the over-supply of labor is not to be settled by a decimation of the laboring class, whether by gunpower or starvation. . . . The giant Labor did not merely turn from one side to the other for an easier position. Rather he rose up, "Like blind Orion hungry for the morn." . . . They had learned by bitter experience that it was on the body of old King Log *Laissez-faire* that King Stork perched to devour them. *Let-alone* is good policy after you have once got your perfect system established to let alone. (Quoted in Scudder, *James Russell Lowell,* Vol. I, pp. 205–206.)

In common with the Abolitionists, Lowell appealed to the Declaration of Independence against the Constitution. He took delight in satirizing his Federalist forebears, who, he asserts, beginning to fear the light of freedom, ingeniously constructed a "Sacred Parasol" for the new Goddess of Liberty, "to prevent her from being tanned":

> A stout machine of parchment was accordingly constructed, and, under the respectable name of a Constitution, was interposed wherever there seemed to be danger from the hostile incursions of light. Whenever this is spread, a dim twilight, more perplexing than absolute darkness, reigns everywhere beneath its shadow. . . . This contrivance of ours, though the work of our own hands, has acquired a superstitious potency in our eyes. (*Ibid.*, Vol. I, p. 210.)

No wonder Lowell later disowned such apostasies, for after Maria White's death in 1853 came the dun professorial period of his life, when Harvard laid hands on him and came near to reducing him to its own ways. It revived the old Brahmin instincts that had lain dormant during the years of his Abolitionism, without reviving the old sanctions. Left without a cause, half ashamed of his youthful indiscretions yet ill content to drift, he turned bookman and for twenty-one years wandered with Norton and Longfellow and Child in the Sahara of medieval scholarship. It was not a happy time with him. There is plenty of evidence of his restlessness and dissatisfaction that occasionally prompted the wish to turn wholly scholar and keep his note-books in order; that prodded him to salvage the mass of his accumulation by turning his lecture-notes into literary essays; and that in other moods induced him to turn half savagely upon his dead enthusiasms and find solace in clever satire. His vigorous salvagings were scarcely worth the trouble. He

456

had nothing important to say about Dante or Pope or Wordsworth, and he said it with a good deal of needless verbal exertion. The essay on Thoreau, written in 1865, was a different matter. Here he was brought face to face with a past which it still hurt him to remember; and the ill nature that colors his comment is sufficient testimony to the painfulness of his memories. Certainly he did not understand Thoreau, was incapable of understanding him; yet might not his dislike have been prodded by the consciousness that Thoreau had refused to make terms with Harvard culture as he had done? An intelligent reading of Thoreau must have been an unpleasant experience in Lowell's mood, keenly aware of certain backslidings of his own; and the essay is suggestive for the light it throws on Lowell, not on Thoreau.

To this period belong most of the essays on which rests Lowell's reputation as a critic of letters and politics. Bright as that reputation long was, it is beginning to show tarnish. Subjected to the scrutiny of eyes unblinded by the congenialities of the Cambridge coterie, it appears that Lowell's brilliancy covered over certain grave shortcomings that unfitted him for serious critical judgment.[5] He had no standards other than ethical, only likes and dislikes; no interest in ideas, only a pottering concern for the text; no historical backgrounds, only isolated figures dwelling in a vacuum. He was puzzled over new schools and unfamiliar technic, and was at ease only in praising established reputations and confirming approved judgments. He scoffed at Taine instead of going to school to him, and made merry over Masson's *Life of Milton;* yet he was wholly incapable of dealing with men from whose fruitful minds came ideas that summoned throngs of followers. In almost the last year of his life he spent weeks rereading Rousseau, and was satisfied to dismiss him with the comment, "a monstrous liar, but always the first dupe of his own lie" (*Letters,* Vol. II, p. 424). *Leaves of Grass* he dismissed as affected, not original. He was shocked at Swinburne's "Adamite" heresy—"When a man begins to lust after the Muse instead of loving her, he may be sure that it is never the Muse that he embraces" (*ibid.,* Vol. I, p. 377). He admired Howell's prose style and loved the man, but he could not bring himself to approve his literary and social theories.

During those sterile professorial years he was closing one

[5] See C. Hartley Grattan, "Lowell," in *The American Mercury,* Vol. II, pp. 63–69.

door after another. Scarcely an important movement of contemporary thought awakened his interest. The hypothesis of evolution he rejected somewhat flabbily. "I think the evolutionists will have to make a fetish of their protoplasm before long," he said in 1879. "Such a mush seems to me a poor substitute for the Rock of Ages—by which I understand a certain set of higher instincts which mankind have found solid under their feet in all weathers" (*ibid.*, Vol. II, p. 245). And as late as 1886 he wrote, "I am a conservative (warranted to wash) and keep on the safe side—with God as against evolution." Naturally so provocative a doctrine as economic determinism never showed its face in his study; Karl Marx was not one of his intellectual companions. Even the homebred knight-errant, Henry George, did not greatly interest him. "Why, who in the world buys such a book as that," he exclaimed of *Progress and Poverty;* and learning that a friend had subscribed for a thousand copies, he remarked, "He *must* be getting eccentric." [6]

The political principles that he discovered in the smoke of his professor's pipe were equally naïve. He took himself seriously as a guide and mentor in matters political. He was fond of talking about the "noble science of politics"; yet he never took the trouble to ground himself in the elements of the subject. He had scarcely read the primer of political theory. Burke was probably the only political writer who ever made any impression on his mind. Of American constitutional history he was as ignorant as a politician, and when in Civil War days he began to scratch the field of politics, he only uncovered certain old Federalist prejudices that lay hidden under his later accumulations. The extreme parochialism of the Brahmin mind is revealed in Lowell's incapacity to understand the South. The comment on Sibley's *Harvard Graduates*—"I do not know when the provincialism of New England has been thrust upon me with so ineradicable a barb"—should be turned upon Lowell's dogmatic essays in American politics. He had not the slightest comprehension of Calhoun's doctrine of majorities; yet he dismissed it contemptuously, after attributing it to one of Calhoun's followers.[7] He speaks of the "weak and wicked element" of states rights—which he supposes the South owed to "the unhappy ingenuity of Mr. Jefferson"—as an unhistorical repudiation of the principle of coercive sover-

---

[6] Five years later he was more sympathetic, but hopelessly confused. See *Democracy,* Vol. VI, p. 35.

[7] See "The Rebellion," in *Prose Works,* Vol. V, p. 134.

eignty established by the fathers, quite overlooking the Hartford Convention. His treatment of Jefferson Davis and Andrew Johnson is marked by the dogmatisms of one who is defending God's will against the devil's sophistries. He will have no other interpretation of history than an ethical interpretation, in which good and evil are eternally at combat; and he closes his volume of political essays with a comment that embodies for him the sum of all political wisdom:

We have only to be unswervingly faithful to what is the true America of our hope and belief, and whatever is American will rise from one end of the country to the other instinctively to our side, with more than ample means of present succour and of final triumph. It is only by being loyal and helpful to Truth that men learn at last how loyal and helpful she can be to them. (*Ibid.,* Vol. V, p. 326.)

Into the stagnant atmosphere of the Elmwood study came on a happy day in the middle sixties the vibrant personality of Edwin Lawrence Godkin, and under the stimulus of his crisp thinking there began for Lowell what may perhaps be reckoned an intellectual renaissance. Godkin was a moderate English liberal, a man of complete self-assurance, whose tart comment on politics and economics was pointed by a conviction of the finality of his own conclusions. Under such teaching Lowell made rapid progress in the new school of criticism fathered by *The Nation.* The delight with which he read Godkin's comment and the eager faith with which he greeted his ideas suggest that his own ethical interpretation of politics was giving way under the strain of postwar experience. From Godkin he got some casual instruction in *laissez faire,* and certain of its teachings snuggled down comfortably in his mind beside the principles of coercive sovereignty and a centralizing state, without awakening any suspicion of their incompatibility of temperament. He never went over wholly to *laisse faire;* he was too strongly Brahmin Federalist for that; but his leanings often carried him into the English camp. It was a tonic to his native conservatism that was troubled about the new theories of collectivism, and it awakened strong doubts about the experiment in democracy. The reaction against the radicalism of his Abolition days became sharp and final. "We have got to work back from a democracy to our original institution as a republic again," he wrote Leslie Stephen in 1879 (*Letters,* Vol. II, p. 161); and in 1888 he asserted that the republic would endure only "so long as the ideas of the men who founded it continue dominant" (*The Independent in Politics,* Vol. VI, p. 207). He warned Thomas Hughes against the extension of suffrage in England,[8] and he was more and more inclined to think that democracy meant a slough of mediocrity underlain with the mud of corruption—that it might prove to be "a Kakistocracy rather, for the benefit of knaves at the cost of fools" (*Letters,* Vol. II, p. 159).

From the vigorous movements of protest of the seventies and eighties, the agrarian uprising of the Middle Border and the proletarian organization in the industrial centers, he drew added confirmation of his fears. In his attitude towards both he was little more than an echo of Godkin, who was laying about him briskly, hitting both farmer and workingman with fine impartiality. He shared the latter's contempt for all agrarian programs, without quite understanding them. He knew little of America. The continent was scarcely more than a hinterland to Cambridge, a hinterland that he explored with some bewilderment on a trip that carried him as far as Cincinnati. Equally ignorant of economics and of the Middle Border, he had no basis for any opinion; a juster man would have put the agrarian question aside as beyond his competency; at least he would have been careful to clear his mind of prejudice. But Lowell was as much a victim of capitalistic prejudice as Thomas Bailey Aldrich and other Boston pseudo-intellectuals. The old Brahminism was close to the surface in those later years, and a scratch would reveal it. In the matter of the "Haymarket Riot" he wrote Howells that "he thought those Chicago ruffians well hanged"—a comment that recalls the Abner Kneeland episode of fifty years before. Physically Lowell was in close proximity to the labor problem, but intellectually he was worlds removed. He looked upon the labor unions with heavy misgivings. He frankly feared the power of the proletariat and was bitter in denunciation of social legislation. In 1869 he wrote Godkin, "Pray give Henry Wilson a broadside for dipping his flag to that piratical craft of the eight-hour men. . . . I have a thorough contempt for a man who pretends to believe that eight is equal to ten" (*Letters,* Vol. II, p. 31). And somewhat later he wrote Norton:

I sometimes feel a little blue over the outlook here, with our penny-paper universal education and our workingmen's parties, with their tremendous lever of suffrage, decrying brains. . . . But the more I learn, the more am I impressed with the wonderful system of checks and balances which history reveals (our

8 See *Letters,* Vol. II, p. 175.

Constitution is a baby-house to it!) and the more my confidence in the general commonsense and honest intention of mankind increases. . . . I take great comfort in God. I think He is considerably amused with us sometimes, but that He likes us, on the whole, and would not let us get at the match-box so carelessly, as He does, unless He knew that the frame of His Universe was fire-proof. How many times have I not seen the fire-engines of Church and State clanging and lumbering along to put out—a false alarm! And when the heavens are cloudy what a glare can be cast by a burning shanty! (*Ibid.*, Vol. II, p. 51.)

The ways of the Gilded Age were a rude shock to Lowell's ill-grounded idealism. The crude post-war exploitation and the political corruption that marked the buccaneer stage of the rising plutocracy filled him with anxiety. As an honest man he was angered by the common scoundrelism of the politicians and the press and troubled at the apathy of the public, but his dislike for economics did him a grave disservice. In seeking out the guilty he went wide of the mark. To trace the source of the virus that was poisoning the public life to an exploiting economics, would have brought him close home. He chose to think it was spread rather by western agrarians and city ringsters, than by respectable New Englanders; yet after passing through the *Crédit Mobilier* scandal he was visited by unpleasant suspicions. "I suspect," he wrote after his return from the Cincinnati Convention in 1876, "that few of our Boston men who have had to do with Western railways have been more scrupulous [than the western Grangers]. I rather think they set the example of tempting legislators with the hope of questionable gains" (*Letters*, Vol. II, p. 170). With the open facts of a Congressional investigation before him, Lowell got no deeper than that. Yet his indignation must find outlet and he contributed two poems to *The Nation*— "The World's Fair, 1876," and "Tempora Mutantur"—in one of which he wrote:

> Show 'em your Civil Service, and explain
> How all men's loss is everybody's gain; . . .
> Show your short cut to cure financial ills
> By making paper-collars current bills;
> Show your new bleaching-process, cheap and brief,
> To wit: a jury chosen by the thief;
> Show your State legislatures; show your Rings;
> And challenge Europe to produce such things
> As high officials sitting half in sight
> To share the plunder and to fix things right;
> If that don't fetch her, why, you only need

Your latest style in Martyrs—Tweed:
She'll find it hard to hide her spiteful tears
At such advance in one poor hundred years.

(Letters, Vol. II, p. 155.)

This is Godkin translated into the Lowell vernacular, and
what issued from his indignation was Godkin also—an apostolic ardor for civil service reform. He had learned at least,
that democracy had not yet been achieved in America; that,
indeed, such spontaneous liberalism as had been bred by
free land was in danger of being destroyed by evils that issued from the loins of this same heedless frontier order.[9] In
1876 he wrote, "Let us all work together (and the task will
need us all) to make Democracy possible. It certainly is no
invention to go of itself any more than the perpetual motion" (Letters, Vol. II, p. 159). Yet in spite of his zeal,
one may be permitted to doubt that Lowell really desired
any other than a Brahmin democracy. In those later years
his conception of an ideal society was unconsciously colored
by memories of Cambridge fifty years before—a simple,
patriarchal world, amenable to the rule of the better sort.
In such a world democracy seemed possible; but in the rising proletarian-plutocratic order, what reasonable hope was
there?

From his growing perplexities Lowell found a happy relief in his mission abroad. The experience was a godsend to
a mind that was growing torpid. In 1869 he had written,
"I fancy if I were suddenly snatched away to London, my
brain would prickle all over, as a foot that has been asleep
when the blood starts in it again. Books are good dry forage;
we can keep alive on them; but, after all, men are the only
fresh pasture" (ibid., Vol. II, p. 24). London, in this mellow
autumn of his life, ripened Lowell. He slipped into the congenial environment as easily as Irving had done a generation
before, and found English society as delightful. He loved
England with unaffected heartiness, and under the stimulating experience he expanded into a kindly English Liberal.
The extreme Liberals—men like Mill and Arnold and John
Morley—he found less sympathetic; and radical thinkers
like William Morris he seems not to have known of. But
English Liberalism of the Gladstone type was own cousin to
Cambridge Brahminism; it united dignity and conscience; it
seemed to him the ideal type of government—the rule of
God-fearing gentlemen who strove to be faithful to their

* See The Independent in Politics, Vol. VI, pp. 204–209.

trusteeship, and who ruled because they were best fitted to rule. Into such a world no other American of the times could have entered more appreciatively than Lowell. If congeniality to the host be a prime requisite in an ambassador, President Hayes made no mistake in sending him to the Court of St. James's. He was a distinguished representative of Brahmin culture; but whether he was a representative of the solid realities of America is not so certain.

CONCLUSION

To the ebullient romanticisms with which the foregoing pages have dealt, the Civil War brought diverse fortunes; and from the titanic conflict emerged an America rid of one of the feculent sources of domestic schism. The romantic imperialisms of the slave economy were gone forever. So much at least was cleared from the path of its destiny, and the field of potential conflict was narrowed to the rival imperialisms of eastern capitalism and western agrarianism. Both had been vastly strengthened by the war. In the eastern centers was a greatly stimulated industrialism, fed from the reservoirs of liquid capital gathered in the process of financing the northern armies, ready to turn to transcontinental railway-building, large-scale manufacture, and a gigantic exploitation of the raw materials of mine and forest and field. Along the Middle Border the old romance of the settlement came to new life as the flood of homesteaders, augmented by disbanded soldiers, poured over the prairie spaces beyond the Mississippi, to repeat there the story of commonwealth building. East and West would eventually clash, for their diverse economic needs were driving towards a collision; but that would not come for a generation till the conflict of interests was thrust into sharper relief.

In the meantime many familiar things were becoming anachronisms over night, though they might linger on for years. As the romantic revolution began with the laying aside of the smallclothes and tie-wig of eighteenth-century aristocratic conservatism, so the new age began with the putting away of the outworn dress of eighteenth-century romantic liberalism. In the hurrying new days there was no time or place for abstract theories of natural rights, for equalitarian democracy, for local home rule—these relics of the past were thrust aside in the scramble for wealth and power. The old philosophies were swept out on the rubbish heap—Jefferson and Lincoln with Calhoun and Stephens— and Hamilton and Marshall came to their own again. The lost cause carried down to defeat much more than slavery, it carried down the old ideal of decentralized democracies, of individual liberty; and with the overthrow of the traditional principles in their last refuge, the nation hurried forward along the path of an unquestioning and uncritical consolidation, that was to throw the coercive powers of a centralizing state into the hands of the new industrialism. Here was a revolution that was to engulf the older romantic America, its dignified literary ideals as well as its democratic political theory. In the world of Jay Cooke and Commodore Vanderbilt, the transcendental dream was as hopelessly a lost cause as the plantation dream; it was in even worse plight, for it left no tragic memories to weave a new romance about the fallen hopes. Emerson in Concord was as much out of date as Lowell in Cambridge, or Gilmore Simms in Charleston. A new age had come and other dreams—the age and the dreams of a middle-class sovereignty, that was busily surveying the fields of its future conquests. From the crude and vast romanticisms of that vigorous sovereignty emerged eventually a spirit of realistic criticism, seeking to evaluate the worth of this new America, and discover if possible other philosophies to take the place of those which had gone down in the fierce battles of the Civil War. What form this critical spirit assumed, and what replies it returned to the strident challenge of the time, are questions not to be answered here.

BIBLIOGRAPHY

Only the more important titles dealt with in the present study are listed hereunder, together with selected biographical and critical material. The invaluable bibliographies in the *Cambridge History of American Literature*, 4 vols., New York, 1917–22, cover most of the writers considered, and the reader is referred to them.

BOOK I: PART I

Information will be found in the *Library of Southern Literature* by E. A. Alderman and others (16 vols., New Orleans, 1908–13) and in Montrose J. Moses, *Literature of the South* (New York, 1910). See also Carl Van Doren, *The American Novel* (New York, 1921).

I. THE OLD DOMINION. See Thomas J. Wertenbaker, *Patrician and Plebeian in Virginia* (Charlottesville, Va., 1910).

II. For the economics of Jeffersonianism, see Charles A. Beard, *The Economic Origins of Jeffersonian Democracy* (New York, 1915; Chapter XII). Also Charles Gide and Charles Rist, *A History of Economic Doctrines* (translated by W. Smart and R. Richards, Boston).

JOHN TAYLOR: His works are out of print. Important titles are: *An Inquiry into the Principles and Policy of the United States* (Fredericksburg, Va., 1814). *New Views of the Constitution of the United States* (Washington, 1823). *Correspondence* (edited by W. E. Dodd, Richmond, 1908).

See "John Taylor, Prophet of Secession" (by William E. Dodd, in *Branch Historical Papers, II*, Richmond, 1908) See also Beard, *Economic Origins of Jeffersonian Democracy*.

III. JOHN MARSHALL: Sufficient materials will be found in Albert J. Beveridge, *Life of John Marshall* (4 vols., New York, 1916–19.)

IV. For the plantation tradition, see Francis Pendleton Gaines, *The Southern Plantation* (New York, 1924).

WILLIAM WIRT: His works are out of print. *Letters of a British Spy* (Richmond, 1803). *The Old Bachelor* (2 vols., Richmond, 1810). *Life and Character of Patrick Henry* (Philadelphia, 1817; also several later editions).

See John P. Kennedy, *Memoirs . . . of William Wirt* (Philadelphia, 1849).

NATHANIEL BEVERLY TUCKER: His works are out of print. *George Balcombe; a Novel* (2 vols., New York, 1836).— *The Partisan Leader; a Tale of the Future*, by Edward William Sidney (printed for the publishers, by J. Caxton, 1856 [*i. e.*, Washington, printed by Duff Green, 1836], 2 vols.); reissued as *A Key to the Disunion Conspiracy: The Partisan Leader* (2 vols. in one, New York, 1861); edition issued at Richmond, 1862.

Some information about Tucker will be found in W. P. Trent, *William Gilmore Simms* (Boston and New York, 1892).

V. WILLIAM ALEXANDER CARUTHERS: *The Kentuckian in New York. Or, the Adventures of Three Southerns. By a Virginian* (2 vols., New York, 1834).—*The Cavaliers of Virginia, or the Recluse of Jamestown. An Historical Romance of the Old Dominion* (2 vols., New York, 1834–1835).— *The Knights of the Horse-Shoe; a Traditionary Tale of the Cocked Hat Gentry in the Old Dominion* (Wetumpka, Ala., 1845; New York, 1882, 1909).

JOHN P. KENNEDY: *Works* (3 vols., New York, 1854; 9 vols., New York, 1871, with life by H. T. Tuckerman, Vol. X). *Swallow Barn, or a Sojourn in the Old Dominion* (2 vols., Philadelphia, 1832; several later editions). *Horse-Shoe Robinson; a Tale of the Tory Ascendency* (2 vols., Philadelphia, 1835; numerous later editions, the latest in 1906). *Rob of the Bowl; a Legend of St. Inigoe's* (2 vols., Philadelphia, 1838; later editions). *Quodlibet: Containing Some Annals Thereof . . .* (Philadelphia, 1840; 1860).

EDGAR ALLAN POE: The bibliography is extensive. See the *Cambridge History of American Literature*.

BOOK I: PART II

II. JOHN C. CALHOUN: *Works* (6 vols., Columbia, S. C., 1851; New York, 1853–55). *Correspondence*, edited by J. F. Jameson (American Historical Association, *Annual Report*, 1899, Vol. II).

Biographies: W. E. Dodd, in *Statesmen of the Old South* (New York, 1911). H. von Holst, *John C. Calhoun* (*American Statesmen Series*, Boston, 1882, 1899). W. M. Meigs, *Life of John Caldwell Calhoun* (2 vols., New York, 1917). G. M. Pinckney, *Life of John C. Calhoun* (Charleston, 1903). W. P. Trent, *Southern Statesmen of the Old Régime* (New York, 1897).

ALEXANDER H. STEPHENS: *Constitutional View of the War between the States* (2 vols., Philadelphia, 1868).

See L. B. Pendleton, *Alexander H. Stephens* (Philadelphia, 1908).

FRANCIS LIEBER: *The Stranger in America* (2 vols. in one

London, 1834). *Political Ethics* (Philadelphia, 1838; edited by Theodore D. Woolsey, Philadelphia, 1890; with introduction by Nicholas Murray Butler, Philadelphia, 1911). *Essays on Property and Labor* (New York, 1841). *Civil Liberty and Self-Government* (2 vols., Philadelphia, 1853; London, 1859; edited by Theodore D. Woolsey, Philadelphia, 1891). *Miscellaneous Writings* (2 vols., Philadelphia, 1881; edited by Daniel C. Gilman, Philadelphia, 1916).

See L. R. Harley, *Francis Lieber: His Life and Political Philosophy* (New York, 1899).

III. For the southern position, see Jeannette Reid Tandy, "Pro-Slavery Propaganda in American Fiction in the Fifties" (in *South Atlantic Quarterly*, January-March, 1922). Francis Pendleton Gaines, *The Southern Plantation* (New York, 1924; Chapter III).

WILLIAM J. GRAYSON: *The Hireling and the Slave* (Charleston, 1856).

IV. WILLIAM CRAFTS: *A Selection in Prose and Poetry, from the Miscellaneous Writings of the Late William Crafts. With Memoir by Samuel Gilman* (Charleston, 1828).

HUGH SWINTON LEGARÉ: *Writings* (2 vols., Charleston, 1846; with memoir).

WILLIAM GILMORE SIMMS: His works have never been collected and most of them are out of print. *Border Romances* (17 vols., New York, 1859, 1866, 1879; 10 vols., New York, 1882; 15 vols., Chicago, 1885; 17 vols., Chicago, 1888; 17 vols., Atlanta, 1901 [?]).

See W. P. Trent, *William Gilmore Simms* (New York, 1892) —an excellent study. Also see J. Erskine, *Leading American Novelists* (New York, 1910).

BOOK I: PART III

Excellent bibliographical material for western literature will be found in Ralph Leslie Rusk, *The Literature of the Middle Western Frontier* (2 vols., New York, 1925). See also W. H. Venable, *The Beginnings of Literary Culture in the Ohio Valley* (Cincinnati, 1891).

II. Interesting material will be found in Claude G. Bowers, *Party Battles of the Jackson Period* (Boston, 1922).

III. TIMOTHY FLINT: His works are out of print and rare. *Recollections of the Last Ten Years* (Boston, 1826). *Francis Berrian, or the Mexican Patriot* (Boston, 1826; Philadelphia and London, 1834). *The Life and Adventures of Arthur Clenning* (Philadelphia, 1828). *George Mason, the Young Backwoodsman; or, "Don't Give up the Ship"* (Boston, 1829; with changed title, London, 1833). *The Shoshonee Valley; a Romance* (Cincinnati, 1830).

468

See John Ervin Kirkpatrick, *Timothy Flint, Pioneer, Missionary, Author, Editor* (Cleveland, 1911)—an excellent study with bibliography.

JAMES HALL: *Works* (4 vols., New York, 1853–56). *Legends of the West* (Philadelphia, 1832, 1833; five later editions). —*The Soldier's Bride; and Other Tales* (Philadelphia, 1833).—*The Harpe's Head; a Legend of Kentucky* (Philadelphia, 1833); as *Kentucky. A Tale* (London, 1834, 2 vols.).—*Tales of the Border* (Philadelphia, 1835). *The Wilderness and the War Path* (New York, 1846; New York and London, 1849).

See J. L. Davis, "Judge James Hall, a Literary Pioneer of the Middle West" (in *Ohio Archæological and Historical Society Publications*, October, 1909).

AUGUSTUS LONGSTREET: *Georgia Scenes* (Atlanta, Ga., 1835; New York, 1840; several later editions).

See John Donald Wade, *Augustus Longstreet, a Study of the Development of Culture in the South* (New York, 1924), an excellent study with bibliographical material.

DAVY CROCKETT: Five titles are grouped under the name of Crockett: *Sketches and Eccentricities of Col. David Crockett, of West Tennessee* (1833). *A Narrative of the Life of David Crockett, of the State of Tennessee* (Philadelphia, 1834; seven editions in one year). *Life of Martin Van Buren* (1835). *An Account of Col. Crockett's Tour to the North and Down East* (1835). *Col. Crockett's Exploits and Adventures in Texas* (1836). The *Narrative* is reprinted with an introduction by Hamlin Garland, in *The Modern Student's Library*, under the title, *The Autobiography of David Crockett* (New York, 1923).

There is no life of Crockett; such so-called works are uncritical jumbles of fact and fiction. Some information will be found in John Donald Wade, "The Authorship of David Crockett's Autobiography" (*Georgia Historical Quarterly*, September, 1922); S. H. Stout, "David Crockett" (*American Historical Magazine*, Vol. VII, No. I, Jan., 1902)— uncritical; Chester T. Crowell, "Davy Crockett" (*American Mercury*, Vol. IV, No. 13).

BOOK II

For Philadelphia, see Ellis Paxson Oberholtzer, *The Literary History of Philadelphia* (Philadelphia, 1906). Also H. M. Ellis, "Joseph Dennie and His Circle" (*University of Texas Bulletin*). For the politics of New York, see Dixon Ryan Fox, *The Decline of Aristocracy in the Politics of New York* (New York, 1918).

I. CHARLES BROCKDEN BROWN: *The Novels of Charles Brockden Brown . . . with a Memoir* (Boston, 1827; Philadelphia, 1857, 1887). *Wieland; or the Transformation* (New

York, 1798; best recent edition in *American Authors Series,* New York, 1926). *Arthur Mervyn; cr, Memoirs of the Year 1793* (Philadelphia, 1799; Second Part, New York, 1800; numerous later editions).

No adequate life has been written. The best is by William Dunlap, *The Life of Charles Brockden Brown* (2 vols., Philadelphia, 1815). See John Erskine, *Leading American Novelists* (New York, 1910), and Annie R. Marble, in *Heralds of American Literature* (Chicago and London, 1907).

ROBERT MONTGOMERY BIRD: For a list of his plays, see A. H. Quinn, *A History of the American Theatre* (New York, 1923).

Calavar; or, the Knight of the Conquest: a Romance of Mexico (2 vols., Philadelphia, 1834; about ten later editions).—*The Hawks of Hawks-Hollow. A Tradition of Pennsylvania* (2 vols., Philadelphia, 1835; two London editions).—*The Infidel; or, The Fall of Mexico* (2 vols., Philadelphia, 1835; London, 1835).—*Nick of the Woods, or, Jibbenainosay. A Tale of Kentucky* (2 vols., Philadelphia, 1837; upward of twenty later editions).

For his life, see Clement Foust, *Life and Dramatic Works of Robert Montgomery Bird* (1919).

II. JAMES KENT: *Commentaries on American Law* (4 vols., New York, 1826–1830; many later editions).

For his life, see William Kent, *Memoirs and Letters of James Kent* (Boston, 1898).

FITZ-GREENE HALLECK: *Poetical Works* (New York and Philadelphia; eight editions between 1847 and 1859). *Poetical Writings with Extracts from those of Joseph Rodman Drake* (edited by J. G. Wilson, New York, 1869, 1885).

For a life, see J. G. Wilson, *The Life and Letters of Fitz-Greene Halleck* (New York, 1869). Also see W. C. Bryant, *Some Notices on the Life and Writings of Fitz-Greene Halleck* (New York, 1869).

III. WASHINGTON IRVING: The standard edition of his works is in forty volumes, New York, 1887.

The standard life is by Pierre M. Irving, *The Life and Letters of Washington Irving* (4 vols., London, 1864; New 1879, 1883).

See also *The Letters of Washington Irving to Henry Brevoort* (edited by George S. Hellman, 2 vols., New York, 1915). A recent study is George S. Hellman, *Washington Irving, Esq.* (New York, 1925).

JAMES KIRKE PAULDING: *Works* (15 vols., New York, 1834–1839; 4 vols., 1867–1868).—*The Diverting History of John Bull and Brother Jonathan* (New York, 1812).—*Letters from the South* (2 vols., New York, 1817).—*The Backwoodsman. A Poem* (Philadelphia, 1818).—*Salmagundi, Second Series* (2 vols., New York, 1820).—*Kon-*

ingsmarke, the Long Finne, A Story of the New World
(New York, 1823; 2 vols., New York, 1834; three London
editions, and a German).—*Westward Ho! A Tale* (2 vols.,
New York, 1832, 1845; three London editions, a French
and a German).—*The Dutchman's Fireside. A Tale* (2
vols., New York, 1831; latest edition, 1900).—*The Puritan
and his Daughter* (New York, 1849, 1850; also London,
1849, two editions, and one German).

No adequate life has been written, but see W. I. Paulding,
Literary Life of James K. Paulding (New York, 1867).

IV. JAMES FENIMORE COOPER: The editions of Cooper's novels
are numerous; as good as any is the one in thirty-two volumes (New York, 1895, 1896–97). Much of his controversial work and critical articles have not been reprinted. See
*Notions of the Americans; Picked up by a Travelling
Bachelor* (2 vols., Philadelphia, 1829). *A Letter to His
Countrymen* (New York, 1834). *The American Democrat;
or Hints on the Social and Civic Relations of the United
States* (Cooperstown, 1838). *The History of the Navy* (2
vols., Philadelphia, 1839). Also his eight volumes of European travels.

No satisfactory life has been written. The best is by T. R.
Lounsbury, *James Fenimore Cooper* (New York, 1883).
See also *Correspondence of James Fenimore-Cooper*
edited by his grandson, James Fenimore Cooper, 2 vols.,
New Haven, 1922). W. C. Brownell, in *American Prose
Masters* (New York, 1909). Carl Van Doren, in *The
American Novel* (New York, 1921).

V. WILLIAM CULLEN BRYANT: The Standard edition is edited by
Parke Godwin (6 vols., New York, 1883–1889; 1–2, *Biography*, 1883; 3–4, *Poetical Works*, 1883, 1901; 5–6,
Prose Writings, 1884–1889). Much information on his
work in journalism will be found in Allan Nevins, *A Century of Journalism* (New York, 1921).

HORACE GREELEY: His works have not been collected. See
Hints towards Reform (New York, 1850). *Recollections of
a Busy Life* (New York, 1868). *Essays Designed to Eluci-
date the Science of Political Economy* (Boston, 1870). *The
American Conflict* (Hartford and Chicago, 1864–1866).
For his life, see James Parton, *The Life of Horace Greeley*
(Boston, 1868). Charles Sotheran, *Horace Greeley* (New
York, 1915). See also John R. Commons, "Horace Greeley
and the Working-Class Origins of the Republican Party"
(*Political Science Quarterly*, Vol. XXIV, pp. 468–488).

HERMAN MELVILLE: The best edition is The Standard (16
vols., London, 1922–23). Also see *Works* (4 vols., edited
by A. Stedman, New York, 1892, 1896; Boston, 1900,
1910). Convenient editions of *Typee, Omoo,* and *Moby
Dick* are plentiful.

The indispensable life is Raymond Weaver's *Herman Mel-*

ville: Mariner and Mystic (New York, 1921), with bibliography. Also see John Freeman, *Herman Melville* (in *English Men of Letters Series*, New York, 1926).

BOOK III: PART I

I. For the political backgrounds, see A. E. Morse, *The Federalist Party in Massachusetts to the Year 1800* (Princeton, 1909). W. A. Robinson, *Jeffersonian Democracy in New England* (New Haven, 1916). Samuel Eliot Morison, *Life and Letters of Harrison Gray Otis* (2 vols., Boston, 1913).

FISHER AMES: *Works* (with memoir by J. T. Kirkland, Boston, 1809). *Works, with a Selection from his Speeches and Correspondence* (edited by his son, Seth Ames, 2 vols., Boston, 1854).

ROBERT TREAT PAINE: *Works in Prose and Verse* (with memoir, Boston, 1812).

II. JOSEPH STORY: *Commentaries on the Constitution of the United States* (3 vols., Boston, 1833; numerous later editions).

See W. W. Story, *Life and Letters of Joseph Story* (2 vols., Boston, 1851).

DANIEL WEBSTER: The best edition of his works is The National—*The Writings and Speeches of Daniel Webster* (18 vols., Boston, 1903). *Private Correspondence of Daniel Webster* (2 vols., Boston, 1857). *Letters* (edited by C. H. Van Tyne, New York, 1902).

See George Ticknor Curtis, *Life of Daniel Webster* (2 vols., New York and London, 1870). For a critical contemporary estimate see Theodore Parker, *Discourse Occasioned by the Death of Daniel Webster* (Boston, 1853). See also Charles A. Beard, *The Economic Basis of Politics* (New York, 1922).

BOOK III: PART II

I. UNITARIANISM: See George Willis Cooke, *Unitarianism in America: A History of its Origin and Development* (Boston, 1902). Williston Walker, *A History of the Congregational Churches in the United States* (New York, 1804).

WILLIAM ELLERY CHANNING: *Works* (5 vols., Boston, 1841; sixth volume added in 1843; numerous later editions).

An excellent life is J. W. Chadwick, *William Ellery Channing, Minister of Religion* (Boston, 1903). See also William H. Channing, *Memoir of William Ellery Channing* (3 vols., Boston, 1848).

II. PERFECTIONISM: For materials see Garrison, *Life of William Lloyd Garrison* (4 vols., New York, 1885–1889).

BROOK FARM: See Lindsay Swift, *Brook Farm; Its Members, Scholars and Visitors* (New York, 1906; contains bibliography). J. T. Codman, *Brook Farm: Historic and Personal Memoirs* (Boston, 1894). Nathaniel Hawthorne, *Blithedale Romance*.

ABOLITIONISM: Sufficient materials will be found in Garrison, *Life of William Lloyd Garrison* (4 vols., New York, 1885–1889). See also Catherine N. Birney, *Sarah and Angelina Grimké* (Boston, 1885); and *James G. Birney and His Times, by His Son, William Birney* (New York, 1890).

III. WILLIAM LLOYD GARRISON: See Garrison, *Life of William Lloyd Garrison* (4 vols., New York, 1885–1889).

JOHN G. WHITTIER: *The Writings of John Greenleaf Whittier* (Riverside Edition, 7 vols., Boston, 1885–1889).

See G. R. Carpenter, *John Greenleaf Whittier* (in *American Men of Letters Series*).—T. S. Pickard, *Life and Letters of John Greenleaf Whittier* (2 vols., Boston, 1894).—F. H. Underwood, *John Greenleaf Whittier. A Biography* (Boston, 1884).

HARRIET BEECHER STOWE: *Works* (Riverside Edition, 16 vols., Boston, 1896; with life by Mrs. Field, 17 vols., 1898).

See Mrs. J. T. Fields, *The Life of Harriet Beecher Stowe* (Boston, 1897).

BOOK III: PART III

I. TRANSCENDENTALISM: The literature is abundant. See *The Dial* (4 vols., Boston, 1840–1844).—*The Harbinger* (4 vols., New York, 1844–1848).—Harold Clarke Goddard, *Studies in New England Transcendentalism* (New York, 1908).—O. B. Frothingham, *Transcendentalism in New England. A History* (New York, 1876).—See also Sylvester Judd, *Margaret. A Tale of the Real and Ideal* (2 vols., Boston, 1845; revised edition, 1851).

II. RALPH WALDO EMERSON: *Works* (Riverside Edition, edited by James Eliot Cabot, 12 vols., Boston, 1884–1893; London, 1884–1893; Centenary Edition, with biographical introduction and notes by E. W. Emerson, 12 vols., Boston, 1903–04; London, 1904).—*Journals of Ralph Waldo Emerson, with Annotations* (edited by Edward Waldo Emerson and Waldo Emerson Forbes, 10 vols., Boston, 1909–1914).—*Uncollected Writings. Essays, Addresses, Poems, Reviews and Letters by Ralph Waldo Emerson* (New York [1912]).

See George Willis Cooke, *Bibliography of Ralph Waldo Emerson* (Boston, 1908). James Eliot Cabot, *A Memoir of Ralph Waldo Emerson* (2 vols., Boston, 1887). George Willis Cooke, *Ralph Waldo Emerson; His Life, Writings, and Philosophy* (Boston, 1881). Oscar W. Firkins, *Ralph Waldo Emerson* (Boston, 1915). W. C. Brownell, *American Prose Masters* (New York, 1909).

III. Henry David Thoreau: *Works* (Riverside Edition, 11 vols., Boston, 1894; Manuscript Edition, 20 vols. [Vols. VII–XX contain the Journals], Boston, 1906).

See Francis H. Allen, *A Bibliography of Henry David Thoreau* (Boston and New York, 1908). William E. Channing, *Thoreau, the Poet-Naturalist* (Boston, 1873, 1902). F. B. Sanborn, *Henry D. Thoreau* (in *American Men of Letters Series*, Boston, 1882, 1910); *The Personality of Thoreau* (Boston, 1901); *The Life of Henry David Thoreau* (Boston and New York, 1917). Léon Bazalgette, *Henry Thoreau—Bachelor of Nature* (translated by Van Wyck Brooks, New York, 1924).

IV. Theodore Parker: *Collected Works* (edited by F. P. Cobbe, 14 vols., London, 1863–71). *The Critical and Miscellaneous Writings of Theodore Parker* (Boston, 1843). *Speeches, Addresses and Occasional Sermons* (2 vols., Boston, 1876). *The American Scholar* (with notes by George Willis Cooke, Boston, 1907).

An excellent study is J. W. Chadwick, *Theodore Parker, a Biography* (Boston, 1900), containing a bibliography. John Weiss, *Life and Correspondence of Theodore Parker* (2 vols., New York, 1864)—indispensable.

V. Margaret Fuller: Her works have not been collected. Important titles are: *Women in the Nineteenth Century* (New York and London, 1845; with additional papers and introduction by Horace Greeley, New York, 1855). *Life Without and Life Within* (Boston, 1860; New York, 1869). *Papers on Literature and Art* (2 vols., New York and London, 1846).

An excellent study is Katharine Anthony, *Margaret Fuller: A Psychological Biography* (New York, 1920). See also R. W. Emerson, W. H. Channing, and J. F. Clarke, *Memoirs of Margaret Fuller Ossoli* (2 vols., Boston, 1852). Thomas Wentworth Higginson, *Margaret Fuller Ossoli* (in *American Men of Letters Series*, Boston, 1884), containing bibliography.

BOOK III: PART IV

I. Henry W. Longfellow: *The Writings of . . . with Bibliographical and Critical Notes* (11 vols., Boston, 1886 [Vols. I–VI, *Foetical Works;* VII–VIII, *Prose Works;* IX–XI, *Dante*]).

See Samuel Longfellow, *Life of Henry Wadsworth Longfellow* (3 vols., Boston and New York, 1891). T. W. Higginson, *Henry Wadsworth Longfellow* (in *American Men of Letters Series*, Boston and New York, 1902).

II. Nathaniel Hawthorne: *Works* (12 vols., Boston, 1871–76; Fireside Edition, 12 vols., Boston, 1879; Riverside Edition,

12 vols., Boston, 1883; Standard Library Edition, 15 vols., Boston, 1891 [contains *Nathaniel Hawthorne and His Wife*, by Julian Hawthorne]; New Wayside Edition, 13 vols., Boston, 1902).

The best-known life is Julian Hawthorne, *Nathaniel Hawthorne and His Wife* (2 vols., Boston, 1885). Henry James, *Nathaniel Hawthorne* (in *English Men of Letters Series*, London, 1879; New York, 1885, 1887). See also W. B. Brownell, *American Prose Masters* (New York, 1909). John Erskine, *Great American Novelists* (New York, 1910). Carl Van Doren, *The American Novel* (New York, 1921). Stuart P. Sherman, *Americans* (New York, 1923).

III. OLIVER WENDELL HOLMES: *Works* (Riverside Edition, 13 vols., Boston, 1891, additional volume, 1892; Autocrat Edition, 13 vols., Boston and New York, 1904).

See George B. Ives, *A Bibliography of Oliver Wendell Holmes* (Boston and New York, 1907).—John T. Morse, *Life and Letters of Oliver Wendell Holmes* (2 vols., Boston and New York, 1896).—Lewis W. Townsend, *Oliver Wendell Holmes. Centenary Biography* (London, 1909).

JAMES RUSSELL LOWELL: *Works* (Riverside Edition, 13 vols., Boston and New York, 1902 [contains Scudder's *Life*]; Elmwood Edition, 16 vols., Boston, 1904 [four volumes of letters]). *Anti-Slavery Papers* (2 vols., Boston and New York, 1902). *Letters of James Russell Lowell* (edited by Charles Eliot Norton, 2 vols., New York, 1893; 3 vols., Boston, 1904). *Early Prose Writings of* . . . (2 vols., New York, 1903).

G. W. Cooke, *A Bibliography of James Russell Lowell* (Boston and New York, 1906). H. E. Scudder, *James Russell Lowell: A Biography* (2 vols., Boston, 1901). Ferris Greenslet, *James Russell Lowell: A Biography* (2 vols., Boston, 1901). Ferris Greenslet, *James Russell Lowell: His Life and Work* (Boston, 1905). See also C. Hartley Grattan, "Lowell" (*The American Mercury*, Vol. II, p. 69); Harry Hayden Clark, *Lowell's Criticism of Romantic Literature* ("Publications of the Modern Language Association," March, 1926); W. D. Howells, *Literary Friends and Acquaintances* (New York, 1902); Henry James, *Essays in London and Elsewhere* (New York, 1893); J. J. Reilly, *James Russell Lowell as a Critic* (New York, 1915); and John M. Robertson, *Lowell as a Critic* (*North American Review*, February, 1919).

INDEX